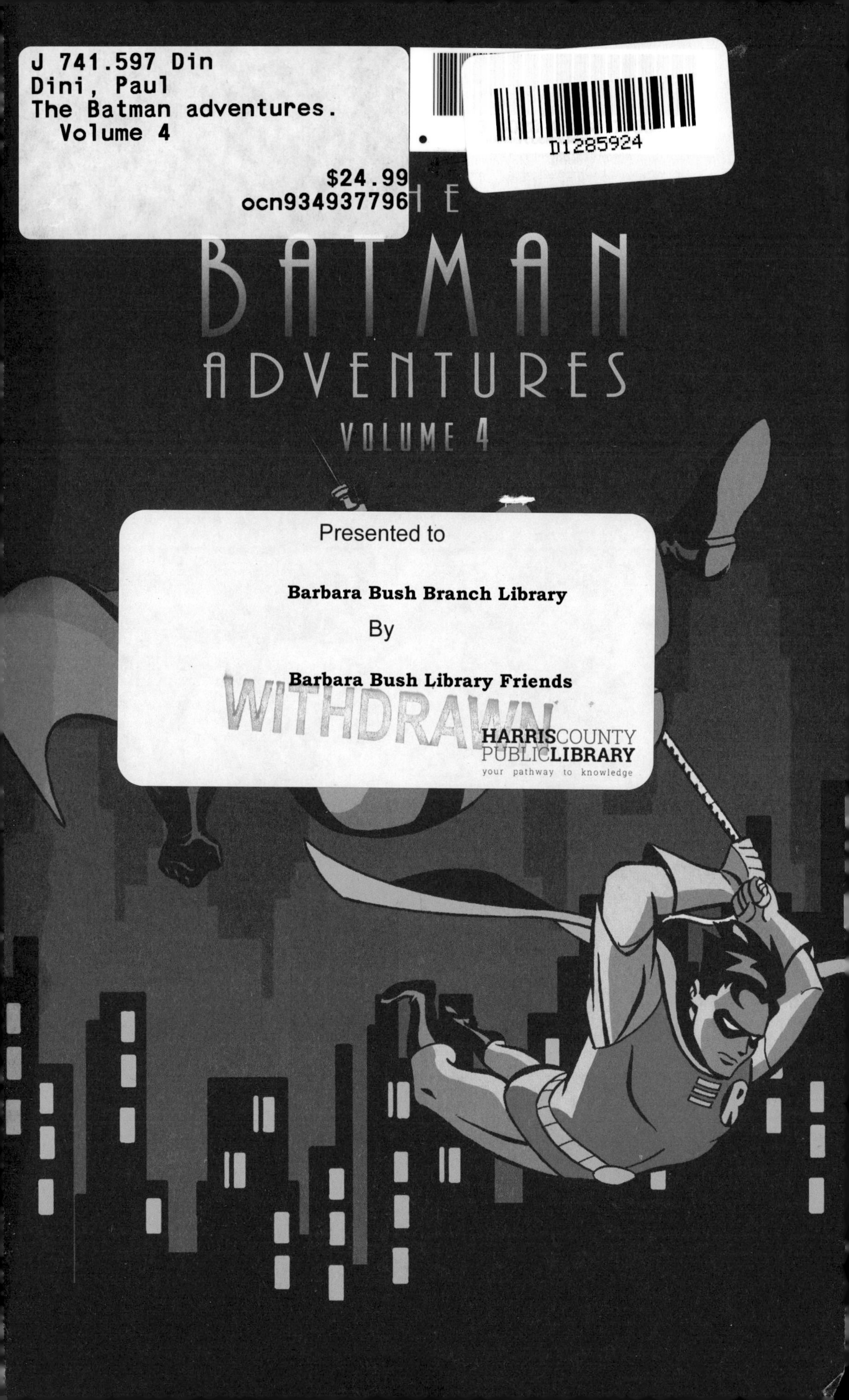
THE
BATMAN
ADVENTURES
VOLUME 4

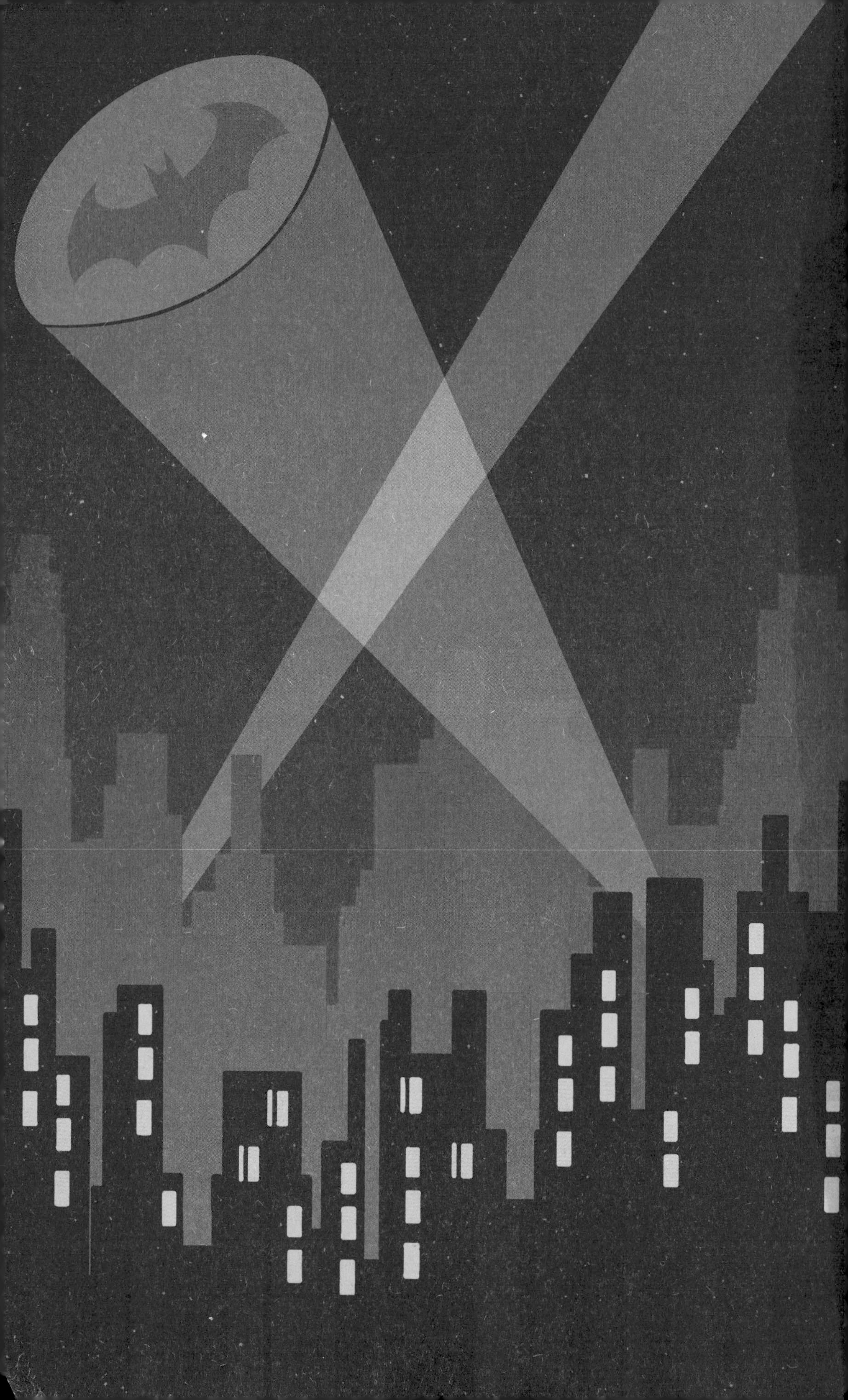

THE BATMAN ADVENTURES

VOLUME 4

PAUL DINI
BRUCE TIMM
KELLEY PUCKETT
ALAN GRANT
DAN RASPLER
TY TEMPLETON
RONNIE DEL CARMEN
writers

BRUCE TIMM
MIKE PAROBECK
RICK BURCHETT
DEV MADAN
GLEN MURAKAMI
DAN RIBA
RONNIE DEL CARMEN
KEVIN ALTIERI
BUTCH LUKIC
artists

RICK TAYLOR
GLEN MURAKAMI
BRUCE TIMM
colorists

RICHARD STARKINGS/COMICRAFT
TIM HARKINS
letterer

BRUCE TIMM
collection cover artist

BATMAN created by
BOB KANE with BILL FINGER

Scott Peterson   Editor – Original Series
Darren Vincenzo   Assistant Editor – Original Series
Jeb Woodard   Group Editor – Collected Editions
Steve Cook   Design Director – Books
Sarabeth Kett   Publication Design

Bob Harras   Senior VP – Editor-in-Chief, DC Comics

Diane Nelson   President
Dan DiDio and Jim Lee   Co-Publishers
Geoff Johns   Chief Creative Officer
Amit Desai   Senior VP – Marketing & Global Franchise Management
Nairi Gardiner   Senior VP – Finance
Sam Ades   VP – Digital Marketing
Bobbie Chase   VP – Talent Development
Mark Chiarello   Senior VP – Art, Design & Collected Editions
John Cunningham   VP – Content Strategy
Anne DePies   VP – Strategy Planning & Reporting
Don Falletti   VP – Manufacturing Operations
Lawrence Ganem   VP – Editorial Administration & Talent Relations
Alison Gill   Senior VP – Manufacturing & Operations
Hank Kanalz   Senior VP – Editorial Strategy & Administration
Jay Kogan   VP – Legal Affairs
Derek Maddalena   Senior VP – Sales & Business Development
Jack Mahan   VP – Business Affairs
Dan Miron   VP – Sales Planning & Trade Development
Nick Napolitano   VP – Manufacturing Administration
Carol Roeder   VP – Marketing
Eddie Scannell   VP – Mass Account & Digital Sales
Courtney Simmons   Senior VP – Publicity & Communications
Jim (Ski) Sokolowski   VP – Comic Book Specialty & Newsstand Sales
Sandy Yi   Senior VP – Global Franchise Management

THE BATMAN ADVENTURES VOLUME 4

Originally published in single magazine form in THE BATMAN ADVENTURES 28-36,
THE BATMAN ADVENTURES HOLIDAY SPECIAL 1, THE BATMAN ADVENTURES ANNUAL
2. Copyright © 1995 DC Comics. All Rights Reserved. All characters, their distinctive
likenesses and related elements featured in this publication are trademarks of DC Comics.
The stories, characters and incidents featured in this publication are entirely fictional.
DC Comics does not read or accept unsolicited ideas, stories or artwork.

DC Comics, 2900 West Alameda Ave., Burbank, CA 91505
Printed by Transcontinental Interglobe, Beauceville, QC, Canada. 3/4/16 First Printing.
ISBN: 978-1-4012-6061-3

Library of Congress Cataloging-in-Publication Data is Available.

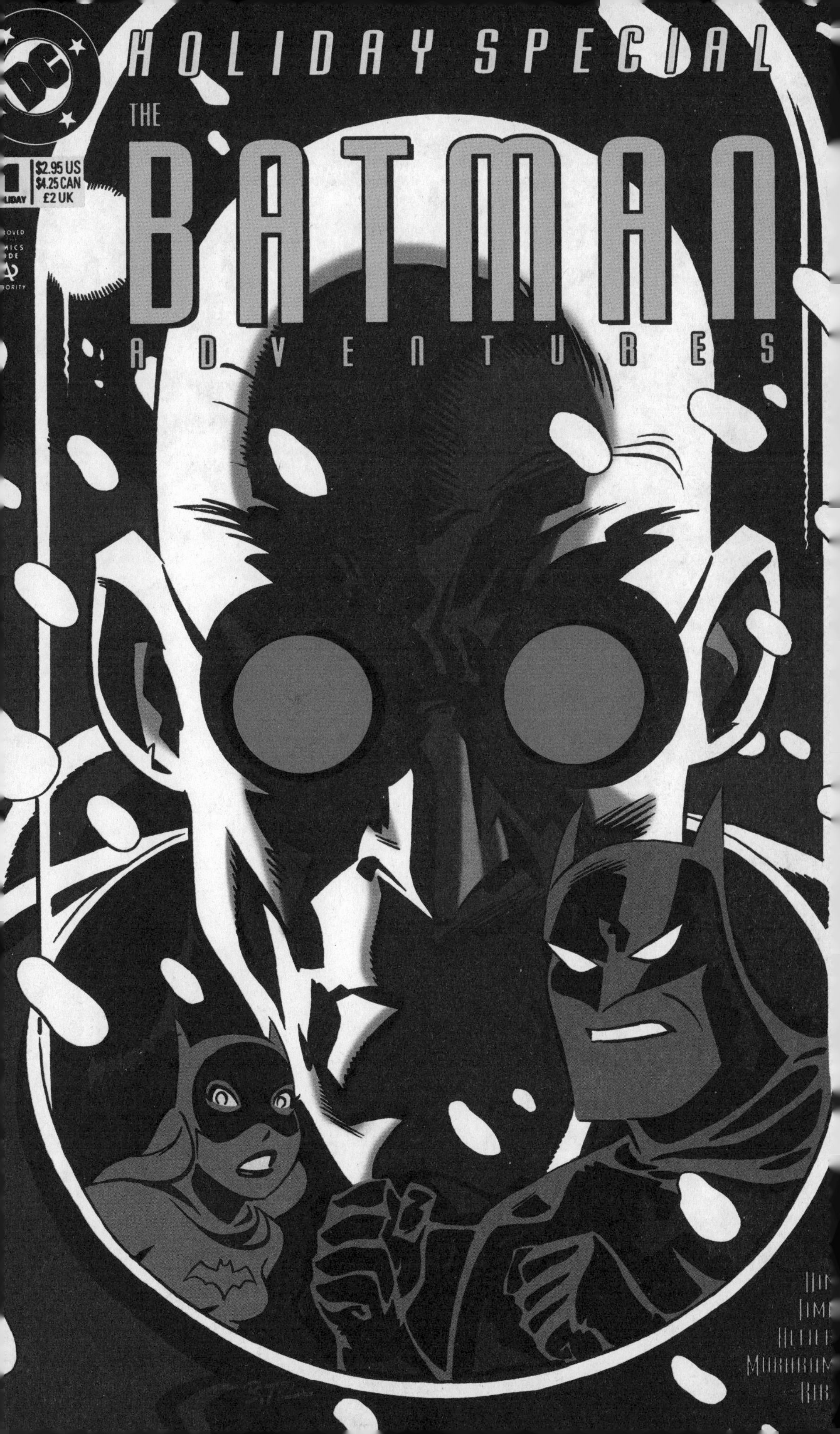
HOLIDAY SPECIAL
THE
BATMAN
ADVENTURES
1
$2.95 US
$4.25 CAN
£2 UK

INTRO

written by PAUL DINI
art by DAN RIBA
colored by BRUCE TIMM
lettered by RICHARD STARKINGS/COMICRAFT

"JOLLY OL' ST. NICHOLAS"

written by PAUL DINI & BRUCE TIMM
art and color by BRUCE TIMM
lettered by RICHARD STARKINGS/COMICRAFT

"THE HARLEY AND THE IVY"

story by PAUL DINI & RONNIE DEL CARMEN
written by PAUL DINI
art and color by RONNIE DEL CARMEN
lettered by RICHARD STARKINGS/COMICRAFT

"WHITE CHRISTMAS"

written by PAUL DINI
art and color by GLEN MURAKAMI
lettered by RICHARD STARKINGS/COMICRAFT

"WHAT ARE YOU DOING NEW YEAR'S EVE?"

story by PAUL DINI & BRUCE TIMM
written by PAUL DINI
art by KEVIN ALTIERI & BUTCH LUKIC
colored by GLEN MURAKAMI
lettered by RICHARD STARKINGS/COMICRAFT

"SHOULD OLD ACQUAINTANCE BE FORGOT"

written by PAUL DINI
art by DAN RIBA
colored by BRUCE TIMM
lettered by RICHARD STARKINGS/COMICRAFT

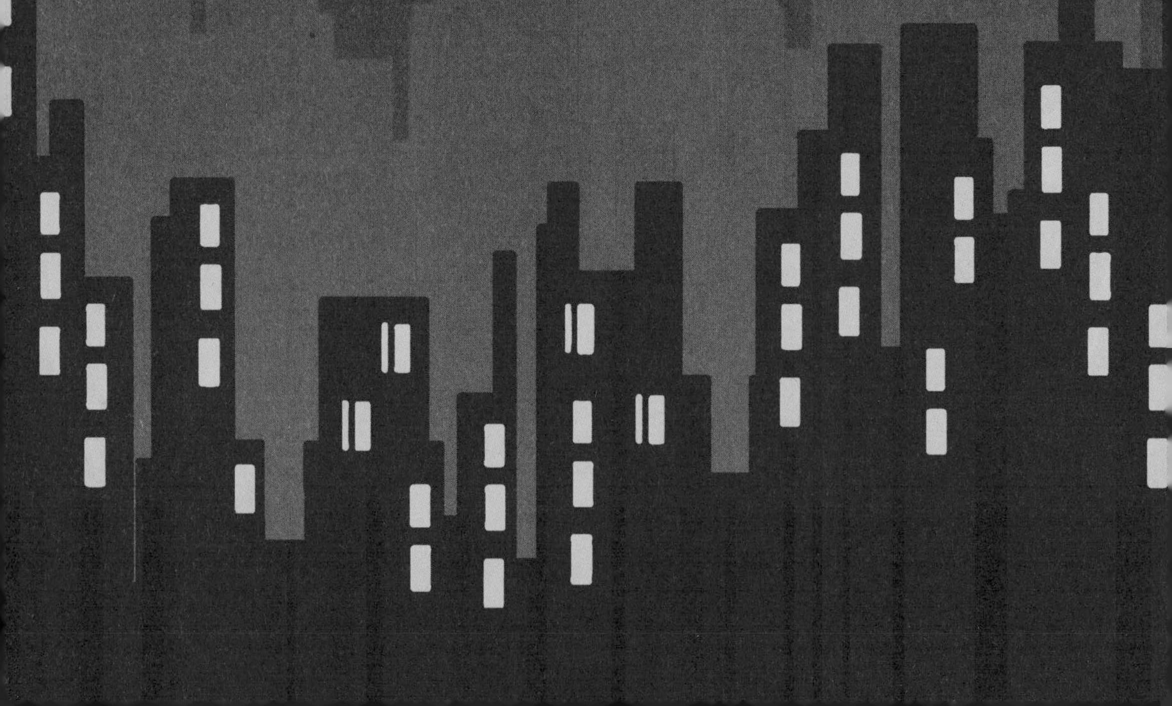

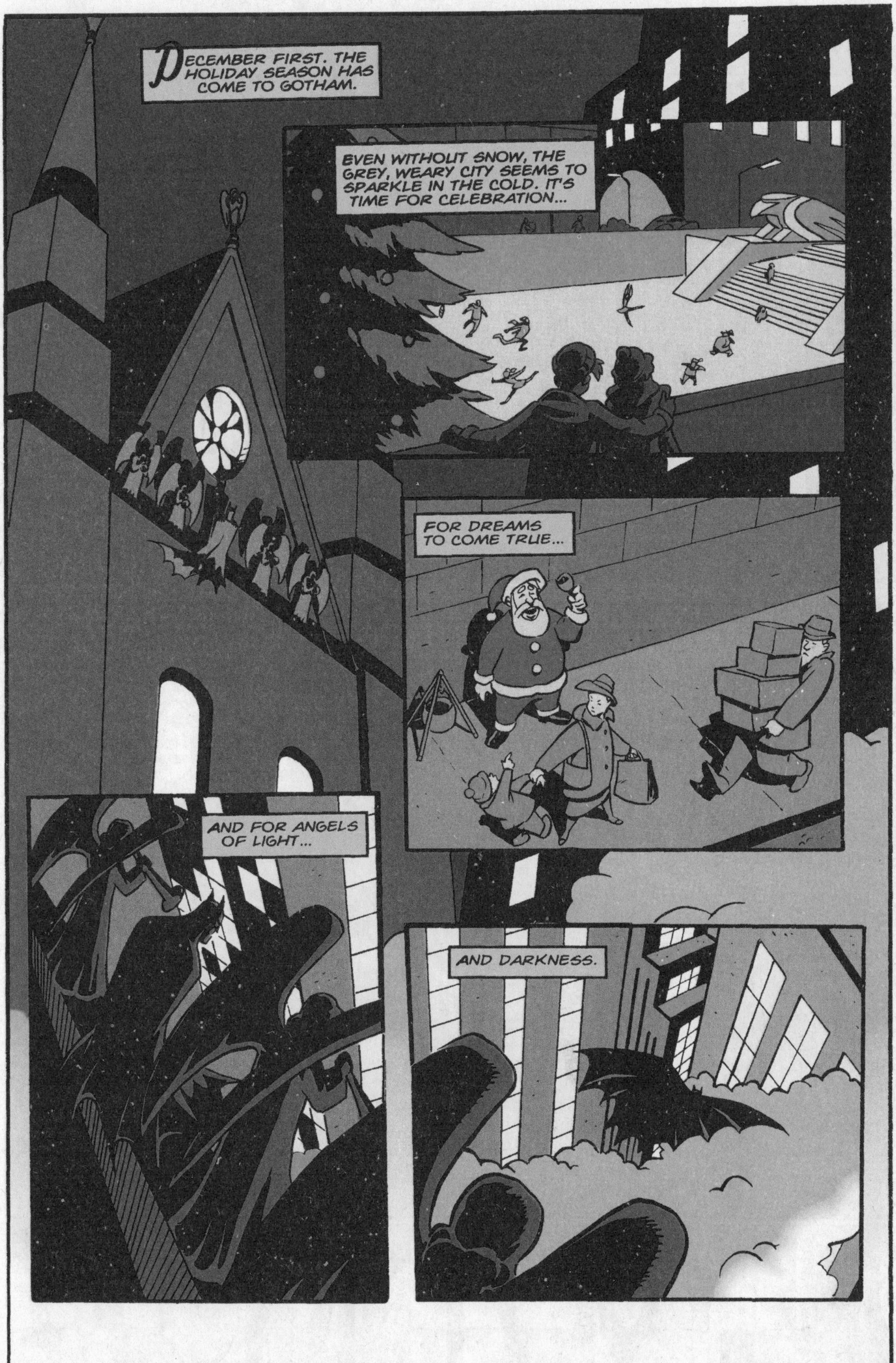
DECEMBER FIRST. THE HOLIDAY SEASON HAS COME TO GOTHAM.
EVEN WITHOUT SNOW, THE GREY, WEARY CITY SEEMS TO SPARKLE IN THE COLD. IT'S TIME FOR CELEBRATION...
FOR DREAMS TO COME TRUE...
AND FOR ANGELS OF LIGHT...
AND DARKNESS.

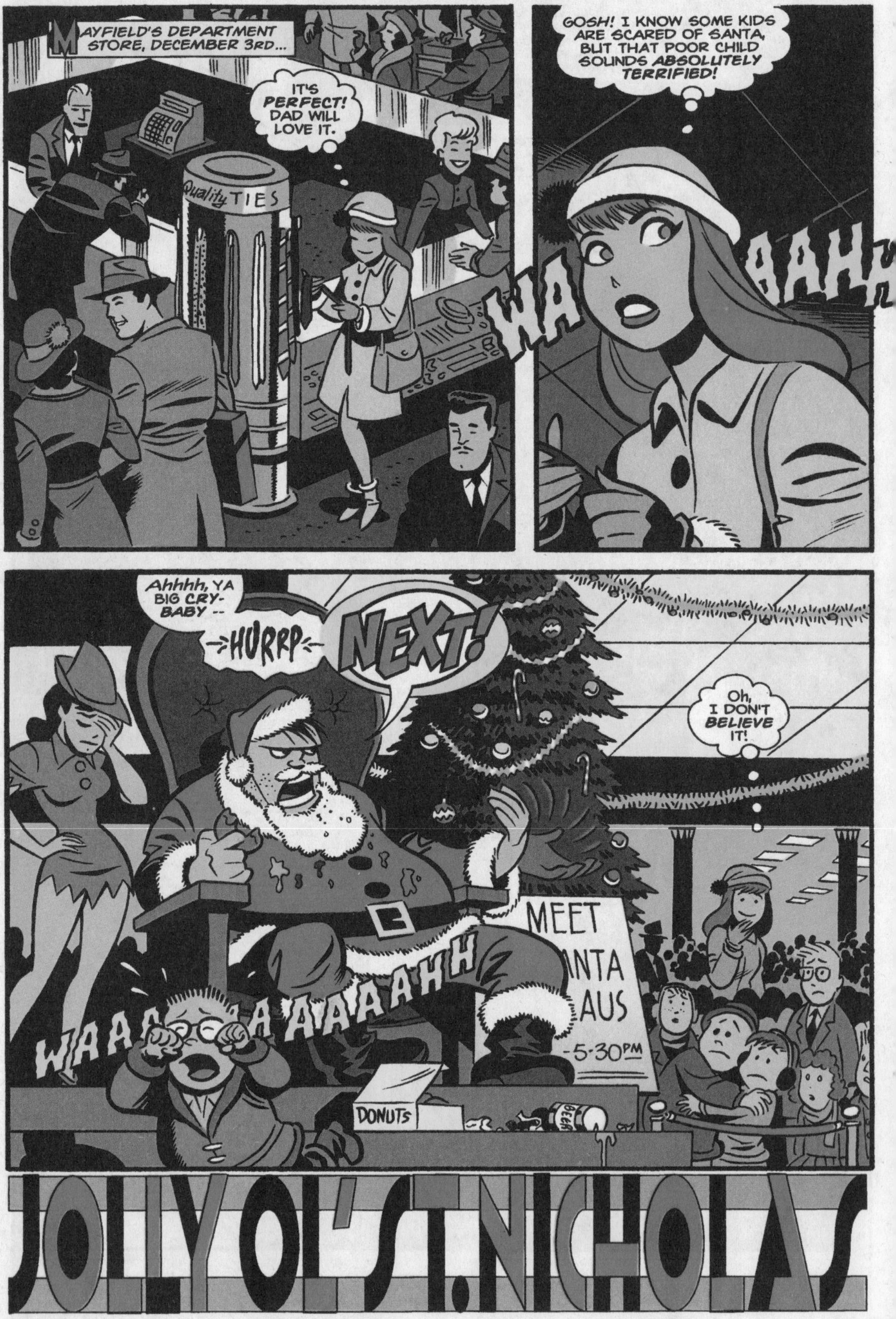
MAYFIELD'S DEPARTMENT STORE, DECEMBER 3RD...
IT'S PERFECT! DAD WILL LOVE IT.
QUALITY TIES
WAAAAAHH
GOSH! I KNOW SOME KIDS ARE SCARED OF SANTA, BUT THAT POOR CHILD SOUNDS ABSOLUTELY TERRIFIED!
Ahhhh, YA BIG CRY-BABY --
HURRP
NEXT!
Oh, I DON'T BELIEVE IT!
WAAAAAAAAAHH
MEET SANTA CLAUS -5:30PM
DONUTS

JOLLY OL' ST. NICHOLAS

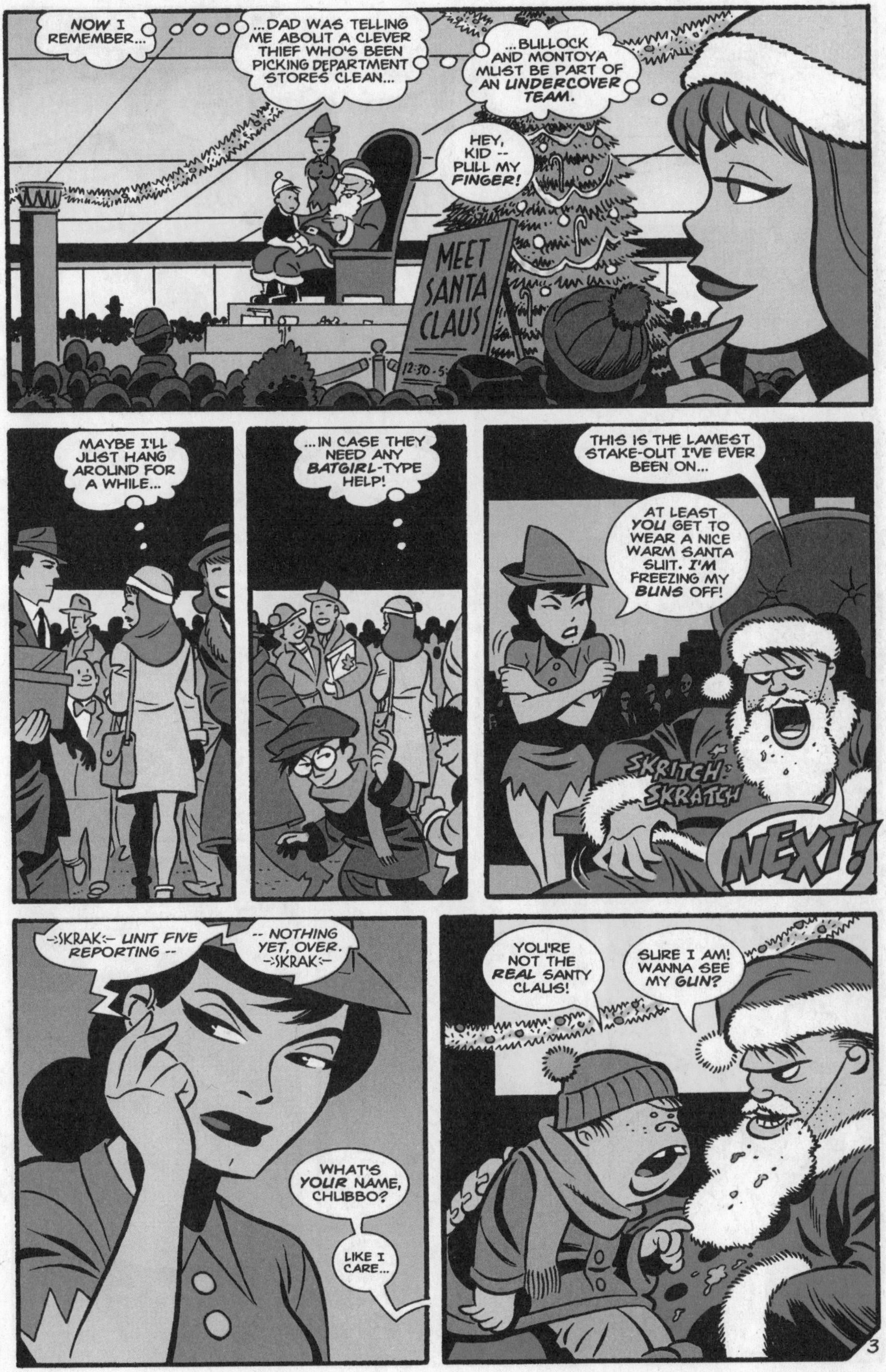
NOW I REMEMBER...
...DAD WAS TELLING ME ABOUT A CLEVER THIEF WHO'S BEEN PICKING DEPARTMENT STORES CLEAN...
...BULLOCK AND MONTOYA MUST BE PART OF AN UNDERCOVER TEAM.
HEY, KID -- PULL MY FINGER!
MEET SANTA CLAUS
12:30-5
MAYBE I'LL JUST HANG AROUND FOR A WHILE...
...IN CASE THEY NEED ANY BATGIRL-TYPE HELP!
THIS IS THE LAMEST STAKE-OUT I'VE EVER BEEN ON...
AT LEAST YOU GET TO WEAR A NICE WARM SANTA SUIT. I'M FREEZING MY BUNS OFF!
SKRITCH SKRATCH
NEXT!
-SKRAK- UNIT FIVE REPORTING --
-- NOTHING YET, OVER. -SKRAK-
WHAT'S YOUR NAME, CHUBBO?
LIKE I CARE...
YOU'RE NOT THE REAL SANTY CLAUS!
SURE I AM! WANNA SEE MY GUN?

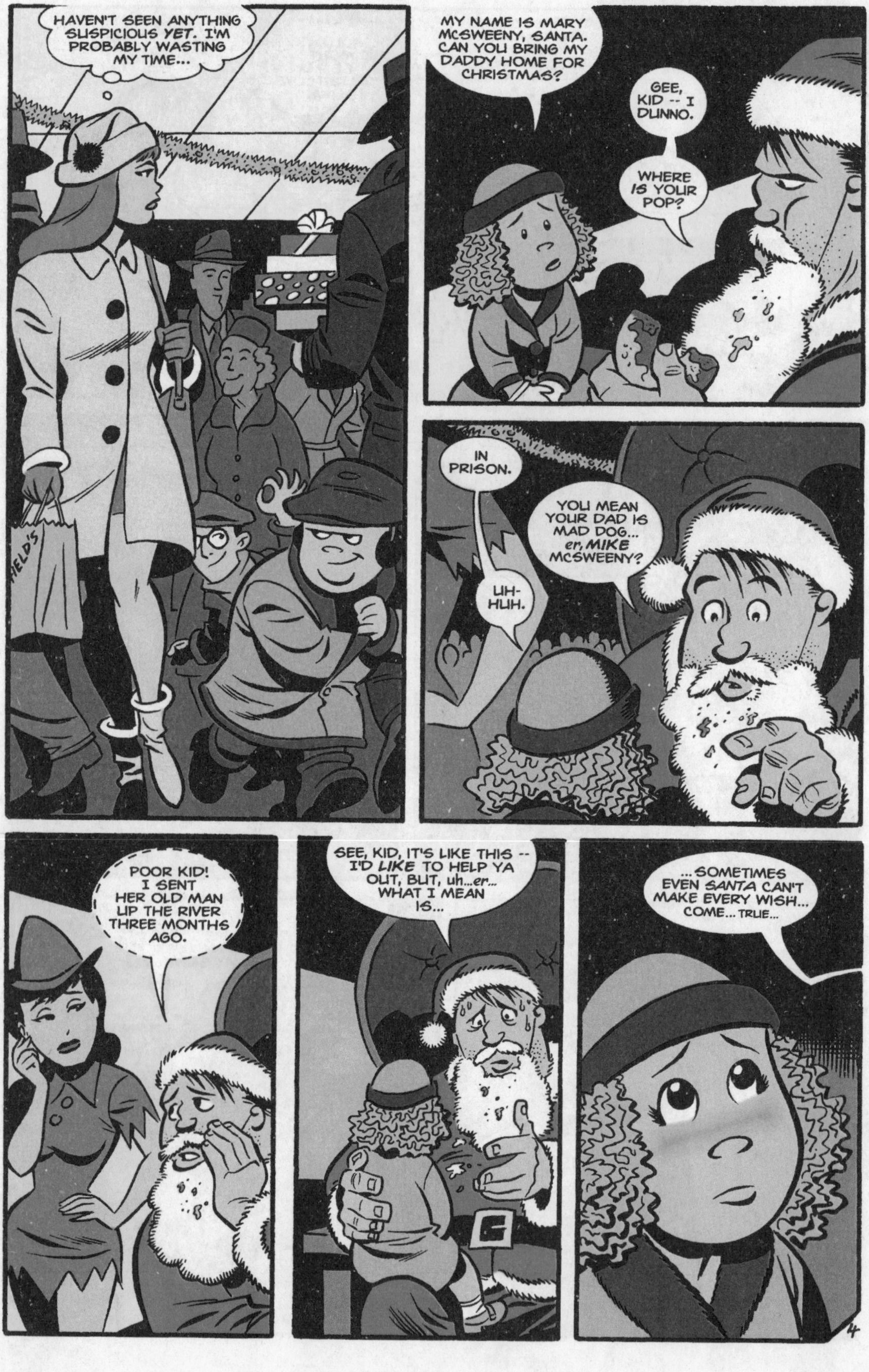
HAVEN'T SEEN ANYTHING SUSPICIOUS *YET*. I'M PROBABLY WASTING MY TIME...
MY NAME IS MARY MCSWEENY, SANTA. CAN YOU BRING MY DADDY HOME FOR CHRISTMAS?
GEE, KID -- I DUNNO.
WHERE *IS* YOUR POP?
IN PRISON.
YOU MEAN YOUR DAD IS MAD DOG... *er, MIKE* MCSWEENY?
UH-HUH.
POOR KID! I SENT HER OLD MAN UP THE RIVER THREE MONTHS AGO.
SEE, KID, IT'S LIKE THIS -- I'D *LIKE* TO HELP YA OUT, BUT, uh...er... WHAT I MEAN IS...
...SOMETIMES EVEN *SANTA* CAN'T MAKE EVERY WISH... COME... TRUE...

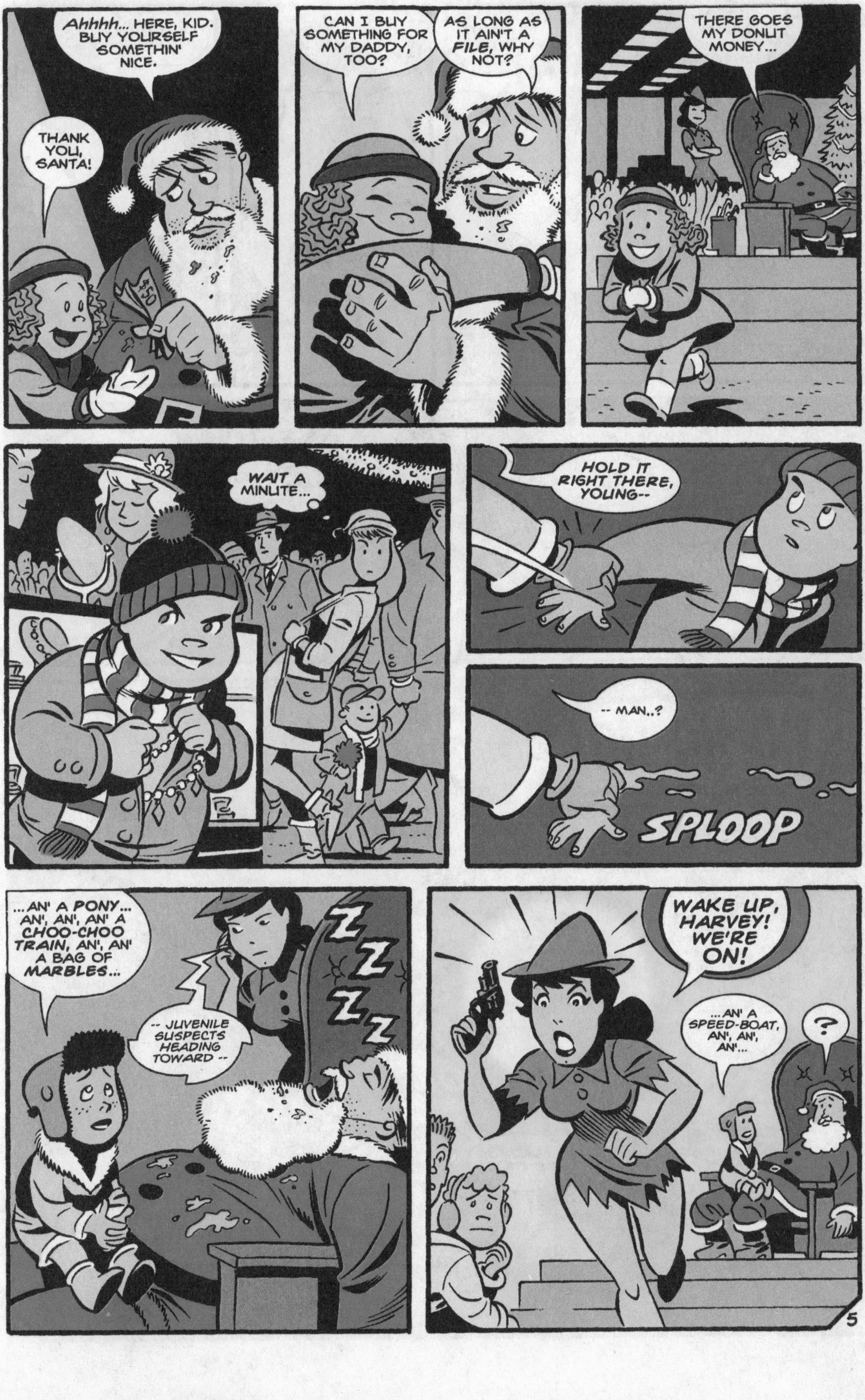
Ahhhh... HERE, KID. BUY YOURSELF SOMETHIN' NICE.
THANK YOU, SANTA!
CAN I BUY SOMETHING FOR MY DADDY, TOO?
AS LONG AS IT AIN'T A FILE, WHY NOT?
THERE GOES MY DONUT MONEY...
WAIT A MINUTE...
HOLD IT RIGHT THERE, YOUNG--
-- MAN..?
SPLOOP
...AN' A PONY... AN', AN', AN' A CHOO-CHOO TRAIN, AN', AN' A BAG OF MARBLES...
-- JUVENILE SUSPECTS HEADING TOWARD --
WAKE UP, HARVEY! WE'RE ON!
...AN' A SPEED-BOAT, AN', AN', AN'...
?

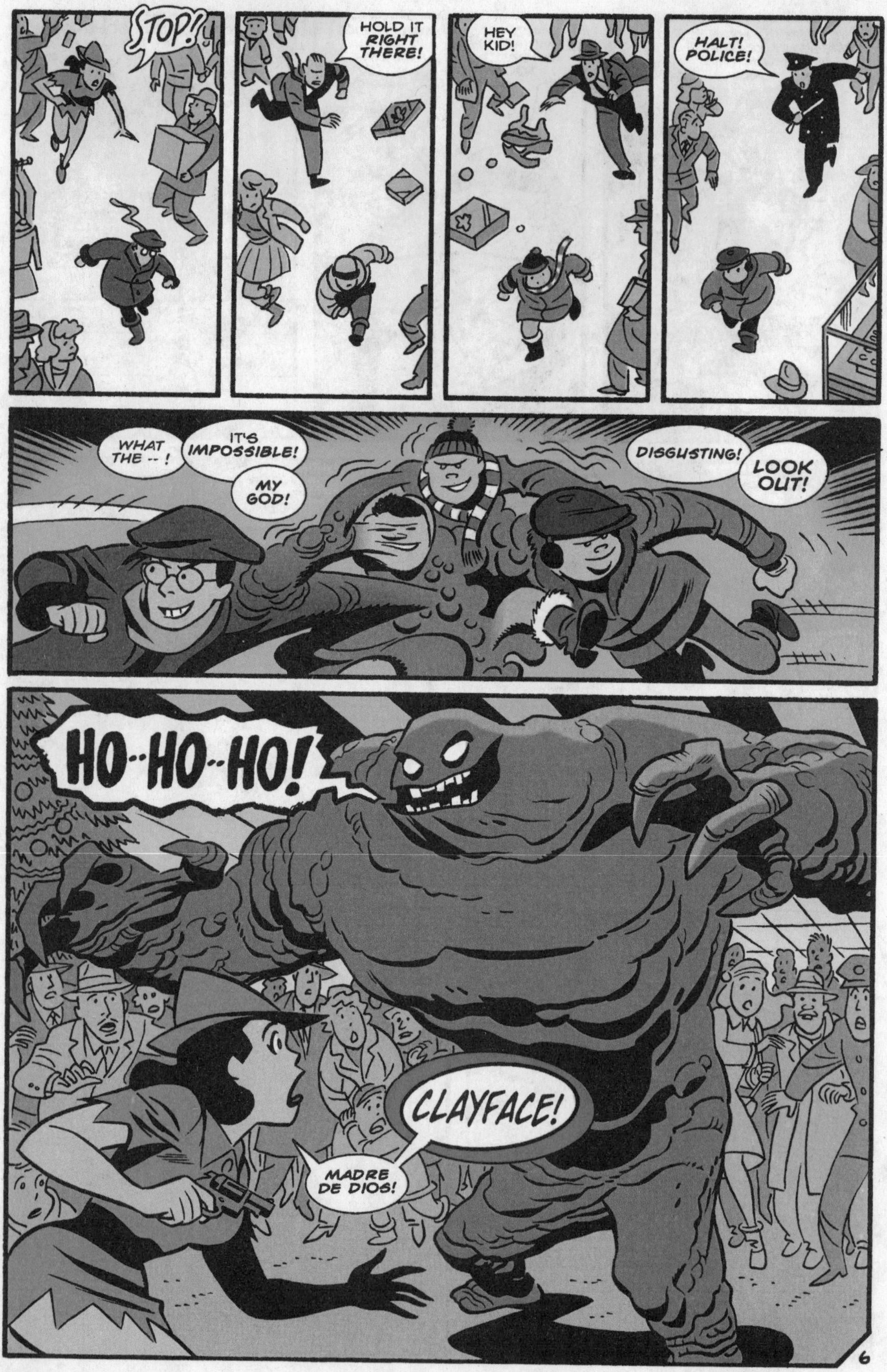
STOP?!
HOLD IT RIGHT THERE!
HEY KID!
HALT! POLICE!
WHAT THE -- !
IT'S IMPOSSIBLE!
MY GOD!
DISGUSTING!
LOOK OUT!
HO-HO-HO!
CLAYFACE!
MADRE DE DIOS!

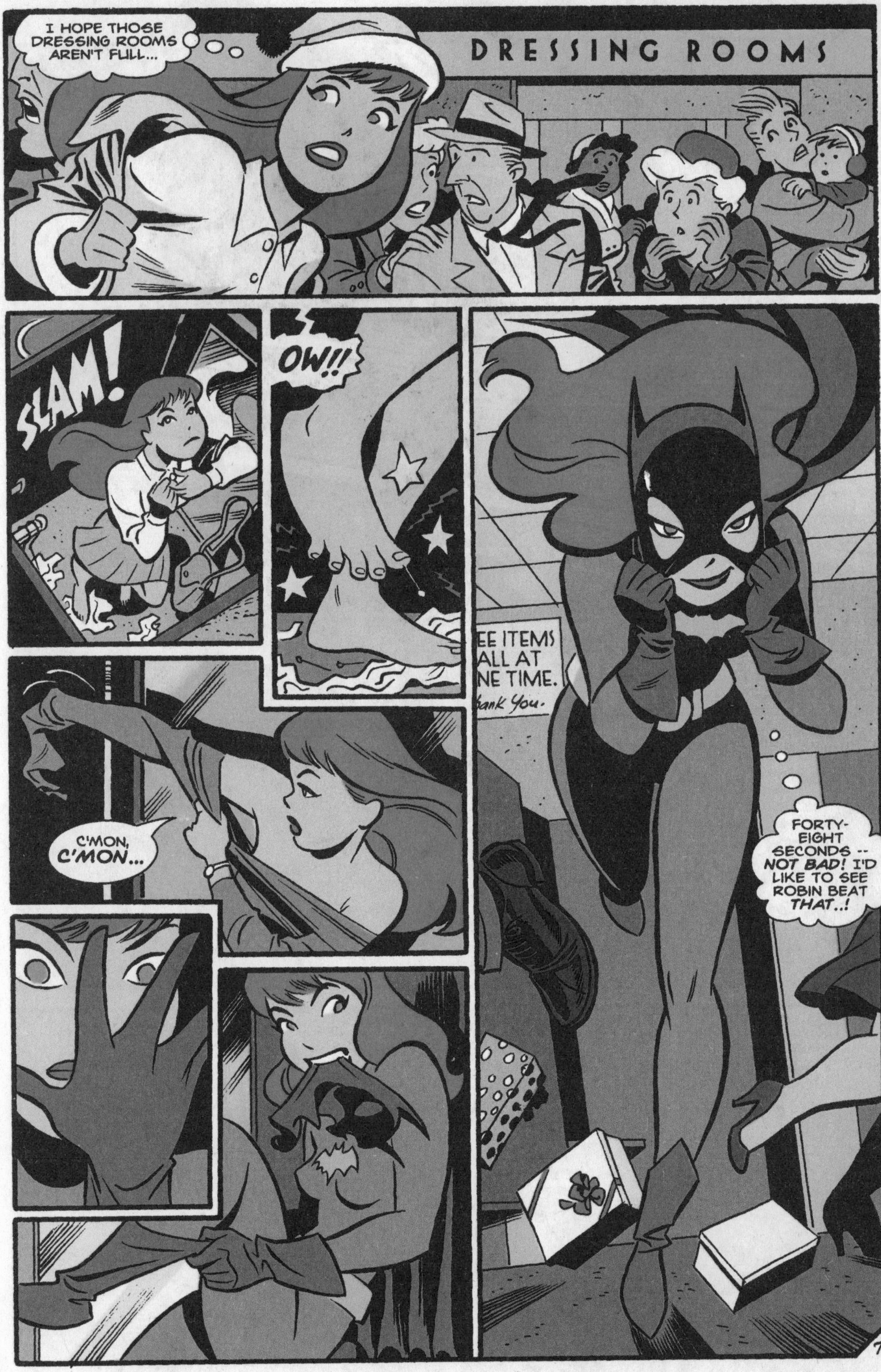
I HOPE THOSE DRESSING ROOMS AREN'T FULL...
DRESSING ROOMS
SLAM!
OW!!
C'MON, C'MON...
EE ITEMS
ALL AT
NE TIME.
hank You.
FORTY-EIGHT SECONDS -- NOT BAD! I'D LIKE TO SEE ROBIN BEAT THAT..!

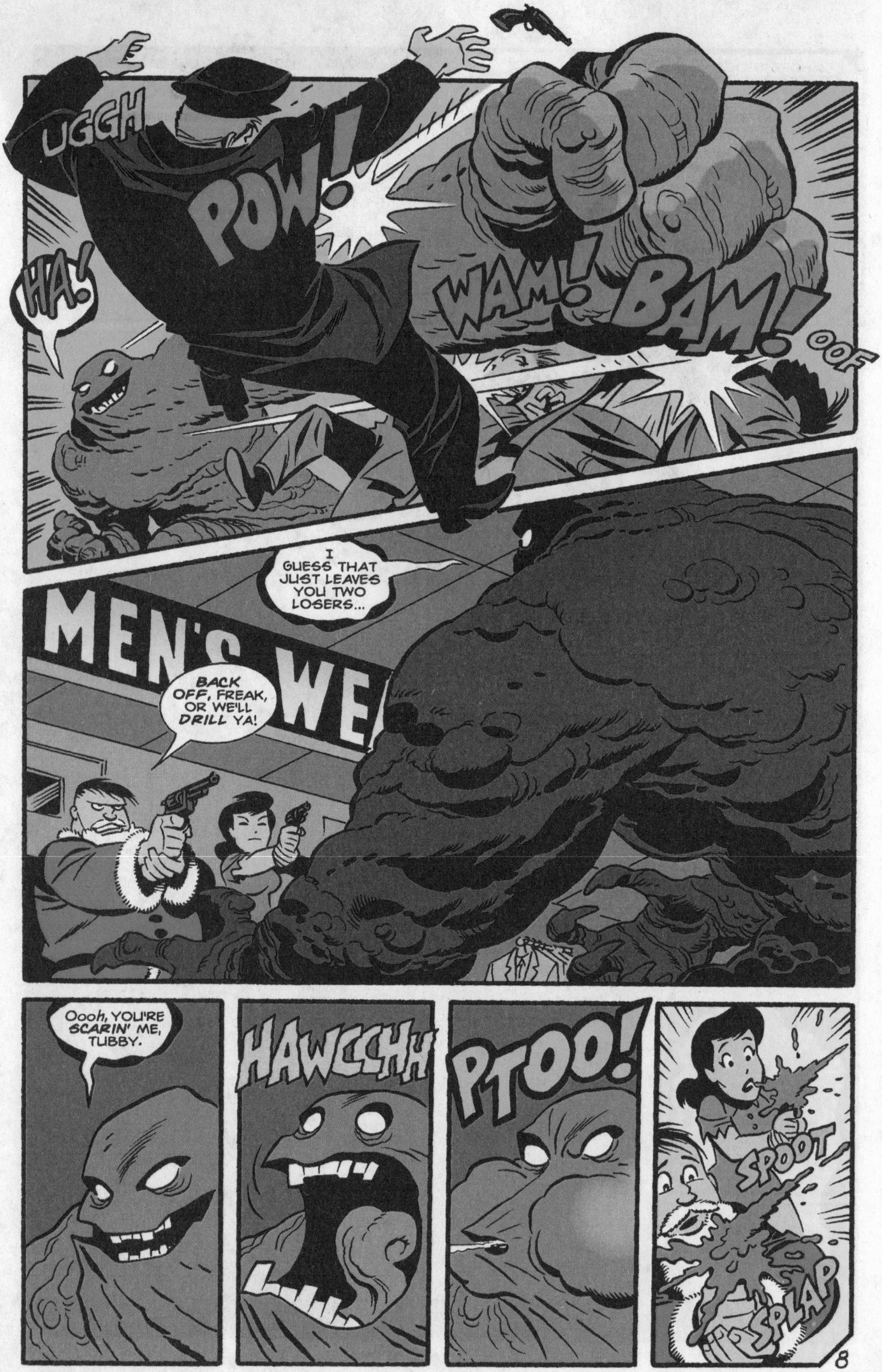

UGGH
POW!
HA!
WAM! BAM!
OOF
I GUESS THAT JUST LEAVES YOU TWO LOSERS...
MEN'S WE
BACK OFF, FREAK, OR WE'LL DRILL YA!
Oooh, YOU'RE SCARIN' ME, TUBBY.
HAWCCHH
PTOO!
!
SPOOT
SPLAP

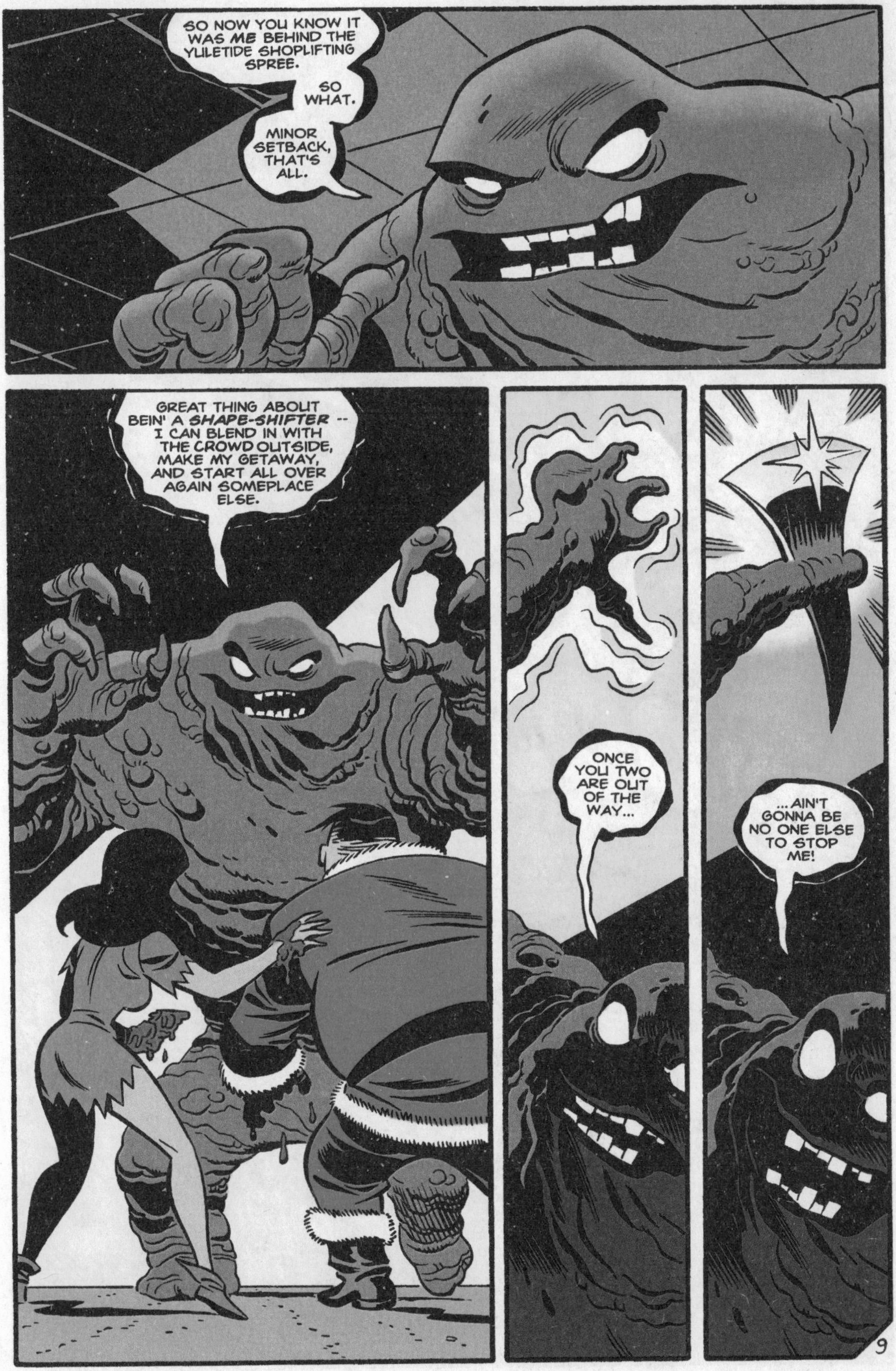
SO NOW YOU KNOW IT WAS ME BEHIND THE YULETIDE SHOPLIFTING SPREE.
SO WHAT.
MINOR SETBACK, THAT'S ALL.
GREAT THING ABOUT BEIN' A SHAPE-SHIFTER -- I CAN BLEND IN WITH THE CROWD OUTSIDE, MAKE MY GETAWAY, AND START ALL OVER AGAIN SOMEPLACE ELSE.
ONCE YOU TWO ARE OUT OF THE WAY...
...AIN'T GONNA BE NO ONE ELSE TO STOP ME!

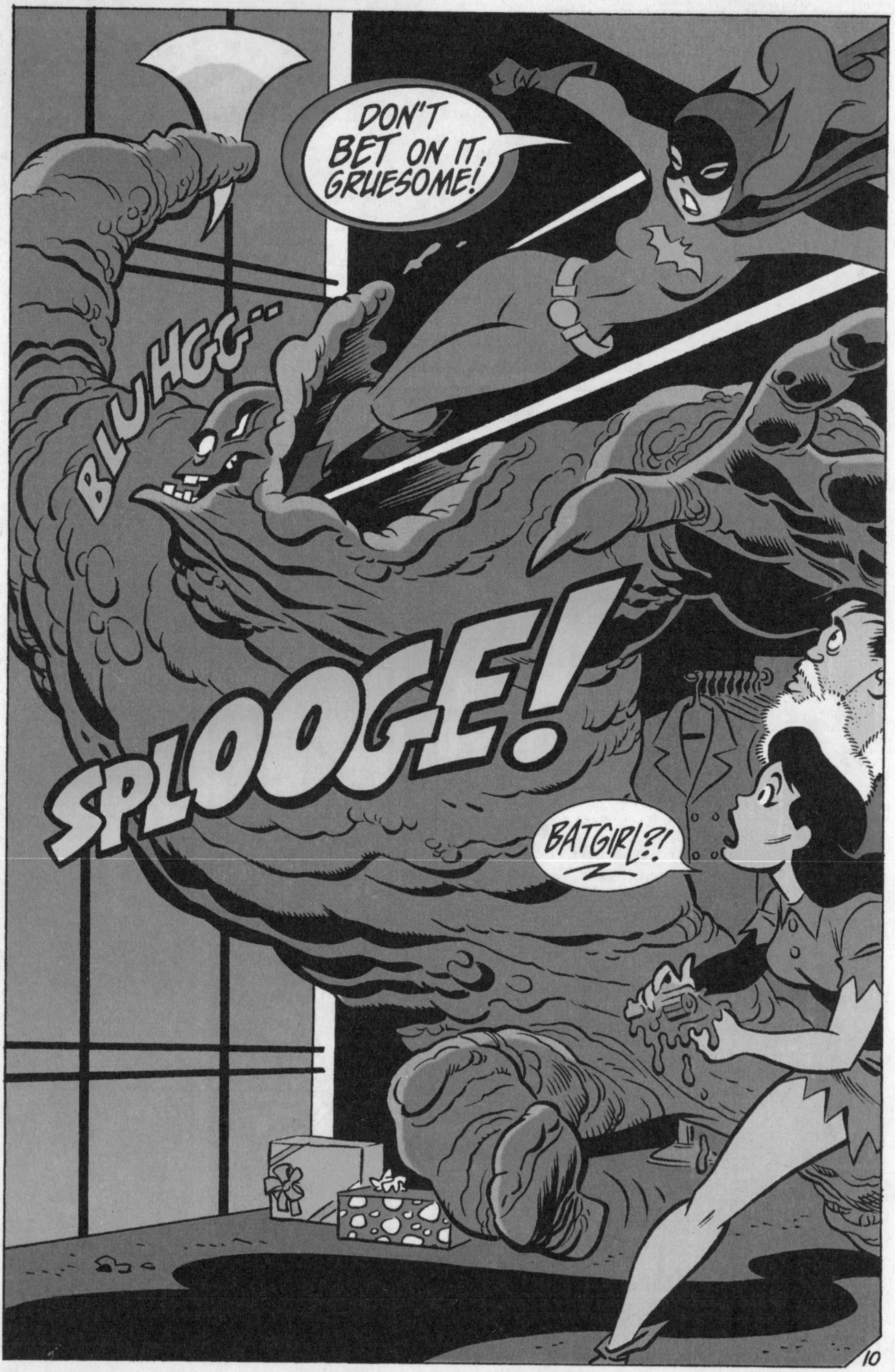
DON'T BET ON IT, GRUESOME!
BLUHGG--
SPLOOGE!
BATGIRL?!

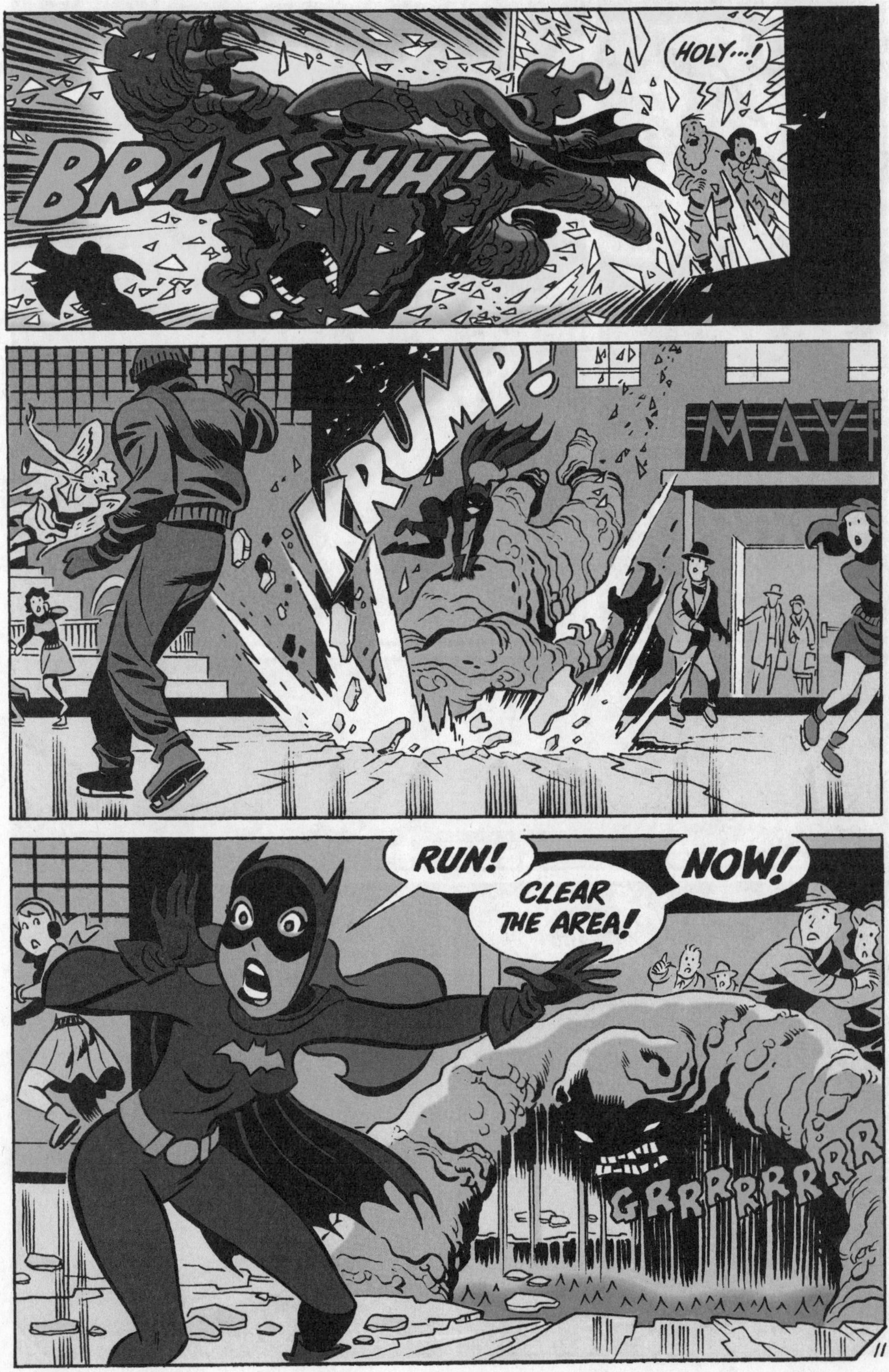

BRASSHH!
HOLY...!
KRUMP!
MAYF
RUN!
CLEAR THE AREA!
NOW!
GRRRRRRRR

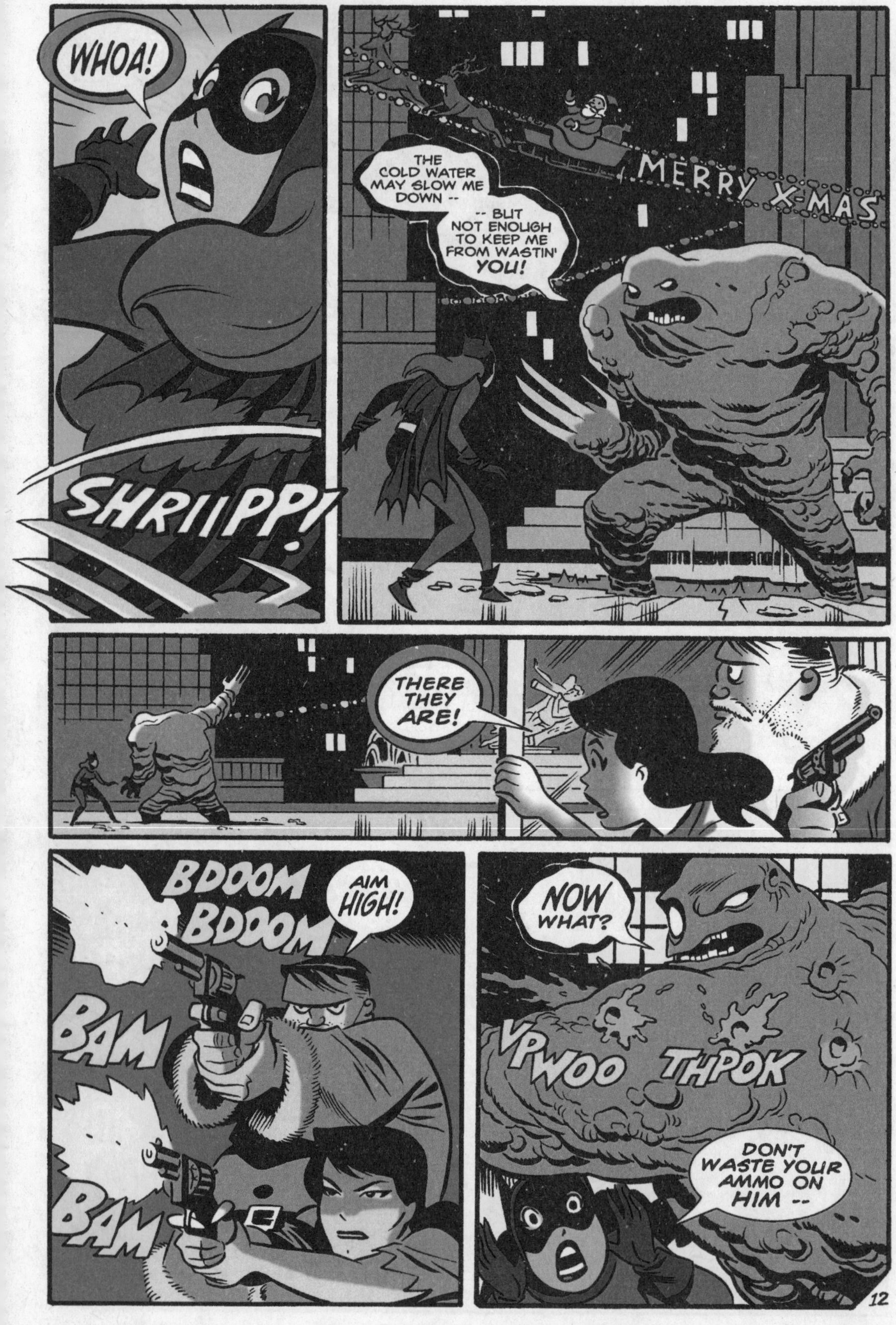
WHOA!
SHRIIPP!
MERRY X-MAS
THE COLD WATER MAY SLOW ME DOWN --
-- BUT NOT ENOUGH TO KEEP ME FROM WASTIN' YOU!
THERE THEY ARE!
BDOOM
BDOOM
AIM HIGH!
BAM
BAM
NOW WHAT?
VPWOO
THPOK
DON'T WASTE YOUR AMMO ON HIM --

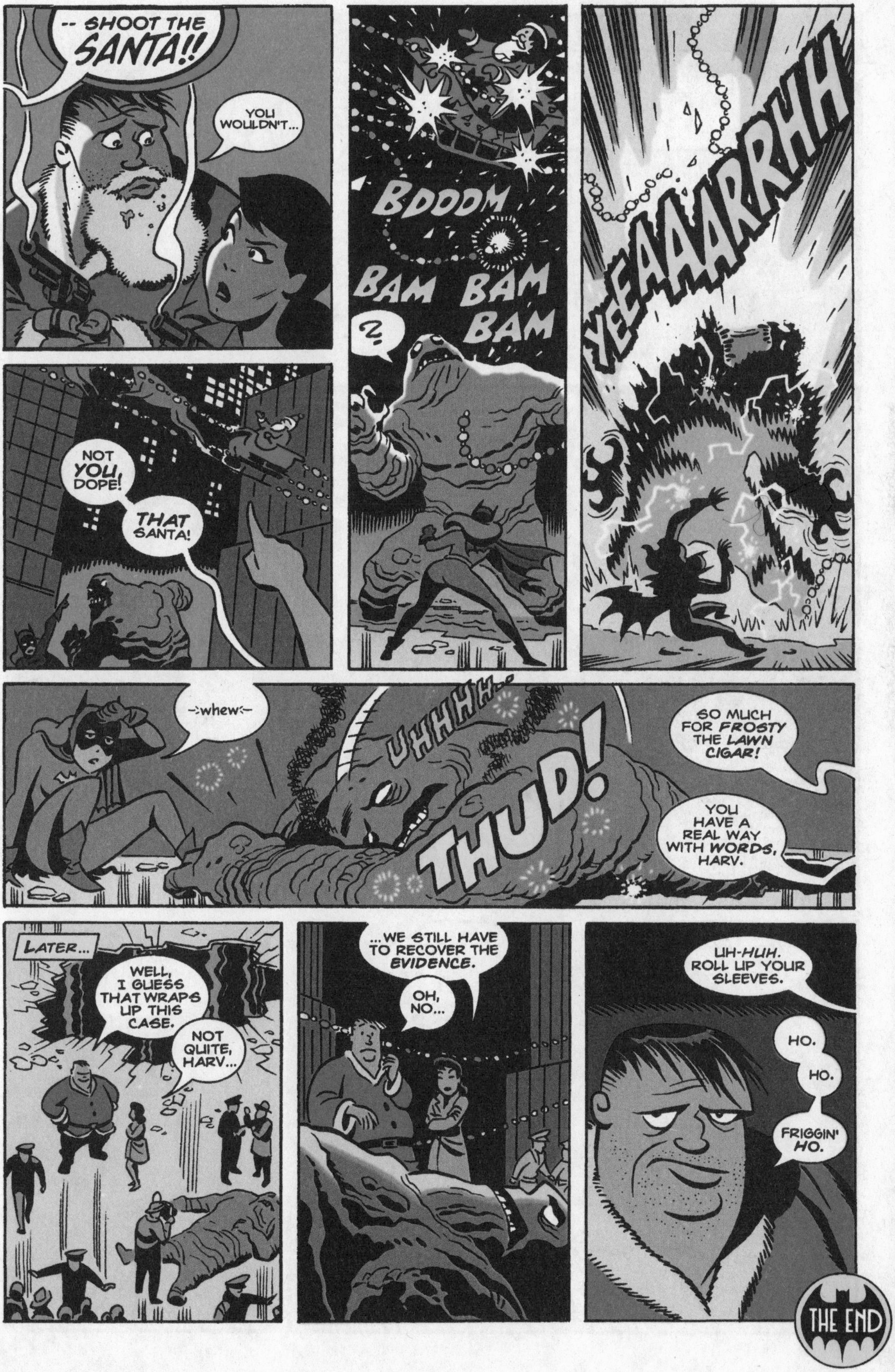
-- SHOOT THE SANTA!!
YOU WOULDN'T...
NOT YOU, DOPE!
THAT SANTA!
BDOOM
BAM BAM BAM
?
YEEAAARRHH
-whew-
UHHHH-
THUD!
SO MUCH FOR FROSTY THE LAWN CIGAR!
YOU HAVE A REAL WAY WITH WORDS, HARV.
LATER...
WELL, I GUESS THAT WRAPS UP THIS CASE.
NOT QUITE, HARV...
...WE STILL HAVE TO RECOVER THE EVIDENCE.
OH, NO...
UH-HUH. ROLL UP YOUR SLEEVES.
HO.
HO.
FRIGGIN' HO.
THE END

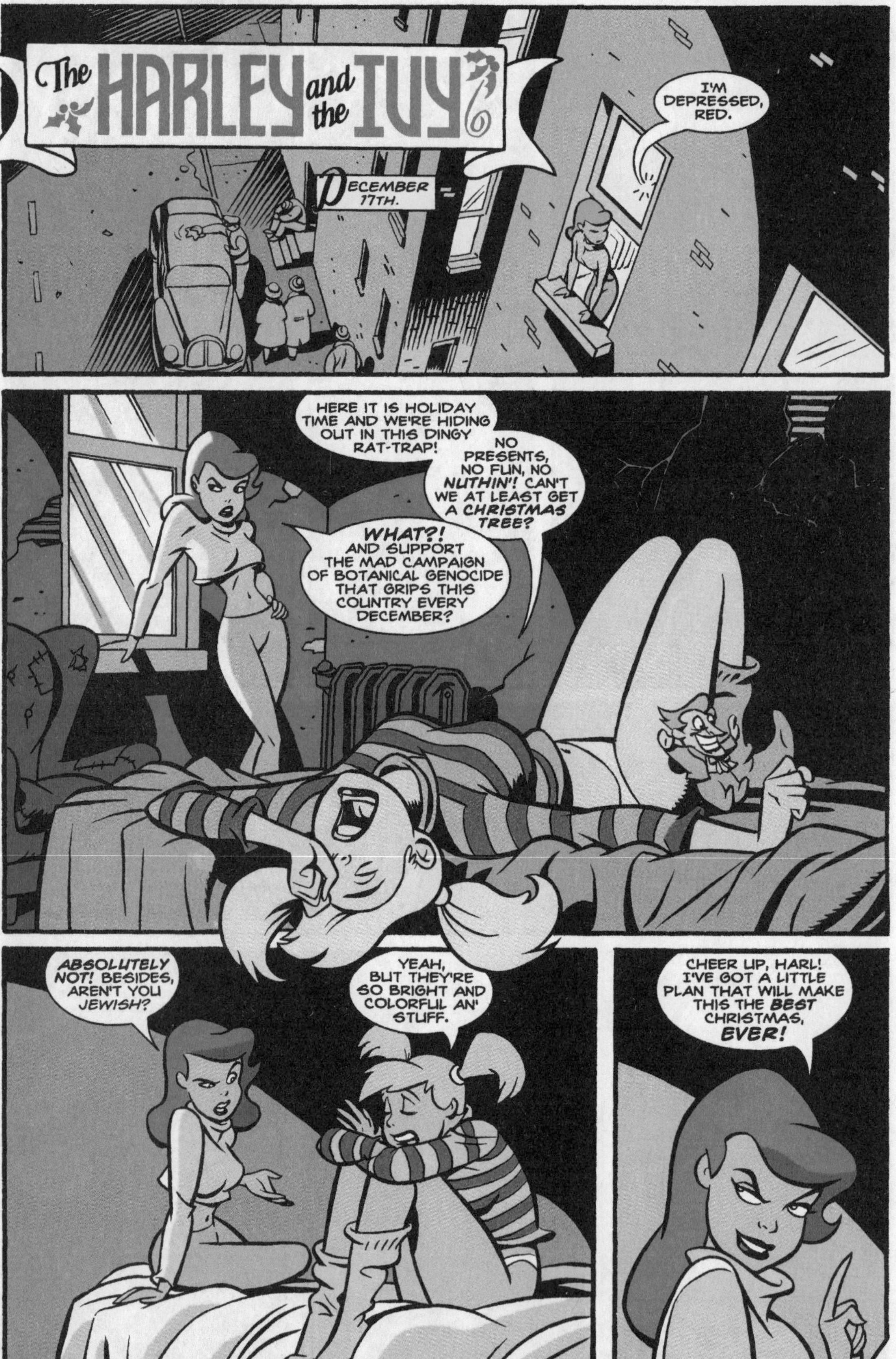
The HARLEY and the IVY
I'M DEPRESSED, RED.
DECEMBER 17TH.
HERE IT IS HOLIDAY TIME AND WE'RE HIDING OUT IN THIS DINGY RAT-TRAP!
NO PRESENTS, NO FUN, NO NUTHIN'! CAN'T WE AT LEAST GET A CHRISTMAS TREE?
WHAT?! AND SUPPORT THE MAD CAMPAIGN OF BOTANICAL GENOCIDE THAT GRIPS THIS COUNTRY EVERY DECEMBER?
ABSOLUTELY NOT! BESIDES, AREN'T YOU JEWISH?
YEAH, BUT THEY'RE SO BRIGHT AND COLORFUL AN' STUFF.
CHEER UP, HARL! I'VE GOT A LITTLE PLAN THAT WILL MAKE THIS THE BEST CHRISTMAS, EVER!

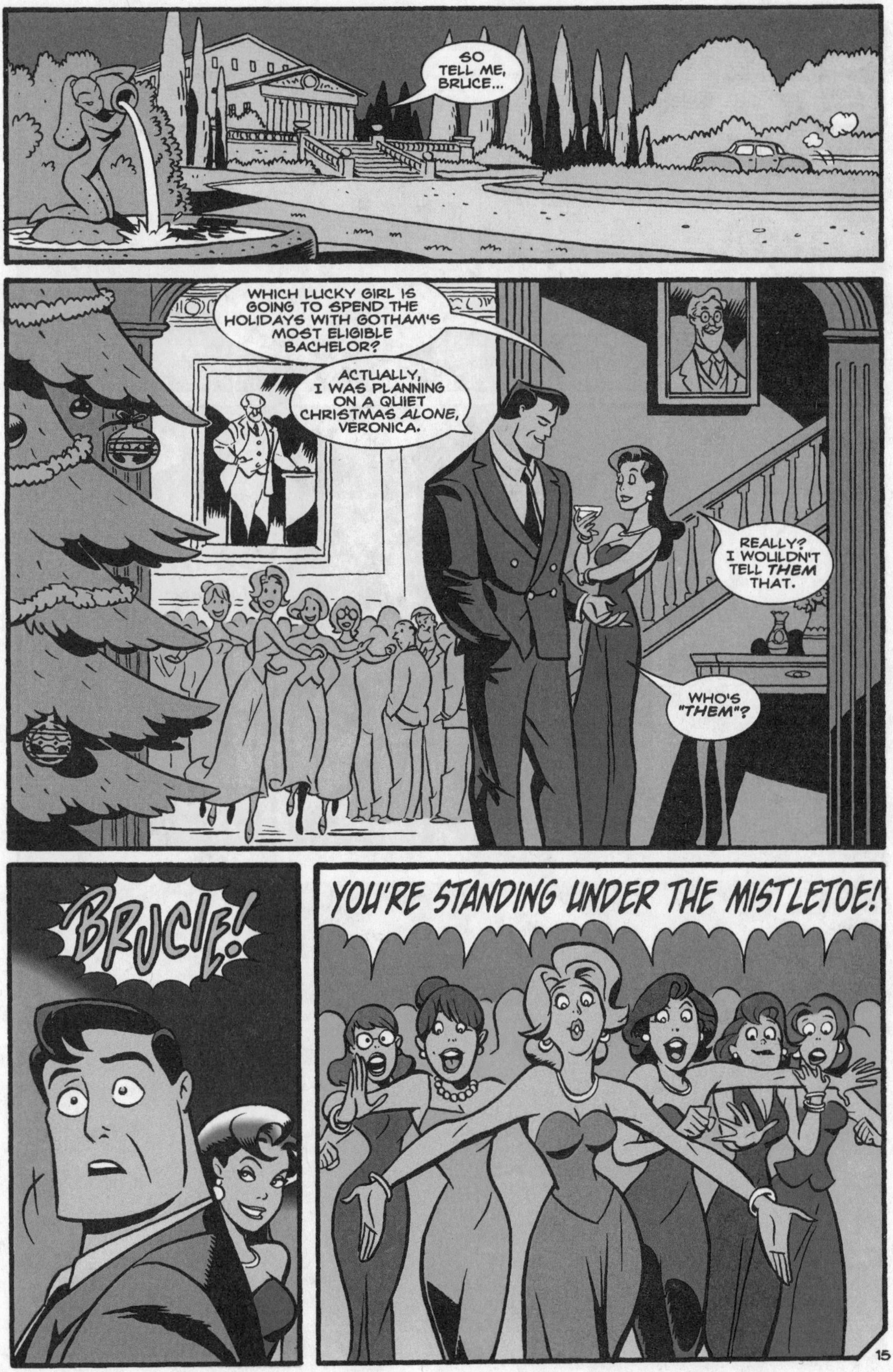
SO TELL ME, BRUCE...
WHICH LUCKY GIRL IS GOING TO SPEND THE HOLIDAYS WITH GOTHAM'S MOST ELIGIBLE BACHELOR?
ACTUALLY, I WAS PLANNING ON A QUIET CHRISTMAS *ALONE*, VERONICA.
REALLY? I WOULDN'T TELL *THEM* THAT.
WHO'S "*THEM*"?
BRUCIE!
YOU'RE STANDING UNDER THE MISTLETOE!

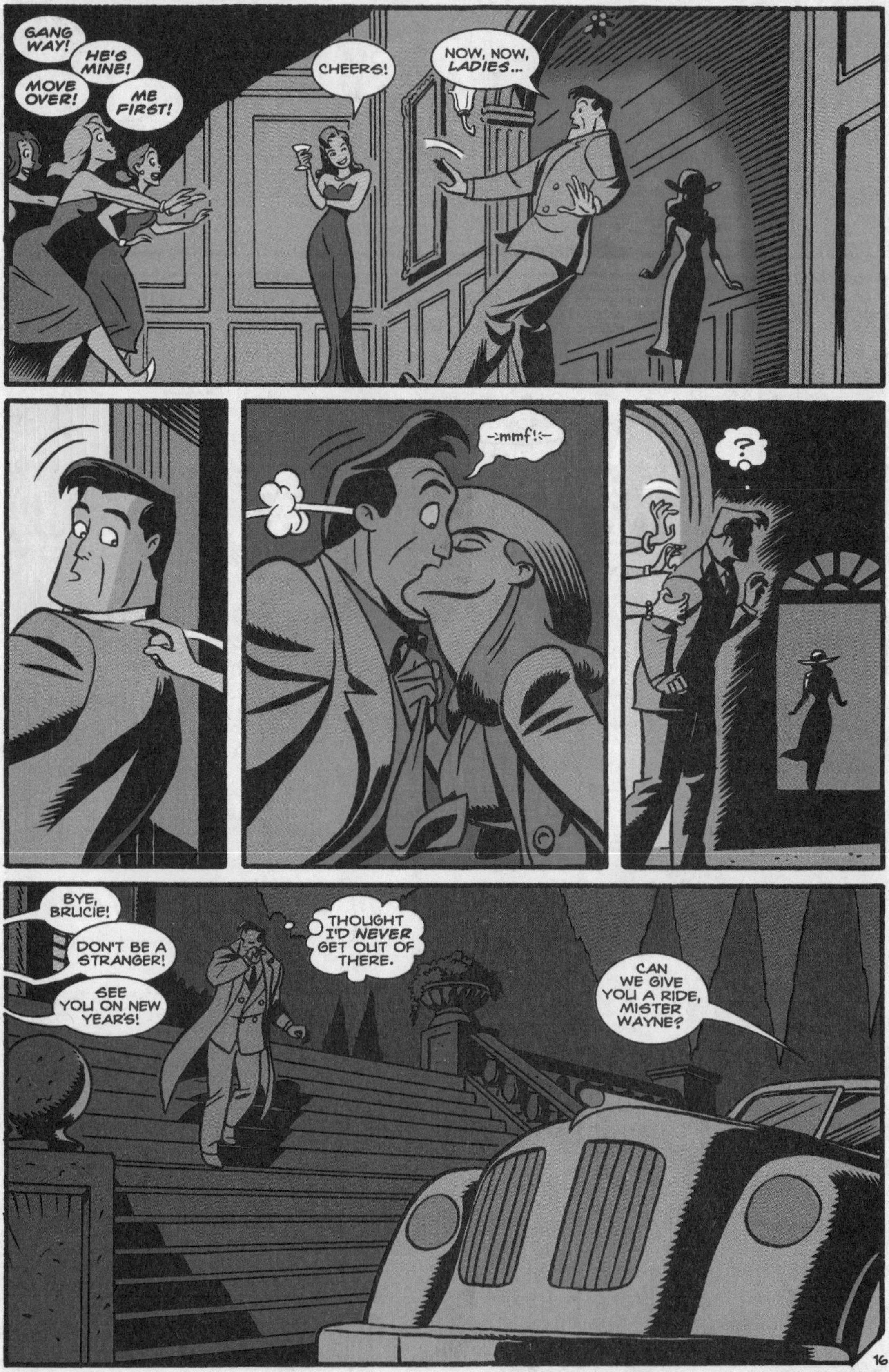
GANG WAY!
HE'S MINE!
MOVE OVER!
ME FIRST!
CHEERS!
NOW, NOW, LADIES...
—mmf!—
?
BYE, BRUCIE!
DON'T BE A STRANGER!
SEE YOU ON NEW YEAR'S!
THOUGHT I'D NEVER GET OUT OF THERE.
CAN WE GIVE YOU A RIDE, MISTER WAYNE?

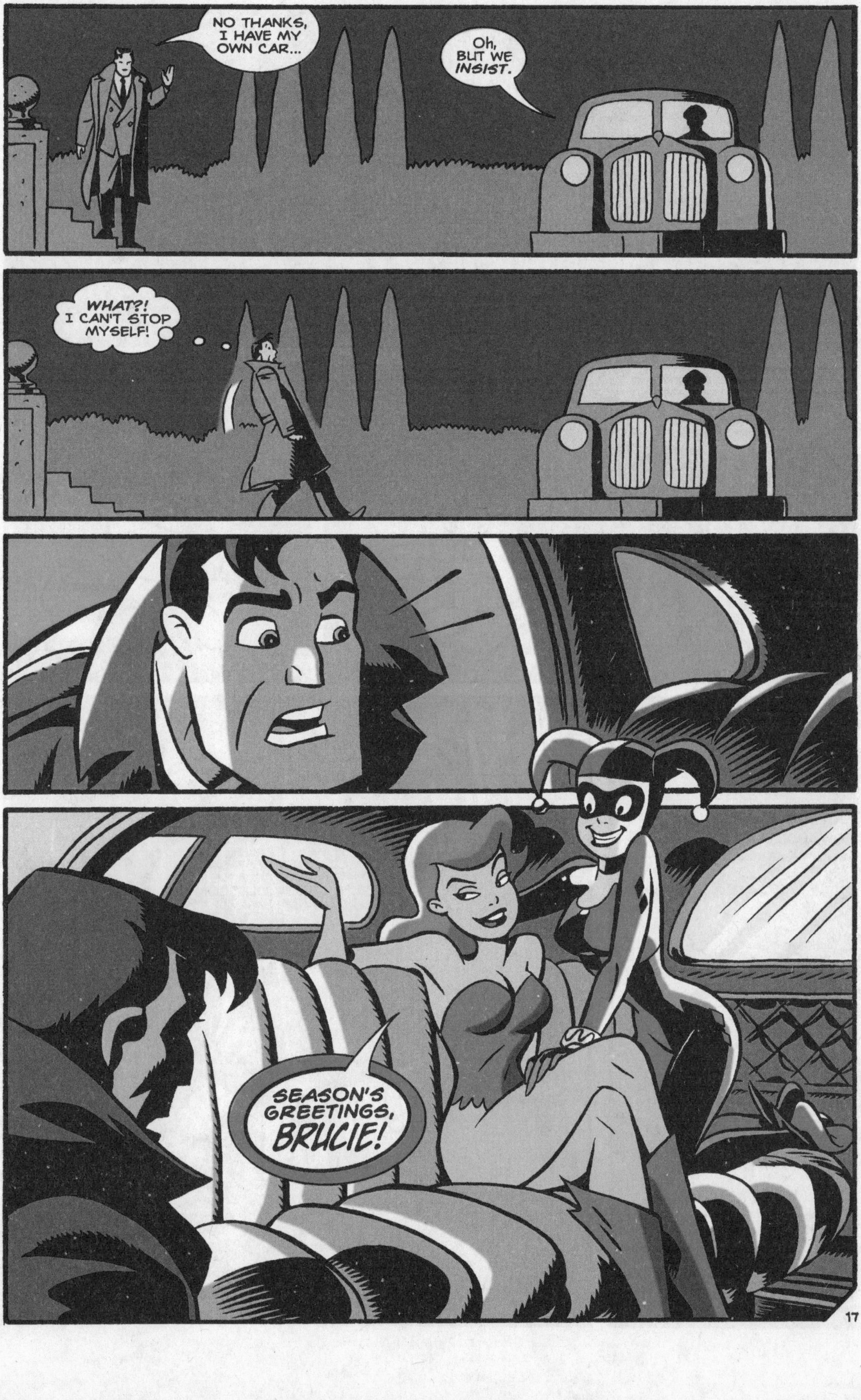
NO THANKS, I HAVE MY OWN CAR...
Oh, BUT WE *INSIST*.
WHAT?! I CAN'T STOP MYSELF!
SEASON'S GREETINGS, BRUCIE!

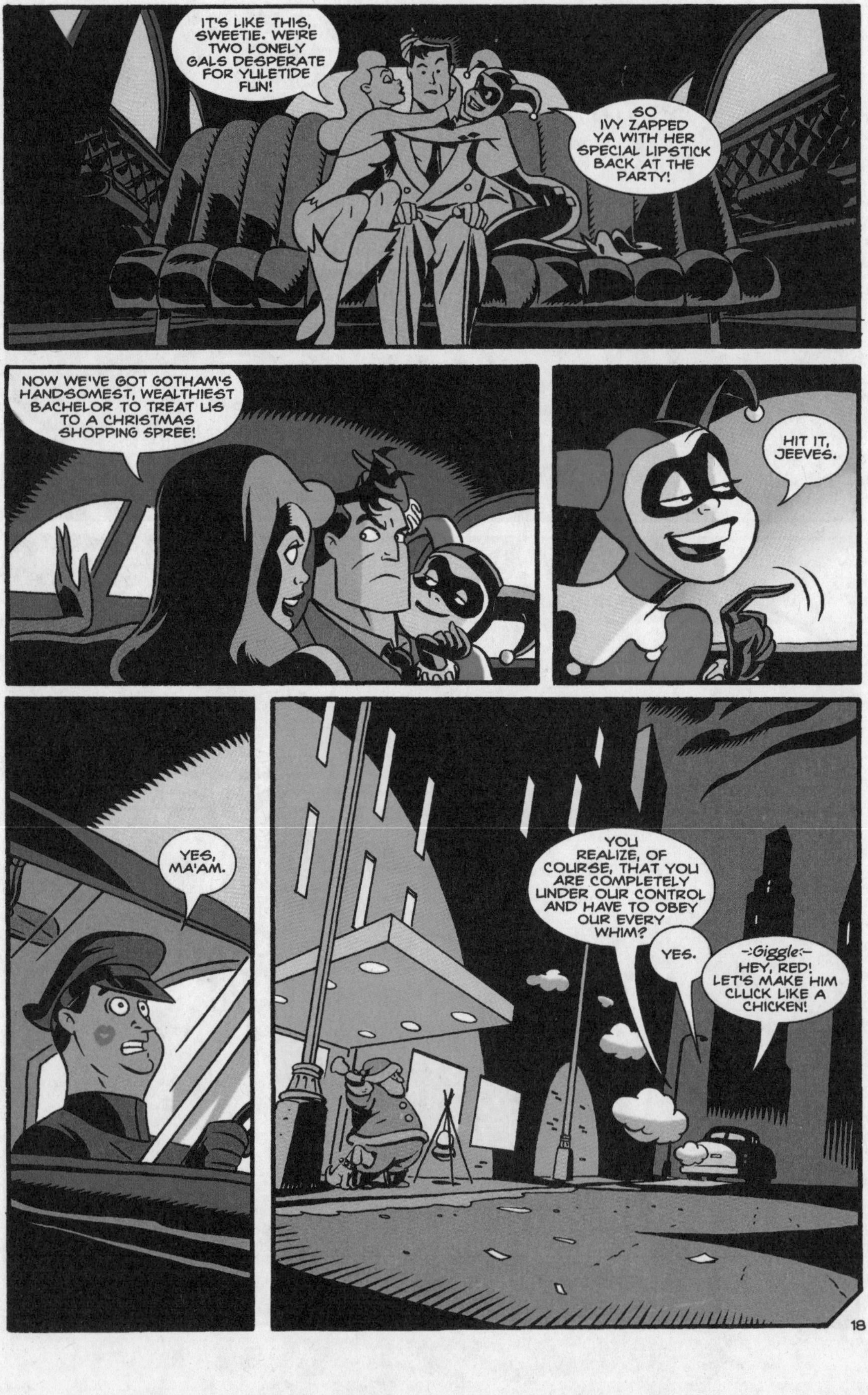
IT'S LIKE THIS, SWEETIE. WE'RE TWO LONELY GALS DESPERATE FOR YULETIDE FUN!
SO IVY ZAPPED YA WITH HER SPECIAL LIPSTICK BACK AT THE PARTY!
NOW WE'VE GOT GOTHAM'S HANDSOMEST, WEALTHIEST BACHELOR TO TREAT US TO A CHRISTMAS SHOPPING SPREE!
HIT IT, JEEVES.
YES, MA'AM.
YOU REALIZE, OF COURSE, THAT YOU ARE COMPLETELY UNDER OUR CONTROL AND HAVE TO OBEY OUR EVERY WHIM?
YES.
-:Giggle:- HEY, RED! LET'S MAKE HIM CLUCK LIKE A CHICKEN!

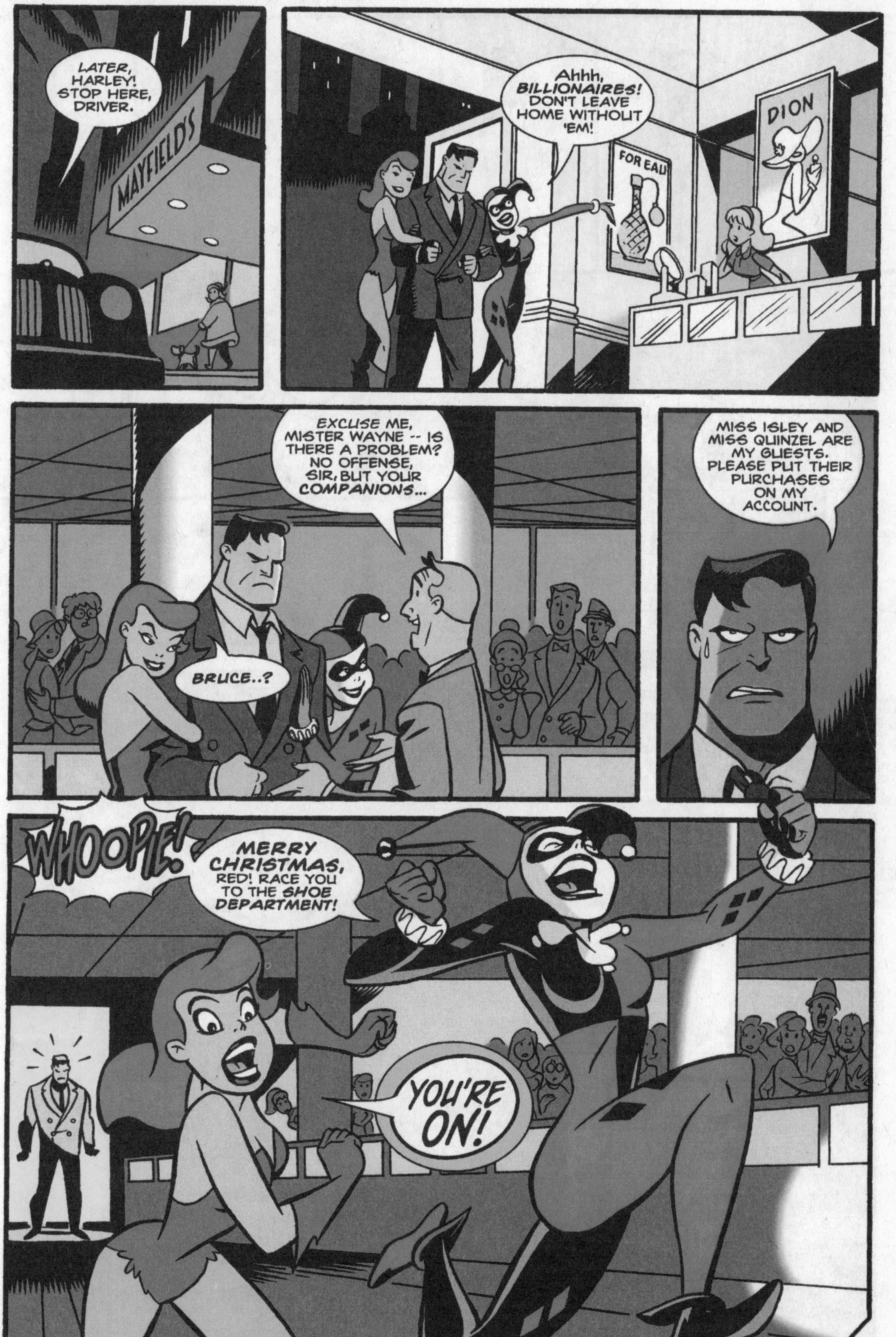
LATER, HARLEY! STOP HERE, DRIVER.
MAYFIELD'S
Ahhh, BILLIONAIRES! DON'T LEAVE HOME WITHOUT 'EM!
FOR EAU
DION
EXCUSE ME, MISTER WAYNE -- IS THERE A PROBLEM? NO OFFENSE, SIR, BUT YOUR COMPANIONS...
BRUCE..?
MISS ISLEY AND MISS QUINZEL ARE MY GUESTS. PLEASE PUT THEIR PURCHASES ON MY ACCOUNT.
WHOOPIE!
MERRY CHRISTMAS, RED! RACE YOU TO THE SHOE DEPARTMENT!
YOU'RE ON!

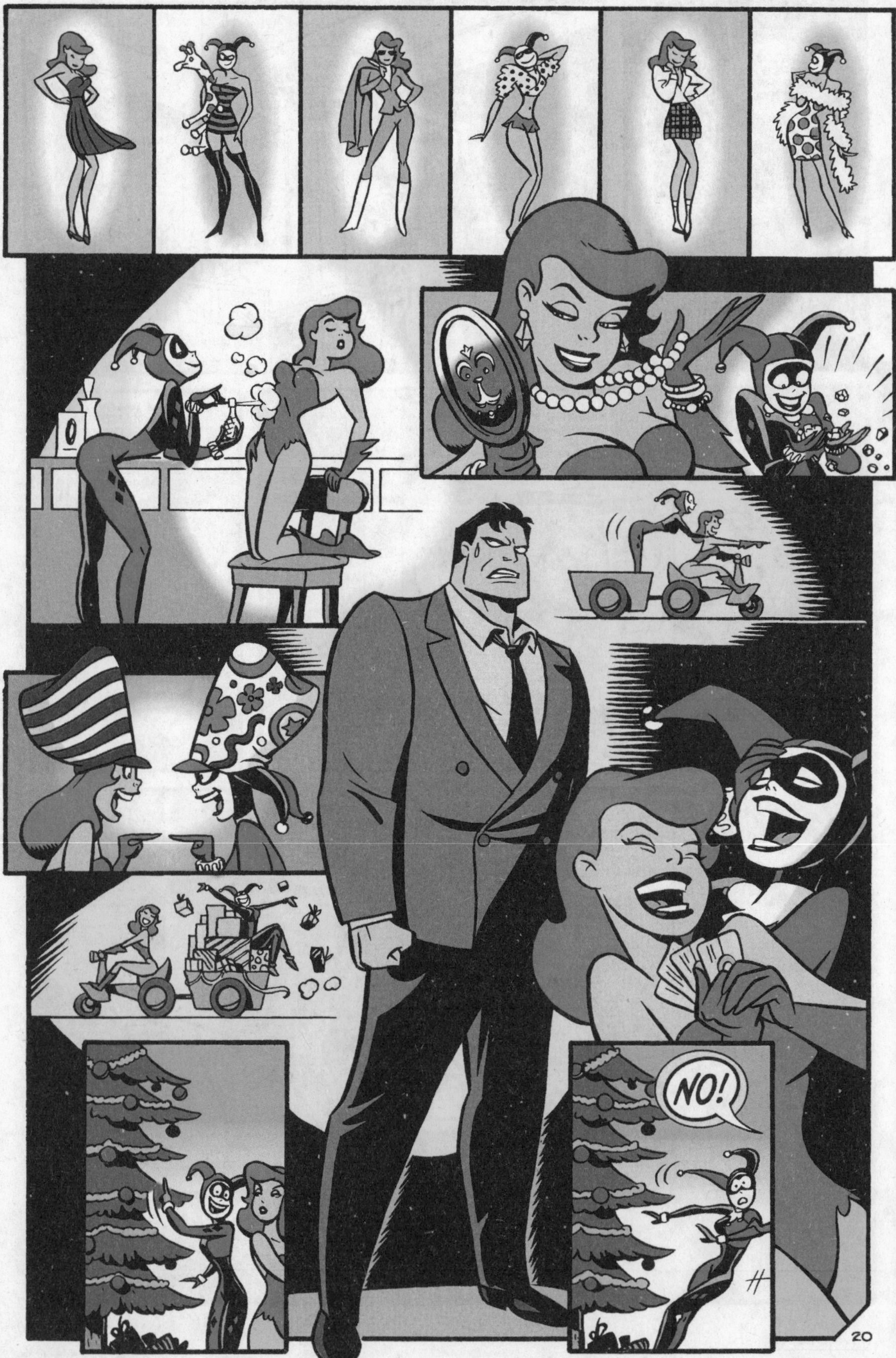
NO!

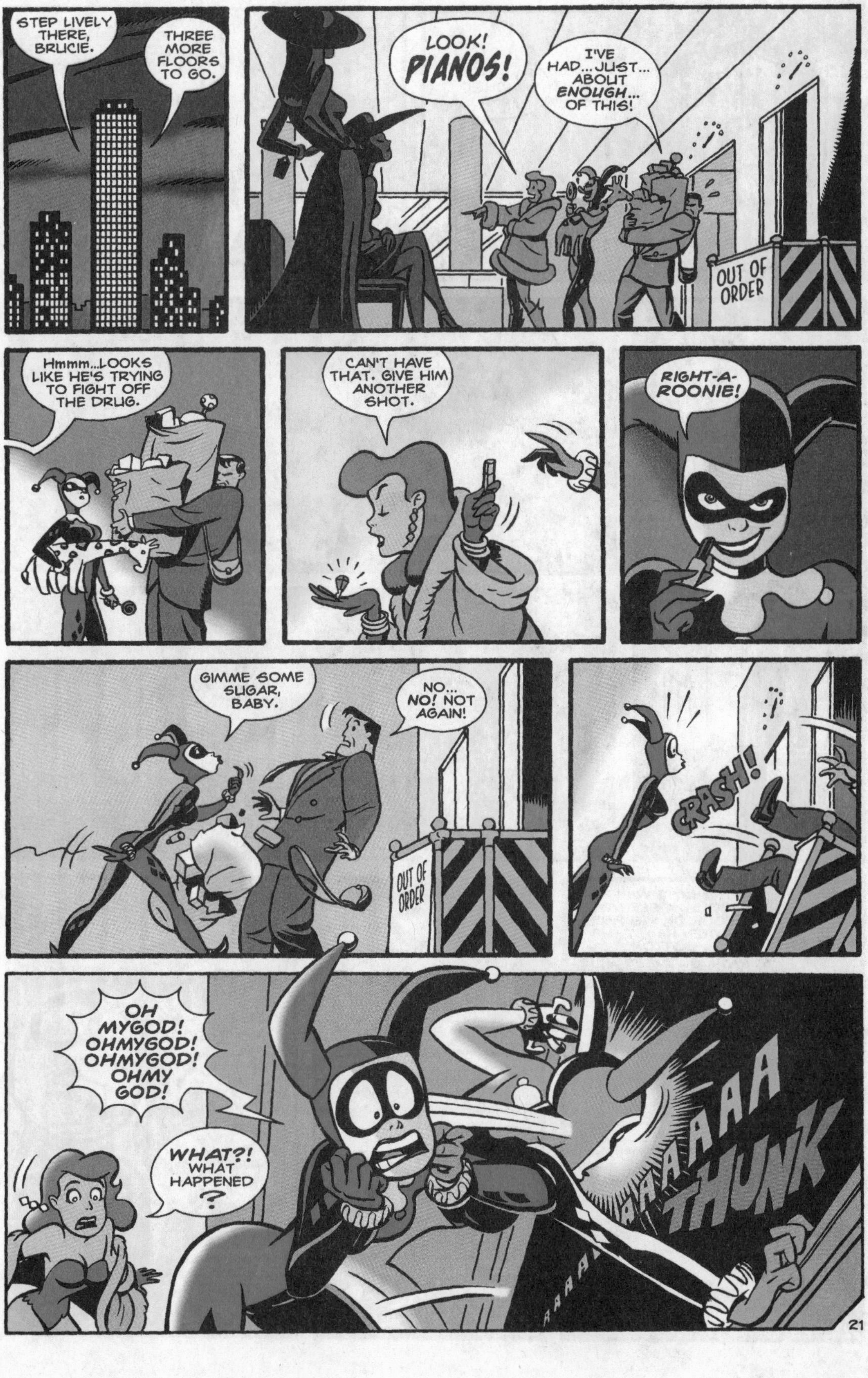
STEP LIVELY THERE, BRUCIE.
THREE MORE FLOORS TO GO.
LOOK! PIANOS!
I'VE HAD... JUST... ABOUT ENOUGH... OF THIS!
OUT OF ORDER
Hmmm...LOOKS LIKE HE'S TRYING TO FIGHT OFF THE DRUG.
CAN'T HAVE THAT. GIVE HIM ANOTHER SHOT.
RIGHT-A-ROONIE!
GIMME SOME SUGAR, BABY.
NO... NO! NOT AGAIN!
OUT OF ORDER
CRASH!
OH MYGOD! OHMYGOD! OHMYGOD! OHMY GOD!
WHAT?! WHAT HAPPENED?
AAAAAAAAAAA
THUNK

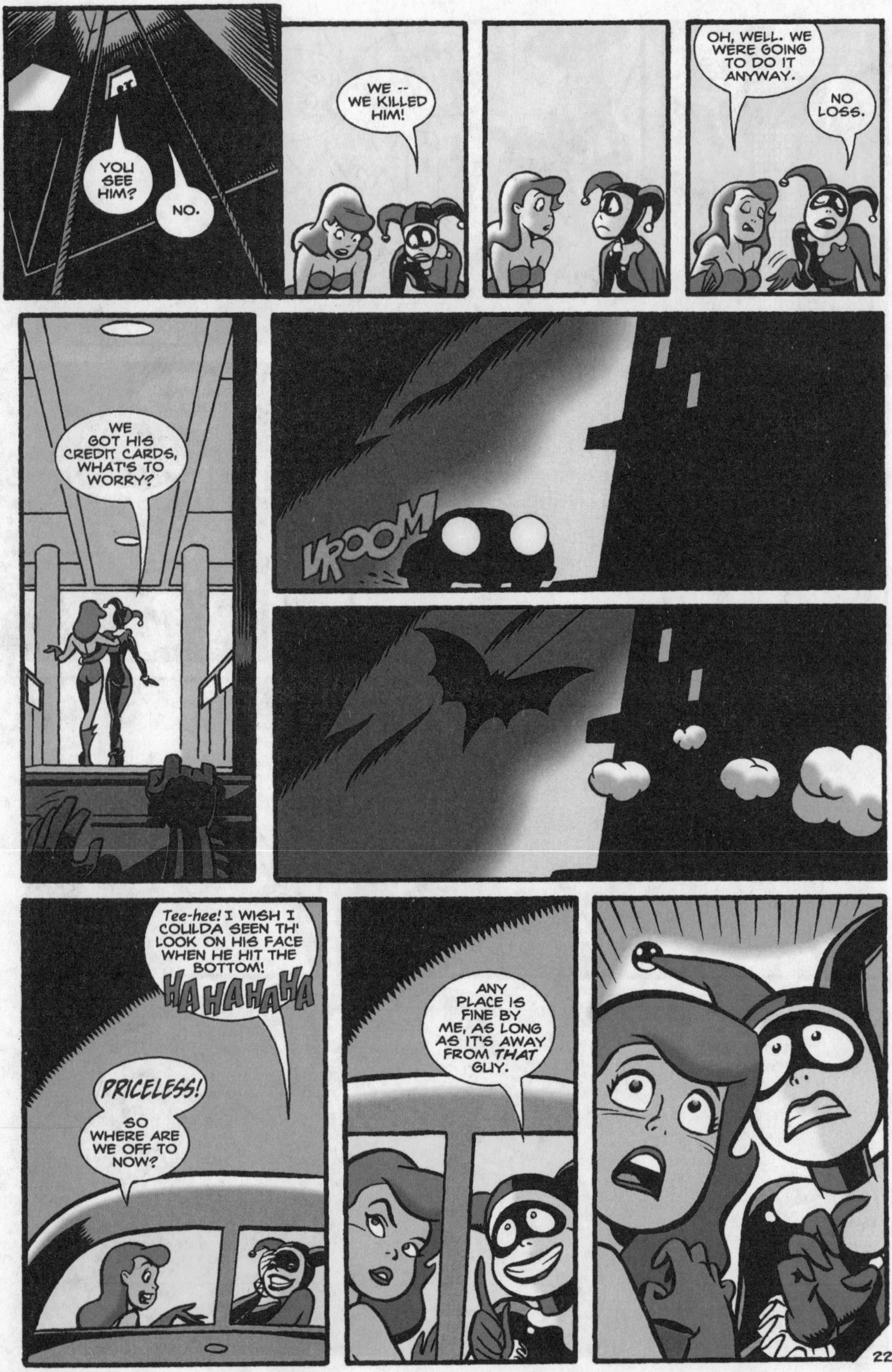
YOU SEE HIM?
NO.
WE -- WE KILLED HIM!
OH, WELL. WE WERE GOING TO DO IT ANYWAY.
NO LOSS.
WE GOT HIS CREDIT CARDS, WHAT'S TO WORRY?
VROOM
Tee-hee! I WISH I COULDA SEEN TH' LOOK ON HIS FACE WHEN HE HIT THE BOTTOM!
HAHAHAHA
PRICELESS!
SO WHERE ARE WE OFF TO NOW?
ANY PLACE IS FINE BY ME, AS LONG AS IT'S AWAY FROM *THAT* GUY.

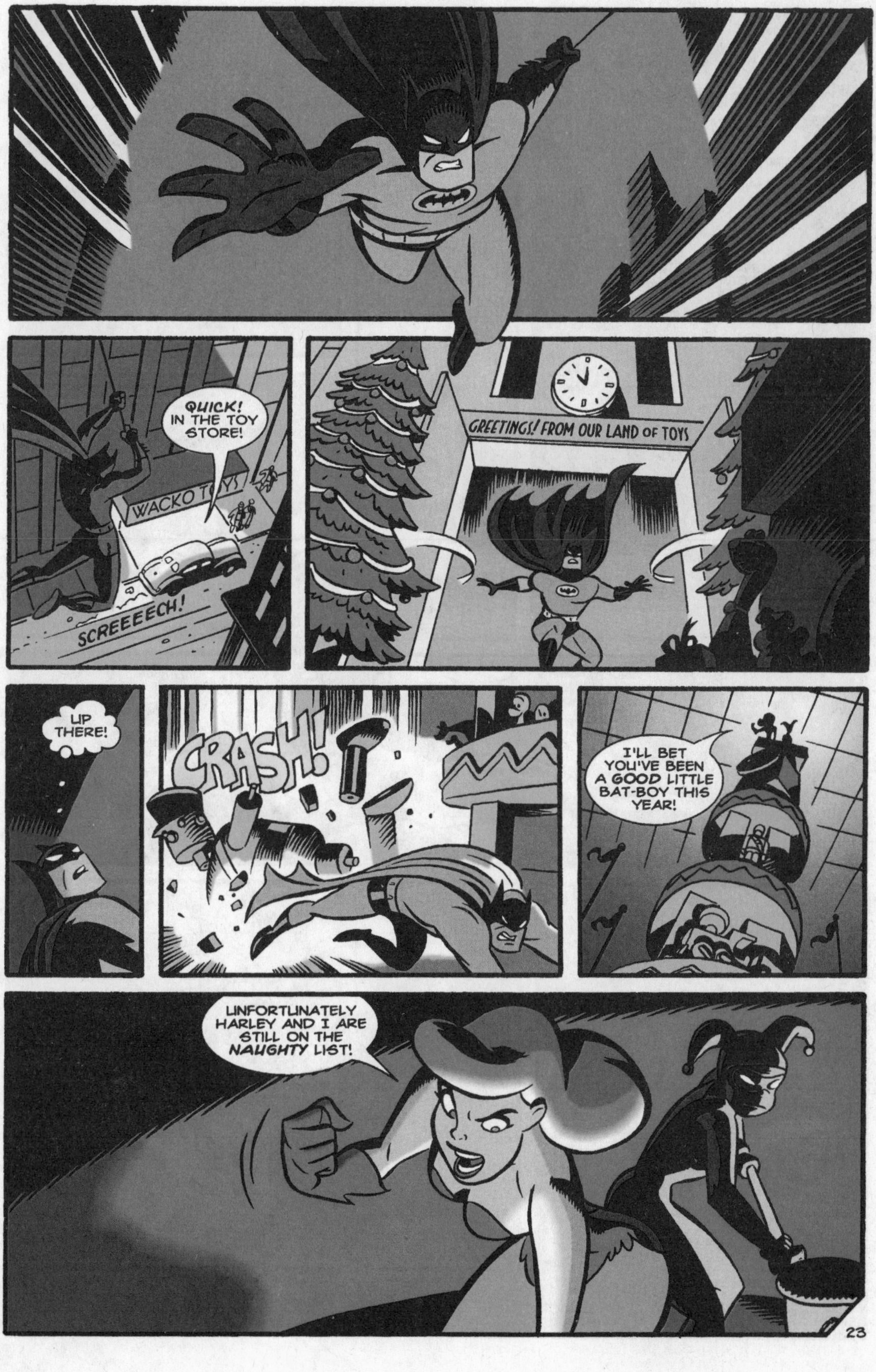
QUICK! IN THE TOY STORE!
WACKO TOYS
SCREEEECH!
GREETINGS! FROM OUR LAND OF TOYS
UP THERE!
CRASH!
I'LL BET YOU'VE BEEN A GOOD LITTLE BAT-BOY THIS YEAR!
UNFORTUNATELY HARLEY AND I ARE STILL ON THE NAUGHTY LIST!

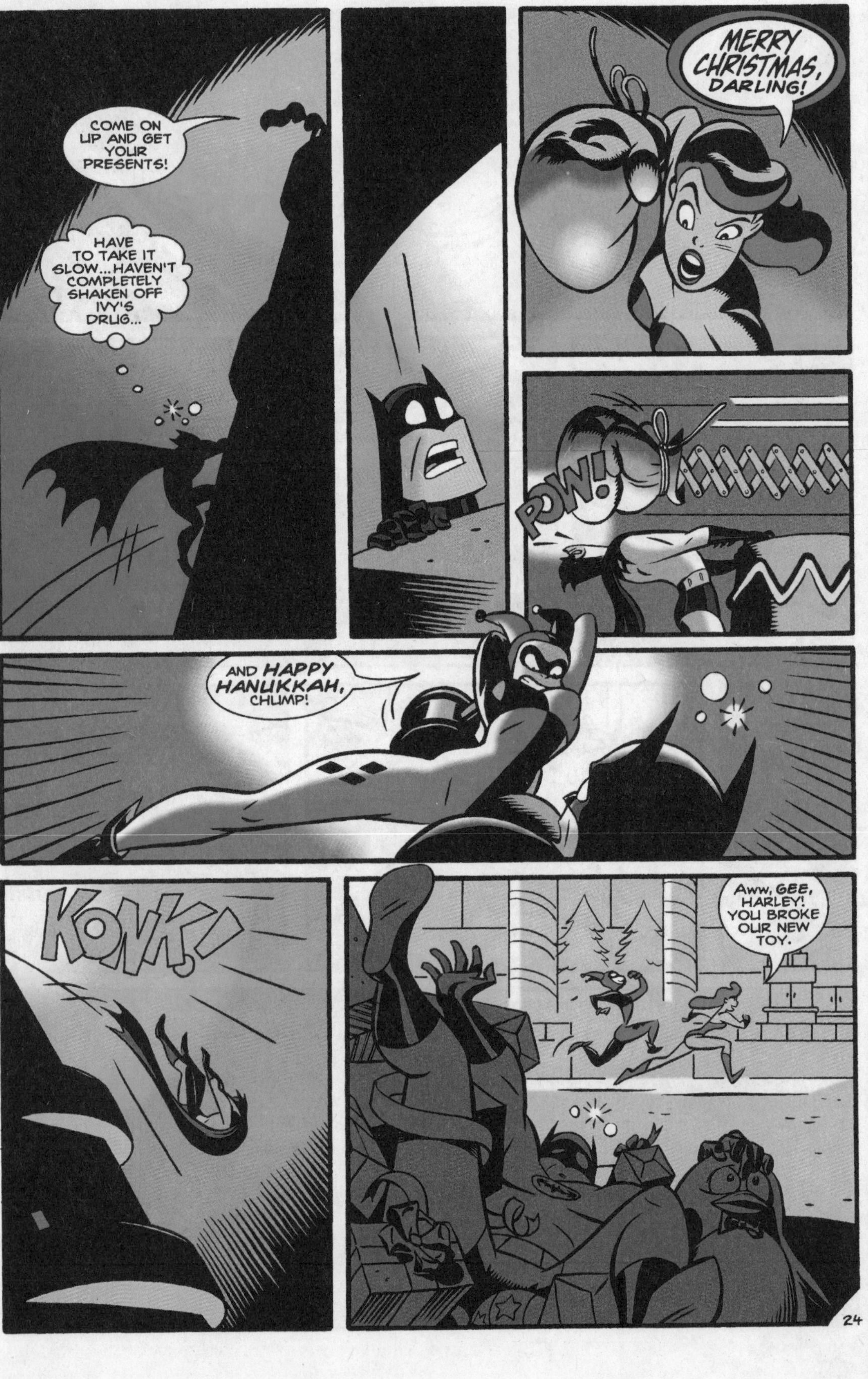

COME ON UP AND GET YOUR PRESENTS!
HAVE TO TAKE IT SLOW... HAVEN'T COMPLETELY SHAKEN OFF IVY'S DRUG...
MERRY CHRISTMAS, DARLING!
POW!
AND HAPPY HANUKKAH, CHUMP!
KONK!
AWW, GEE, HARLEY! YOU BROKE OUR NEW TOY.

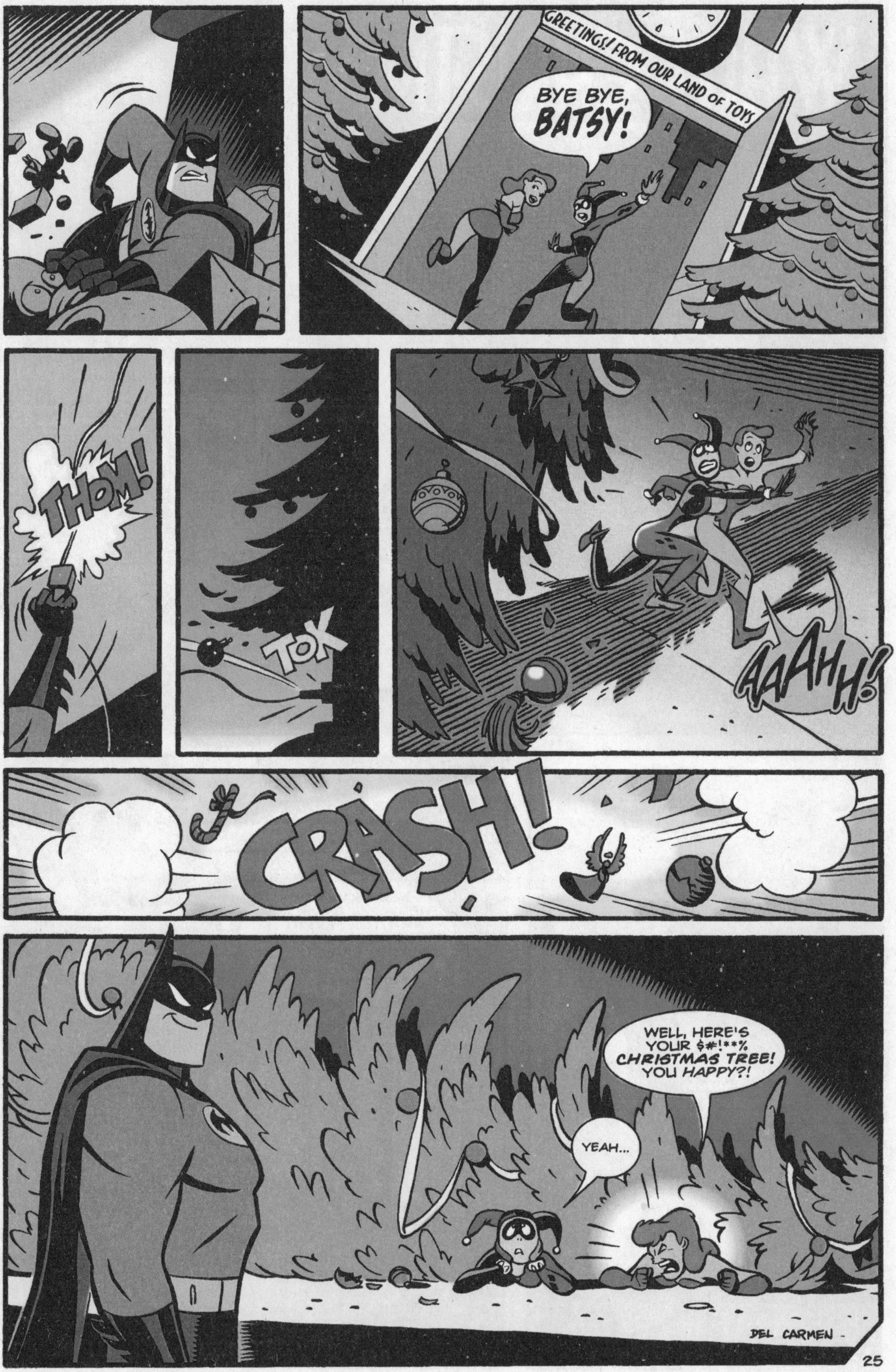
GREETINGS! FROM OUR LAND OF TOYS
BYE BYE, BATSY!
THOM!
TOK
AAAHH!
CRASH!
WELL, HERE'S YOUR $#!**% CHRISTMAS TREE! YOU HAPPY?!
YEAH...
DEL CARMEN

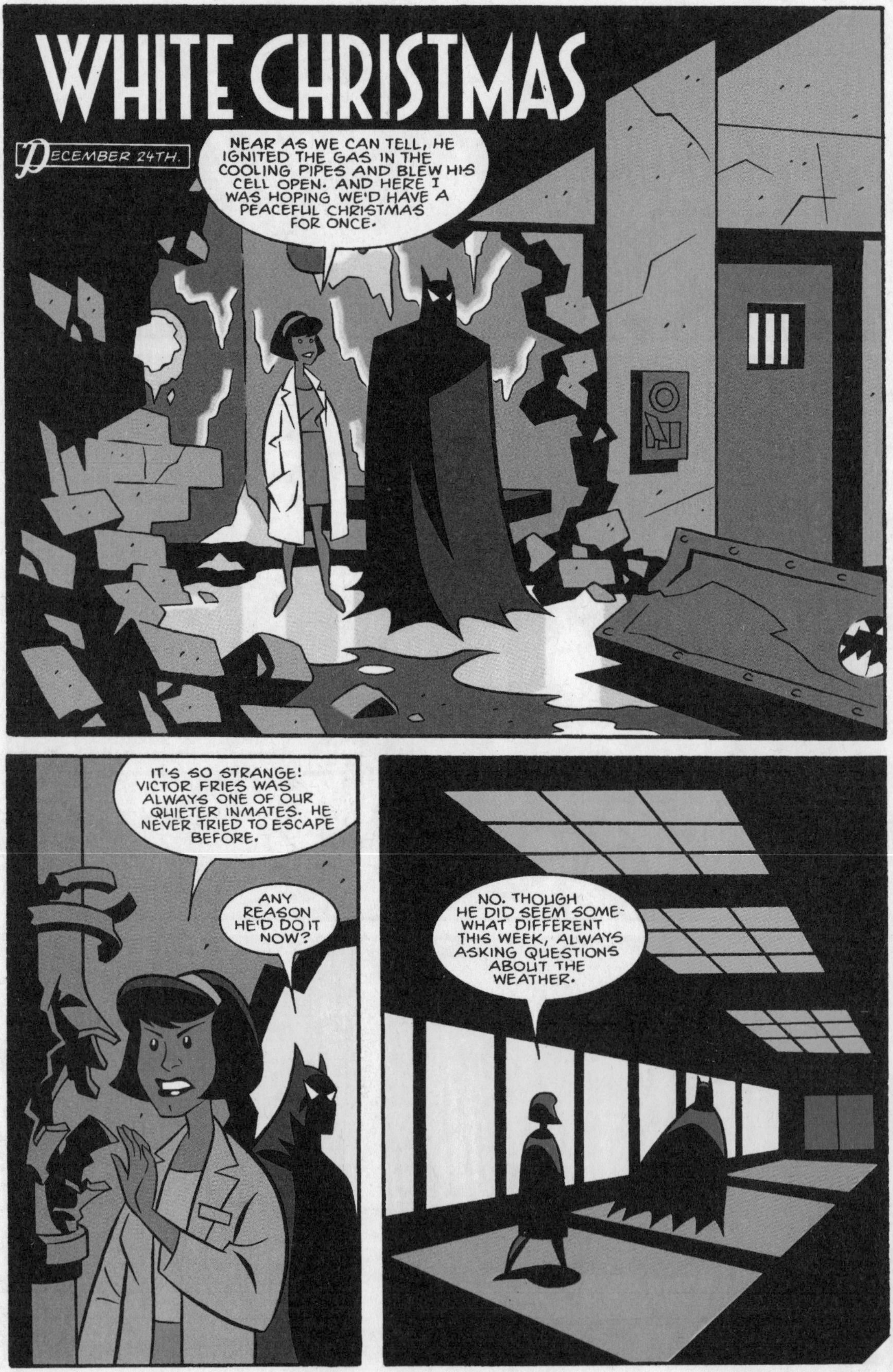
WHITE CHRISTMAS
DECEMBER 24TH.
NEAR AS WE CAN TELL, HE IGNITED THE GAS IN THE COOLING PIPES AND BLEW HIS CELL OPEN. AND HERE I WAS HOPING WE'D HAVE A PEACEFUL CHRISTMAS FOR ONCE.
IT'S SO STRANGE! VICTOR FRIES WAS ALWAYS ONE OF OUR QUIETER INMATES. HE NEVER TRIED TO ESCAPE BEFORE.
ANY REASON HE'D DO IT NOW?
NO. THOUGH HE DID SEEM SOME-WHAT DIFFERENT THIS WEEK, ALWAYS ASKING QUESTIONS ABOUT THE WEATHER.

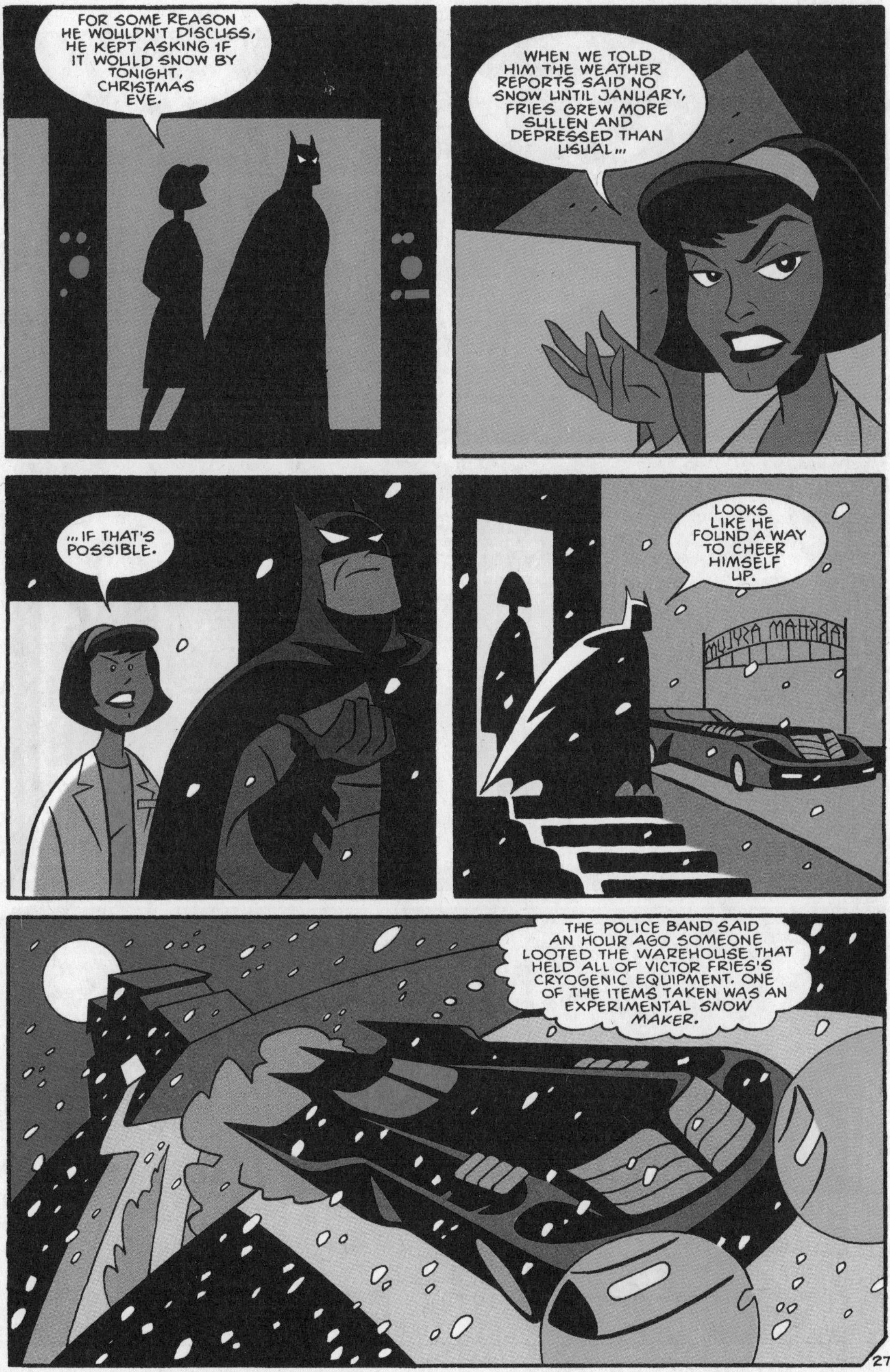
FOR SOME REASON HE WOULDN'T DISCUSS, HE KEPT ASKING IF IT WOULD SNOW BY TONIGHT, CHRISTMAS EVE.
WHEN WE TOLD HIM THE WEATHER REPORTS SAID NO SNOW UNTIL JANUARY, FRIES GREW MORE SULLEN AND DEPRESSED THAN USUAL...
...IF THAT'S POSSIBLE.
LOOKS LIKE HE FOUND A WAY TO CHEER HIMSELF UP.
ARKHAM ASYLUM
THE POLICE BAND SAID AN HOUR AGO SOMEONE LOOTED THE WAREHOUSE THAT HELD ALL OF VICTOR FRIES'S CRYOGENIC EQUIPMENT. ONE OF THE ITEMS TAKEN WAS AN EXPERIMENTAL SNOW MAKER.

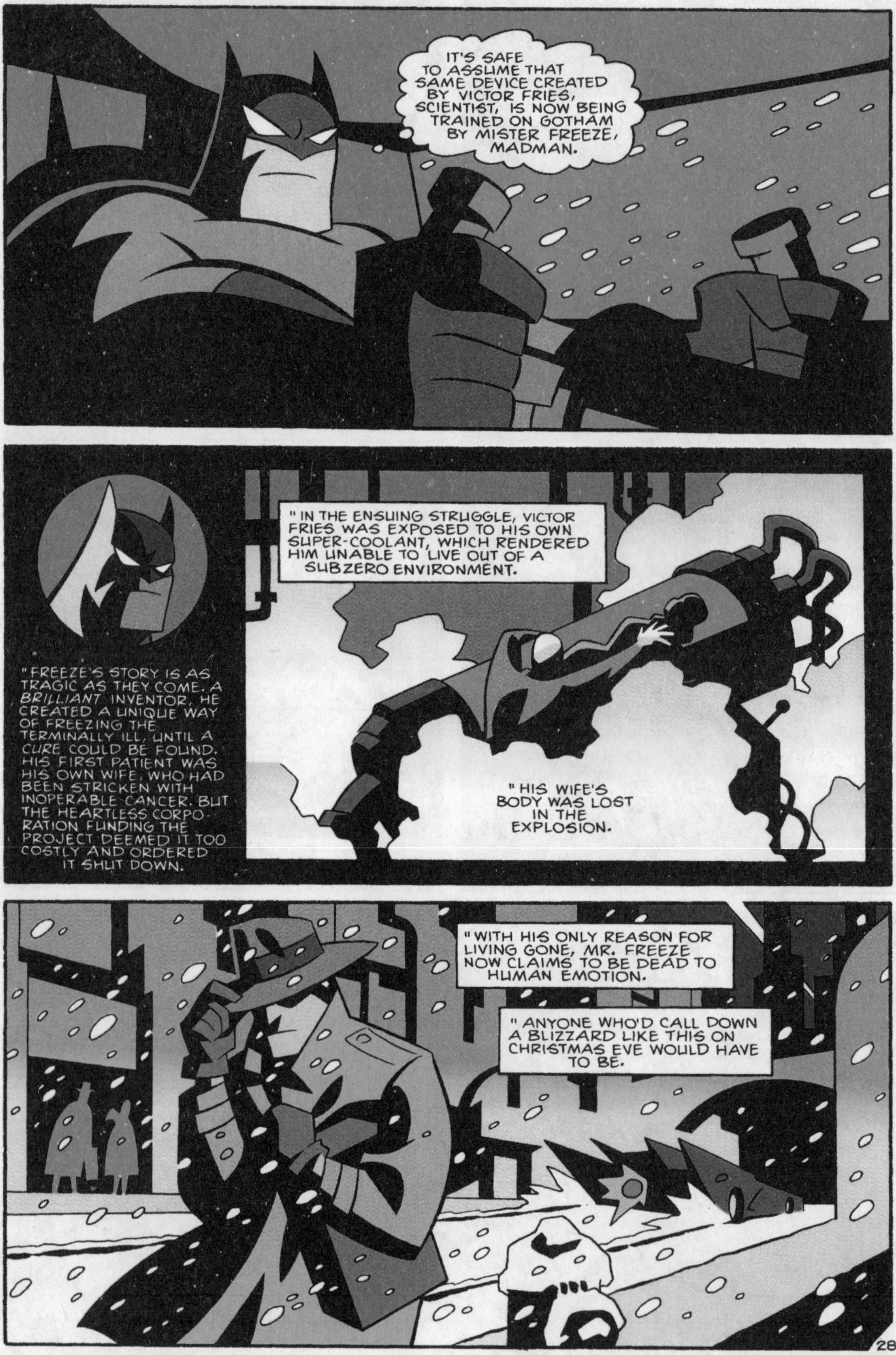

IT'S SAFE TO ASSUME THAT SAME DEVICE CREATED BY VICTOR FRIES, SCIENTIST, IS NOW BEING TRAINED ON GOTHAM BY MISTER FREEZE, MADMAN.
"FREEZE'S STORY IS AS TRAGIC AS THEY COME. A BRILLIANT INVENTOR, HE CREATED A UNIQUE WAY OF FREEZING THE TERMINALLY ILL, UNTIL A CURE COULD BE FOUND. HIS FIRST PATIENT WAS HIS OWN WIFE, WHO HAD BEEN STRICKEN WITH INOPERABLE CANCER. BUT THE HEARTLESS CORPORATION FUNDING THE PROJECT DEEMED IT TOO COSTLY AND ORDERED IT SHUT DOWN.
"IN THE ENSUING STRUGGLE, VICTOR FRIES WAS EXPOSED TO HIS OWN SUPER-COOLANT, WHICH RENDERED HIM UNABLE TO LIVE OUT OF A SUBZERO ENVIRONMENT.
"HIS WIFE'S BODY WAS LOST IN THE EXPLOSION.
"WITH HIS ONLY REASON FOR LIVING GONE, MR. FREEZE NOW CLAIMS TO BE DEAD TO HUMAN EMOTION.
"ANYONE WHO'D CALL DOWN A BLIZZARD LIKE THIS ON CHRISTMAS EVE WOULD HAVE TO BE.

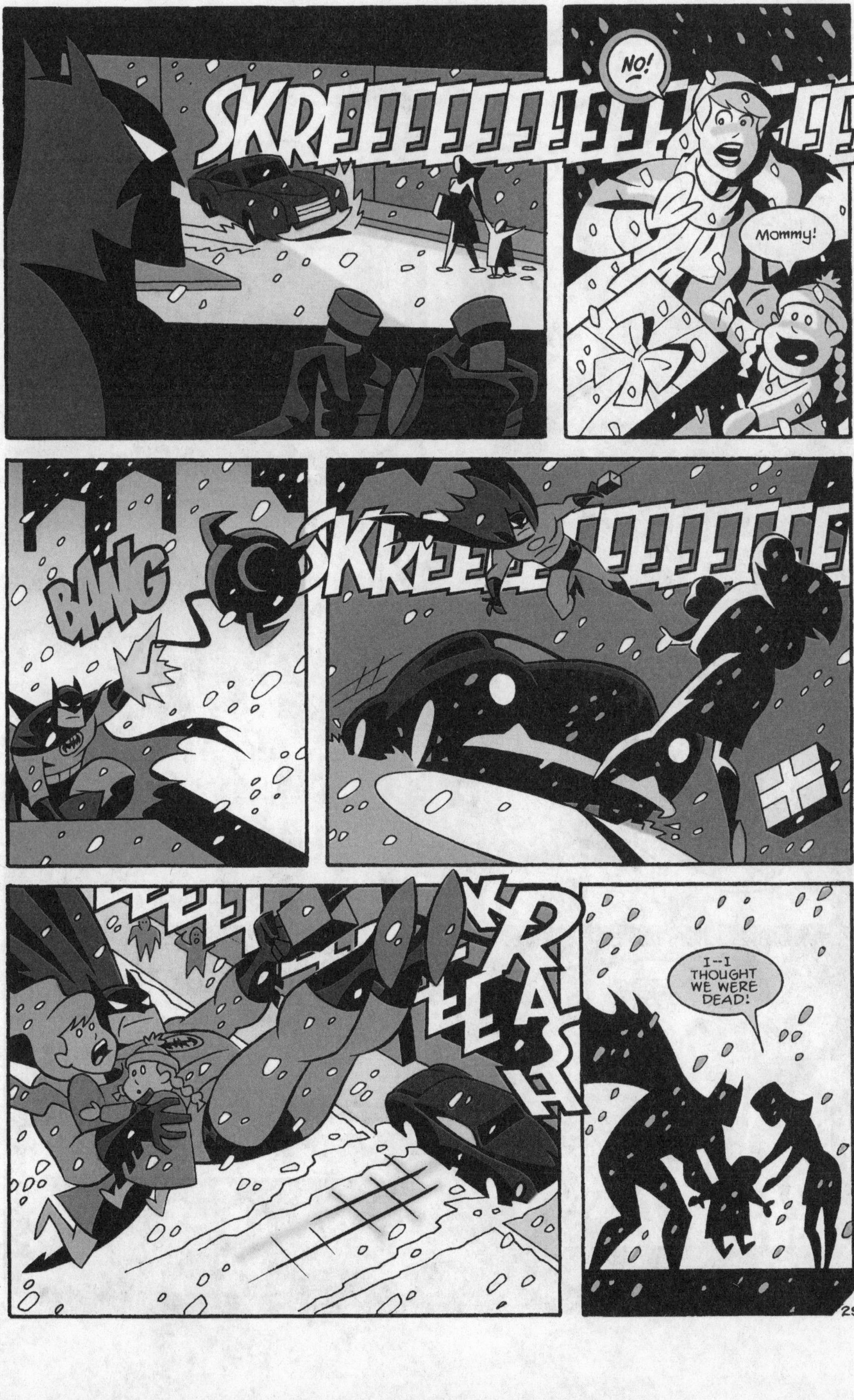
SKREEEEEEEEEEEEEEE
NO!
Mommy!
BANG
SKREEEEEEEEEEEE
RASH
I--I THOUGHT WE WERE DEAD!

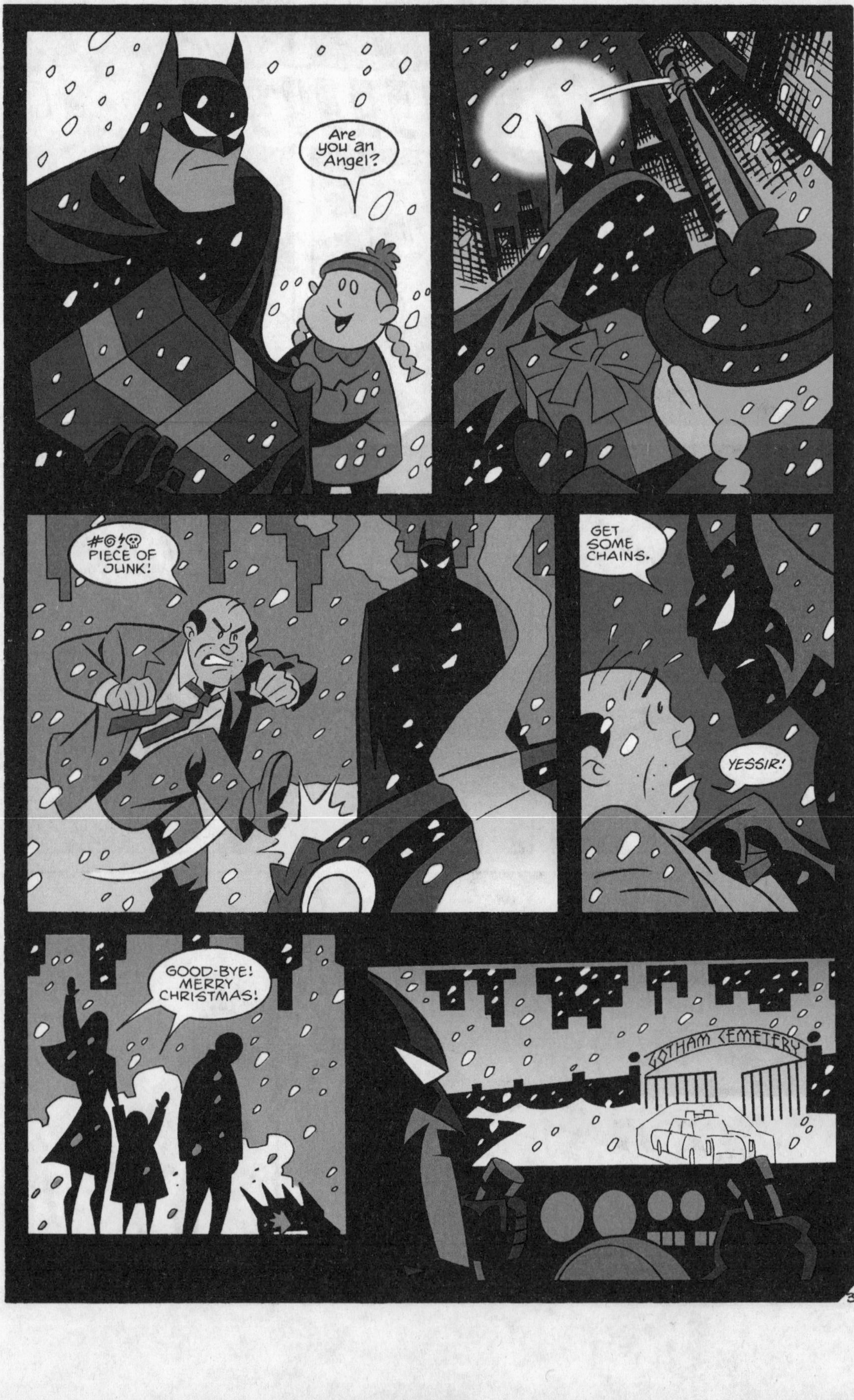
Are you an Angel?
#@⚡💀 PIECE OF JUNK!
GET SOME CHAINS.
YESSIR!
GOOD-BYE! MERRY CHRISTMAS!
GOTHAM CEMETERY

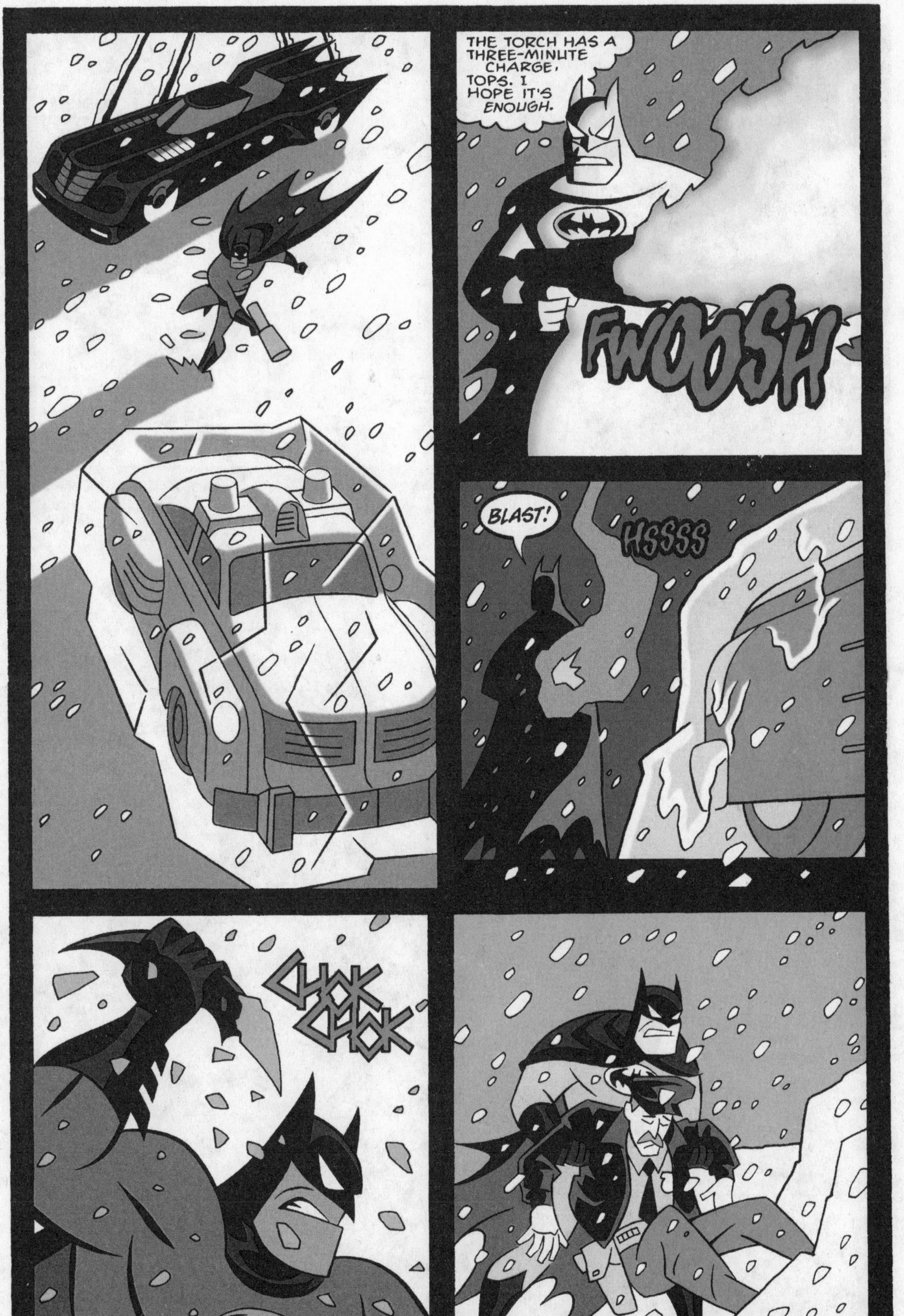
THE TORCH HAS A THREE-MINUTE CHARGE, TOPS. I HOPE IT'S ENOUGH.
FWOOSH
BLAST!
HSSSS
CHOK CHOK

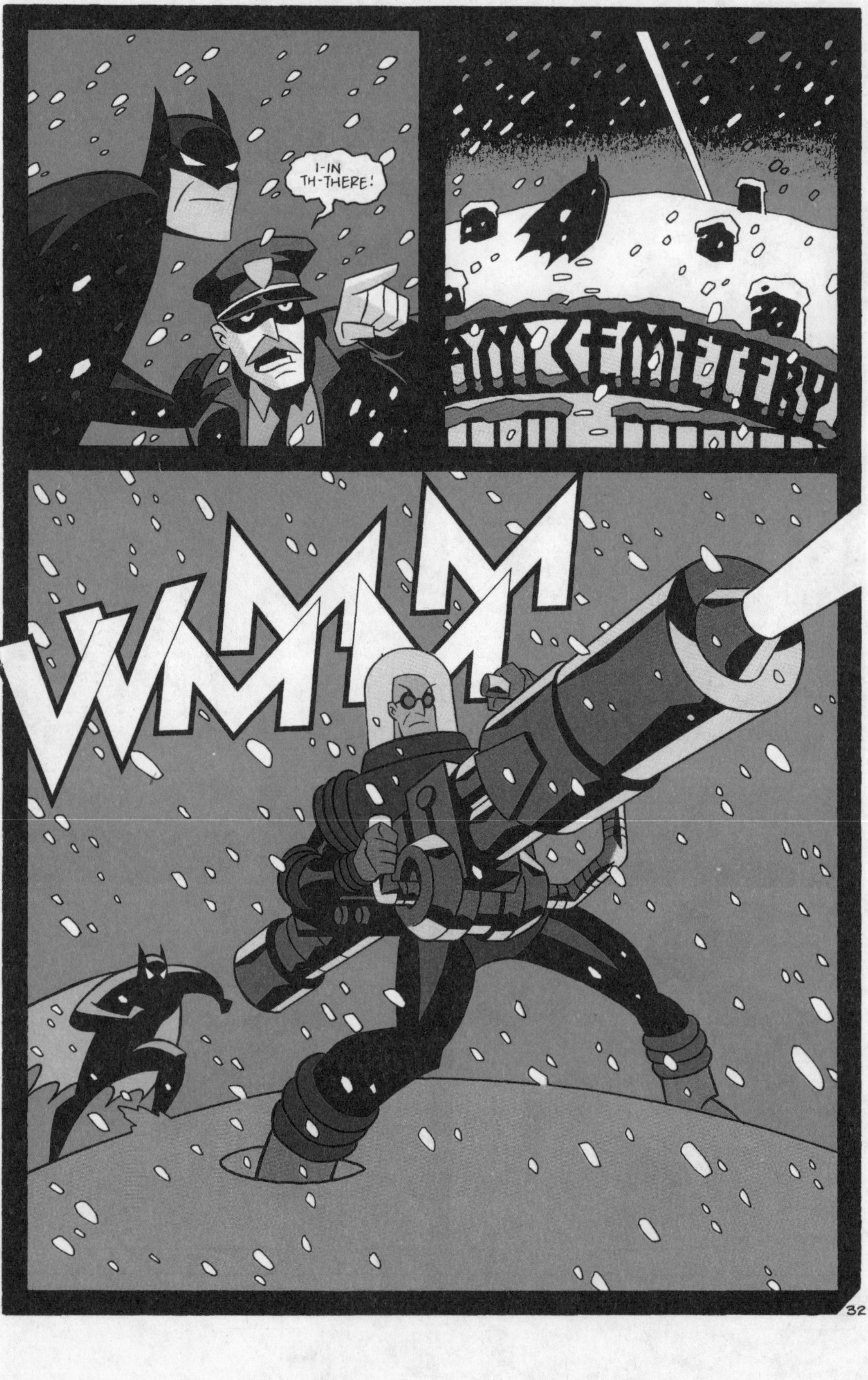
I-IN
TH-THERE!
...MY CEMETERY
VWMMM

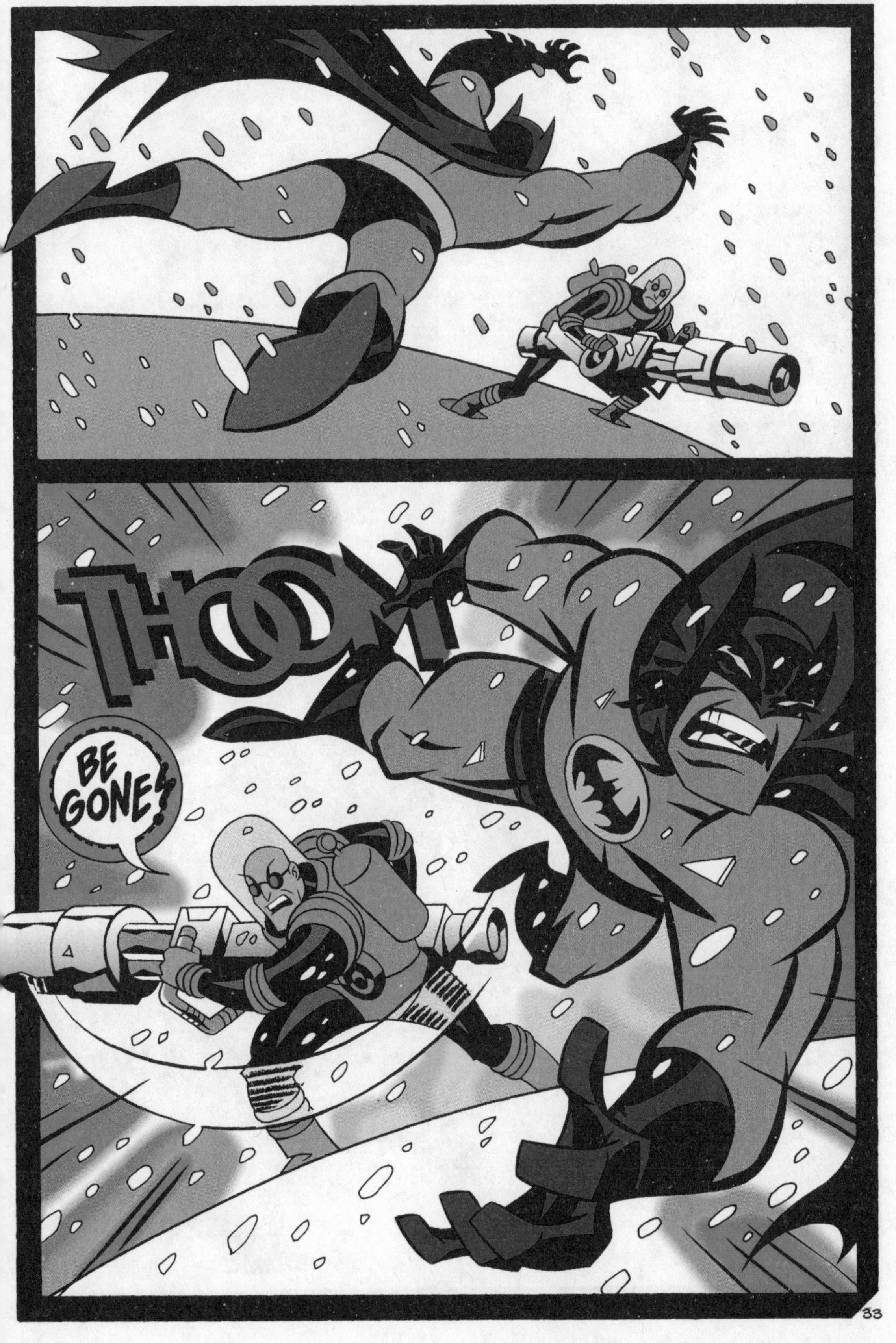
THOOM
BE GONE!

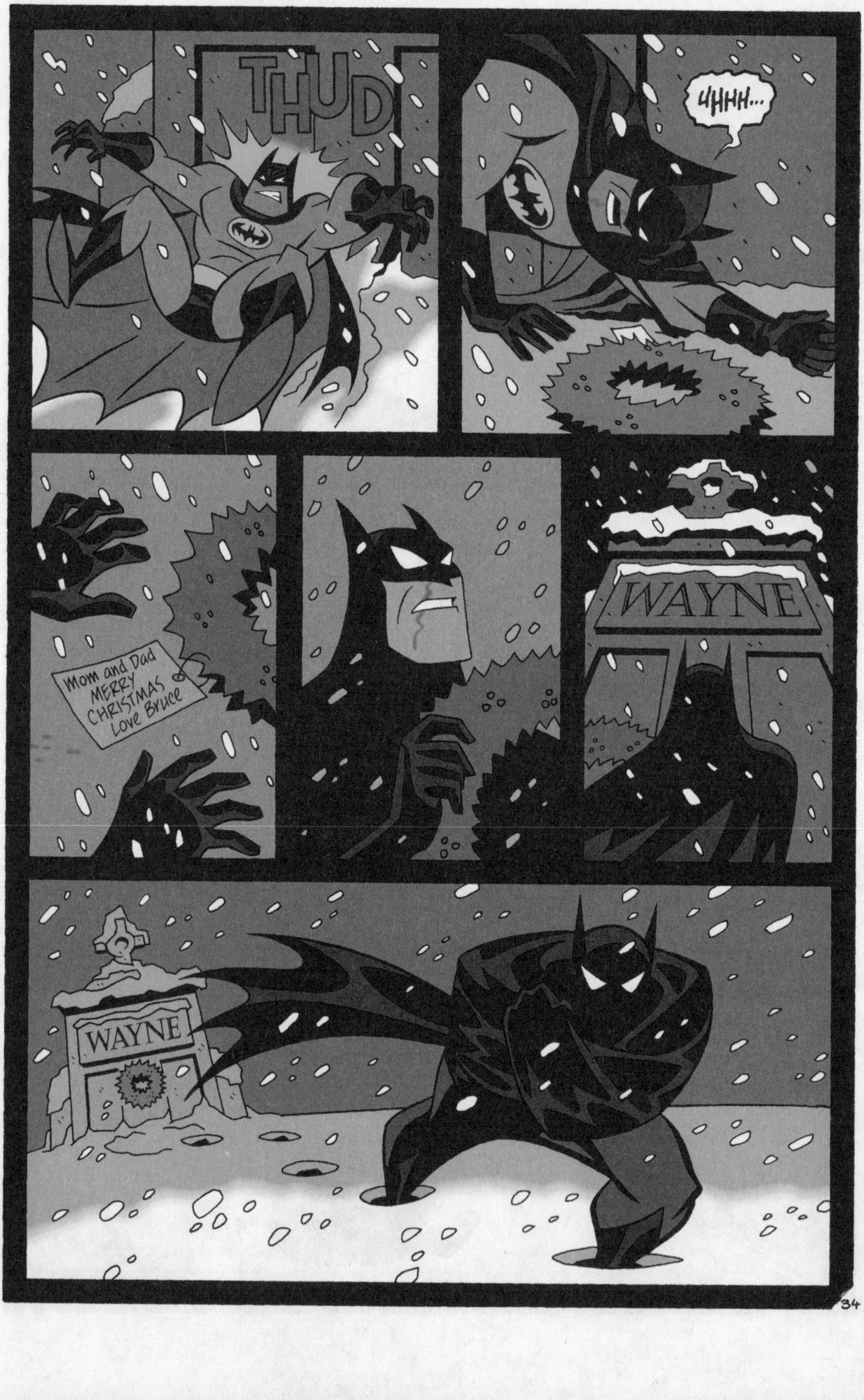
THUD
UHHH...
Mom and Dad
MERRY
CHRISTMAS
Love Bruce
WAYNE
WAYNE

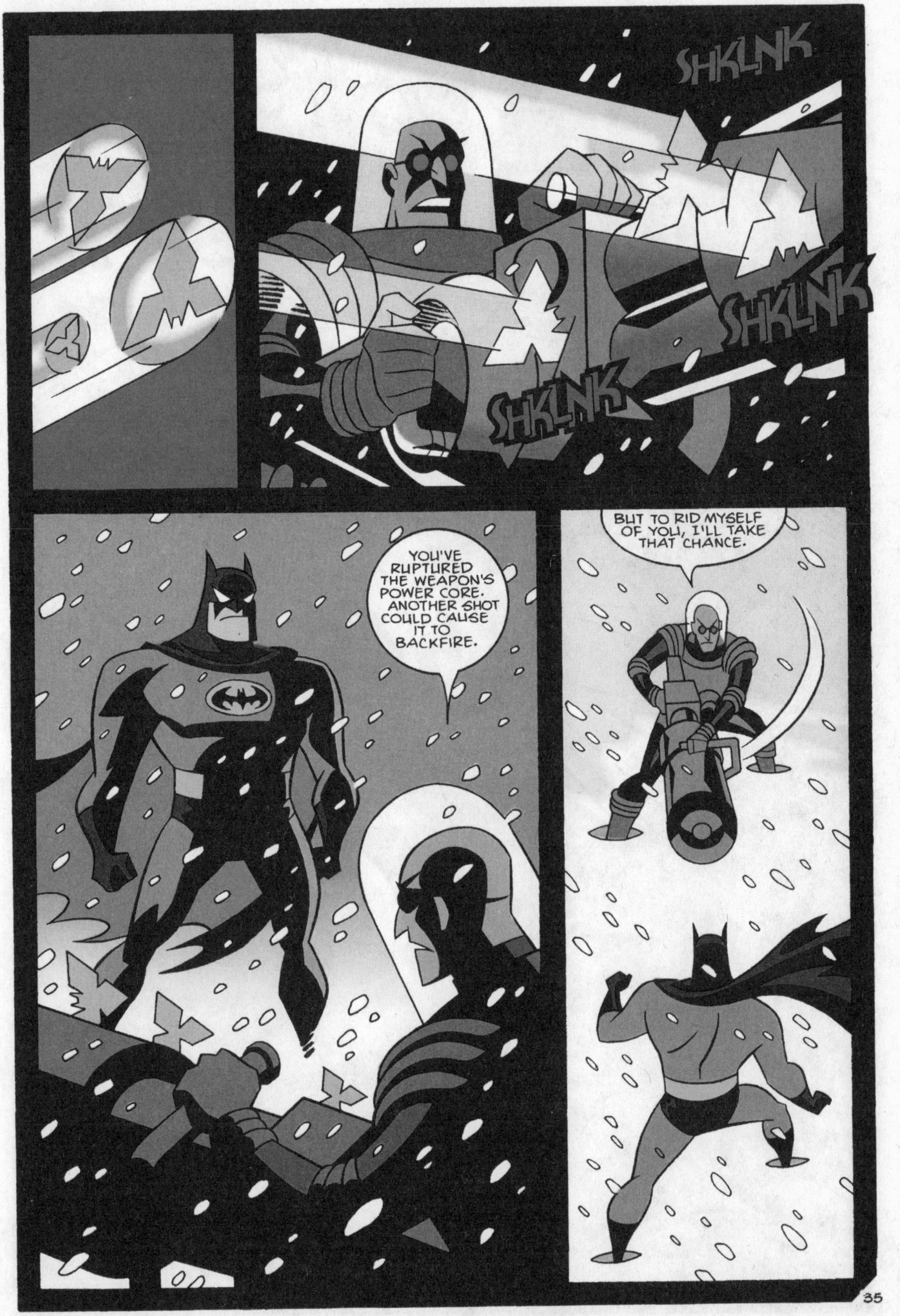
SHKLNK
SHKLNK
SHKLNK
YOU'VE RUPTURED THE WEAPON'S POWER CORE. ANOTHER SHOT COULD CAUSE IT TO BACKFIRE.
BUT TO RID MYSELF OF YOU, I'LL TAKE THAT CHANCE.

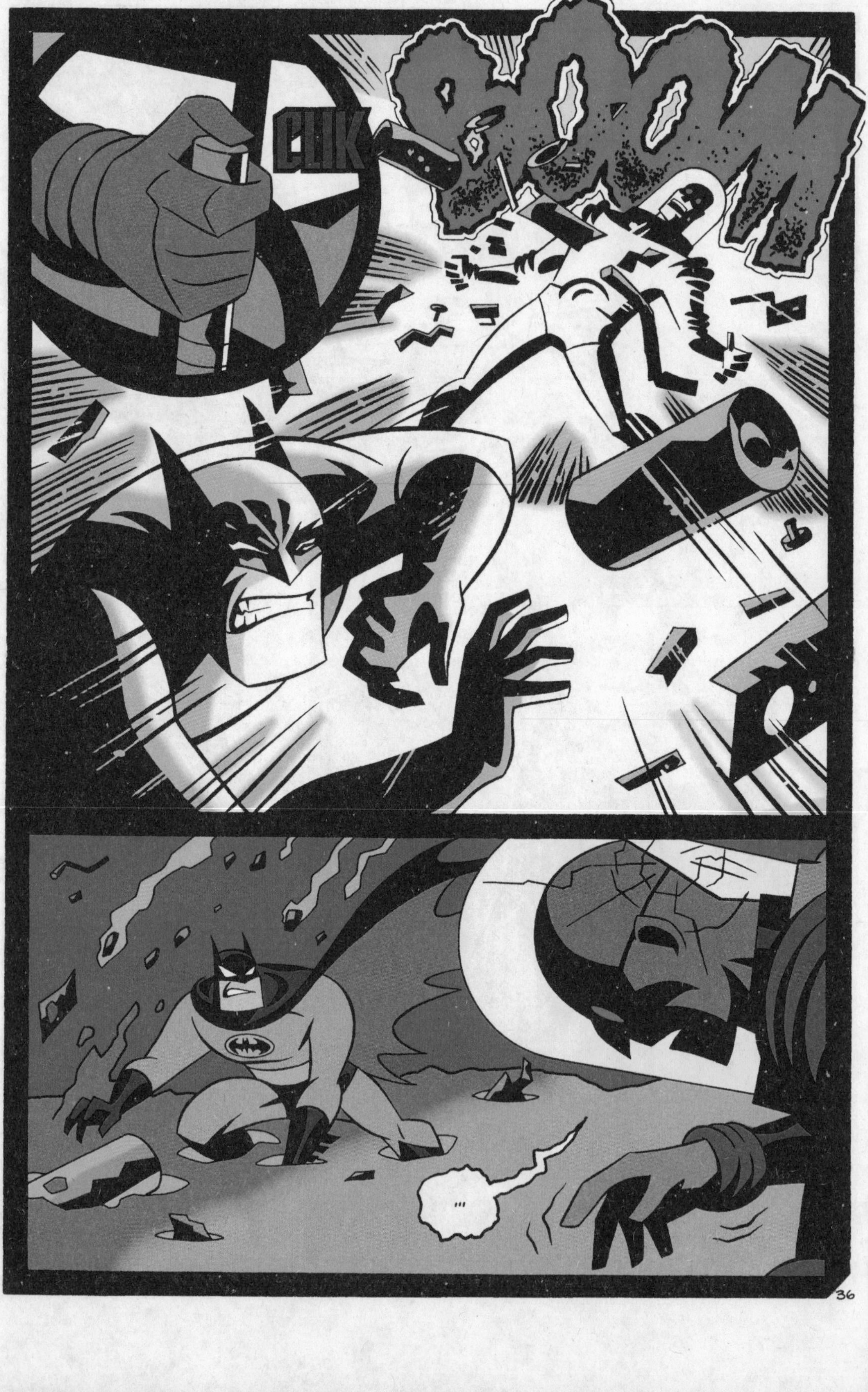
CLIK
BOOM
...

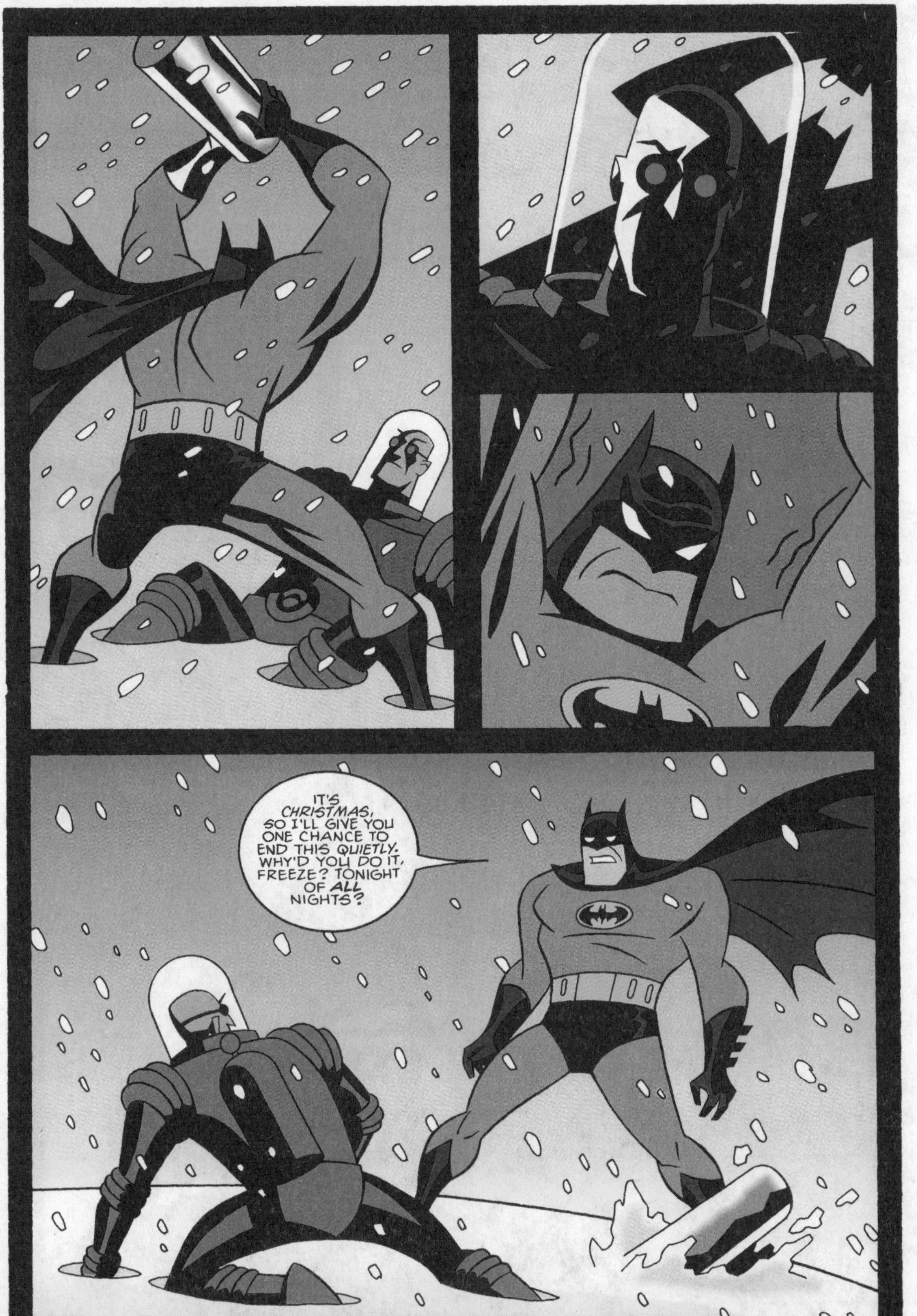
IT'S CHRISTMAS, SO I'LL GIVE YOU ONE CHANCE TO END THIS QUIETLY. WHY'D YOU DO IT, FREEZE? TONIGHT OF ALL NIGHTS?

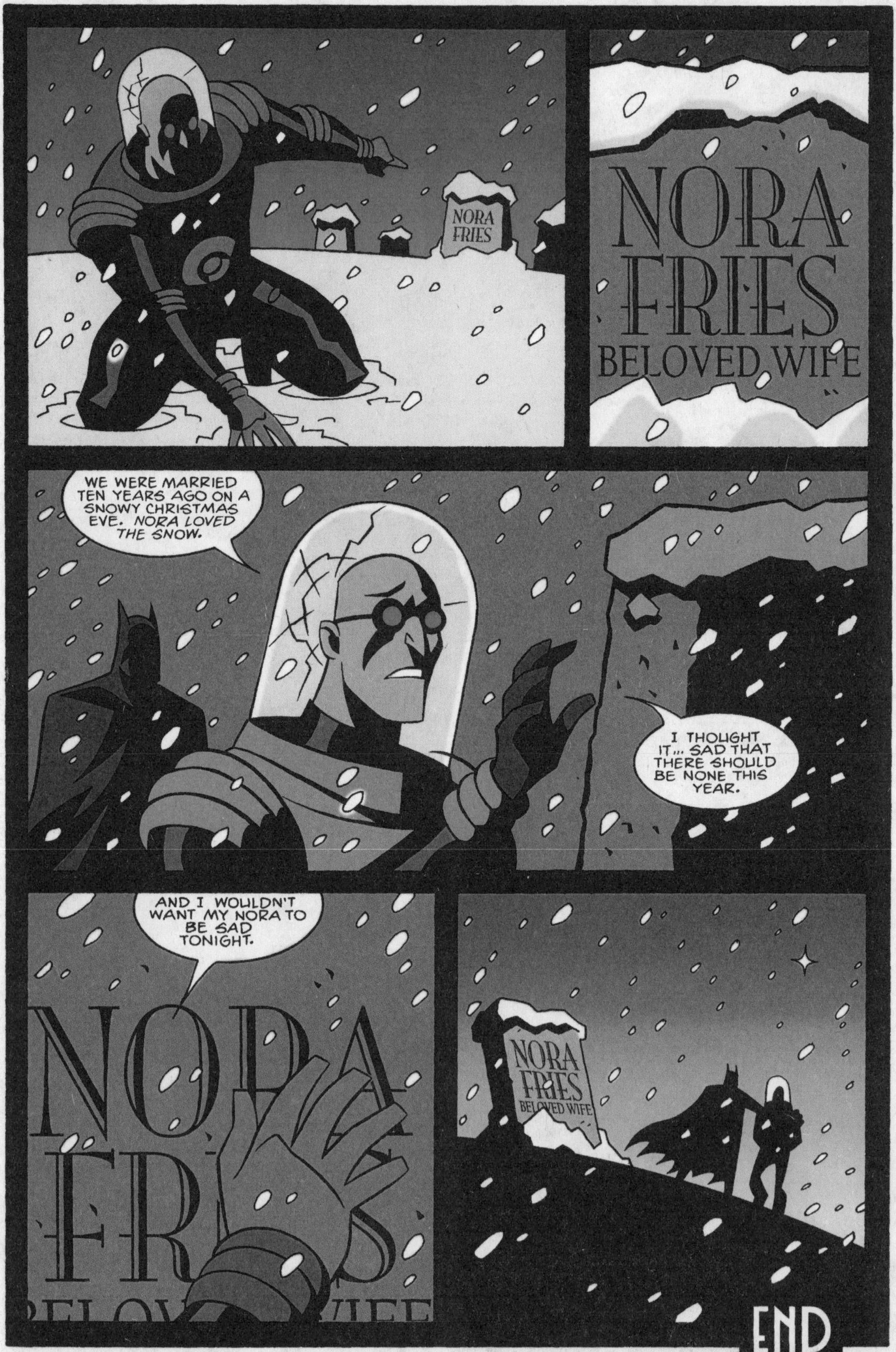

NORA FRIES
NORA FRIES BELOVED WIFE
WE WERE MARRIED TEN YEARS AGO ON A SNOWY CHRISTMAS EVE. NORA LOVED THE SNOW.
I THOUGHT IT... SAD THAT THERE SHOULD BE NONE THIS YEAR.
AND I WOULDN'T WANT MY NORA TO BE SAD TONIGHT.
NORA FRIES BELOVED WIFE
END

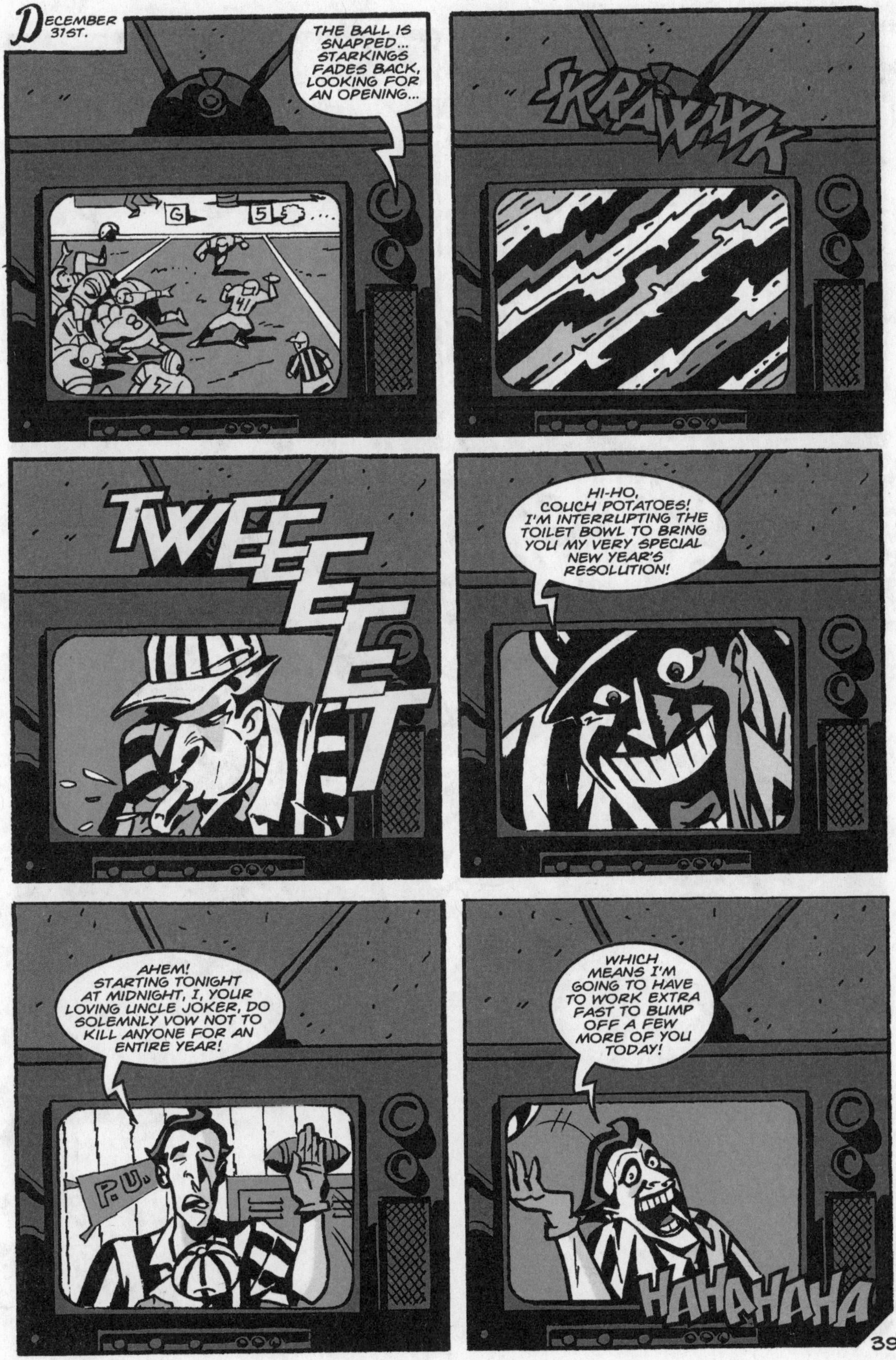
DECEMBER 31ST.
THE BALL IS SNAPPED... STARKINGS FADES BACK, LOOKING FOR AN OPENING...
SKRAWWK
TWEEEEET
HI-HO, COUCH POTATOES! I'M INTERRUPTING THE TOILET BOWL TO BRING YOU MY VERY SPECIAL NEW YEAR'S RESOLUTION!
AHEM! STARTING TONIGHT AT MIDNIGHT, I, YOUR LOVING UNCLE JOKER, DO SOLEMNLY VOW NOT TO KILL ANYONE FOR AN ENTIRE YEAR!
P.U.
WHICH MEANS I'M GOING TO HAVE TO WORK EXTRA FAST TO BUMP OFF A FEW MORE OF YOU TODAY!
HAHAHAHA

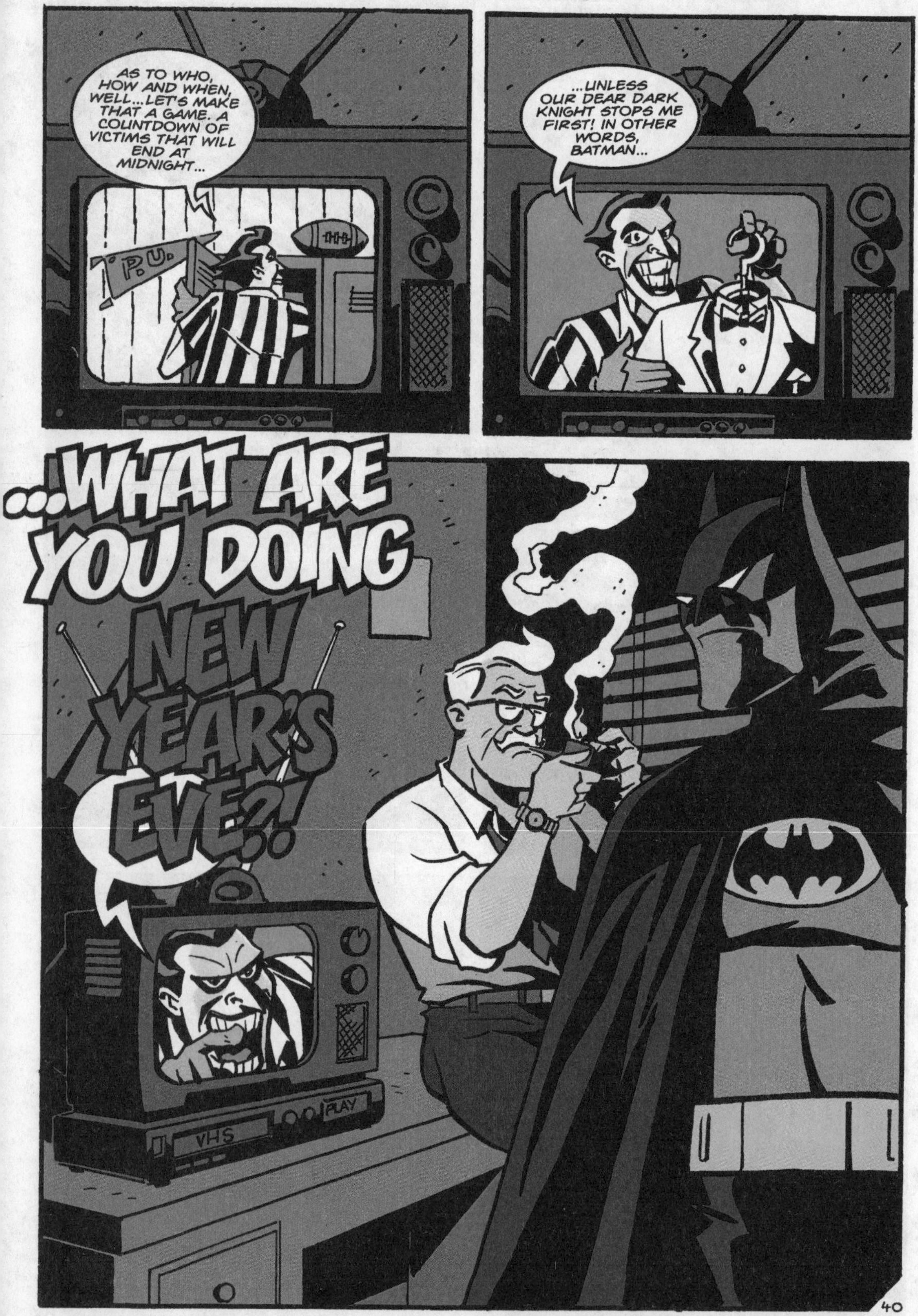

AS TO WHO, HOW AND WHEN, WELL... LET'S MAKE THAT A GAME. A COUNTDOWN OF VICTIMS THAT WILL END AT MIDNIGHT...
P.U.
...UNLESS OUR DEAR DARK KNIGHT STOPS ME FIRST! IN OTHER WORDS, BATMAN...
...WHAT ARE YOU DOING NEW YEAR'S EVE?!
VHS
PLAY

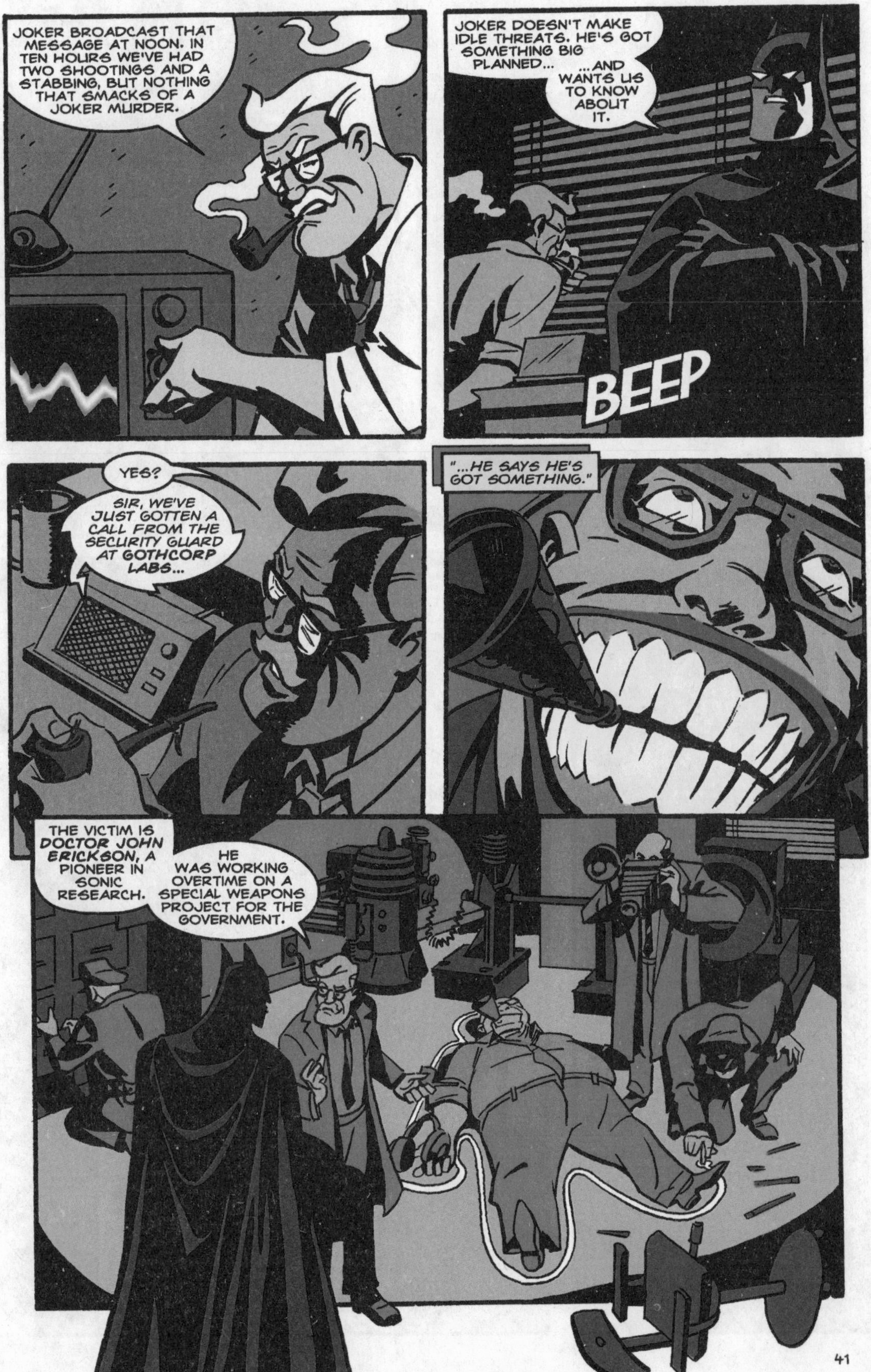

JOKER BROADCAST THAT MESSAGE AT NOON. IN TEN HOURS WE'VE HAD TWO SHOOTINGS AND A STABBING, BUT NOTHING THAT SMACKS OF A JOKER MURDER.
JOKER DOESN'T MAKE IDLE THREATS. HE'S GOT SOMETHING BIG PLANNED...
...AND WANTS US TO KNOW ABOUT IT.
BEEP
YES?
SIR, WE'VE JUST GOTTEN A CALL FROM THE SECURITY GUARD AT GOTHCORP LABS...
"...HE SAYS HE'S GOT SOMETHING."
THE VICTIM IS DOCTOR JOHN ERICKSON, A PIONEER IN SONIC RESEARCH.
HE WAS WORKING OVERTIME ON A SPECIAL WEAPONS PROJECT FOR THE GOVERNMENT.

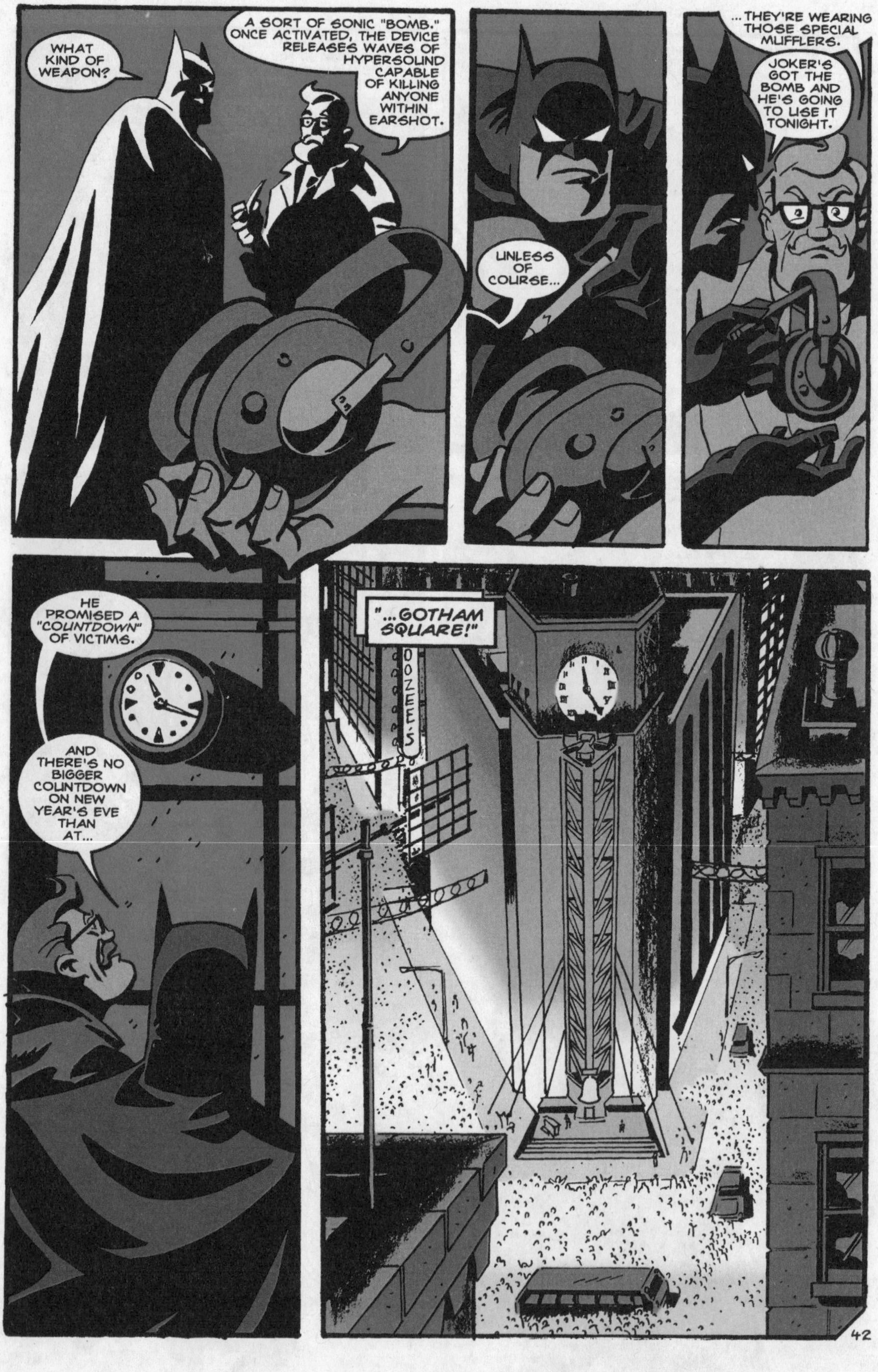
WHAT KIND OF WEAPON?
A SORT OF SONIC "BOMB." ONCE ACTIVATED, THE DEVICE RELEASES WAVES OF HYPERSOUND CAPABLE OF KILLING ANYONE WITHIN EARSHOT.
UNLESS OF COURSE...
...THEY'RE WEARING THOSE SPECIAL MUFFLERS.
JOKER'S GOT THE BOMB AND HE'S GOING TO USE IT TONIGHT.
HE PROMISED A "COUNTDOWN" OF VICTIMS.
AND THERE'S NO BIGGER COUNTDOWN ON NEW YEAR'S EVE THAN AT...
"...GOTHAM SQUARE!"
OOZEE'S

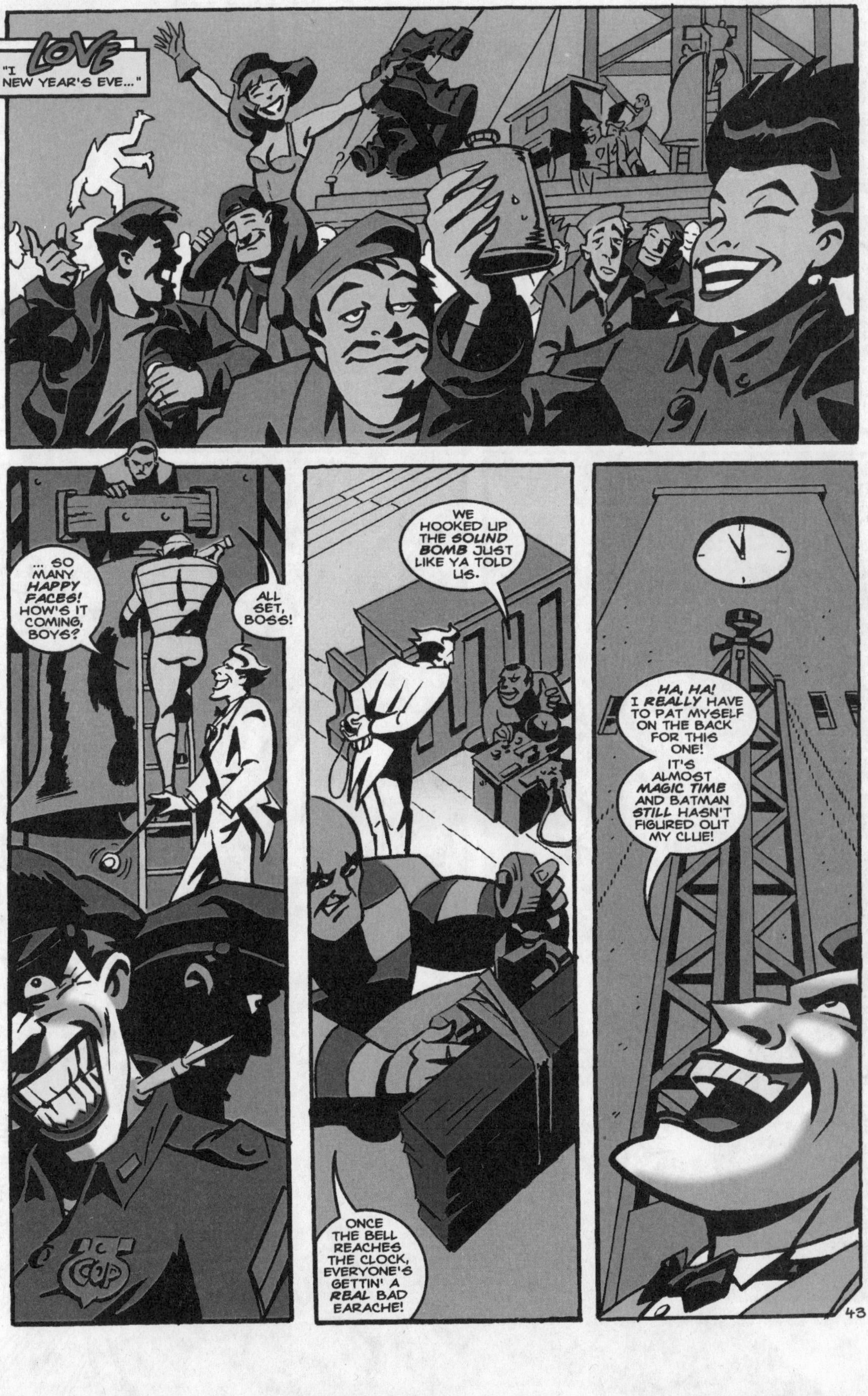
"I LOVE NEW YEAR'S EVE..."
... SO MANY HAPPY FACES! HOW'S IT COMING, BOYS?
ALL SET, BOSS!
COP
WE HOOKED UP THE SOUND BOMB JUST LIKE YA TOLD US.
ONCE THE BELL REACHES THE CLOCK, EVERYONE'S GETTIN' A REAL BAD EARACHE!
HA, HA! I REALLY HAVE TO PAT MYSELF ON THE BACK FOR THIS ONE!
IT'S ALMOST MAGIC TIME AND BATMAN STILL HASN'T FIGURED OUT MY CLUE!

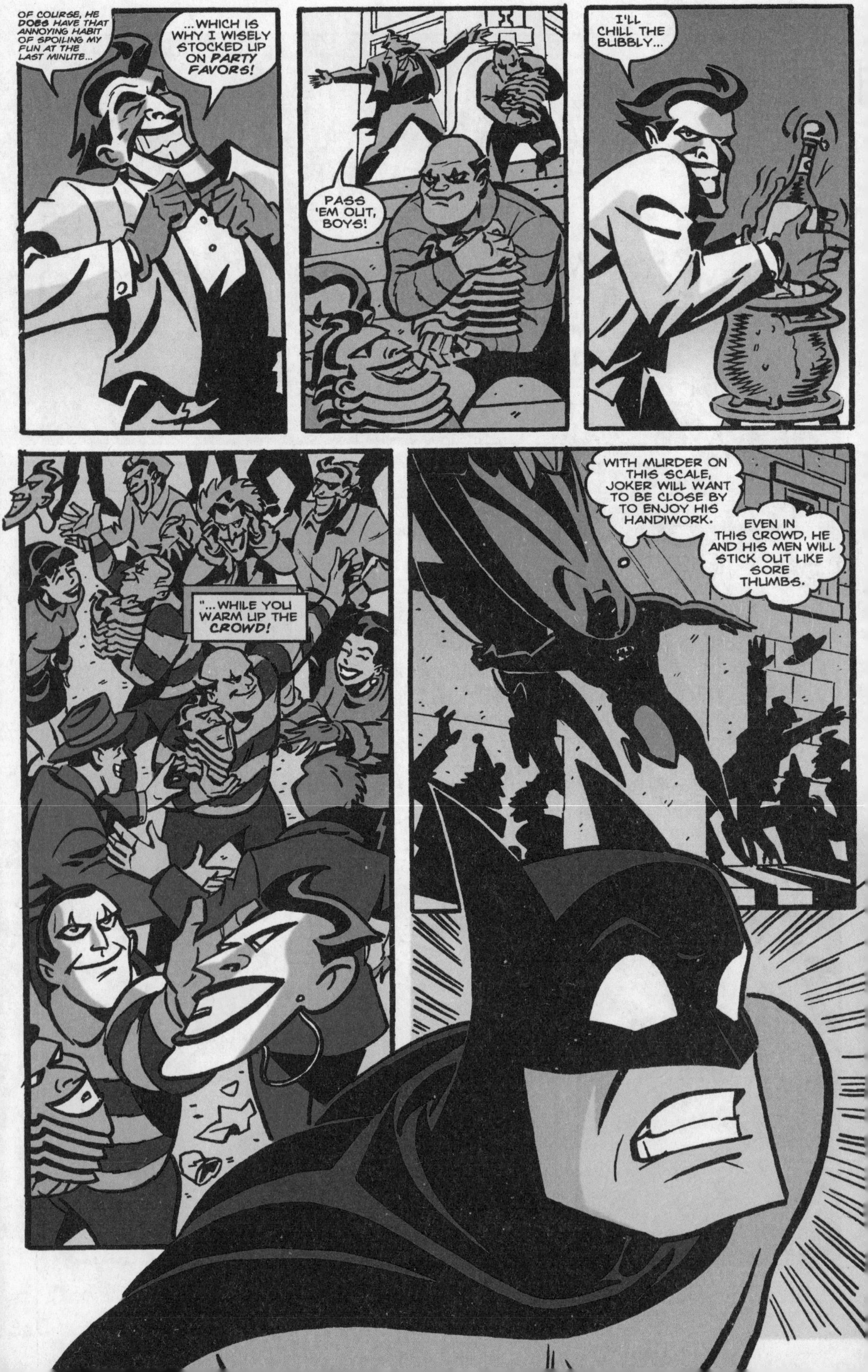
OF COURSE, HE DOES HAVE THAT ANNOYING HABIT OF SPOILING MY FUN AT THE LAST MINUTE...
...WHICH IS WHY I WISELY STOCKED UP ON PARTY FAVORS!
PASS 'EM OUT, BOYS!
I'LL CHILL THE BUBBLY...
"...WHILE YOU WARM UP THE CROWD!
WITH MURDER ON THIS SCALE, JOKER WILL WANT TO BE CLOSE BY TO ENJOY HIS HANDIWORK.
EVEN IN THIS CROWD, HE AND HIS MEN WILL STICK OUT LIKE SORE THUMBS.

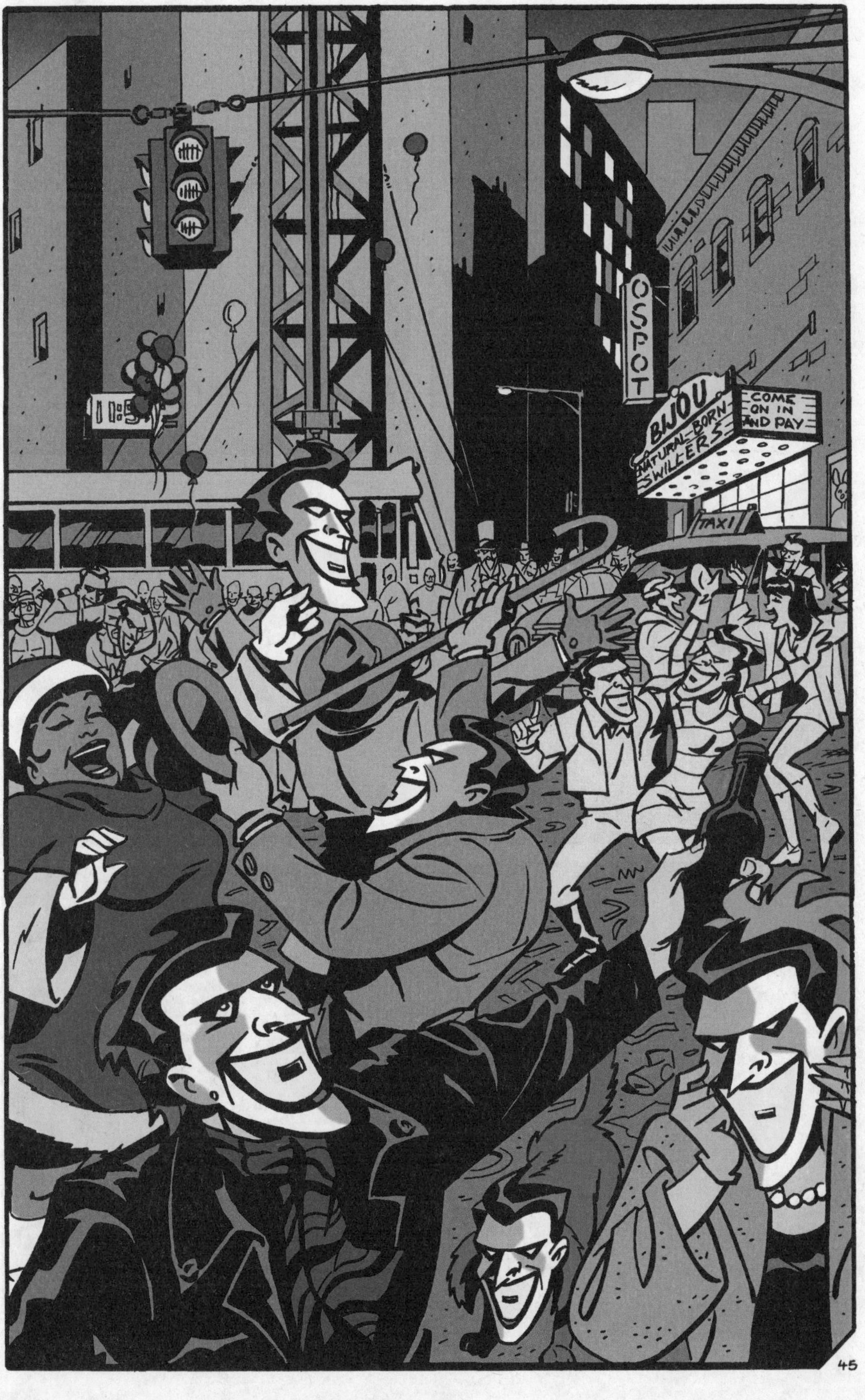
OSPOT
BIJOU
NATURAL-BORN SWILLERS
COME ON IN AND PAY
TAXI

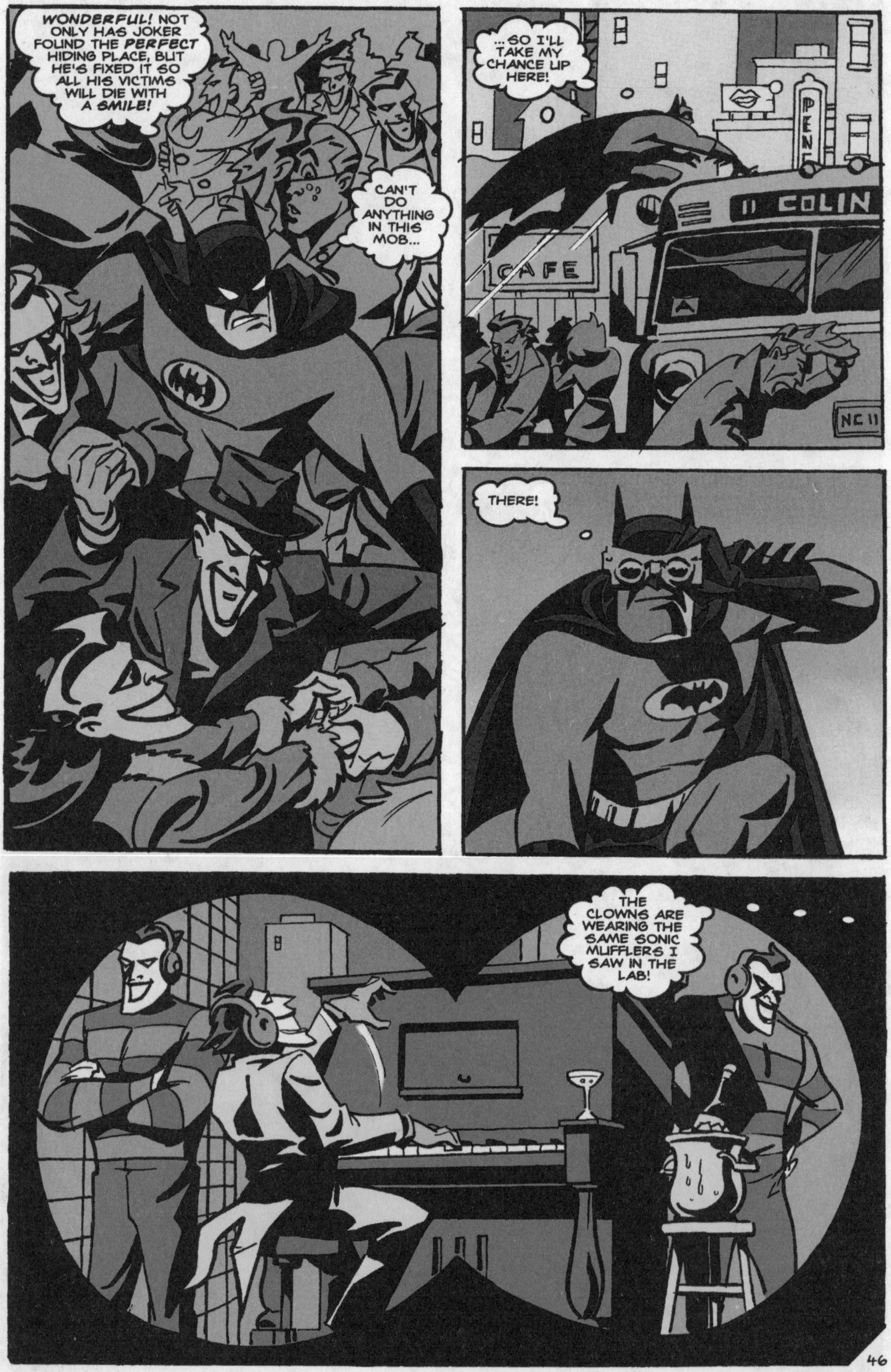
WONDERFUL! NOT ONLY HAS JOKER FOUND THE PERFECT HIDING PLACE, BUT HE'S FIXED IT SO ALL HIS VICTIMS WILL DIE WITH A SMILE!
CAN'T DO ANYTHING IN THIS MOB...
...SO I'LL TAKE MY CHANCE UP HERE!
COLIN
CAFE
NC 11
THERE!
THE CLOWNS ARE WEARING THE SAME SONIC MUFFLERS I SAW IN THE LAB!

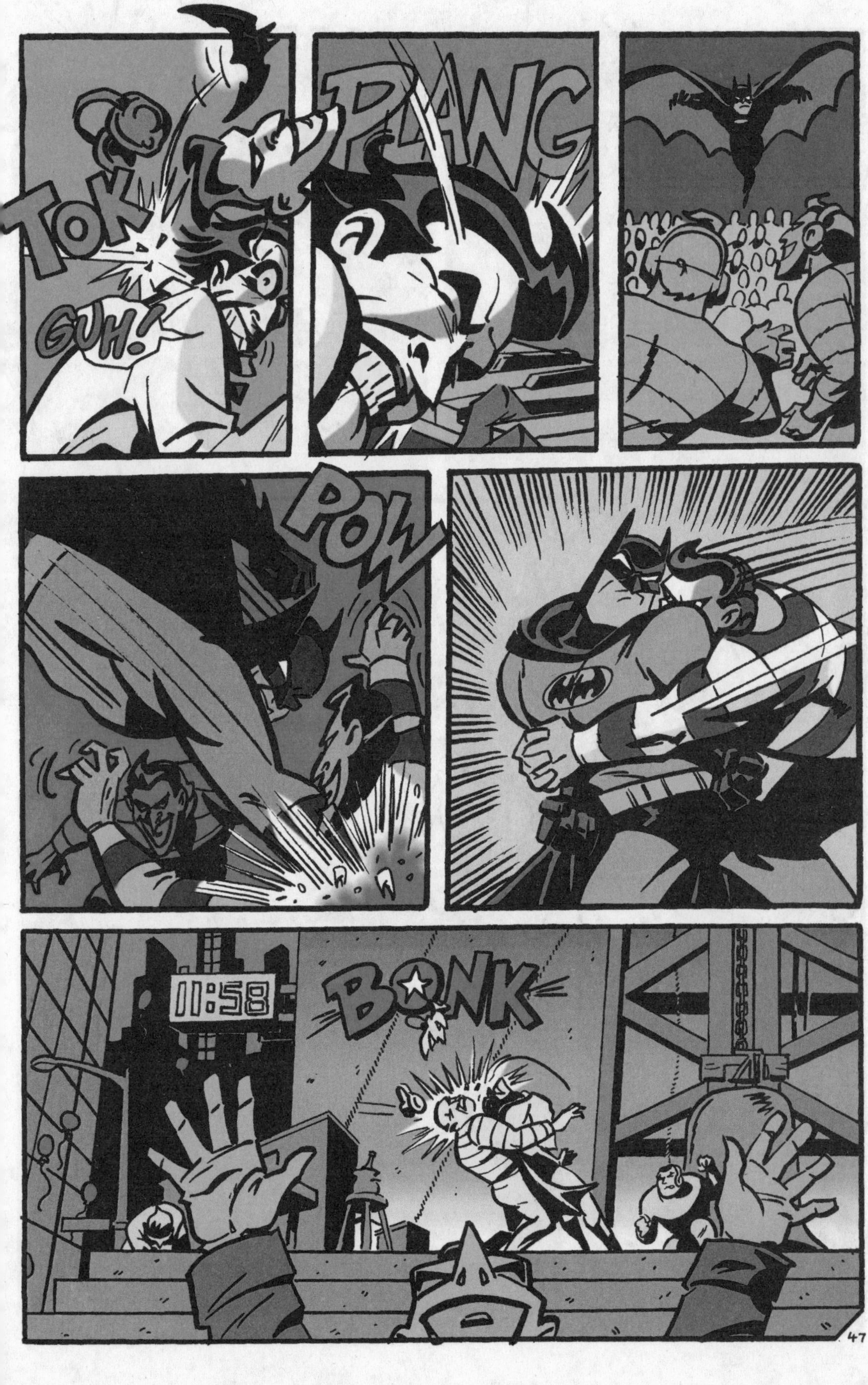
TOK
GUH!
PLANG
POW
11:58
BONK

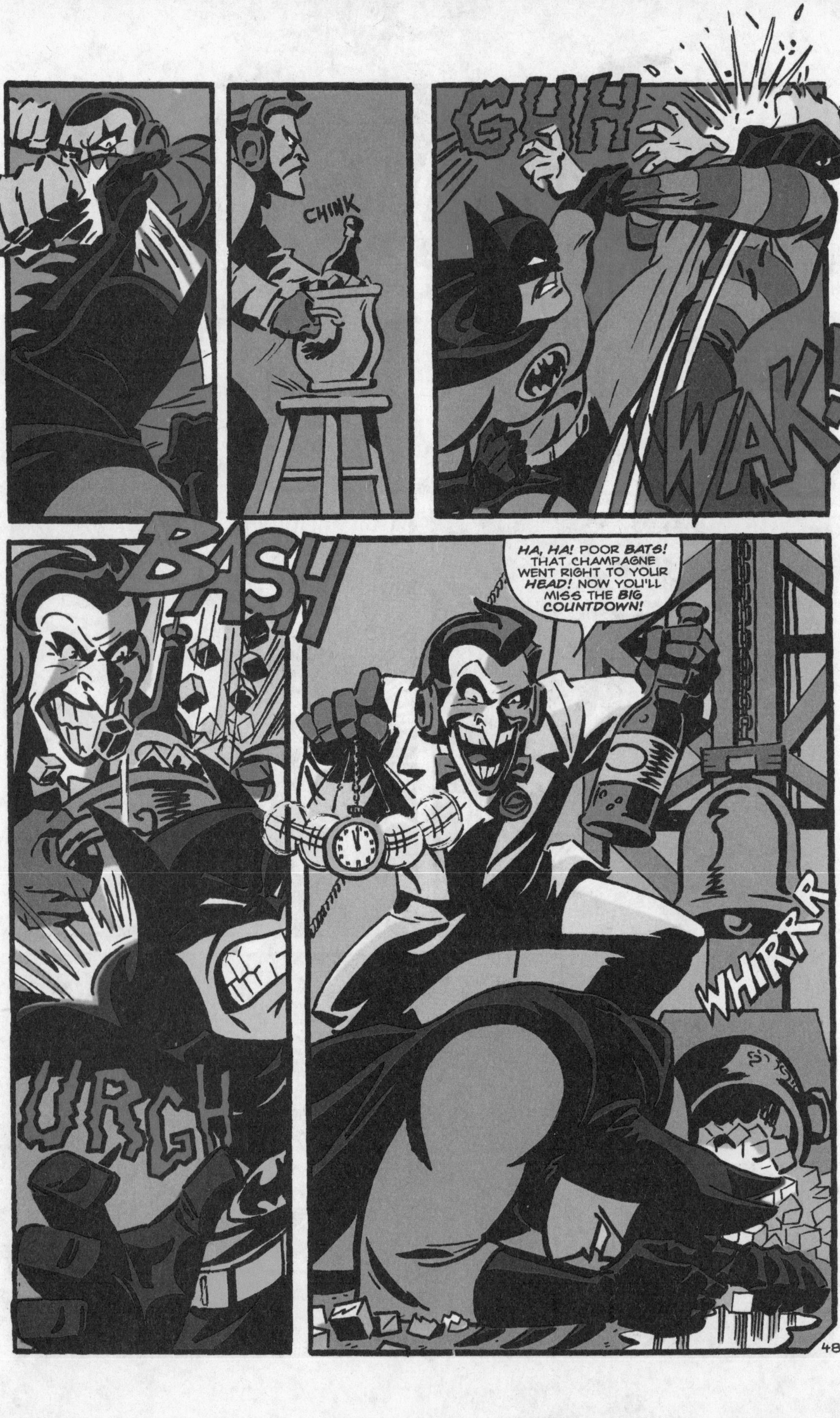
CHINK
GUH
WAK!
BASH
HA, HA! POOR BATS! THAT CHAMPAGNE WENT RIGHT TO YOUR HEAD! NOW YOU'LL MISS THE BIG COUNTDOWN!
WHIRRR
URGH

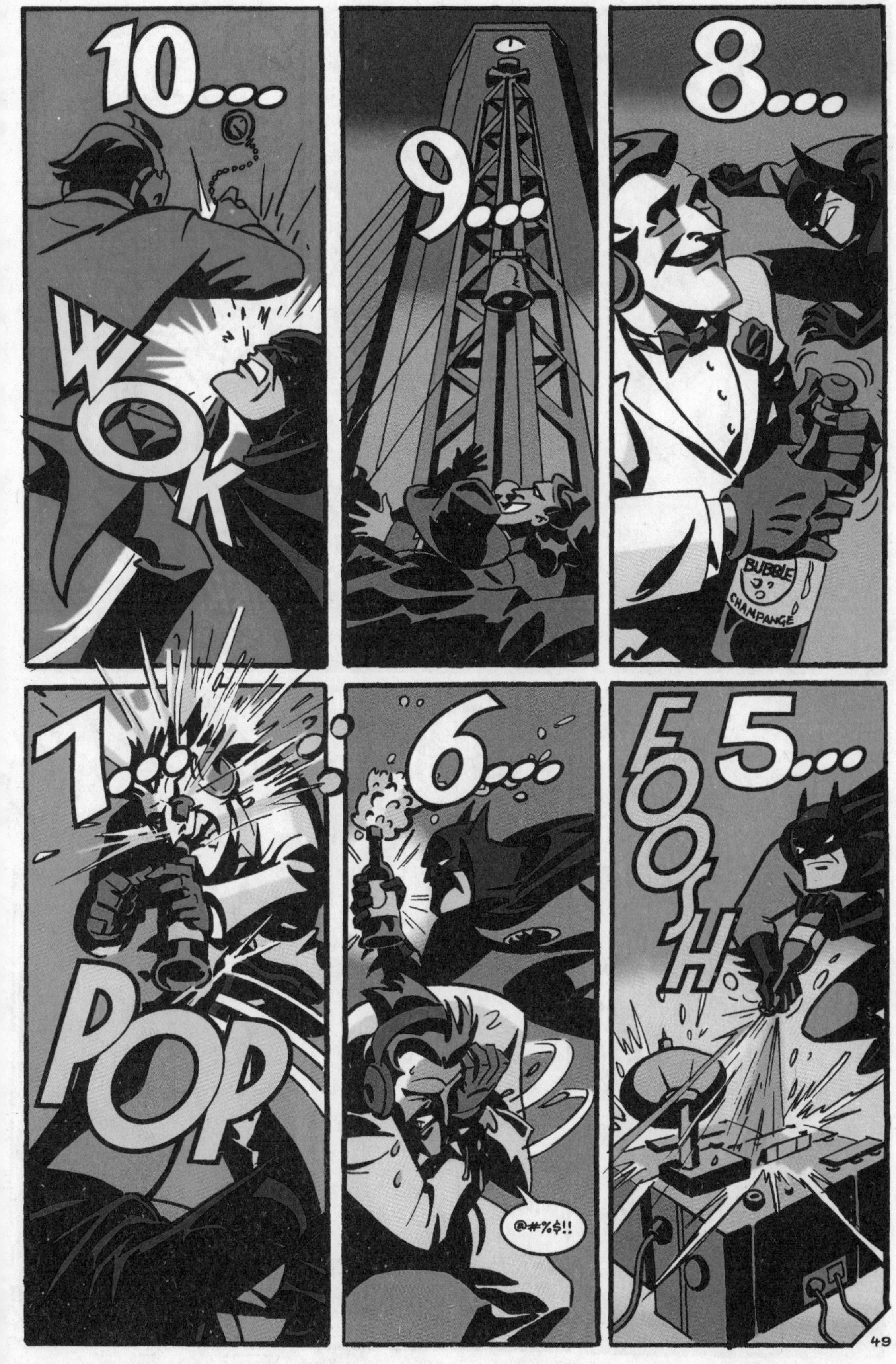
10...
WOK
9...
8...
BUBBLE
CHAMPANGE
7...
POP
6...
@#%$!!
FOOSH
5...

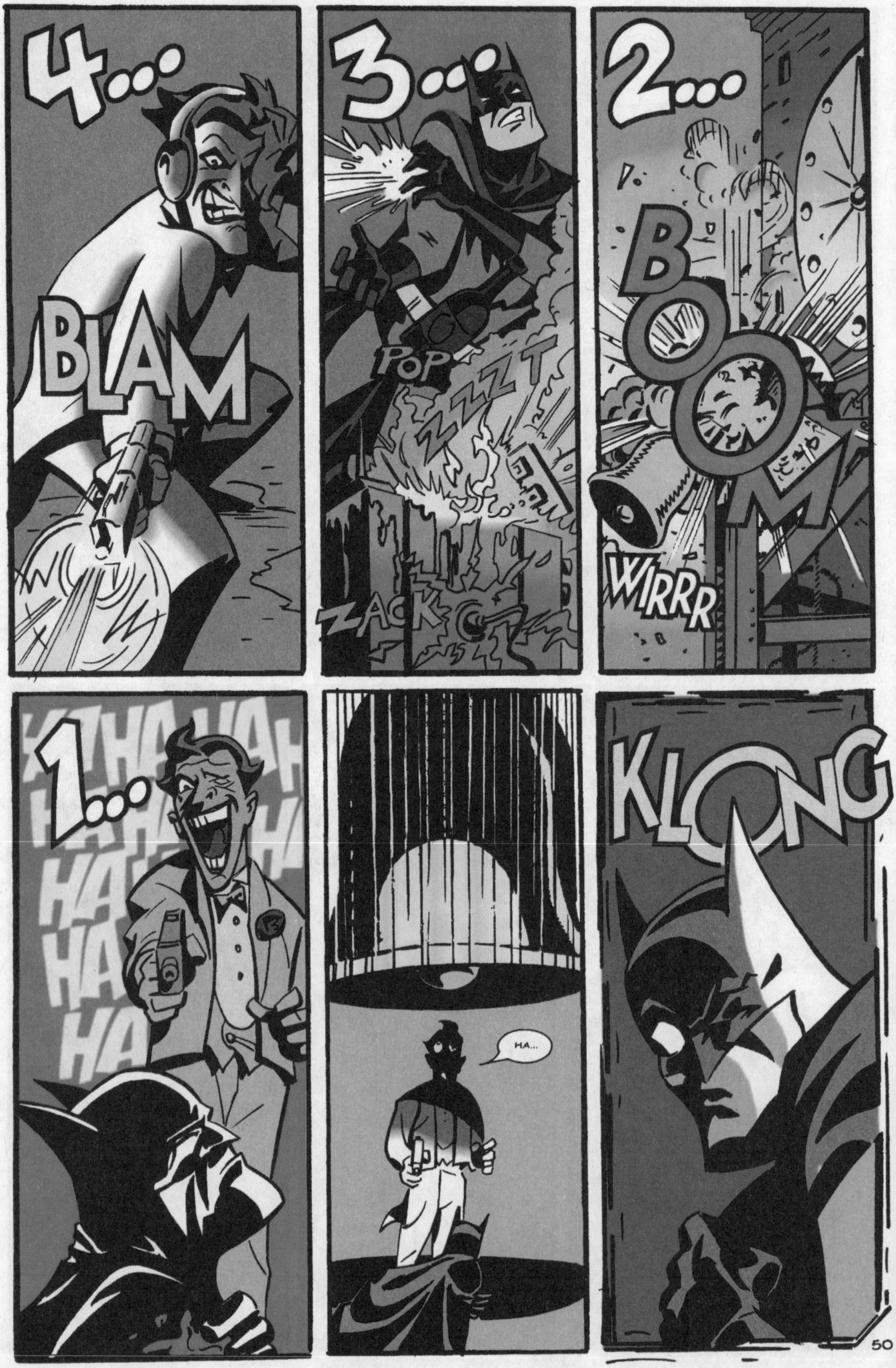
4...
BLAM
3...
POP
ZZZZT
ZACK
2...
BOOM
WIRRR
1...
HA HA HA HA HA HA
HA...
KLONG

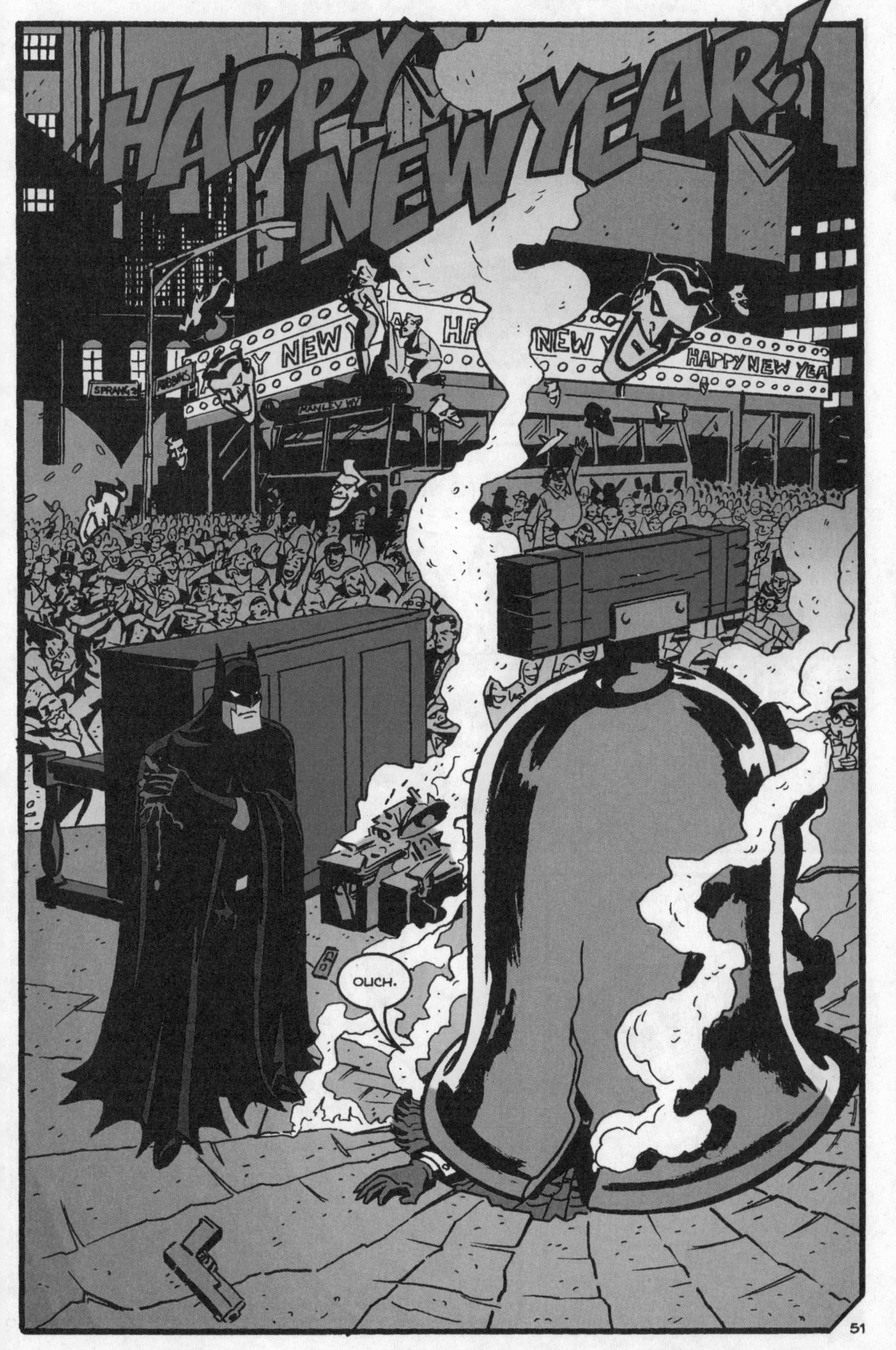
HAPPY NEW YEAR!
HAPPY NEW YEA
MANLEY WY
OUCH.

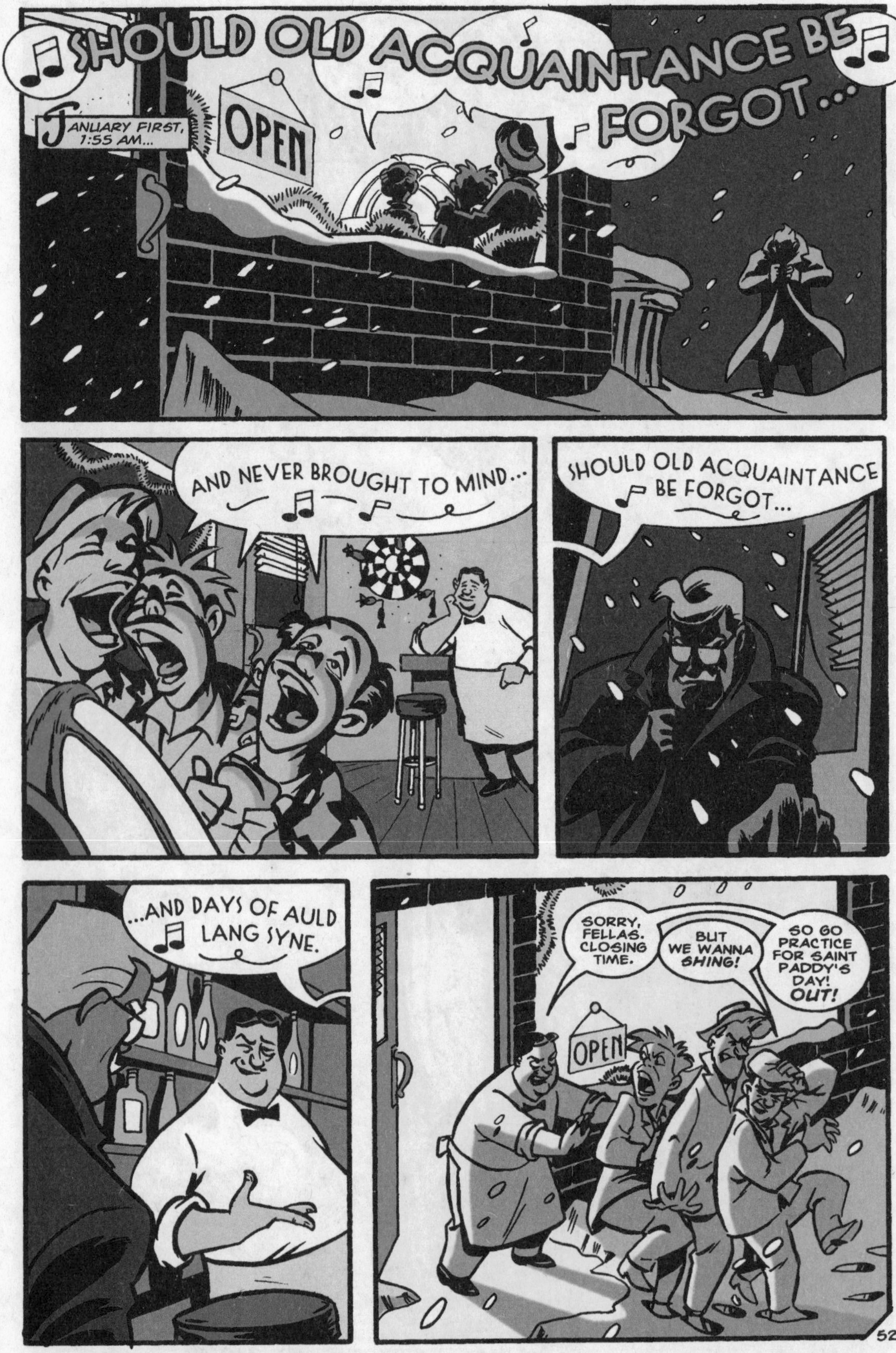
SHOULD OLD ACQUAINTANCE BE FORGOT...
JANUARY FIRST, 1:55 AM...
OPEN
AND NEVER BROUGHT TO MIND...
SHOULD OLD ACQUAINTANCE BE FORGOT...
...AND DAYS OF AULD LANG SYNE.
SORRY, FELLAS. CLOSING TIME.
BUT WE WANNA SHING!
SO GO PRACTICE FOR SAINT PADDY'S DAY! OUT!
OPEN

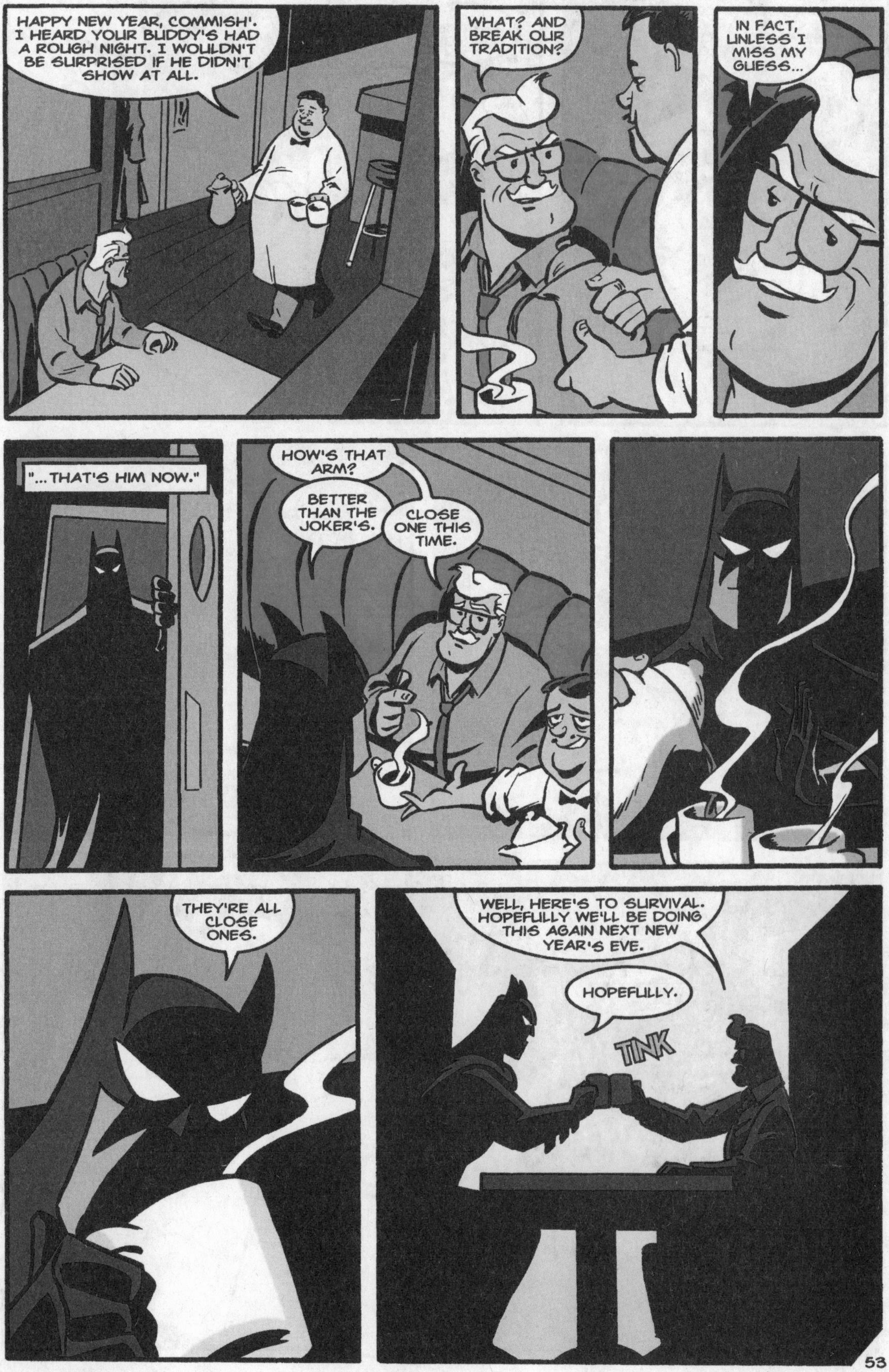
HAPPY NEW YEAR, COMMISH'. I HEARD YOUR BUDDY'S HAD A ROUGH NIGHT. I WOULDN'T BE SURPRISED IF HE DIDN'T SHOW AT ALL.
WHAT? AND BREAK OUR TRADITION?
IN FACT, UNLESS I MISS MY GUESS...
"...THAT'S HIM NOW."
HOW'S THAT ARM?
BETTER THAN THE JOKER'S.
CLOSE ONE THIS TIME.
THEY'RE ALL CLOSE ONES.
WELL, HERE'S TO SURVIVAL. HOPEFULLY WE'LL BE DOING THIS AGAIN NEXT NEW YEAR'S EVE.
HOPEFULLY.
TINK

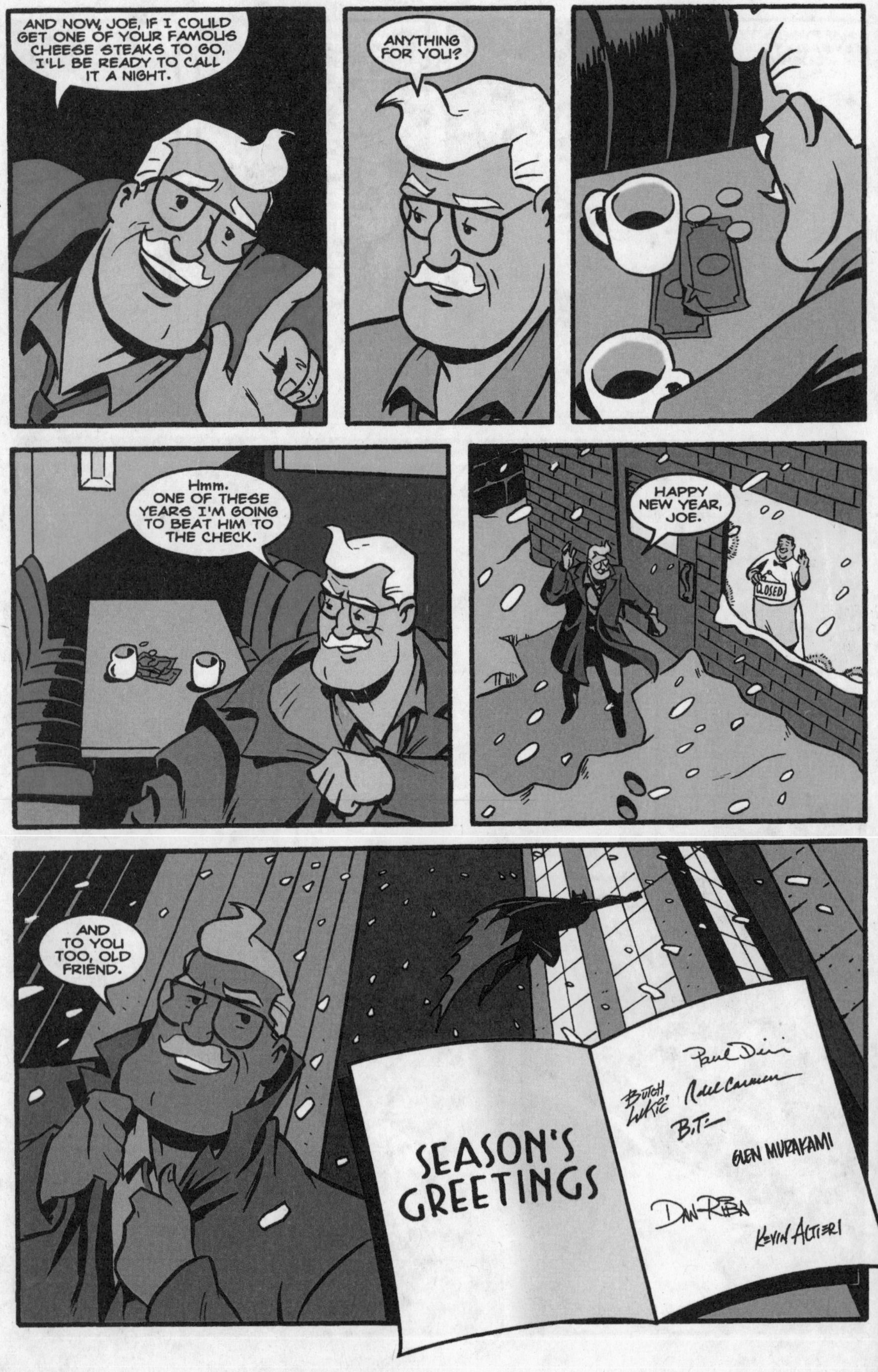
AND NOW, JOE, IF I COULD GET ONE OF YOUR FAMOUS CHEESE STEAKS TO GO, I'LL BE READY TO CALL IT A NIGHT.
ANYTHING FOR YOU?
Hmm. ONE OF THESE YEARS I'M GOING TO BEAT HIM TO THE CHECK.
HAPPY NEW YEAR, JOE.
CLOSED
AND TO YOU TOO, OLD FRIEND.
SEASON'S GREETINGS
Paul Dini
BUTCH LUKIC
GLEN MURAKAMI
KEVIN ALTIERI

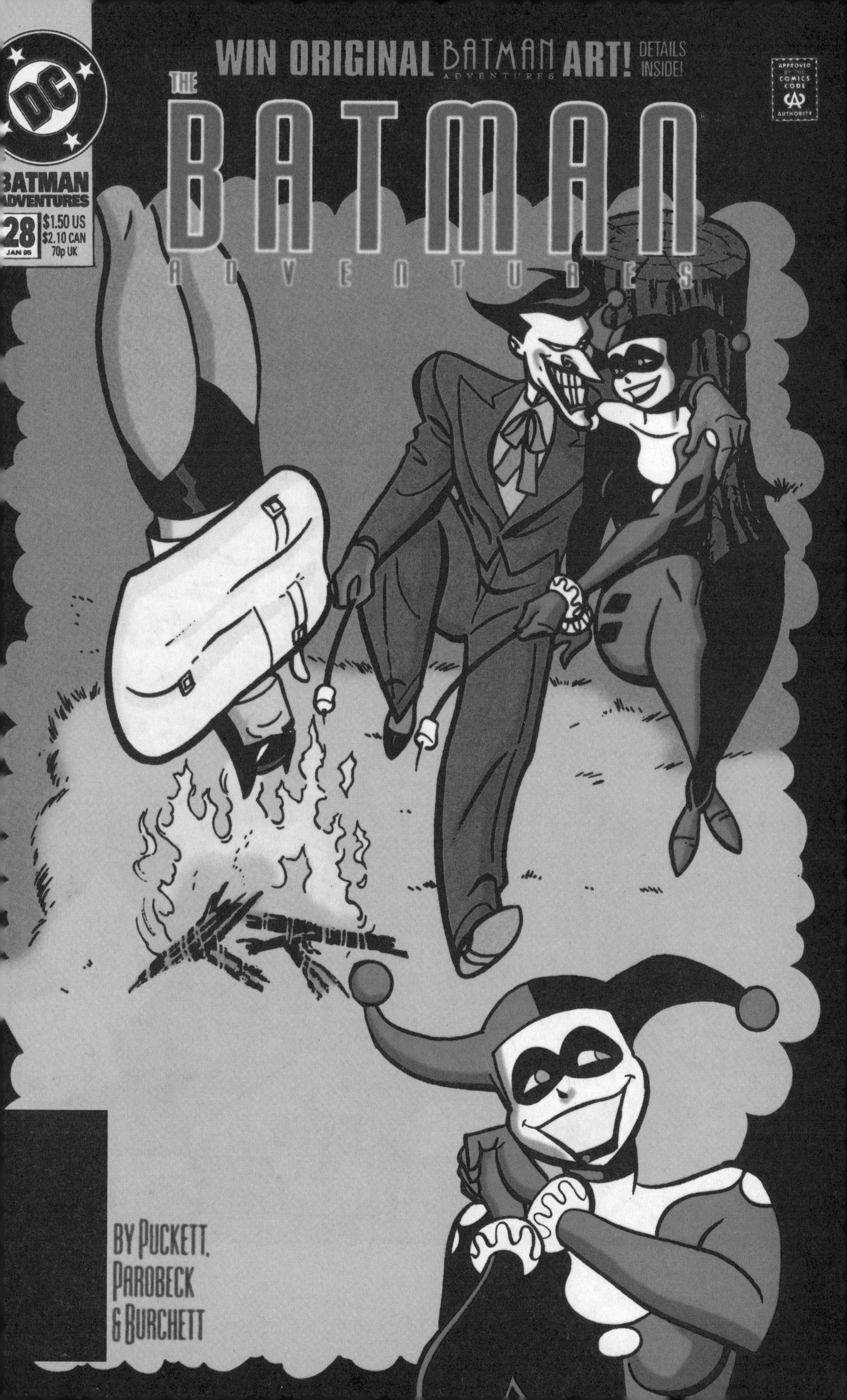

WIN ORIGINAL BATMAN ADVENTURES ART! DETAILS INSIDE!
APPROVED BY THE COMICS CODE AUTHORITY
DC
BATMAN ADVENTURES
28
JAN 95
$1.50 US
$2.10 CAN
70p UK
THE BATMAN ADVENTURES
BY PUCKETT, PAROBECK & BURCHETT

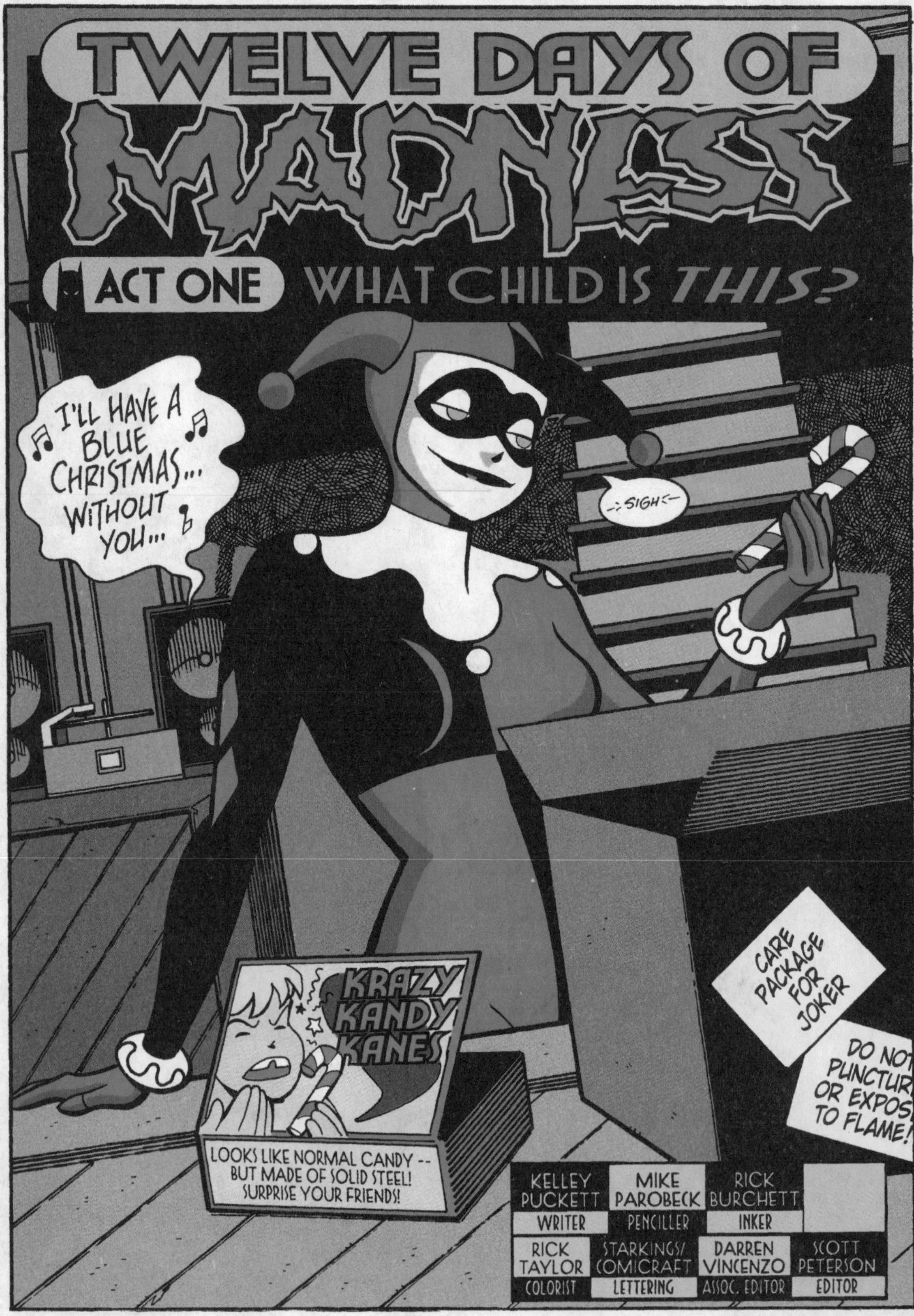
TWELVE DAYS OF
MADNESS
ACT ONE WHAT CHILD IS THIS?
I'LL HAVE A BLUE CHRISTMAS... WITHOUT YOU...
SIGH
KRAZY KANDY KANES
LOOKS LIKE NORMAL CANDY -- BUT MADE OF SOLID STEEL! SURPRISE YOUR FRIENDS!
CARE PACKAGE FOR JOKER
DO NOT PUNCTURE OR EXPOSE TO FLAME!
KELLEY PUCKETT WRITER
MIKE PAROBECK PENCILLER
RICK BURCHETT INKER
RICK TAYLOR COLORIST
STARKINGS/COMICRAFT LETTERING
DARREN VINCENZO ASSOC. EDITOR
SCOTT PETERSON EDITOR

ROSES ARE RED, VIOLETS ARE BLUE, YOU'RE TIED UP IN YOUR CELL, I WISH I WAS —

BRRRING

CHORUS ONE

JINGLE BELLS, JINGLE BELLS,

JINGLE ALL THE WAY

SING OUT, EVERYBODY! ONLY A WEEK OF PRACTICE LEFT TILL THE BIG CHRISTMAS SHOW!

SAVE ME, HARLEY! I'M GOING INSANE WITH BOREDOM!

SAY NO MORE, MISTER J! GIMME A SEC TO FIND THE FORM AND I'LL COMMIT MYSELF!

CHORUS ONE

BATMAN SMELLS

BELLS, JINGLE BELLS,

ROBIN LAID AN EGG

LL THE WAY

NO, NO, NO. I'VE GOT SOMETHING ELSE IN MIND...

HA HA HA

2

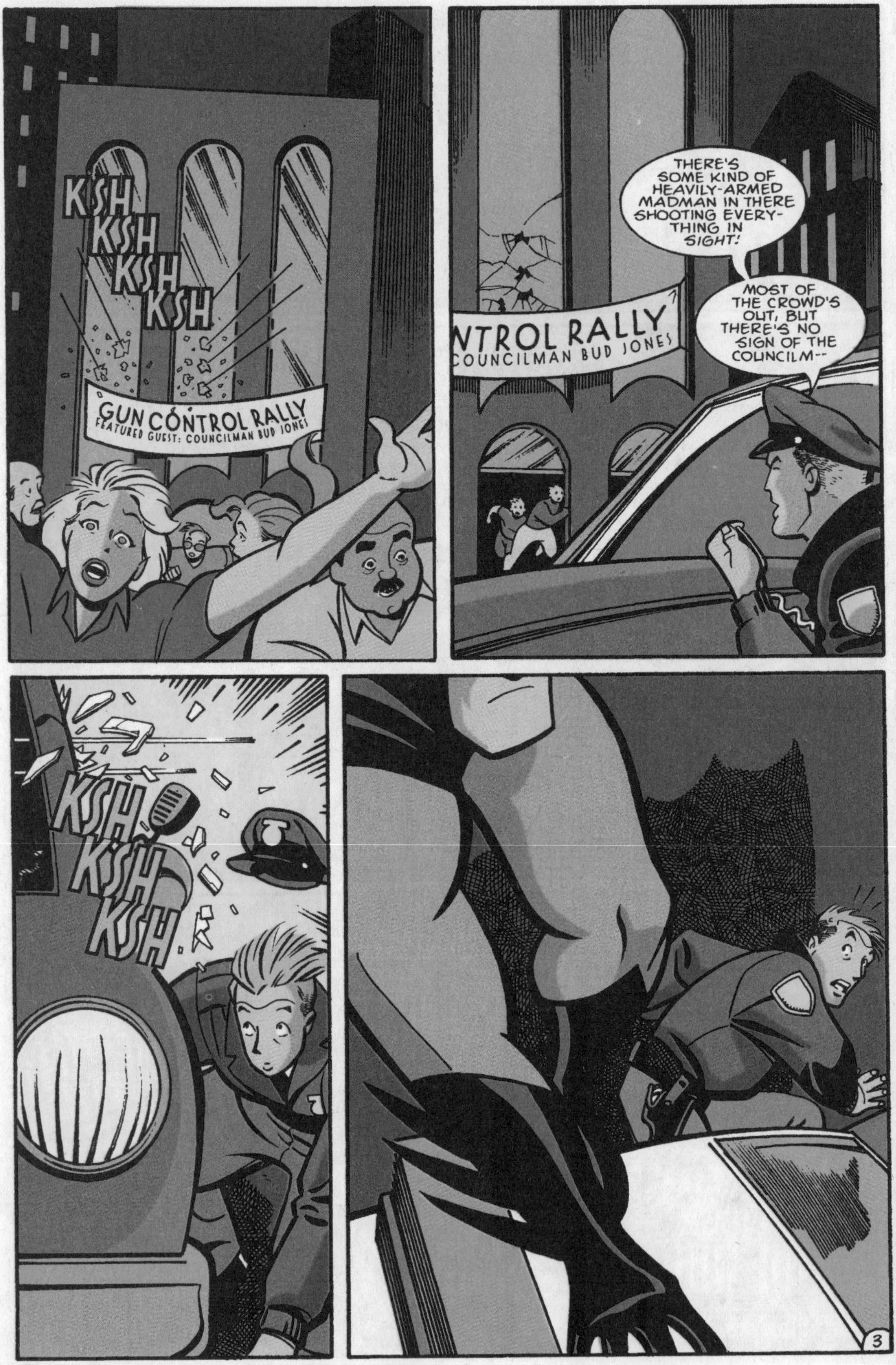
KSH KSH KSH KSH
GUN CONTROL RALLY
FEATURED GUEST: COUNCILMAN BUD JONES
NTROL RALLY
COUNCILMAN BUD JONES
THERE'S SOME KIND OF HEAVILY-ARMED MADMAN IN THERE SHOOTING EVERY-THING IN SIGHT!
MOST OF THE CROWD'S OUT, BUT THERE'S NO SIGN OF THE COUNCILM--
KSH KSH KSH
3

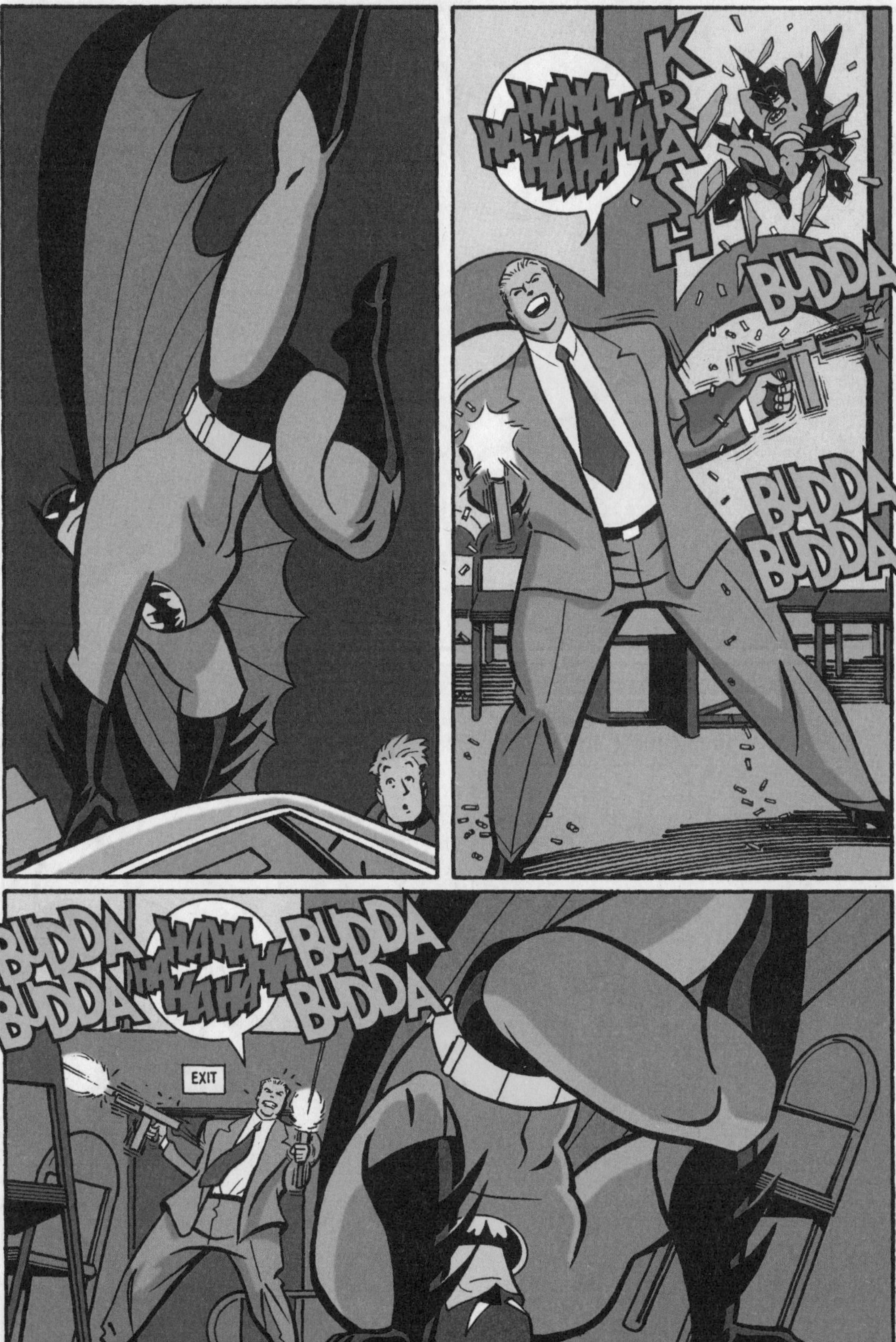

HAHAHAHA HAHAHA
KRASH
BUDDA
BUDDA BUDDA
BUDDA BUDDA
HAHAHAHAHA
BUDDA BUDDA
EXIT

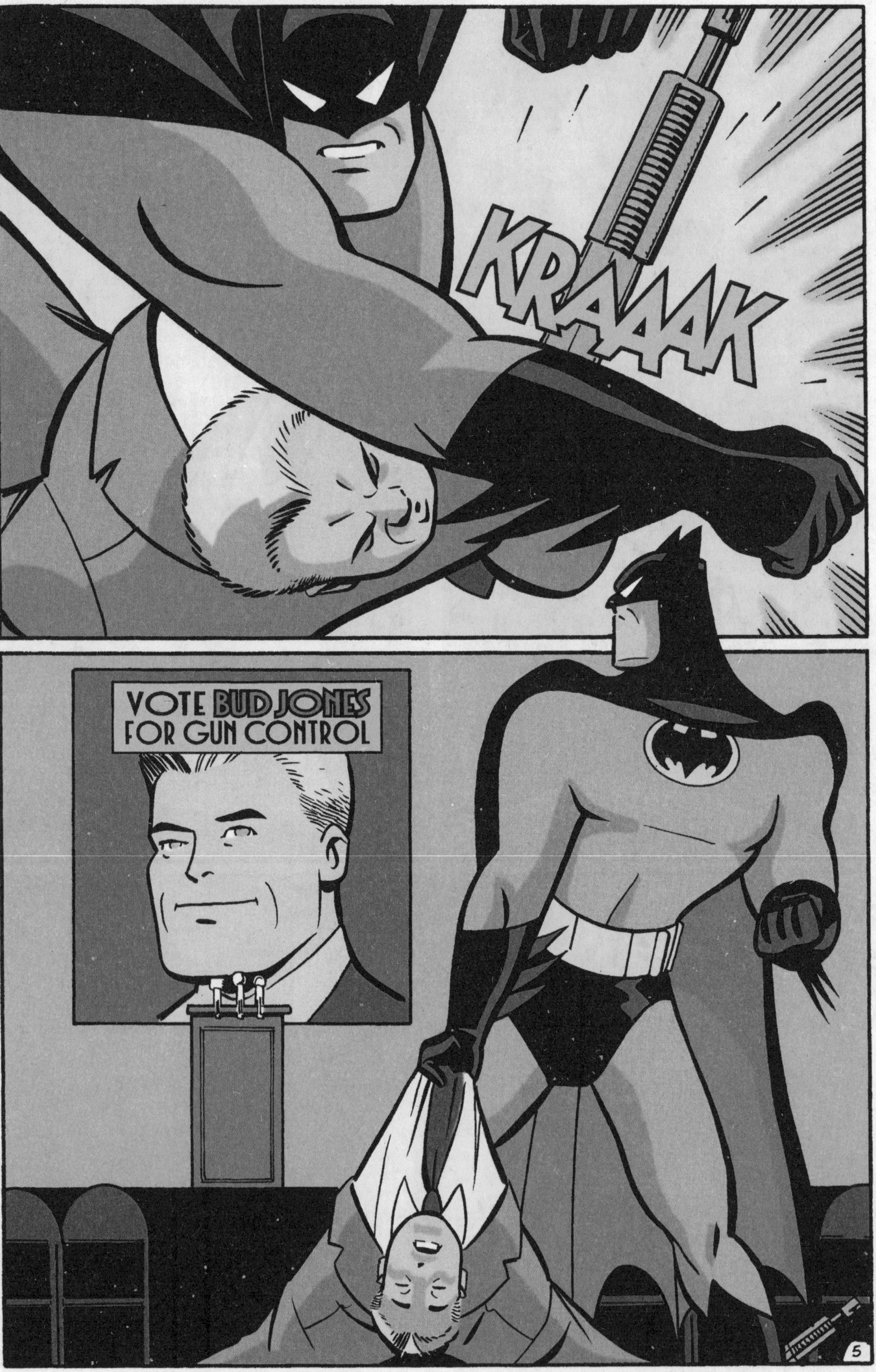
KRAAAK
VOTE BUD JONES
FOR GUN CONTROL
5

I CAN'T TELL YOU HOW *HONORED* I AM TO HAVE SOMEONE FROM THE DUSSELDORF INSTITUTE VISITING US HERE AT ARKHAM, DOCTOR HEIMLICH!

JA, VELL -- YOU SHOULD BE.

VAT IS ZIS?

DR M. MEDVED
DIRECTOR GENERAL

NOT *NOW*, DOCTOR LELAND! CAN'T YOU SEE I'M *BUSY*?

EMERGENCY ADMITTANCE, DOCTOR MEDVED. YOUR *SIGNATURE'S* REQUIRED.

VERRRY INTERESTING ...

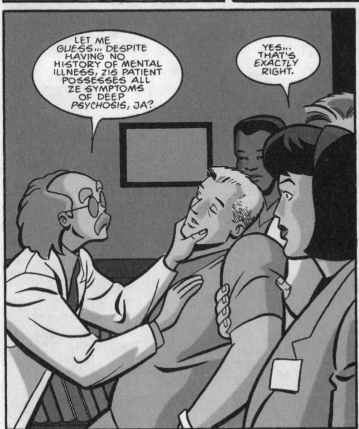

LET ME *GUESS*... DESPITE HAVING NO HISTORY OF MENTAL ILLNESS, ZIS PATIENT POSSESSES ALL ZE SYMPTOMS OF DEEP PSYCHOSIS, JA?

YES... THAT'S *EXACTLY* RIGHT.

AS I SUSPECTED. I VILL STAY HERE UND SEE TO ZIS PATIENT MYSELF.

HE VILL BE COMPLETELY CURED IN ONE VEEK, OR MY NAME ISN'T *HEINRIK HEIMLICH*!

6

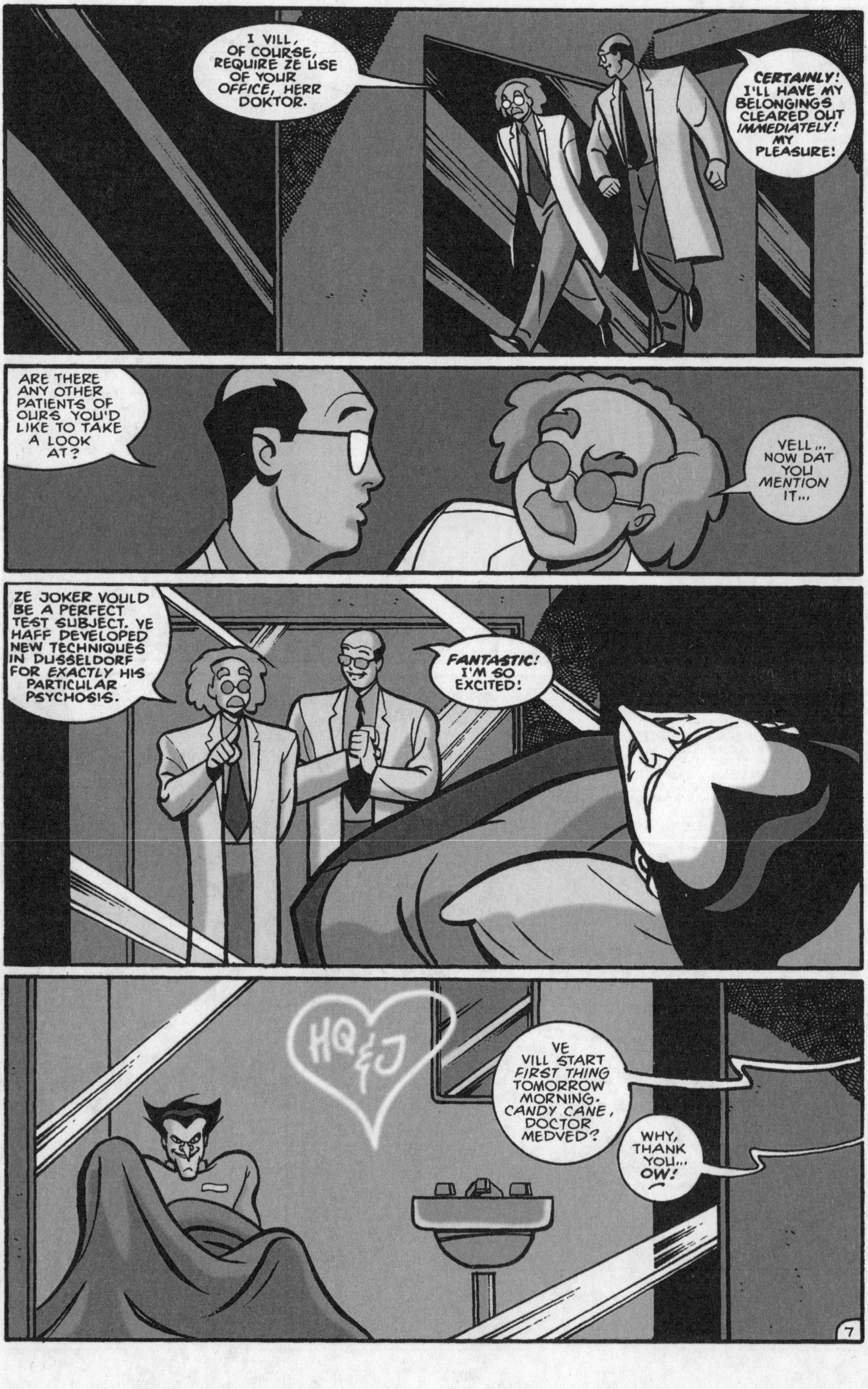
I VILL, OF COURSE, REQUIRE ZE USE OF YOUR OFFICE, HERR DOKTOR.
CERTAINLY! I'LL HAVE MY BELONGINGS CLEARED OUT IMMEDIATELY! MY PLEASURE!
ARE THERE ANY OTHER PATIENTS OF OURS YOU'D LIKE TO TAKE A LOOK AT?
VELL... NOW DAT YOU MENTION IT...
ZE JOKER VOULD BE A PERFECT TEST SUBJECT. VE HAFF DEVELOPED NEW TECHNIQUES IN DUSSELDORF FOR EXACTLY HIS PARTICULAR PSYCHOSIS.
FANTASTIC! I'M SO EXCITED!
HQ & J
VE VILL START FIRST THING TOMORROW MORNING. CANDY CANE, DOCTOR MEDVED?
WHY, THANK YOU... OW!

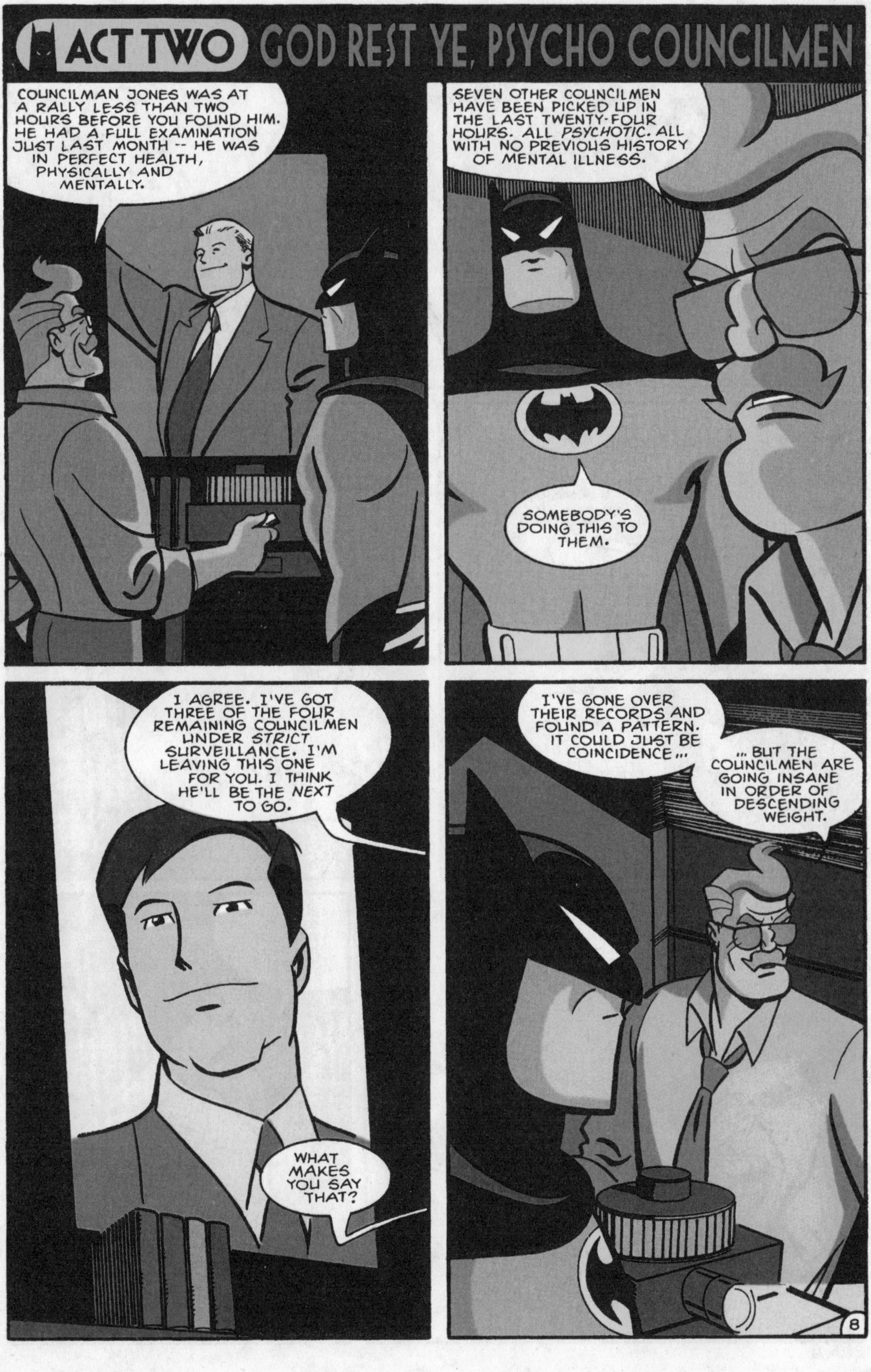
ACT TWO GOD REST YE, PSYCHO COUNCILMEN
COUNCILMAN JONES WAS AT A RALLY LESS THAN TWO HOURS BEFORE YOU FOUND HIM. HE HAD A FULL EXAMINATION JUST LAST MONTH -- HE WAS IN PERFECT HEALTH, PHYSICALLY AND MENTALLY.
SEVEN OTHER COUNCILMEN HAVE BEEN PICKED UP IN THE LAST TWENTY-FOUR HOURS. ALL *PSYCHOTIC*. ALL WITH NO PREVIOUS HISTORY OF MENTAL ILLNESS.
SOMEBODY'S DOING THIS TO THEM.
I AGREE. I'VE GOT THREE OF THE FOUR REMAINING COUNCILMEN UNDER *STRICT* SURVEILLANCE. I'M LEAVING THIS ONE FOR YOU. I THINK HE'LL BE THE *NEXT* TO GO.
WHAT MAKES YOU SAY THAT?
I'VE GONE OVER THEIR RECORDS AND FOUND A PATTERN. IT COULD JUST BE COINCIDENCE...
... BUT THE COUNCILMEN ARE GOING INSANE IN ORDER OF DESCENDING WEIGHT.
8

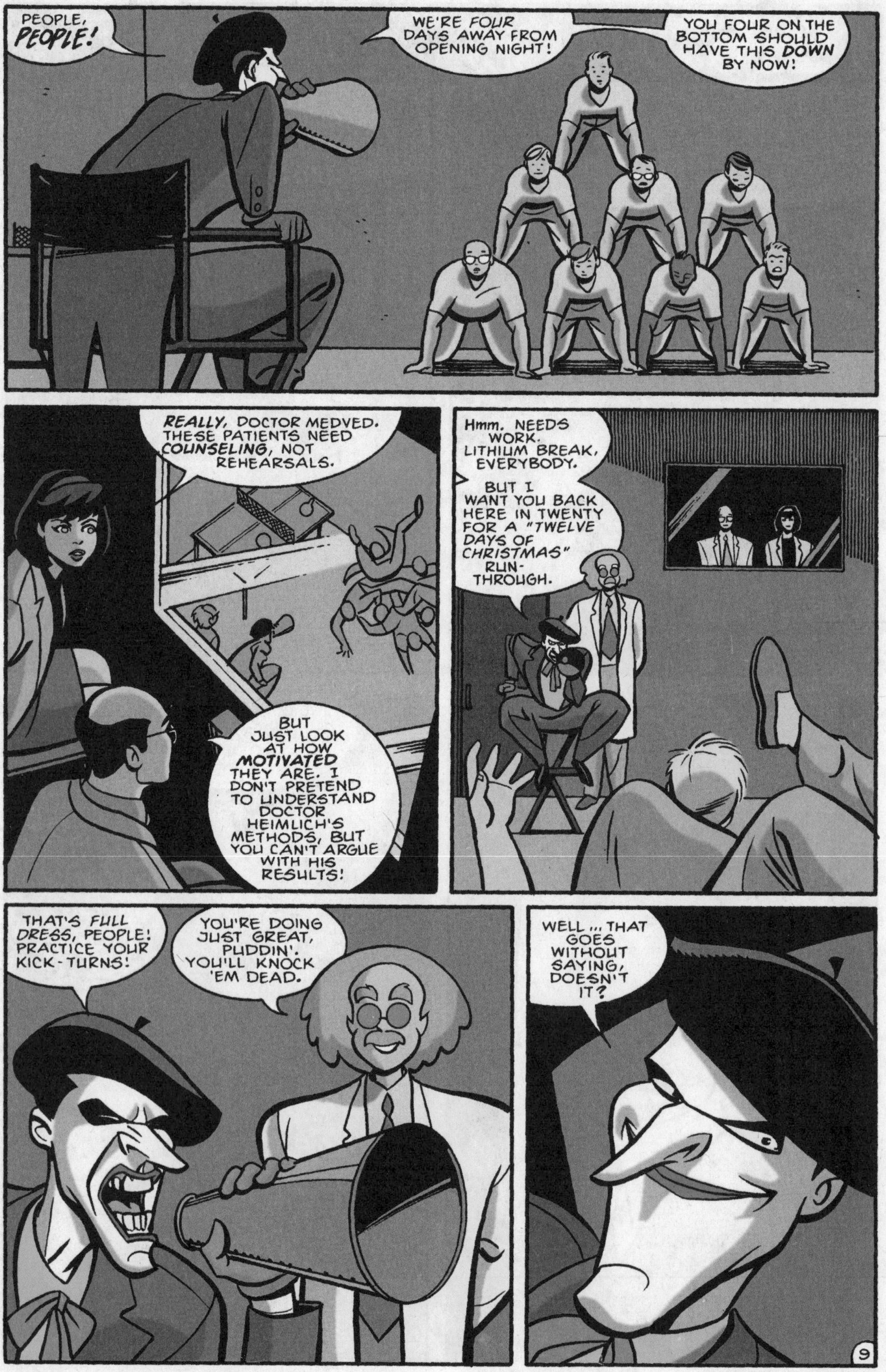
PEOPLE, PEOPLE!
WE'RE FOUR DAYS AWAY FROM OPENING NIGHT!
YOU FOUR ON THE BOTTOM SHOULD HAVE THIS DOWN BY NOW!
REALLY, DOCTOR MEDVED. THESE PATIENTS NEED COUNSELING, NOT REHEARSALS.
BUT JUST LOOK AT HOW MOTIVATED THEY ARE. I DON'T PRETEND TO UNDERSTAND DOCTOR HEIMLICH'S METHODS, BUT YOU CAN'T ARGUE WITH HIS RESULTS!
Hmm. NEEDS WORK. LITHIUM BREAK, EVERYBODY.
BUT I WANT YOU BACK HERE IN TWENTY FOR A "TWELVE DAYS OF CHRISTMAS" RUN-THROUGH.
THAT'S FULL DRESS, PEOPLE! PRACTICE YOUR KICK-TURNS!
YOU'RE DOING JUST GREAT, PUDDIN'. YOU'LL KNOCK 'EM DEAD.
WELL ... THAT GOES WITHOUT SAYING, DOESN'T IT?
9

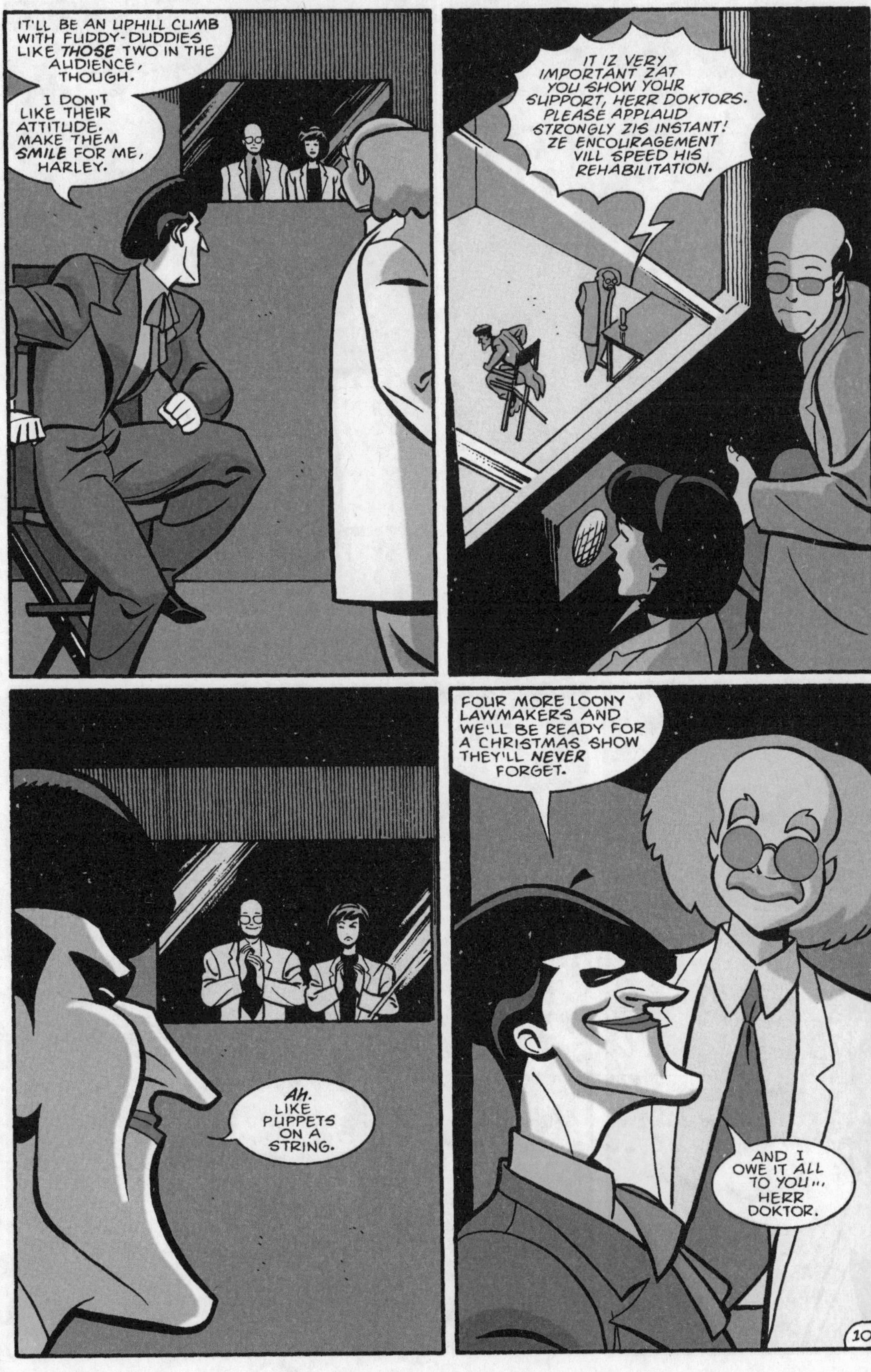

IT'LL BE AN UPHILL CLIMB WITH FUDDY-DUDDIES LIKE *THOSE* TWO IN THE AUDIENCE, THOUGH.
I DON'T LIKE THEIR ATTITUDE. MAKE THEM *SMILE* FOR ME, HARLEY.
IT IZ VERY IMPORTANT ZAT YOU SHOW YOUR SUPPORT, HERR DOKTORS. PLEASE APPLAUD STRONGLY ZIS INSTANT! ZE ENCOURAGEMENT VILL SPEED HIS REHABILITATION.
Ah. LIKE PUPPETS ON A STRING.
FOUR MORE LOONY LAWMAKERS AND WE'LL BE READY FOR A CHRISTMAS SHOW THEY'LL *NEVER* FORGET.
AND I OWE IT ALL TO YOU... HERR DOKTOR.

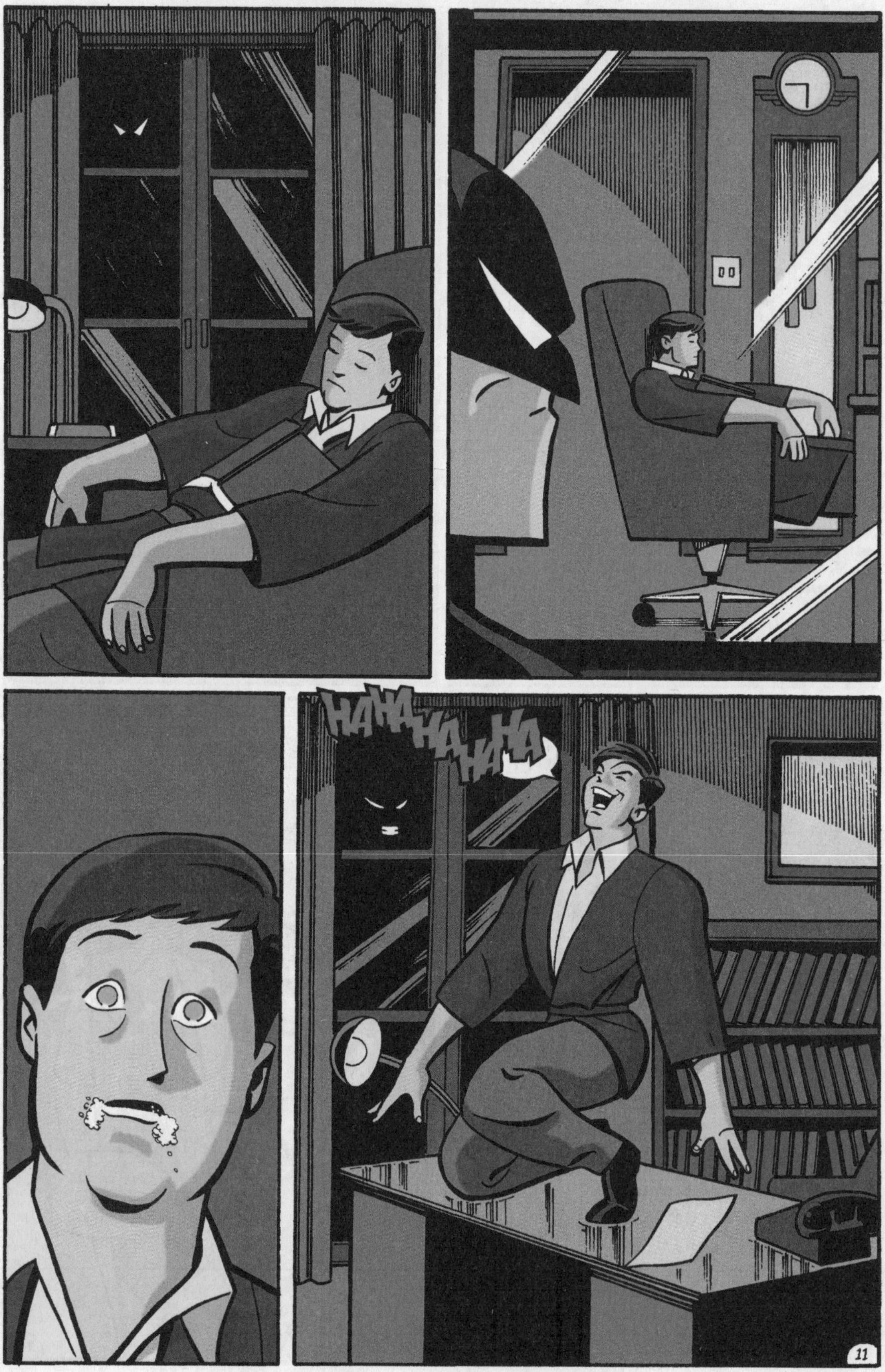
HA HA HA HA HA

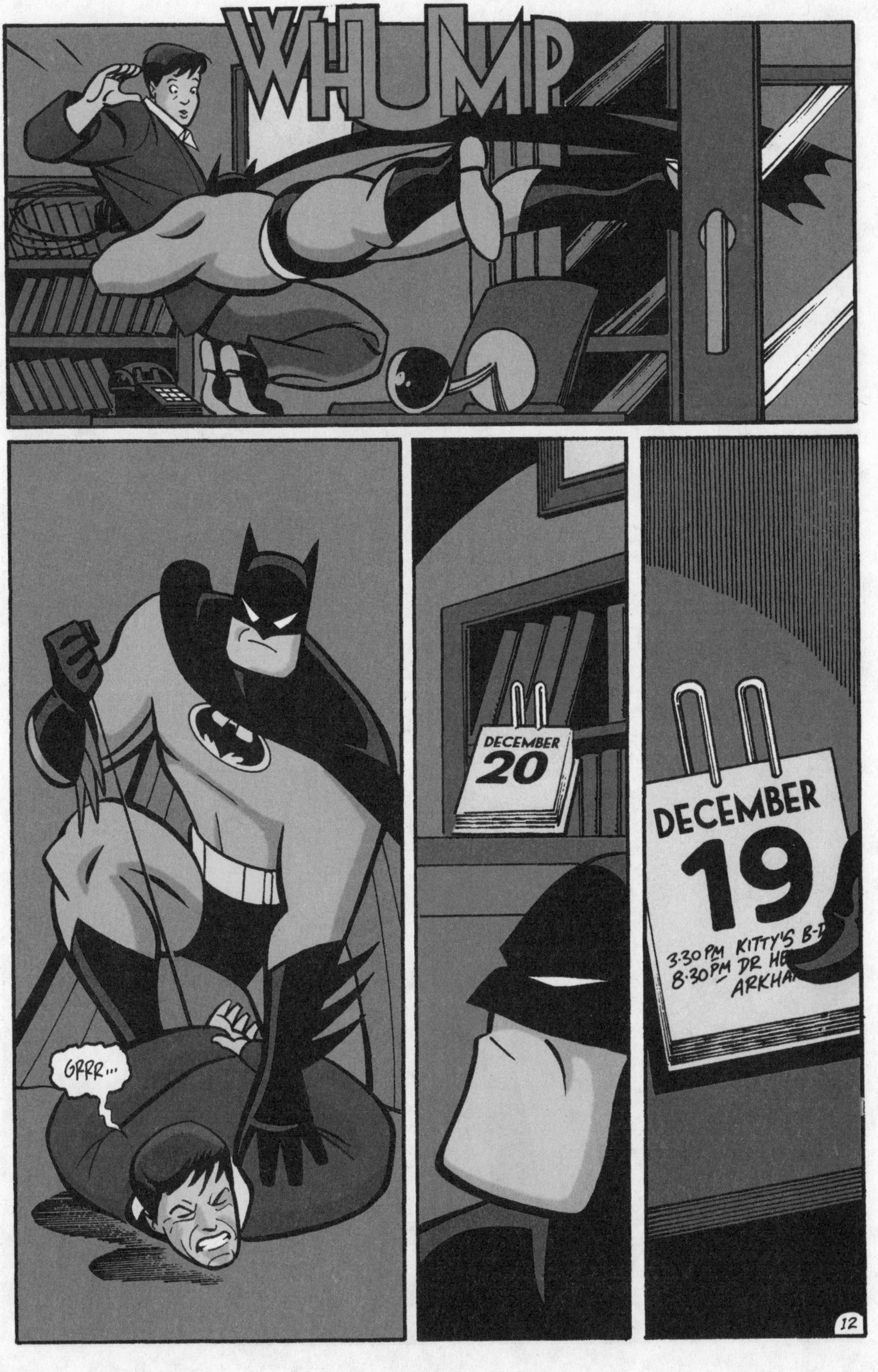
WHUMP
GRRR...
DECEMBER
20
DECEMBER
19
3:30 PM KITTY'S B-D
8:30 PM DR HE
ARKHA

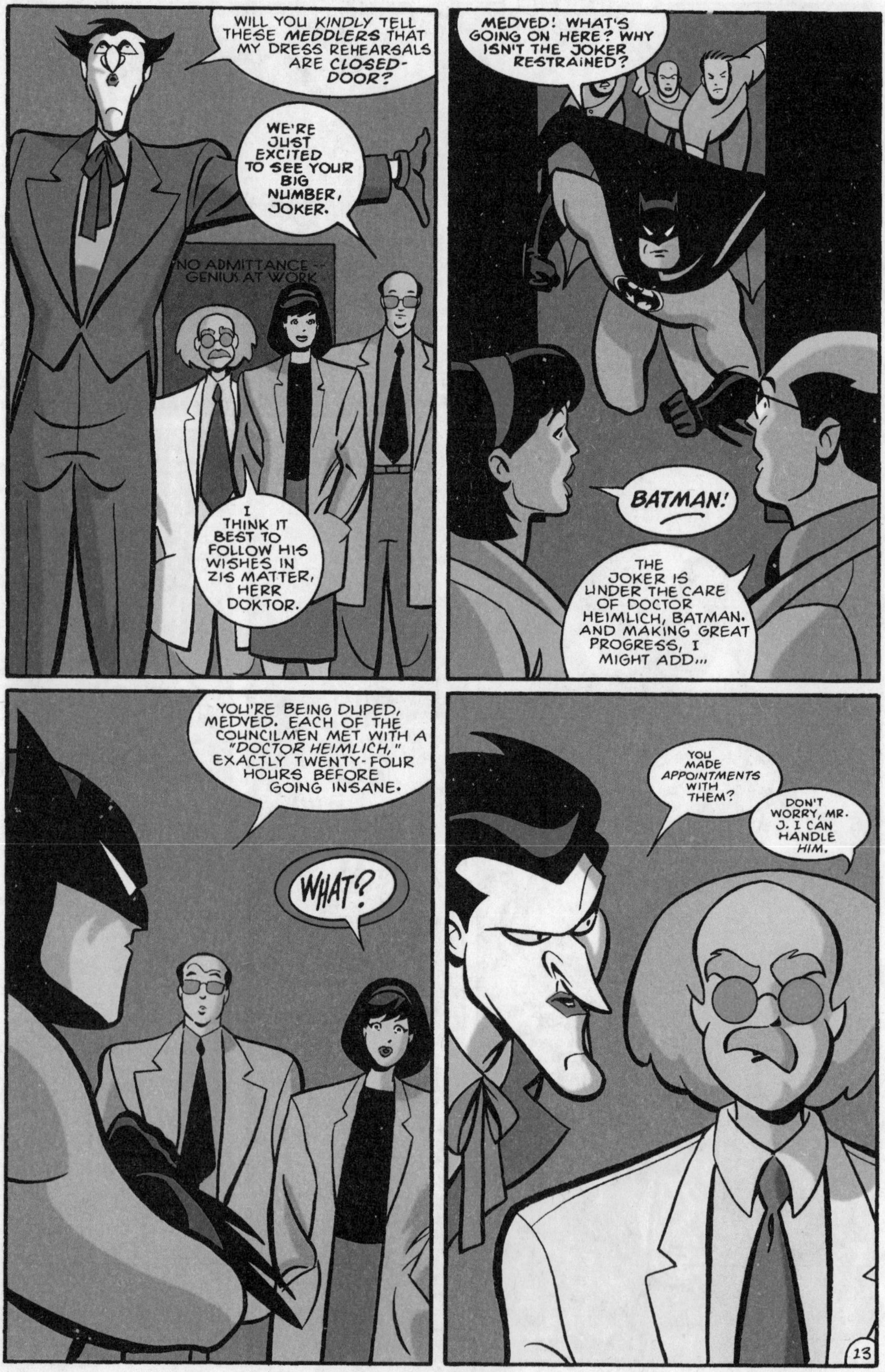
WILL YOU *KINDLY* TELL THESE *MEDDLERS* THAT MY DRESS REHEARSALS ARE *CLOSED-DOOR?*
WE'RE JUST EXCITED TO SEE YOUR BIG NUMBER, JOKER.
NO ADMITTANCE -- GENIUS AT WORK
I THINK IT BEST TO FOLLOW HIS WISHES IN ZIS MATTER, HERR DOKTOR.
MEDVED! WHAT'S GOING ON *HERE?* WHY ISN'T THE JOKER RESTRAINED?
BATMAN!
THE JOKER IS UNDER THE CARE OF DOCTOR HEIMLICH, BATMAN. AND MAKING GREAT PROGRESS, I MIGHT ADD...
YOU'RE BEING DUPED, MEDVED. EACH OF THE COUNCILMEN MET WITH A *"DOCTOR HEIMLICH,"* EXACTLY TWENTY-FOUR HOURS BEFORE GOING INSANE.
WHAT?
YOU MADE *APPOINTMENTS* WITH THEM?
DON'T WORRY, MR. J. I CAN HANDLE *HIM.*

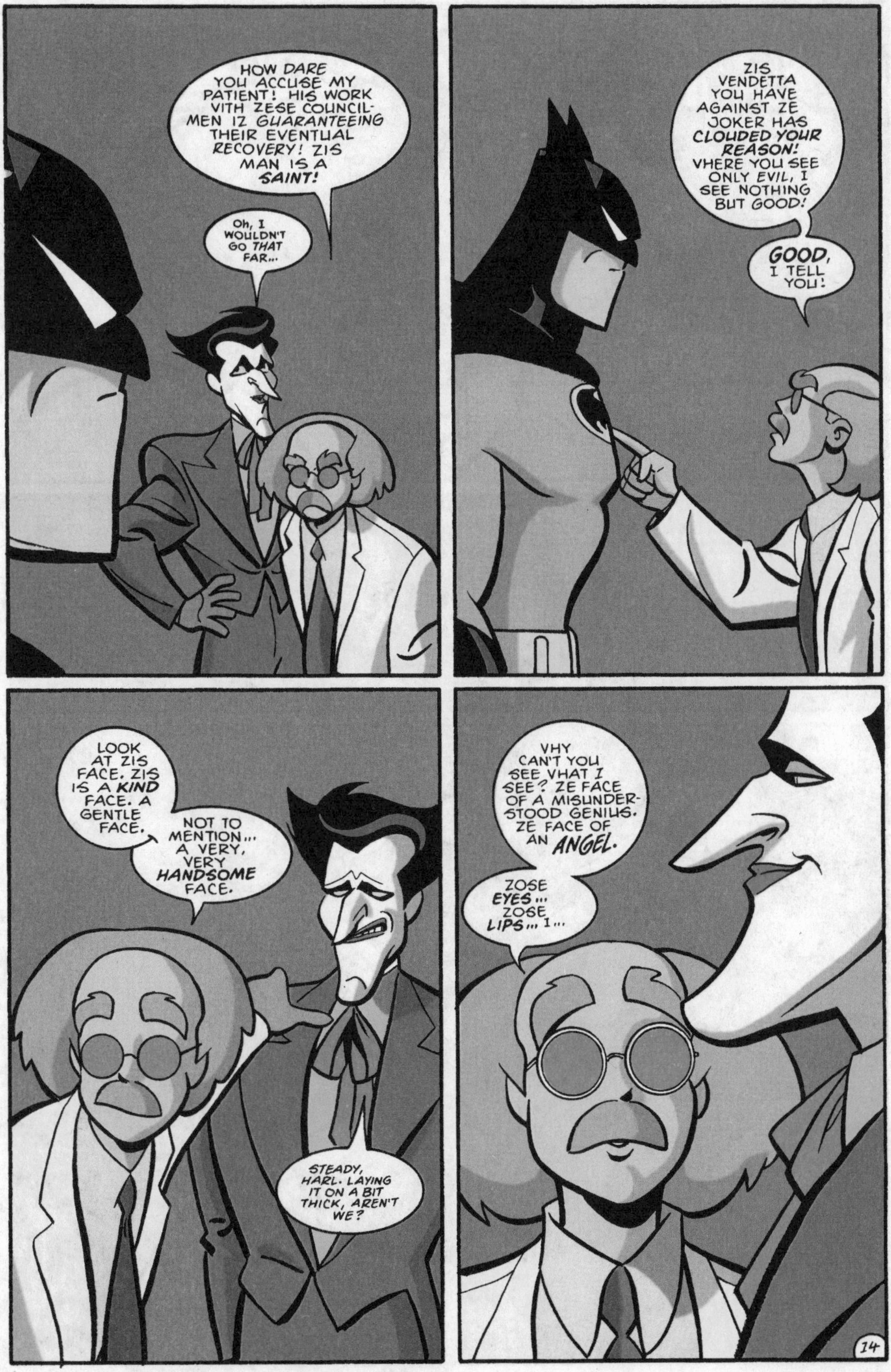
HOW DARE YOU ACCUSE MY PATIENT! HIS WORK VITH ZESE COUNCILMEN IZ GUARANTEEING THEIR EVENTUAL RECOVERY! ZIS MAN IS A SAINT!
Oh, I WOULDN'T GO THAT FAR...
ZIS VENDETTA YOU HAVE AGAINST ZE JOKER HAS CLOUDED YOUR REASON! VHERE YOU SEE ONLY EVIL, I SEE NOTHING BUT GOOD!
GOOD, I TELL YOU!
LOOK AT ZIS FACE. ZIS IS A KIND FACE. A GENTLE FACE.
NOT TO MENTION... A VERY, VERY HANDSOME FACE.
STEADY, HARL. LAYING IT ON A BIT THICK, AREN'T WE?
VHY CAN'T YOU SEE VHAT I SEE? ZE FACE OF A MISUNDERSTOOD GENIUS. ZE FACE OF AN ANGEL.
ZOSE EYES... ZOSE LIPS... I...

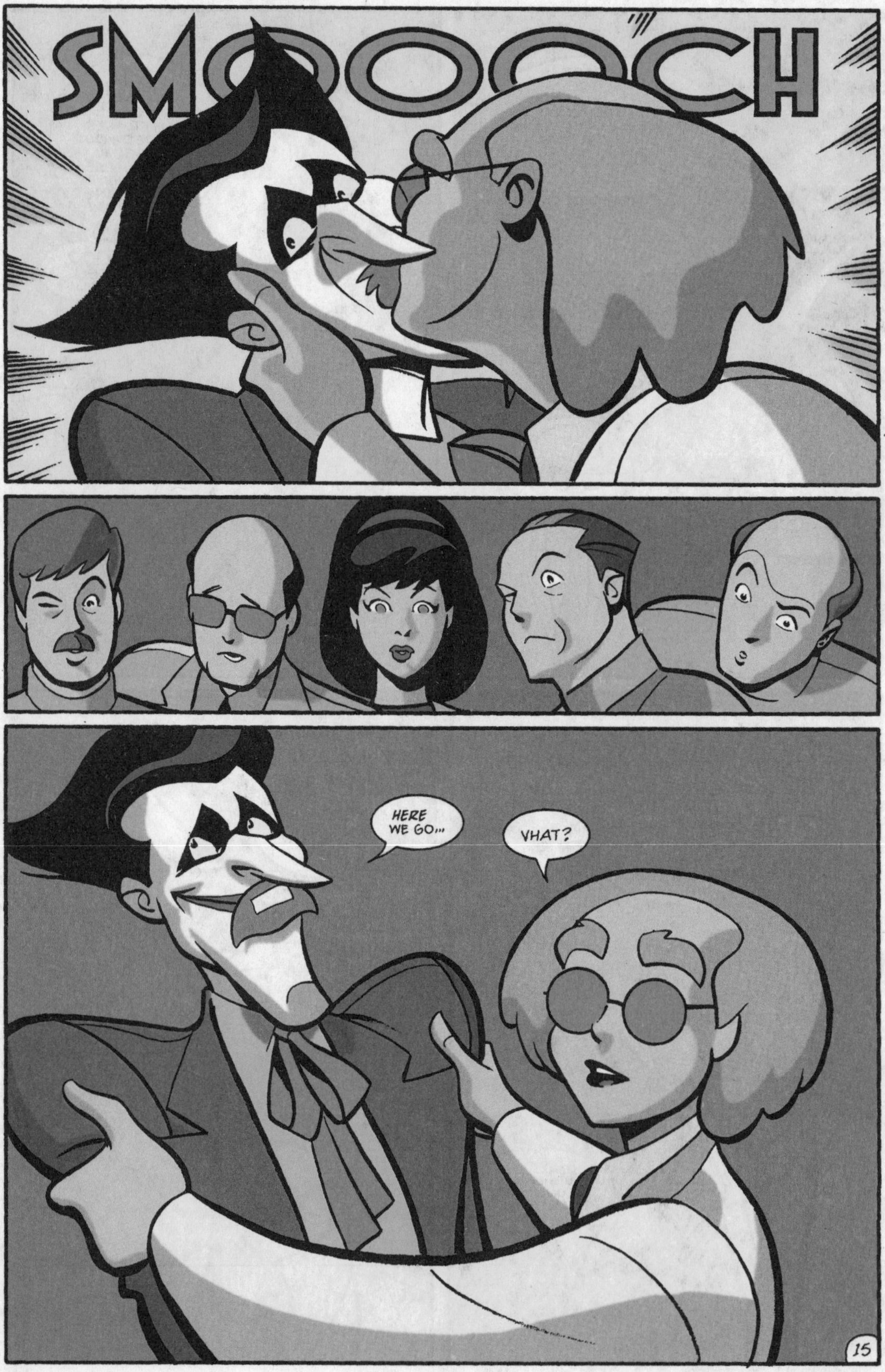
SMOOOCH
HERE WE GO...
VHAT?

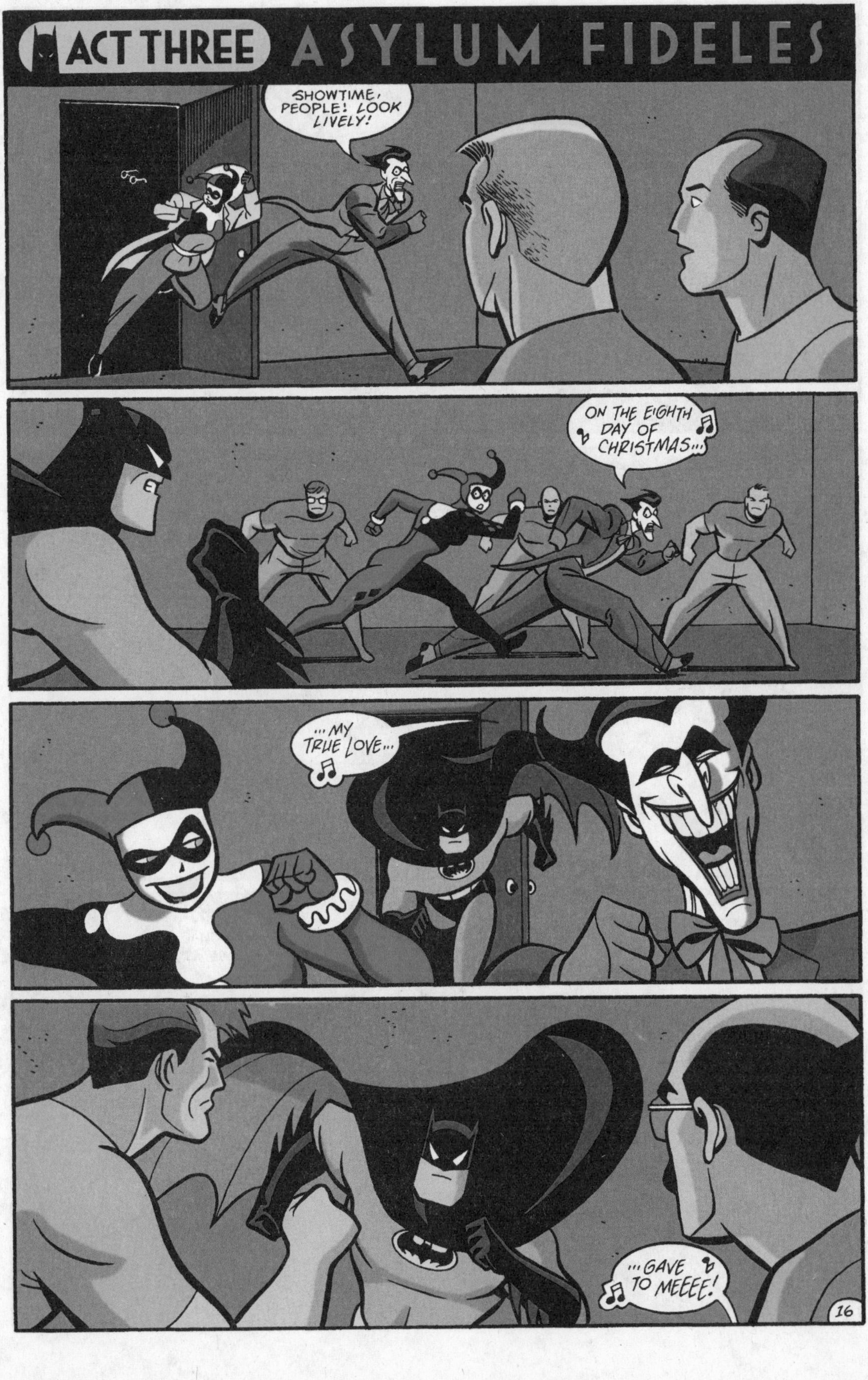
ACT THREE
ASYLUM FIDELES
SHOWTIME, PEOPLE! LOOK LIVELY!
ON THE EIGHTH DAY OF CHRISTMAS...
...MY TRUE LOVE...
...GAVE TO MEEEE!

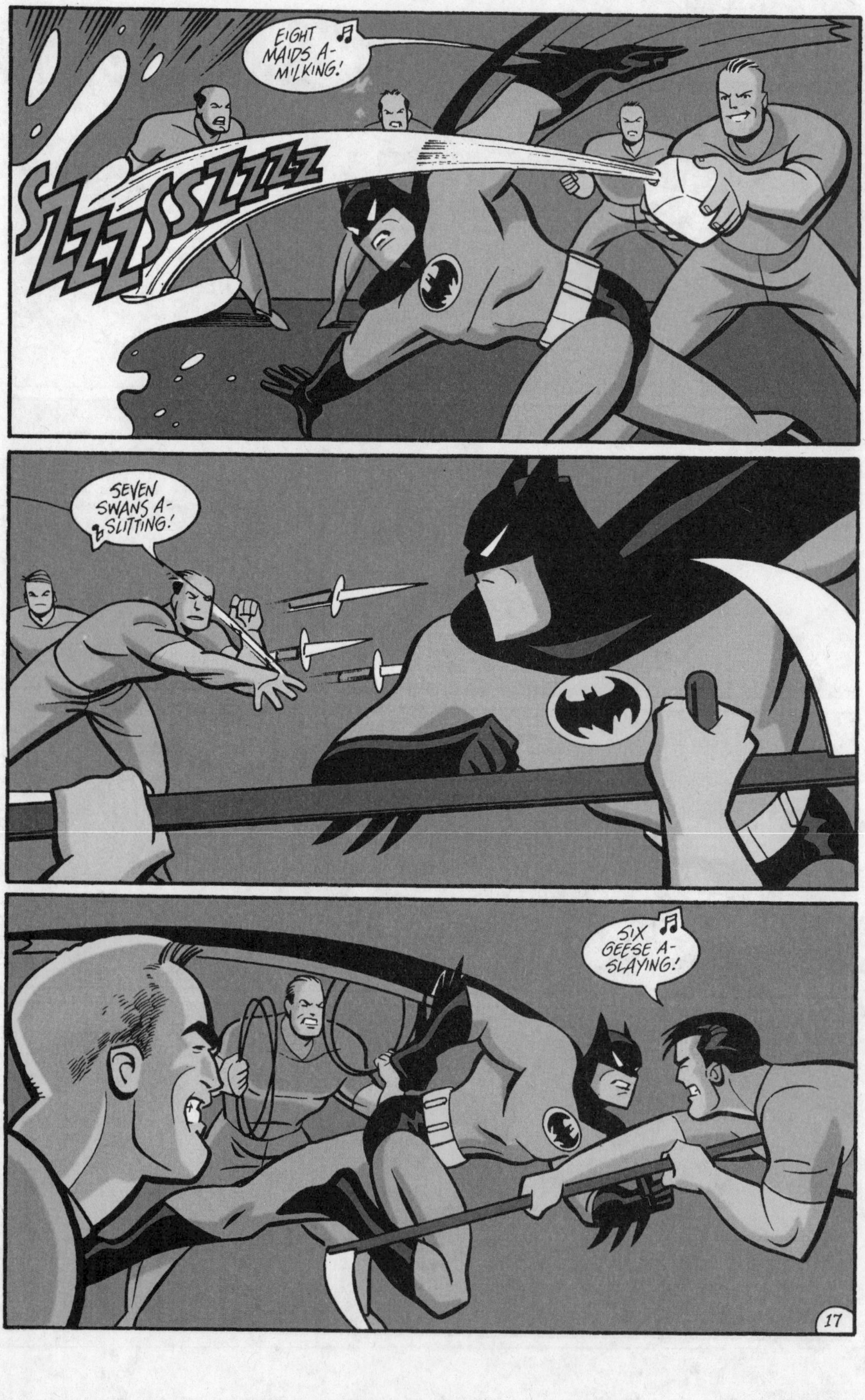
EIGHT MAIDS A-MILKING!
SZZZSSZZZZZ
SEVEN SWANS A-SLITTING!
SIX GEESE A-SLAYING!

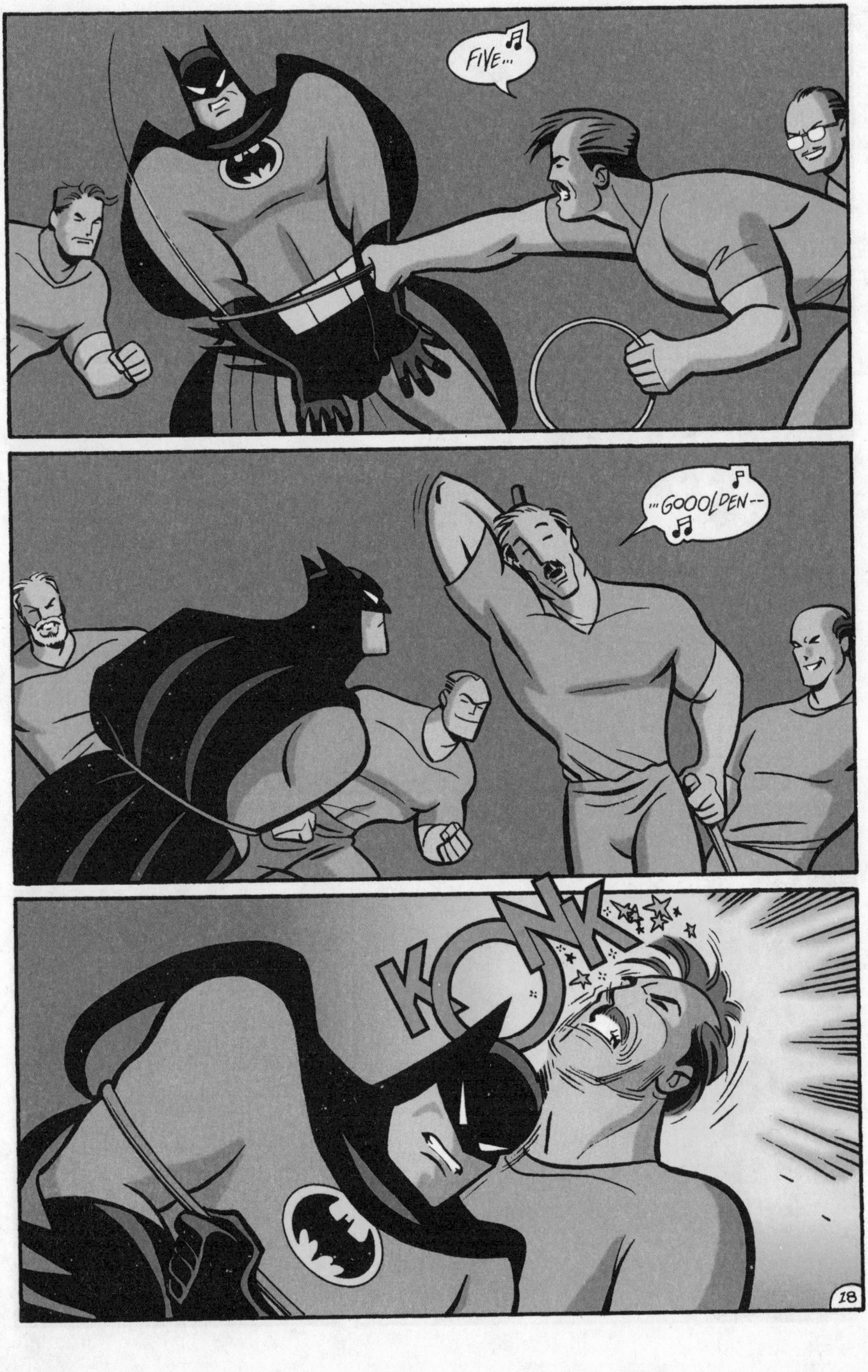
FIVE...
...GOOOLDEN--
KONK

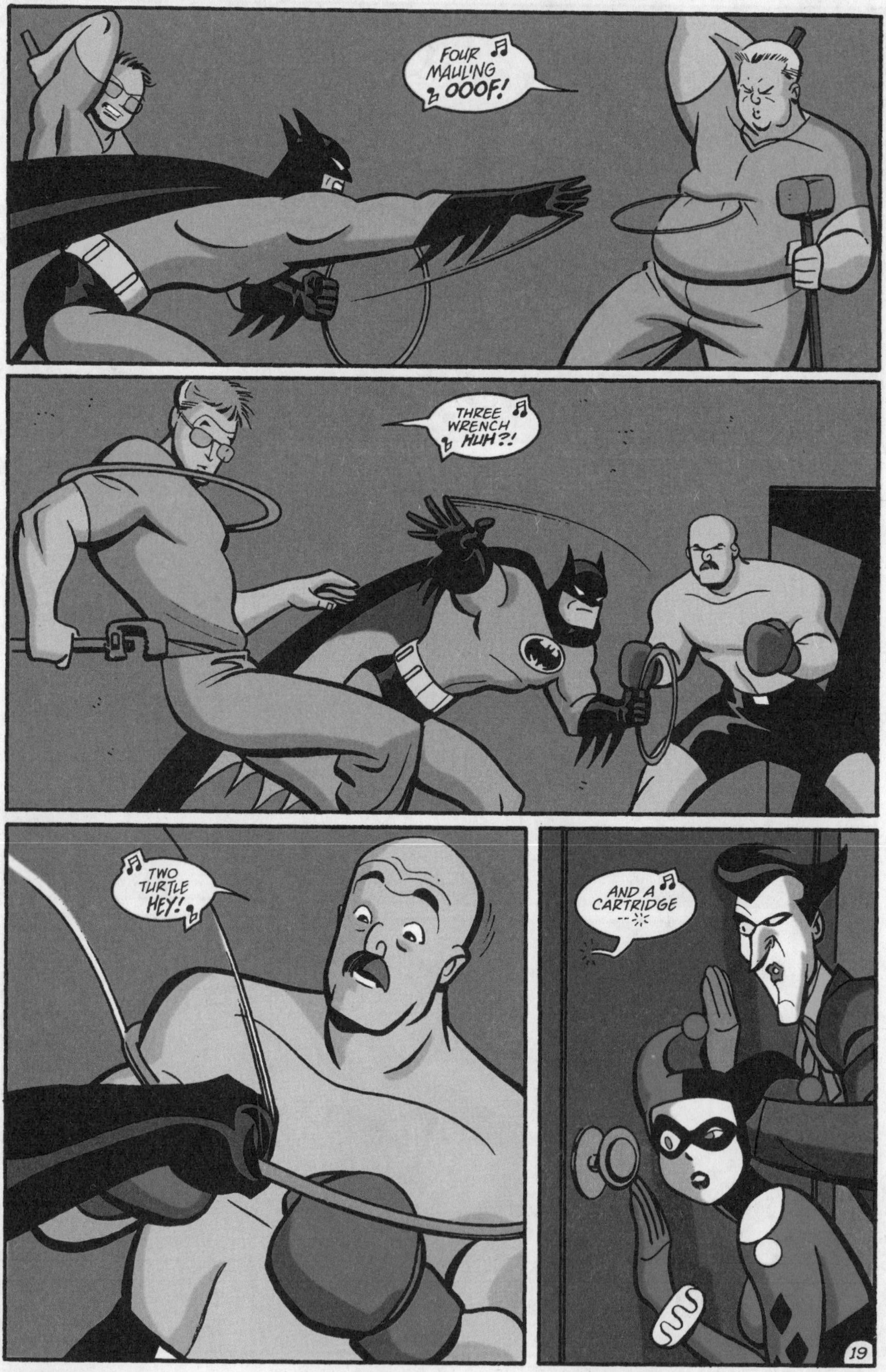
FOUR MAULING OOOF!
THREE WRENCH HUH?!
TWO TURTLE HEY!
AND A CARTRIDGE
19

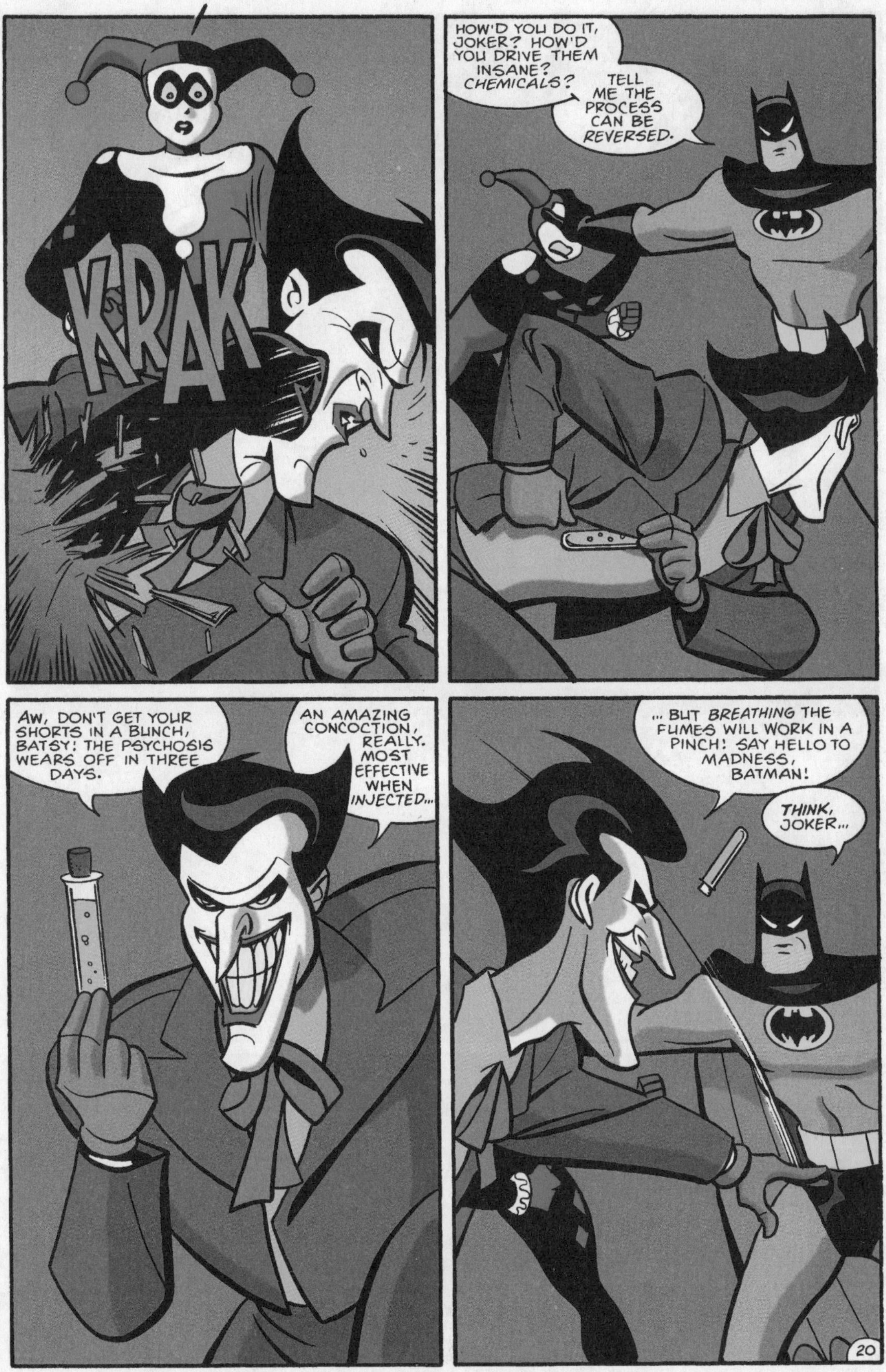
KRAK
HOW'D YOU DO IT, JOKER? HOW'D YOU DRIVE THEM INSANE? CHEMICALS?
TELL ME THE PROCESS CAN BE REVERSED.
AW, DON'T GET YOUR SHORTS IN A BUNCH, BATSY: THE PSYCHOSIS WEARS OFF IN THREE DAYS.
AN AMAZING CONCOCTION, REALLY. MOST EFFECTIVE WHEN INJECTED...
... BUT BREATHING THE FUMES WILL WORK IN A PINCH! SAY HELLO TO MADNESS, BATMAN!
THINK, JOKER...
20

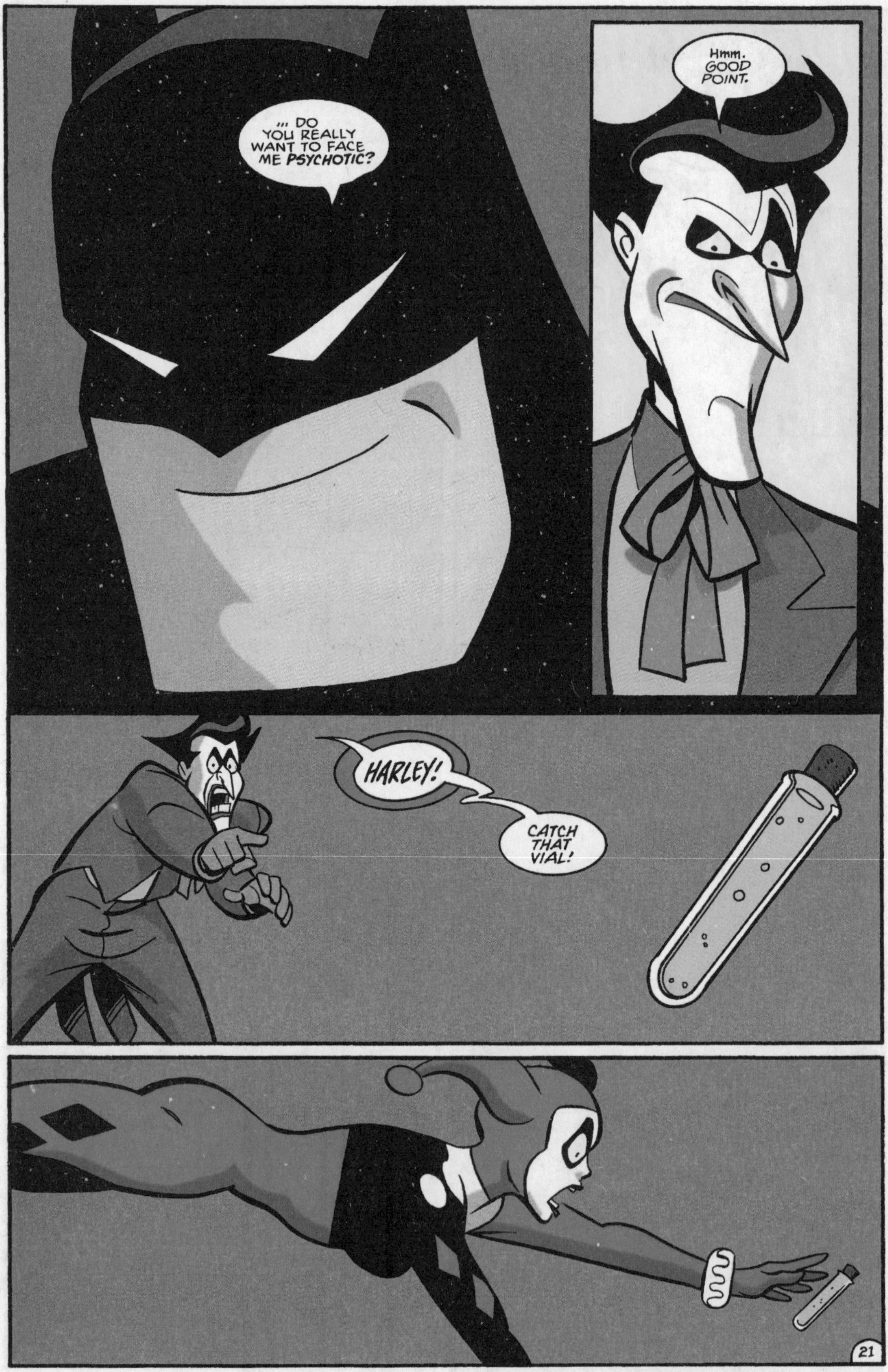
... DO YOU REALLY WANT TO FACE ME PSYCHOTIC?
Hmm. GOOD POINT.
HARLEY!
CATCH THAT VIAL!

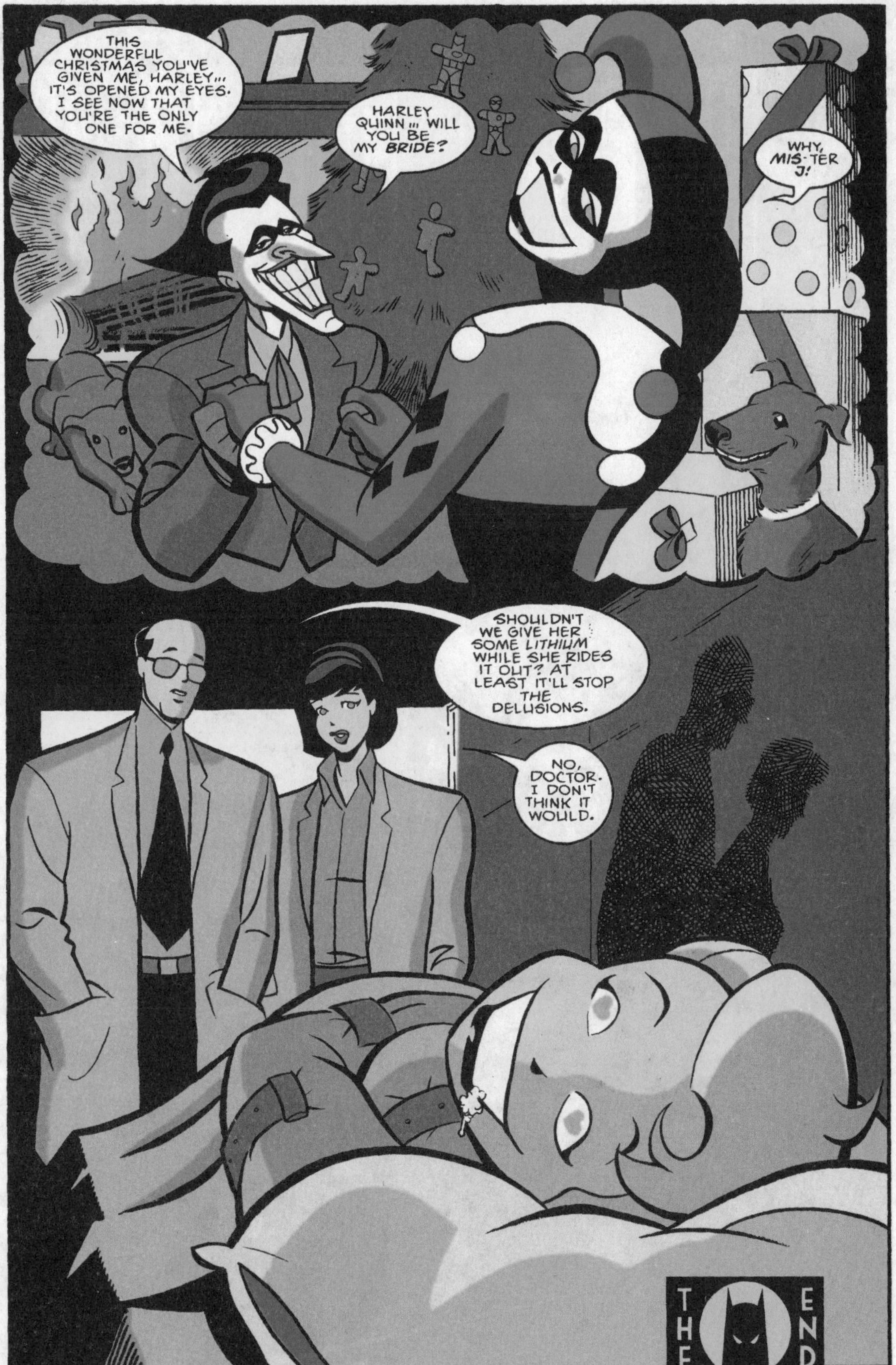
THIS WONDERFUL CHRISTMAS YOU'VE GIVEN ME, HARLEY... IT'S OPENED MY EYES. I SEE NOW THAT YOU'RE THE ONLY ONE FOR ME.
HARLEY QUINN... WILL YOU BE MY BRIDE?
WHY, MIS-TER J!
SHOULDN'T WE GIVE HER SOME LITHIUM WHILE SHE RIDES IT OUT? AT LEAST IT'LL STOP THE DELUSIONS.
NO, DOCTOR. I DON'T THINK IT WOULD.
THE END

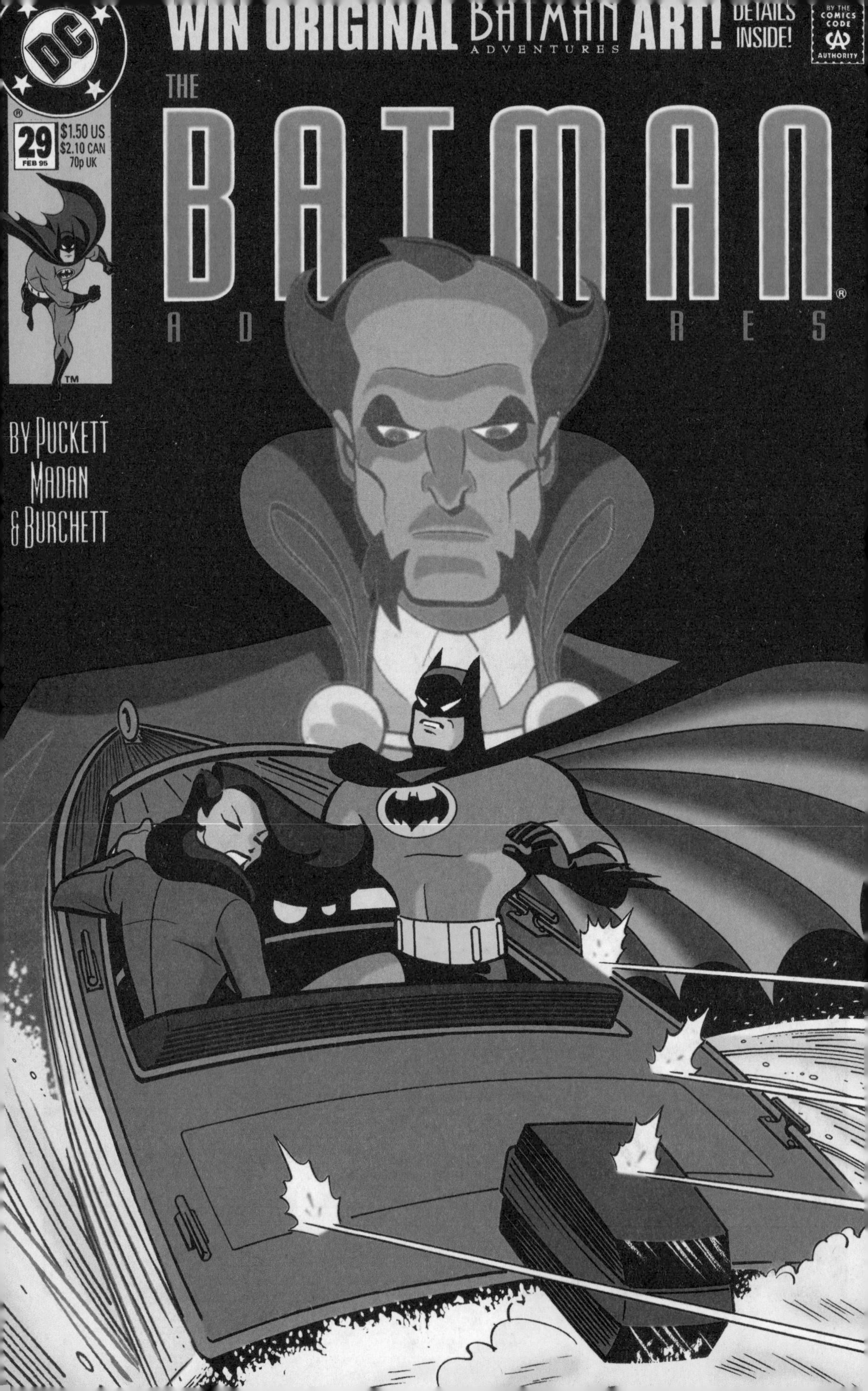
WIN ORIGINAL BATMAN ADVENTURES ART!
DETAILS INSIDE!
BY THE COMICS CODE AUTHORITY
DC
29
FEB 95
$1.50 US
$2.10 CAN
70p UK
THE BATMAN®
BY PUCKETT
MADAN
& BURCHETT

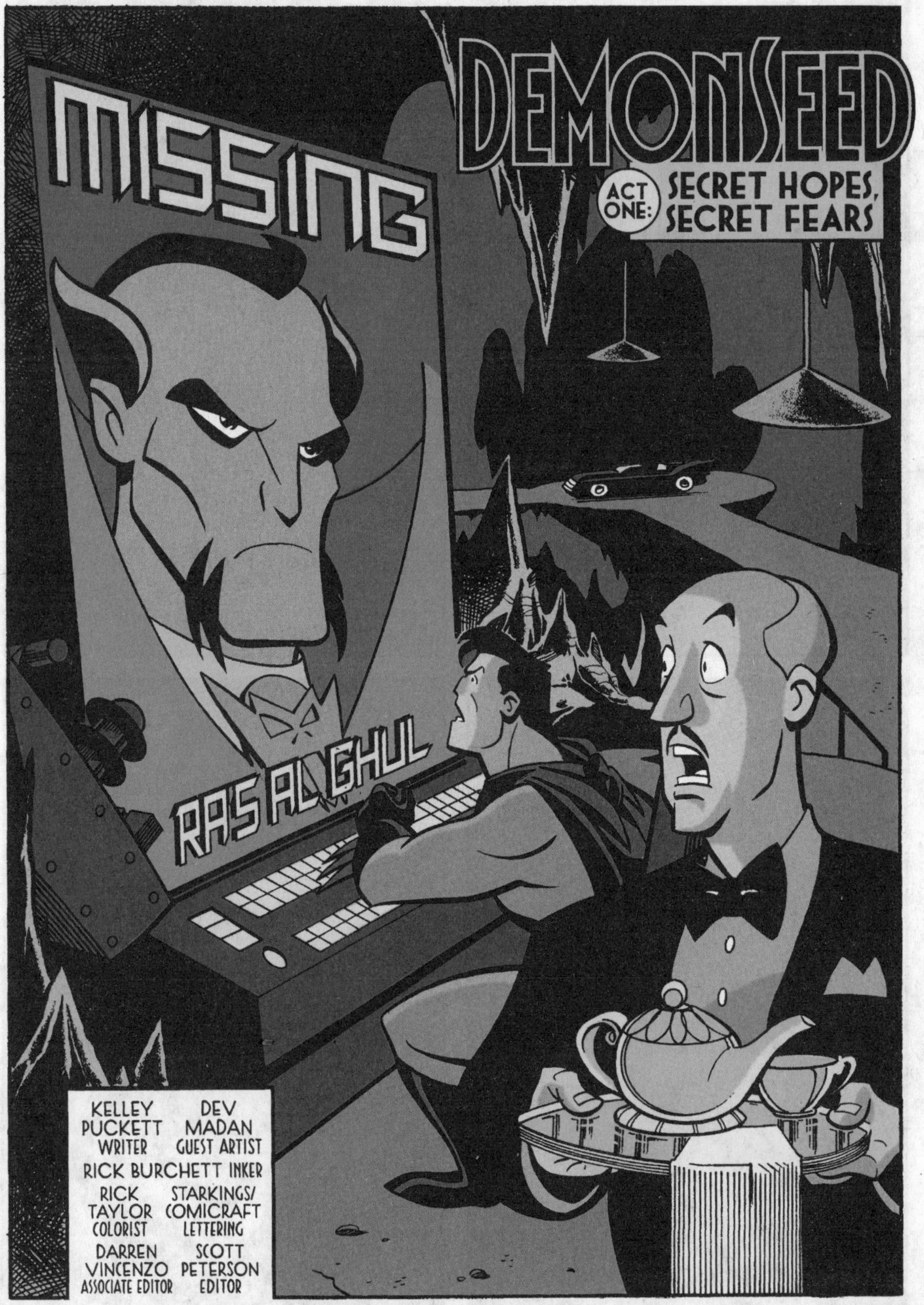

MISSING
DEMONSEED
ACT ONE: SECRET HOPES, SECRET FEARS
RA'S AL GHUL
KELLEY PUCKETT WRITER
DEV MADAN GUEST ARTIST
RICK BURCHETT INKER
RICK TAYLOR COLORIST
STARKINGS/ COMICRAFT LETTERING
DARREN VINCENZO ASSOCIATE EDITOR
SCOTT PETERSON EDITOR

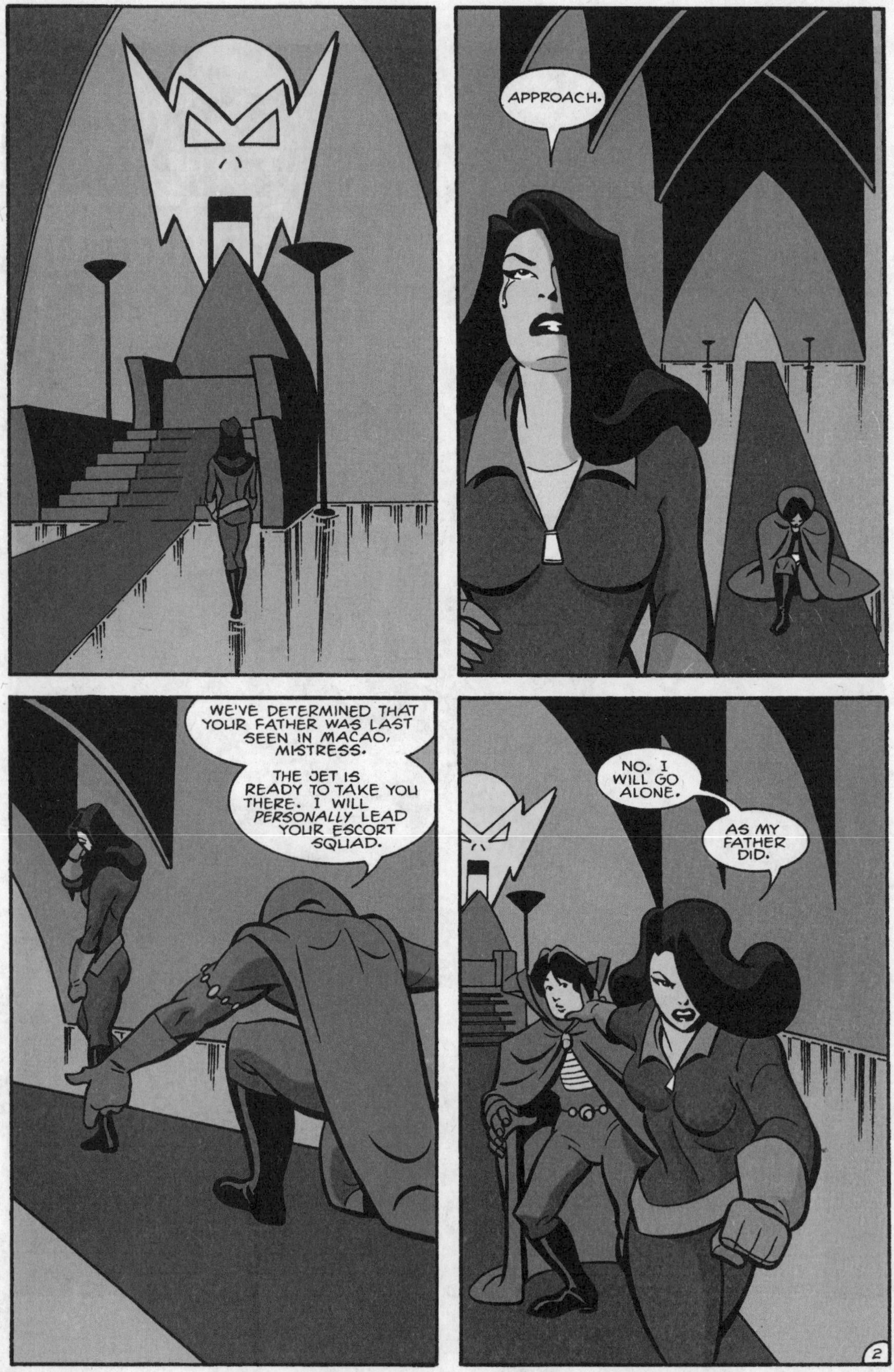
APPROACH.
WE'VE DETERMINED THAT YOUR FATHER WAS LAST SEEN IN MACAO, MISTRESS.
THE JET IS READY TO TAKE YOU THERE. I WILL *PERSONALLY* LEAD YOUR ESCORT SQUAD.
NO. I WILL GO ALONE.
AS MY FATHER DID.

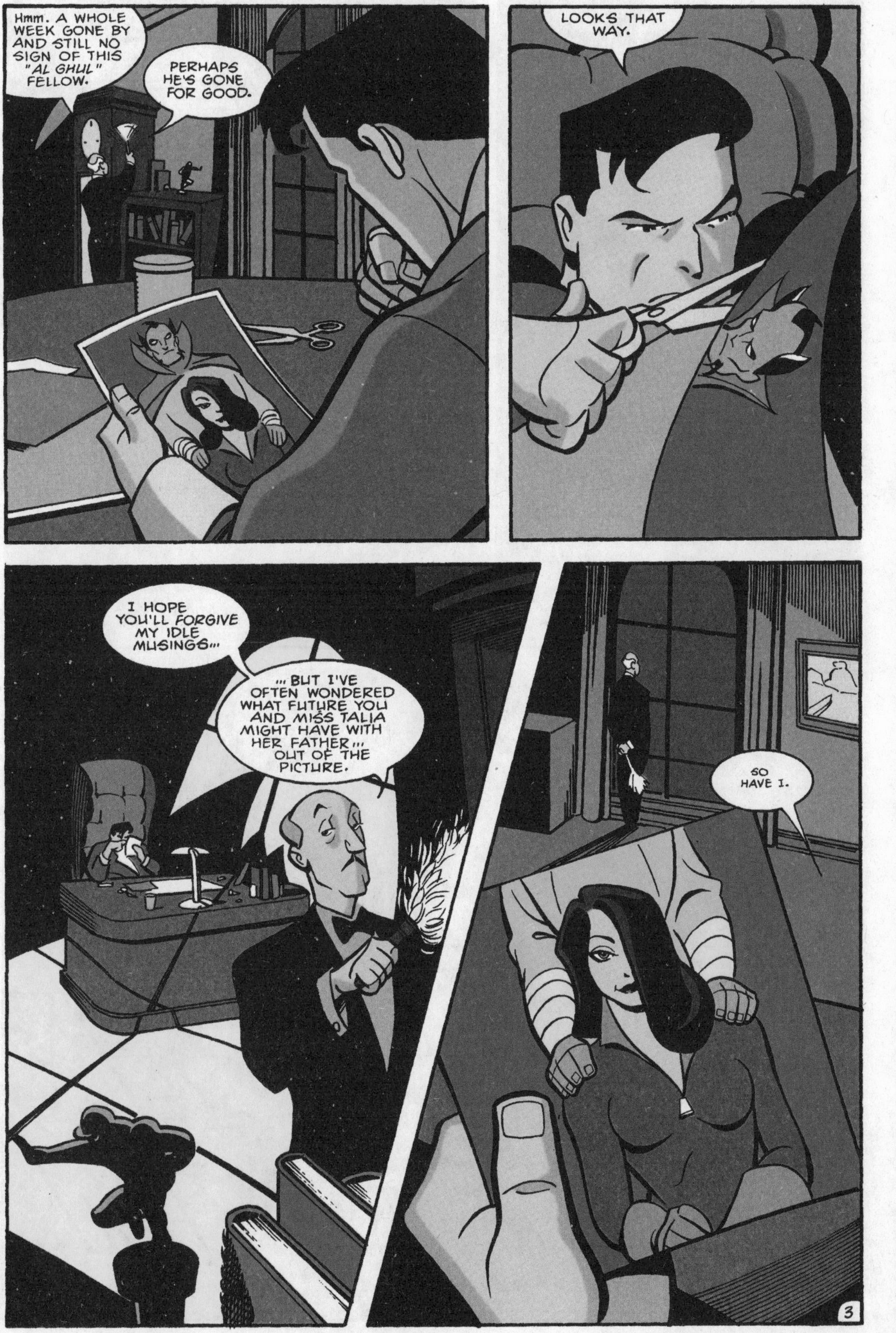
Hmm. A WHOLE WEEK GONE BY AND STILL NO SIGN OF THIS "AL GHUL" FELLOW.
PERHAPS HE'S GONE FOR GOOD.
LOOKS THAT WAY.
I HOPE YOU'LL FORGIVE MY IDLE MUSINGS...
...BUT I'VE OFTEN WONDERED WHAT FUTURE YOU AND MISS TALIA MIGHT HAVE WITH HER FATHER... OUT OF THE PICTURE.
SO HAVE I.
3

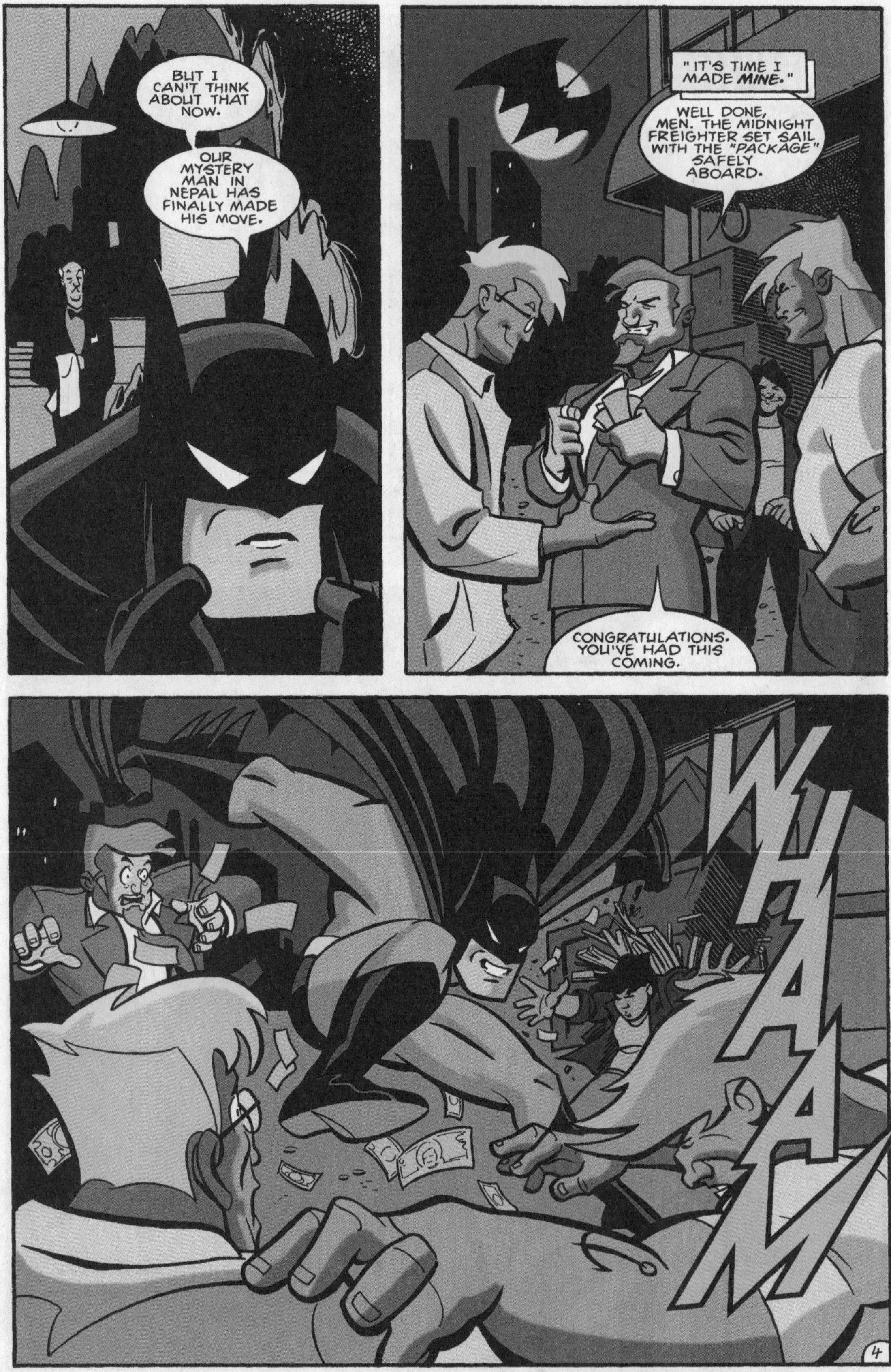
BUT I CAN'T THINK ABOUT THAT NOW.
OUR MYSTERY MAN IN NEPAL HAS FINALLY MADE HIS MOVE.
"IT'S TIME I MADE MINE."
WELL DONE, MEN. THE MIDNIGHT FREIGHTER SET SAIL WITH THE "PACKAGE" SAFELY ABOARD.
CONGRATULATIONS. YOU'VE HAD THIS COMING.
WHAAM
4

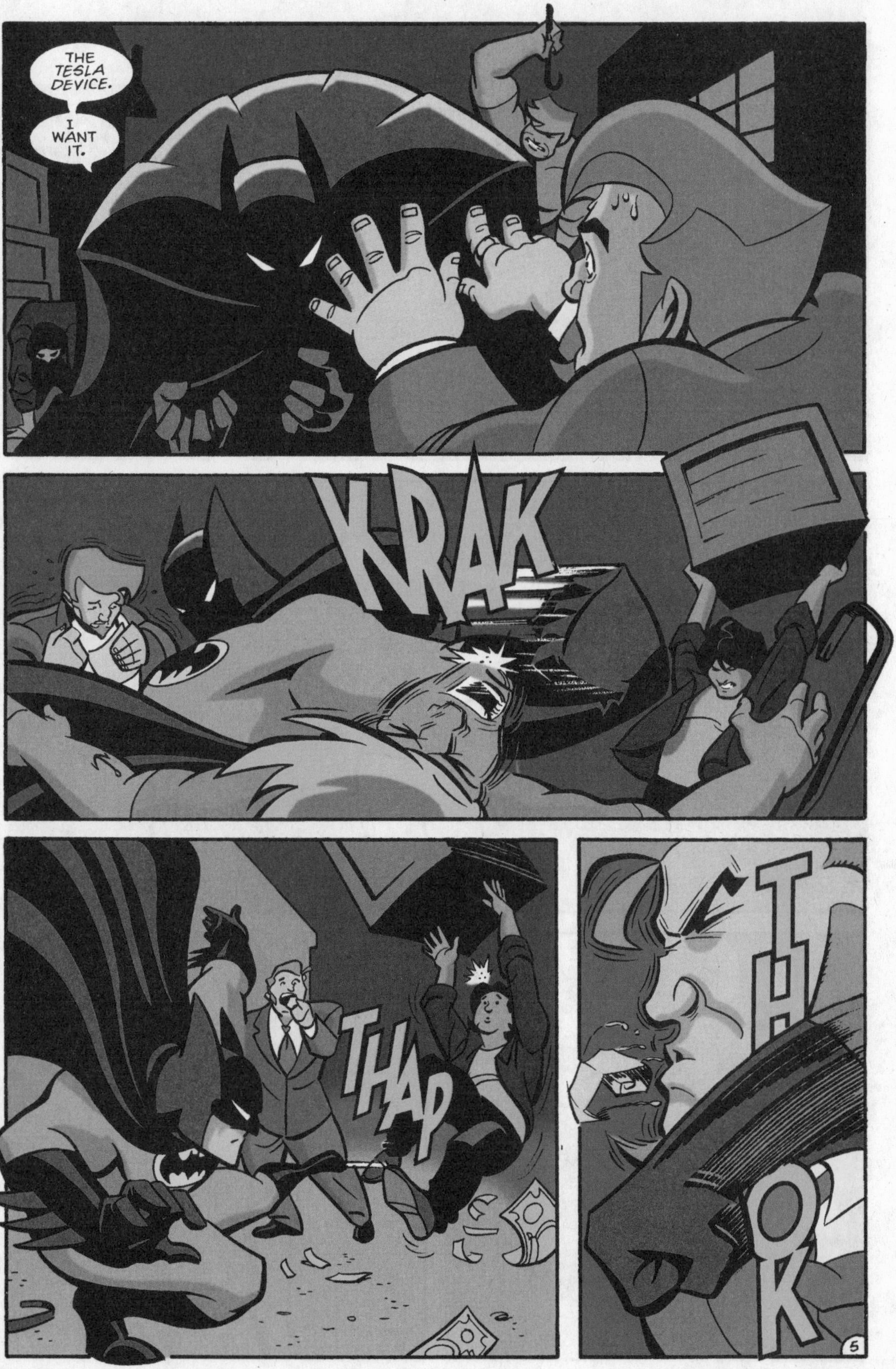
THE TESLA DEVICE.
I WANT IT.
KRAK
THAP
CTHOK

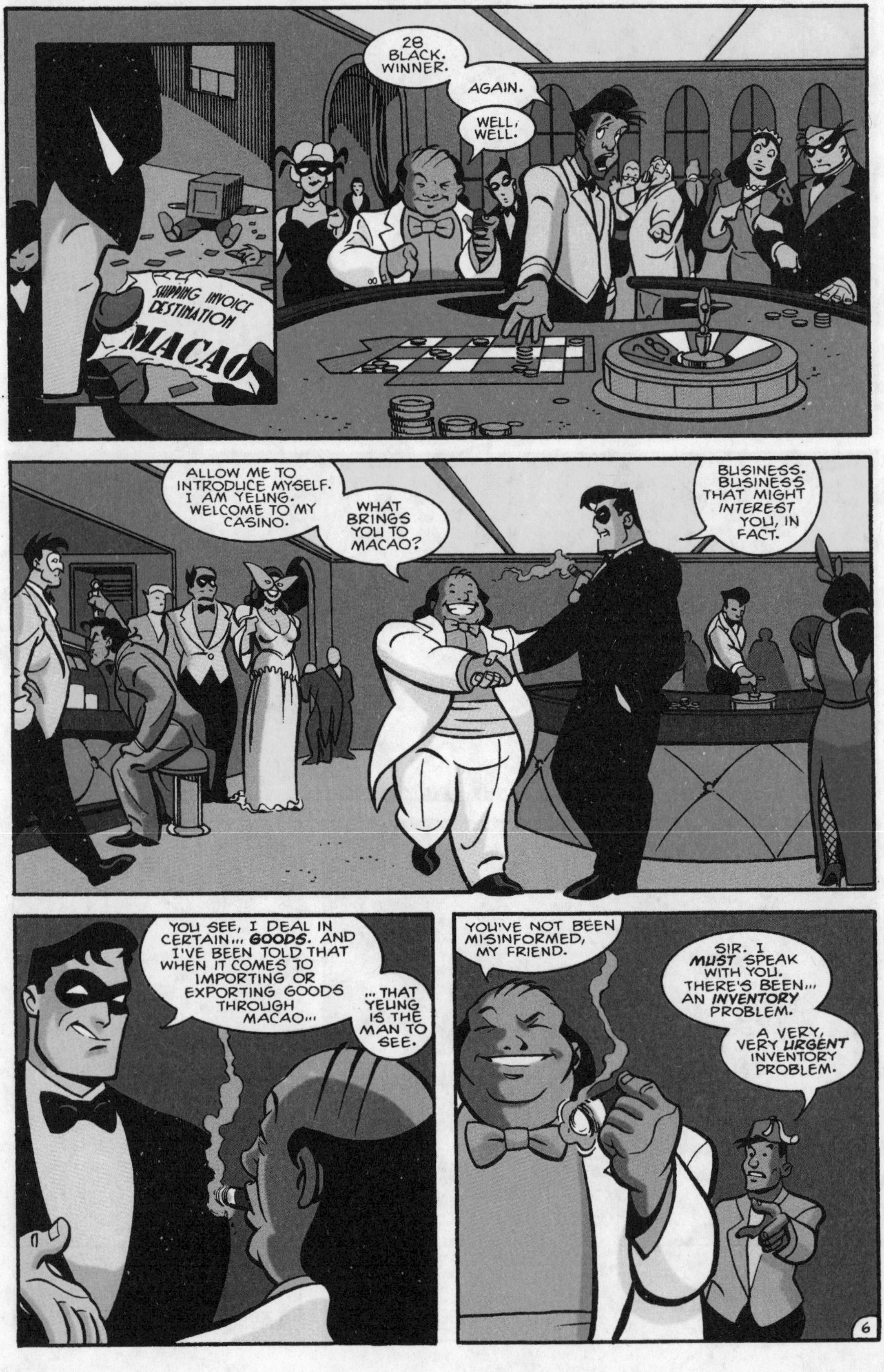

SHIPPING INVOICE
DESTINATION
MACAO
28 BLACK. WINNER.
AGAIN.
WELL, WELL.
ALLOW ME TO INTRODUCE MYSELF. I AM YEUNG. WELCOME TO MY CASINO.
WHAT BRINGS YOU TO MACAO?
BUSINESS. BUSINESS THAT MIGHT INTEREST YOU, IN FACT.
YOU SEE, I DEAL IN CERTAIN... GOODS. AND I'VE BEEN TOLD THAT WHEN IT COMES TO IMPORTING OR EXPORTING GOODS THROUGH MACAO...
...THAT YEUNG IS THE MAN TO SEE.
YOU'VE NOT BEEN MISINFORMED, MY FRIEND.
SIR. I MUST SPEAK WITH YOU. THERE'S BEEN... AN INVENTORY PROBLEM.
A VERY, VERY URGENT INVENTORY PROBLEM.

PLEASE, ENJOY YOUR WINNINGS. I'LL BE BUT A MOMENT.

PRIVATE

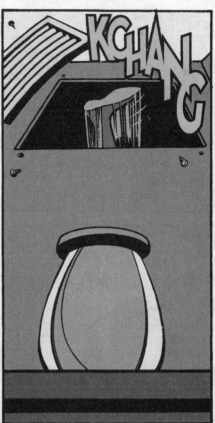

KCHANG

WHAT CURRENCY WOULD YOU LIKE THESE IN, SIR?

SIR?

7

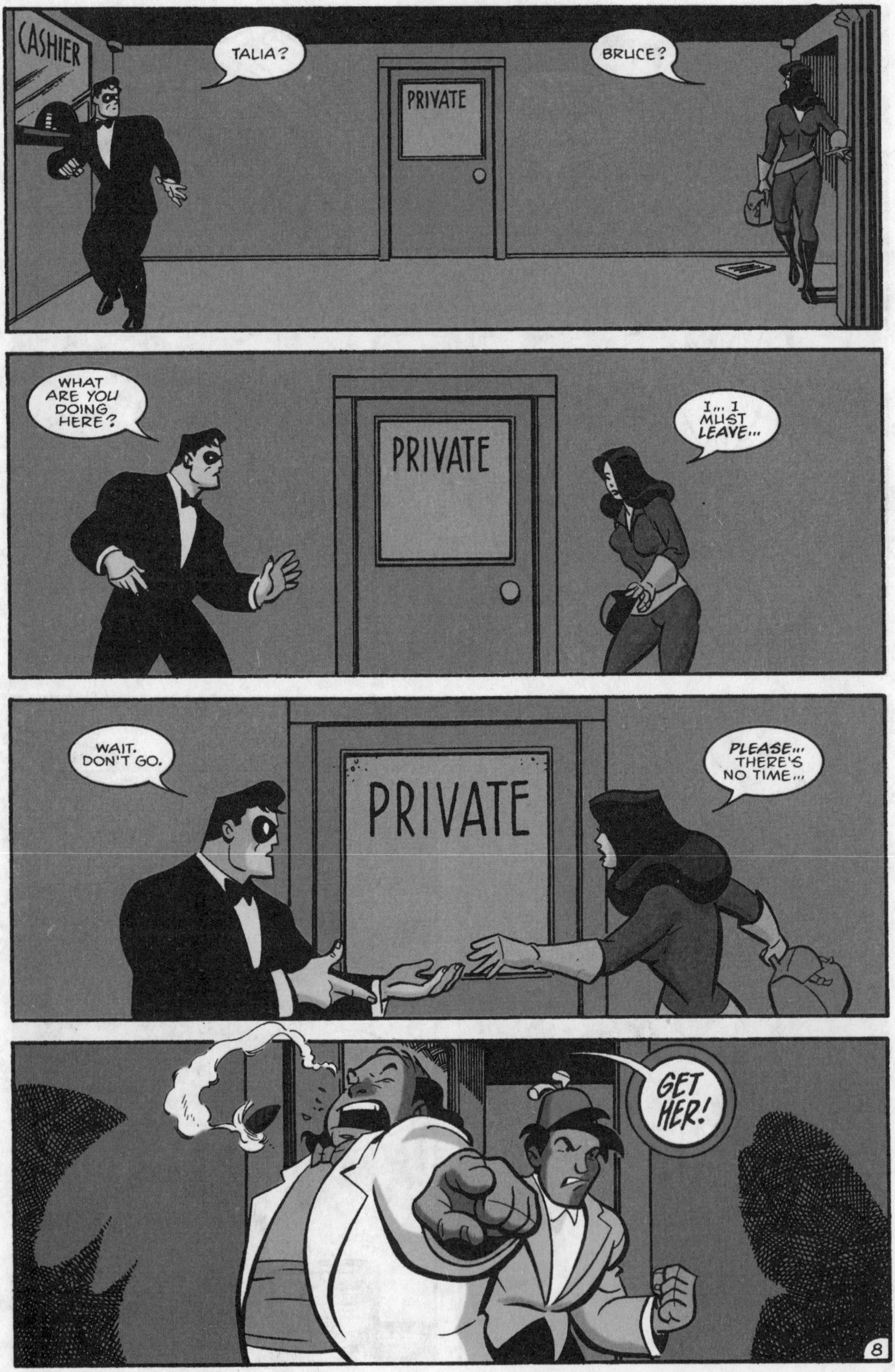
CASHIER
TALIA?
BRUCE?
PRIVATE
WHAT ARE YOU DOING HERE?
PRIVATE
I... I MUST LEAVE...
WAIT. DON'T GO.
PRIVATE
PLEASE... THERE'S NO TIME...
GET HER!
8

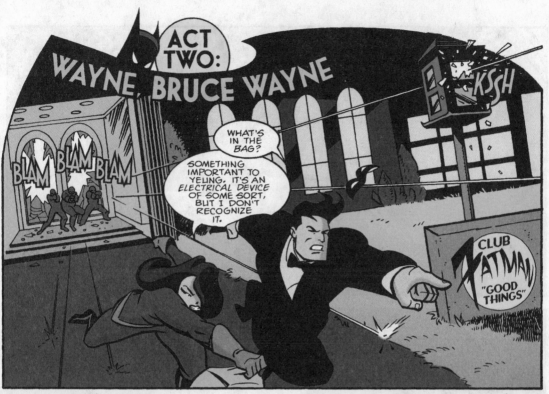

ACT TWO:
WAYNE, BRUCE WAYNE

KSSH

WHAT'S IN THE BAG?

SOMETHING IMPORTANT TO YEUNG. IT'S AN *ELECTRICAL DEVICE* OF SOME SORT, BUT I DON'T RECOGNIZE IT.

BLAM BLAM BLAM

CLUB *BATMAN* "GOOD THINGS"

TO BOATS

FEW WOULD. IT'S AN EXPERIMENTAL *FIELD GENERATOR* STOLEN FROM THE GOTHAM INSTITUTE. A MAN NAMED *NARAYAN* IS TRYING DESPERATELY TO SMUGGLE IT INTO NEPAL.

WHY?

KTHUD

I'M NOT SURE. I THINK HE PLANS TO RULE THE WORLD WITH IT.

9

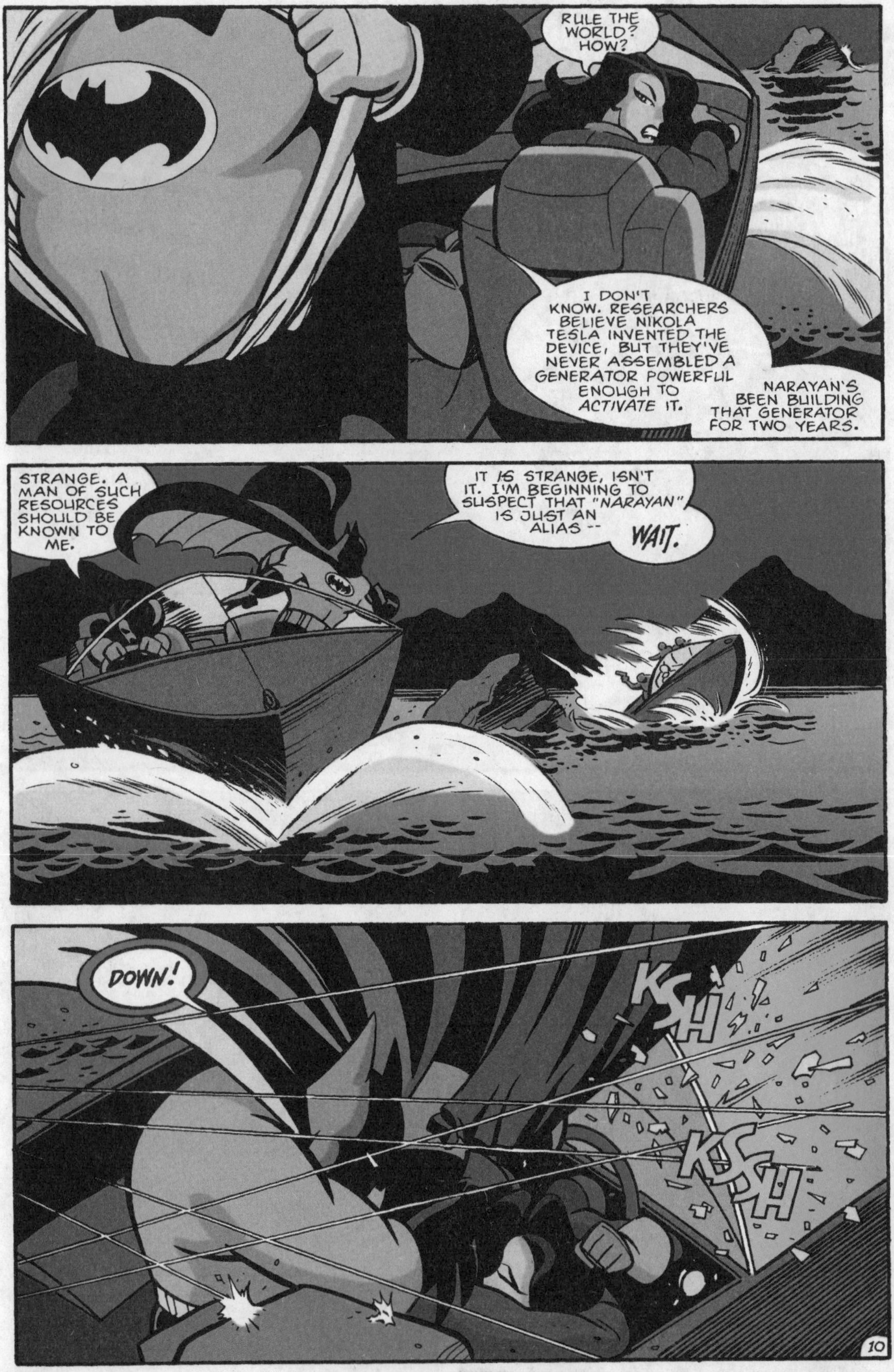
RULE THE WORLD? HOW?
I DON'T KNOW. RESEARCHERS BELIEVE NIKOLA TESLA INVENTED THE DEVICE, BUT THEY'VE NEVER ASSEMBLED A GENERATOR POWERFUL ENOUGH TO ACTIVATE IT.
NARAYAN'S BEEN BUILDING THAT GENERATOR FOR TWO YEARS.
STRANGE. A MAN OF SUCH RESOURCES SHOULD BE KNOWN TO ME.
IT IS STRANGE, ISN'T IT. I'M BEGINNING TO SUSPECT THAT "NARAYAN" IS JUST AN ALIAS --
WAIT.
DOWN!
KSH
KSSH
10

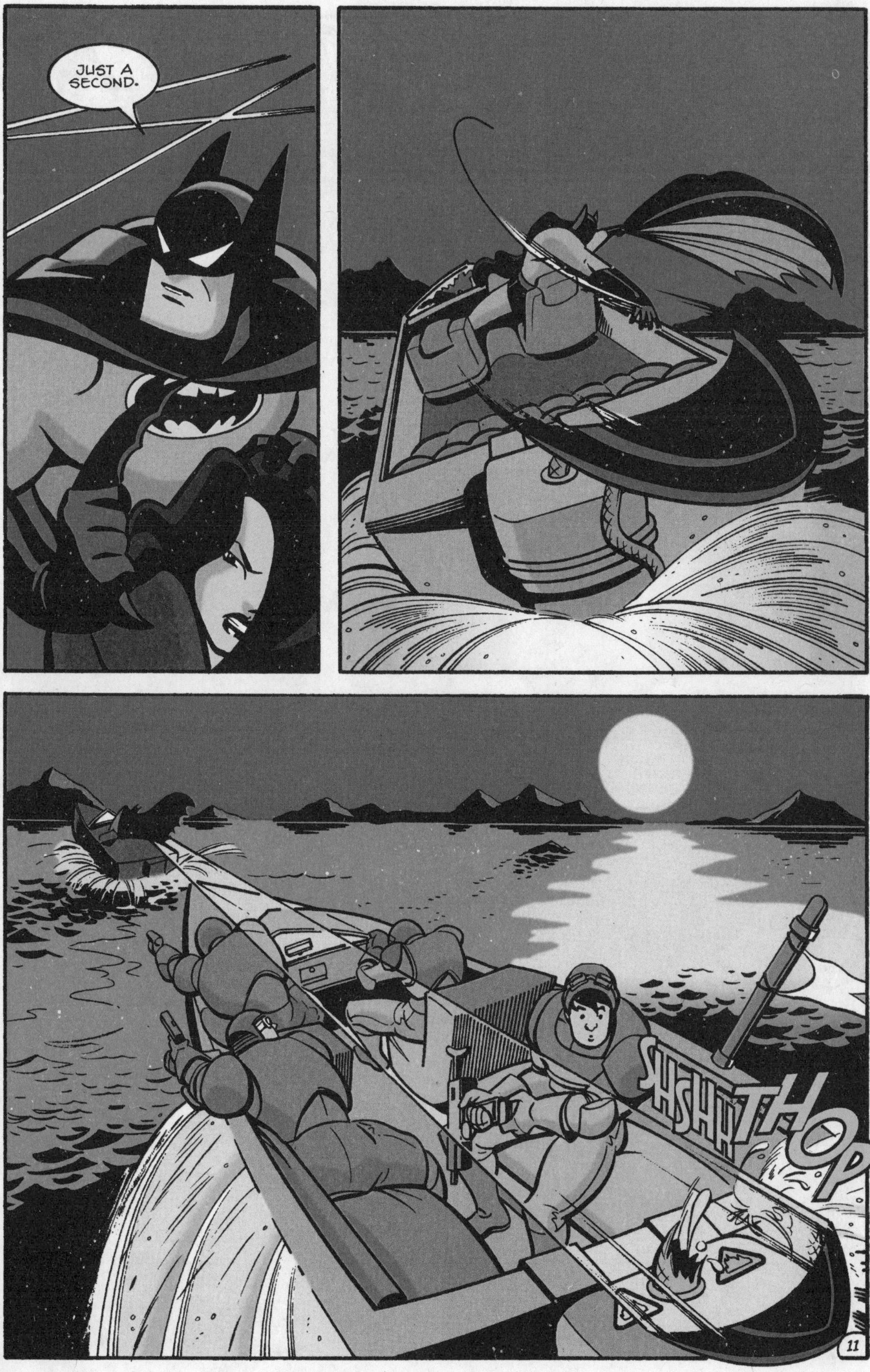
JUST A SECOND.
SHSHHTHOP

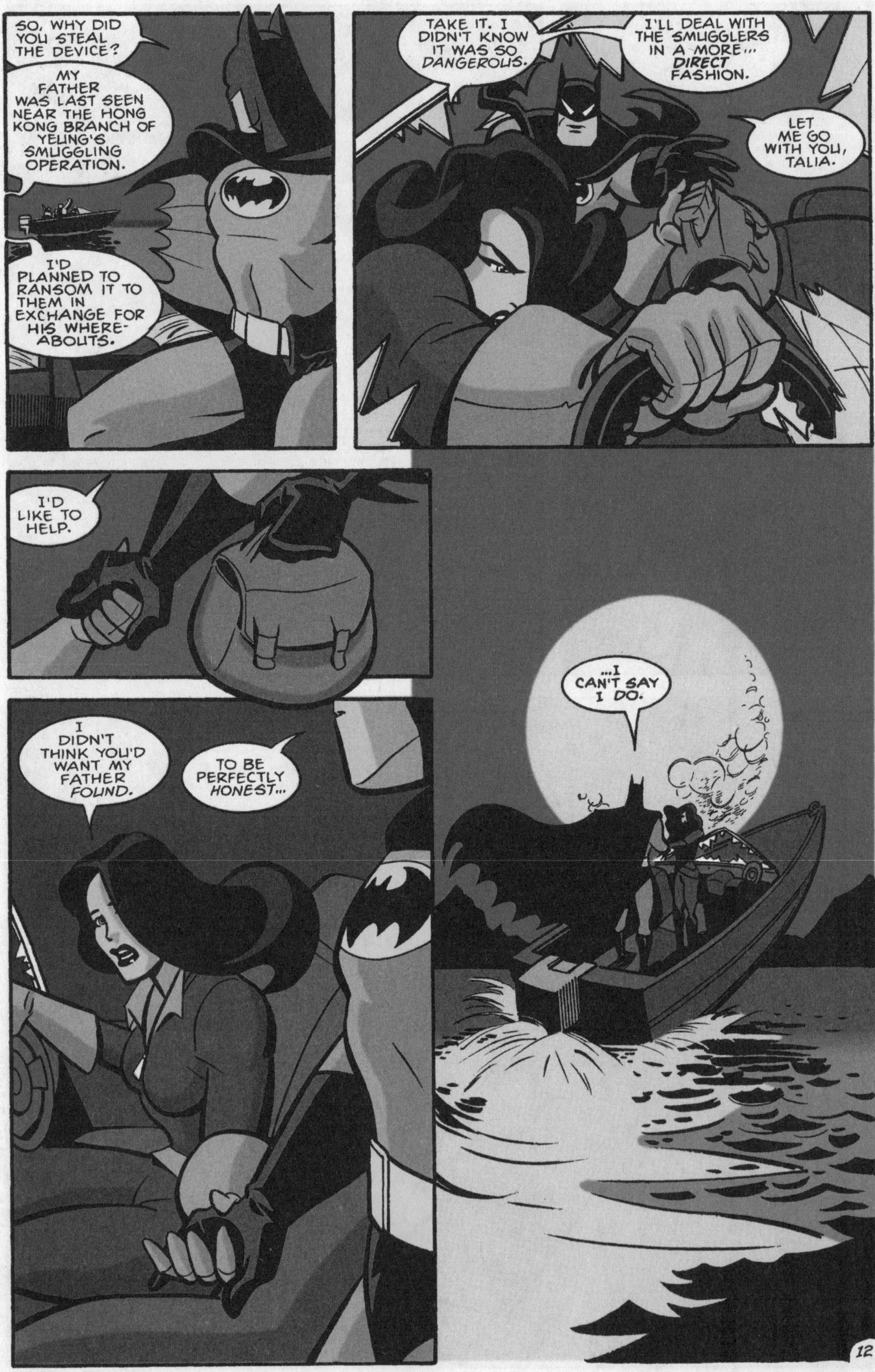
SO, WHY DID YOU STEAL THE DEVICE?
MY FATHER WAS LAST SEEN NEAR THE HONG KONG BRANCH OF YELING'S SMUGGLING OPERATION.
I'D PLANNED TO RANSOM IT TO THEM IN EXCHANGE FOR HIS WHERE-ABOUTS.
TAKE IT. I DIDN'T KNOW IT WAS SO DANGEROUS.
I'LL DEAL WITH THE SMUGGLERS IN A MORE... DIRECT FASHION.
LET ME GO WITH YOU, TALIA.
I'D LIKE TO HELP.
I DIDN'T THINK YOU'D WANT MY FATHER FOUND.
TO BE PERFECTLY HONEST...
...I CAN'T SAY I DO.

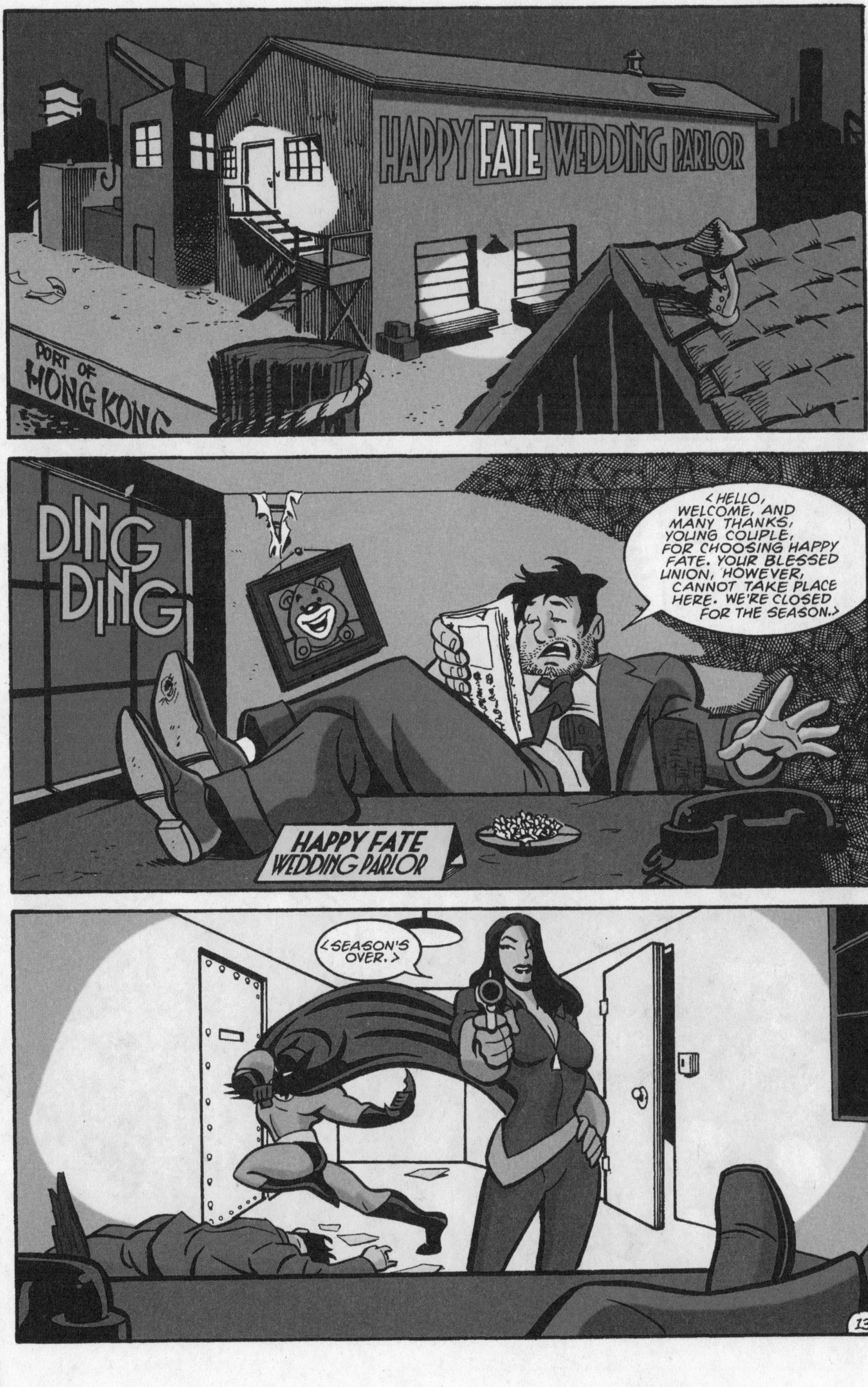
HAPPY FATE WEDDING PARLOR
PORT OF HONG KONG
DING DING
<HELLO, WELCOME, AND MANY THANKS, YOUNG COUPLE, FOR CHOOSING HAPPY FATE. YOUR BLESSED UNION, HOWEVER, CANNOT TAKE PLACE HERE. WE'RE CLOSED FOR THE SEASON.>
HAPPY FATE WEDDING PARLOR
<SEASON'S OVER.>

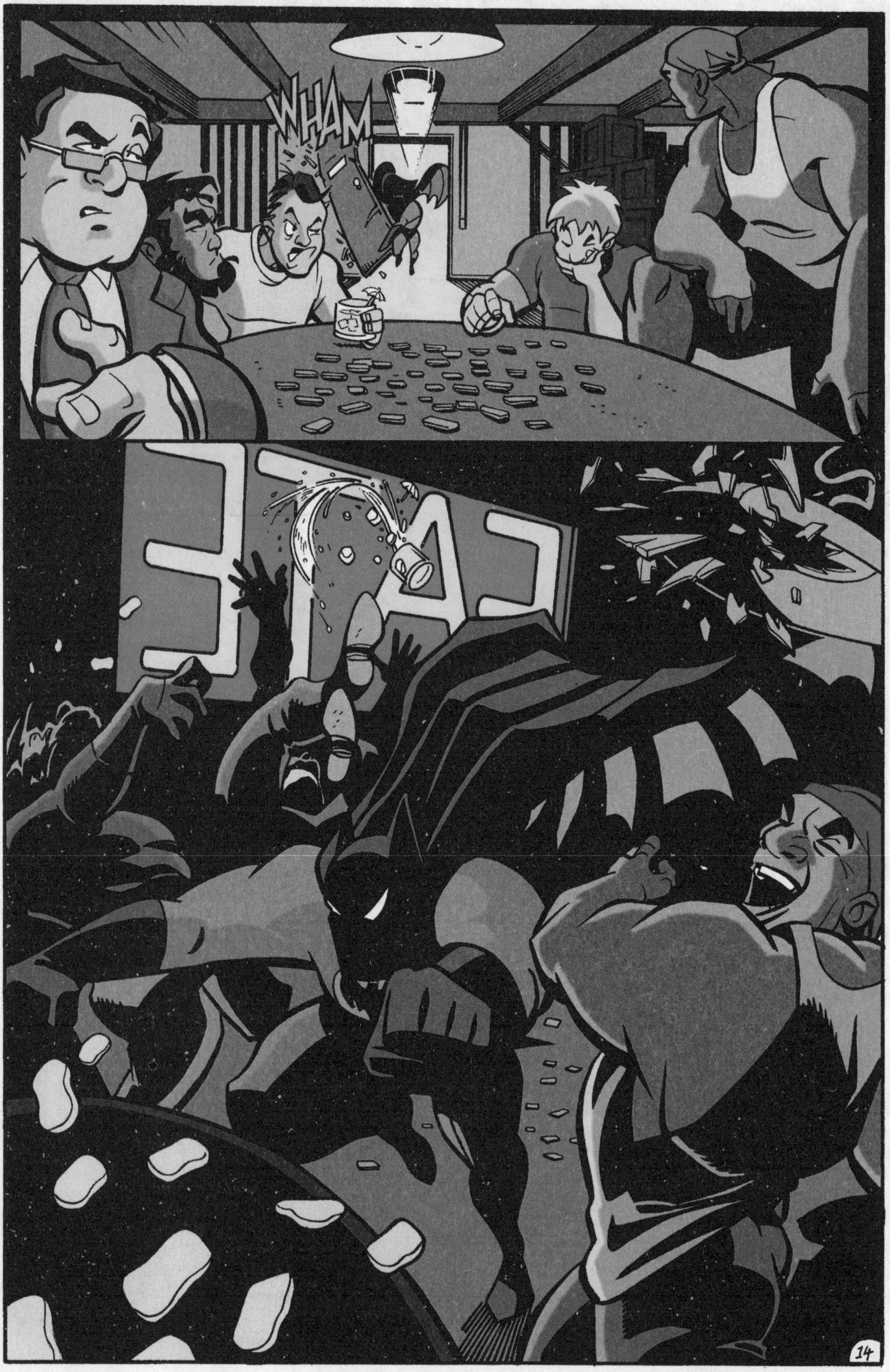
WHAM

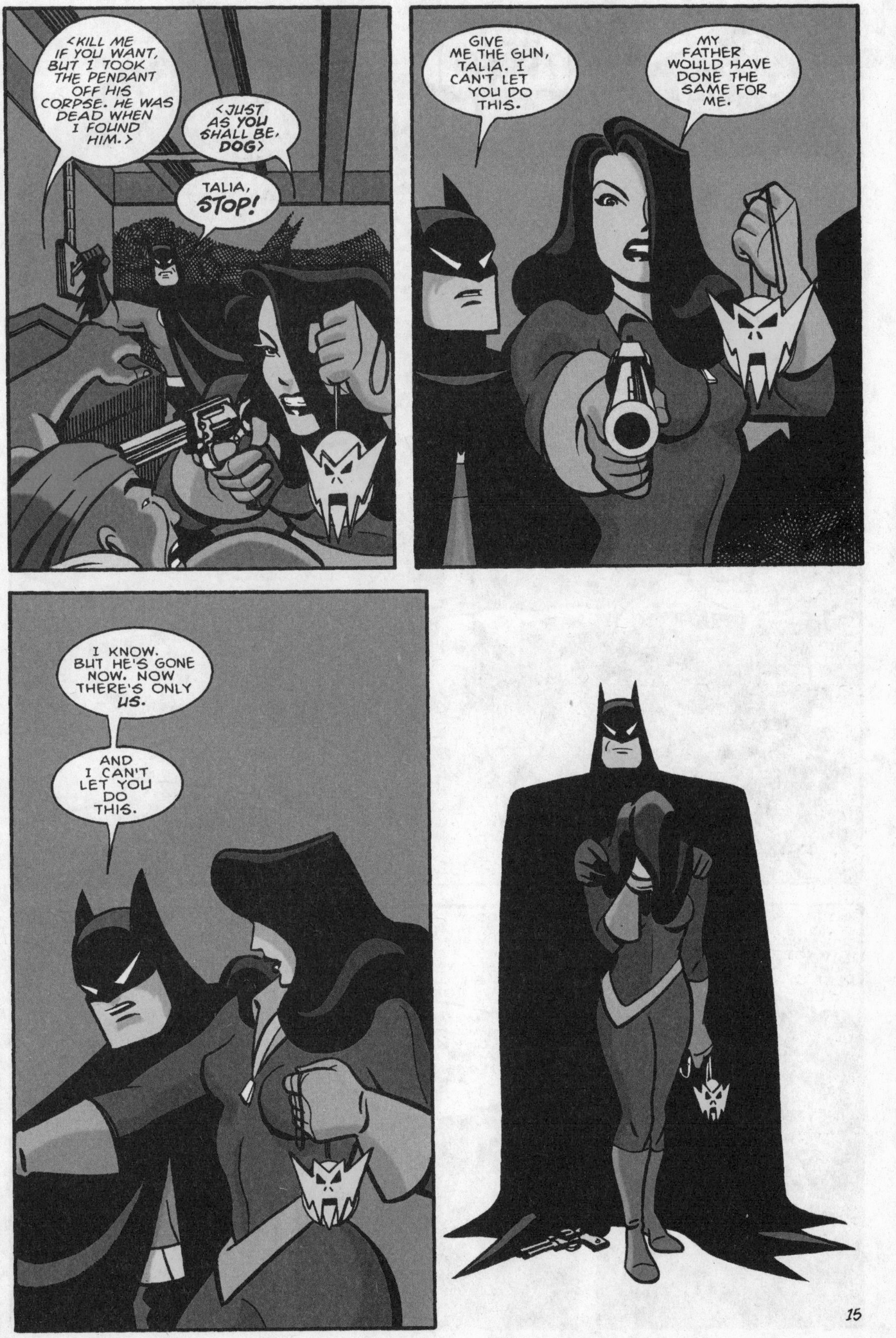
<KILL ME IF YOU WANT, BUT I TOOK THE PENDANT OFF HIS CORPSE. HE WAS DEAD WHEN I FOUND HIM.>
<JUST AS YOU SHALL BE, DOG>
TALIA, STOP!
GIVE ME THE GUN, TALIA. I CAN'T LET YOU DO THIS.
MY FATHER WOULD HAVE DONE THE SAME FOR ME.
I KNOW. BUT HE'S GONE NOW. NOW THERE'S ONLY US.
AND I CAN'T LET YOU DO THIS.

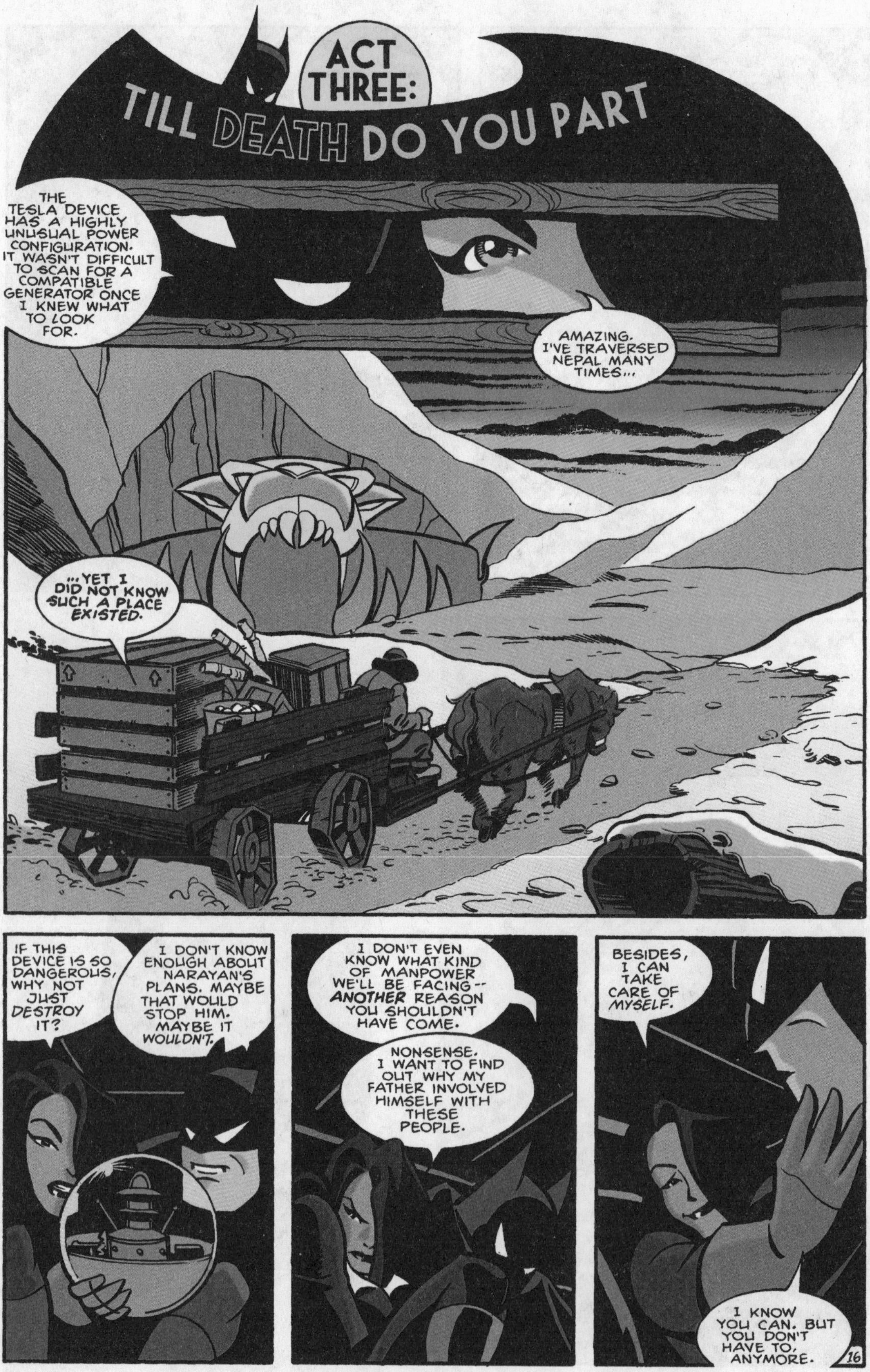
ACT THREE:
TILL DEATH DO YOU PART
THE TESLA DEVICE HAS A HIGHLY UNUSUAL POWER CONFIGURATION. IT WASN'T DIFFICULT TO SCAN FOR A COMPATIBLE GENERATOR ONCE I KNEW WHAT TO LOOK FOR.
AMAZING. I'VE TRAVERSED NEPAL MANY TIMES...
...YET I DID NOT KNOW SUCH A PLACE EXISTED.
IF THIS DEVICE IS SO DANGEROUS, WHY NOT JUST DESTROY IT?
I DON'T KNOW ENOUGH ABOUT NARAYAN'S PLANS. MAYBE THAT WOULD STOP HIM. MAYBE IT WOULDN'T.
I DON'T EVEN KNOW WHAT KIND OF MANPOWER WE'LL BE FACING-- ANOTHER REASON YOU SHOULDN'T HAVE COME.
NONSENSE. I WANT TO FIND OUT WHY MY FATHER INVOLVED HIMSELF WITH THESE PEOPLE.
BESIDES, I CAN TAKE CARE OF MYSELF.
I KNOW YOU CAN. BUT YOU DON'T HAVE TO, ANYMORE.
16

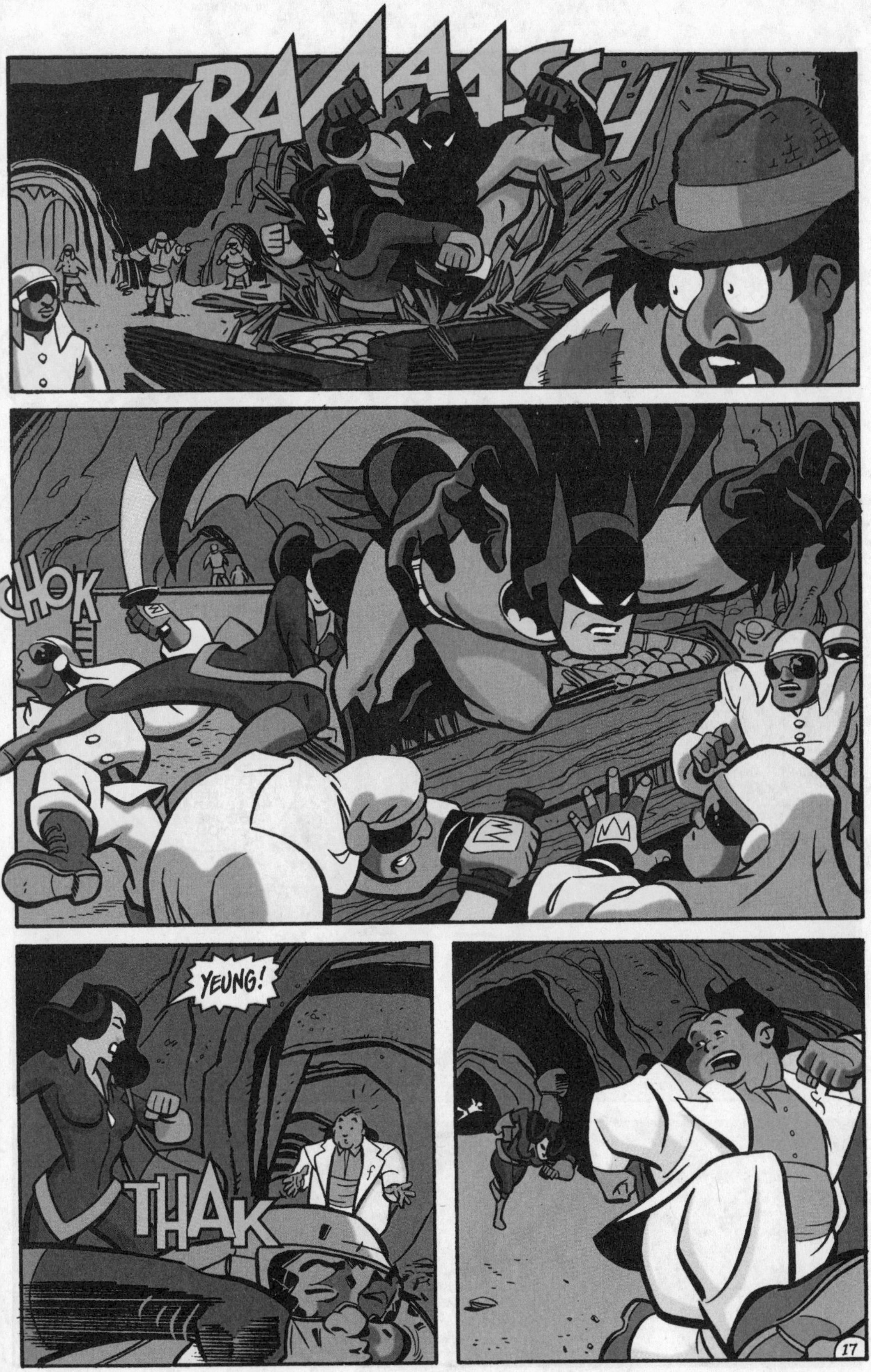
KRAAAASSH
CHOK
YEUNG!
THAK

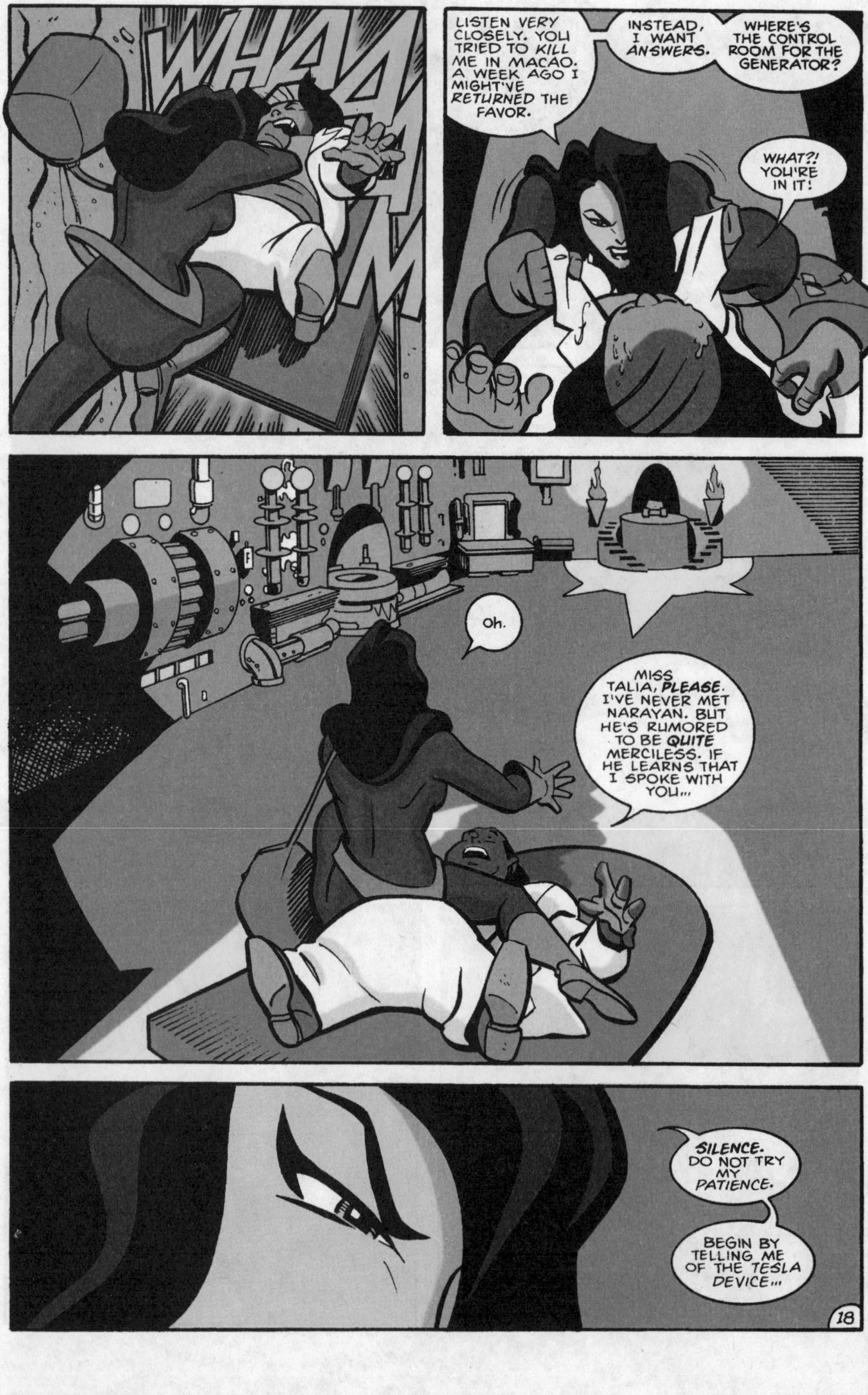
WHAAAM
LISTEN VERY CLOSELY. YOU TRIED TO KILL ME IN MACAO. A WEEK AGO I MIGHT'VE RETURNED THE FAVOR.
INSTEAD, I WANT ANSWERS.
WHERE'S THE CONTROL ROOM FOR THE GENERATOR?
WHAT?! YOU'RE IN IT!
Oh.
MISS TALIA, PLEASE. I'VE NEVER MET NARAYAN. BUT HE'S RUMORED TO BE QUITE MERCILESS. IF HE LEARNS THAT I SPOKE WITH YOU...
SILENCE. DO NOT TRY MY PATIENCE.
BEGIN BY TELLING ME OF THE TESLA DEVICE...
18

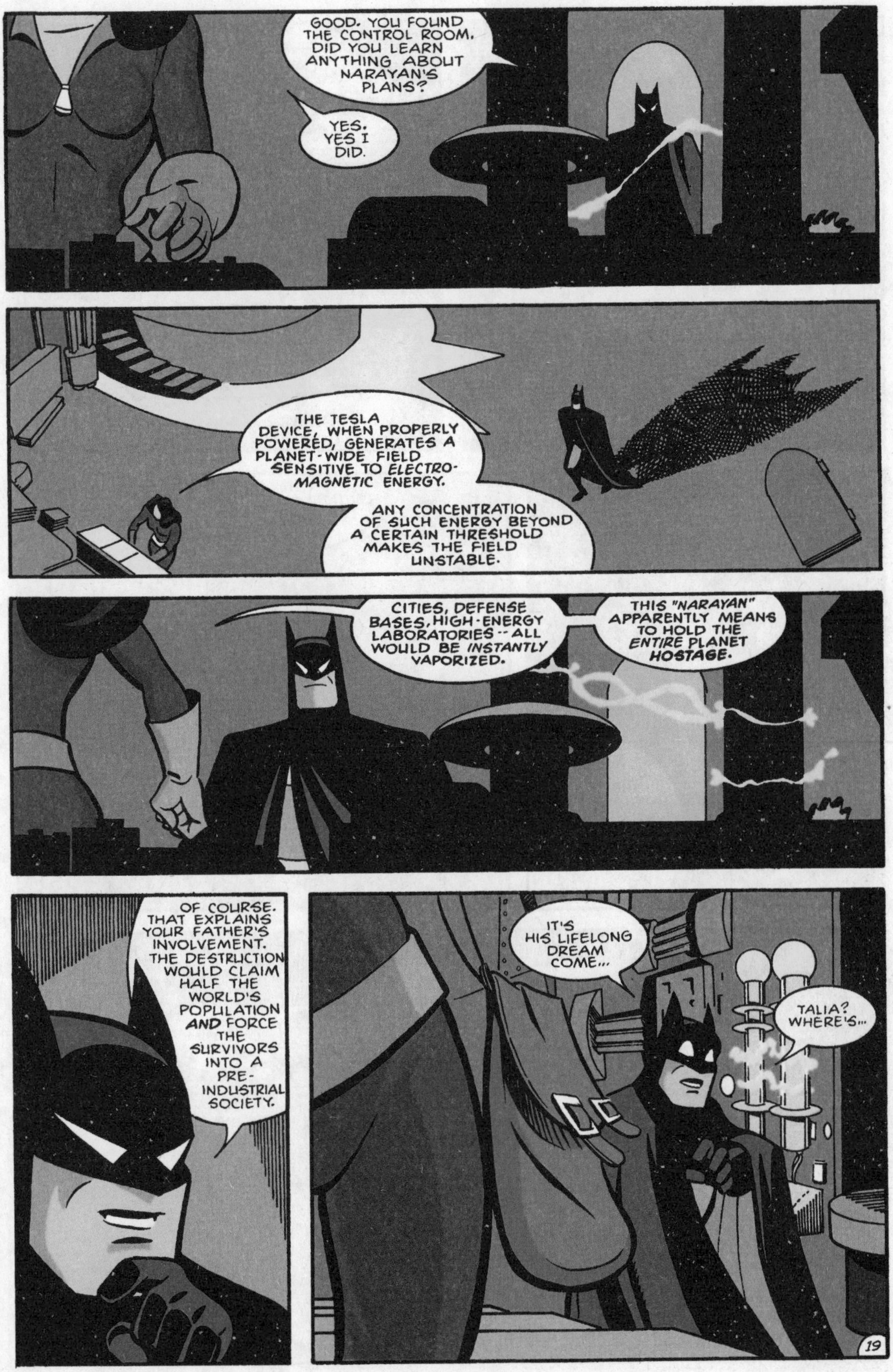
GOOD. YOU FOUND THE CONTROL ROOM. DID YOU LEARN ANYTHING ABOUT NARAYAN'S PLANS?
YES. YES I DID.
THE TESLA DEVICE, WHEN PROPERLY POWERED, GENERATES A PLANET-WIDE FIELD SENSITIVE TO *ELECTRO-MAGNETIC* ENERGY.
ANY CONCENTRATION OF SUCH ENERGY BEYOND A CERTAIN THRESHOLD MAKES THE FIELD UNSTABLE.
CITIES, DEFENSE BASES, HIGH-ENERGY LABORATORIES -- ALL WOULD BE *INSTANTLY* VAPORIZED.
THIS *"NARAYAN"* APPARENTLY MEANS TO HOLD THE *ENTIRE* PLANET **HOSTAGE**.
OF COURSE. THAT EXPLAINS YOUR FATHER'S INVOLVEMENT. THE DESTRUCTION WOULD CLAIM HALF THE WORLD'S POPULATION **AND** FORCE THE SURVIVORS INTO A PRE-INDUSTRIAL SOCIETY.
IT'S HIS LIFELONG DREAM COME...
TALIA? WHERE'S...
19

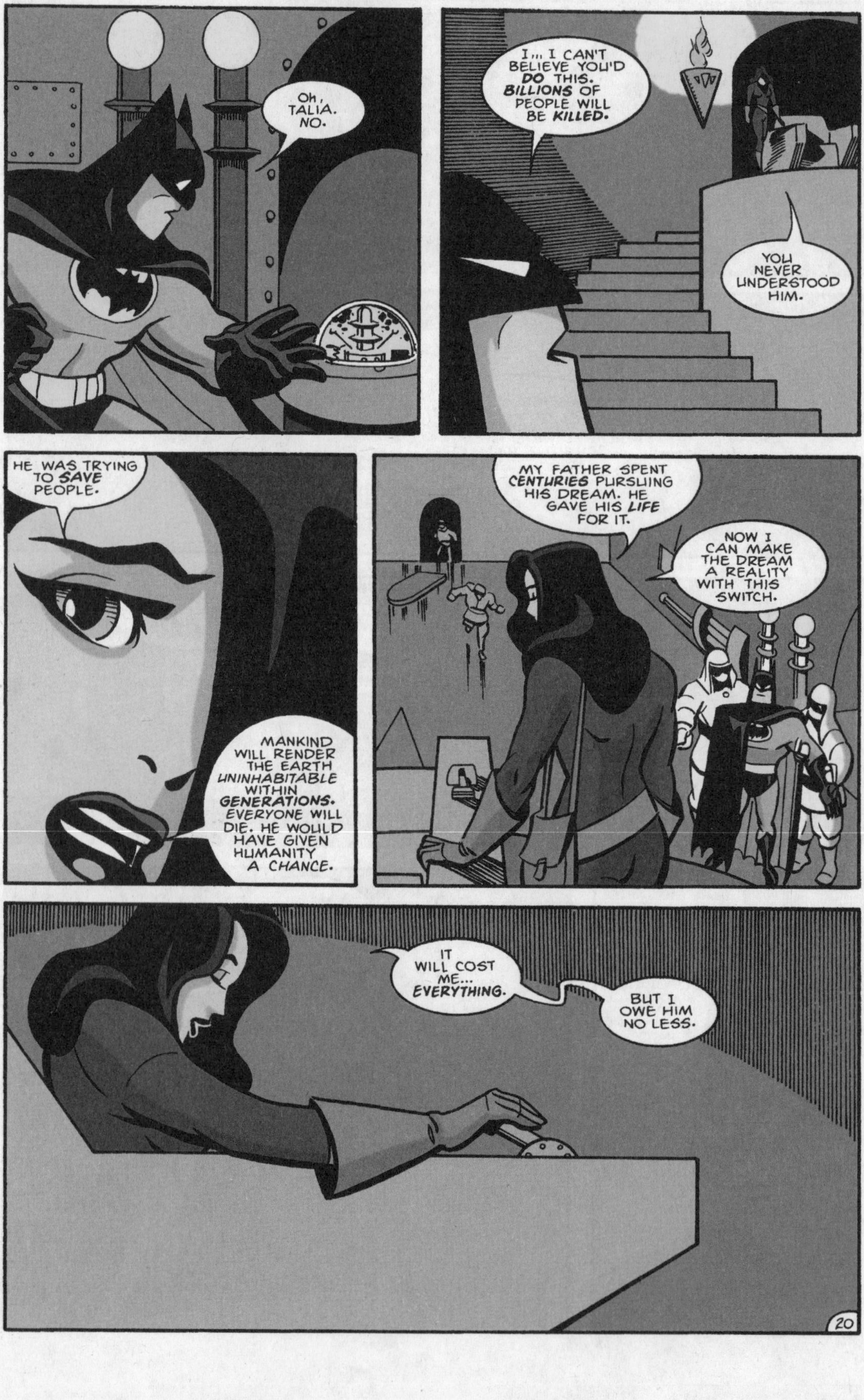

Oh, TALIA. NO.
I... I CAN'T BELIEVE YOU'D DO THIS. BILLIONS OF PEOPLE WILL BE KILLED.
YOU NEVER UNDERSTOOD HIM.
HE WAS TRYING TO SAVE PEOPLE.
MANKIND WILL RENDER THE EARTH UNINHABITABLE WITHIN GENERATIONS. EVERYONE WILL DIE. HE WOULD HAVE GIVEN HUMANITY A CHANCE.
MY FATHER SPENT CENTURIES PURSUING HIS DREAM. HE GAVE HIS LIFE FOR IT.
NOW I CAN MAKE THE DREAM A REALITY WITH THIS SWITCH.
IT WILL COST ME... EVERYTHING.
BUT I OWE HIM NO LESS.

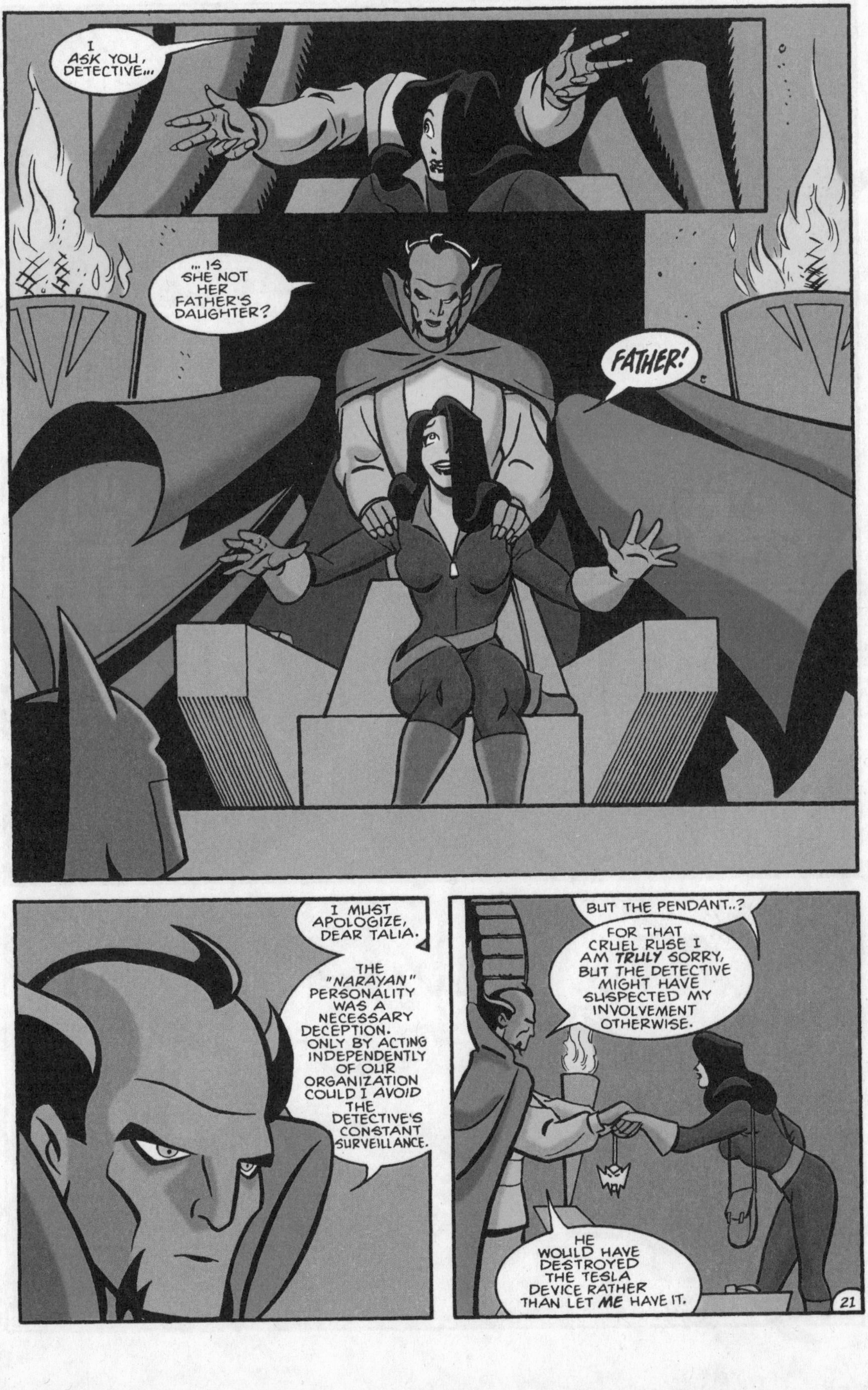
I ASK YOU, DETECTIVE...
... IS SHE NOT HER FATHER'S DAUGHTER?
FATHER!
I MUST APOLOGIZE, DEAR TALIA.
THE "NARAYAN" PERSONALITY WAS A NECESSARY DECEPTION. ONLY BY ACTING INDEPENDENTLY OF OUR ORGANIZATION COULD I AVOID THE DETECTIVE'S CONSTANT SURVEILLANCE.
BUT THE PENDANT..?
FOR THAT CRUEL RUSE I AM TRULY SORRY, BUT THE DETECTIVE MIGHT HAVE SUSPECTED MY INVOLVEMENT OTHERWISE.
HE WOULD HAVE DESTROYED THE TESLA DEVICE RATHER THAN LET ME HAVE IT.

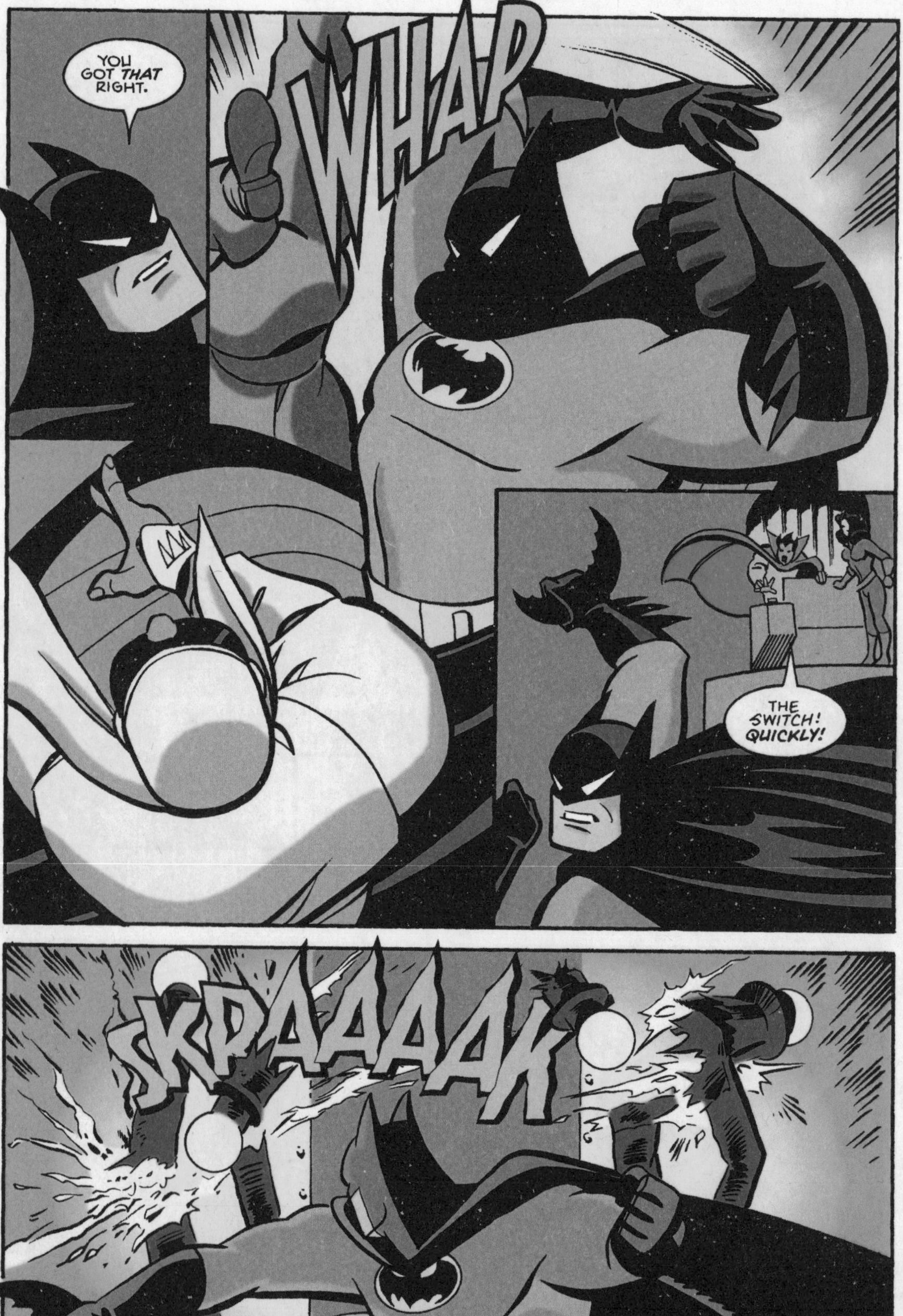
YOU GOT THAT RIGHT.
WHAP
THE SWITCH! QUICKLY!
SKRAAAAK

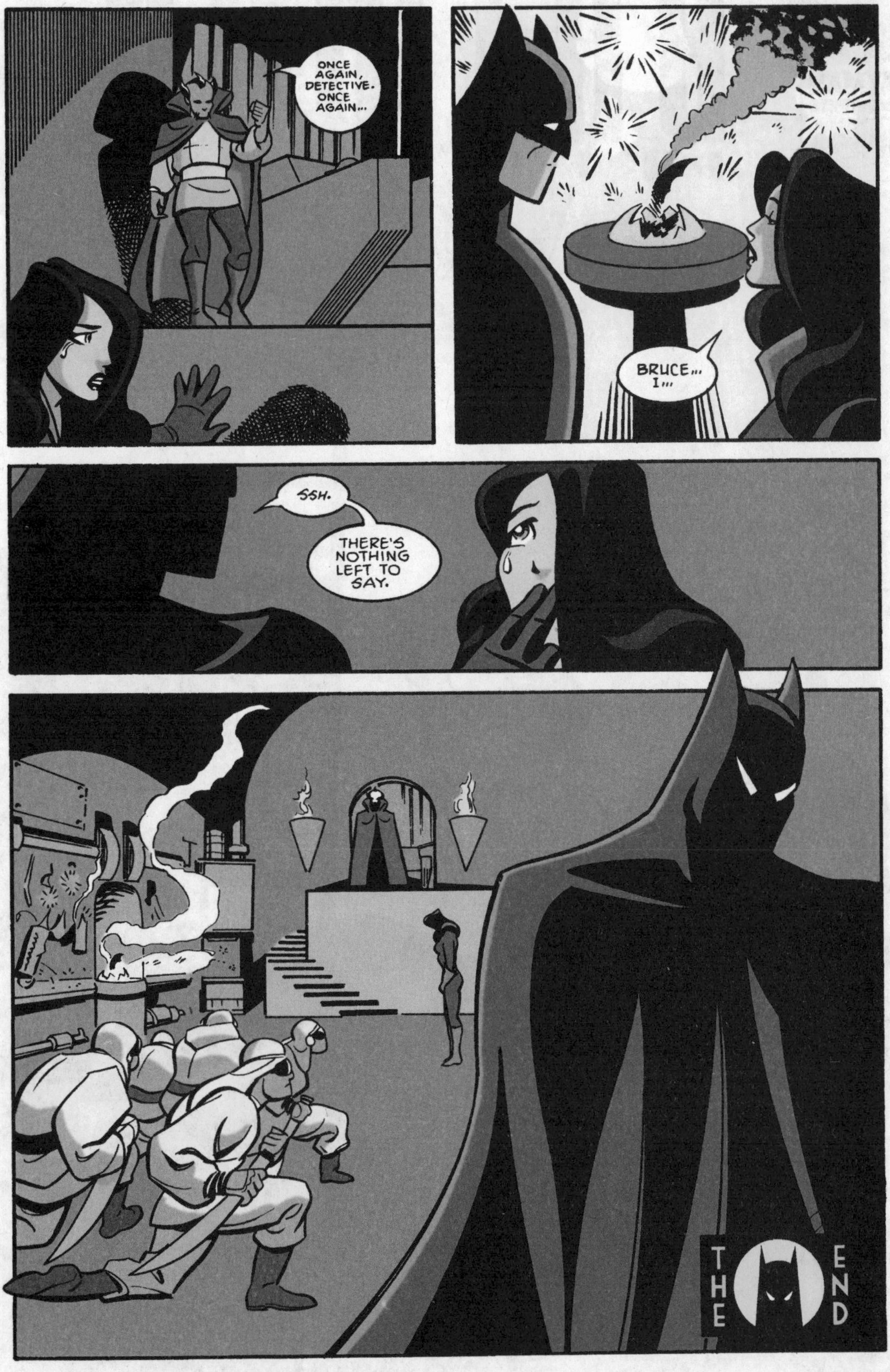
ONCE AGAIN, DETECTIVE. ONCE AGAIN...
BRUCE... I...
SSH.
THERE'S NOTHING LEFT TO SAY.
THE END

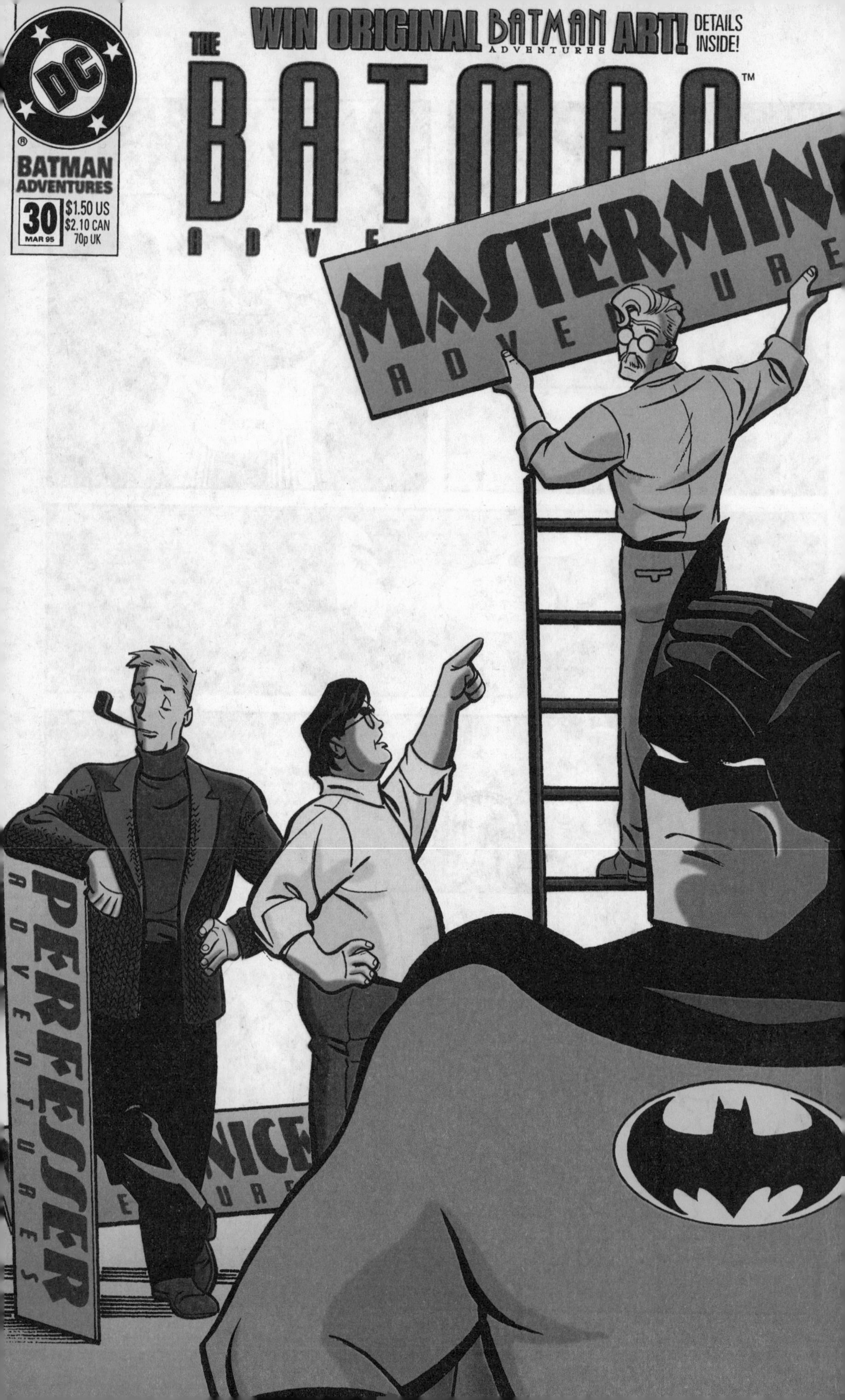
WIN ORIGINAL BATMAN ADVENTURES ART! DETAILS INSIDE!
THE BATMAN ADVE
DC
BATMAN ADVENTURES
30 MAR 95
$1.50 US
$2.10 CAN
70p UK
MASTERMIN
ADVE TURE
PERFESSER
ADVENTURES

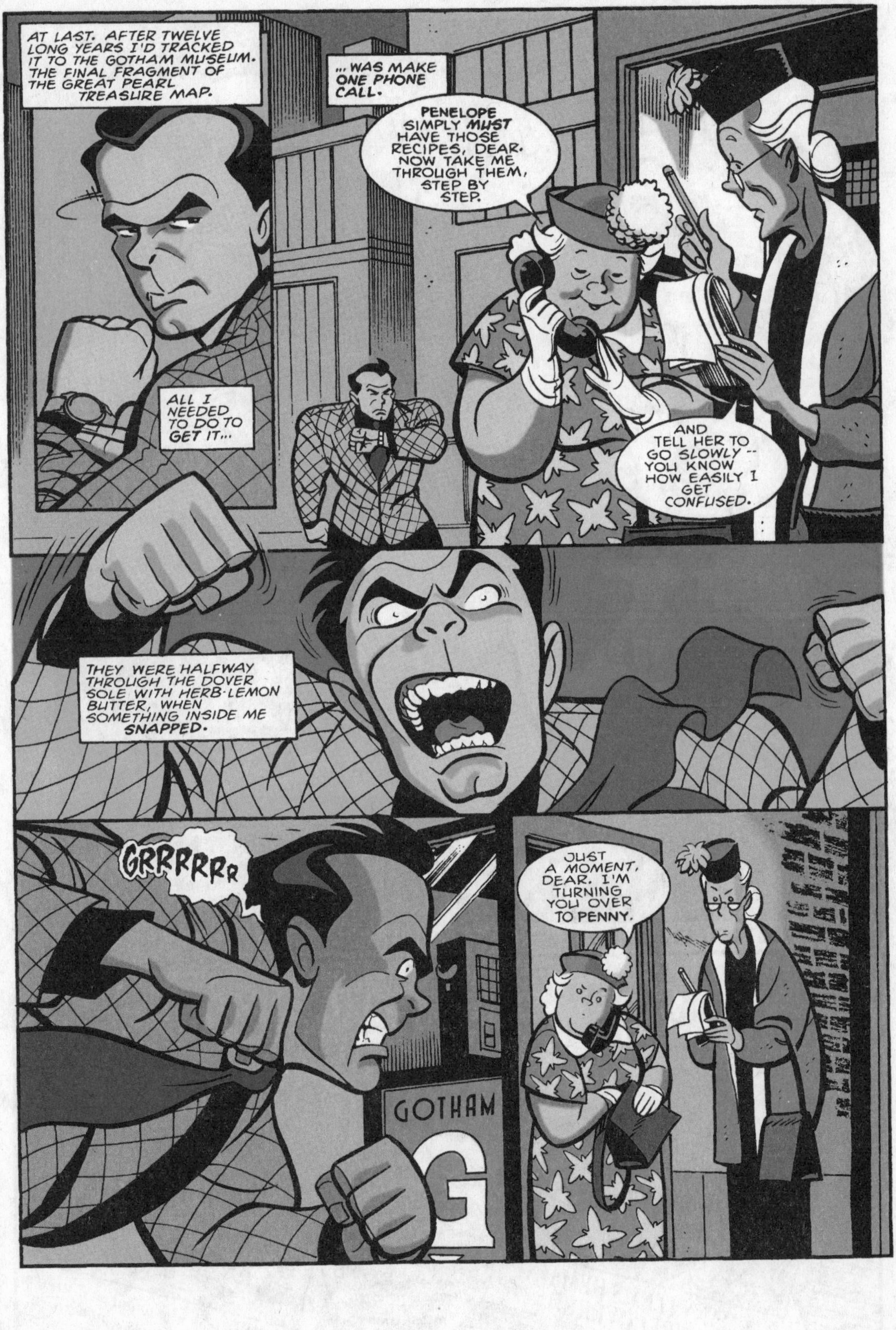
AT LAST. AFTER TWELVE LONG YEARS I'D TRACKED IT TO THE GOTHAM MUSEUM. THE FINAL FRAGMENT OF THE GREAT PEARL TREASURE MAP.
ALL I NEEDED TO DO TO GET IT...
...WAS MAKE ONE PHONE CALL.
PENELOPE SIMPLY MUST HAVE THOSE RECIPES, DEAR. NOW TAKE ME THROUGH THEM, STEP BY STEP.
AND TELL HER TO GO SLOWLY -- YOU KNOW HOW EASILY I GET CONFUSED.
THEY WERE HALFWAY THROUGH THE DOVER SOLE WITH HERB-LEMON BUTTER, WHEN SOMETHING INSIDE ME SNAPPED.
GRRRRRR
GOTHAM
G
JUST A MOMENT, DEAR. I'M TURNING YOU OVER TO PENNY.

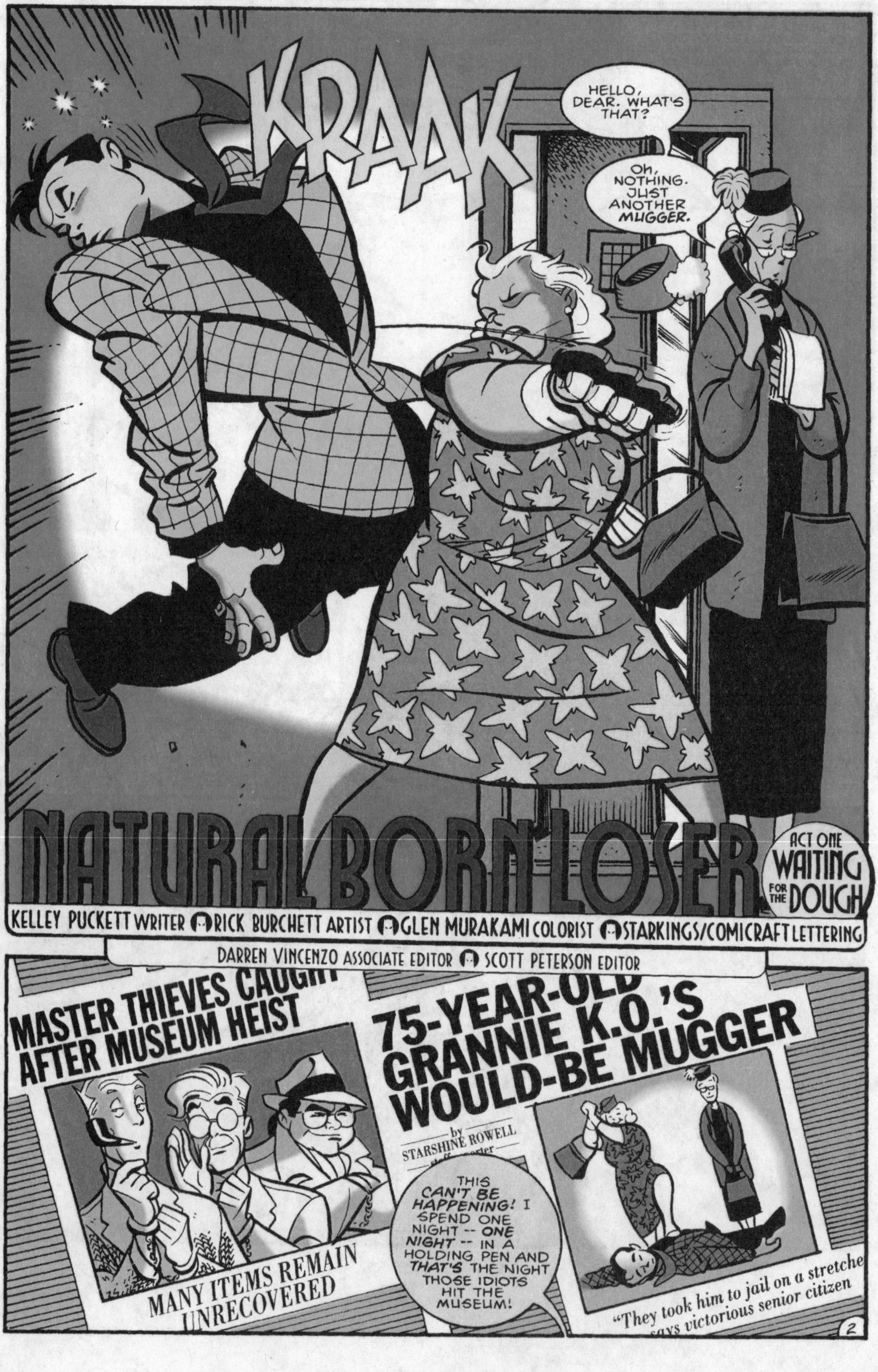
KRAAK
HELLO, DEAR. WHAT'S THAT?
Oh, NOTHING. JUST ANOTHER MUGGER.
NATURAL BORN LOSER
ACT ONE WAITING FOR THE DOUGH
KELLEY PUCKETT WRITER RICK BURCHETT ARTIST GLEN MURAKAMI COLORIST STARKINGS/COMICRAFT LETTERING
DARREN VINCENZO ASSOCIATE EDITOR SCOTT PETERSON EDITOR
MASTER THIEVES CAUGHT AFTER MUSEUM HEIST
MANY ITEMS REMAIN UNRECOVERED
75-YEAR-OLD GRANNIE K.O.'S WOULD-BE MUGGER
by STARSHINE ROWELL
THIS CAN'T BE HAPPENING! I SPEND ONE NIGHT -- ONE NIGHT -- IN A HOLDING PEN AND THAT'S THE NIGHT THOSE IDIOTS HIT THE MUSEUM!
"They took him to jail on a stretche
says victorious senior citizen
2

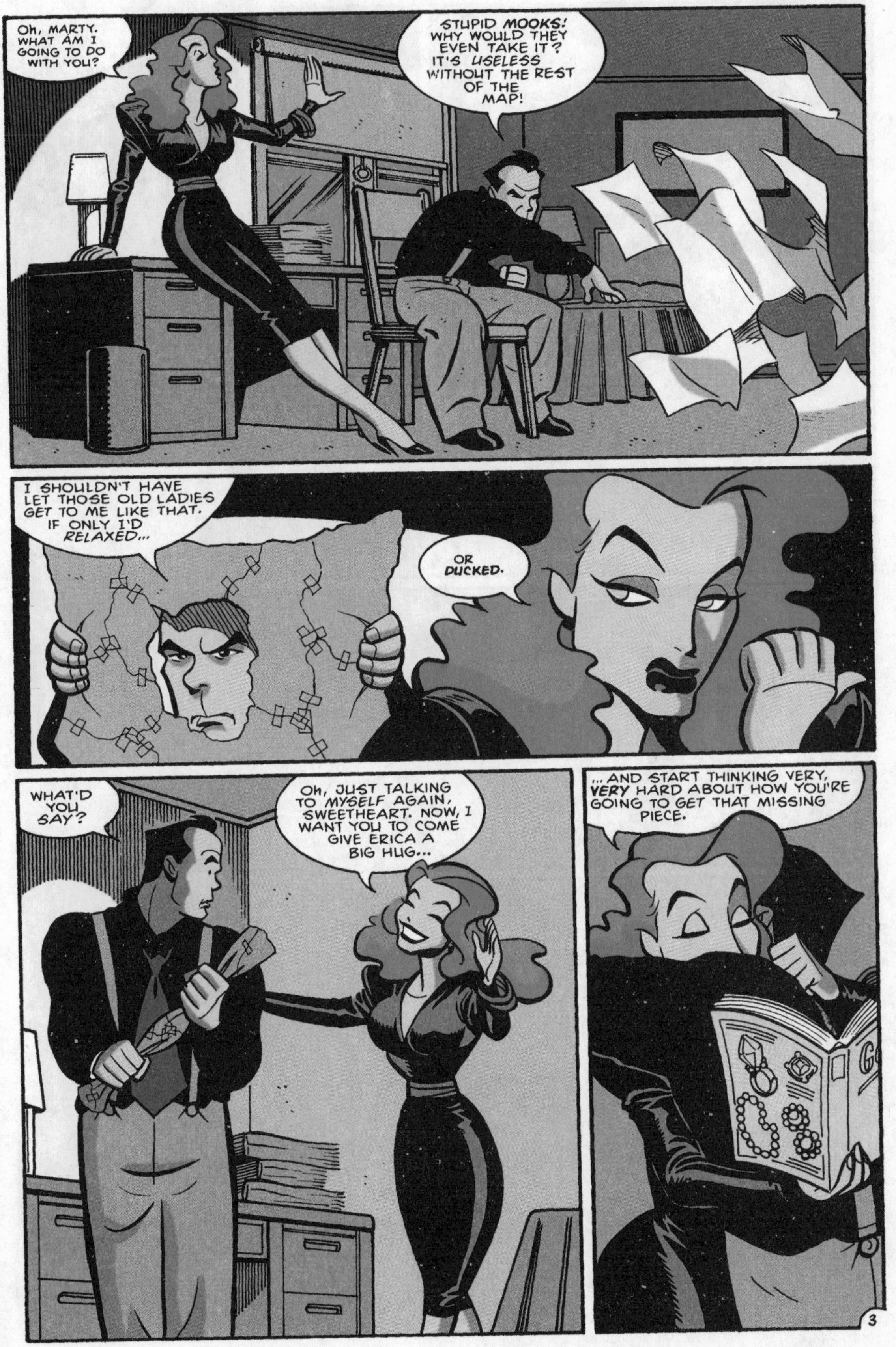
Oh, MARTY. WHAT AM I GOING TO DO WITH YOU?
STUPID MOOKS! WHY WOULD THEY EVEN TAKE IT? IT'S USELESS WITHOUT THE REST OF THE MAP!
I SHOULDN'T HAVE LET THOSE OLD LADIES GET TO ME LIKE THAT. IF ONLY I'D RELAXED...
OR DUCKED.
WHAT'D YOU SAY?
Oh, JUST TALKING TO MYSELF AGAIN, SWEETHEART. NOW, I WANT YOU TO COME GIVE ERICA A BIG HUG...
...AND START THINKING VERY, VERY HARD ABOUT HOW YOU'RE GOING TO GET THAT MISSING PIECE.

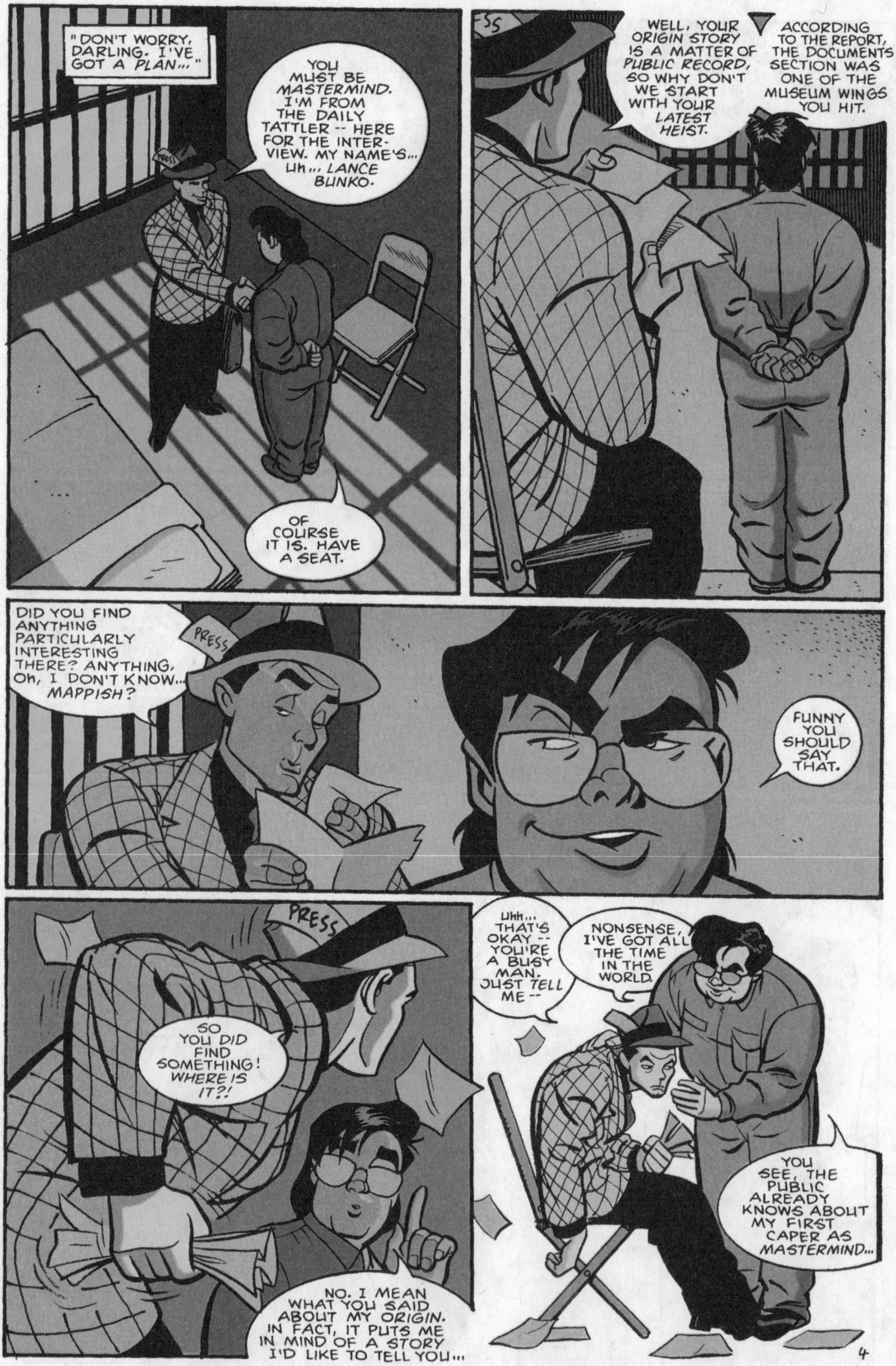
"DON'T WORRY, DARLING. I'VE GOT A PLAN..."
YOU MUST BE MASTERMIND. I'M FROM THE DAILY TATTLER -- HERE FOR THE INTERVIEW. MY NAME'S... UH... LANCE BUNKO.
OF COURSE IT IS. HAVE A SEAT.
WELL, YOUR ORIGIN STORY IS A MATTER OF PUBLIC RECORD, SO WHY DON'T WE START WITH YOUR LATEST HEIST.
ACCORDING TO THE REPORT, THE DOCUMENTS SECTION WAS ONE OF THE MUSEUM WINGS YOU HIT.
DID YOU FIND ANYTHING PARTICULARLY INTERESTING THERE? ANYTHING, OH, I DON'T KNOW... MAPPISH?
FUNNY YOU SHOULD SAY THAT.
SO YOU DID FIND SOMETHING! WHERE IS IT?!
NO. I MEAN WHAT YOU SAID ABOUT MY ORIGIN. IN FACT, IT PUTS ME IN MIND OF A STORY I'D LIKE TO TELL YOU...
UHH... THAT'S OKAY -- YOU'RE A BUSY MAN. JUST TELL ME --
NONSENSE, I'VE GOT ALL THE TIME IN THE WORLD.
YOU SEE, THE PUBLIC ALREADY KNOWS ABOUT MY FIRST CAPER AS MASTERMIND...

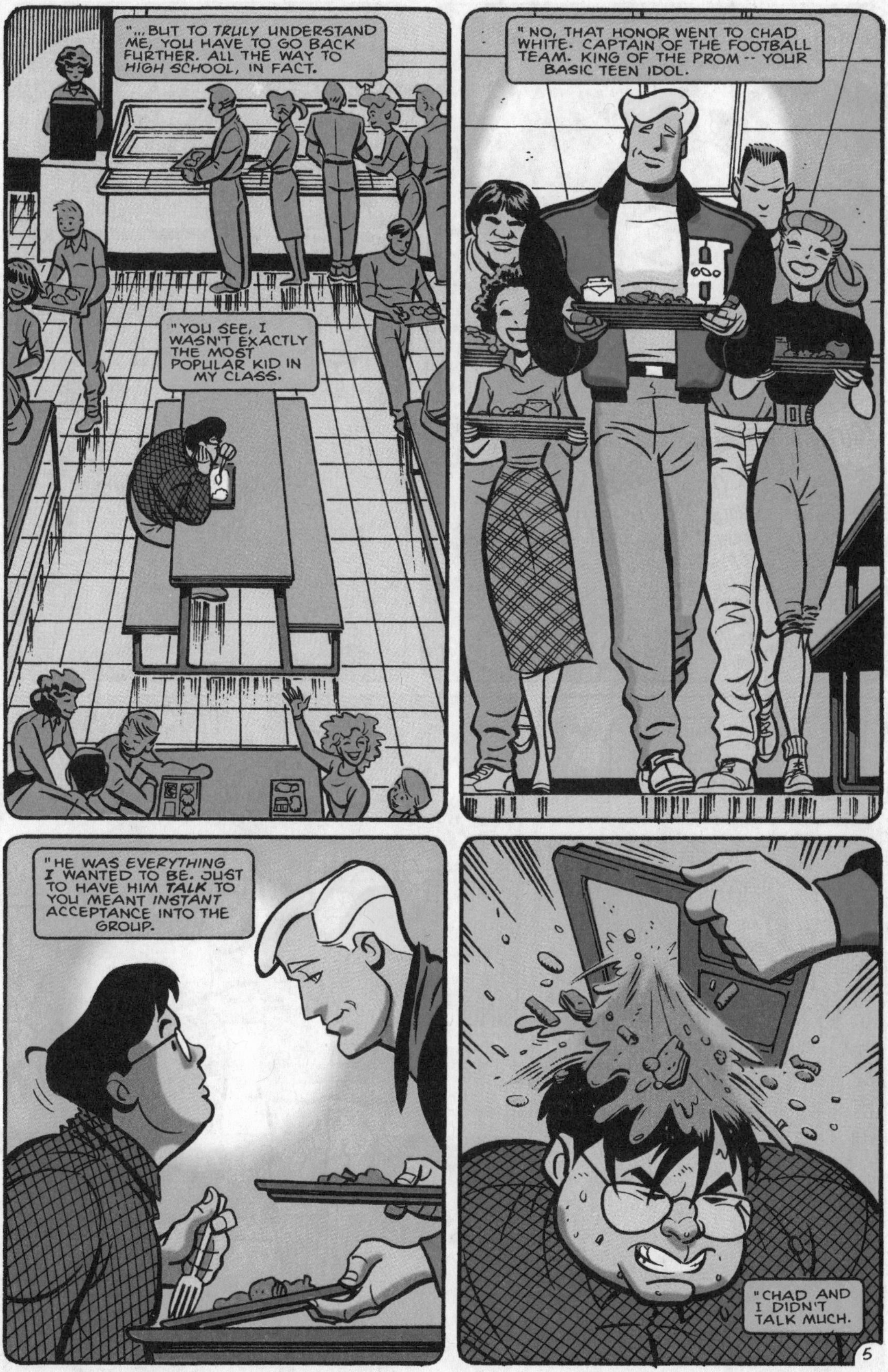
"...BUT TO TRULY UNDERSTAND ME, YOU HAVE TO GO BACK FURTHER. ALL THE WAY TO HIGH SCHOOL, IN FACT.
"YOU SEE, I WASN'T EXACTLY THE MOST POPULAR KID IN MY CLASS.
"NO, THAT HONOR WENT TO CHAD WHITE. CAPTAIN OF THE FOOTBALL TEAM. KING OF THE PROM -- YOUR BASIC TEEN IDOL.
"HE WAS EVERYTHING I WANTED TO BE. JUST TO HAVE HIM TALK TO YOU MEANT INSTANT ACCEPTANCE INTO THE GROUP.
"CHAD AND I DIDN'T TALK MUCH.

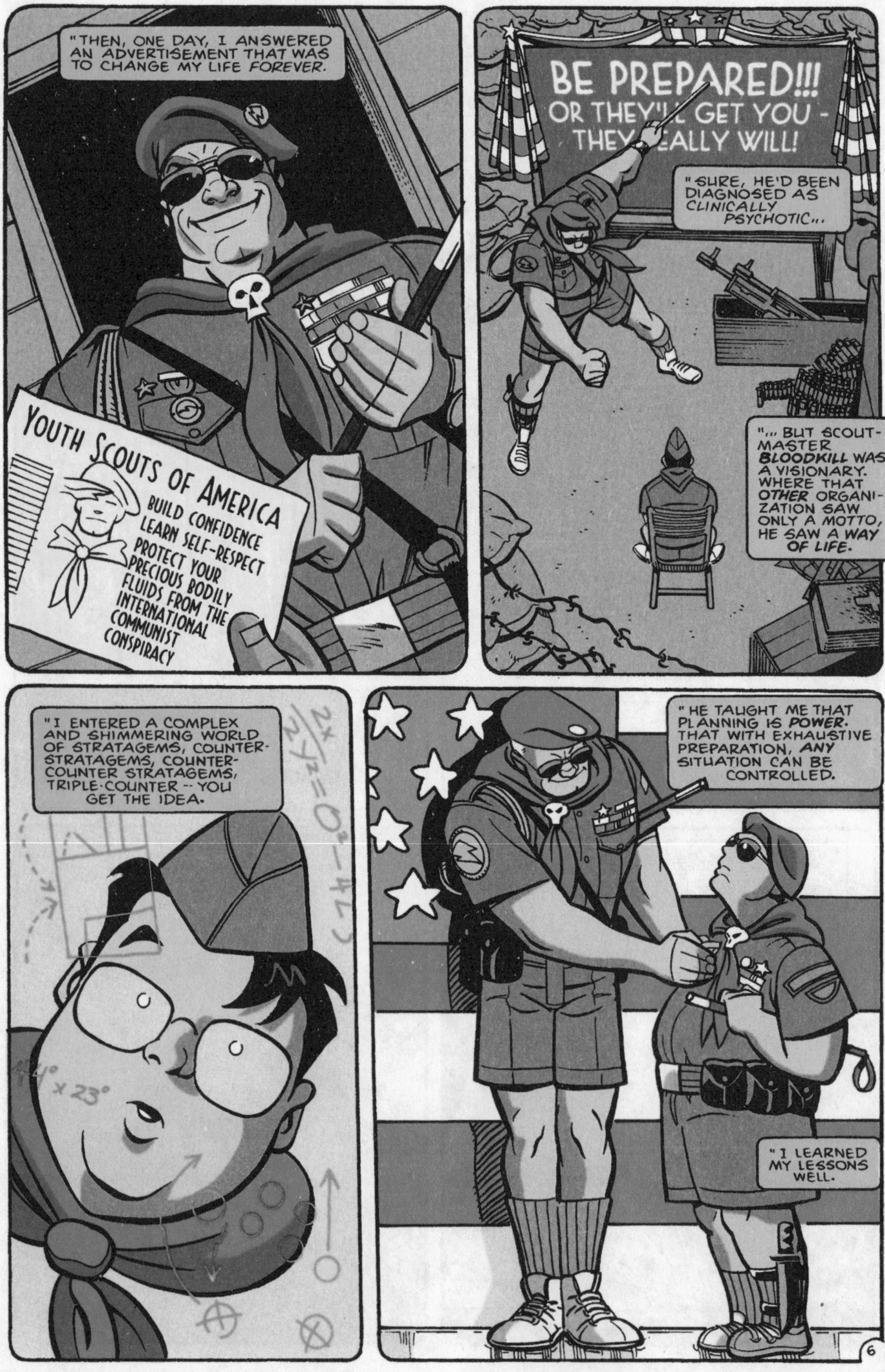
"THEN, ONE DAY, I ANSWERED AN ADVERTISEMENT THAT WAS TO CHANGE MY LIFE *FOREVER*.
YOUTH SCOUTS OF AMERICA
BUILD CONFIDENCE
LEARN SELF-RESPECT
PROTECT YOUR PRECIOUS BODILY FLUIDS FROM THE INTERNATIONAL COMMUNIST CONSPIRACY
BE PREPARED!!!
OR THEY'LL GET YOU - THEY REALLY WILL!
"SURE, HE'D BEEN DIAGNOSED AS *CLINICALLY PSYCHOTIC*...
"... BUT SCOUTMASTER **BLOODKILL** WAS A VISIONARY. WHERE THAT ***OTHER*** ORGANIZATION SAW ONLY A *MOTTO*, HE SAW A ***WAY OF LIFE***.
"I ENTERED A COMPLEX AND SHIMMERING WORLD OF STRATAGEMS, COUNTER-STRATAGEMS, COUNTER-COUNTER STRATAGEMS, TRIPLE-COUNTER -- YOU GET THE IDEA.
"HE TAUGHT ME THAT PLANNING IS ***POWER***. THAT WITH EXHAUSTIVE PREPARATION, ***ANY*** SITUATION CAN BE CONTROLLED.
"I LEARNED MY LESSONS WELL.

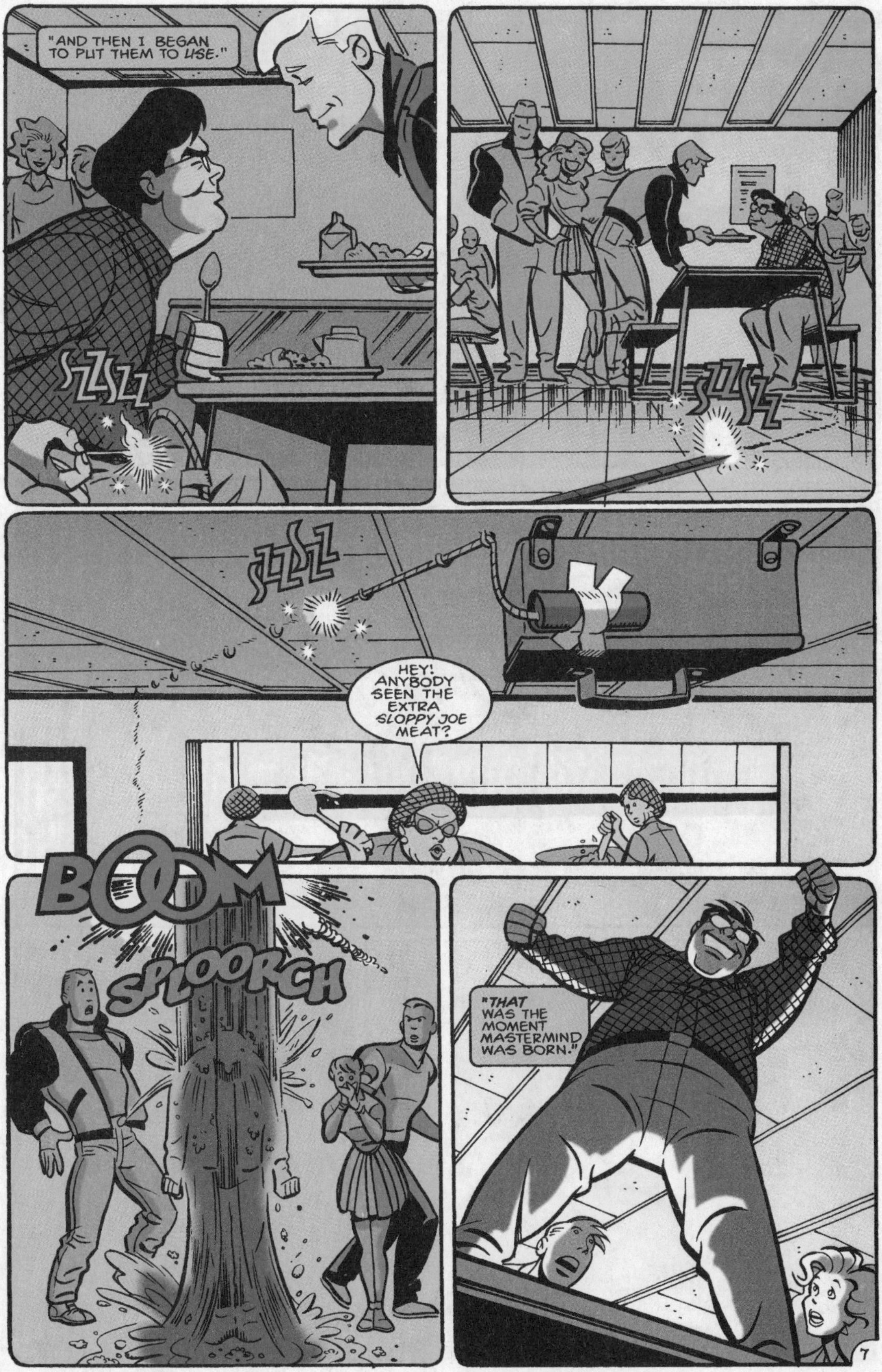
"AND THEN I BEGAN TO PUT THEM TO USE."
SZZSZZ
SZZSZZ
SZZSZZ
HEY! ANYBODY SEEN THE EXTRA SLOPPY JOE MEAT?
BOOM
SPLOORCH
"THAT WAS THE MOMENT MASTERMIND WAS BORN."

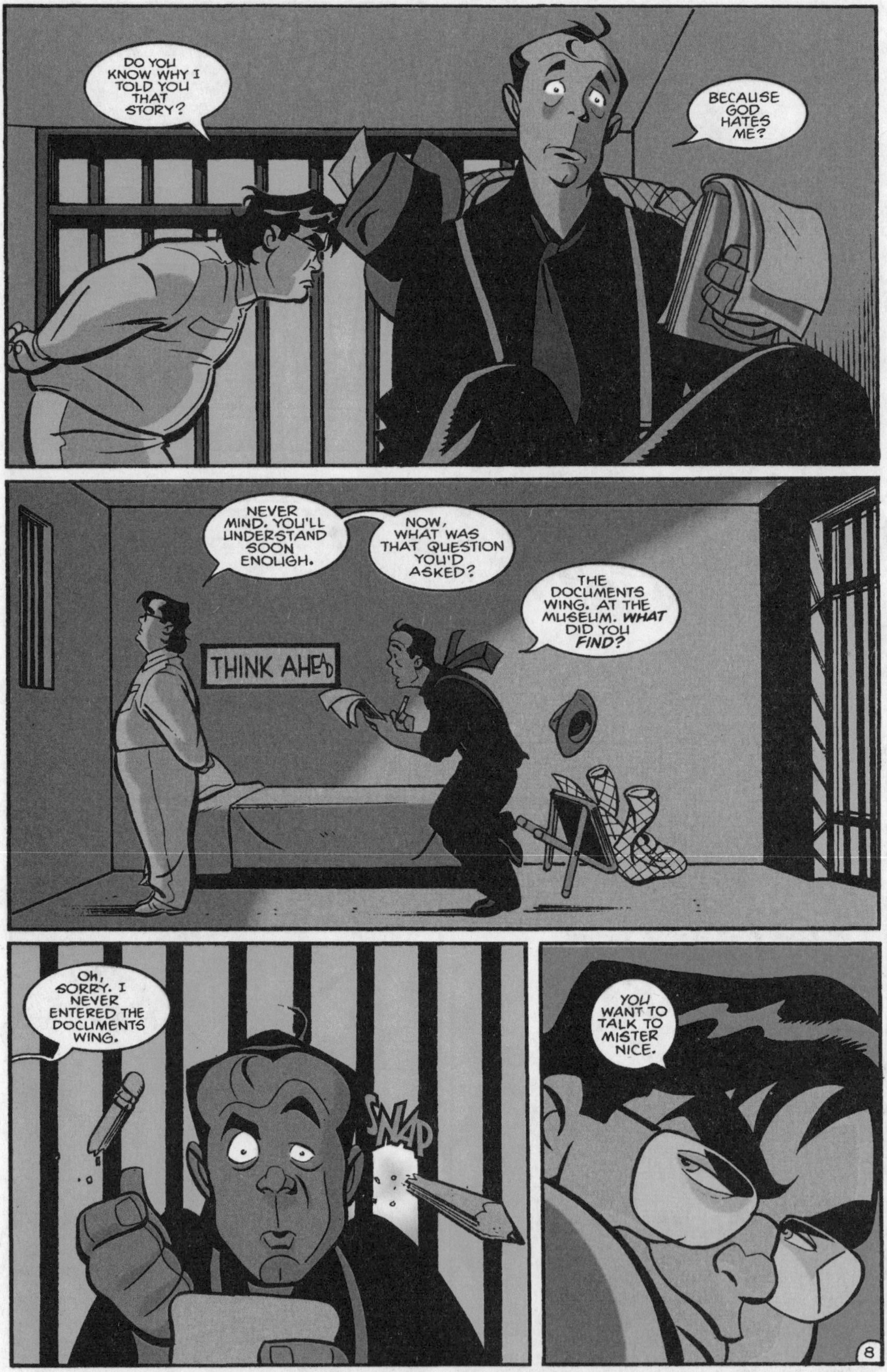

DO YOU KNOW WHY I TOLD YOU THAT STORY?
BECAUSE GOD HATES ME?
NEVER MIND. YOU'LL UNDERSTAND SOON ENOUGH.
NOW, WHAT WAS THAT QUESTION YOU'D ASKED?
THE DOCUMENTS WING. AT THE MUSEUM. WHAT DID YOU FIND?
THINK AHEAD
Oh, SORRY. I NEVER ENTERED THE DOCUMENTS WING.
SNAP
YOU WANT TO TALK TO MISTER NICE.

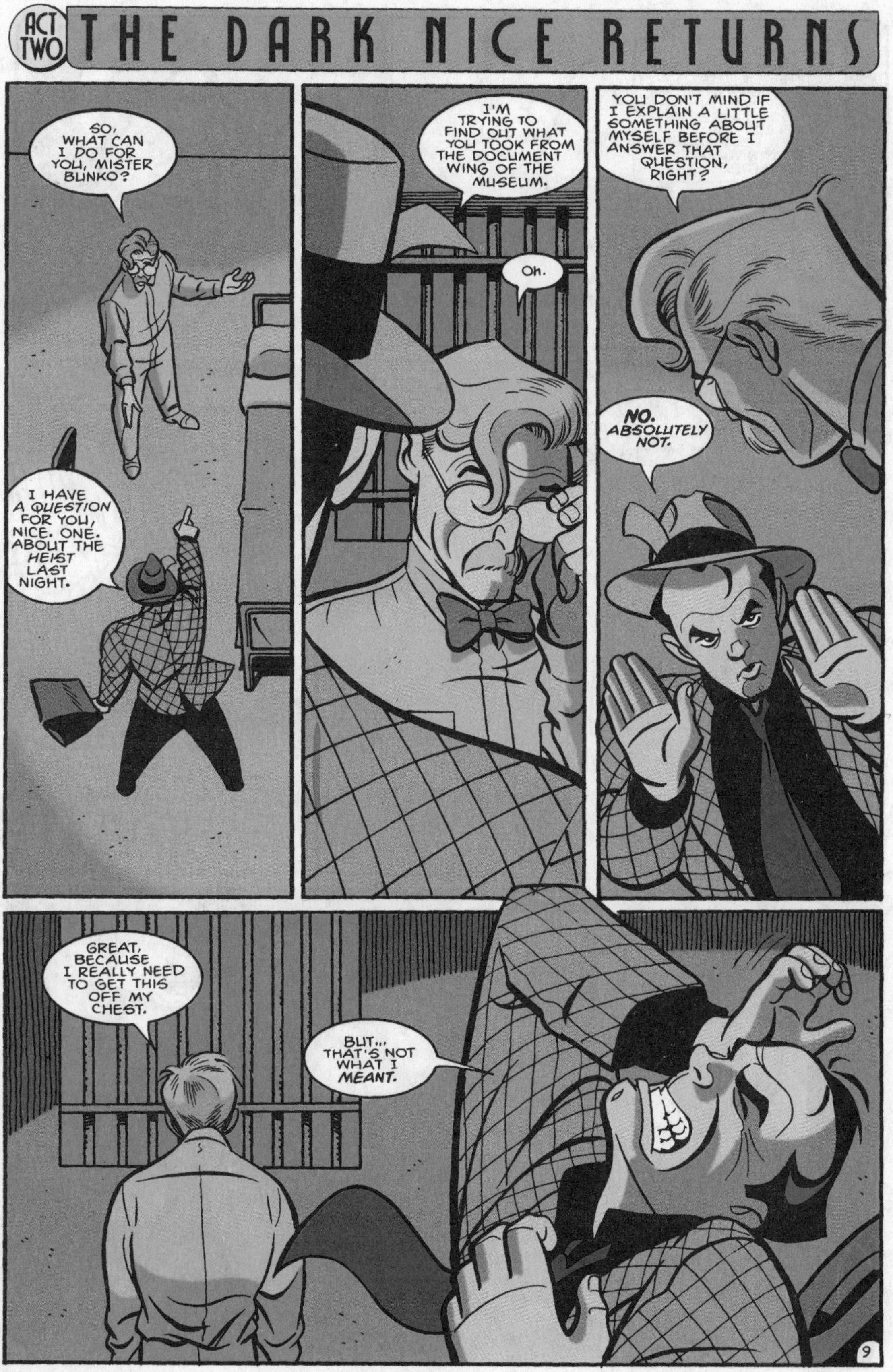

ACT TWO
THE DARK NICE RETURNS
SO, WHAT CAN I DO FOR YOU, MISTER BUNKO?
I HAVE A *QUESTION* FOR YOU, NICE. ONE. ABOUT THE *HEIST* LAST NIGHT.
I'M TRYING TO FIND OUT WHAT YOU TOOK FROM THE DOCUMENT WING OF THE MUSEUM.
Oh.
YOU DON'T MIND IF I EXPLAIN A LITTLE SOMETHING ABOUT MYSELF BEFORE I ANSWER THAT QUESTION, RIGHT?
NO. ABSOLUTELY NOT.
GREAT, BECAUSE I REALLY NEED TO GET THIS OFF MY CHEST.
BUT... THAT'S NOT WHAT I *MEANT*.

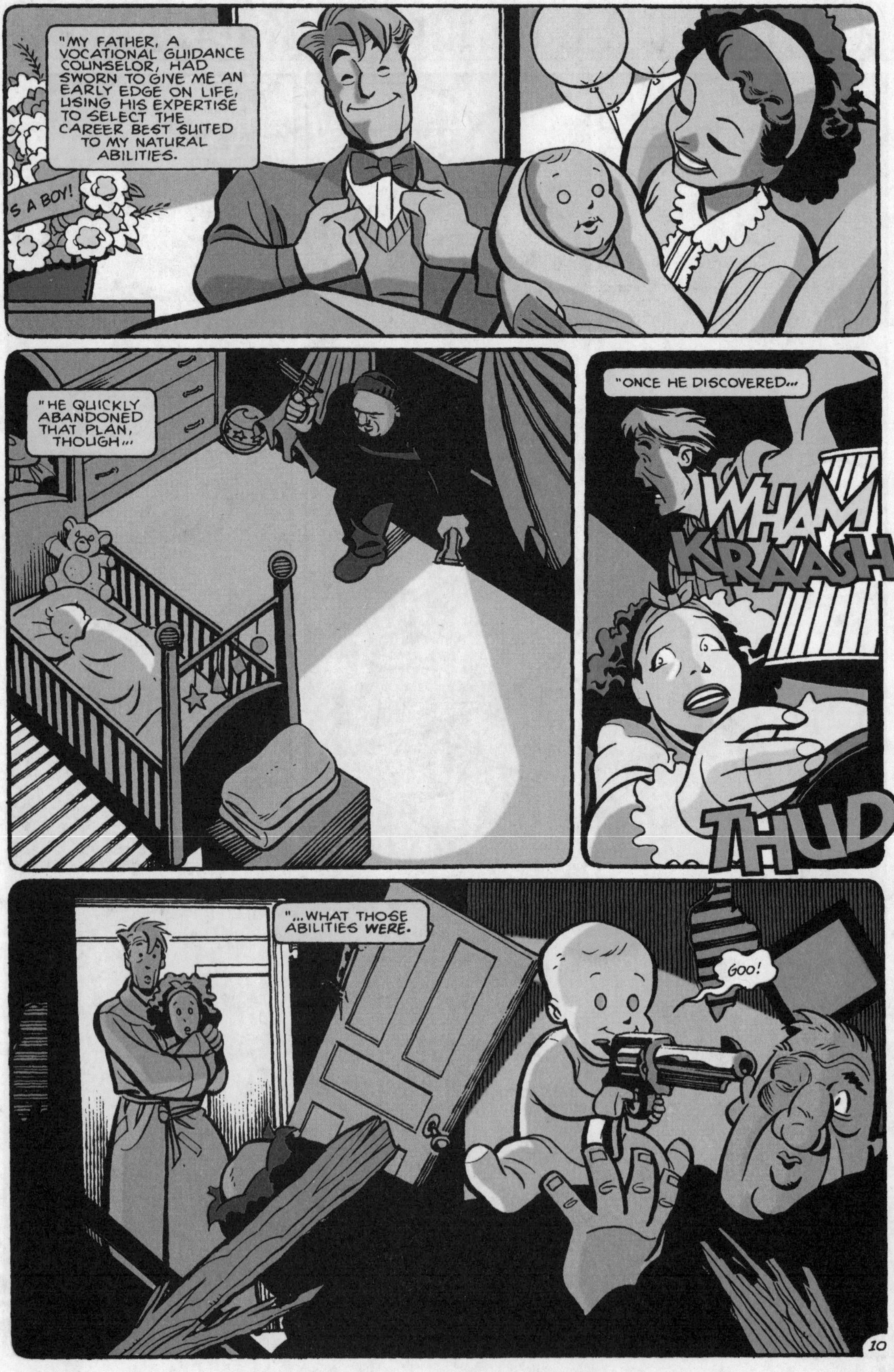
"MY FATHER, A VOCATIONAL GUIDANCE COUNSELOR, HAD SWORN TO GIVE ME AN EARLY EDGE ON LIFE, USING HIS EXPERTISE TO SELECT THE CAREER BEST SUITED TO MY NATURAL ABILITIES.
S A BOY!
"HE QUICKLY ABANDONED THAT PLAN, THOUGH...
"ONCE HE DISCOVERED...
WHAM
KRAASH
THUD
"...WHAT THOSE ABILITIES WERE.
GOO!

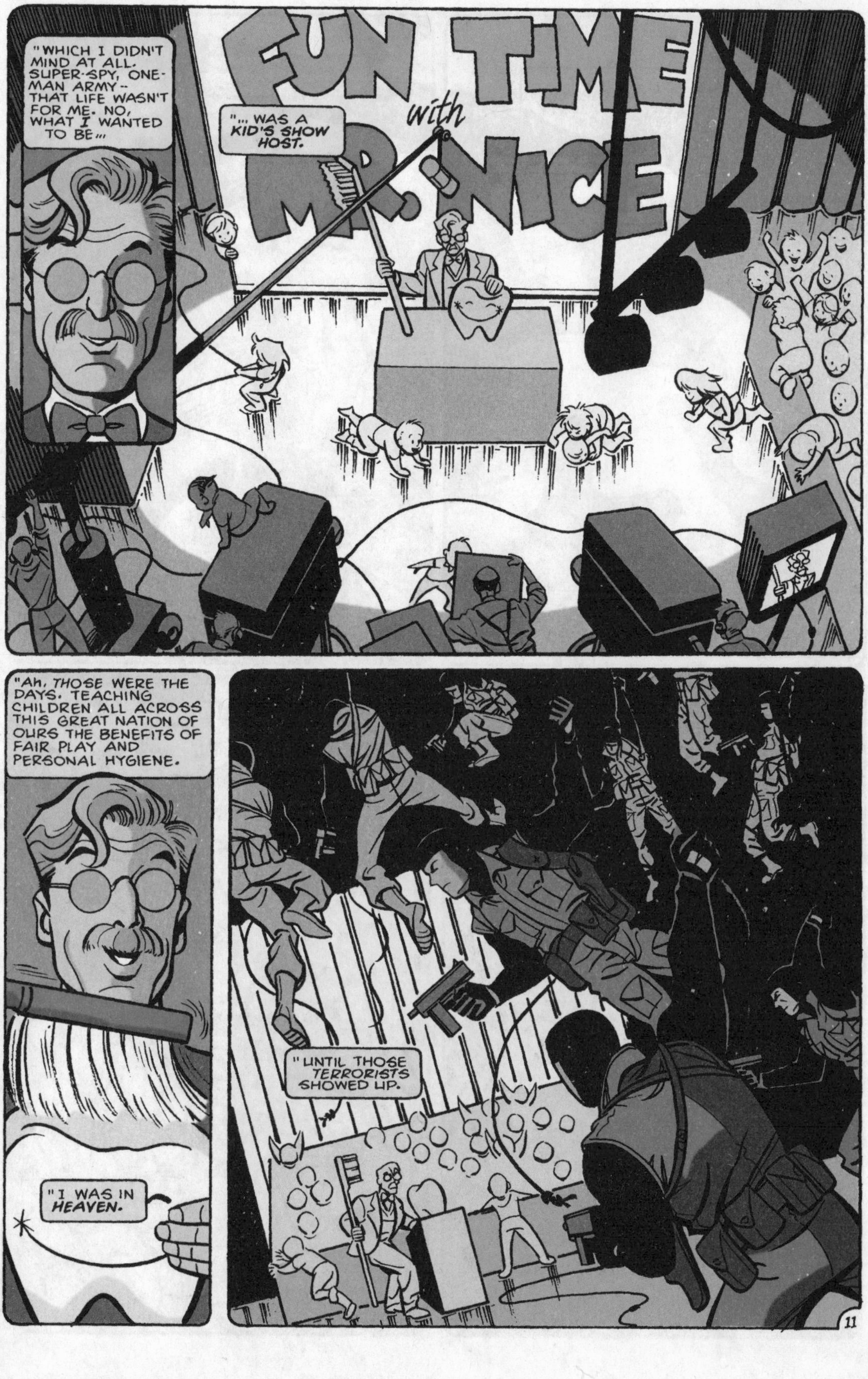
FUN TIME with MR. NICE
"WHICH I DIDN'T MIND AT ALL. SUPER-SPY, ONE-MAN ARMY -- THAT LIFE WASN'T FOR ME. NO, WHAT I WANTED TO BE...
"... WAS A KID'S SHOW HOST.
"Ah, THOSE WERE THE DAYS. TEACHING CHILDREN ALL ACROSS THIS GREAT NATION OF OURS THE BENEFITS OF FAIR PLAY AND PERSONAL HYGIENE.
"I WAS IN HEAVEN.
"UNTIL THOSE TERRORISTS SHOWED UP.

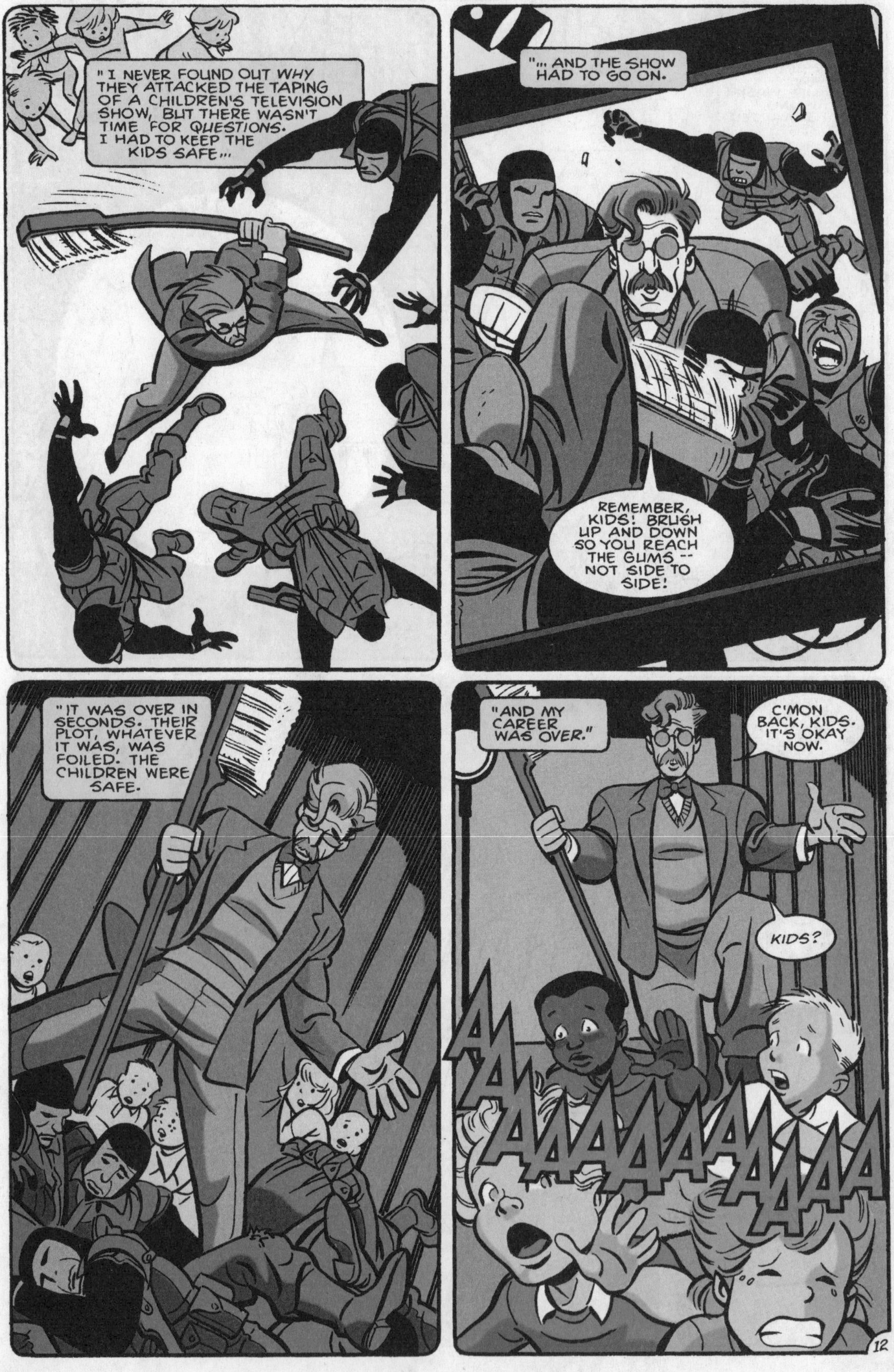
"I NEVER FOUND OUT WHY THEY ATTACKED THE TAPING OF A CHILDREN'S TELEVISION SHOW, BUT THERE WASN'T TIME FOR QUESTIONS. I HAD TO KEEP THE KIDS SAFE...
"... AND THE SHOW HAD TO GO ON.
REMEMBER, KIDS: BRUSH UP AND DOWN SO YOU REACH THE GUMS -- NOT SIDE TO SIDE!
"IT WAS OVER IN SECONDS. THEIR PLOT, WHATEVER IT WAS, WAS FOILED. THE CHILDREN WERE SAFE.
"AND MY CAREER WAS OVER."
C'MON BACK, KIDS. IT'S OKAY NOW.
KIDS?
AAAAAAAAAAAAA

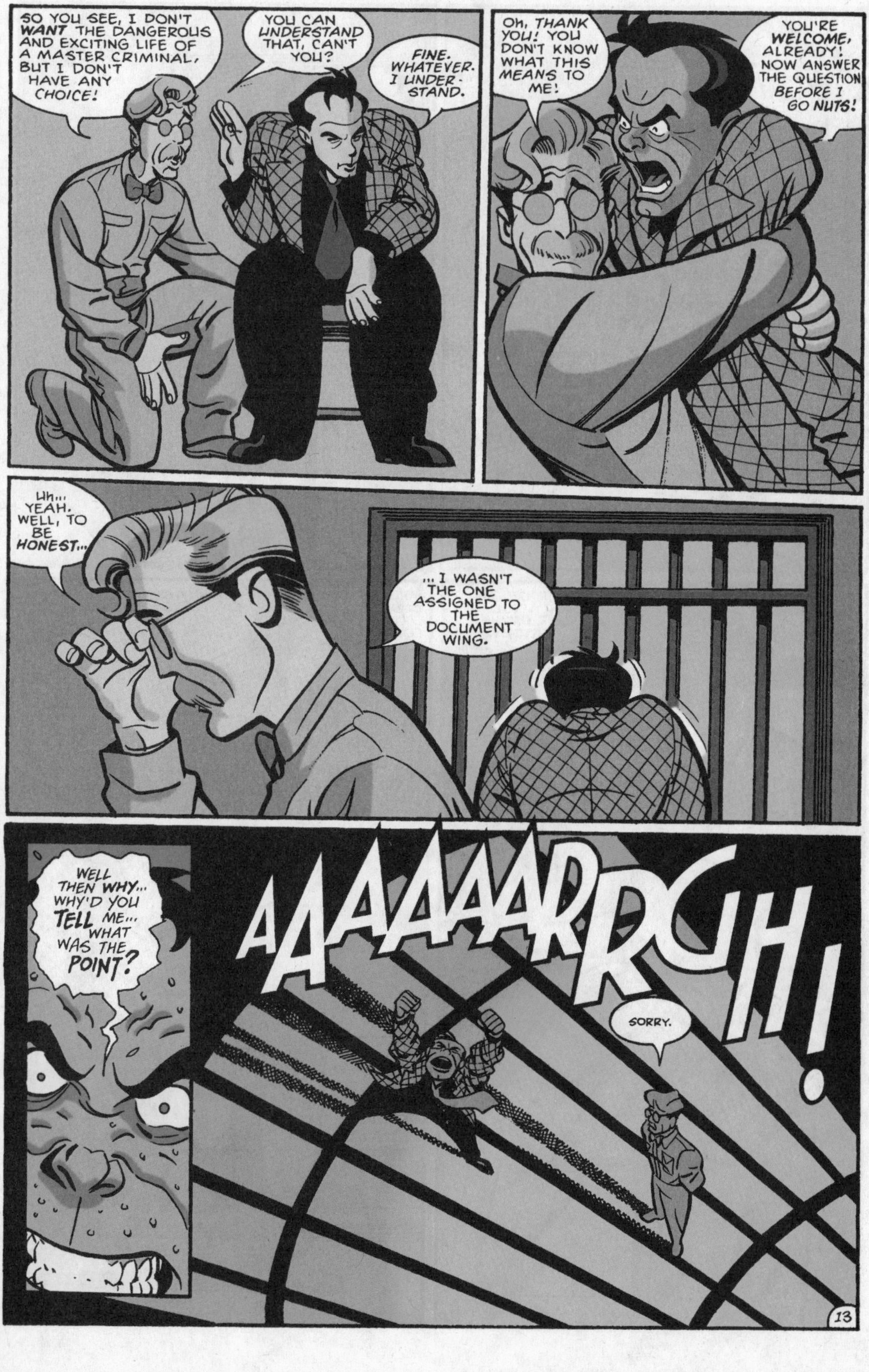
SO YOU SEE, I DON'T WANT THE DANGEROUS AND EXCITING LIFE OF A MASTER CRIMINAL, BUT I DON'T HAVE ANY CHOICE!
YOU CAN UNDERSTAND THAT, CAN'T YOU?
FINE. WHATEVER. I UNDERSTAND.
OH, THANK YOU! YOU DON'T KNOW WHAT THIS MEANS TO ME!
YOU'RE WELCOME, ALREADY! NOW ANSWER THE QUESTION BEFORE I GO NUTS!
UH... YEAH. WELL, TO BE HONEST...
...I WASN'T THE ONE ASSIGNED TO THE DOCUMENT WING.
WELL THEN WHY... WHY'D YOU TELL ME... WHAT WAS THE POINT?
AAAAAARRGH!
SORRY.

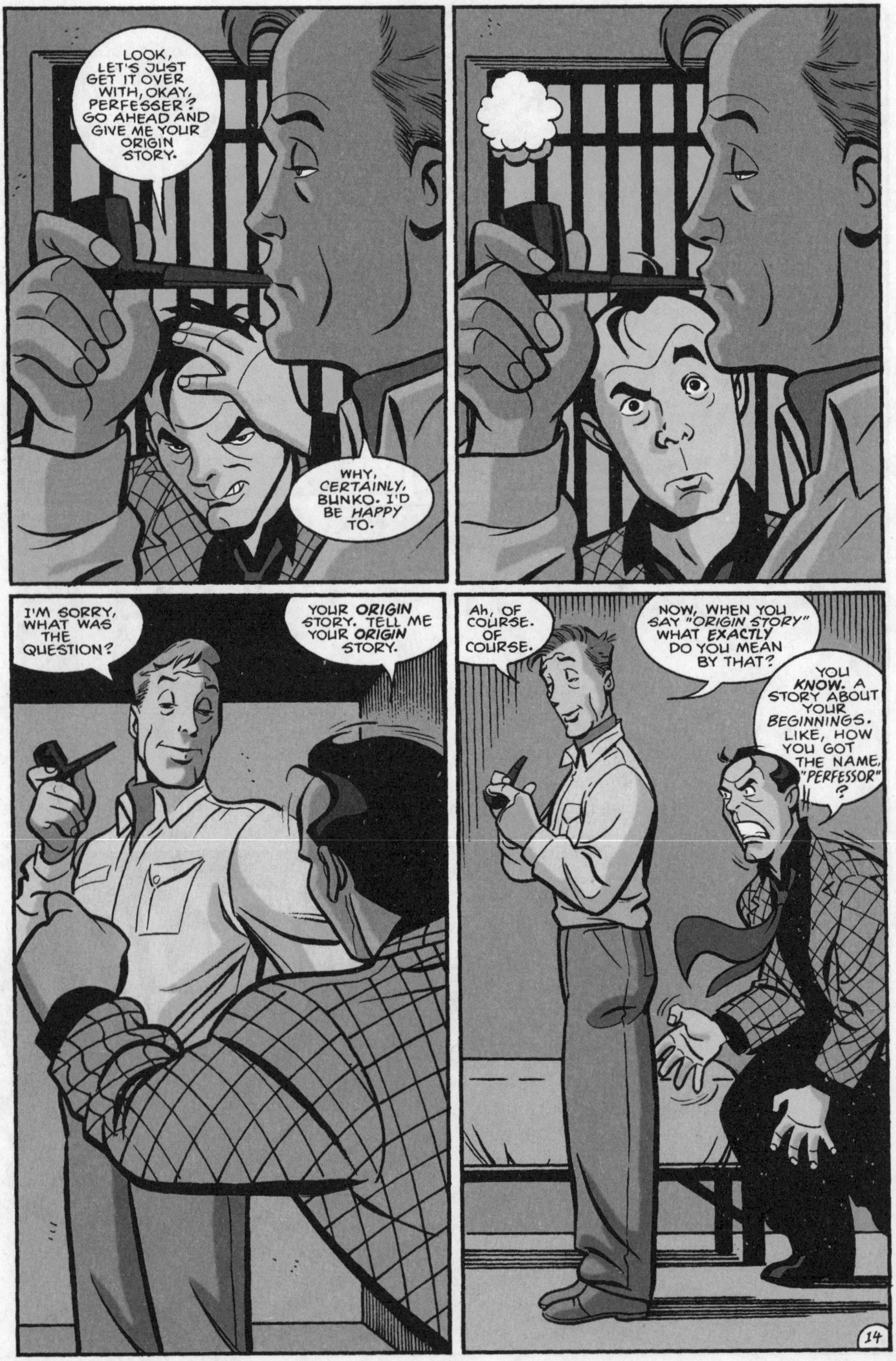
LOOK, LET'S JUST GET IT OVER WITH, OKAY, PERFESSER? GO AHEAD AND GIVE ME YOUR ORIGIN STORY.
WHY, CERTAINLY, BUNKO. I'D BE *HAPPY* TO.
I'M SORRY, WHAT WAS THE QUESTION?
YOUR **ORIGIN** STORY. TELL ME YOUR **ORIGIN** STORY.
Ah, OF COURSE. OF COURSE.
NOW, WHEN YOU SAY *"ORIGIN STORY"* WHAT **EXACTLY** DO YOU MEAN BY THAT?
YOU **KNOW.** A STORY ABOUT YOUR *BEGINNINGS.* LIKE, HOW YOU GOT THE NAME, *"PERFESSOR"*?

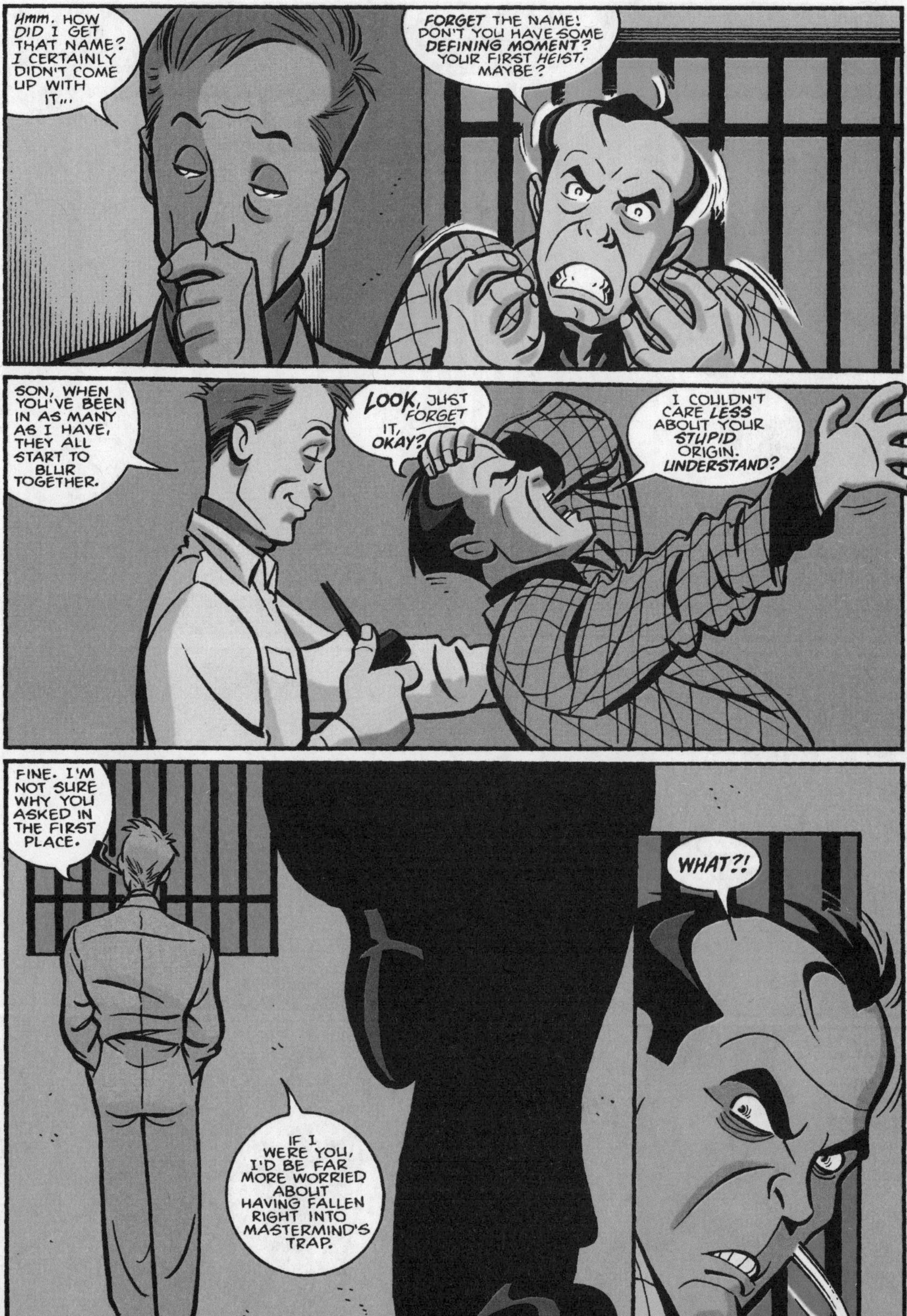
Hmm. HOW DID I GET THAT NAME? I CERTAINLY DIDN'T COME UP WITH IT...
FORGET THE NAME! DON'T YOU HAVE SOME DEFINING MOMENT? YOUR FIRST HEIST, MAYBE?
SON, WHEN YOU'VE BEEN IN AS MANY AS I HAVE, THEY ALL START TO BLUR TOGETHER.
LOOK, JUST FORGET IT, OKAY?
I COULDN'T CARE LESS ABOUT YOUR STUPID ORIGIN. UNDERSTAND?
FINE. I'M NOT SURE WHY YOU ASKED IN THE FIRST PLACE.
WHAT?!
IF I WERE YOU, I'D BE FAR MORE WORRIED ABOUT HAVING FALLEN RIGHT INTO MASTERMIND'S TRAP.

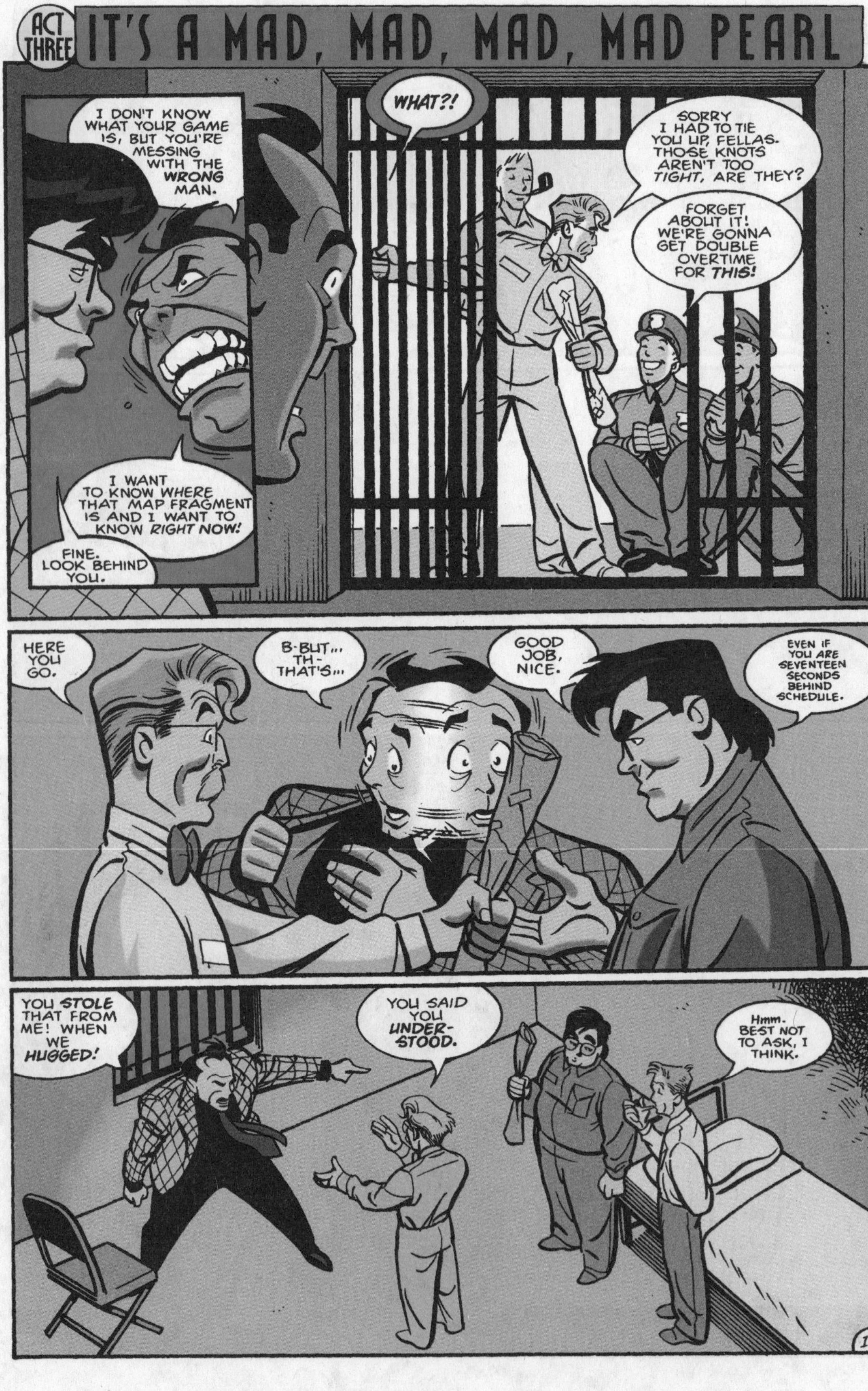

ACT THREE
IT'S A MAD, MAD, MAD, MAD PEARL
I DON'T KNOW WHAT YOUR GAME IS, BUT YOU'RE MESSING WITH THE WRONG MAN.
I WANT TO KNOW WHERE THAT MAP FRAGMENT IS AND I WANT TO KNOW RIGHT NOW!
FINE. LOOK BEHIND YOU.
WHAT?!
SORRY I HAD TO TIE YOU UP, FELLAS. THOSE KNOTS AREN'T TOO TIGHT, ARE THEY?
FORGET ABOUT IT! WE'RE GONNA GET DOUBLE OVERTIME FOR THIS!
HERE YOU GO.
B-BUT... TH-THAT'S...
GOOD JOB, NICE.
EVEN IF YOU ARE SEVENTEEN SECONDS BEHIND SCHEDULE.
YOU STOLE THAT FROM ME! WHEN WE HUGGED!
YOU SAID YOU UNDERSTOOD.
Hmm. BEST NOT TO ASK, I THINK.

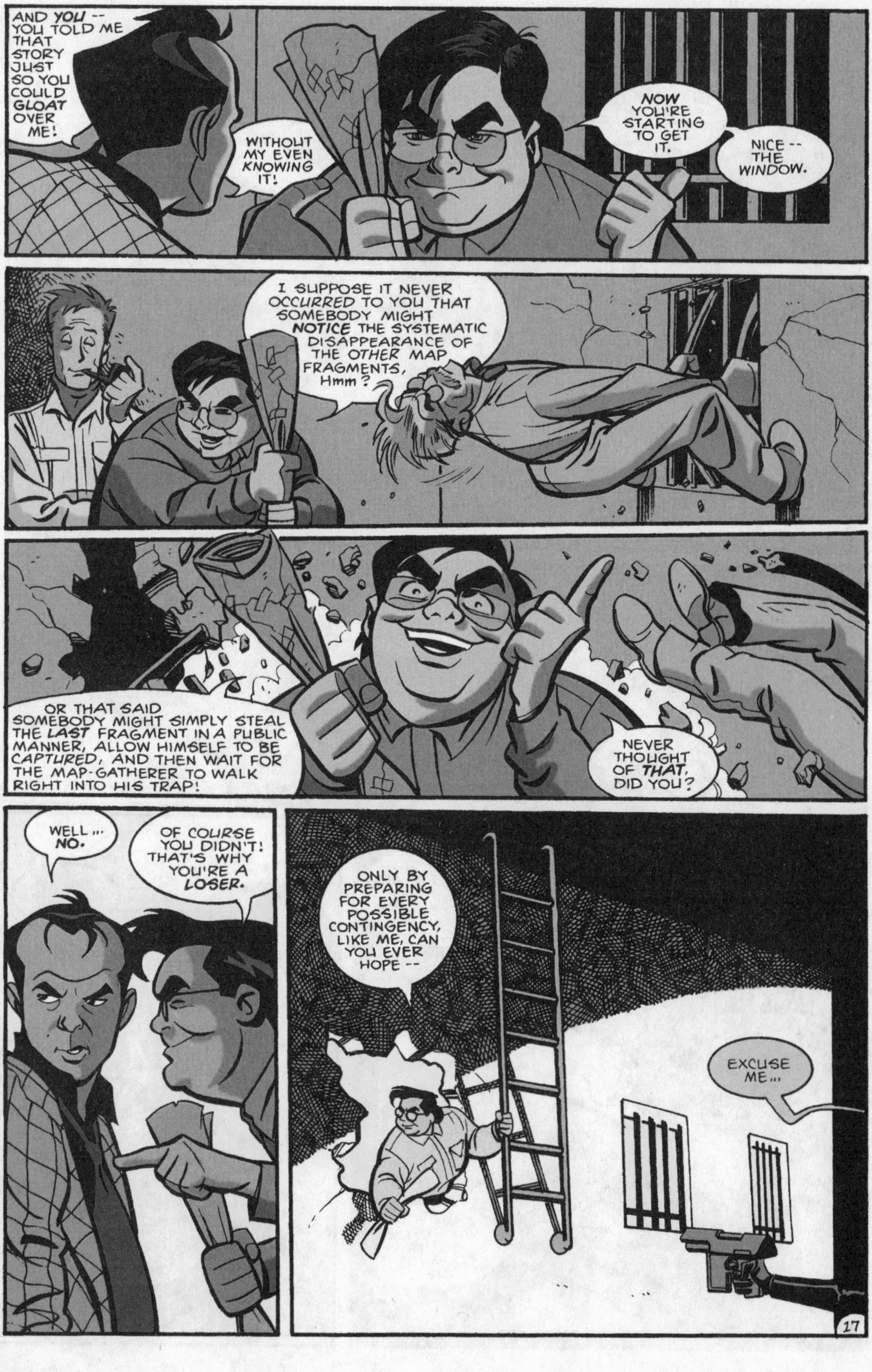
AND YOU -- YOU TOLD ME THAT STORY JUST SO YOU COULD GLOAT OVER ME!
WITHOUT MY EVEN KNOWING IT!
NOW YOU'RE STARTING TO GET IT.
NICE -- THE WINDOW.
I SUPPOSE IT NEVER OCCURRED TO YOU THAT SOMEBODY MIGHT NOTICE THE SYSTEMATIC DISAPPEARANCE OF THE OTHER MAP FRAGMENTS, Hmm?
OR THAT SAID SOMEBODY MIGHT SIMPLY STEAL THE LAST FRAGMENT IN A PUBLIC MANNER, ALLOW HIMSELF TO BE CAPTURED, AND THEN WAIT FOR THE MAP-GATHERER TO WALK RIGHT INTO HIS TRAP!
NEVER THOUGHT OF THAT, DID YOU?
WELL... NO.
OF COURSE YOU DIDN'T! THAT'S WHY YOU'RE A LOSER.
ONLY BY PREPARING FOR EVERY POSSIBLE CONTINGENCY, LIKE ME, CAN YOU EVER HOPE --
EXCUSE ME...
17

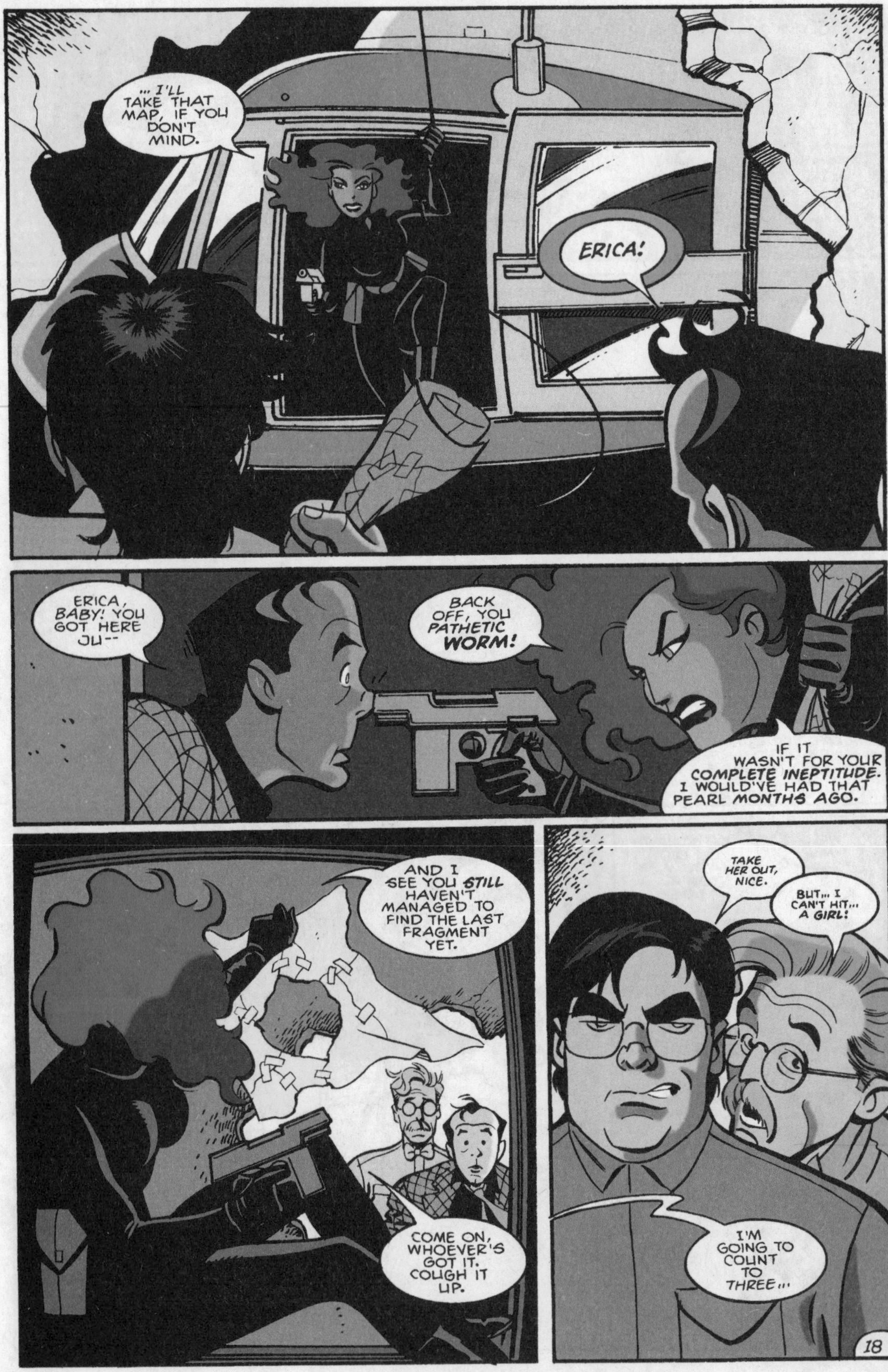
...I'LL TAKE THAT MAP, IF YOU DON'T MIND.
ERICA!
ERICA, BABY! YOU GOT HERE JU--
BACK OFF, YOU PATHETIC WORM!
IF IT WASN'T FOR YOUR COMPLETE INEPTITUDE. I WOULD'VE HAD THAT PEARL MONTHS AGO.
AND I SEE YOU STILL HAVEN'T MANAGED TO FIND THE LAST FRAGMENT YET.
COME ON, WHOEVER'S GOT IT. COUGH IT UP.
TAKE HER OUT, NICE.
BUT... I CAN'T HIT... A GIRL!
I'M GOING TO COUNT TO THREE...
18

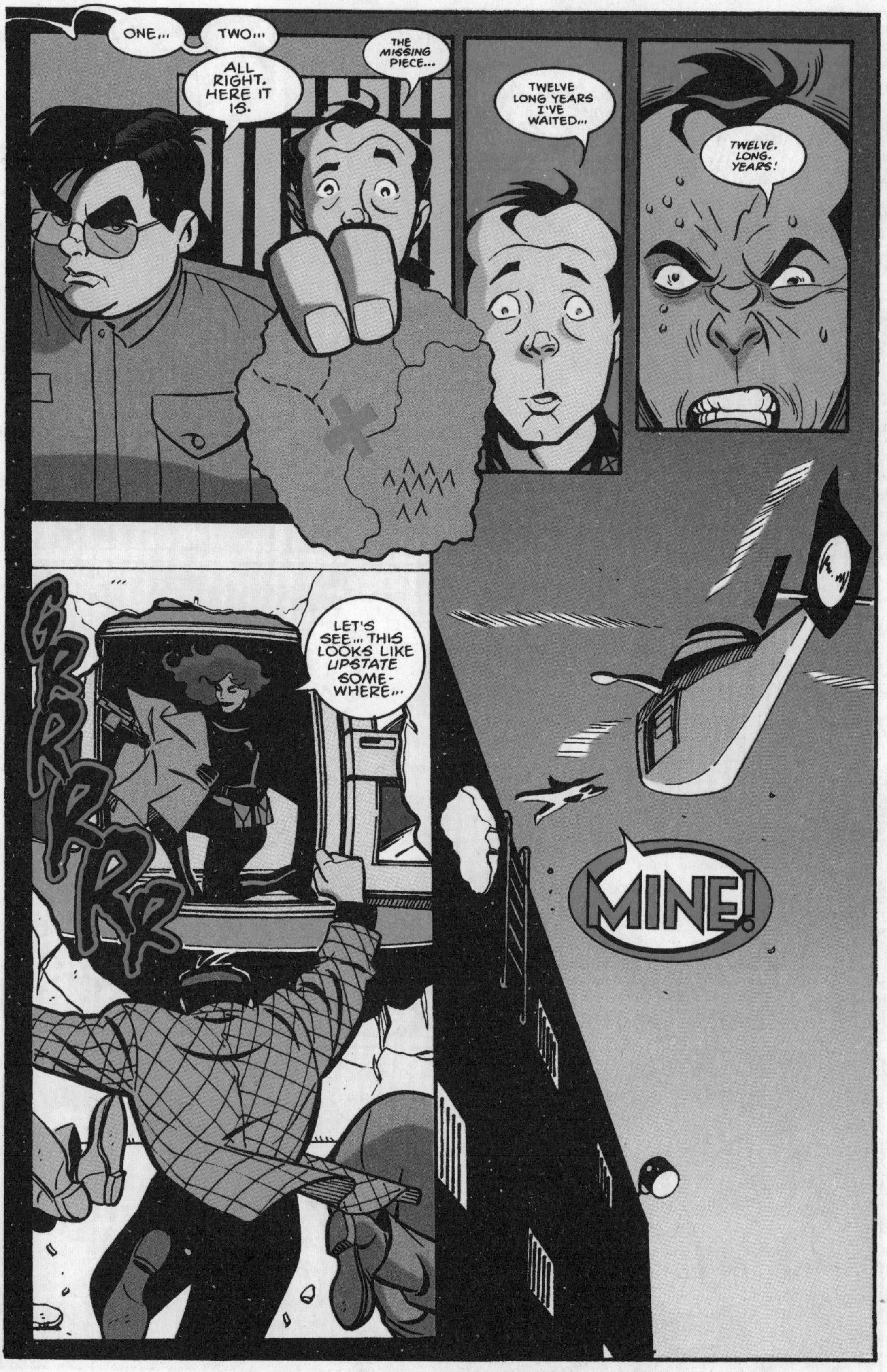
ONE...
TWO...
ALL RIGHT. HERE IT IS.
THE MISSING PIECE...
TWELVE LONG YEARS I'VE WAITED...
TWELVE. LONG. YEARS!
LET'S SEE... THIS LOOKS LIKE UPSTATE SOMEWHERE...
GRRRRR
MINE!

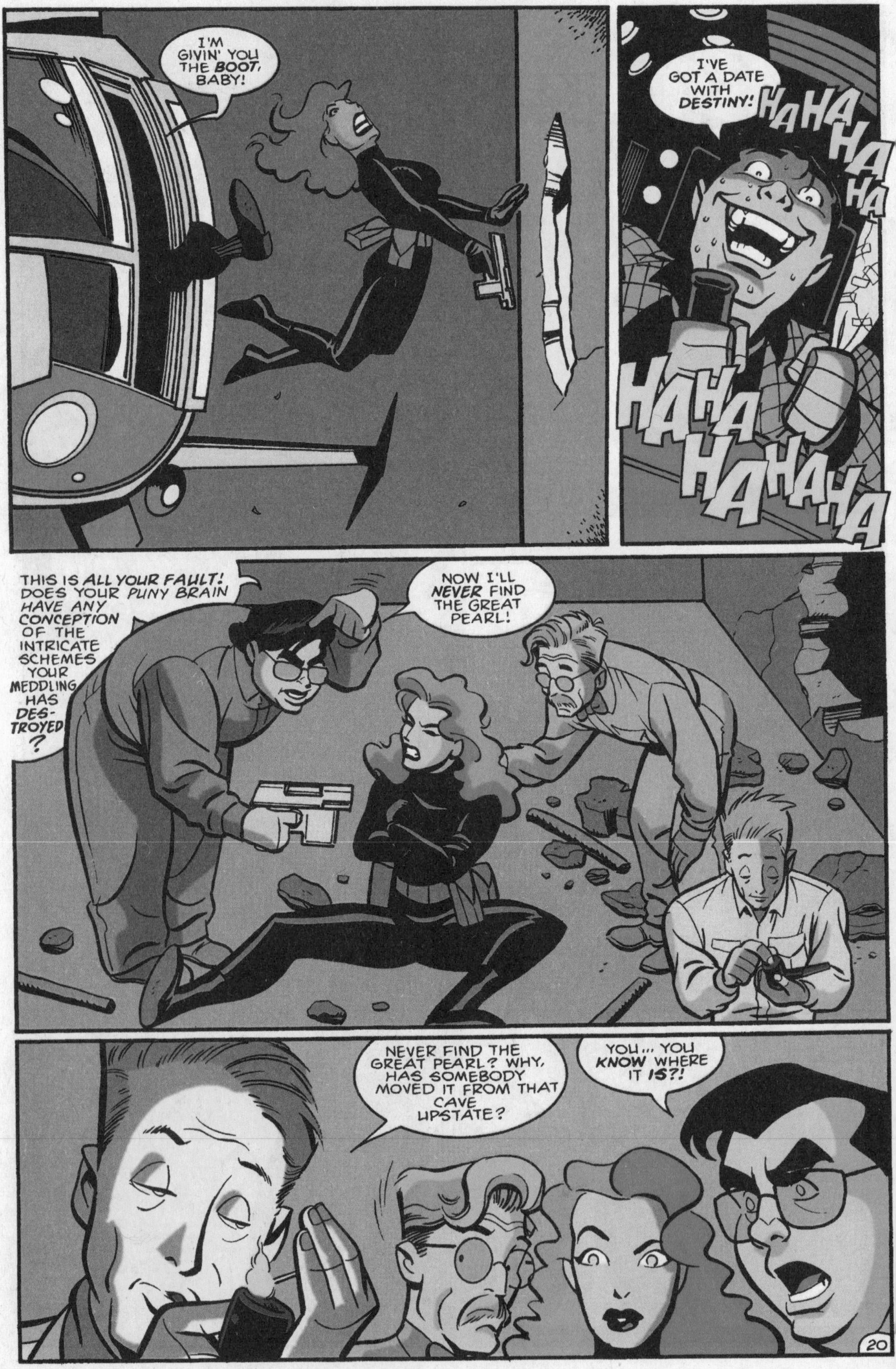
I'M GIVIN' YOU THE *BOOT*, BABY!
I'VE GOT A DATE WITH *DESTINY!*
HA HA HA HA HA HA
HA HA HA HA HA HA HA HA
THIS IS *ALL YOUR FAULT!* DOES YOUR *PUNY BRAIN* HAVE ANY *CONCEPTION* OF THE *INTRICATE SCHEMES* YOUR *MEDDLING* HAS *DES-TROYED*?
NOW I'LL *NEVER* FIND THE GREAT PEARL!
NEVER FIND THE GREAT PEARL? WHY, HAS SOMEBODY MOVED IT FROM THAT CAVE UPSTATE?
YOU... YOU *KNOW* WHERE IT *IS*?!

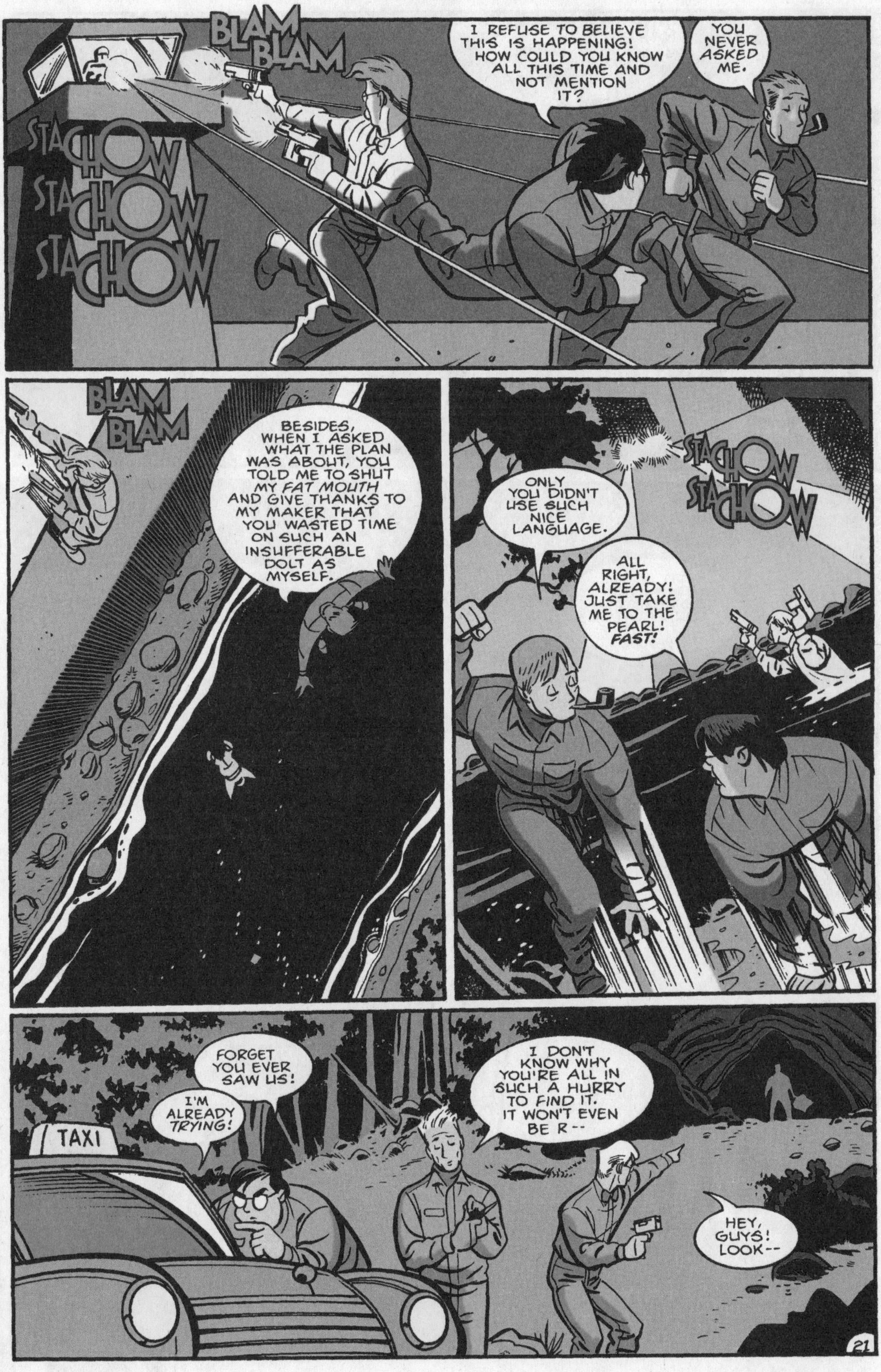
BLAM BLAM
STACHOW STACHOW STACHOW
I REFUSE TO BELIEVE THIS IS HAPPENING! HOW COULD YOU KNOW ALL THIS TIME AND NOT MENTION IT?
YOU NEVER ASKED ME.
BLAM BLAM
BESIDES, WHEN I ASKED WHAT THE PLAN WAS ABOUT, YOU TOLD ME TO SHUT MY FAT MOUTH AND GIVE THANKS TO MY MAKER THAT YOU WASTED TIME ON SUCH AN INSUFFERABLE DOLT AS MYSELF.
STACHOW STACHOW
ONLY YOU DIDN'T USE SUCH NICE LANGUAGE.
ALL RIGHT, ALREADY! JUST TAKE ME TO THE PEARL! FAST!
FORGET YOU EVER SAW US!
I'M ALREADY TRYING!
TAXI
I DON'T KNOW WHY YOU'RE ALL IN SUCH A HURRY TO FIND IT. IT WON'T EVEN BE R--
HEY, GUYS! LOOK--

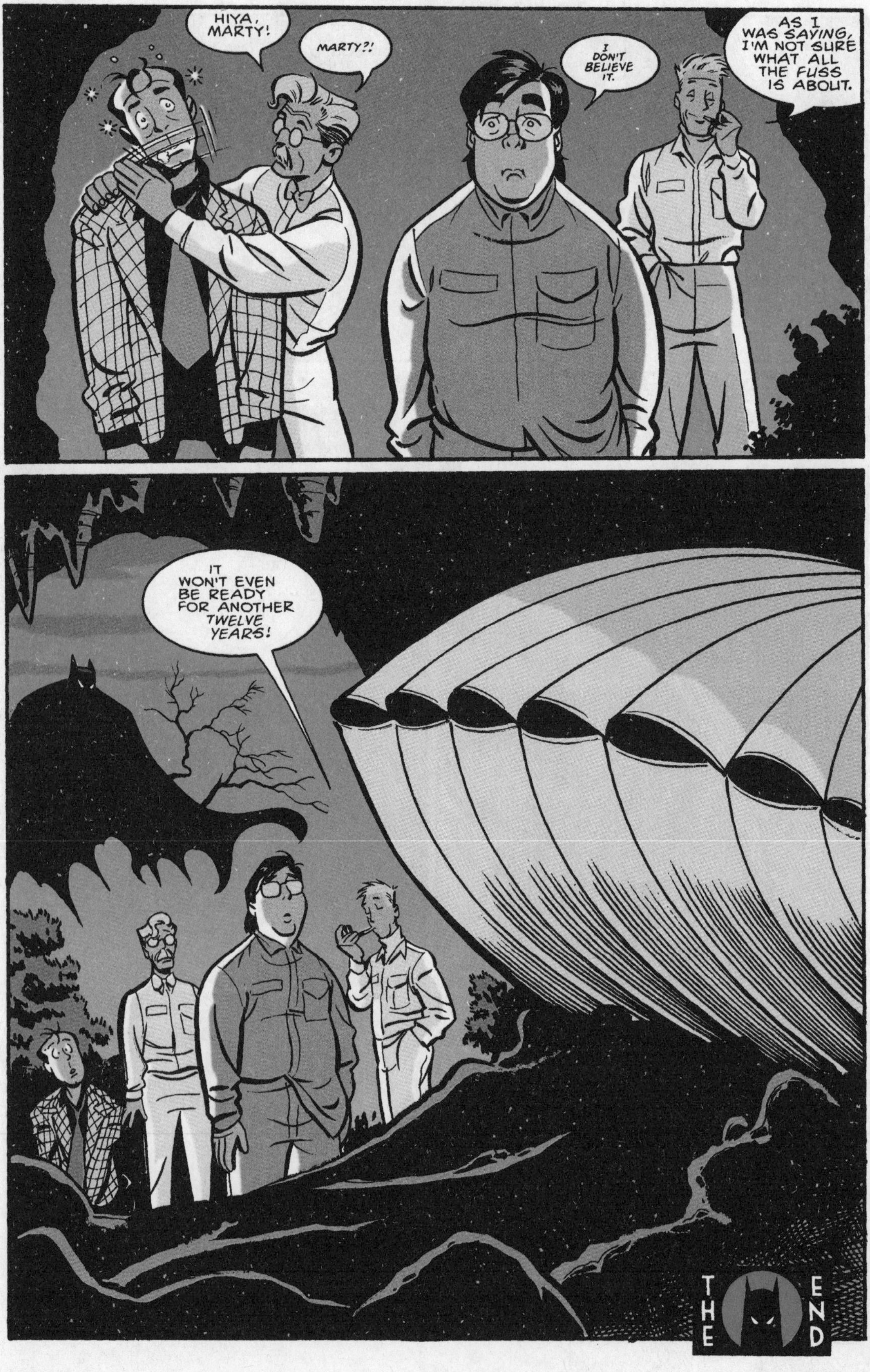
HIYA, MARTY!
MARTY?!
I DON'T BELIEVE IT.
AS I WAS SAYING, I'M NOT SURE WHAT ALL THE FUSS IS ABOUT.
IT WON'T EVEN BE READY FOR ANOTHER TWELVE YEARS!
THE END

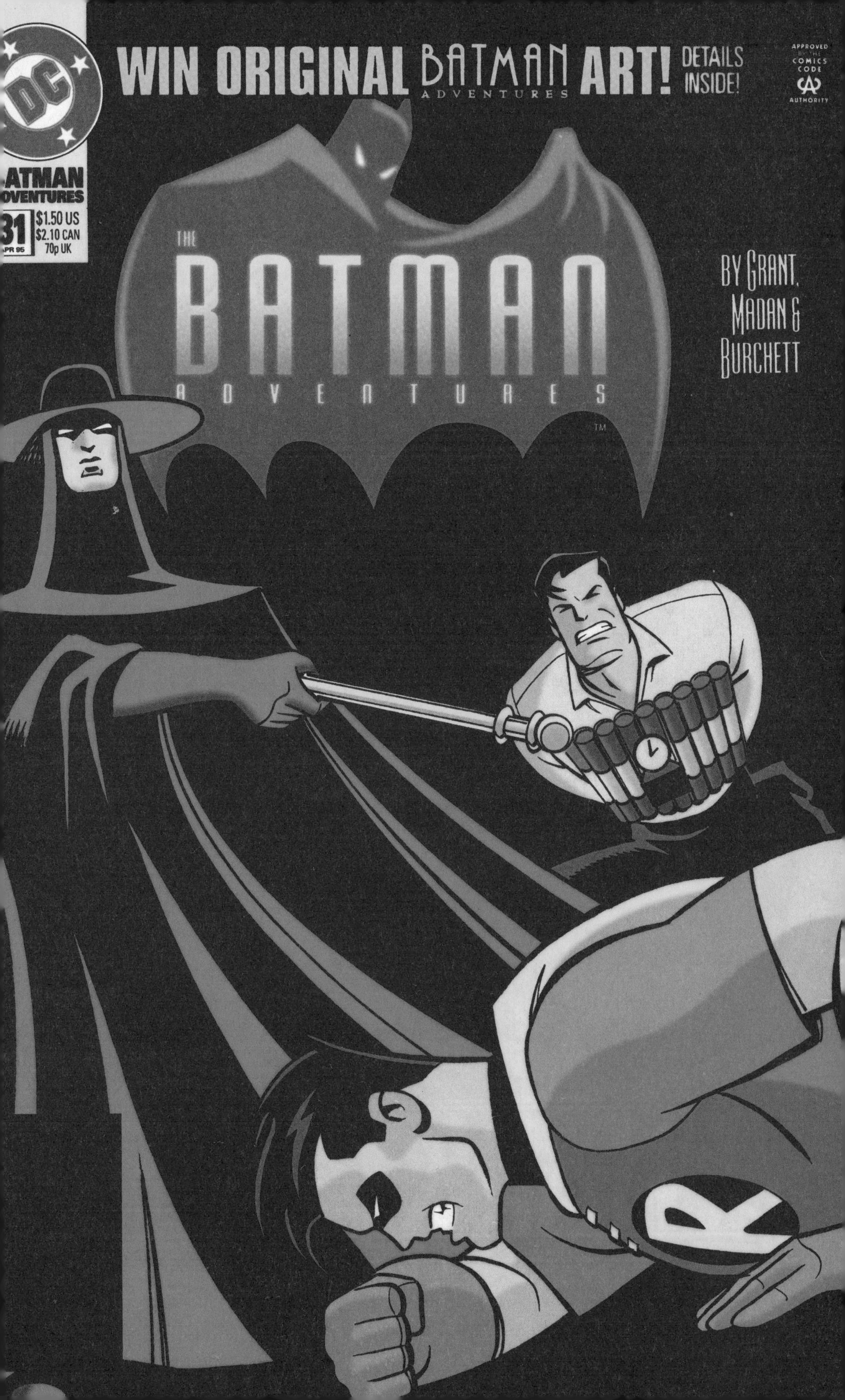

DC
WIN ORIGINAL BATMAN ADVENTURES ART!
DETAILS INSIDE!
APPROVED BY THE COMICS CODE AUTHORITY
ATMAN
OVENTURES
31
$1.50 US
$2.10 CAN
70p UK
APR 95
THE BATMAN ADVENTURES™
BY GRANT, MADAN & BURCHETT

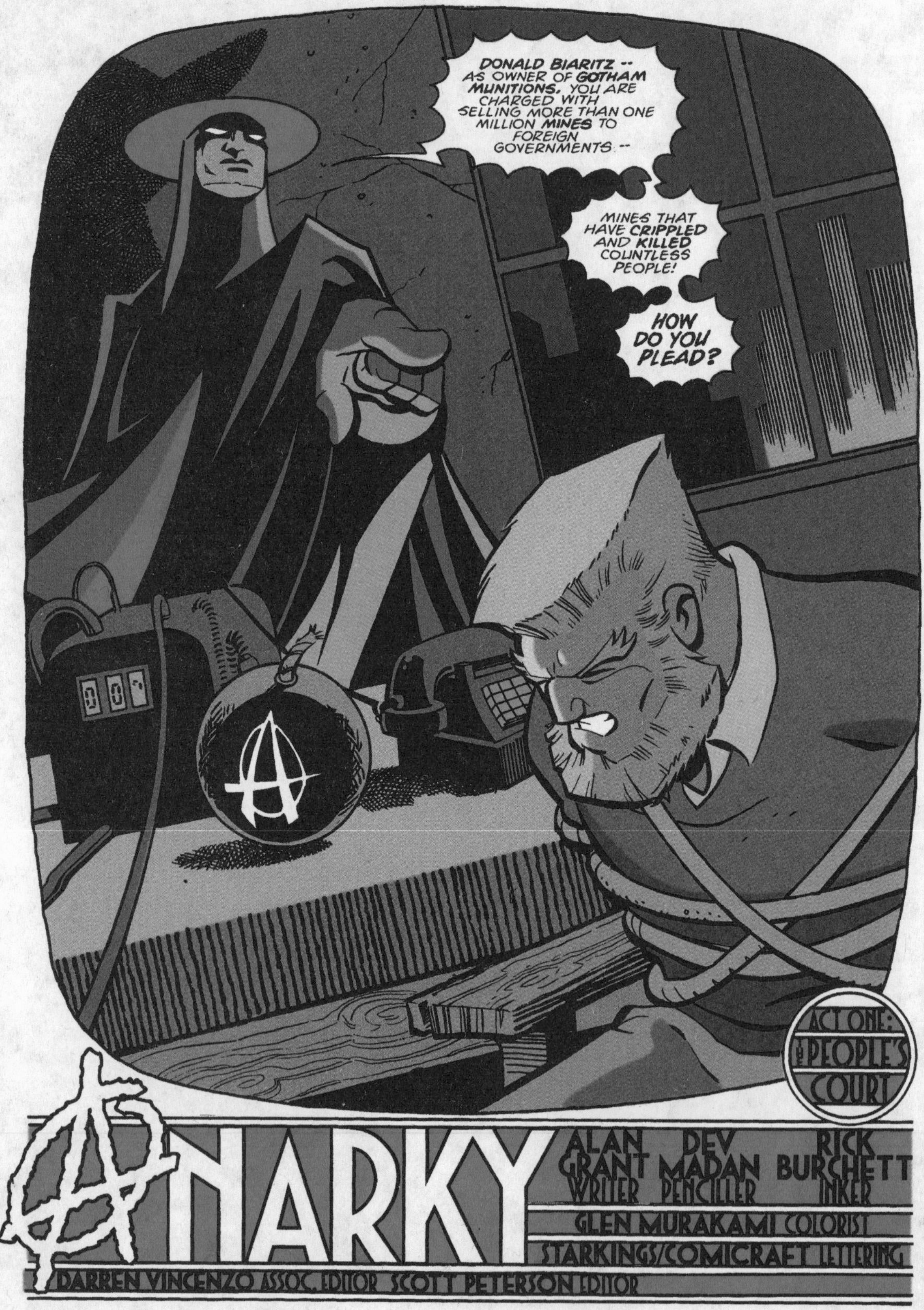

DONALD BIARITZ -- AS OWNER OF GOTHAM MUNITIONS, YOU ARE CHARGED WITH SELLING MORE THAN ONE MILLION MINES TO FOREIGN GOVERNMENTS --
MINES THAT HAVE CRIPPLED AND KILLED COUNTLESS PEOPLE!
HOW DO YOU PLEAD?
ACT ONE: THE PEOPLE'S COURT
ANARKY
ALAN GRANT WRITER
DEV MADAN PENCILLER
RICK BURCHETT INKER
GLEN MURAKAMI COLORIST
STARKINGS/COMICRAFT LETTERING
DARREN VINCENZO ASSOC. EDITOR SCOTT PETERSON EDITOR

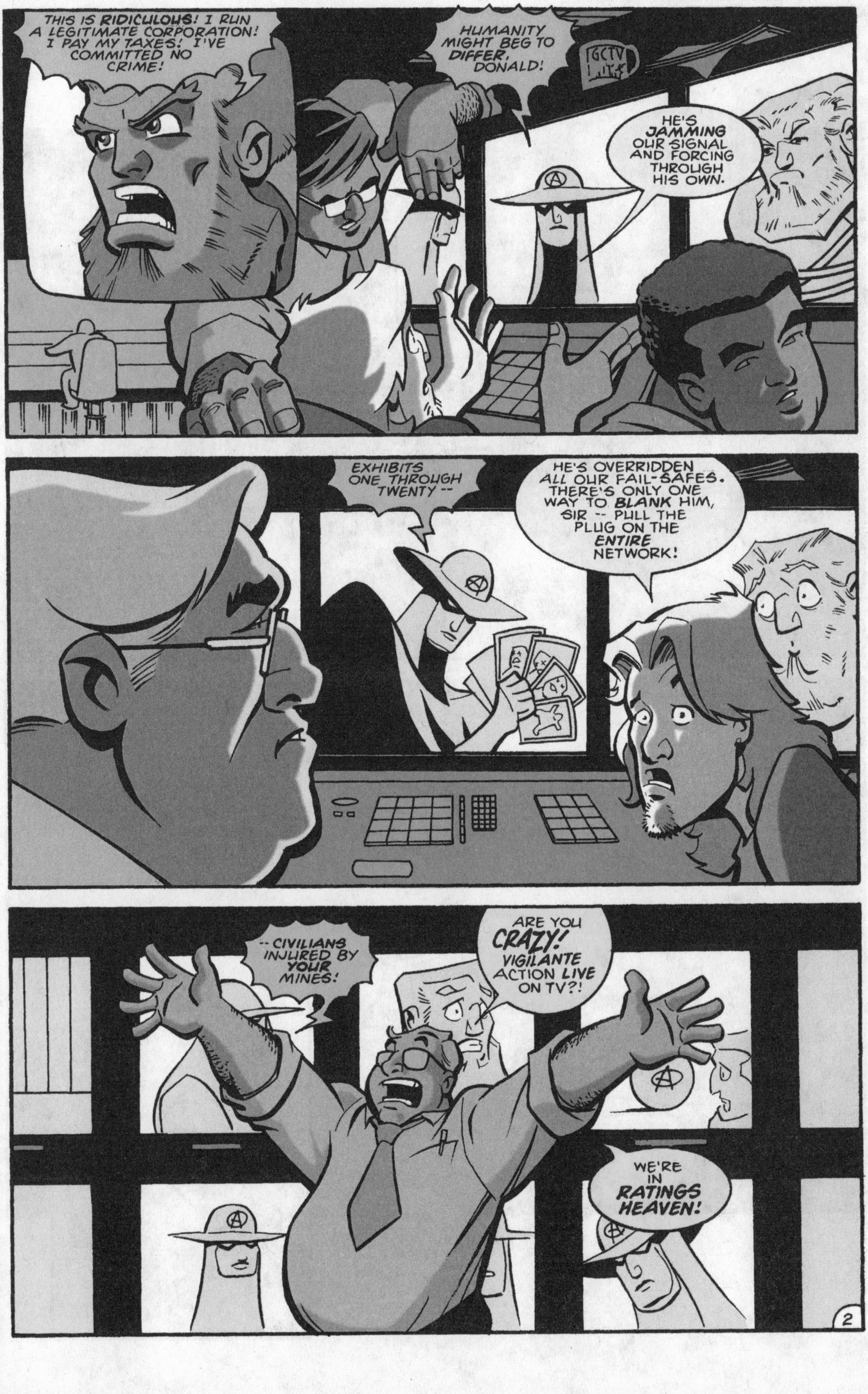
THIS IS RIDICULOUS! I RUN A LEGITIMATE CORPORATION! I PAY MY TAXES! I'VE COMMITTED NO CRIME!
HUMANITY MIGHT BEG TO DIFFER, DONALD!
GCTV
HE'S JAMMING OUR SIGNAL AND FORCING THROUGH HIS OWN.
EXHIBITS ONE THROUGH TWENTY --
HE'S OVERRIDDEN ALL OUR FAIL-SAFES. THERE'S ONLY ONE WAY TO BLANK HIM, SIR -- PULL THE PLUG ON THE ENTIRE NETWORK!
-- CIVILIANS INJURED BY YOUR MINES!
ARE YOU CRAZY! VIGILANTE ACTION LIVE ON TV?!
WE'RE IN RATINGS HEAVEN!

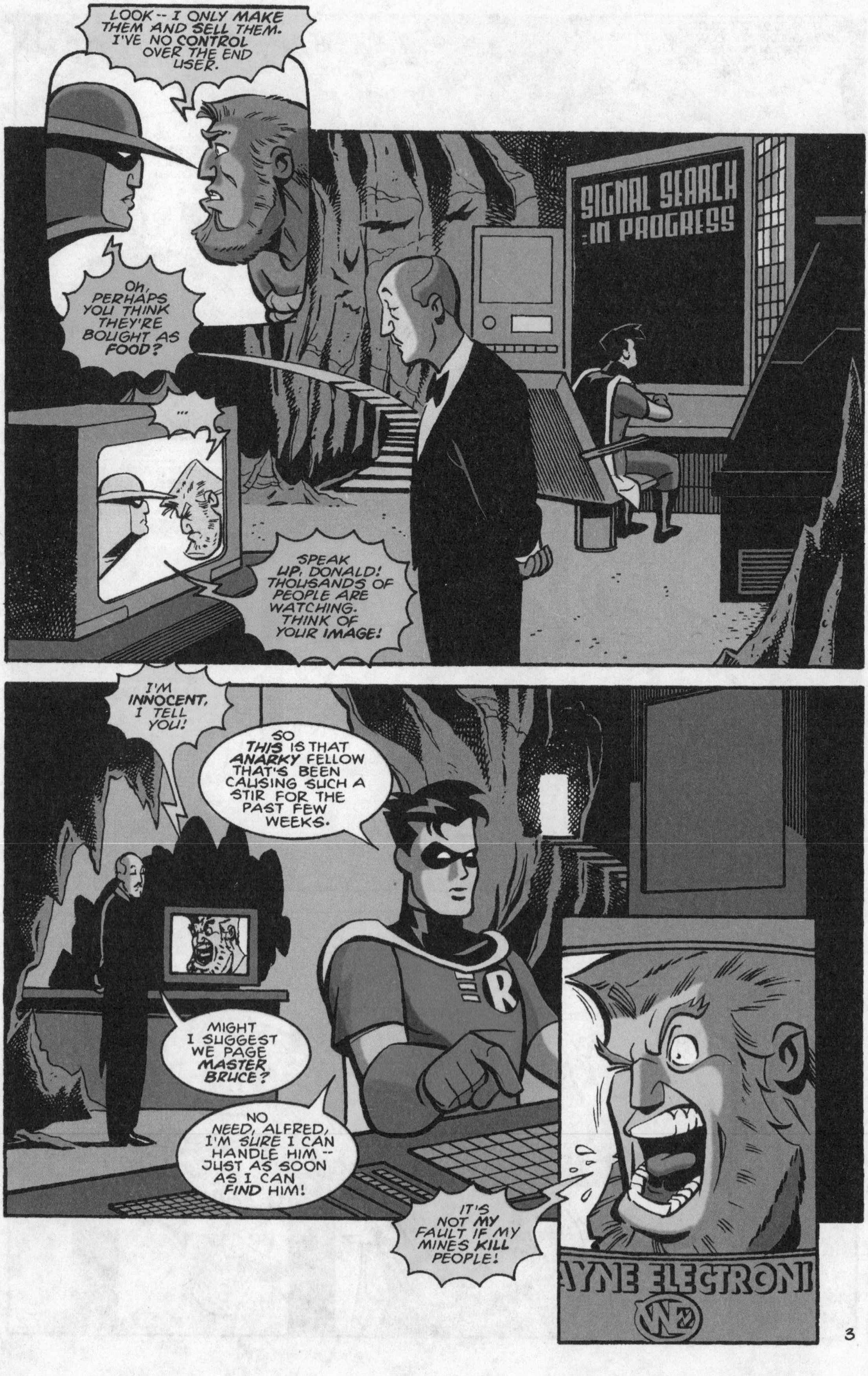
LOOK -- I ONLY MAKE THEM AND SELL THEM. I'VE NO CONTROL OVER THE END USER.
OH, PERHAPS YOU THINK THEY'RE BOUGHT AS FOOD?
SIGNAL SEARCH IN PROGRESS
...
SPEAK UP, DONALD! THOUSANDS OF PEOPLE ARE WATCHING. THINK OF YOUR IMAGE!
I'M INNOCENT, I TELL YOU!
SO THIS IS THAT ANARKY FELLOW THAT'S BEEN CAUSING SUCH A STIR FOR THE PAST FEW WEEKS.
MIGHT I SUGGEST WE PAGE MASTER BRUCE?
NO NEED, ALFRED, I'M SURE I CAN HANDLE HIM -- JUST AS SOON AS I CAN FIND HIM!
IT'S NOT MY FAULT IF MY MINES KILL PEOPLE!
AYNE ELECTRONI

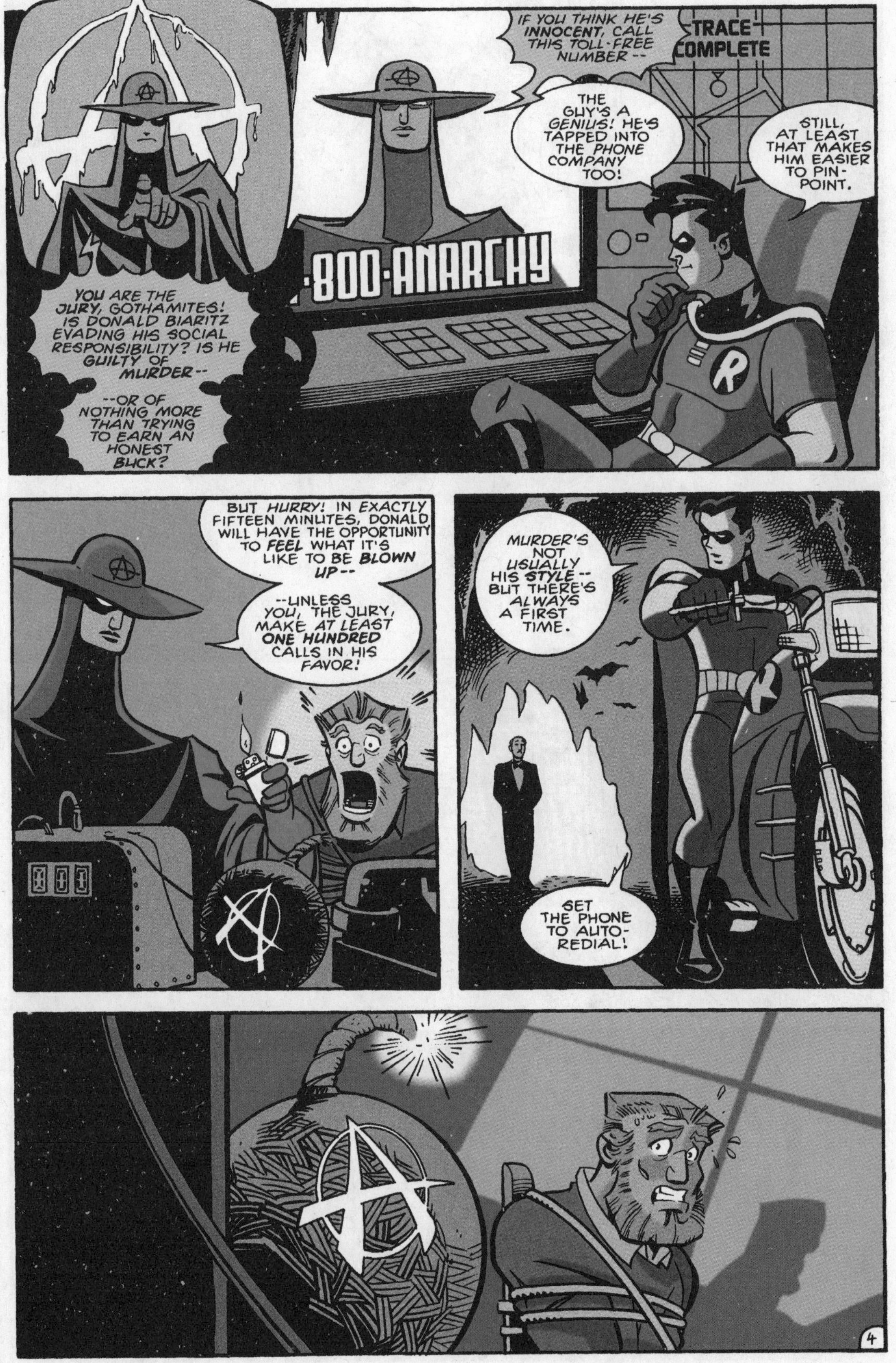

YOU ARE THE JURY, GOTHAMITES! IS DONALD BIARITZ EVADING HIS SOCIAL RESPONSIBILITY? IS HE GUILTY OF MURDER--
--OR OF NOTHING MORE THAN TRYING TO EARN AN HONEST BUCK?
IF YOU THINK HE'S INNOCENT, CALL THIS TOLL-FREE NUMBER--
-800-ANARCHY
TRACE COMPLETE
THE GUY'S A GENIUS! HE'S TAPPED INTO THE PHONE COMPANY TOO!
STILL, AT LEAST THAT MAKES HIM EASIER TO PIN-POINT.
BUT HURRY! IN EXACTLY FIFTEEN MINUTES, DONALD WILL HAVE THE OPPORTUNITY TO FEEL WHAT IT'S LIKE TO BE BLOWN UP--
--UNLESS YOU, THE JURY, MAKE AT LEAST ONE HUNDRED CALLS IN HIS FAVOR!
MURDER'S NOT USUALLY HIS STYLE--BUT THERE'S ALWAYS A FIRST TIME.
SET THE PHONE TO AUTO-REDIAL!

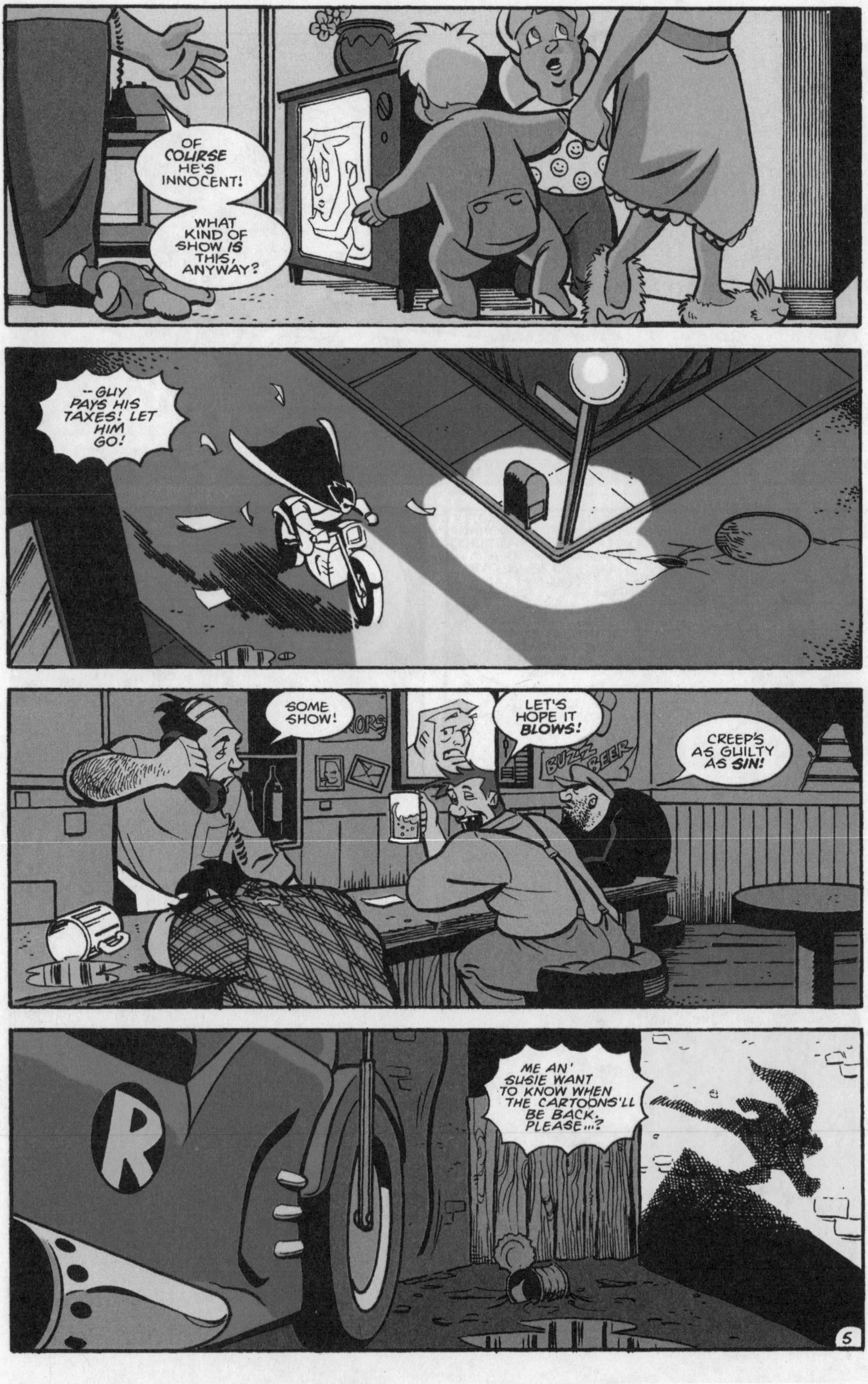
OF COURSE HE'S INNOCENT!
WHAT KIND OF SHOW IS THIS, ANYWAY?
--GUY PAYS HIS TAXES! LET HIM GO!
SOME SHOW!
LET'S HOPE IT BLOWS!
CREEP'S AS GUILTY AS SIN!
BUZZ BEER
ME AN' SUSIE WANT TO KNOW WHEN THE CARTOONS'LL BE BACK. PLEASE...?

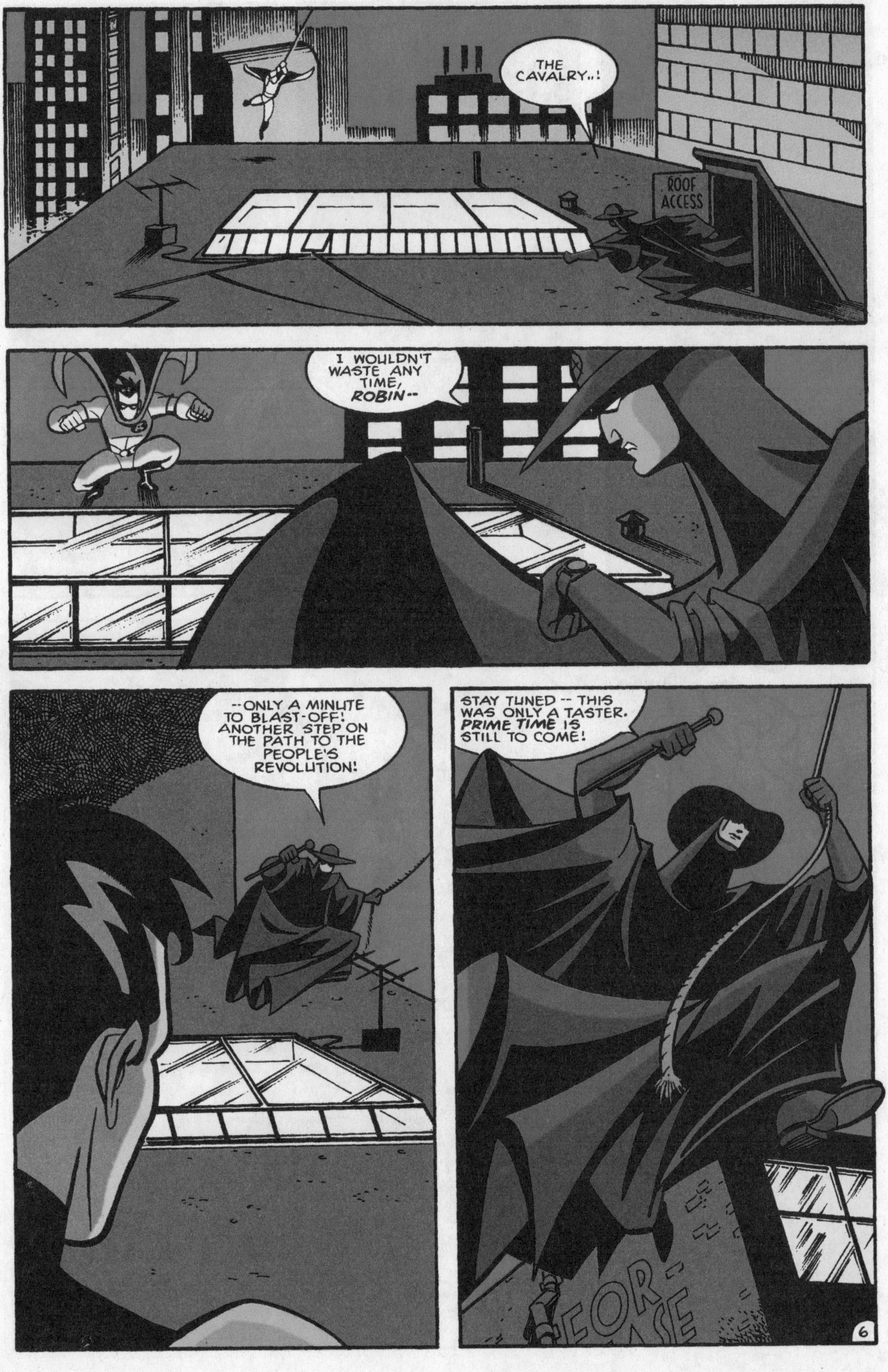
THE CAVALRY..!
ROOF ACCESS
I WOULDN'T WASTE ANY TIME, *ROBIN*--
--ONLY A MINUTE TO BLAST-OFF! ANOTHER STEP ON THE PATH TO THE PEOPLE'S REVOLUTION!
STAY TUNED -- THIS WAS ONLY A TASTER. *PRIME TIME* IS STILL TO COME!

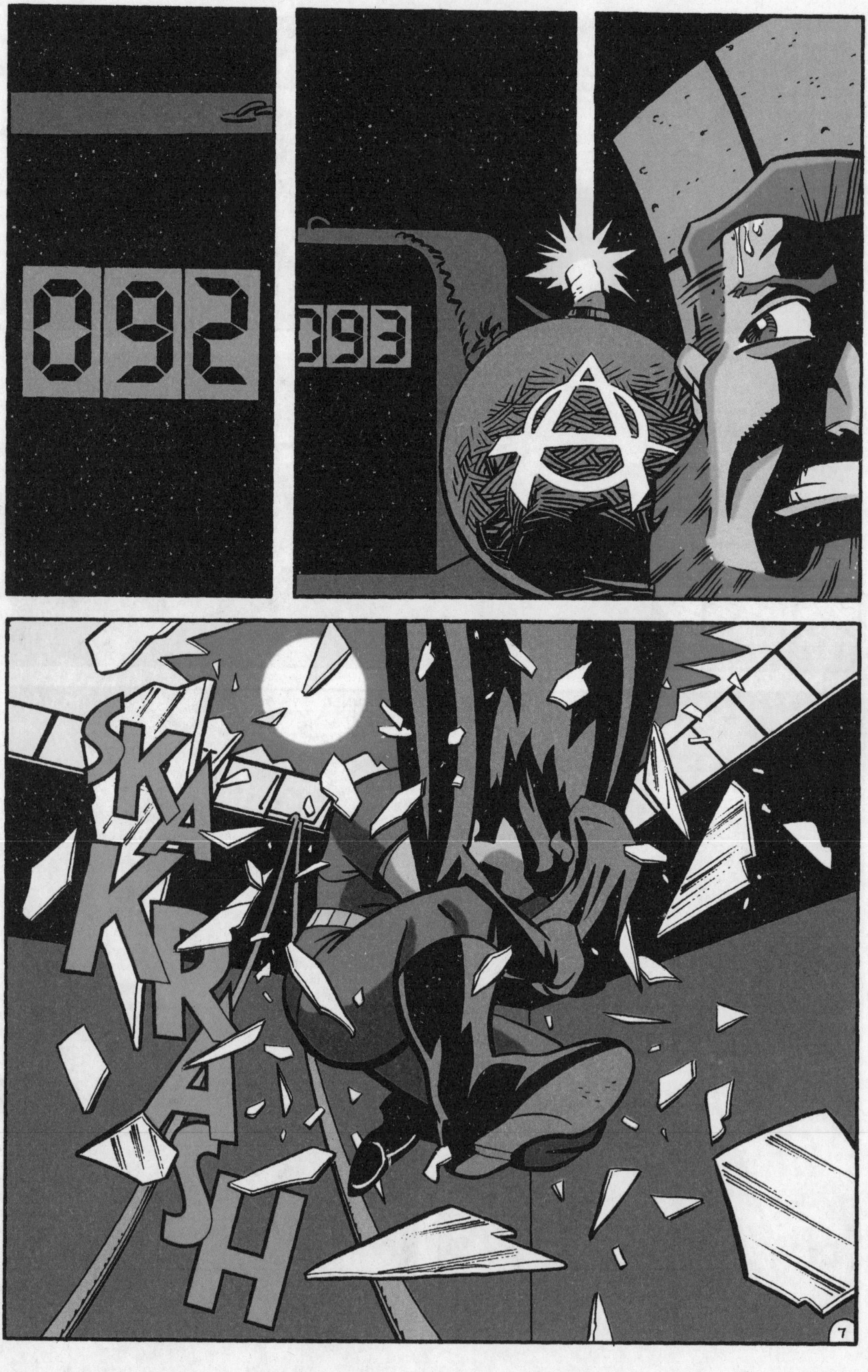

092
093
SKAKRASH

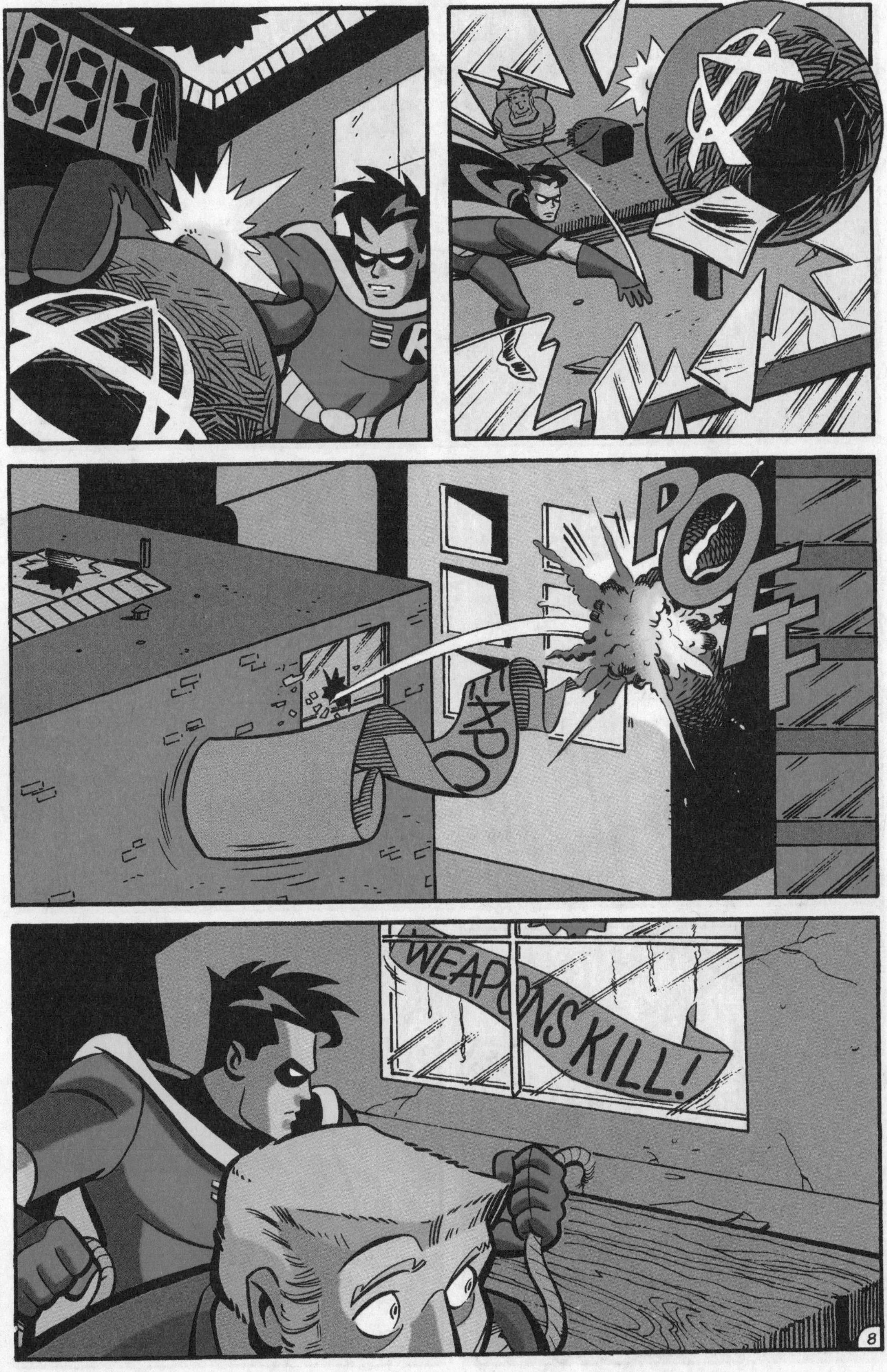
094
POFF
WEAPONS KILL!

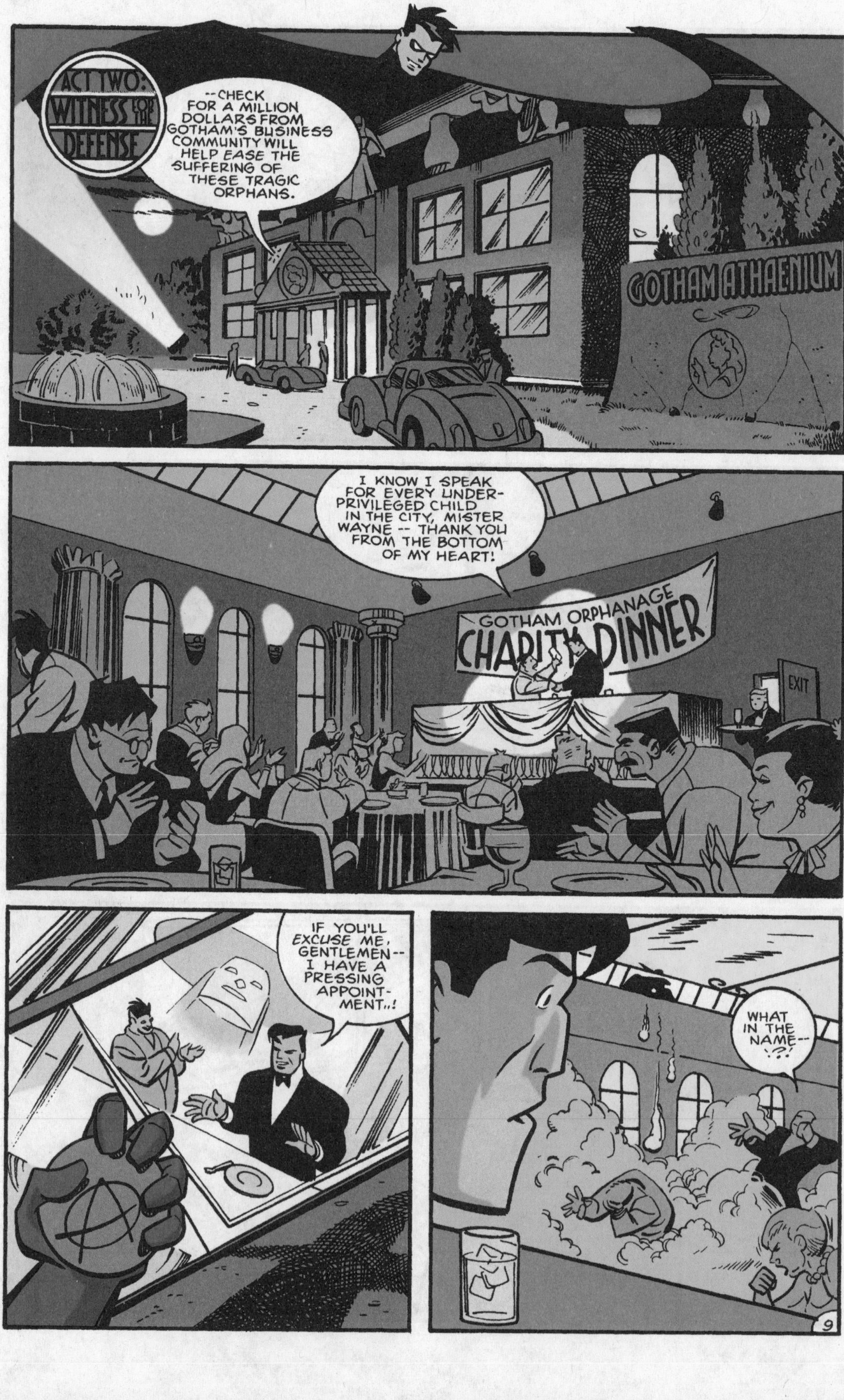
ACT TWO:
WITNESS FOR THE DEFENSE
--CHECK FOR A MILLION DOLLARS FROM GOTHAM'S BUSINESS COMMUNITY WILL HELP EASE THE SUFFERING OF THESE TRAGIC ORPHANS.
GOTHAM ATHAENIUM
I KNOW I SPEAK FOR EVERY UNDER-PRIVILEGED CHILD IN THE CITY, MISTER WAYNE -- THANK YOU FROM THE BOTTOM OF MY HEART!
GOTHAM ORPHANAGE
CHARITY DINNER
EXIT
IF YOU'LL EXCUSE ME, GENTLEMEN-- I HAVE A PRESSING APPOINT-MENT..!
WHAT IN THE NAME--?!

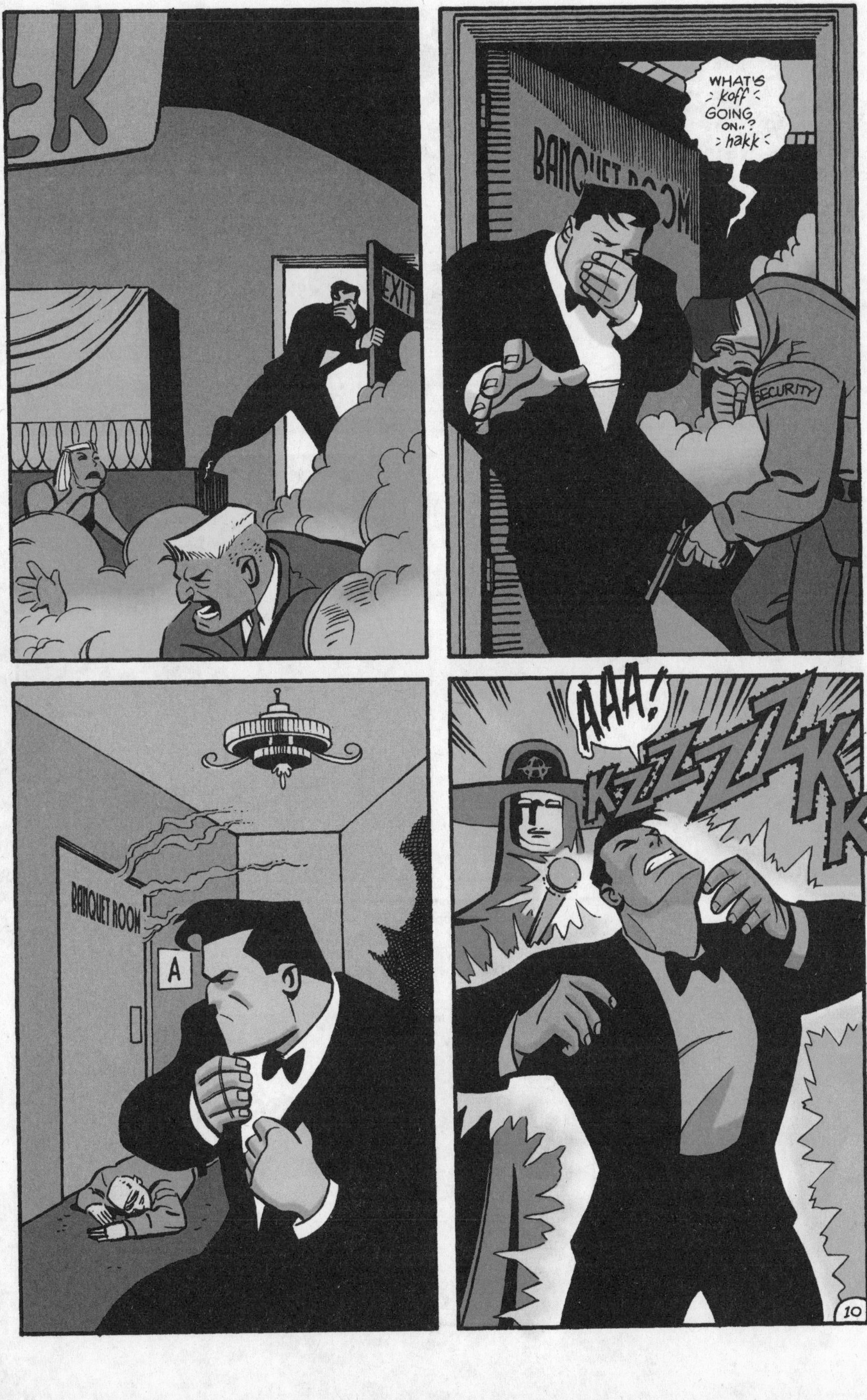
EXIT
BANQUET ROOM
WHAT'S koff GOING ON..? hakk
SECURITY
BANQUET ROOM
A
AAA!
KZZZZZKK

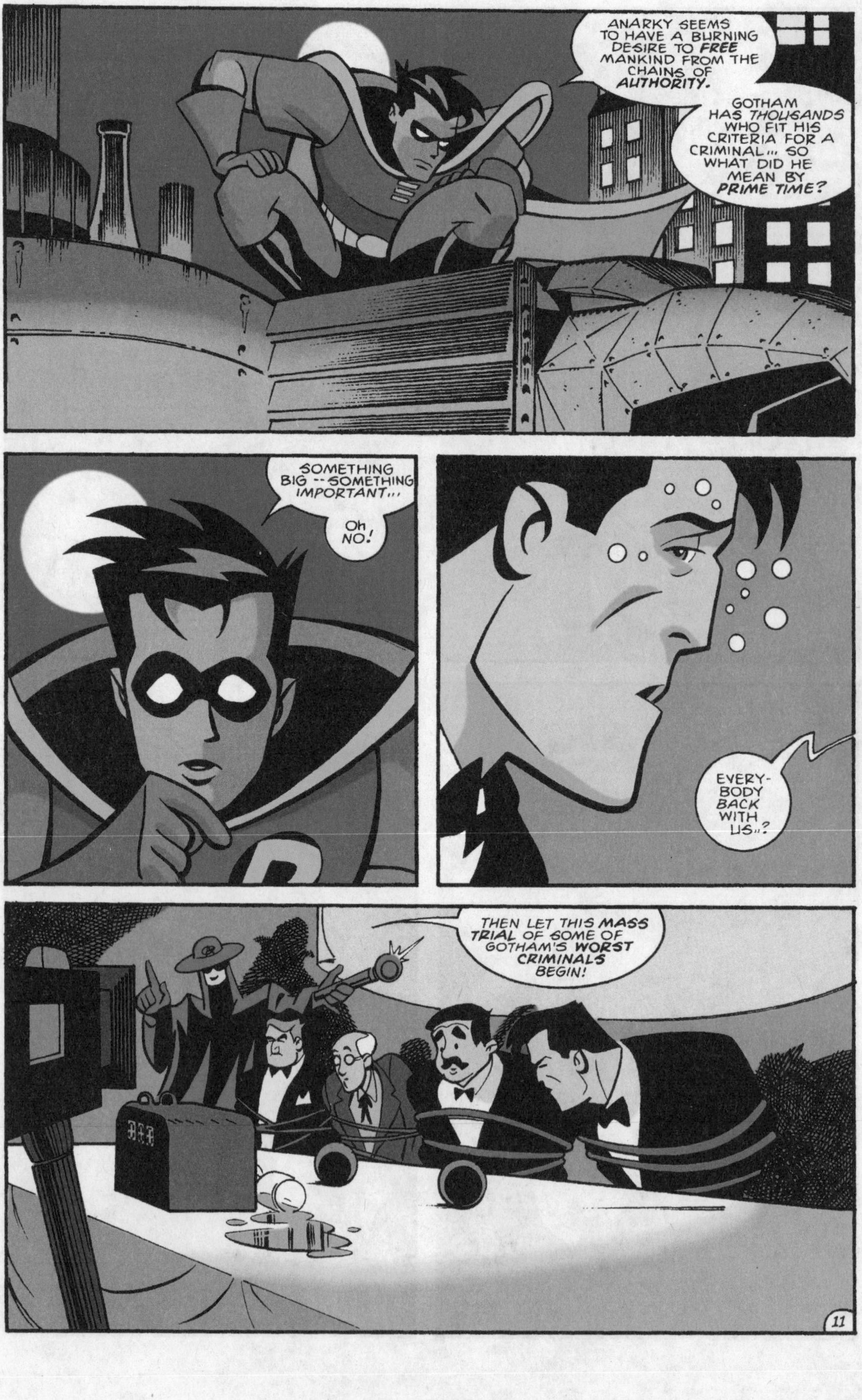

ANARKY SEEMS TO HAVE A BURNING DESIRE TO FREE MANKIND FROM THE CHAINS OF AUTHORITY.
GOTHAM HAS THOUSANDS WHO FIT HIS CRITERIA FOR A CRIMINAL... SO WHAT DID HE MEAN BY PRIME TIME?
SOMETHING BIG --SOMETHING IMPORTANT...
Oh NO!
EVERY-BODY BACK WITH US..?
THEN LET THIS MASS TRIAL OF SOME OF GOTHAM'S WORST CRIMINALS BEGIN!

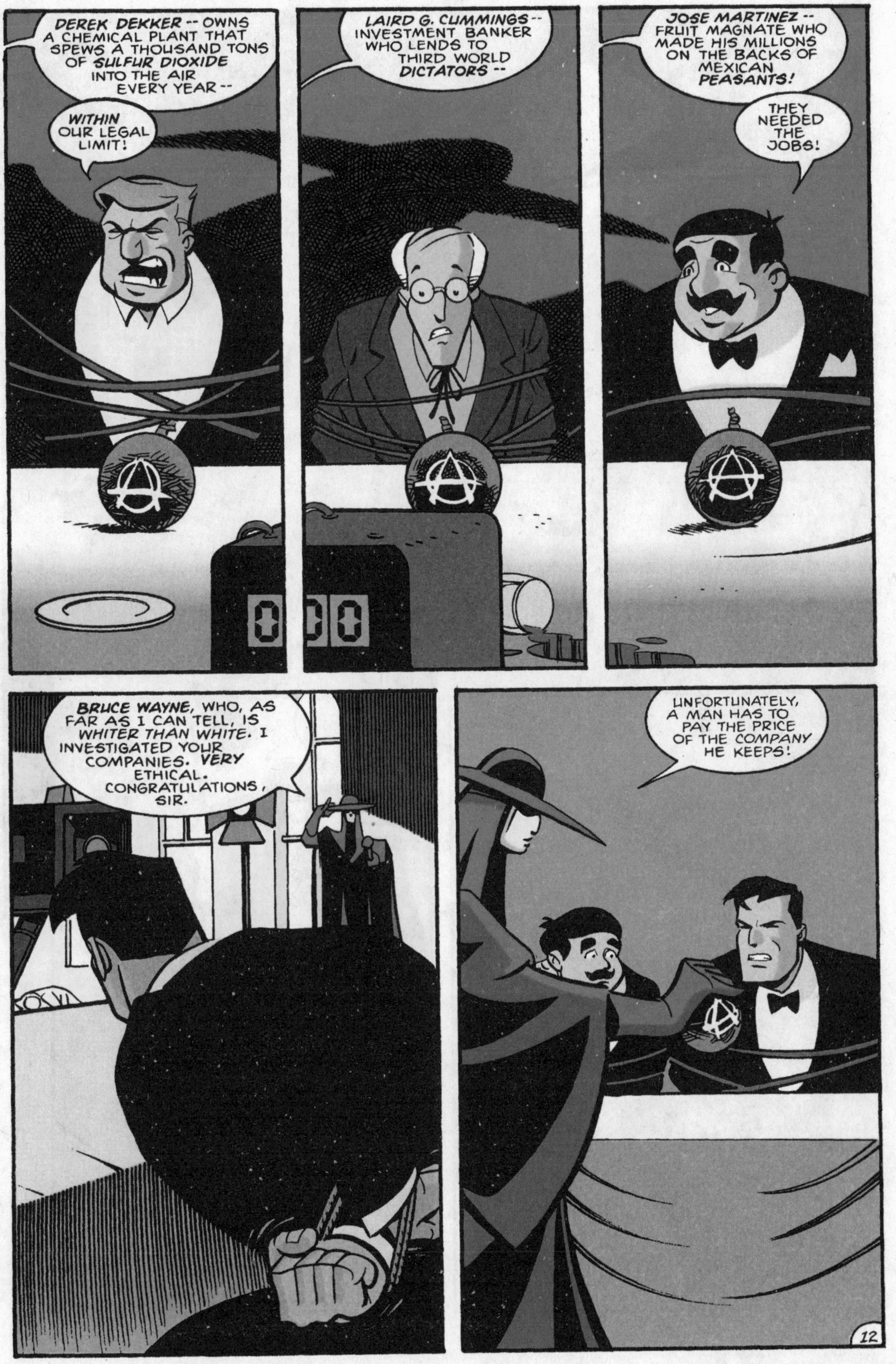

DEREK DEKKER -- OWNS A CHEMICAL PLANT THAT SPEWS A THOUSAND TONS OF SULFUR DIOXIDE INTO THE AIR EVERY YEAR --
WITHIN OUR LEGAL LIMIT!
LAIRD G. CUMMINGS -- INVESTMENT BANKER WHO LENDS TO THIRD WORLD DICTATORS --
JOSE MARTINEZ -- FRUIT MAGNATE WHO MADE HIS MILLIONS ON THE BACKS OF MEXICAN PEASANTS!
THEY NEEDED THE JOBS!
BRUCE WAYNE, WHO, AS FAR AS I CAN TELL, IS WHITER THAN WHITE. I INVESTIGATED YOUR COMPANIES. VERY ETHICAL. CONGRATULATIONS, SIR.
UNFORTUNATELY, A MAN HAS TO PAY THE PRICE OF THE COMPANY HE KEEPS!
12

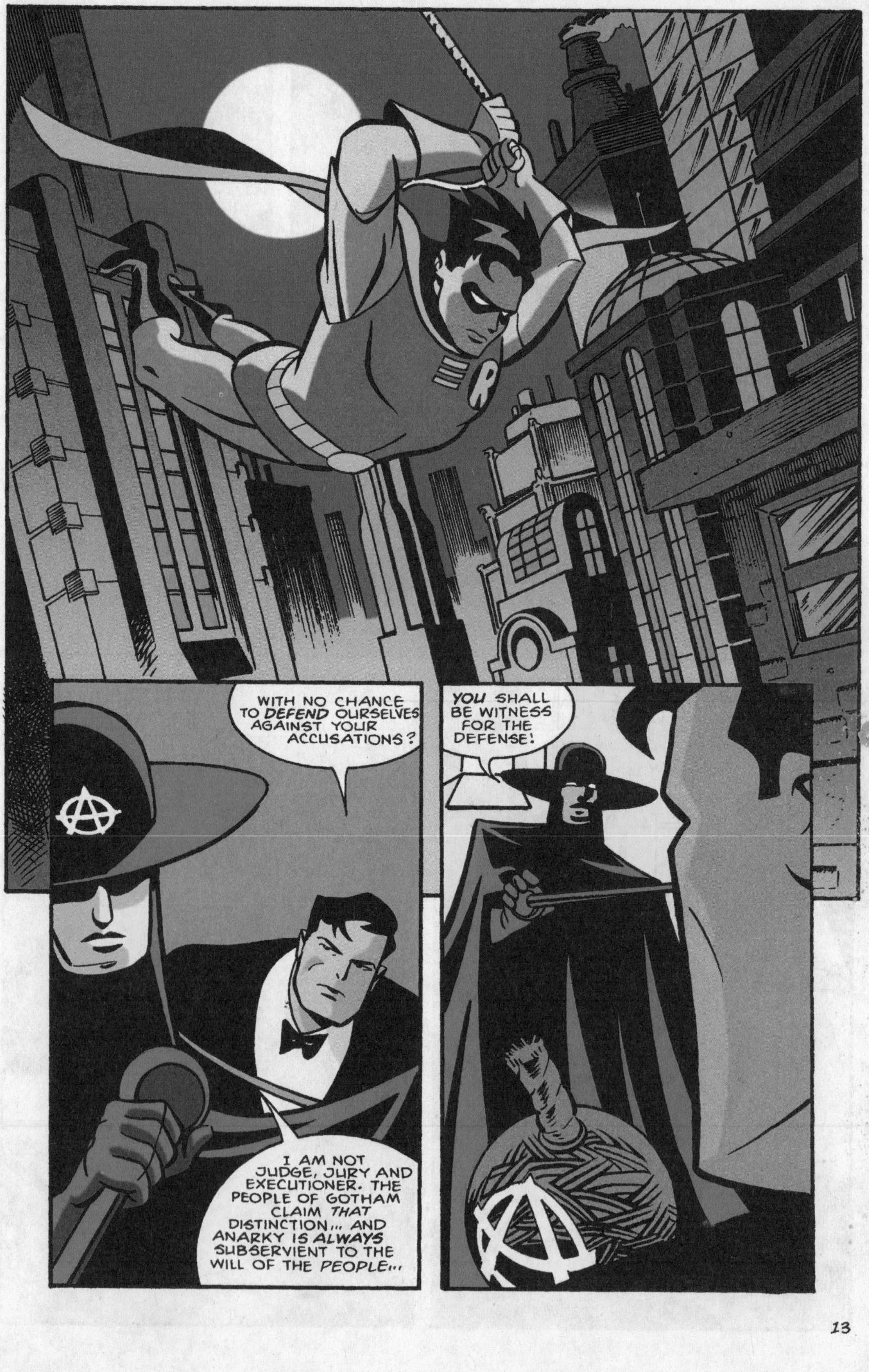

WITH NO CHANCE TO *DEFEND* OURSELVES AGAINST YOUR ACCUSATIONS?
I AM NOT JUDGE, JURY AND EXECUTIONER. THE PEOPLE OF GOTHAM CLAIM *THAT* DISTINCTION... AND ANARKY IS *ALWAYS* SUBSERVIENT TO THE WILL OF THE *PEOPLE*...
YOU SHALL BE WITNESS FOR THE DEFENSE!

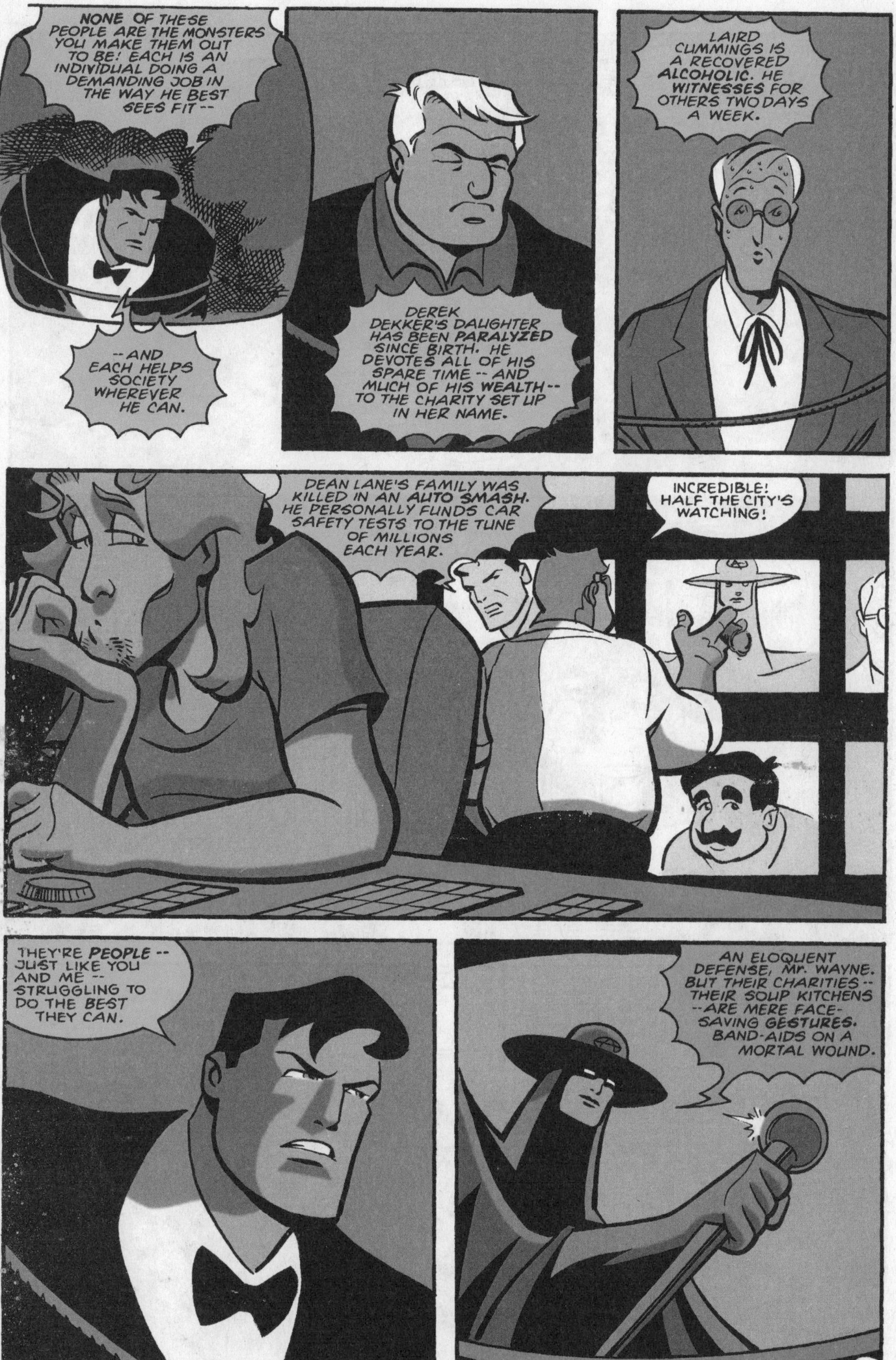

NONE OF THESE PEOPLE ARE THE MONSTERS YOU MAKE THEM OUT TO BE! EACH IS AN INDIVIDUAL DOING A DEMANDING JOB IN THE WAY HE BEST SEES FIT --
-- AND EACH HELPS SOCIETY WHEREVER HE CAN.
DEREK DEKKER'S DAUGHTER HAS BEEN PARALYZED SINCE BIRTH. HE DEVOTES ALL OF HIS SPARE TIME -- AND MUCH OF HIS WEALTH -- TO THE CHARITY SET UP IN HER NAME.
LAIRD CUMMINGS IS A RECOVERED ALCOHOLIC. HE WITNESSES FOR OTHERS TWO DAYS A WEEK.
DEAN LANE'S FAMILY WAS KILLED IN AN AUTO SMASH. HE PERSONALLY FUNDS CAR SAFETY TESTS TO THE TUNE OF MILLIONS EACH YEAR.
INCREDIBLE! HALF THE CITY'S WATCHING!
THEY'RE PEOPLE -- JUST LIKE YOU AND ME -- STRUGGLING TO DO THE BEST THEY CAN.
AN ELOQUENT DEFENSE, Mr. WAYNE. BUT THEIR CHARITIES -- THEIR SOUP KITCHENS -- ARE MERE FACE-SAVING GESTURES. BAND-AIDS ON A MORTAL WOUND.
14

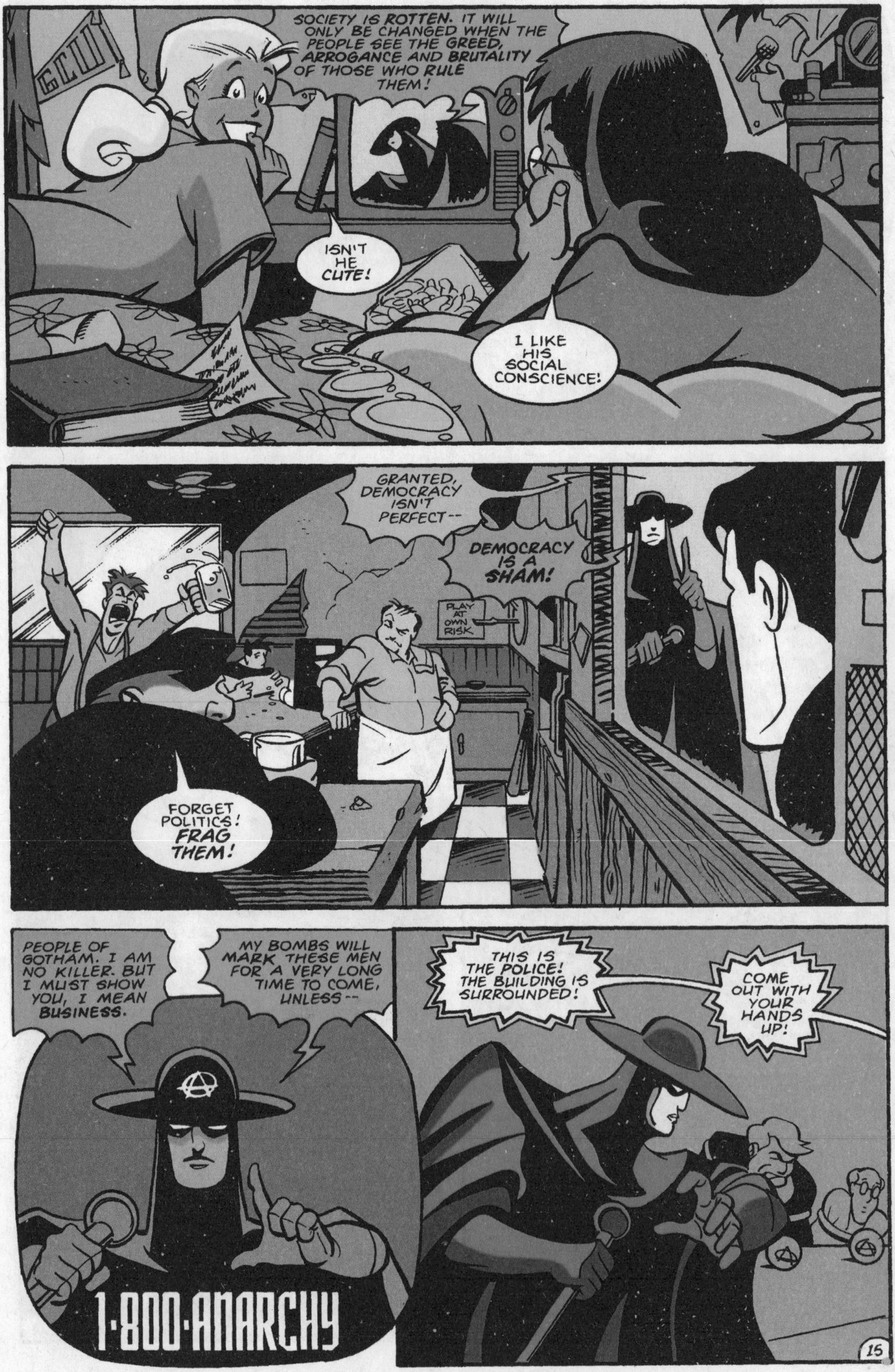
SOCIETY IS ROTTEN. IT WILL ONLY BE CHANGED WHEN THE PEOPLE SEE THE GREED, ARROGANCE AND BRUTALITY OF THOSE WHO RULE THEM!
ISN'T HE CUTE!
I LIKE HIS SOCIAL CONSCIENCE!
GRANTED, DEMOCRACY ISN'T PERFECT--
DEMOCRACY IS A SHAM!
PLAY AT OWN RISK
FORGET POLITICS! FRAG THEM!
PEOPLE OF GOTHAM. I AM NO KILLER. BUT I MUST SHOW YOU, I MEAN BUSINESS.
MY BOMBS WILL MARK THESE MEN FOR A VERY LONG TIME TO COME, UNLESS--
1-800-ANARCHY
THIS IS THE POLICE! THE BUILDING IS SURROUNDED!
COME OUT WITH YOUR HANDS UP!

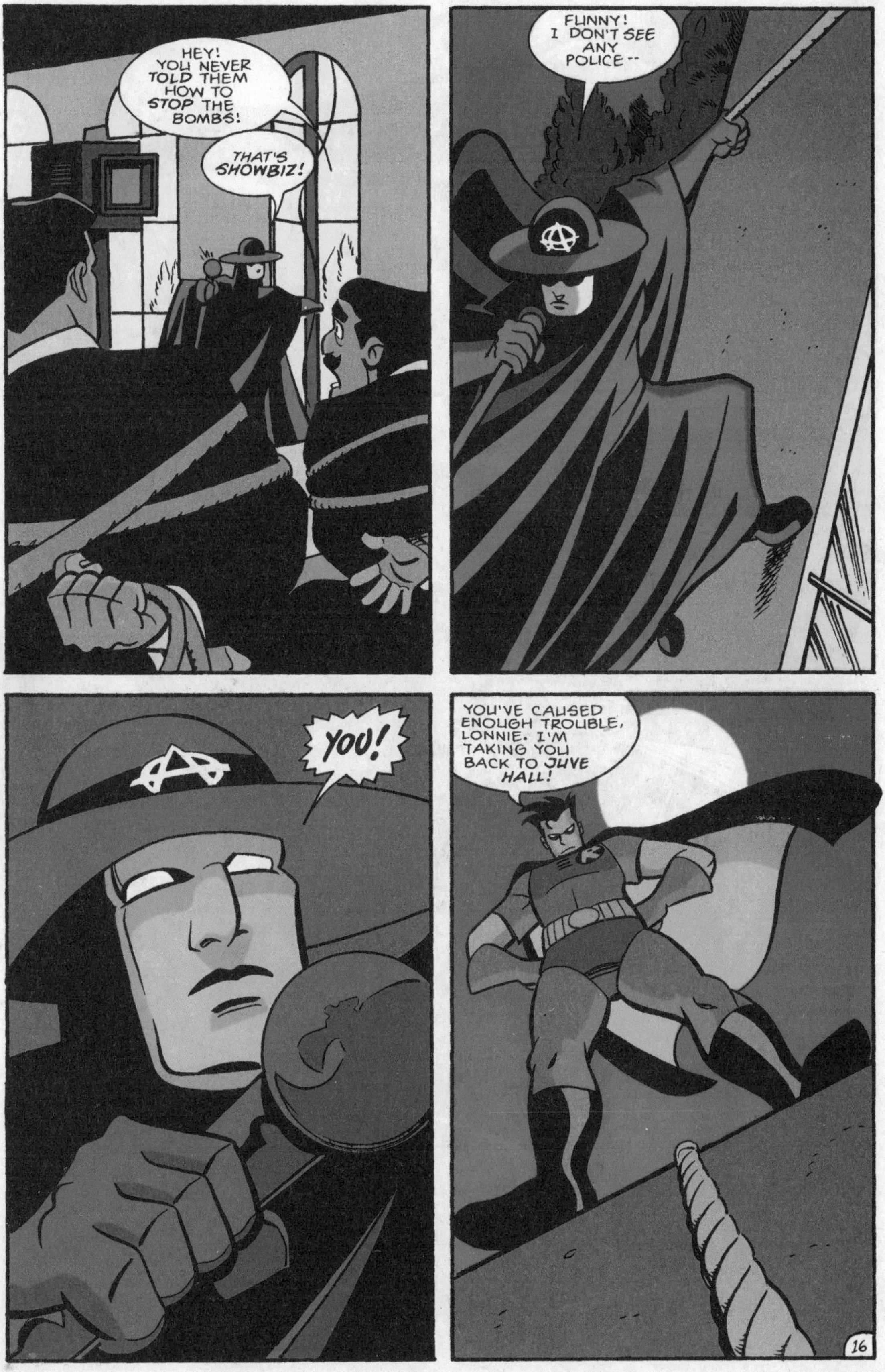
HEY! YOU NEVER TOLD THEM HOW TO STOP THE BOMBS!
THAT'S SHOWBIZ!
FUNNY! I DON'T SEE ANY POLICE --
YOU!
YOU'VE CAUSED ENOUGH TROUBLE, LONNIE. I'M TAKING YOU BACK TO JUVE HALL!
16

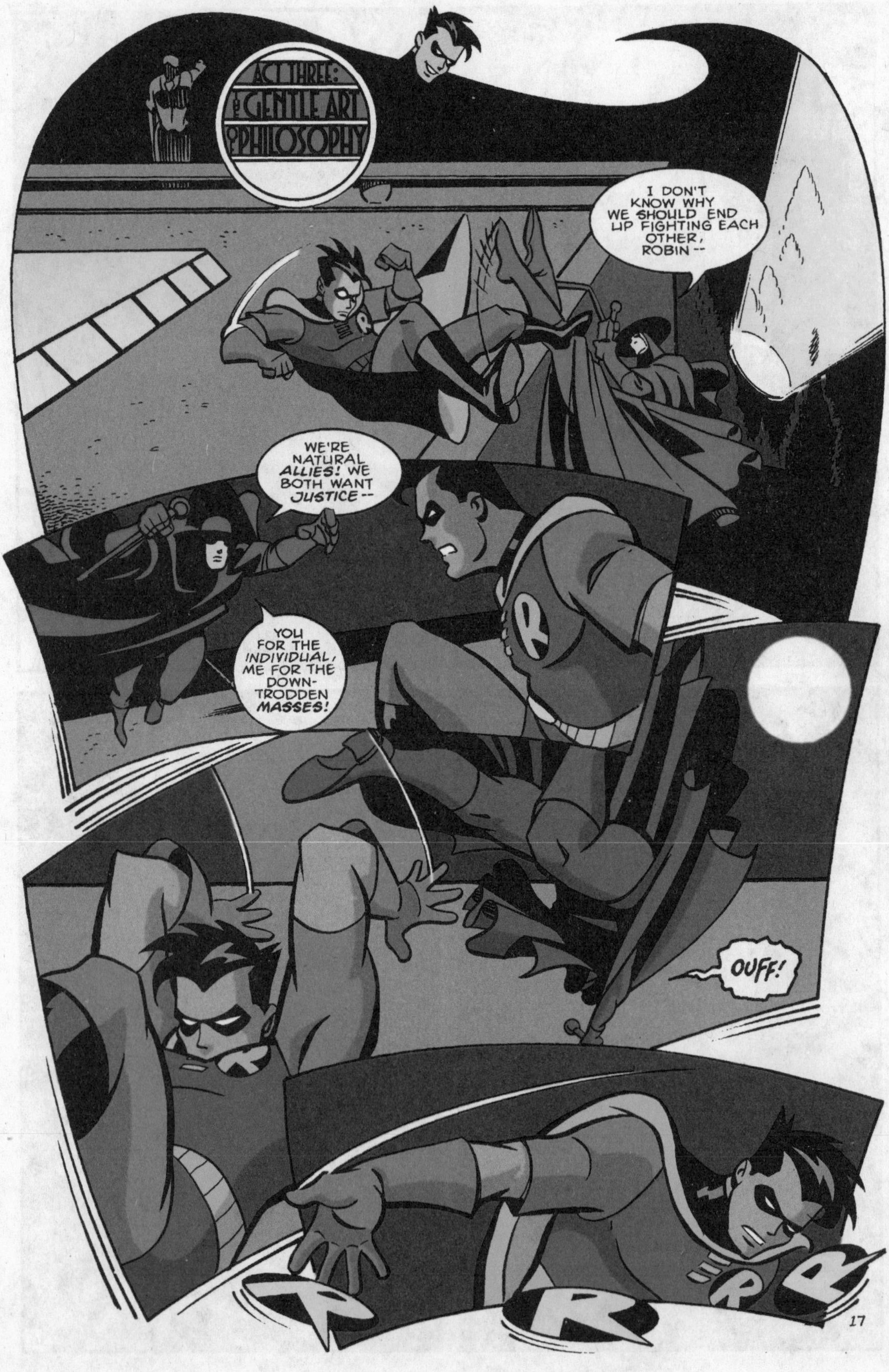
ACT THREE:
THE GENTLE ART OF PHILOSOPHY
I DON'T KNOW WHY WE SHOULD END UP FIGHTING EACH OTHER, ROBIN --
WE'RE NATURAL ALLIES! WE BOTH WANT JUSTICE --
YOU FOR THE INDIVIDUAL, ME FOR THE DOWN-TRODDEN MASSES!
OUFF!

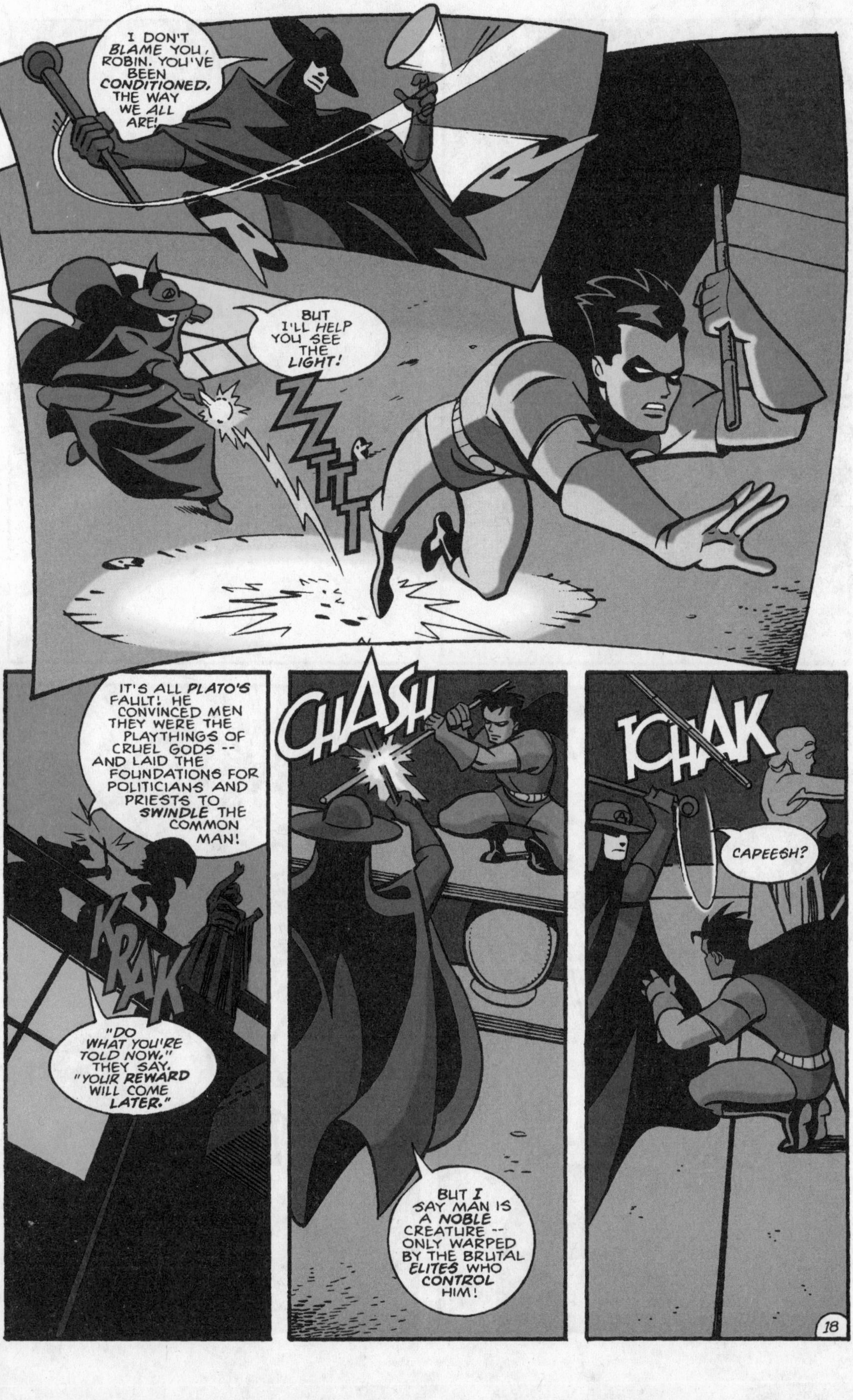

I DON'T BLAME YOU, ROBIN. YOU'VE BEEN CONDITIONED, THE WAY WE ALL ARE!
BUT I'LL HELP YOU SEE THE LIGHT!
ZZTTT
IT'S ALL PLATO'S FAULT! HE CONVINCED MEN THEY WERE THE PLAYTHINGS OF CRUEL GODS -- AND LAID THE FOUNDATIONS FOR POLITICIANS AND PRIESTS TO SWINDLE THE COMMON MAN!
KRAK
"DO WHAT YOU'RE TOLD NOW," THEY SAY. "YOUR REWARD WILL COME LATER."
CHASH
BUT I SAY MAN IS A NOBLE CREATURE -- ONLY WARPED BY THE BRUTAL ELITES WHO CONTROL HIM!
TCHAK
CAPEESH?

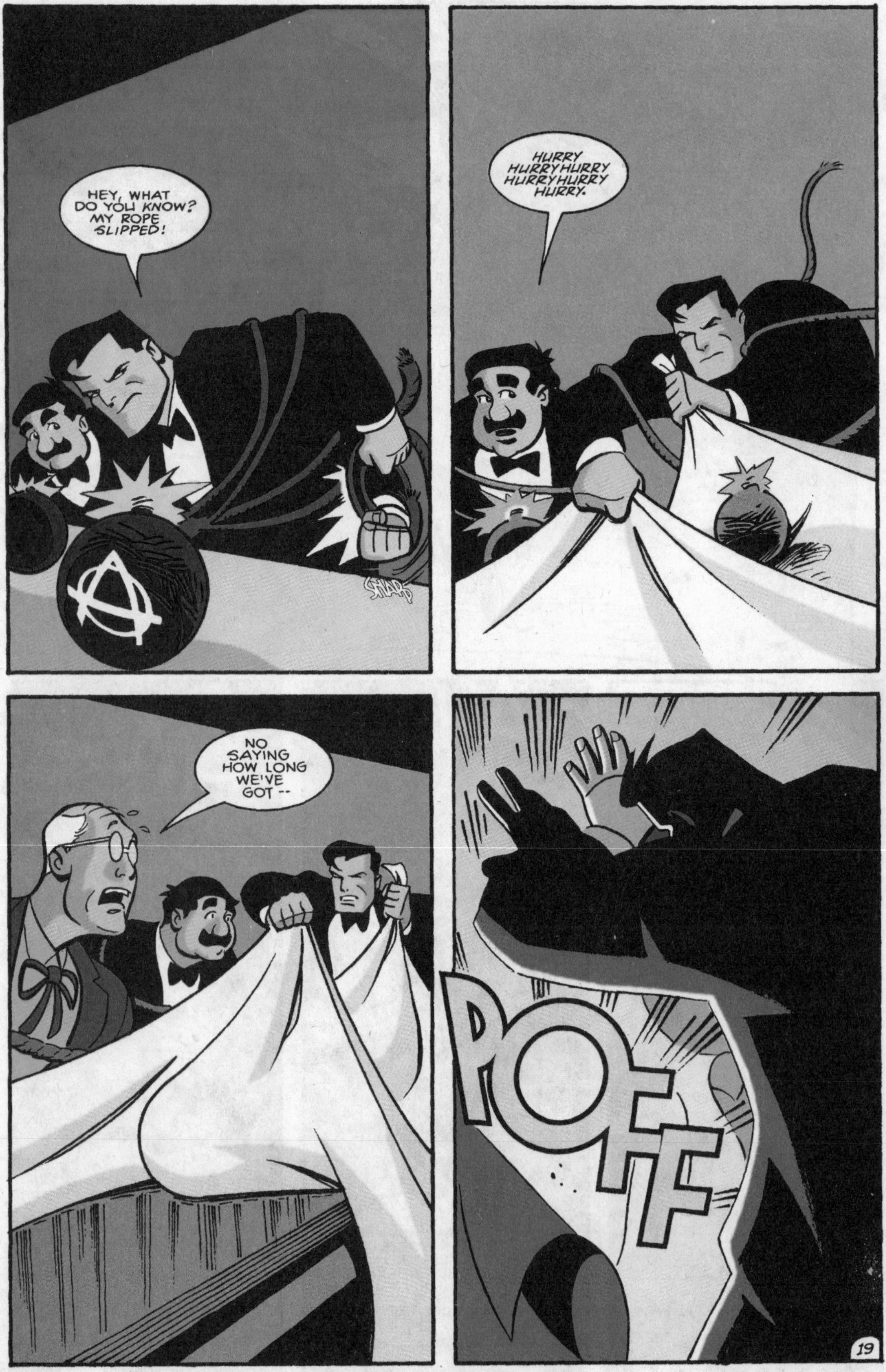
HEY, WHAT DO YOU KNOW? MY ROPE SLIPPED!
HURRY HURRY HURRY HURRY HURRY HURRY.
NO SAYING HOW LONG WE'VE GOT --
POOFF

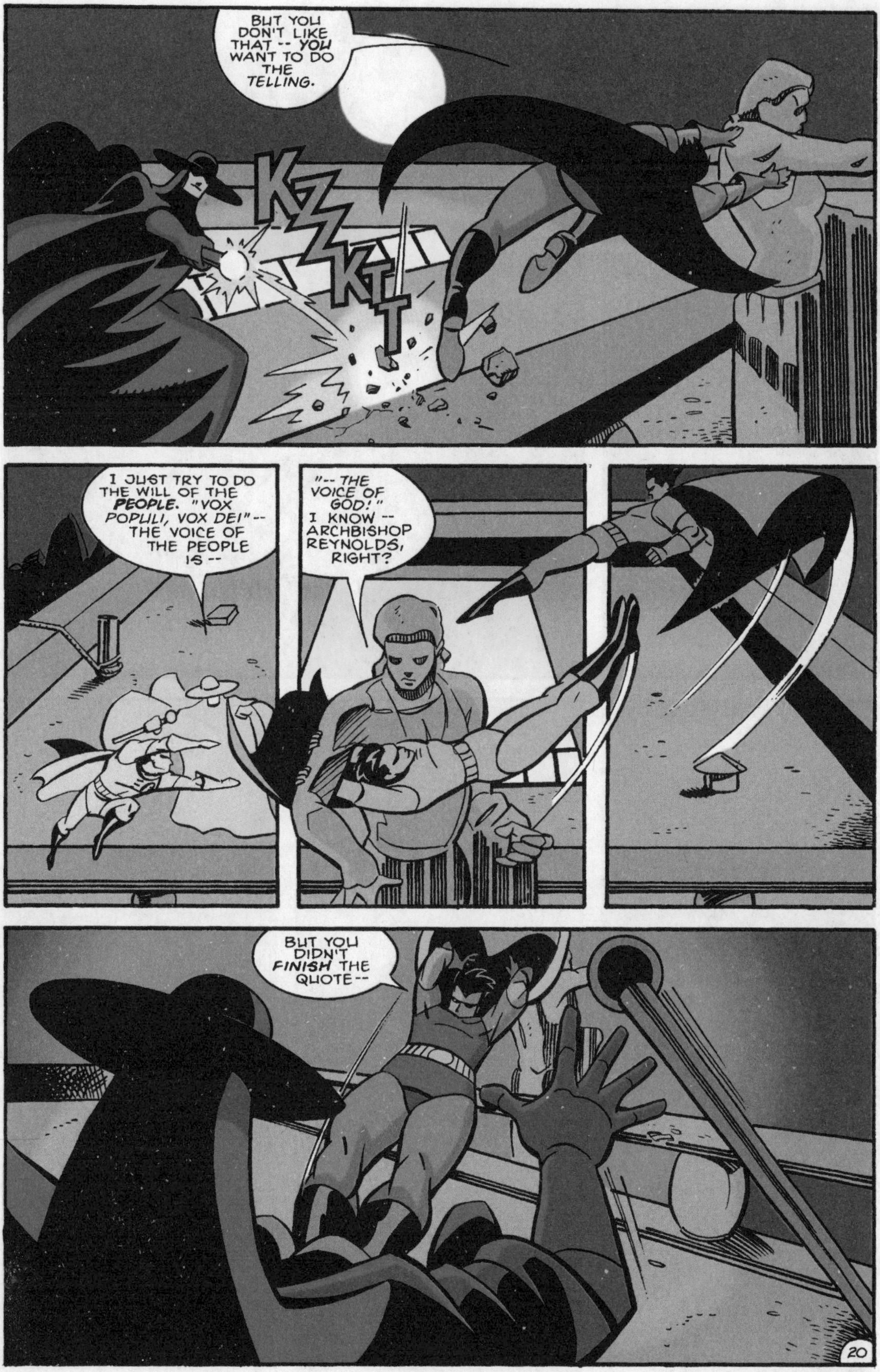

BUT YOU DON'T LIKE THAT -- *YOU* WANT TO DO THE *TELLING*.
KZZKTT
I JUST TRY TO DO THE WILL OF THE *PEOPLE*. "VOX POPULI, VOX DEI" -- THE VOICE OF THE PEOPLE IS --
"-- THE VOICE OF GOD!" I KNOW -- ARCHBISHOP REYNOLDS, RIGHT?
BUT YOU DIDN'T *FINISH* THE QUOTE --

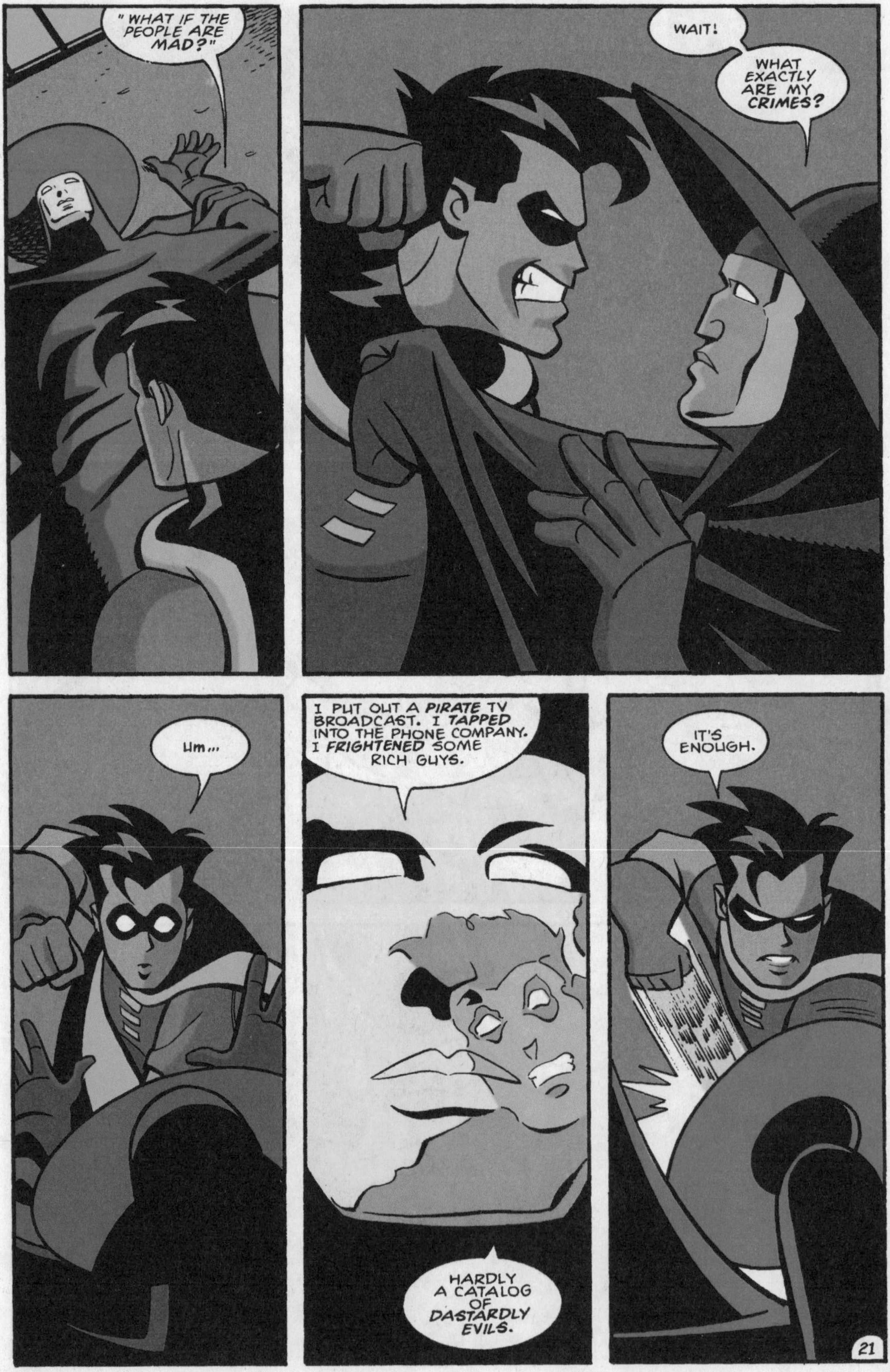
"WHAT IF THE PEOPLE ARE MAD?"
WAIT!
WHAT EXACTLY ARE MY CRIMES?
UM...
I PUT OUT A PIRATE TV BROADCAST. I TAPPED INTO THE PHONE COMPANY. I FRIGHTENED SOME RICH GUYS.
HARDLY A CATALOG OF DASTARDLY EVILS.
IT'S ENOUGH.

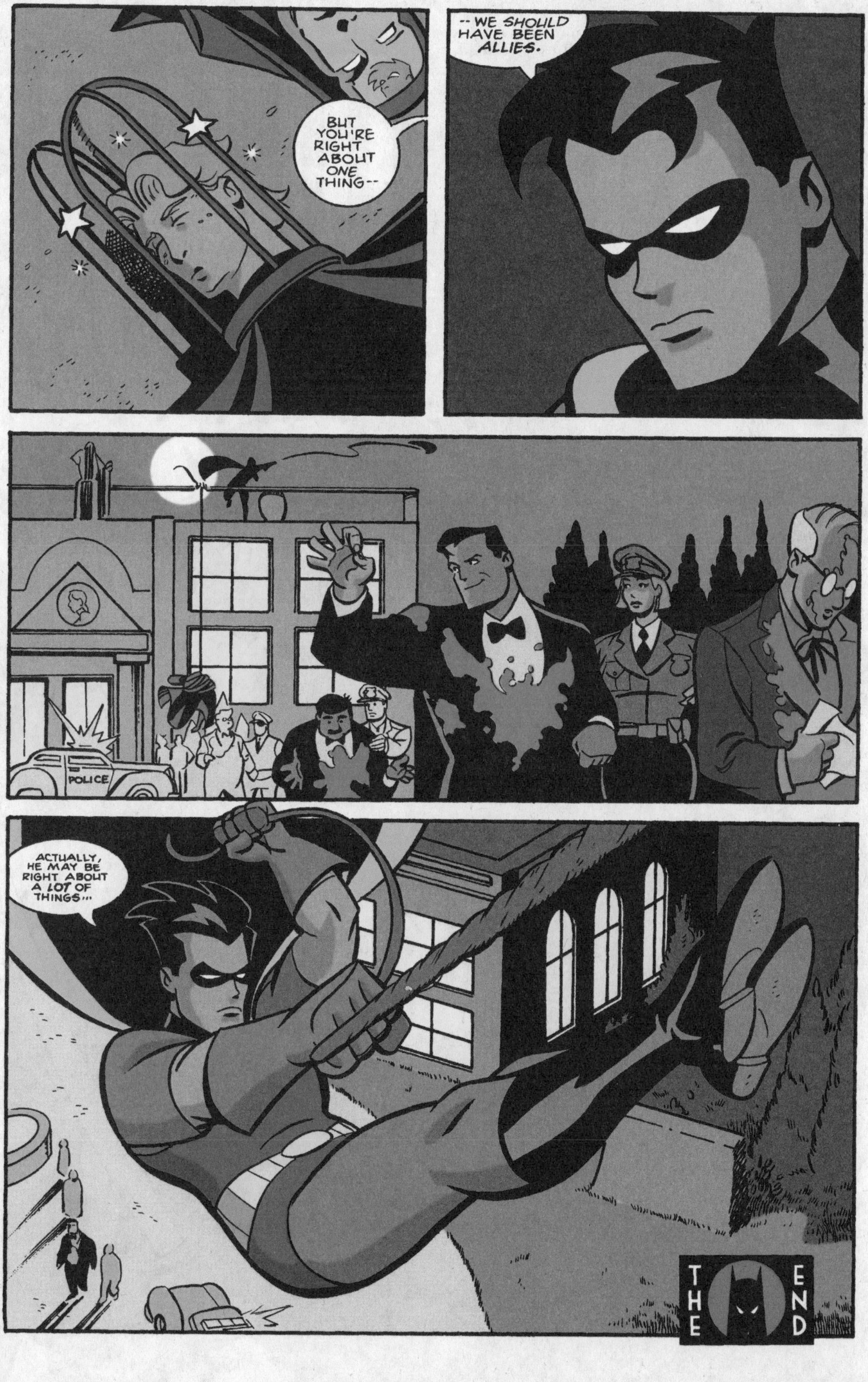
BUT YOU'RE RIGHT ABOUT ONE THING--
--WE SHOULD HAVE BEEN ALLIES.
POLICE
ACTUALLY, HE MAY BE RIGHT ABOUT A LOT OF THINGS...
THE END

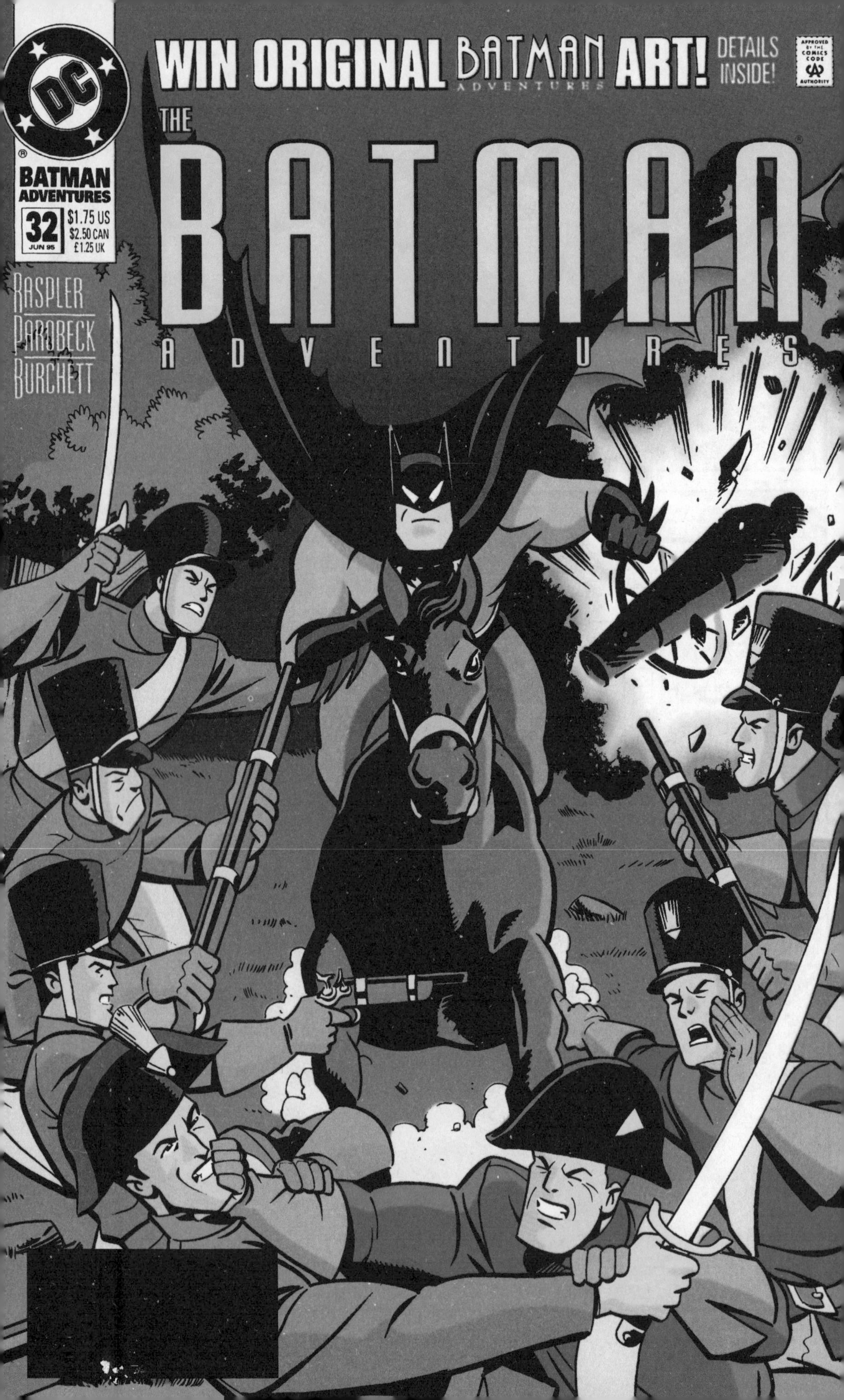

DC
BATMAN ADVENTURES
32
JUN 95
$1.75 US
$2.50 CAN
£1.25 UK
WIN ORIGINAL BATMAN ADVENTURES ART!
DETAILS INSIDE!
APPROVED BY THE COMICS CODE AUTHORITY
THE BATMAN ADVENTURES
RASPLER
PAROBECK
BURCHETT

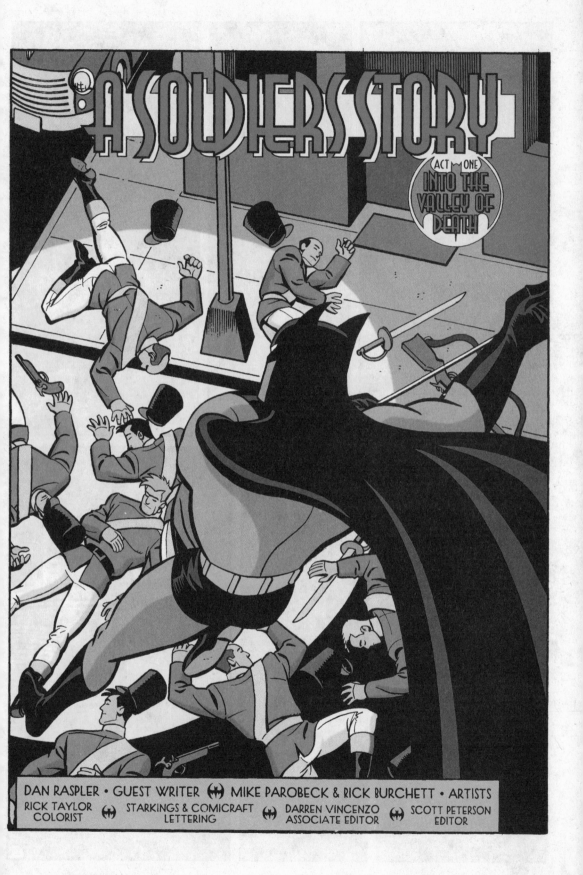

A SOLDIERS STORY

ACT ONE
INTO THE VALLEY OF DEATH

DAN RASPLER • GUEST WRITER ⬤ MIKE PAROBECK & RICK BURCHETT • ARTISTS

RICK TAYLOR
COLORIST ⬤ STARKINGS & COMICRAFT
LETTERING ⬤ DARREN VINCENZO
ASSOCIATE EDITOR ⬤ SCOTT PETERSON
EDITOR

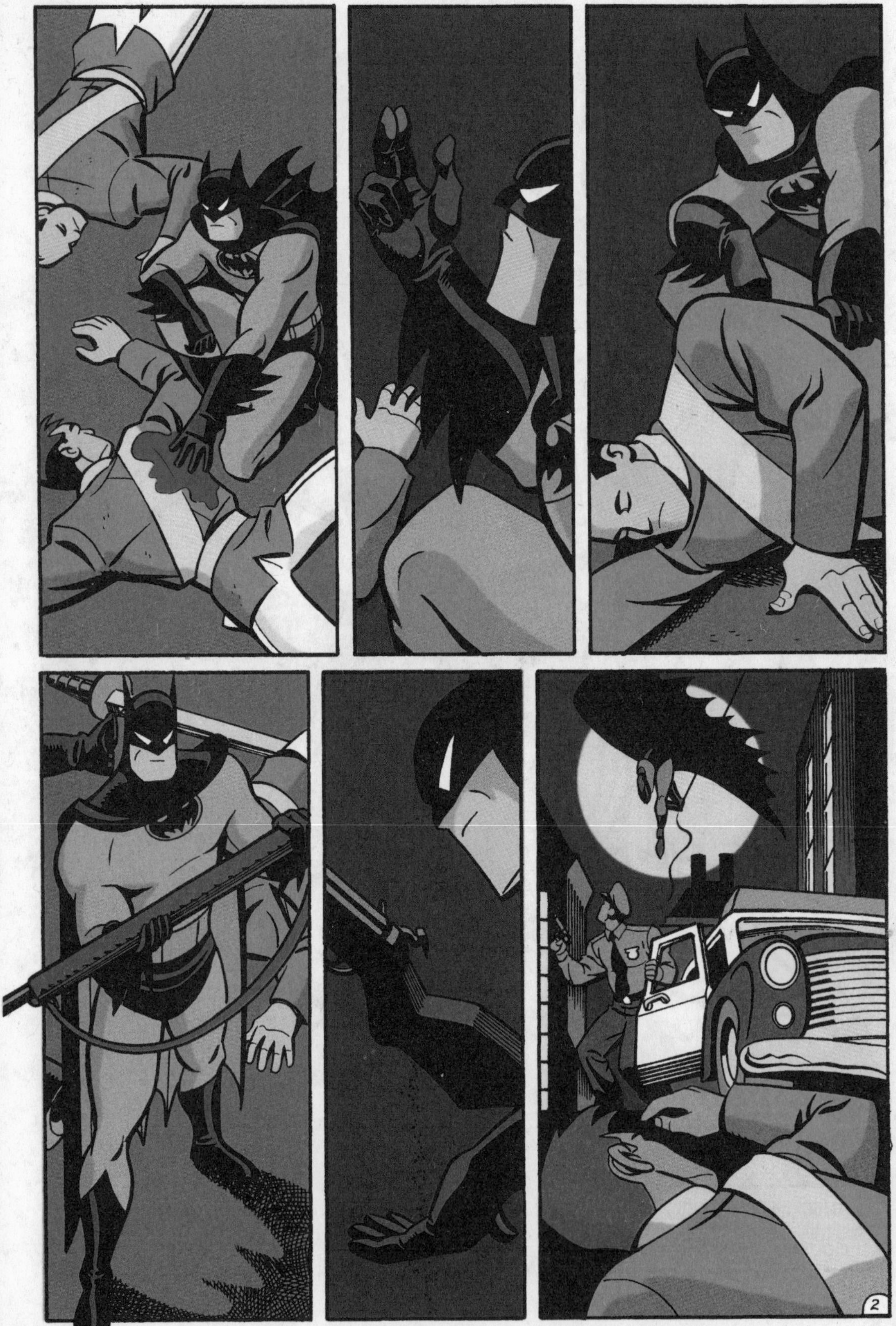

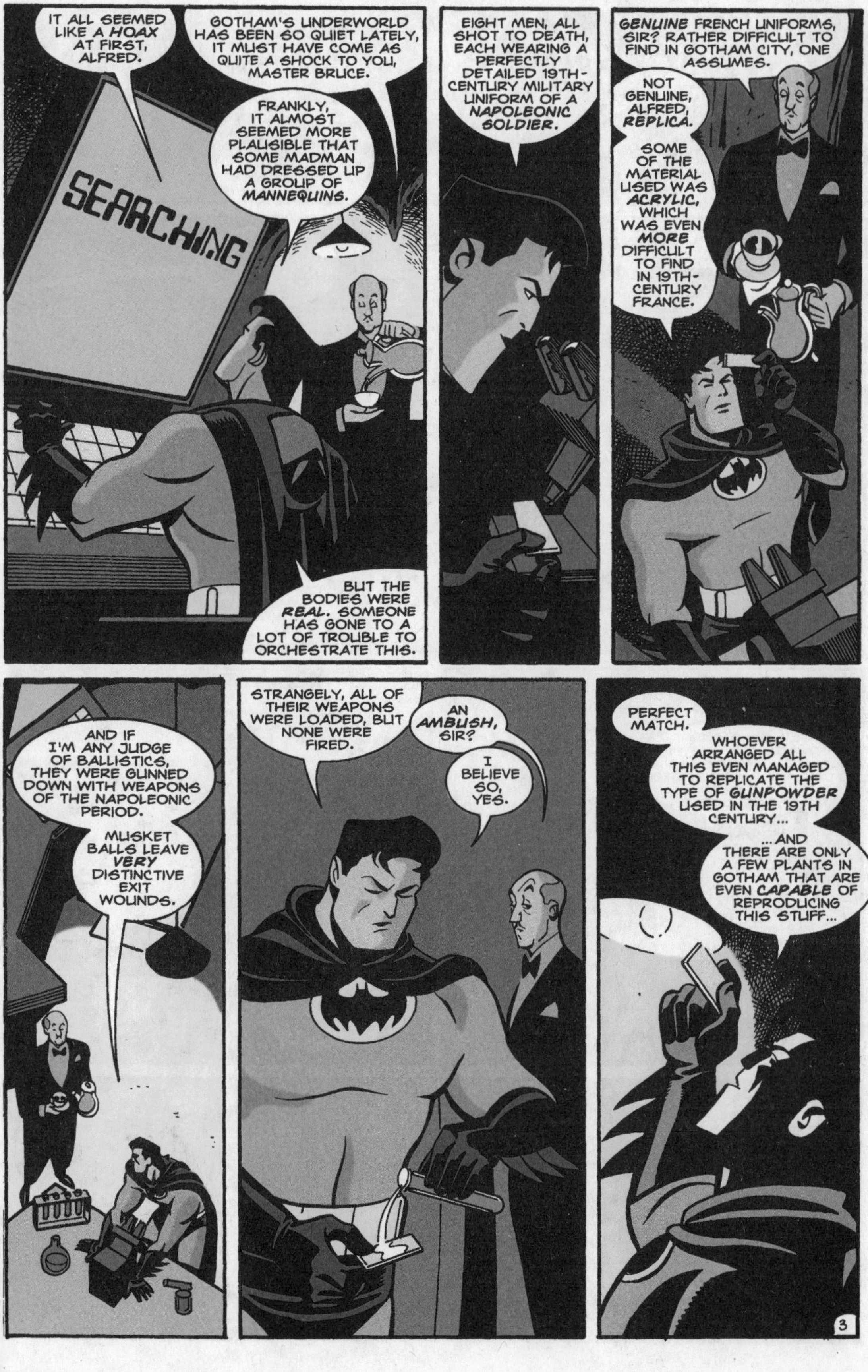

IT ALL SEEMED LIKE A HOAX AT FIRST, ALFRED.
GOTHAM'S UNDERWORLD HAS BEEN SO QUIET LATELY, IT MUST HAVE COME AS QUITE A SHOCK TO YOU, MASTER BRUCE.
FRANKLY, IT ALMOST SEEMED MORE PLAUSIBLE THAT SOME MADMAN HAD DRESSED UP A GROUP OF MANNEQUINS.
SEARCHING
BUT THE BODIES WERE REAL. SOMEONE HAS GONE TO A LOT OF TROUBLE TO ORCHESTRATE THIS.
EIGHT MEN, ALL SHOT TO DEATH, EACH WEARING A PERFECTLY DETAILED 19TH-CENTURY MILITARY UNIFORM OF A NAPOLEONIC SOLDIER.
GENUINE FRENCH UNIFORMS, SIR? RATHER DIFFICULT TO FIND IN GOTHAM CITY, ONE ASSUMES.
NOT GENUINE, ALFRED, REPLICA.
SOME OF THE MATERIAL USED WAS ACRYLIC, WHICH WAS EVEN MORE DIFFICULT TO FIND IN 19TH-CENTURY FRANCE.
AND IF I'M ANY JUDGE OF BALLISTICS, THEY WERE GUNNED DOWN WITH WEAPONS OF THE NAPOLEONIC PERIOD.
MUSKET BALLS LEAVE VERY DISTINCTIVE EXIT WOUNDS.
STRANGELY, ALL OF THEIR WEAPONS WERE LOADED, BUT NONE WERE FIRED.
AN AMBUSH, SIR?
I BELIEVE SO, YES.
PERFECT MATCH.
WHOEVER ARRANGED ALL THIS EVEN MANAGED TO REPLICATE THE TYPE OF GUNPOWDER USED IN THE 19TH CENTURY...
...AND THERE ARE ONLY A FEW PLANTS IN GOTHAM THAT ARE EVEN CAPABLE OF REPRODUCING THIS STUFF...

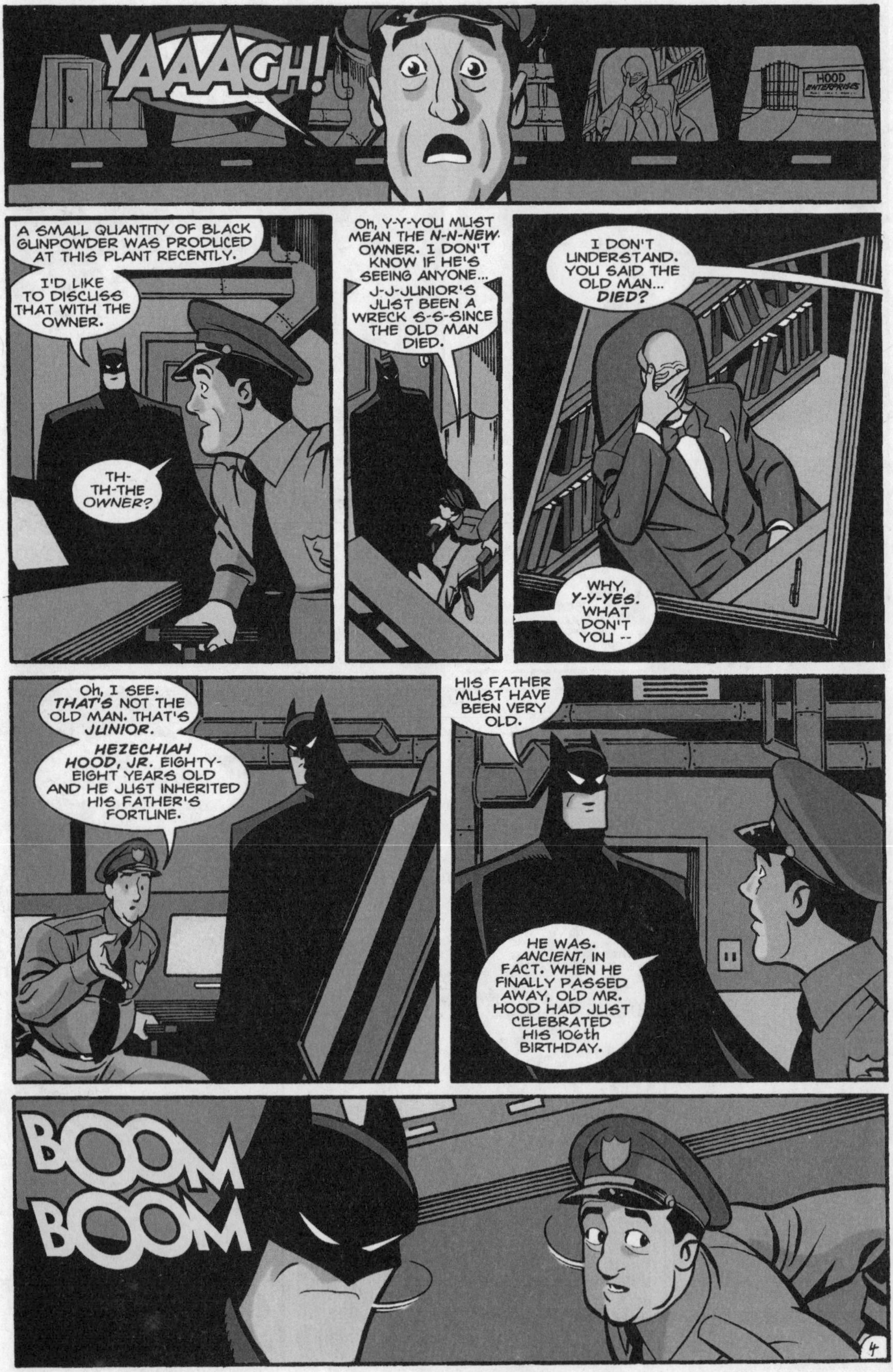
YAAAGH!
HOOD ENTERPRISES
A SMALL QUANTITY OF BLACK GUNPOWDER WAS PRODUCED AT THIS PLANT RECENTLY.
I'D LIKE TO DISCUSS THAT WITH THE OWNER.
TH- TH-THE OWNER?
Oh, Y-Y-YOU MUST MEAN THE N-N-NEW OWNER. I DON'T KNOW IF HE'S SEEING ANYONE...
J-J-JUNIOR'S JUST BEEN A WRECK S-S-SINCE THE OLD MAN DIED.
I DON'T UNDERSTAND. YOU SAID THE OLD MAN... DIED?
WHY, Y-Y-YES. WHAT DON'T YOU --
Oh, I SEE. THAT'S NOT THE OLD MAN. THAT'S JUNIOR.
HEZECHIAH HOOD, JR. EIGHTY-EIGHT YEARS OLD AND HE JUST INHERITED HIS FATHER'S FORTUNE.
HIS FATHER MUST HAVE BEEN VERY OLD.
HE WAS. ANCIENT, IN FACT. WHEN HE FINALLY PASSED AWAY, OLD MR. HOOD HAD JUST CELEBRATED HIS 106th BIRTHDAY.
BOOM BOOM
4

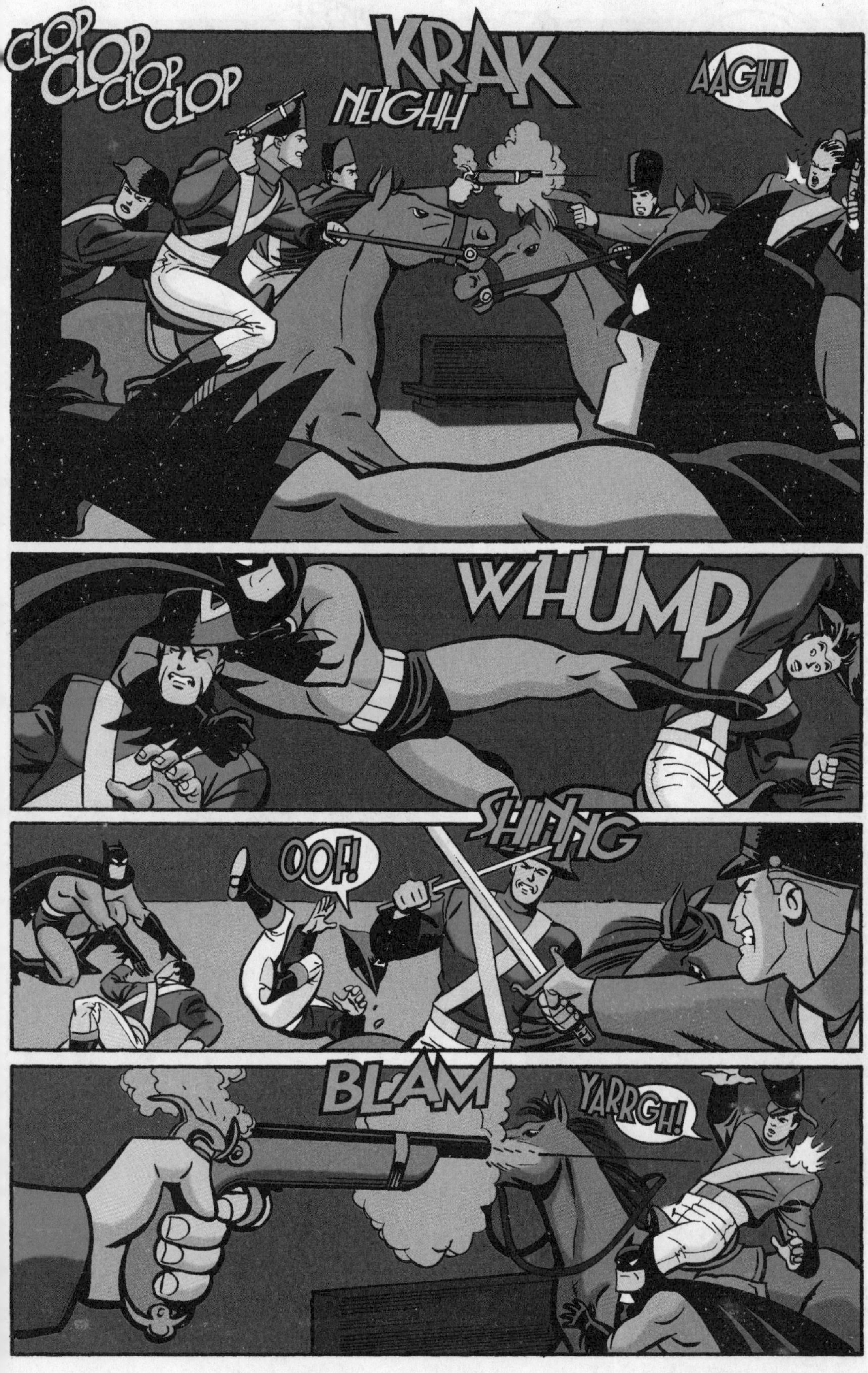

CLOP CLOP CLOP CLOP
KRAK
NEIGHH
AAGH!
WHUMP
SHING
OOF!
BLAM
YARRGH!

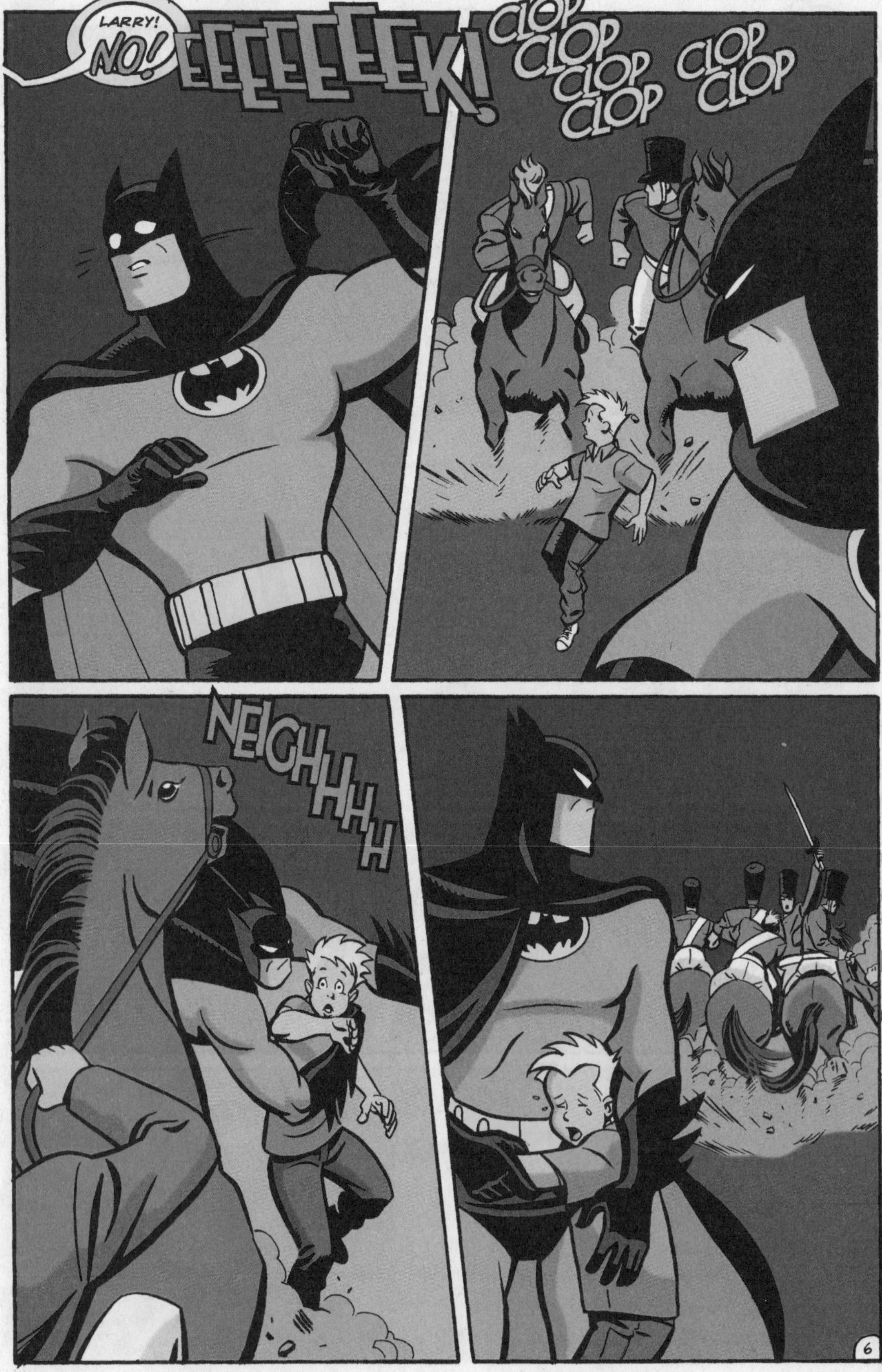

LARRY! NO!
EEEEEEEEEK!
CLOP CLOP CLOP CLOP CLOP CLOP
NEIGHHHHH
6

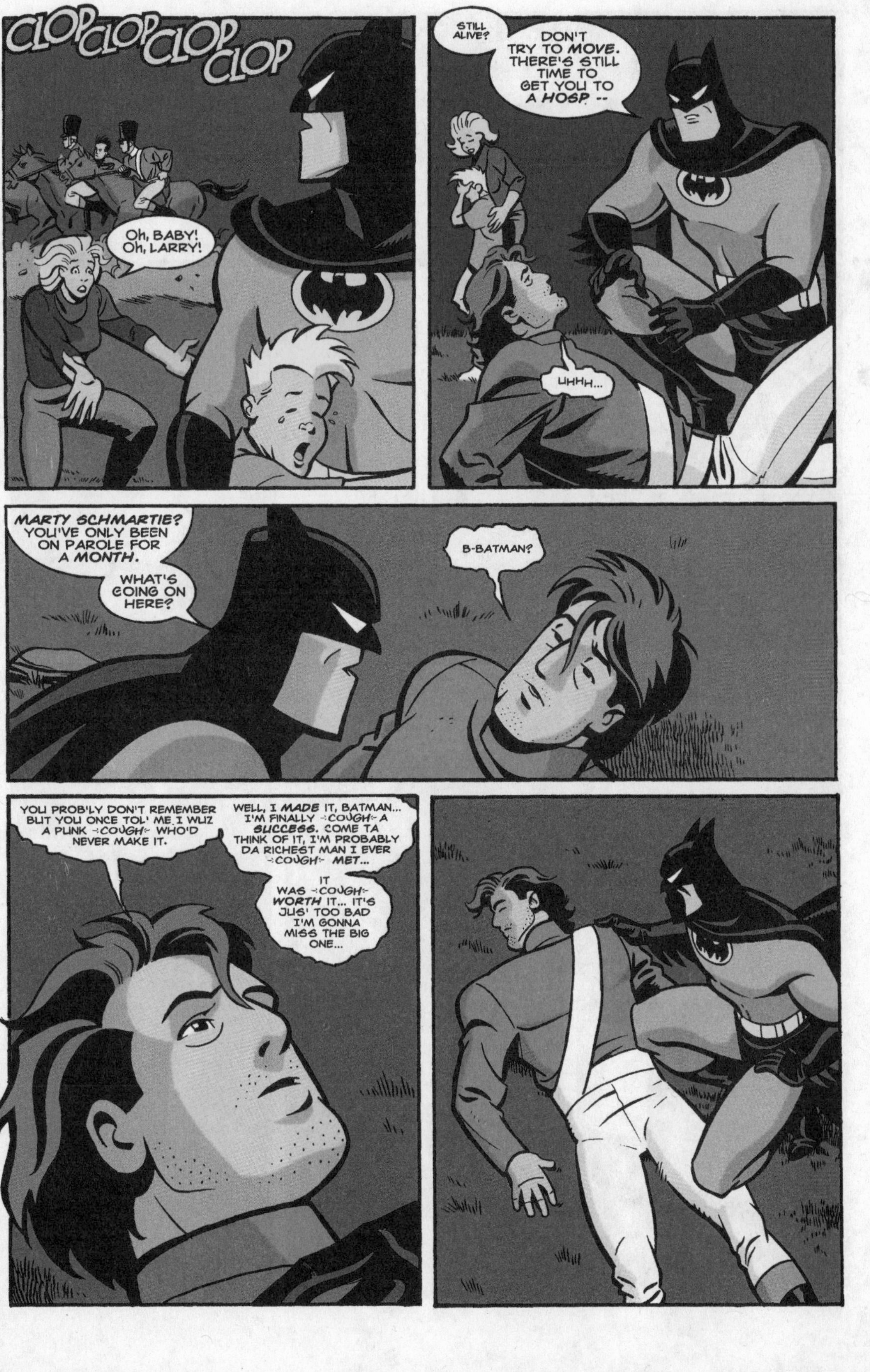
CLOP CLOP CLOP CLOP
Oh, BABY! Oh, LARRY!
STILL ALIVE?
DON'T TRY TO MOVE. THERE'S STILL TIME TO GET YOU TO A HOSP. --
UHHH...
MARTY SCHMARTIE? YOU'VE ONLY BEEN ON PAROLE FOR A MONTH.
WHAT'S GOING ON HERE?
B-BATMAN?
YOU PROB'LY DON'T REMEMBER BUT YOU ONCE TOL' ME I WUZ A PUNK -COUGH- WHO'D NEVER MAKE IT.
WELL, I MADE IT, BATMAN... I'M FINALLY -COUGH- A SUCCESS. COME TA THINK OF IT, I'M PROBABLY DA RICHEST MAN I EVER -COUGH- MET...
IT WAS -COUGH- WORTH IT... IT'S JUS' TOO BAD I'M GONNA MISS THE BIG ONE...

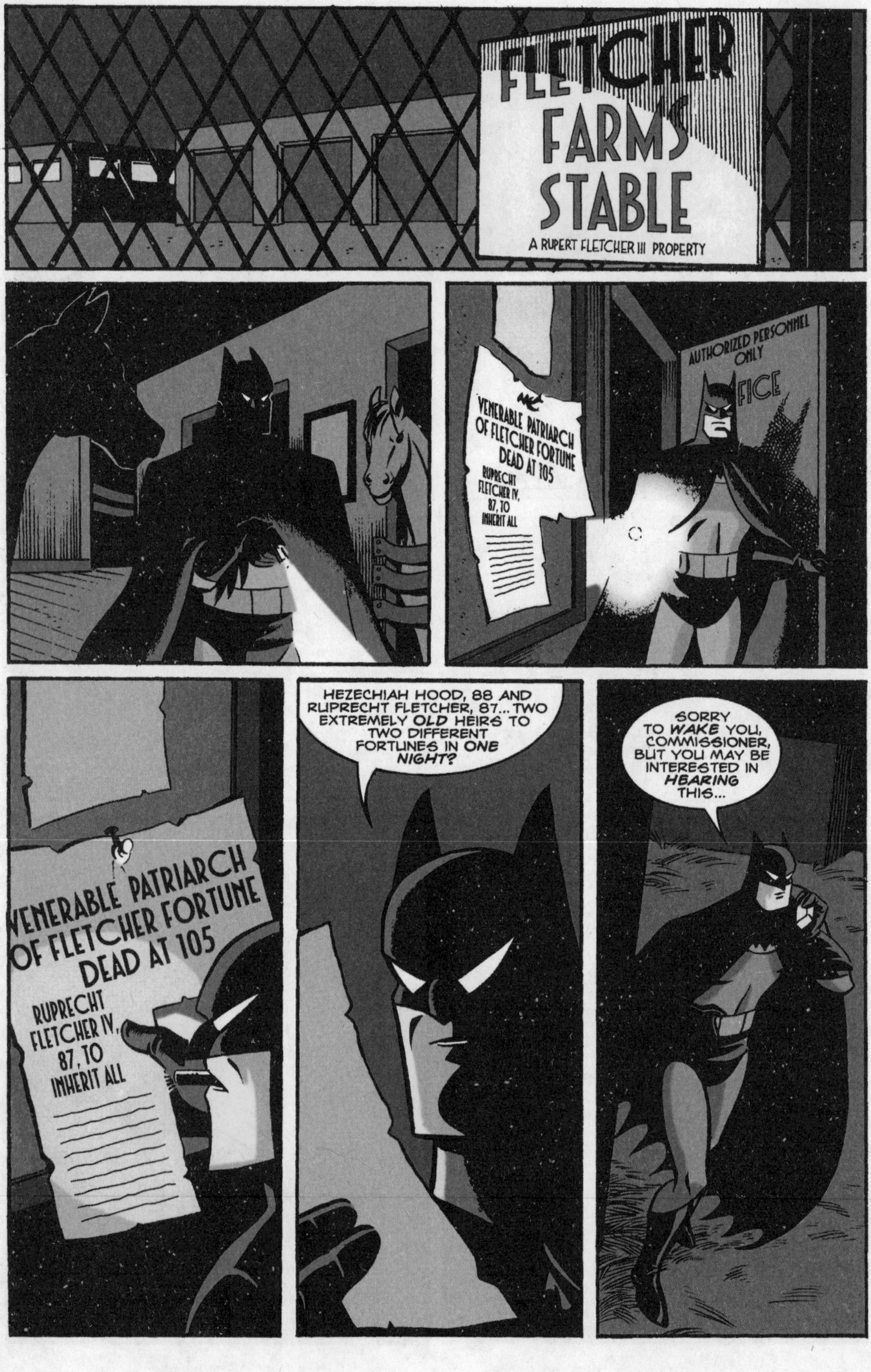
FLETCHER FARMS STABLE
A RUPERT FLETCHER III PROPERTY
VENERABLE PATRIARCH OF FLETCHER FORTUNE DEAD AT 105
RUPRECHT FLETCHER IV, 87, TO INHERIT ALL
AUTHORIZED PERSONNEL ONLY
FICE
VENERABLE PATRIARCH OF FLETCHER FORTUNE DEAD AT 105
RUPRECHT FLETCHER IV, 87, TO INHERIT ALL
HEZECHIAH HOOD, 88 AND RUPRECHT FLETCHER, 87... TWO EXTREMELY OLD HEIRS TO TWO DIFFERENT FORTUNES IN ONE NIGHT?
SORRY TO WAKE YOU, COMMISSIONER, BUT YOU MAY BE INTERESTED IN HEARING THIS...

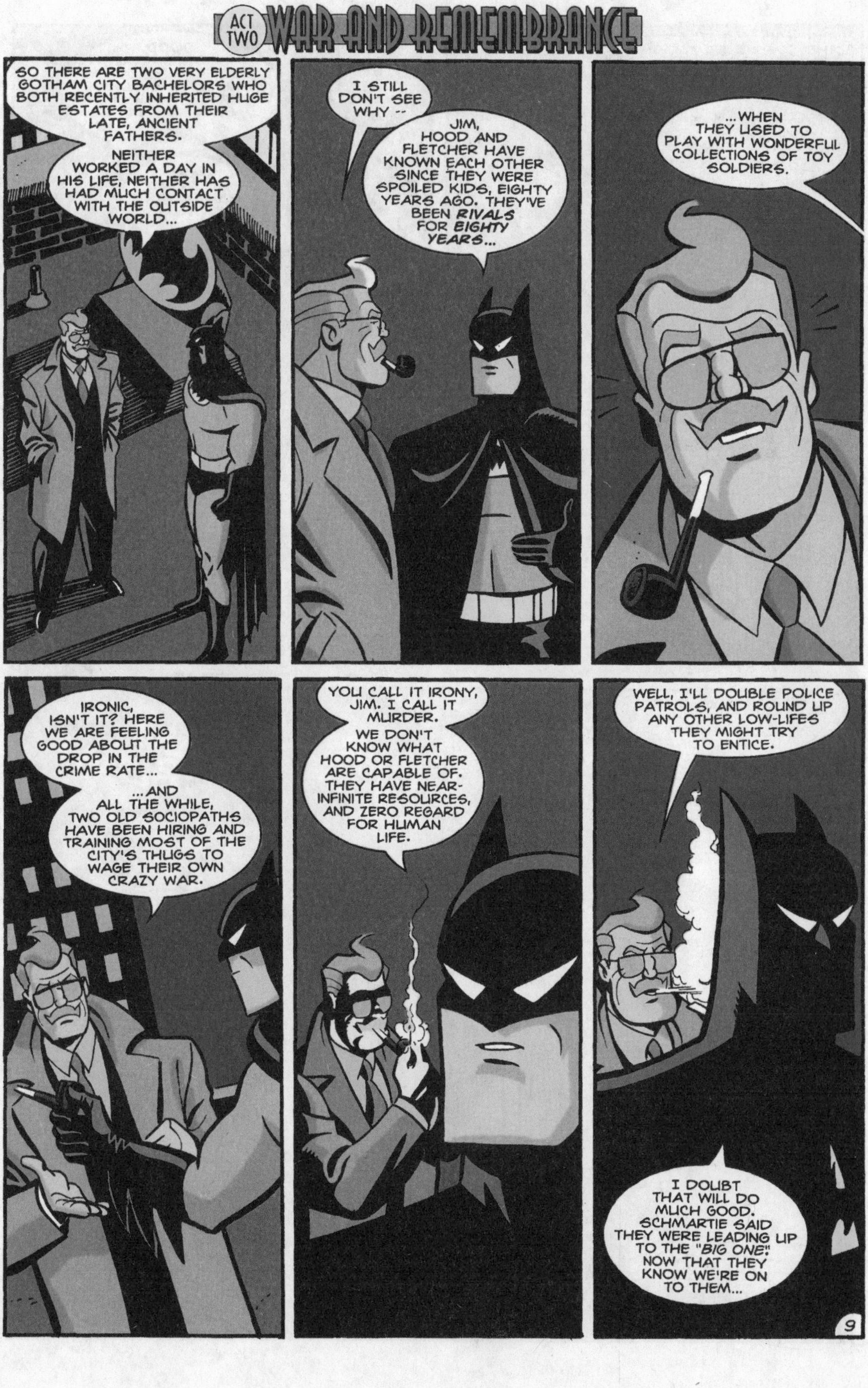
ACT TWO WAR AND REMEMBRANCE
SO THERE ARE TWO VERY ELDERLY GOTHAM CITY BACHELORS WHO BOTH RECENTLY INHERITED HUGE ESTATES FROM THEIR LATE, ANCIENT FATHERS.
NEITHER WORKED A DAY IN HIS LIFE, NEITHER HAS HAD MUCH CONTACT WITH THE OUTSIDE WORLD...
I STILL DON'T SEE WHY --
JIM, HOOD AND FLETCHER HAVE KNOWN EACH OTHER SINCE THEY WERE SPOILED KIDS, EIGHTY YEARS AGO. THEY'VE BEEN RIVALS FOR EIGHTY YEARS...
...WHEN THEY USED TO PLAY WITH WONDERFUL COLLECTIONS OF TOY SOLDIERS.
IRONIC, ISN'T IT? HERE WE ARE FEELING GOOD ABOUT THE DROP IN THE CRIME RATE...
...AND ALL THE WHILE, TWO OLD SOCIOPATHS HAVE BEEN HIRING AND TRAINING MOST OF THE CITY'S THUGS TO WAGE THEIR OWN CRAZY WAR.
YOU CALL IT IRONY, JIM. I CALL IT MURDER.
WE DON'T KNOW WHAT HOOD OR FLETCHER ARE CAPABLE OF. THEY HAVE NEAR-INFINITE RESOURCES, AND ZERO REGARD FOR HUMAN LIFE.
WELL, I'LL DOUBLE POLICE PATROLS, AND ROUND UP ANY OTHER LOW-LIFES THEY MIGHT TRY TO ENTICE.
I DOUBT THAT WILL DO MUCH GOOD. SCHMARTIE SAID THEY WERE LEADING UP TO THE "BIG ONE." NOW THAT THEY KNOW WE'RE ON TO THEM...
9

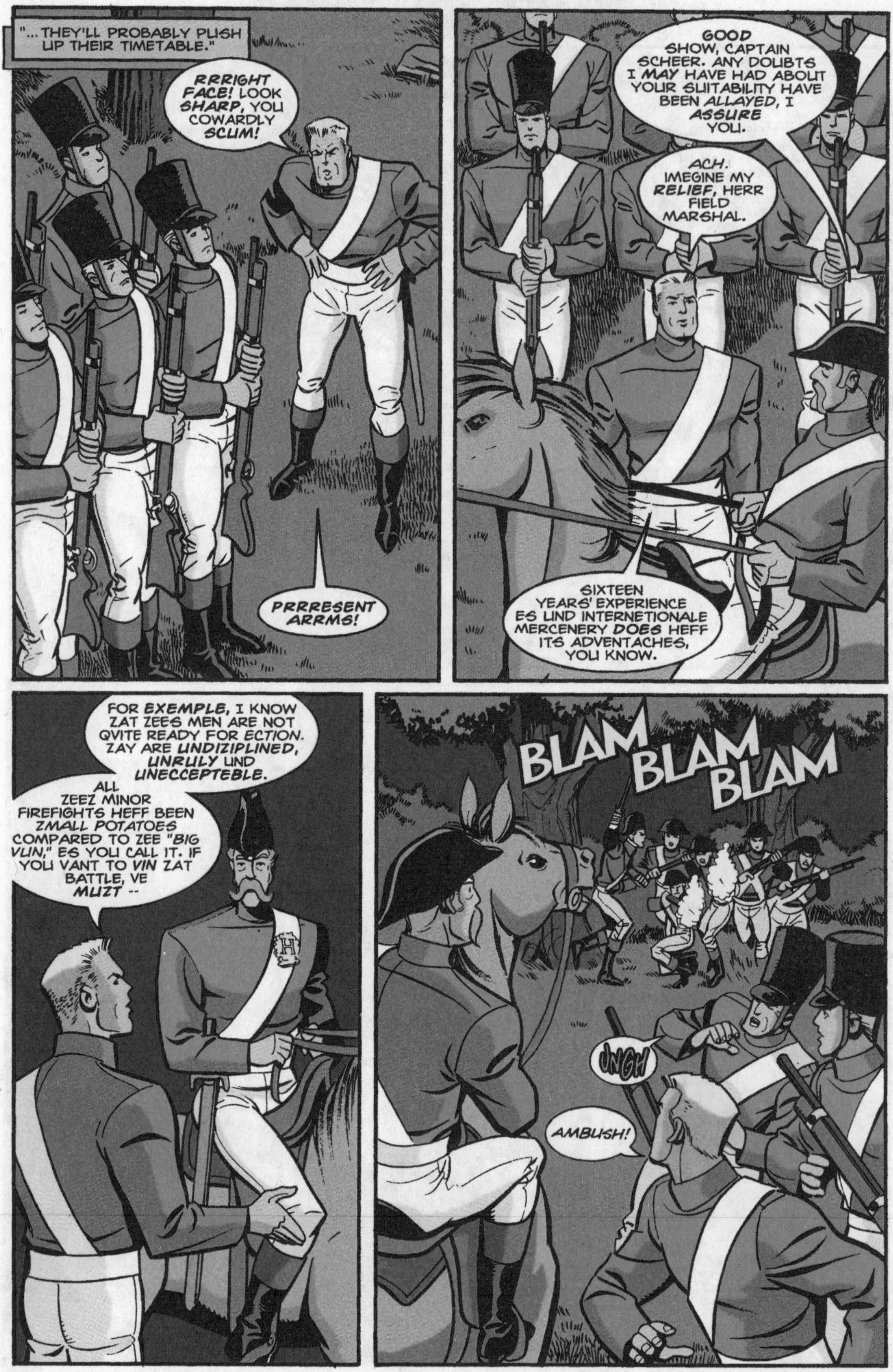
"... THEY'LL PROBABLY PUSH UP THEIR TIMETABLE."
RRRIGHT FACE! LOOK SHARP, YOU COWARDLY SCUM!
PRRRESENT ARRMS!
GOOD SHOW, CAPTAIN SCHEER. ANY DOUBTS I MAY HAVE HAD ABOUT YOUR SUITABILITY HAVE BEEN ALLAYED, I ASSURE YOU.
ACH. IMEGINE MY RELIEF, HERR FIELD MARSHAL.
SIXTEEN YEARS' EXPERIENCE ES UND INTERNETIONALE MERCENERY DOES HEFF ITS ADVENTACHES, YOU KNOW.
FOR EXEMPLE, I KNOW ZAT ZEES MEN ARE NOT QVITE READY FOR ECTION. ZAY ARE UNDIZIPLINED, UNRULY UND UNECCEPTEBLE.
ALL ZEEZ MINOR FIREFIGHTS HEFF BEEN ZMALL POTATOES COMPARED TO ZEE "BIG VUN," ES YOU CALL IT. IF YOU VANT TO VIN ZAT BATTLE, VE MUZT --
BLAM BLAM BLAM
UNGH
AMBUSH!

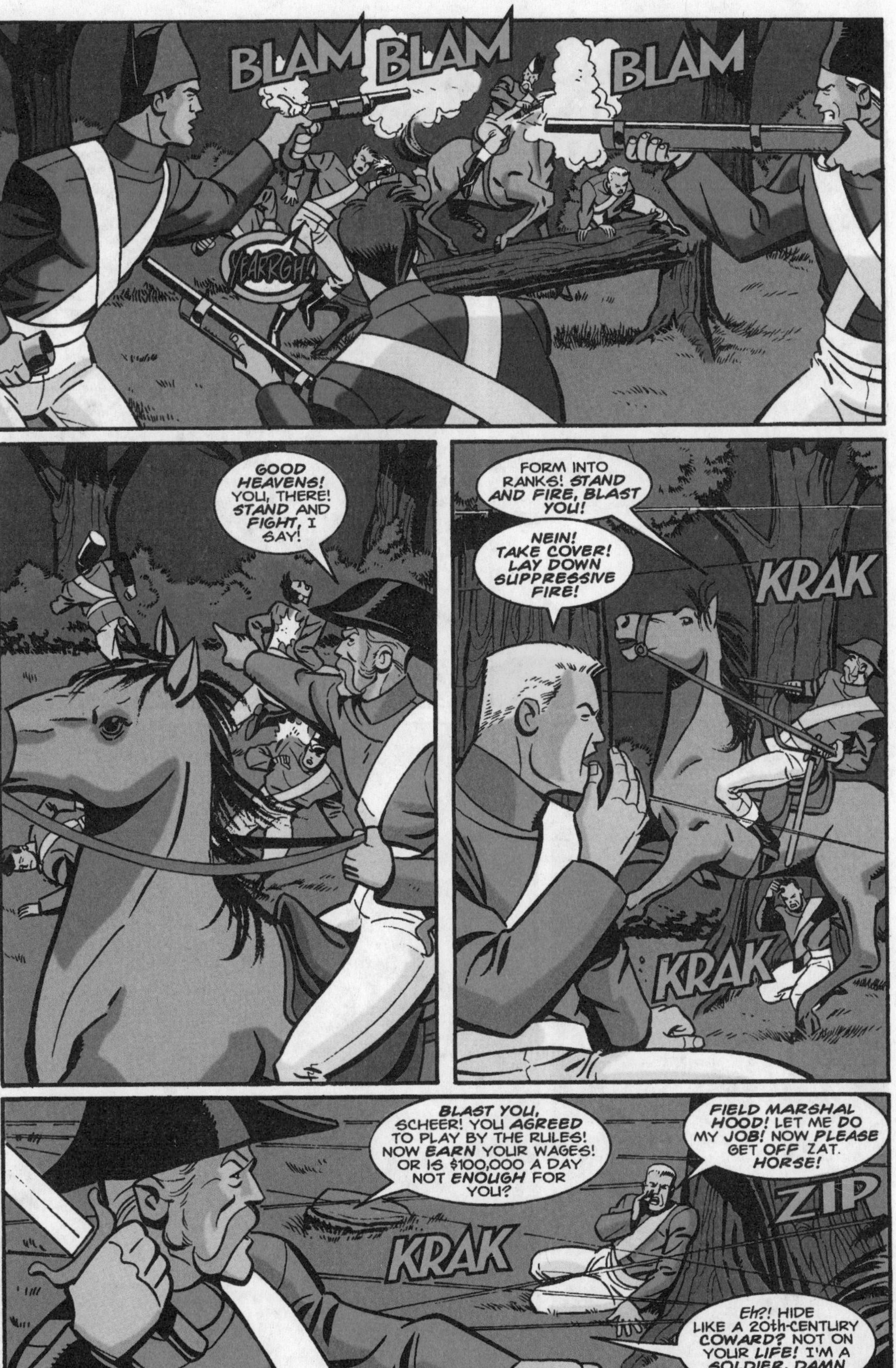
BLAM BLAM
BLAM
YEARRGH!
GOOD HEAVENS! YOU, THERE! STAND AND FIGHT, I SAY!
FORM INTO RANKS! STAND AND FIRE, BLAST YOU!
NEIN! TAKE COVER! LAY DOWN SUPPRESSIVE FIRE!
KRAK
KRAK
BLAST YOU, SCHEER! YOU AGREED TO PLAY BY THE RULES! NOW EARN YOUR WAGES! OR IS $100,000 A DAY NOT ENOUGH FOR YOU?
FIELD MARSHAL HOOD! LET ME DO MY JOB! NOW PLEASE GET OFF ZAT HORSE!
ZIP
KRAK
Eh?! HIDE LIKE A 20th-CENTURY COWARD? NOT ON YOUR LIFE! I'M A SOLDIER, DAMN YOU!

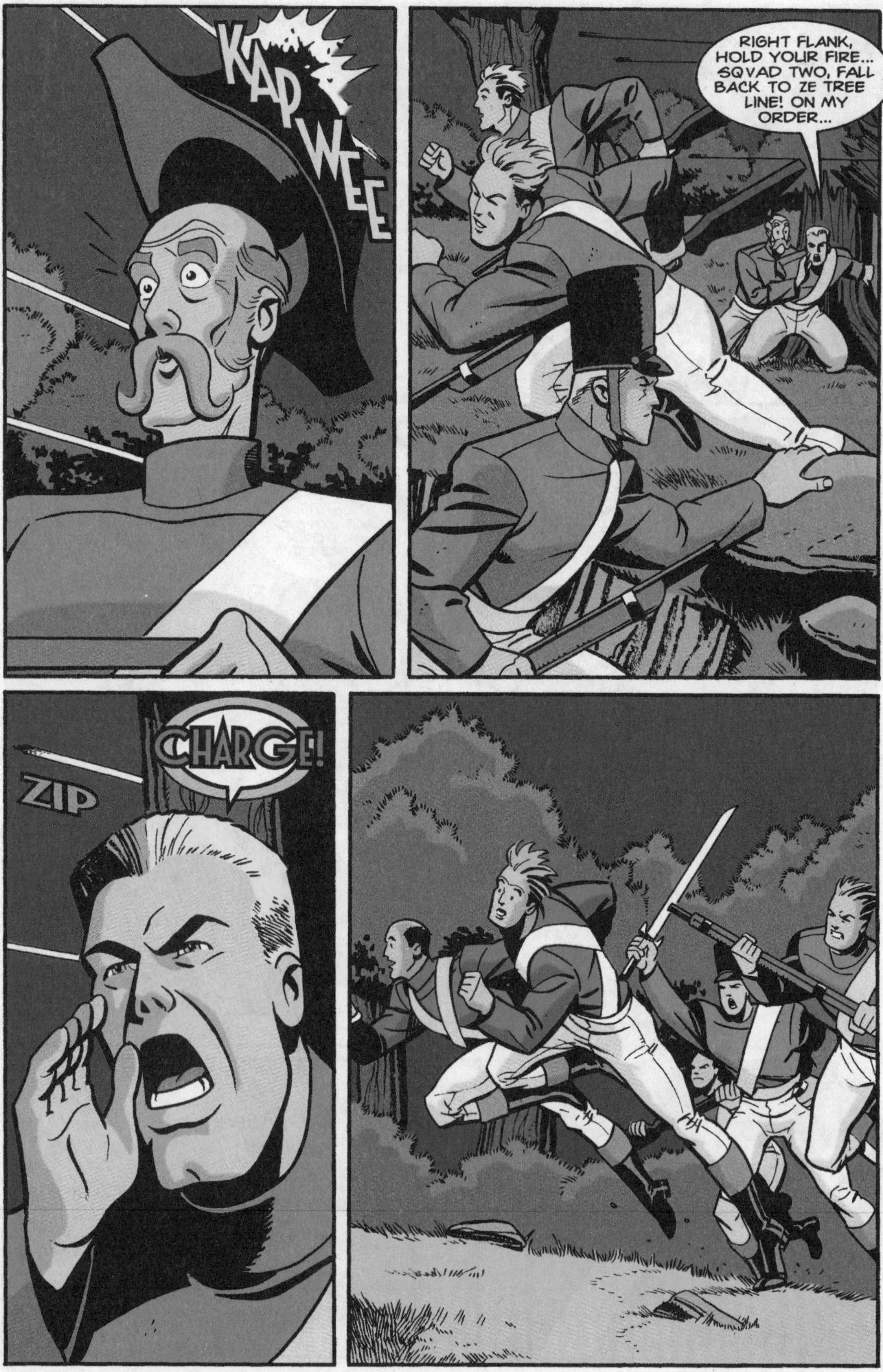
KAP WEEE
RIGHT FLANK, HOLD YOUR FIRE... SQVAD TWO, FALL BACK TO ZE TREE LINE! ON MY ORDER...
ZIP
CHARGE!

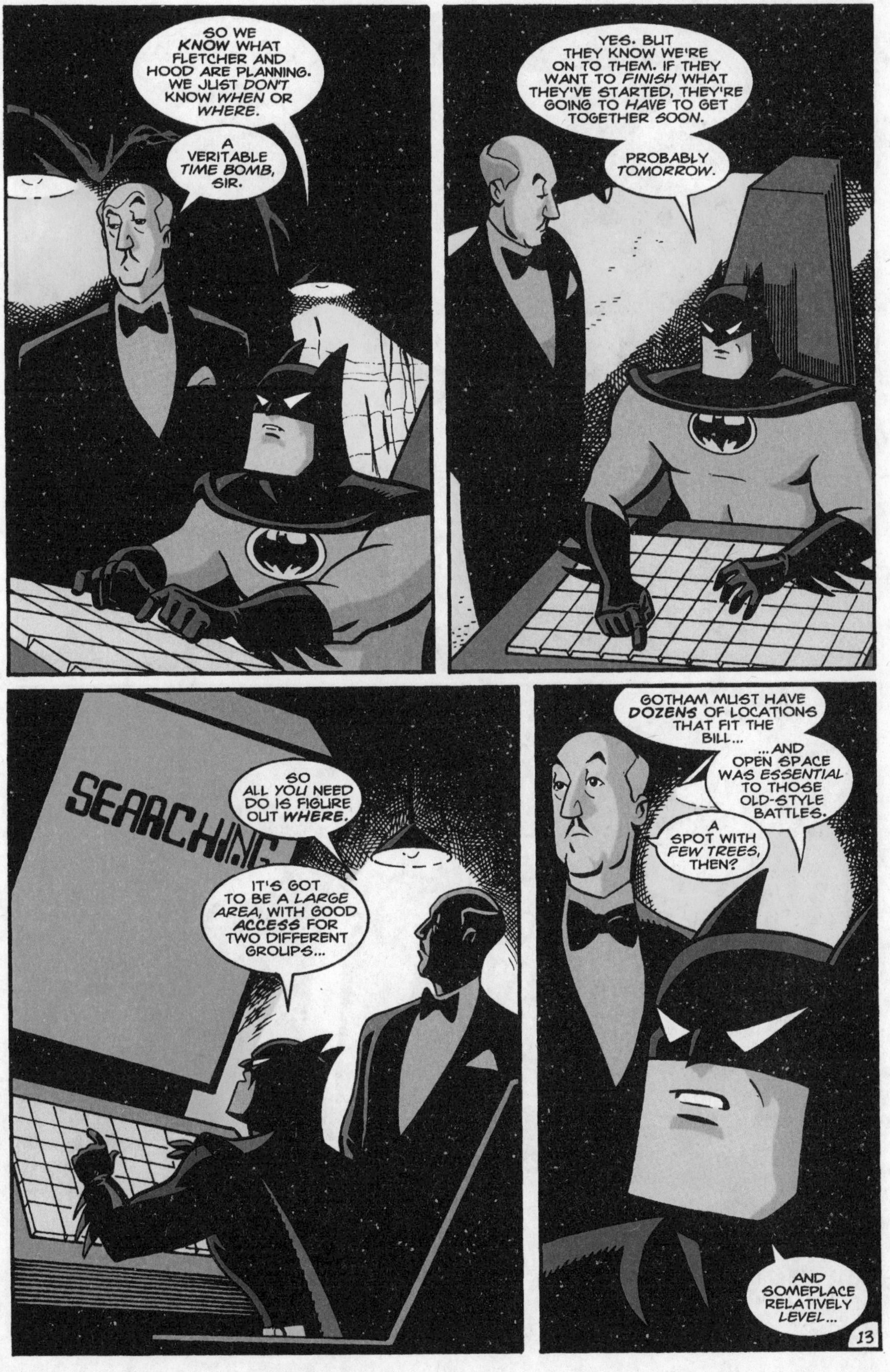
SO WE KNOW WHAT FLETCHER AND HOOD ARE PLANNING. WE JUST DON'T KNOW WHEN OR WHERE.
A VERITABLE TIME BOMB, SIR.
YES. BUT THEY KNOW WE'RE ON TO THEM. IF THEY WANT TO FINISH WHAT THEY'VE STARTED, THEY'RE GOING TO HAVE TO GET TOGETHER SOON.
PROBABLY TOMORROW.
SEARCHING
SO ALL YOU NEED DO IS FIGURE OUT WHERE.
IT'S GOT TO BE A LARGE AREA, WITH GOOD ACCESS FOR TWO DIFFERENT GROUPS...
GOTHAM MUST HAVE DOZENS OF LOCATIONS THAT FIT THE BILL...
...AND OPEN SPACE WAS ESSENTIAL TO THOSE OLD-STYLE BATTLES.
A SPOT WITH FEW TREES, THEN?
AND SOMEPLACE RELATIVELY LEVEL...

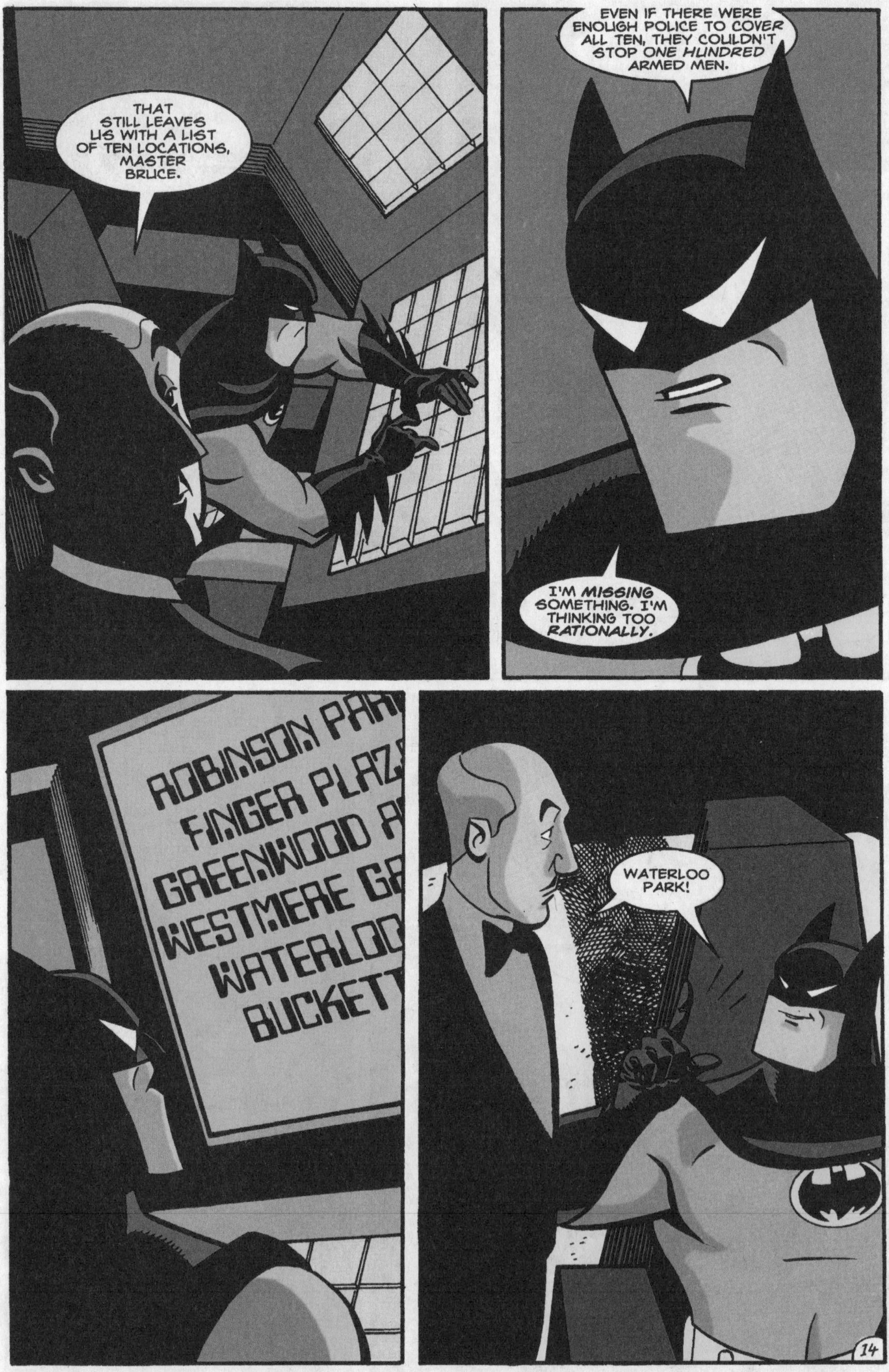
THAT STILL LEAVES US WITH A LIST OF TEN LOCATIONS, MASTER BRUCE.
EVEN IF THERE WERE ENOUGH POLICE TO COVER ALL TEN, THEY COULDN'T STOP ONE *HUNDRED* ARMED MEN.
I'M *MISSING* SOMETHING. I'M THINKING TOO *RATIONALLY*.
ROBINSON PAR
FINGER PLAZ
GREENWOOD A
WESTMERE G
WATERLOO
BUCKETT
WATERLOO PARK!

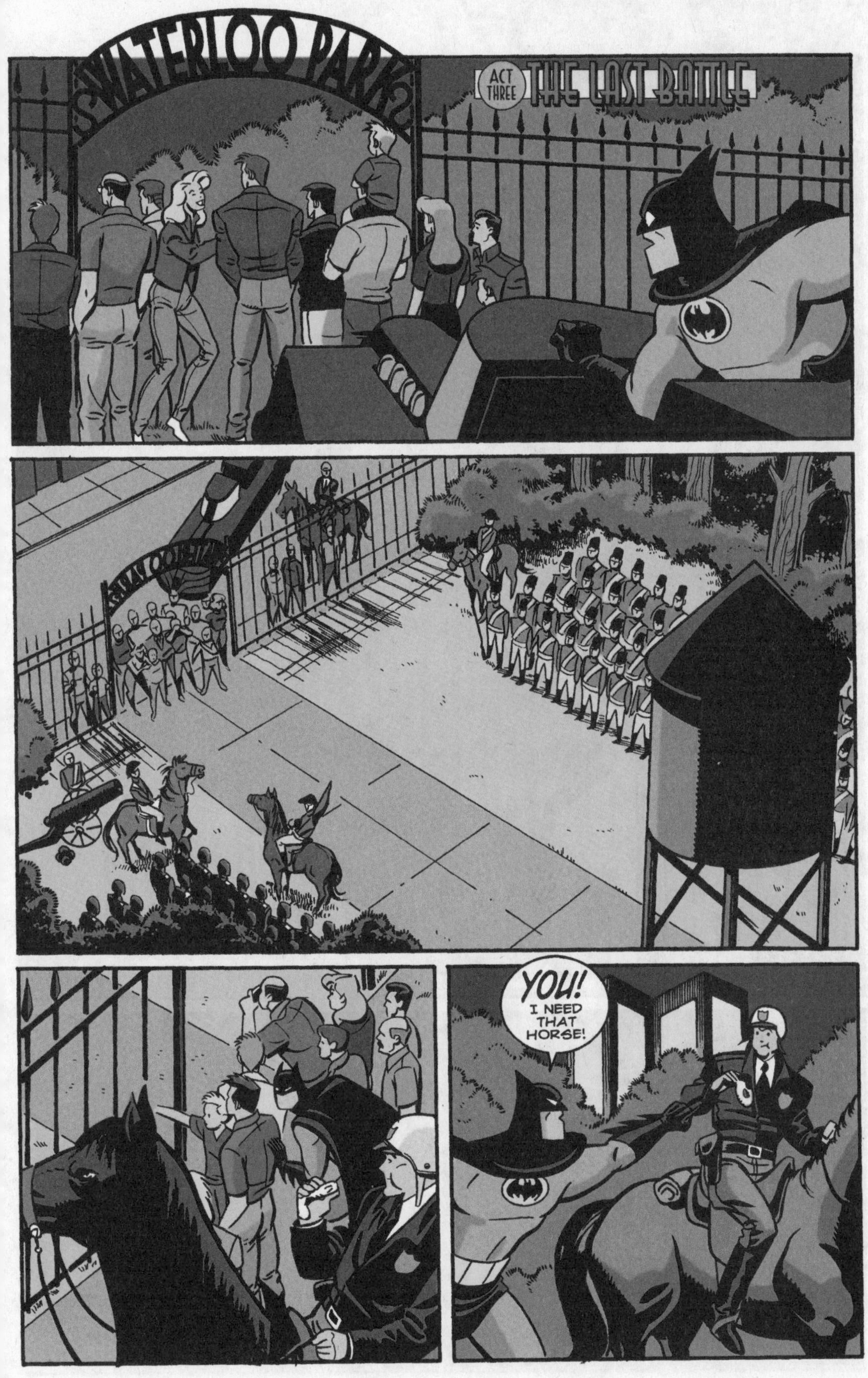
WATERLOO PARK
ACT THREE
THE LAST BATTLE
YOU!
I NEED THAT HORSE!

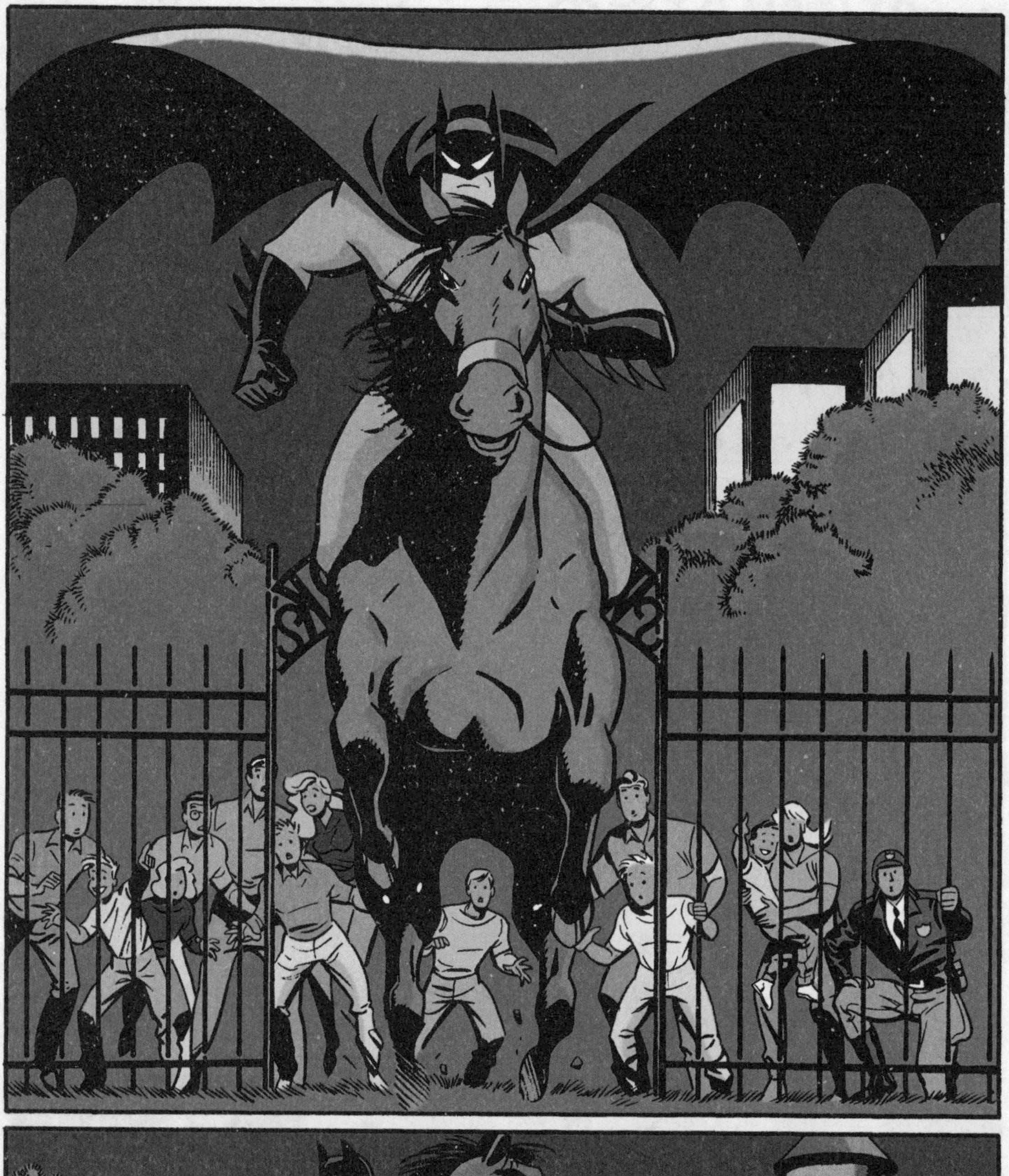
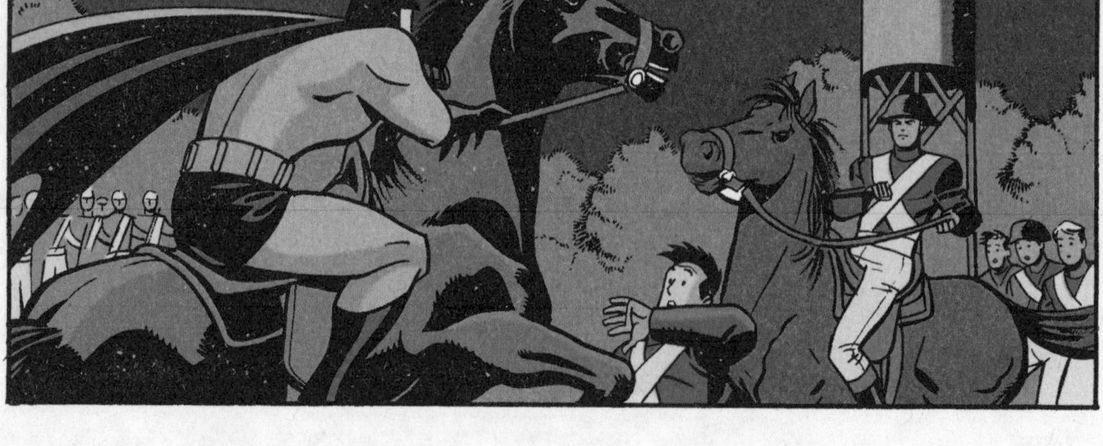

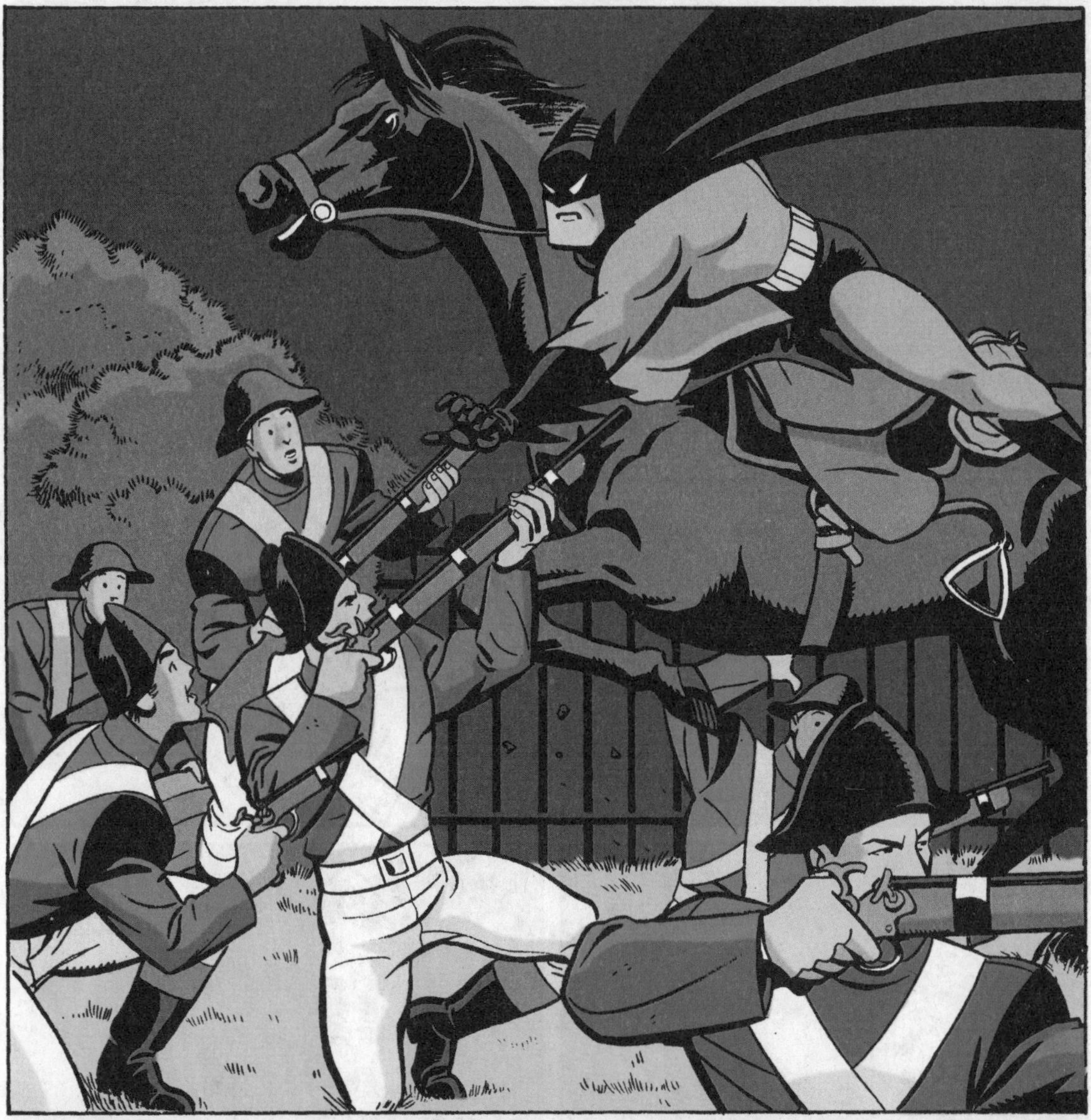

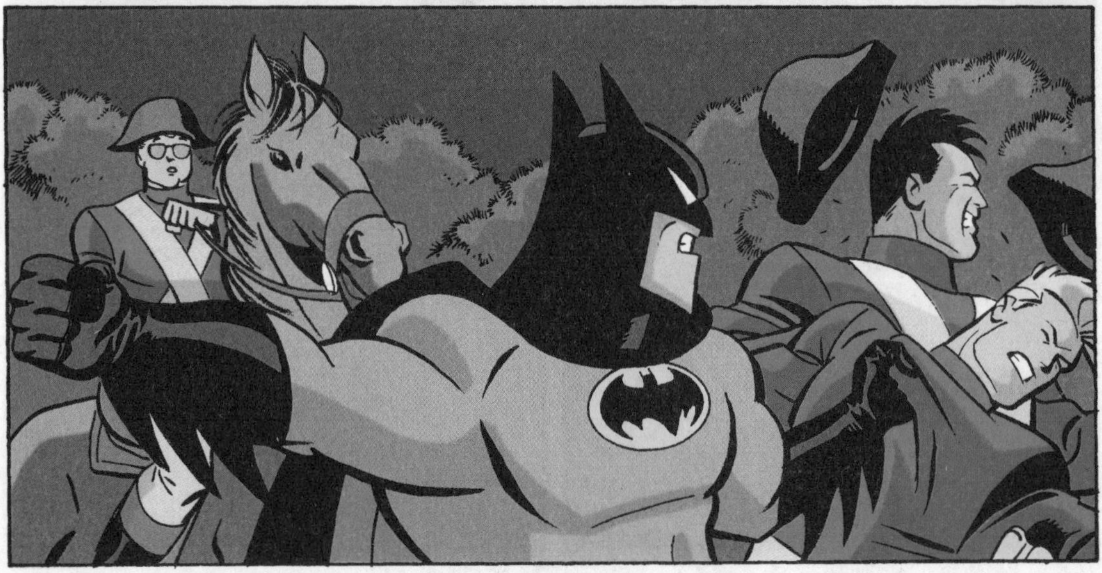

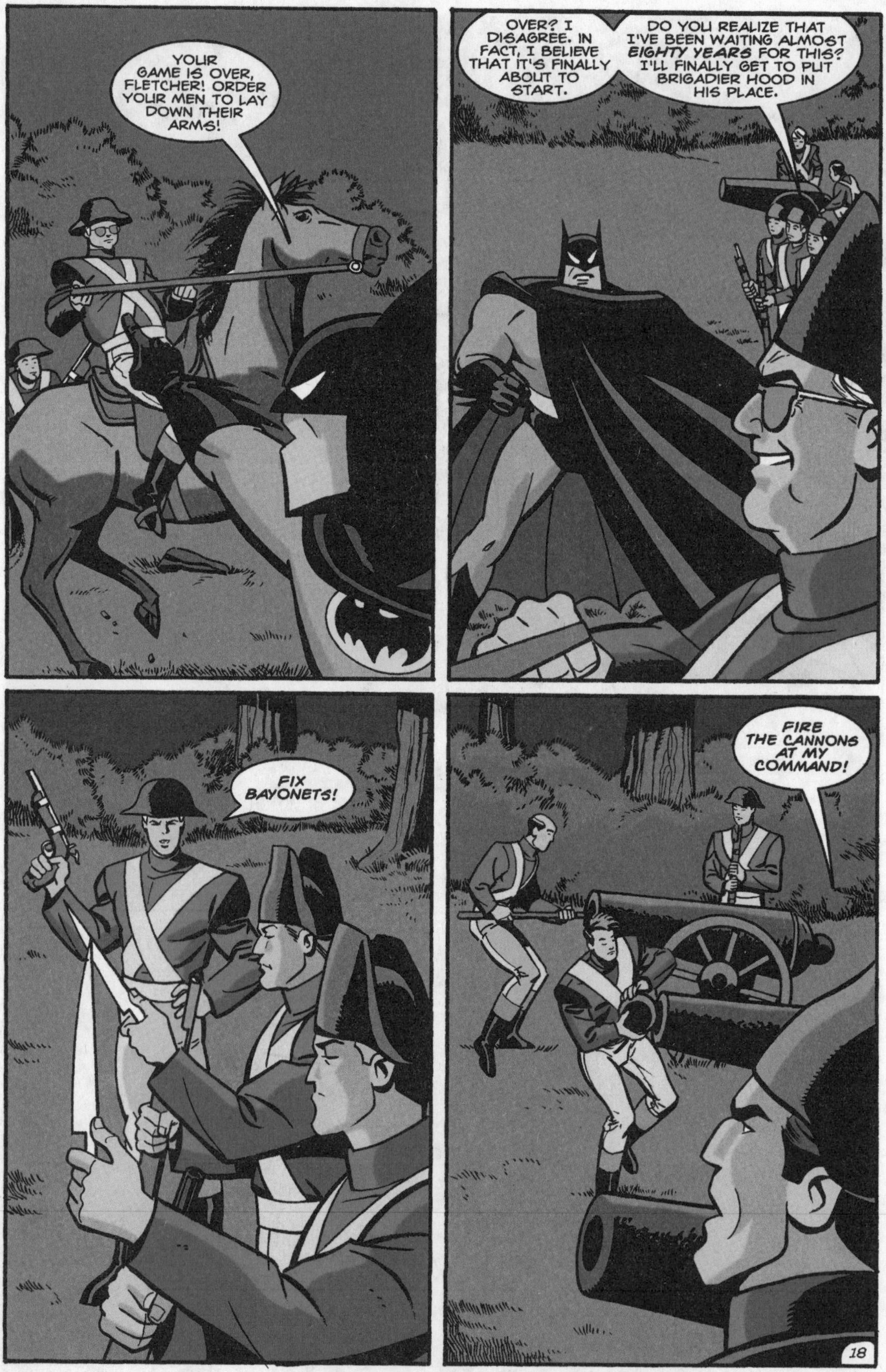
YOUR GAME IS OVER, FLETCHER! ORDER YOUR MEN TO LAY DOWN THEIR ARMS!
OVER? I DISAGREE. IN FACT, I BELIEVE THAT IT'S FINALLY ABOUT TO START.
DO YOU REALIZE THAT I'VE BEEN WAITING ALMOST EIGHTY YEARS FOR THIS? I'LL FINALLY GET TO PUT BRIGADIER HOOD IN HIS PLACE.
FIX BAYONETS!
FIRE THE CANNONS AT MY COMMAND!

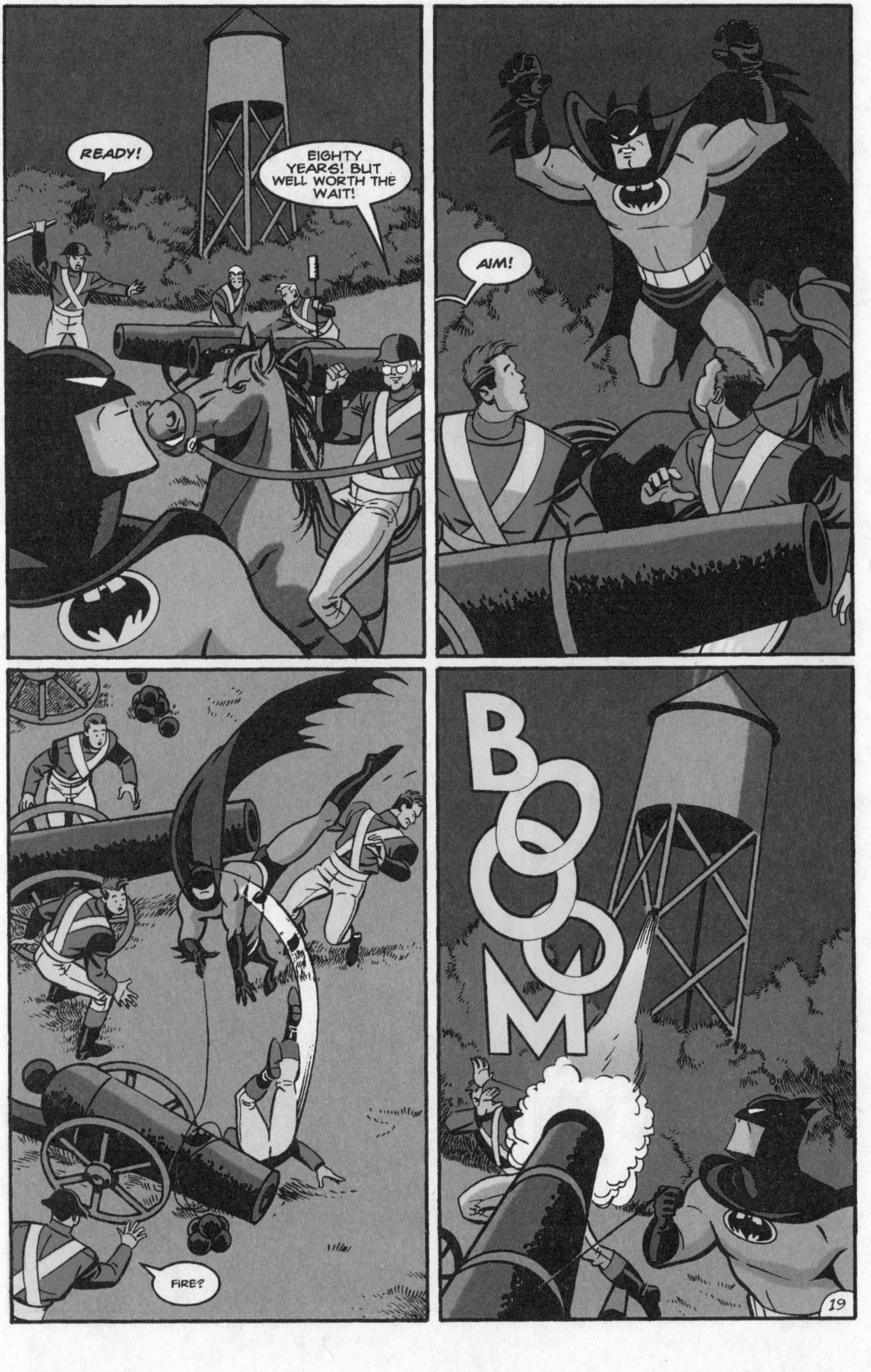
READY!
EIGHTY YEARS! BUT WELL WORTH THE WAIT!
AIM!
FIRE?
BOOOM

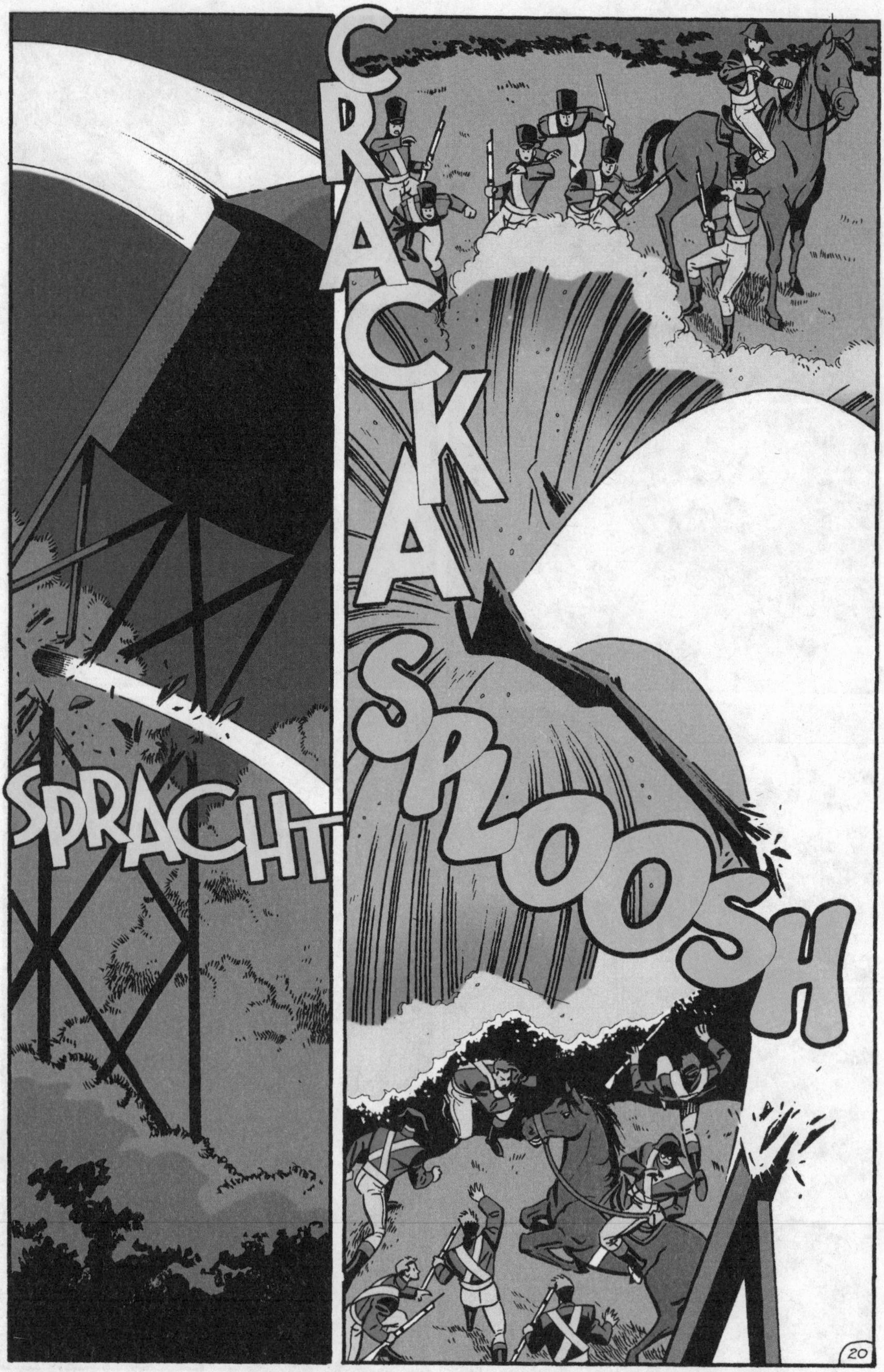
SPRACHT
CRACKA
SPLOOSH

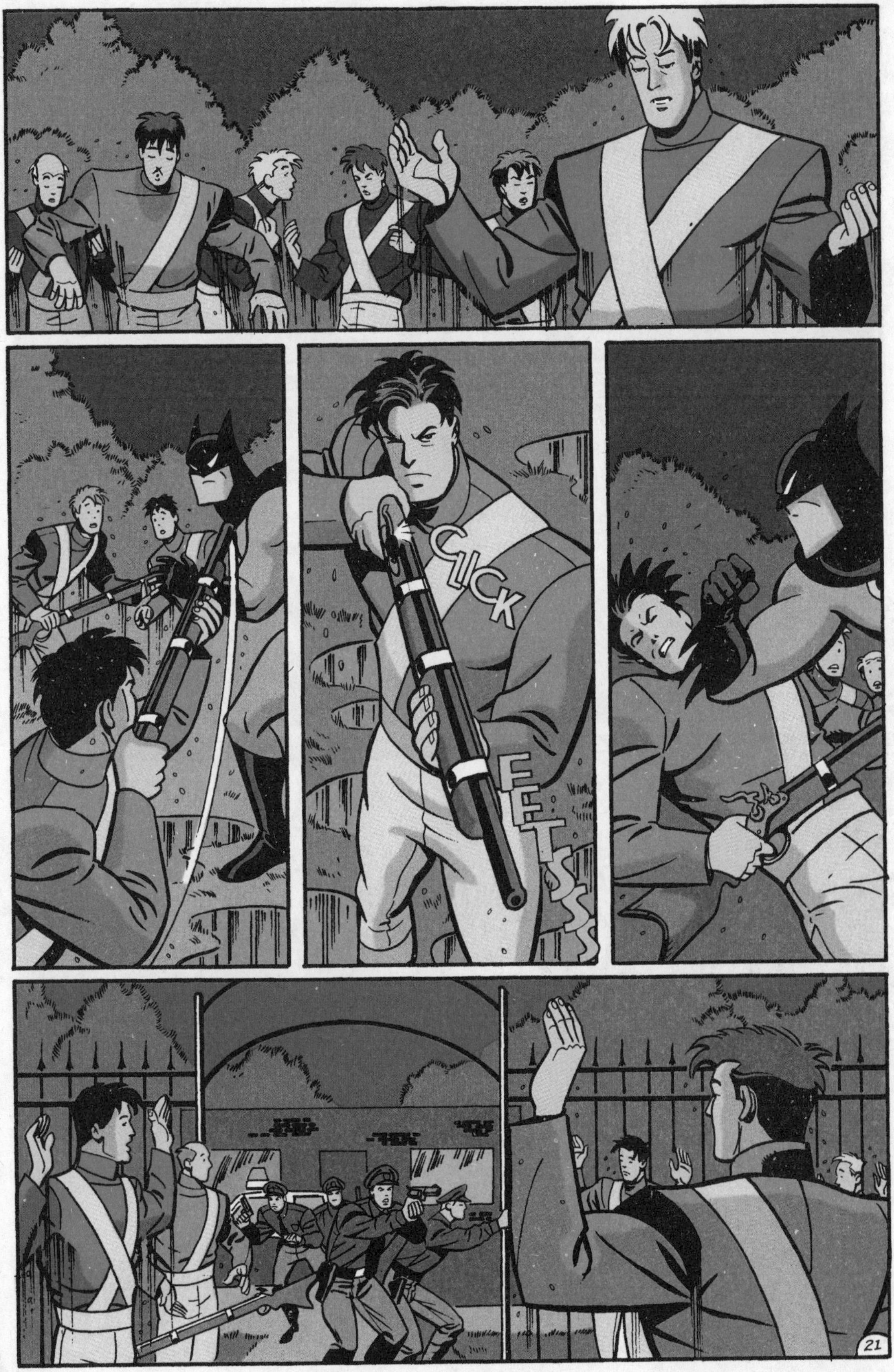
CLICK
FFTSSS

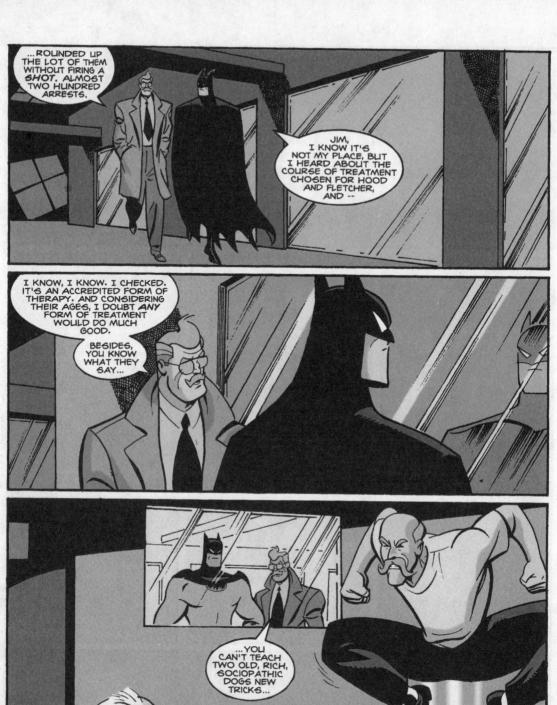

...ROUNDED UP THE LOT OF THEM WITHOUT FIRING A *SHOT*. ALMOST TWO HUNDRED ARRESTS.

JIM, I KNOW IT'S NOT MY PLACE, BUT I HEARD ABOUT THE COURSE OF TREATMENT CHOSEN FOR HOOD AND FLETCHER, AND --

I KNOW, I KNOW. I CHECKED. IT'S AN ACCREDITED FORM OF THERAPY. AND CONSIDERING THEIR AGES, I DOUBT *ANY* FORM OF TREATMENT WOULD DO MUCH GOOD.

BESIDES, YOU KNOW WHAT THEY SAY...

...YOU CAN'T TEACH TWO OLD, RICH, SOCIOPATHIC DOGS NEW TRICKS...

THE END

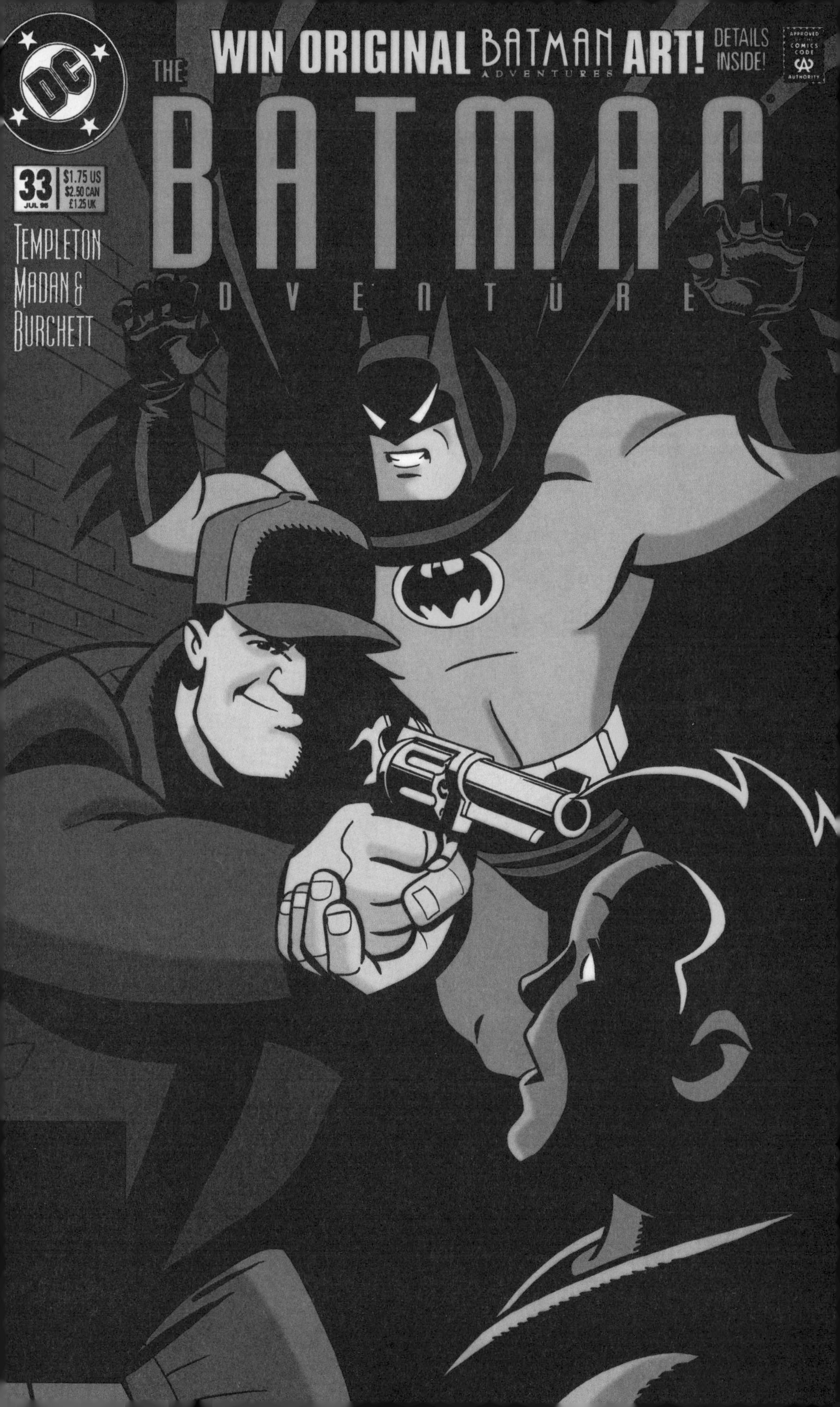

WIN ORIGINAL BATMAN ADVENTURES ART!
DETAILS INSIDE!
APPROVED BY THE COMICS CODE AUTHORITY
THE BATMAN ADVENTURES
33
$1.75 US
$2.50 CAN
£1.25 UK
TEMPLETON
MADAN &
BURCHETT

"HAVE YOU SET A DATE, SIR?"

"A DATE? FOR *WHAT?*"

"WELL THIS IS THE FOURTH TIME YOU AND MS. THOMAS HAVE GONE OUT SINCE YOU MET HER AT THE HOSPITAL FUND-RAISER THREE WEEKS AGO. FOR YOU, MASTER BRUCE, THAT IS PRACTICALLY *ENGAGED.*"

"SLOW DOWN, ALFRED. VERONICA AND I ARE STILL GETTING TO KNOW EACH OTHER; DON'T MARRY ME OFF *YET.*"

"YES, SIR. IT'S JUST THAT IT'S A PLEASANT SURPRISE TO SEE YOU TAKE AN INTEREST IN A WOMAN WHO'S SO... SUBSTANTIAL. AND HER SON JUST ADORES YOU."

JUST ANOTHER NIGHT

ACT ONE: DEJA VU

TY TEMPLETON	DEV MADAN	RICK BURCHETT
WRITER	PENCILLER	INKER

RICK TAYLOR	RICHARD STARKINGS AND COMICRAFT	DARREN VINCENZO	SCOTT PETERSON
COLORIST	LETTERING	ASSOCIATE EDITOR	EDITOR

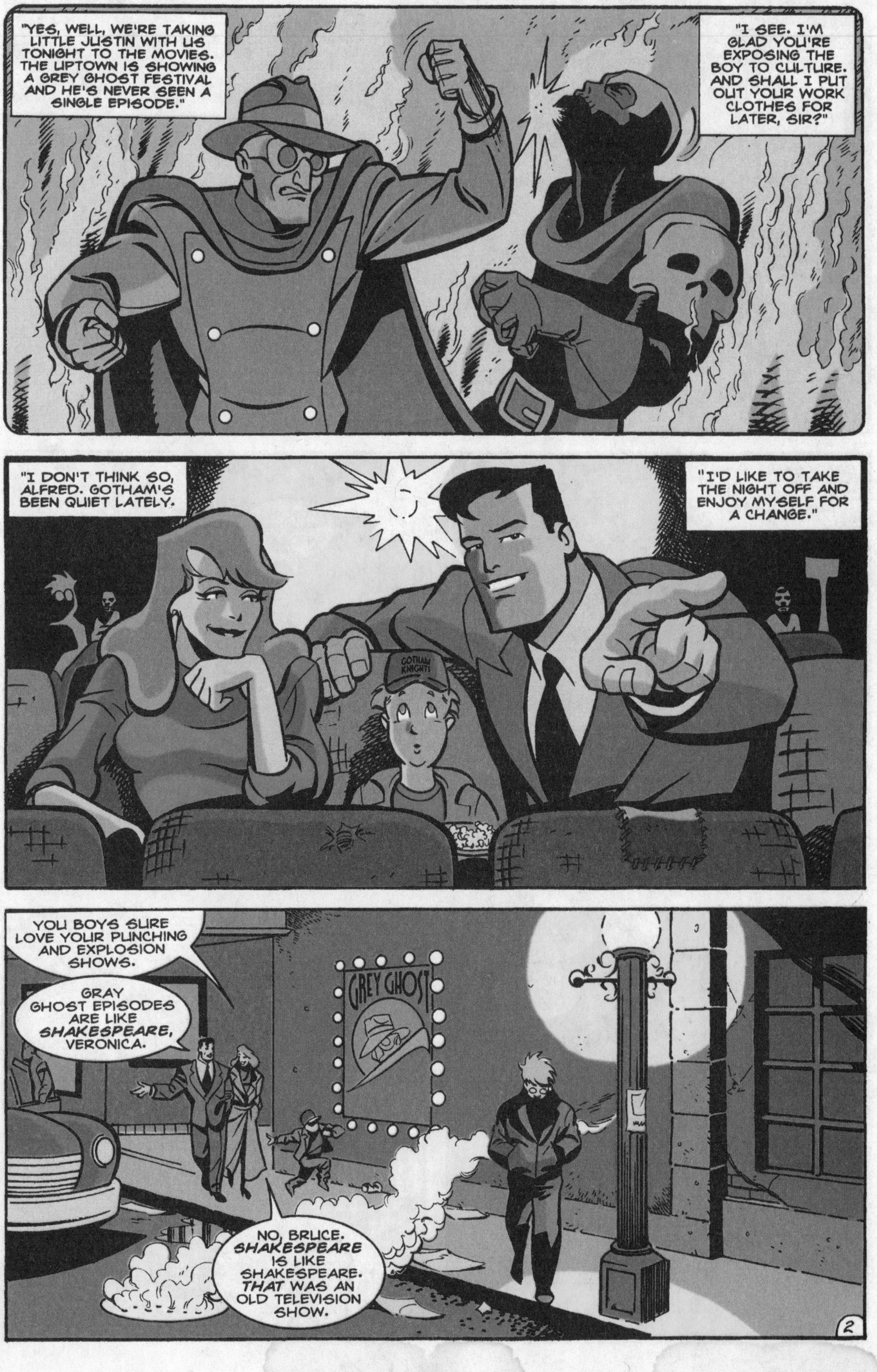
"YES, WELL, WE'RE TAKING LITTLE JUSTIN WITH US TONIGHT TO THE MOVIES. THE UPTOWN IS SHOWING A GREY GHOST FESTIVAL AND HE'S NEVER SEEN A SINGLE EPISODE."
"I SEE. I'M GLAD YOU'RE EXPOSING THE BOY TO CULTURE. AND SHALL I PUT OUT YOUR WORK CLOTHES FOR LATER, SIR?"
"I DON'T THINK SO, ALFRED. GOTHAM'S BEEN QUIET LATELY.
"I'D LIKE TO TAKE THE NIGHT OFF AND ENJOY MYSELF FOR A CHANGE."
GOTHAM KNIGHTS
YOU BOYS SURE LOVE YOUR PUNCHING AND EXPLOSION SHOWS.
GRAY GHOST EPISODES ARE LIKE *SHAKESPEARE,* VERONICA.
GREY GHOST
NO, BRUCE. *SHAKESPEARE* IS LIKE SHAKESPEARE. *THAT* WAS AN OLD TELEVISION SHOW.
2

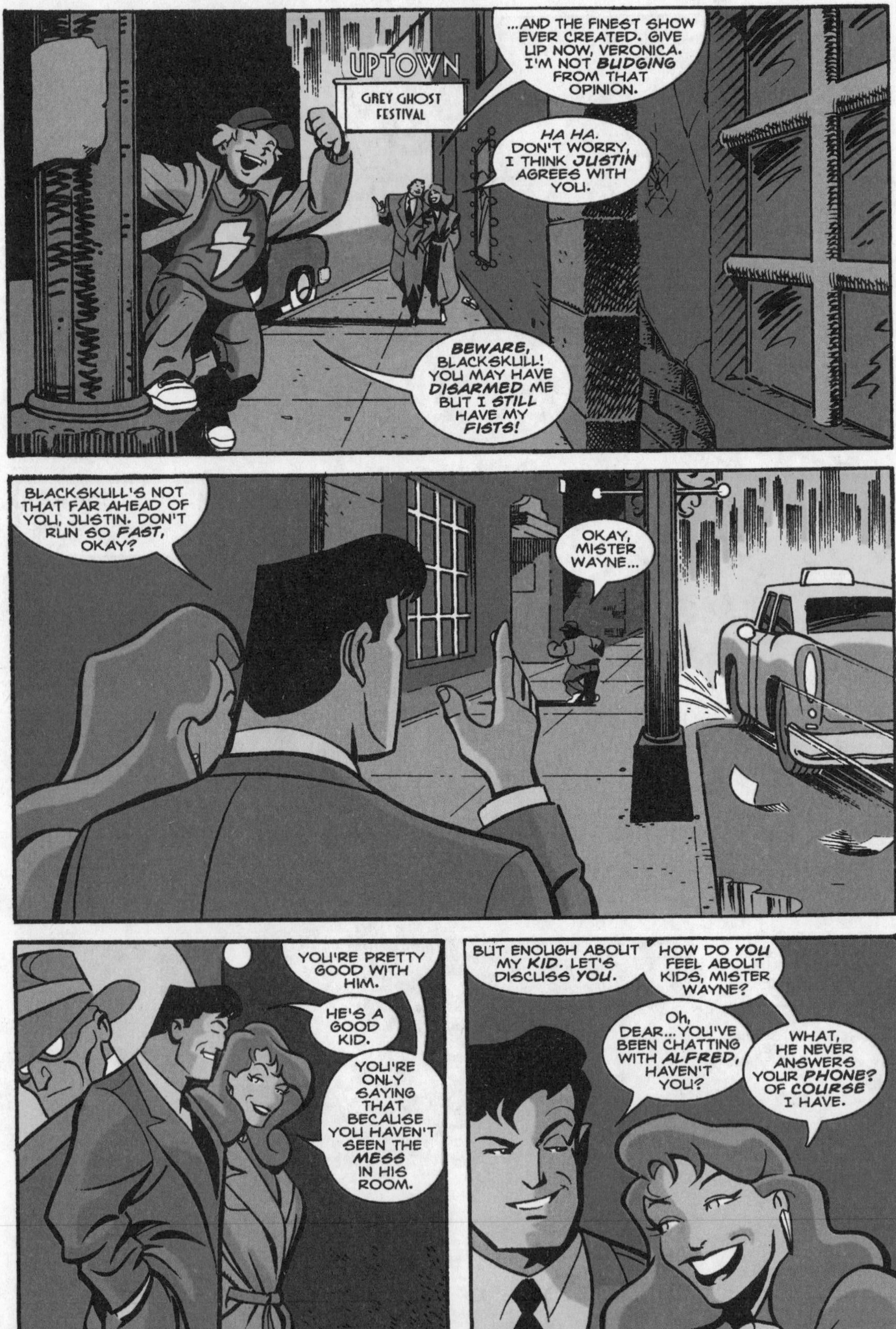
UPTOWN
GREY GHOST FESTIVAL
...AND THE FINEST SHOW EVER CREATED. GIVE UP NOW, VERONICA. I'M NOT BUDGING FROM THAT OPINION.
HA HA. DON'T WORRY, I THINK JUSTIN AGREES WITH YOU.
BEWARE, BLACKSKULL! YOU MAY HAVE DISARMED ME BUT I STILL HAVE MY FISTS!
BLACKSKULL'S NOT THAT FAR AHEAD OF YOU, JUSTIN. DON'T RUN SO FAST, OKAY?
OKAY, MISTER WAYNE...
YOU'RE PRETTY GOOD WITH HIM.
HE'S A GOOD KID.
YOU'RE ONLY SAYING THAT BECAUSE YOU HAVEN'T SEEN THE MESS IN HIS ROOM.
BUT ENOUGH ABOUT MY KID. LET'S DISCUSS YOU.
HOW DO YOU FEEL ABOUT KIDS, MISTER WAYNE?
Oh, DEAR...YOU'VE BEEN CHATTING WITH ALFRED, HAVEN'T YOU?
WHAT, HE NEVER ANSWERS YOUR PHONE? OF COURSE I HAVE.

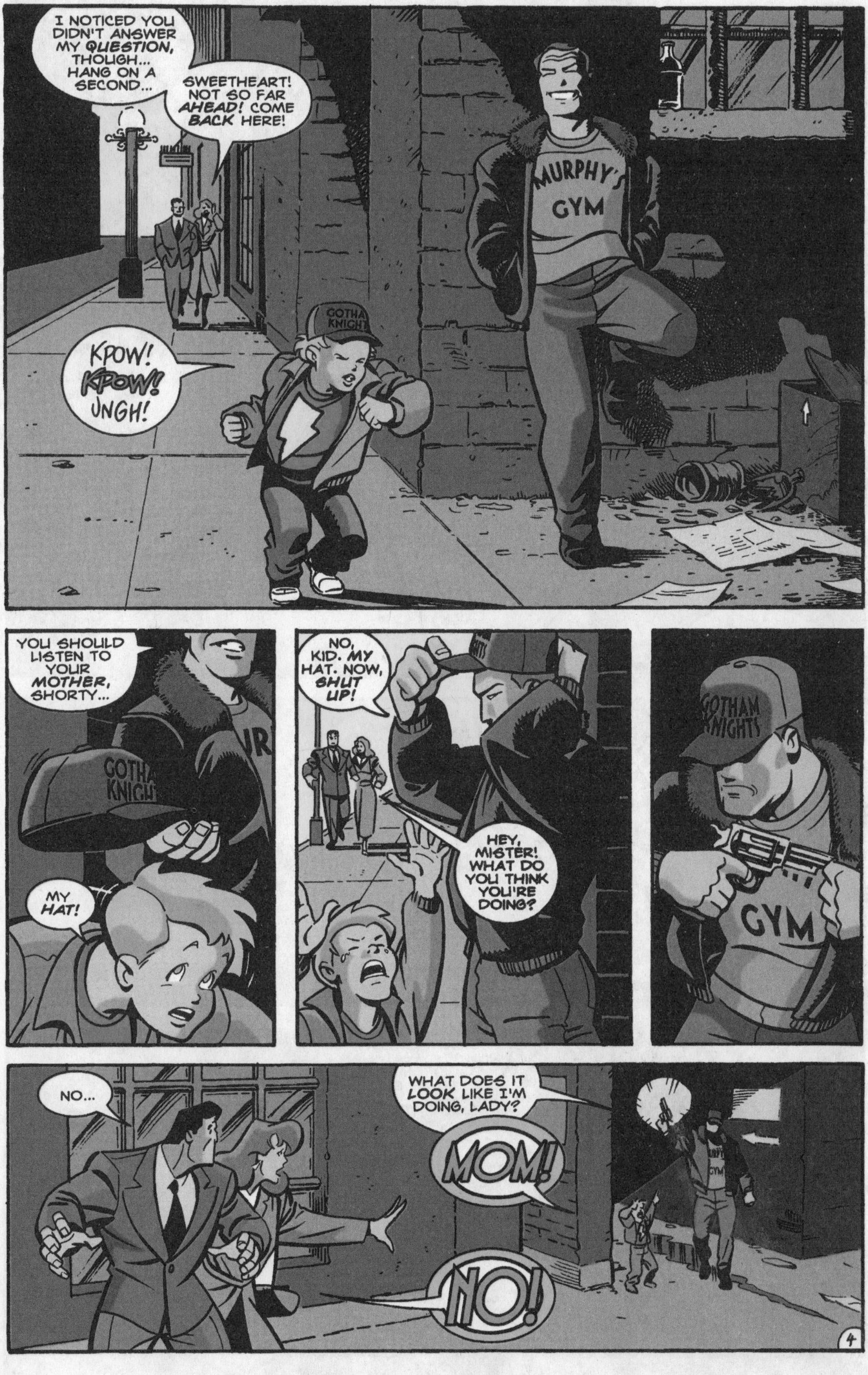
I NOTICED YOU DIDN'T ANSWER MY QUESTION, THOUGH... HANG ON A SECOND...
SWEETHEART! NOT SO FAR AHEAD! COME BACK HERE!
MURPHY'S GYM
GOTHAM KNIGHT
KPOW! KPOW! UNGH!
YOU SHOULD LISTEN TO YOUR MOTHER, SHORTY...
GOTHAM KNIGHT
MY HAT!
NO, KID. MY HAT. NOW, SHUT UP!
HEY, MISTER! WHAT DO YOU THINK YOU'RE DOING?
GOTHAM KNIGHTS
GYM
NO...
WHAT DOES IT LOOK LIKE I'M DOING, LADY?
MOM!
NO!
4

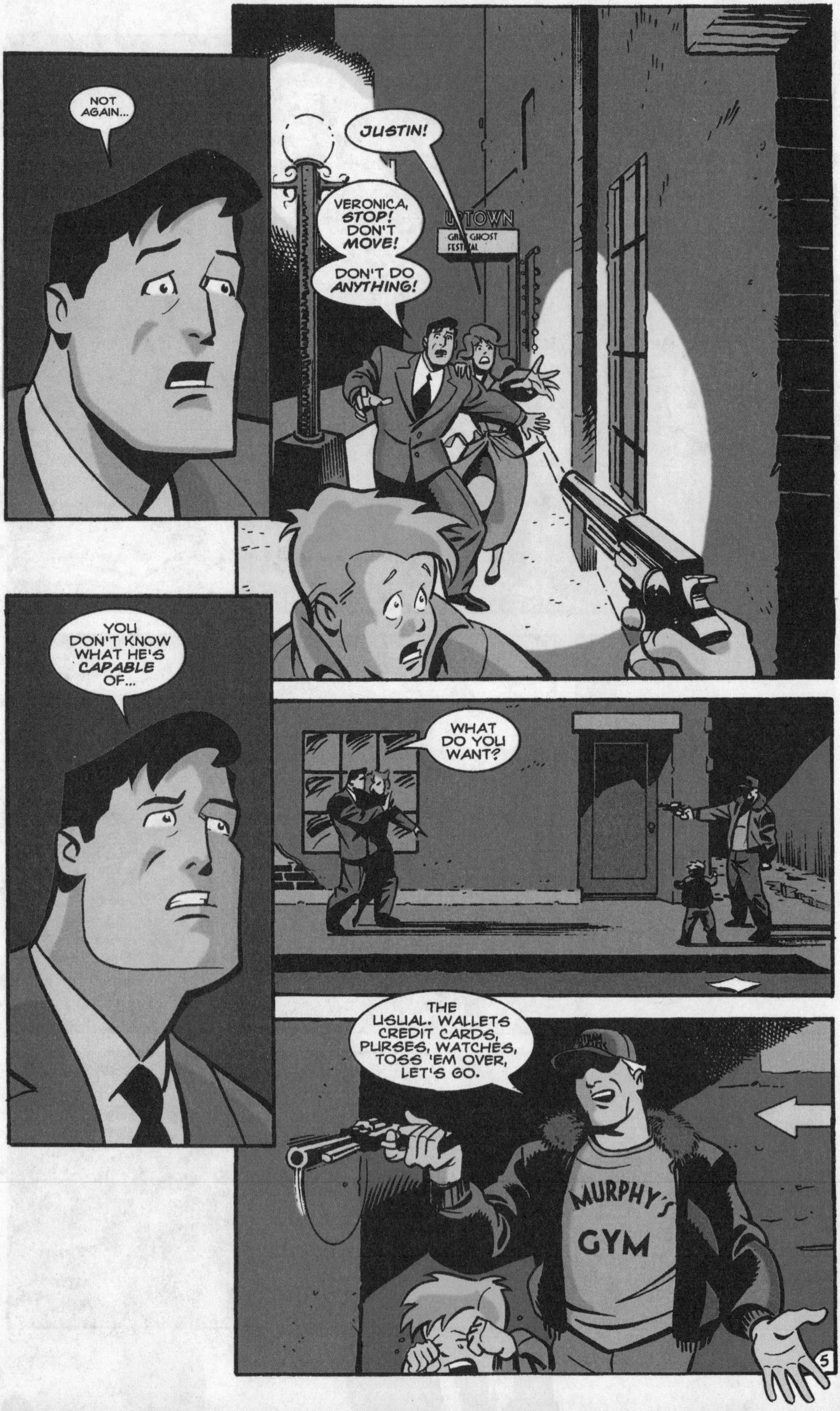
NOT AGAIN...
JUSTIN!
VERONICA, STOP! DON'T MOVE!
DON'T DO ANYTHING!
UPTOWN
GRAY GHOST FESTIVAL
YOU DON'T KNOW WHAT HE'S CAPABLE OF...
WHAT DO YOU WANT?
THE USUAL. WALLETS CREDIT CARDS, PURSES, WATCHES, TOSS 'EM OVER, LET'S GO.
MURPHY'S GYM
5

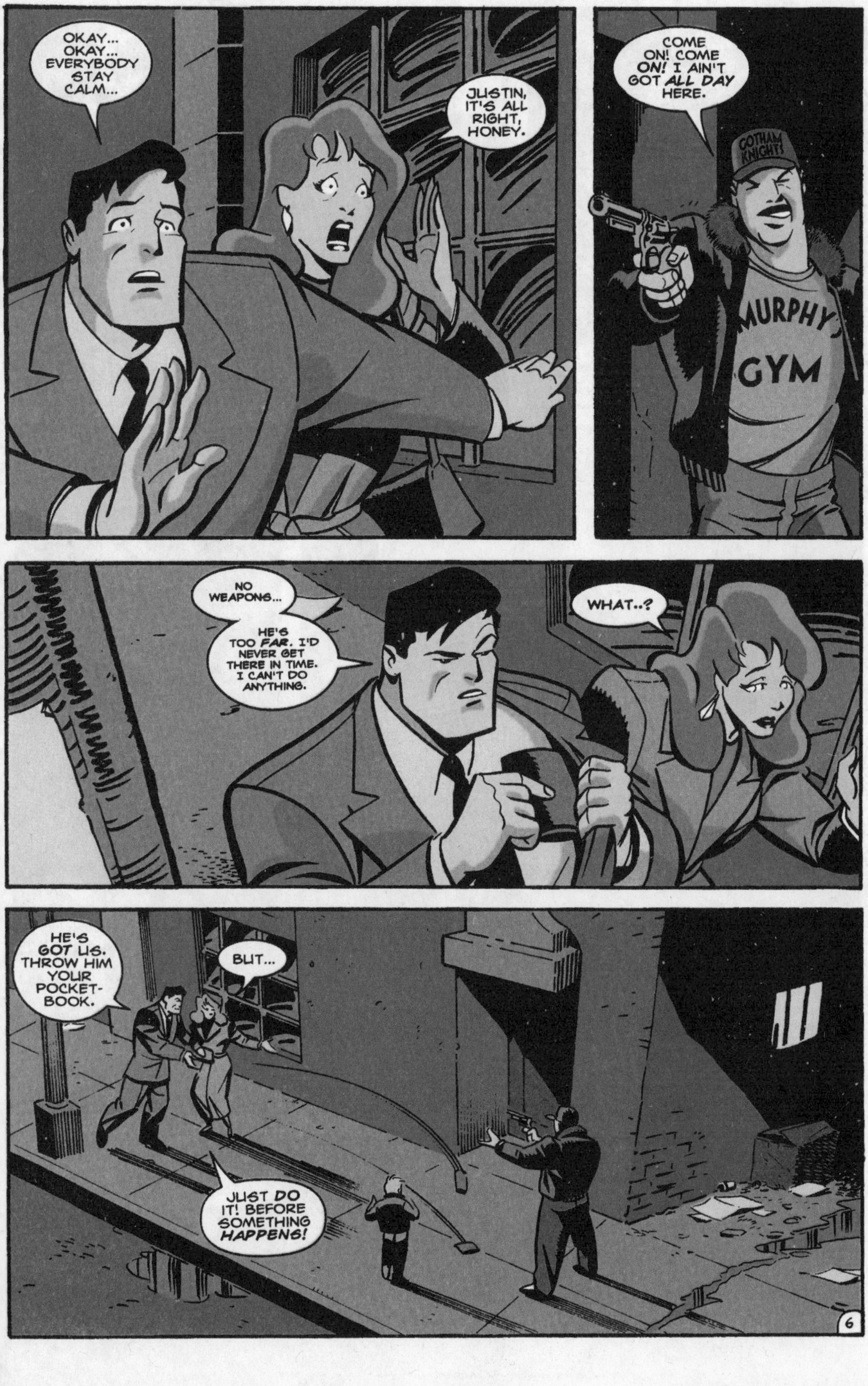

OKAY... OKAY... EVERYBODY STAY CALM...
JUSTIN, IT'S ALL RIGHT, HONEY.
COME ON! COME ON! I AIN'T GOT ALL DAY HERE.
GOTHAM KNIGHTS
MURPHY'S GYM
NO WEAPONS...
HE'S TOO FAR. I'D NEVER GET THERE IN TIME. I CAN'T DO ANYTHING.
WHAT..?
HE'S GOT US. THROW HIM YOUR POCKET-BOOK.
BUT...
JUST DO IT! BEFORE SOMETHING HAPPENS!

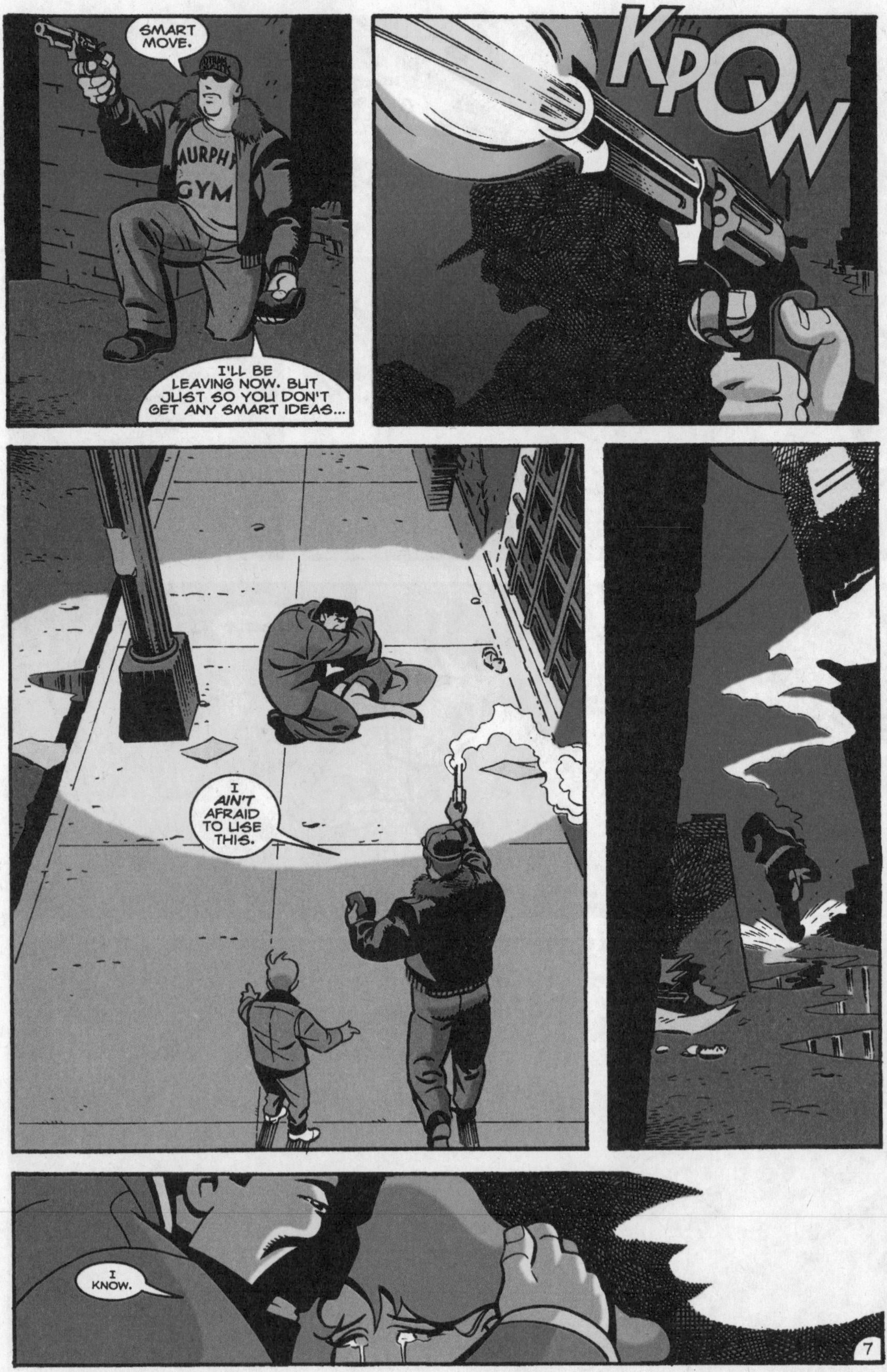
SMART MOVE.
I'LL BE LEAVING NOW. BUT JUST SO YOU DON'T GET ANY SMART IDEAS...
MURPHY GYM
KPOW
I AIN'T AFRAID TO USE THIS.
I KNOW.

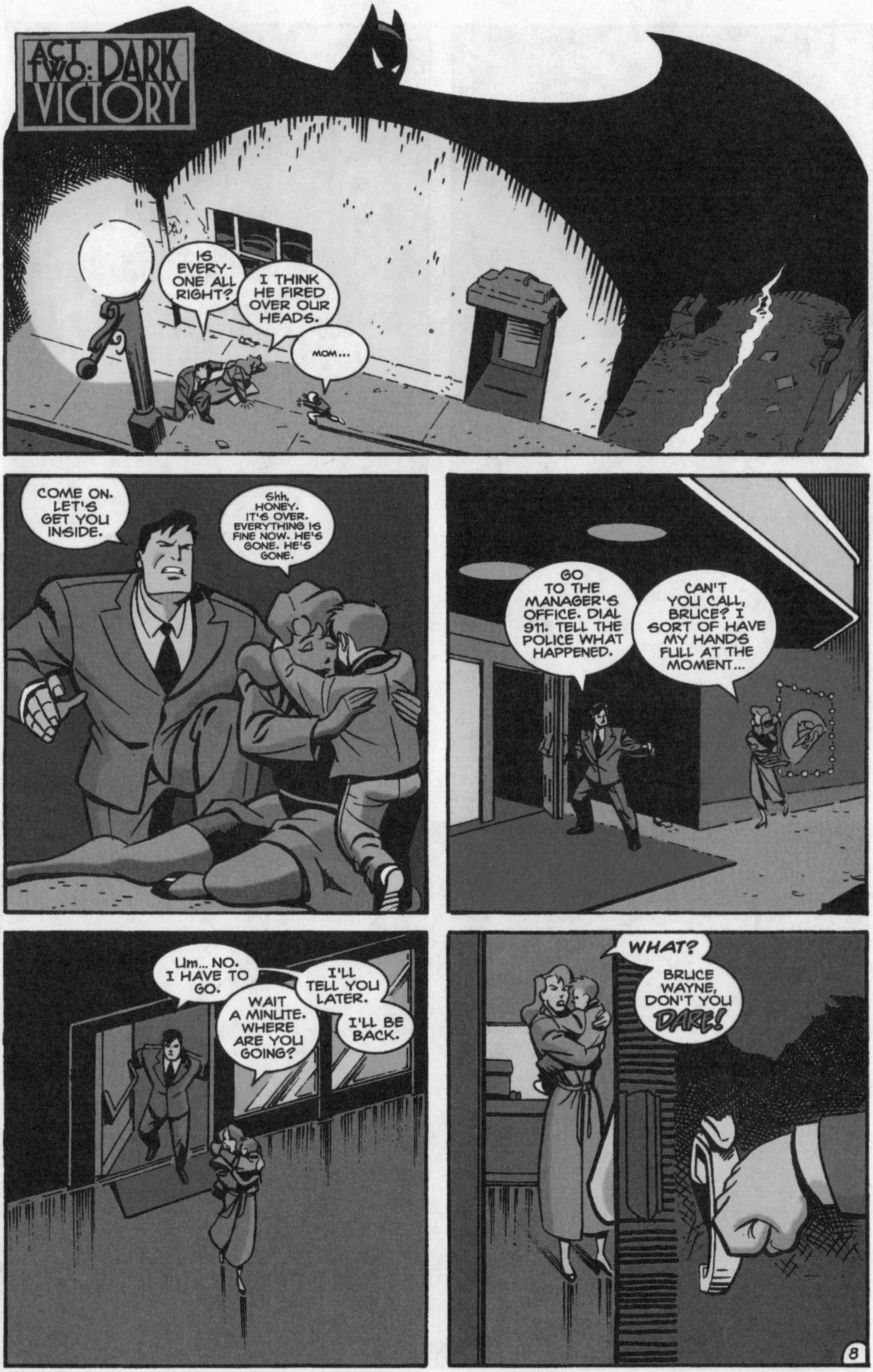
ACT TWO: DARK VICTORY
IS EVERY-ONE ALL RIGHT?
I THINK HE FIRED OVER OUR HEADS.
MOM...
COME ON. LET'S GET YOU INSIDE.
Shh, HONEY. IT'S OVER. EVERYTHING IS FINE NOW. HE'S GONE. HE'S GONE.
GO TO THE MANAGER'S OFFICE. DIAL 911. TELL THE POLICE WHAT HAPPENED.
CAN'T YOU CALL, BRUCE? I SORT OF HAVE MY HANDS FULL AT THE MOMENT...
Um... NO. I HAVE TO GO.
WAIT A MINUTE. WHERE ARE YOU GOING?
I'LL TELL YOU LATER.
I'LL BE BACK.
WHAT?
BRUCE WAYNE, DON'T YOU DARE!
8

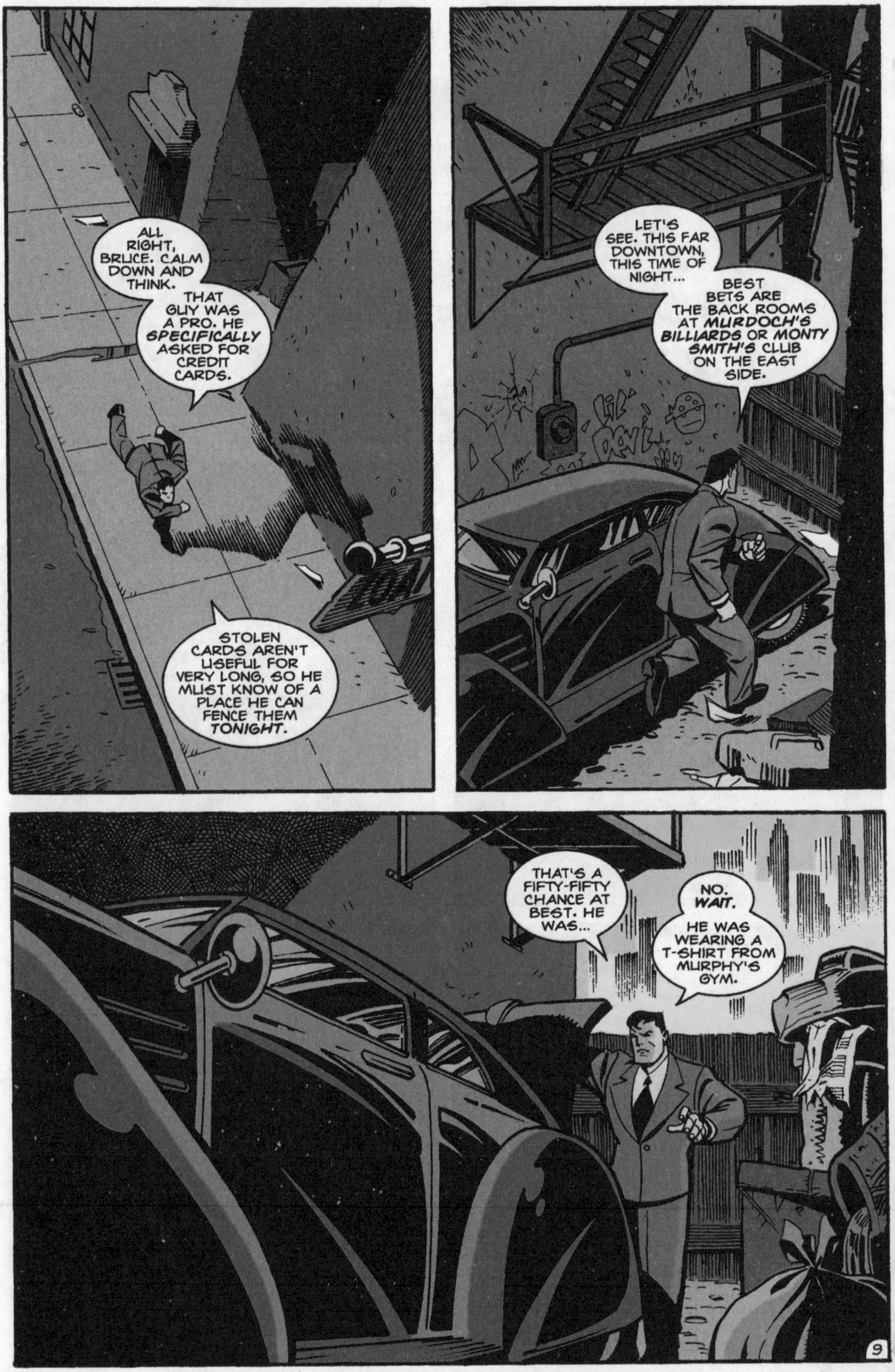
ALL RIGHT, BRUCE. CALM DOWN AND THINK.
THAT GUY WAS A PRO. HE SPECIFICALLY ASKED FOR CREDIT CARDS.
STOLEN CARDS AREN'T USEFUL FOR VERY LONG, SO HE MUST KNOW OF A PLACE HE CAN FENCE THEM TONIGHT.
LET'S SEE. THIS FAR DOWNTOWN, THIS TIME OF NIGHT...
BEST BETS ARE THE BACK ROOMS AT MURDOCH'S BILLIARDS OR MONTY SMITH'S CLUB ON THE EAST SIDE.
THAT'S A FIFTY-FIFTY CHANCE AT BEST. HE WAS...
NO. WAIT.
HE WAS WEARING A T-SHIRT FROM MURPHY'S GYM.

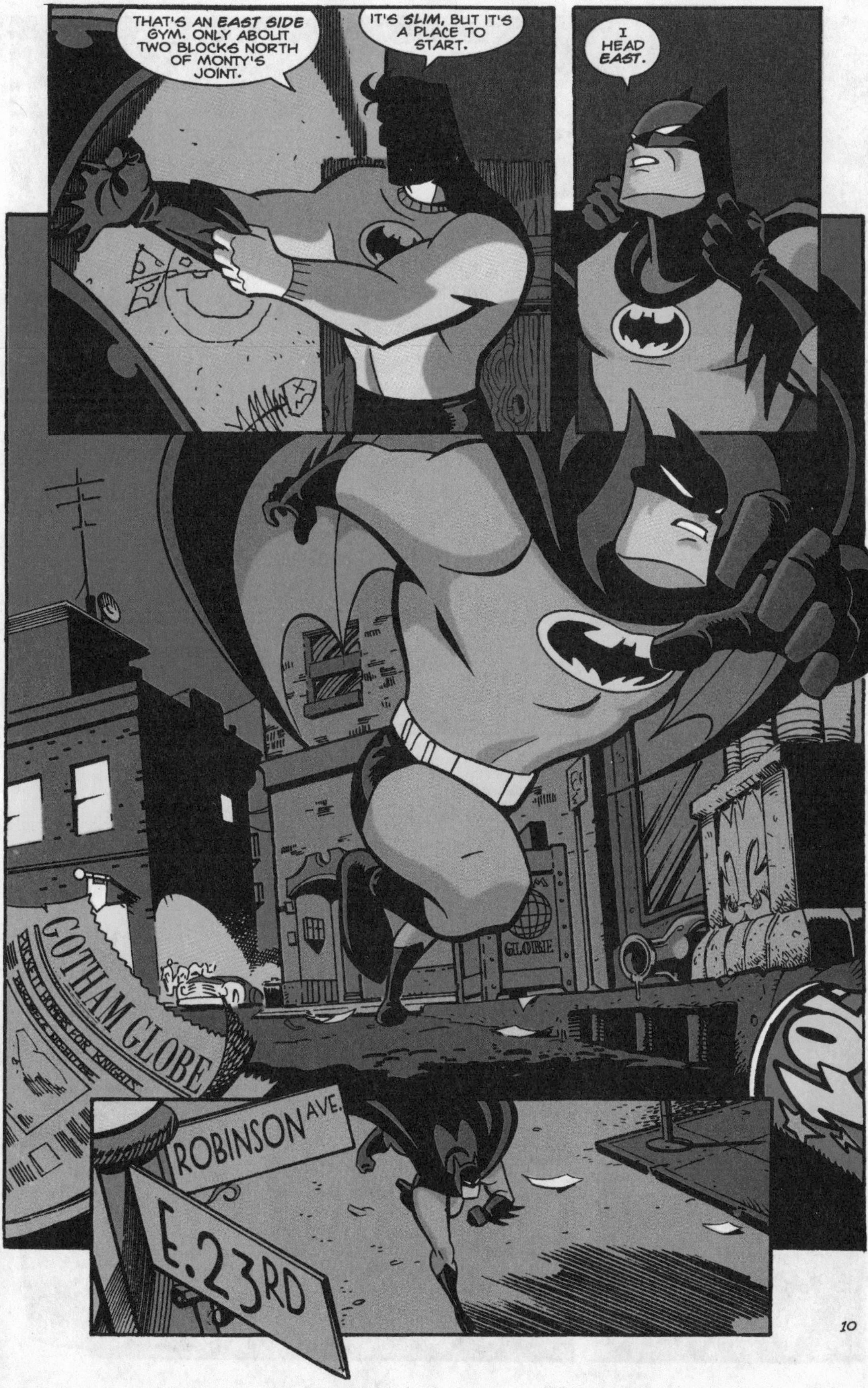
THAT'S AN EAST SIDE GYM. ONLY ABOUT TWO BLOCKS NORTH OF MONTY'S JOINT.
IT'S SLIM, BUT IT'S A PLACE TO START.
I HEAD EAST.
GLOBE
GOTHAM GLOBE
ROBINSON AVE.
E. 23RD

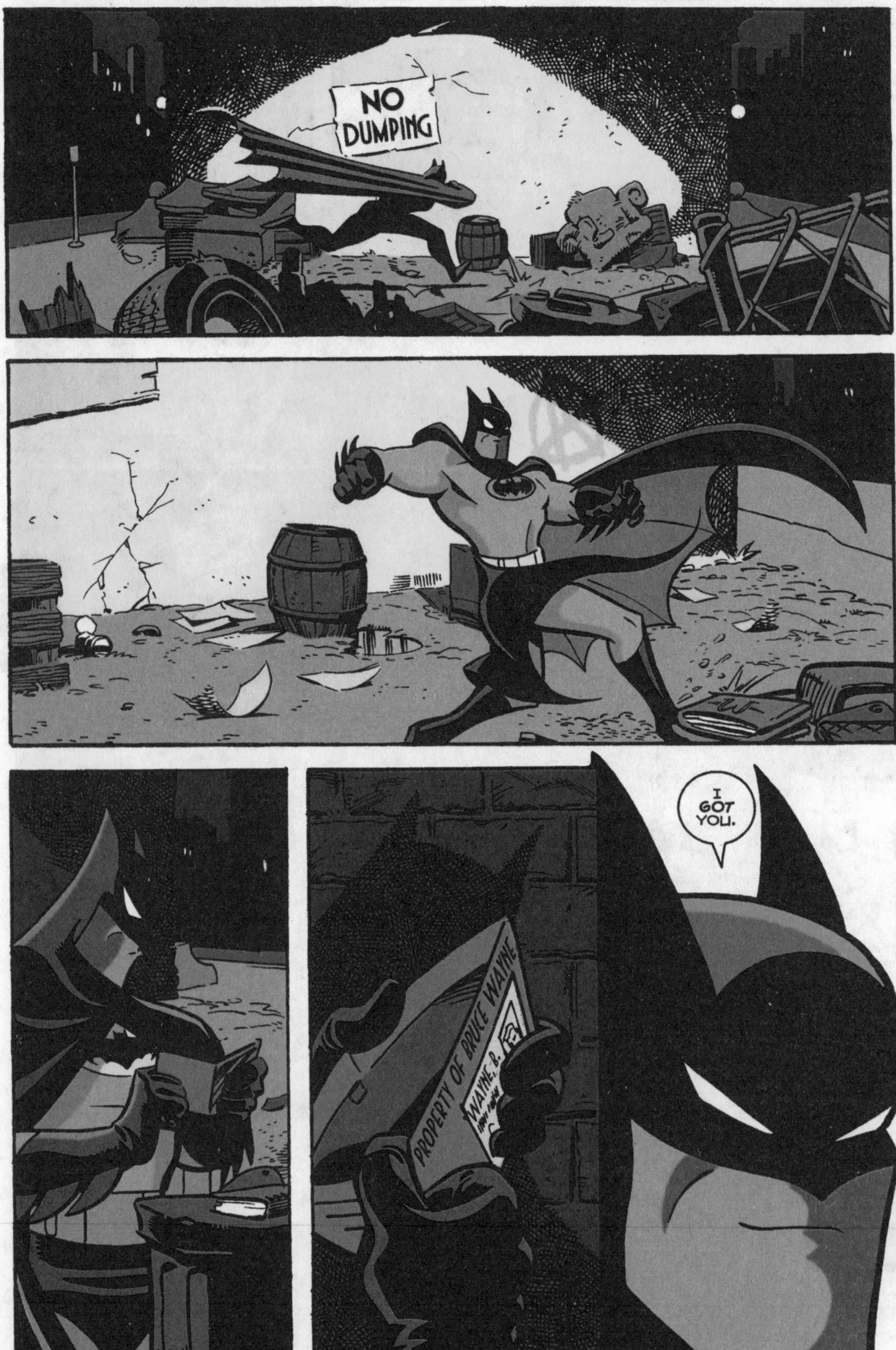
NO DUMPING
PROPERTY OF BRUCE WAYNE
WAYNE, B.
I GOT YOU.

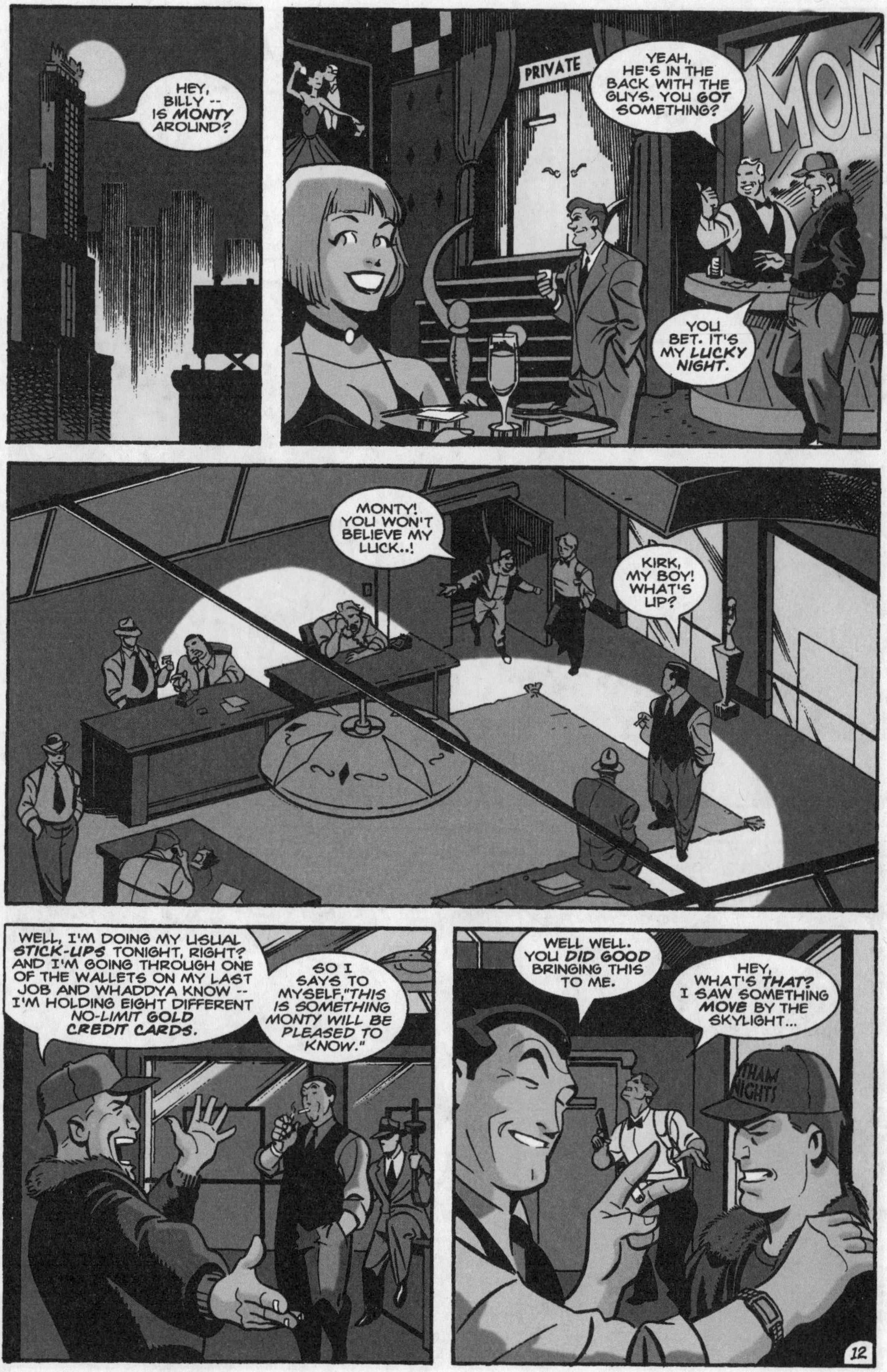
HEY, BILLY -- IS MONTY AROUND?
PRIVATE
YEAH, HE'S IN THE BACK WITH THE GUYS. YOU GOT SOMETHING?
YOU BET. IT'S MY LUCKY NIGHT.
MONTY! YOU WON'T BELIEVE MY LUCK..!
KIRK, MY BOY! WHAT'S UP?
WELL, I'M DOING MY USUAL STICK-UPS TONIGHT, RIGHT? AND I'M GOING THROUGH ONE OF THE WALLETS ON MY LAST JOB AND WHADDYA KNOW -- I'M HOLDING EIGHT DIFFERENT NO-LIMIT GOLD CREDIT CARDS.
SO I SAYS TO MYSELF, "THIS IS SOMETHING MONTY WILL BE PLEASED TO KNOW."
WELL WELL. YOU DID GOOD BRINGING THIS TO ME.
HEY, WHAT'S THAT? I SAW SOMETHING MOVE BY THE SKYLIGHT...

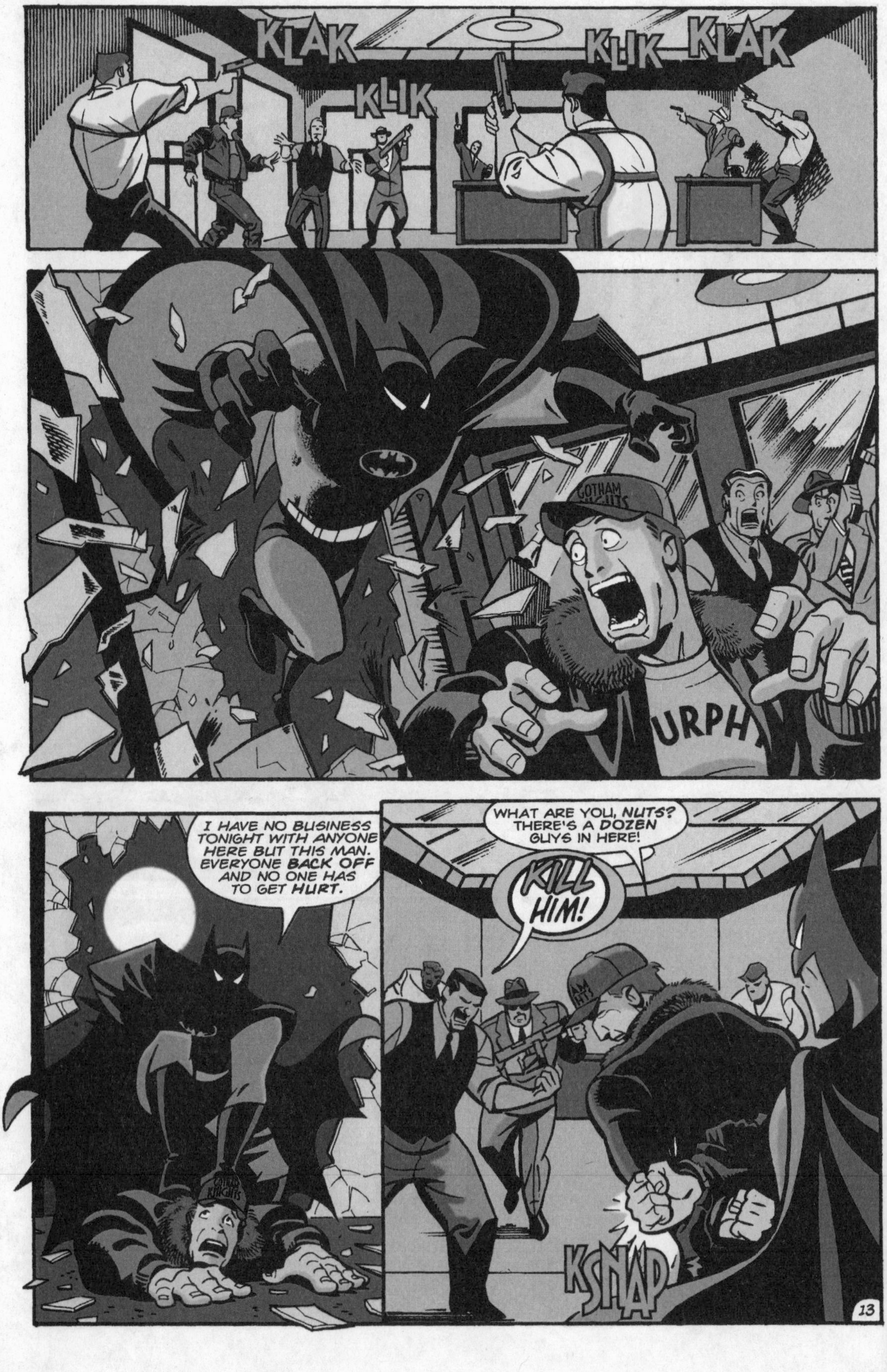

KLAK
KLIK
KLIK KLAK
GOTHAM KNIGHTS
URPH
I HAVE NO BUSINESS TONIGHT WITH ANYONE HERE BUT THIS MAN. EVERYONE BACK OFF AND NO ONE HAS TO GET HURT.
GOTHAM KNIGHTS
WHAT ARE YOU, NUTS? THERE'S A DOZEN GUYS IN HERE!
KILL HIM!
KSNAP

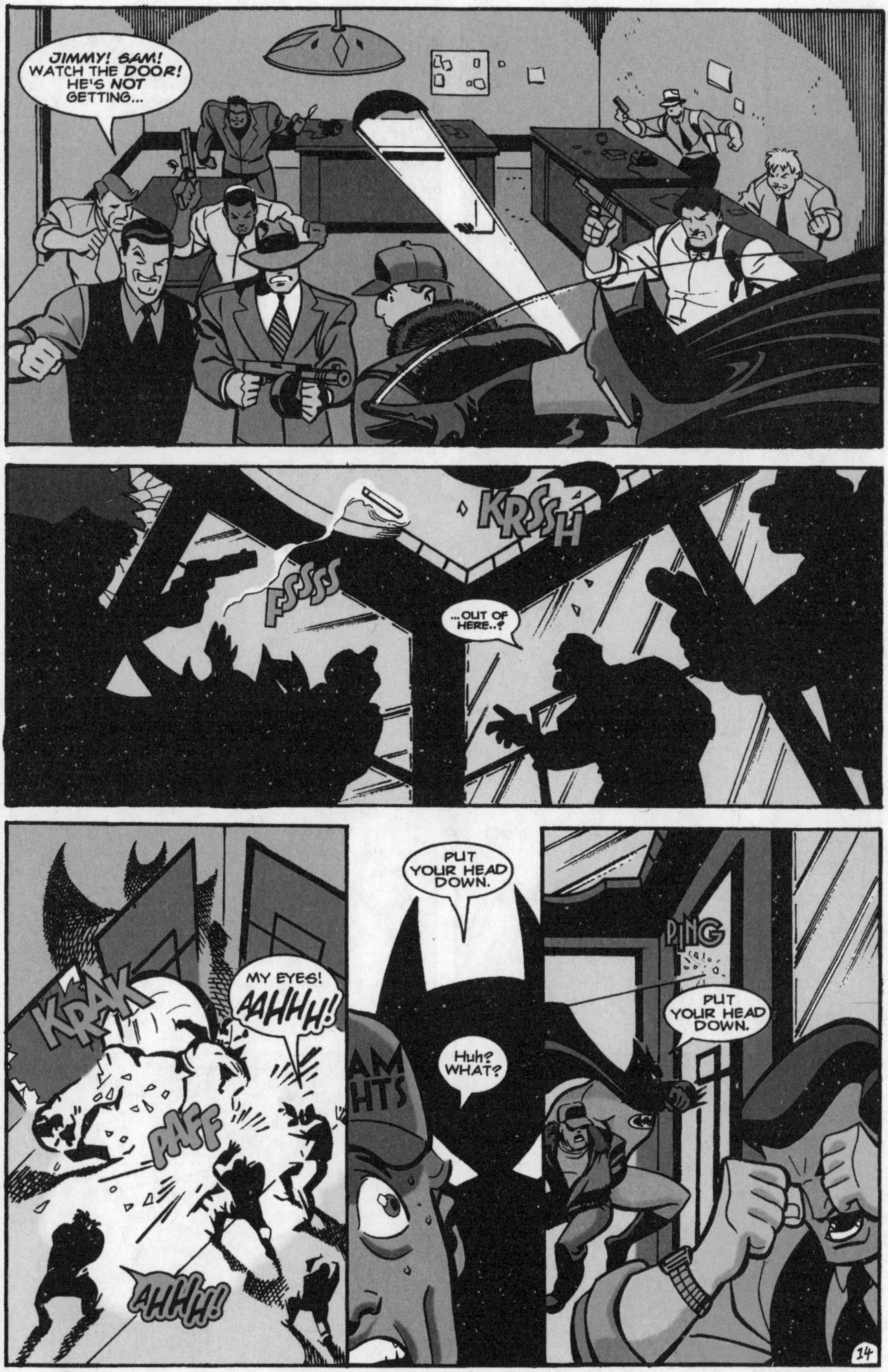
JIMMY! SAM! WATCH THE DOOR! HE'S NOT GETTING...
KRSSH
FSSSS
...OUT OF HERE..?
KRAK
MY EYES! AAHHH!
PAFF
AHHH!
PUT YOUR HEAD DOWN.
Huh? WHAT?
PING
PUT YOUR HEAD DOWN.

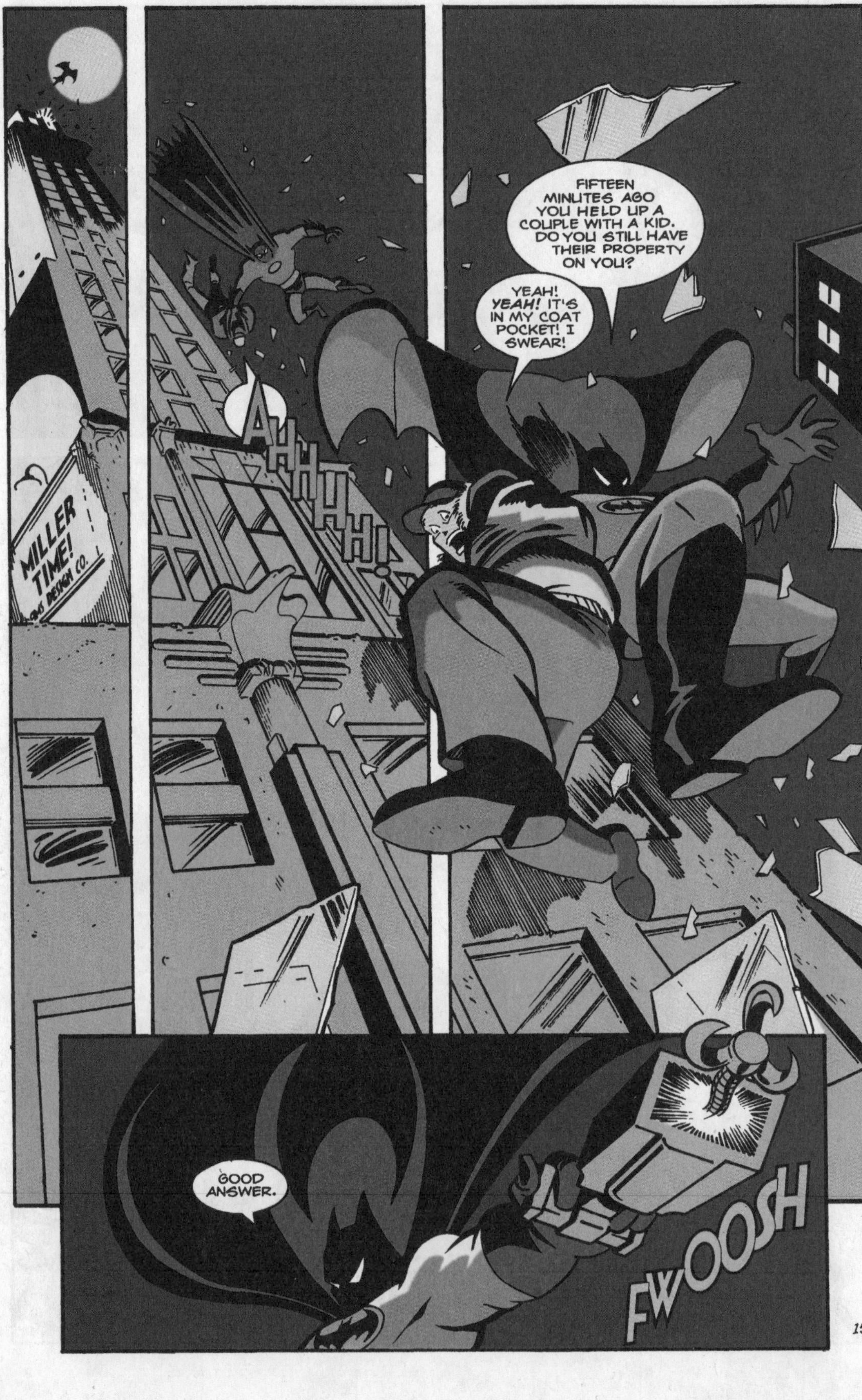

MILLER TIME!
GMS DESIGN CO.
AHHHHHH!
FIFTEEN MINUTES AGO YOU HELD UP A COUPLE WITH A KID. DO YOU STILL HAVE THEIR PROPERTY ON YOU?
YEAH! YEAH! IT'S IN MY COAT POCKET! I SWEAR!
GOOD ANSWER.
FWOOSH

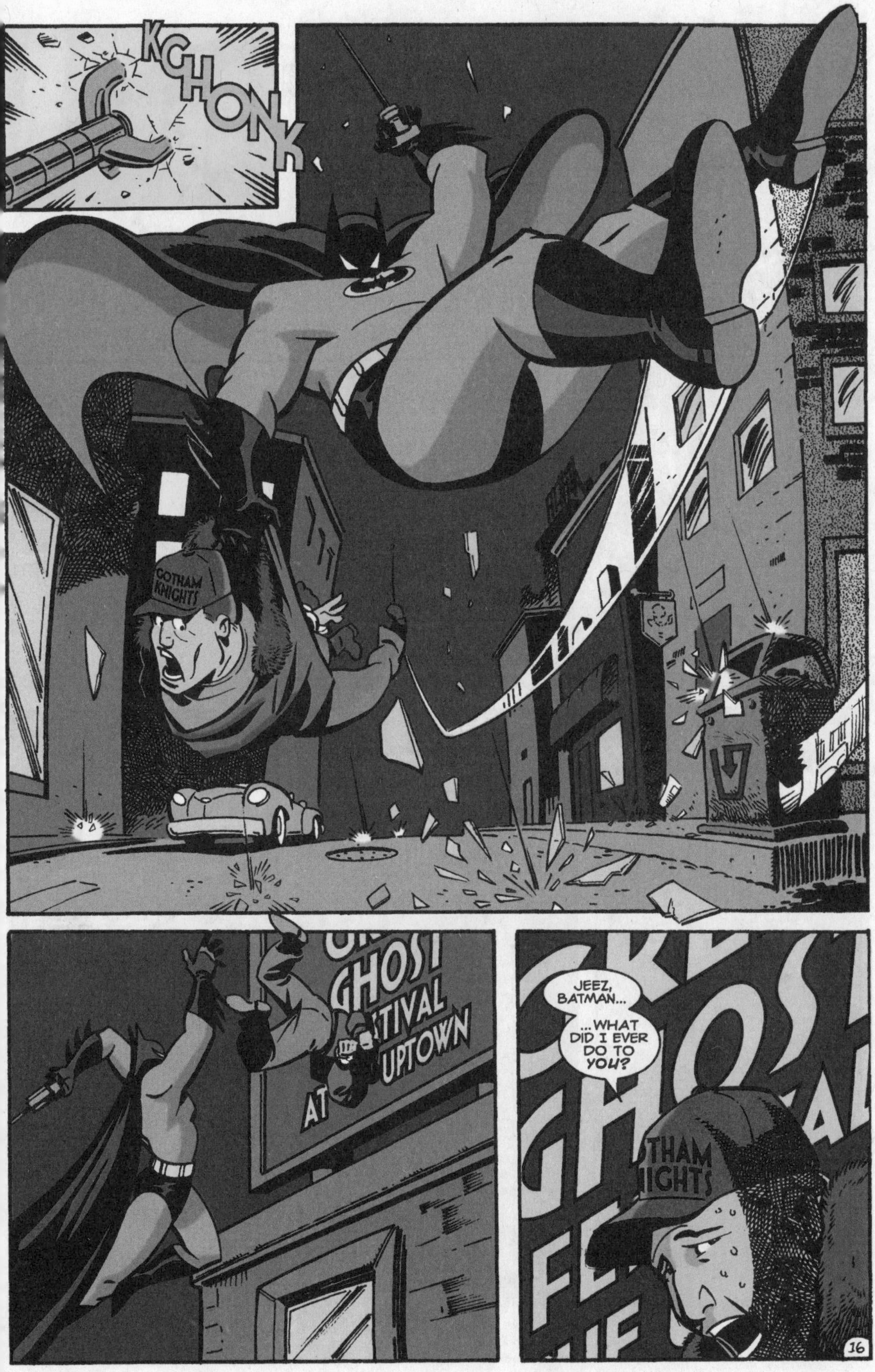
KCHONK
GOTHAM KNIGHTS
GHOST
TIVAL
AT UPTOWN
JEEZ, BATMAN...
...WHAT DID I EVER DO TO YOU?
GOTHAM KNIGHTS
16

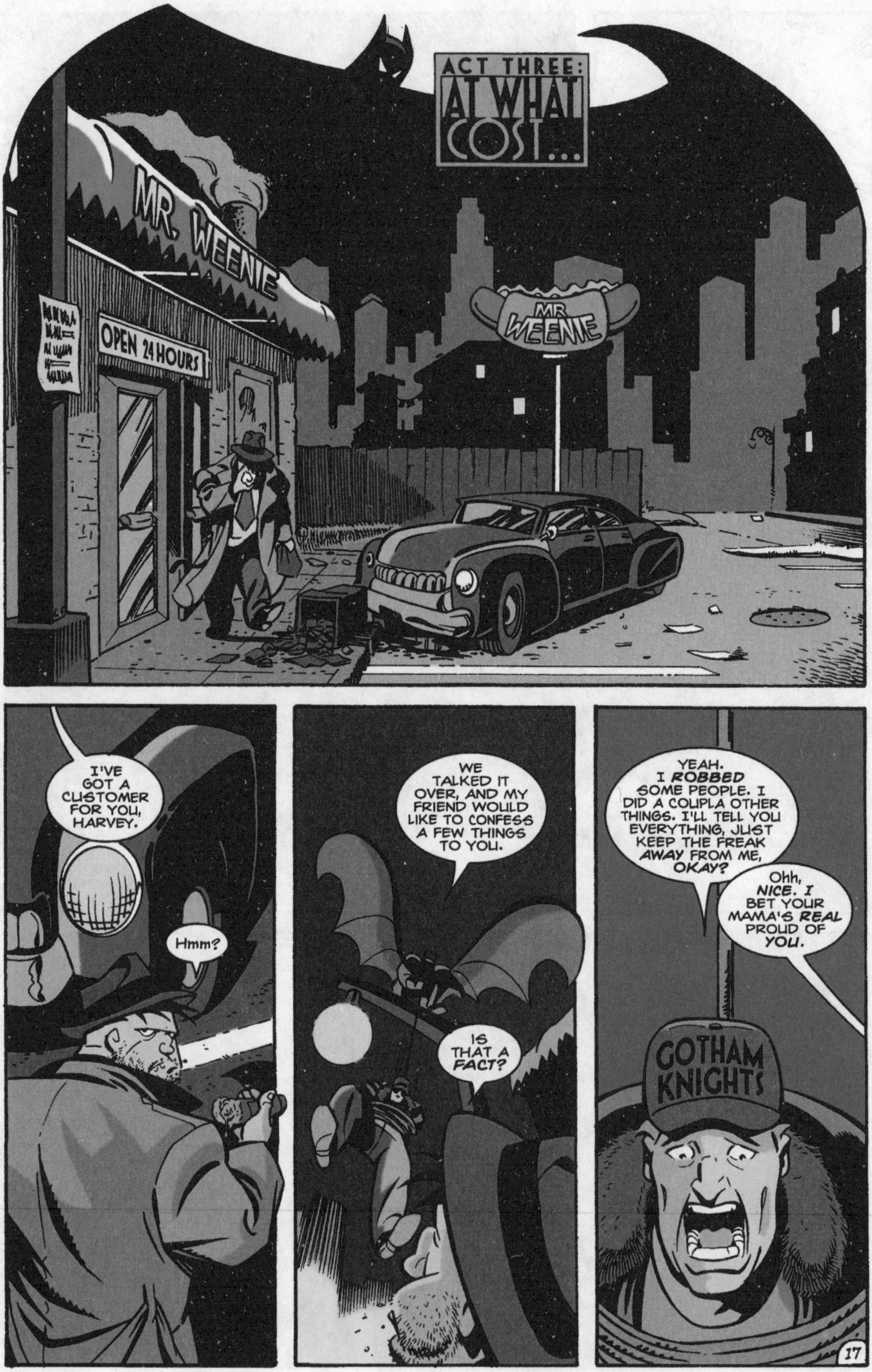
ACT THREE:
AT WHAT COST...
MR. WEENIE
OPEN 24 HOURS
MR WEENIE
I'VE GOT A CUSTOMER FOR YOU, HARVEY.
Hmm?
WE TALKED IT OVER, AND MY FRIEND WOULD LIKE TO CONFESS A FEW THINGS TO YOU.
IS THAT A FACT?
YEAH. I ROBBED SOME PEOPLE. I DID A COUPLA OTHER THINGS. I'LL TELL YOU EVERYTHING, JUST KEEP THE FREAK AWAY FROM ME, OKAY?
Ohh, NICE. I BET YOUR MAMA'S REAL PROUD OF YOU.
GOTHAM KNIGHTS

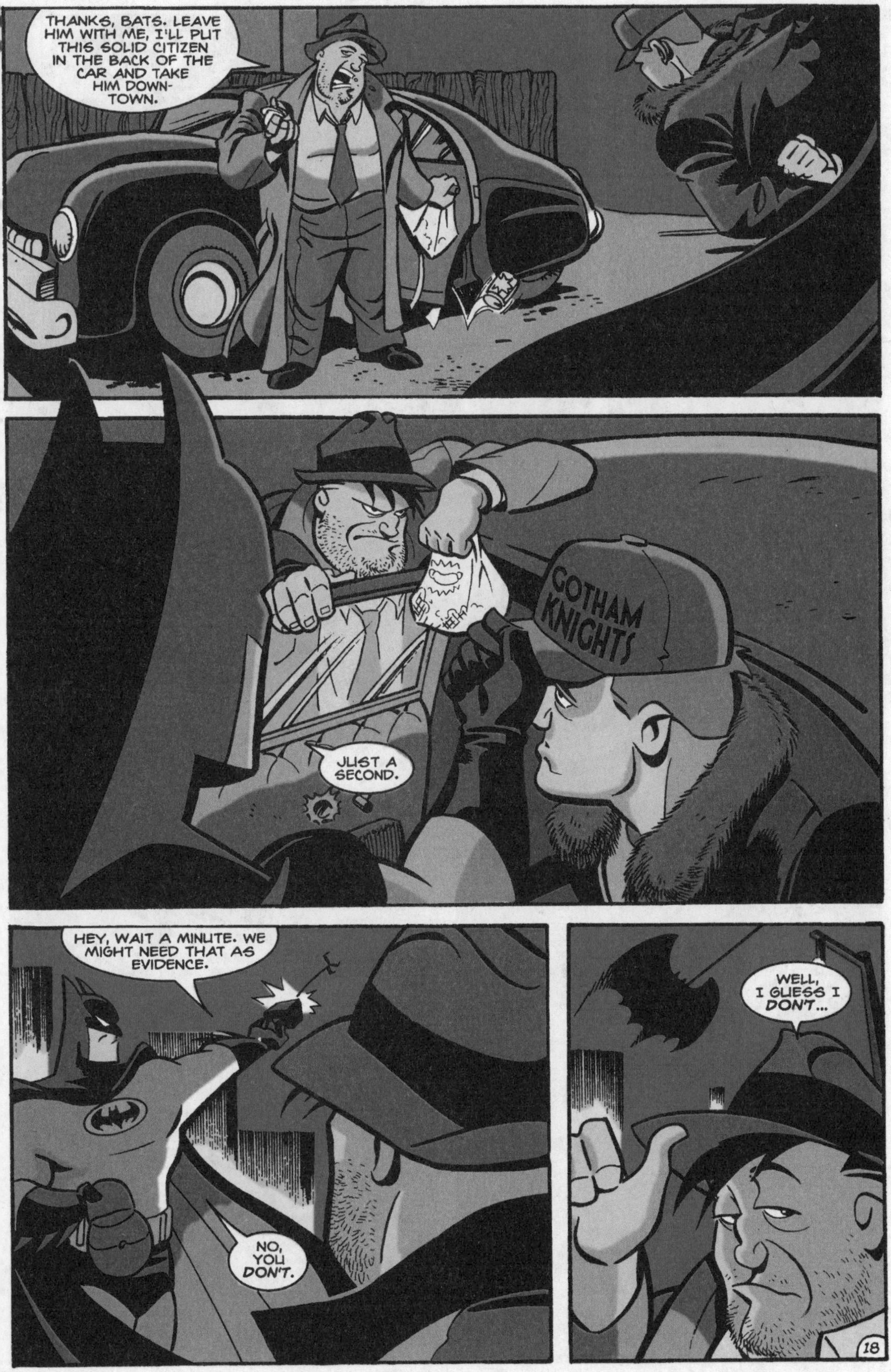
THANKS, BATS. LEAVE HIM WITH ME, I'LL PUT THIS SOLID CITIZEN IN THE BACK OF THE CAR AND TAKE HIM DOWN-TOWN.
GOTHAM KNIGHTS
JUST A SECOND.
HEY, WAIT A MINUTE. WE MIGHT NEED THAT AS EVIDENCE.
NO, YOU DON'T.
WELL, I GUESS I DON'T...

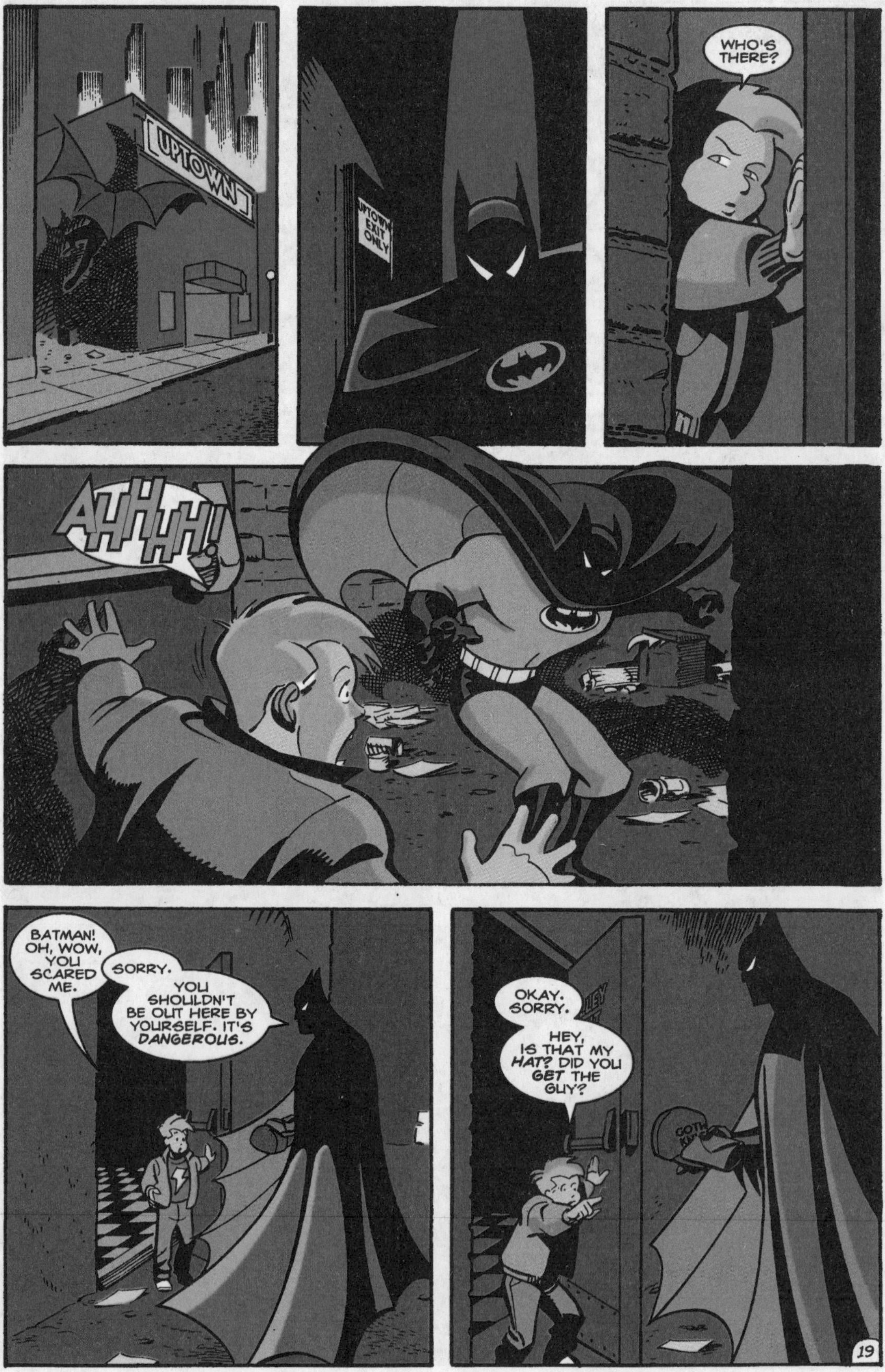

UPTOWN
UPTOWN EXIT ONLY
WHO'S THERE?
AHHHH!
BATMAN! OH, WOW, YOU SCARED ME.
SORRY.
YOU SHOULDN'T BE OUT HERE BY YOURSELF. IT'S DANGEROUS.
OKAY. SORRY.
HEY, IS THAT MY HAT? DID YOU GET THE GUY?

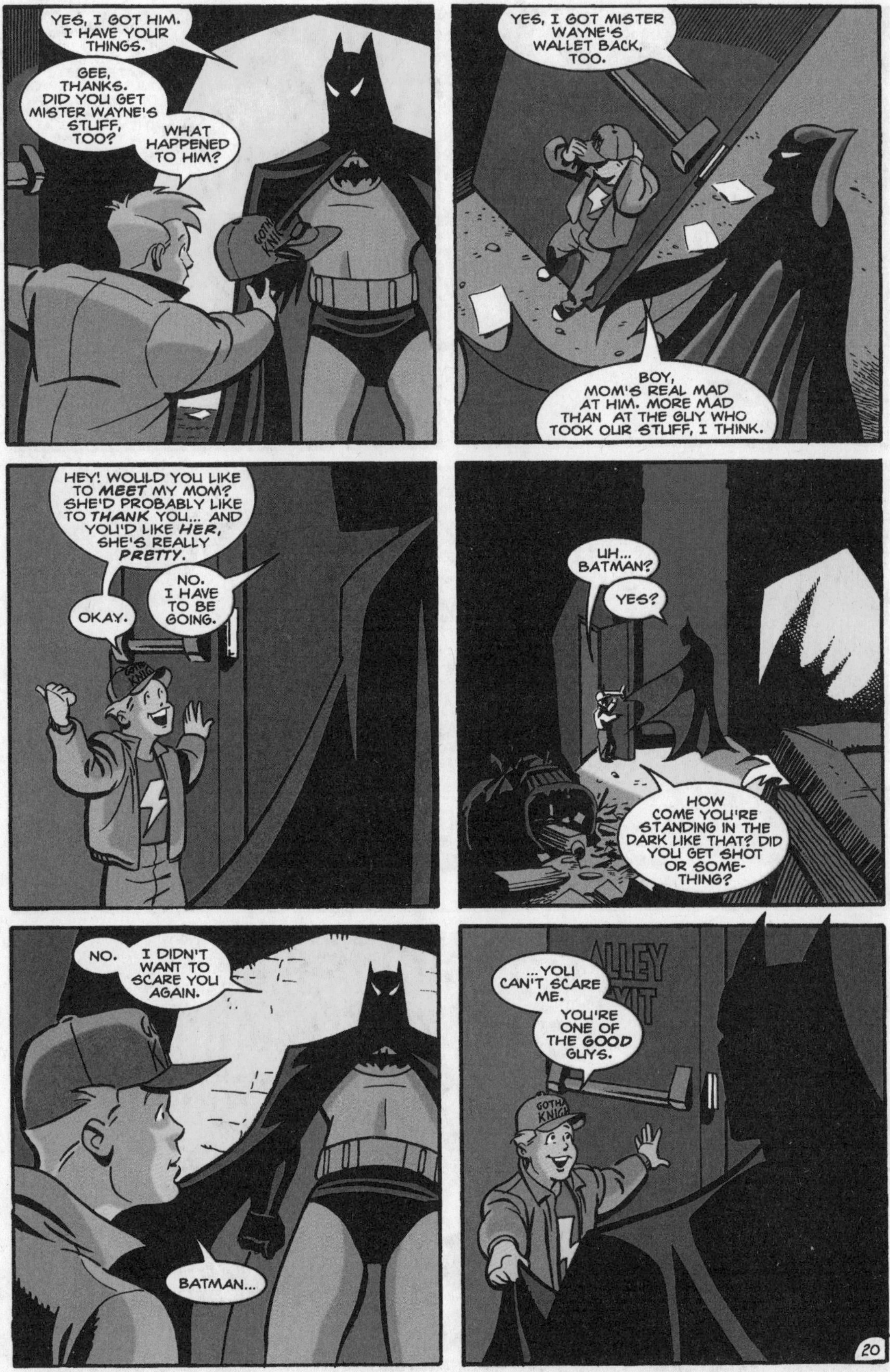
YES, I GOT HIM. I HAVE YOUR THINGS.
GEE, THANKS. DID YOU GET MISTER WAYNE'S STUFF, TOO?
WHAT HAPPENED TO HIM?
YES, I GOT MISTER WAYNE'S WALLET BACK, TOO.
BOY, MOM'S REAL MAD AT HIM. MORE MAD THAN AT THE GUY WHO TOOK OUR STUFF, I THINK.
HEY! WOULD YOU LIKE TO MEET MY MOM? SHE'D PROBABLY LIKE TO THANK YOU... AND YOU'D LIKE HER, SHE'S REALLY PRETTY.
NO. I HAVE TO BE GOING.
OKAY.
UH... BATMAN?
YES?
HOW COME YOU'RE STANDING IN THE DARK LIKE THAT? DID YOU GET SHOT OR SOME-THING?
NO.
I DIDN'T WANT TO SCARE YOU AGAIN.
BATMAN...
...YOU CAN'T SCARE ME.
YOU'RE ONE OF THE GOOD GUYS.
20

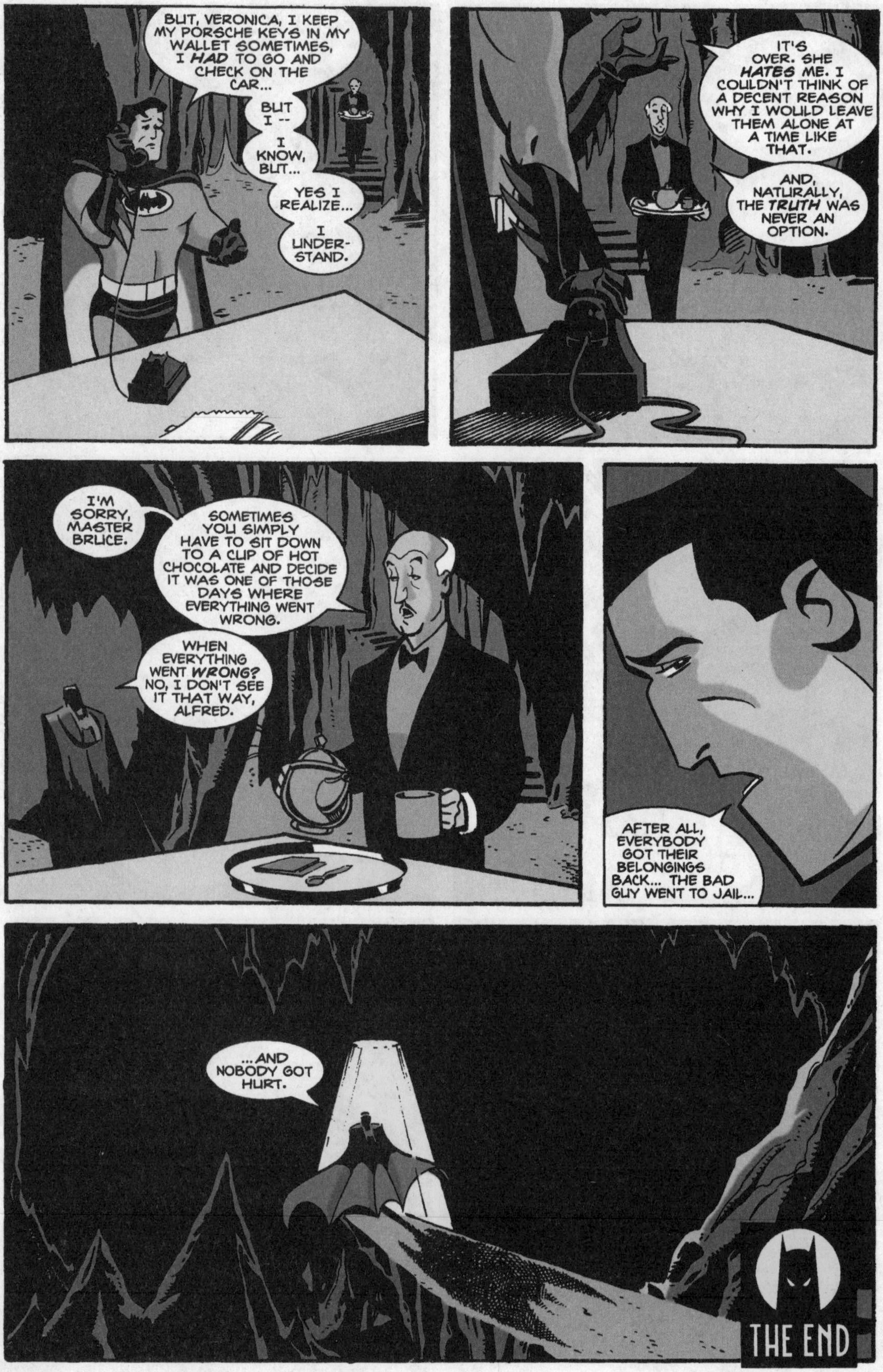
BUT, VERONICA, I KEEP MY PORSCHE KEYS IN MY WALLET SOMETIMES, I HAD TO GO AND CHECK ON THE CAR...
BUT I --
I KNOW, BUT...
YES I REALIZE...
I UNDER-STAND.
IT'S OVER. SHE HATES ME. I COULDN'T THINK OF A DECENT REASON WHY I WOULD LEAVE THEM ALONE AT A TIME LIKE THAT.
AND, NATURALLY, THE TRUTH WAS NEVER AN OPTION.
I'M SORRY, MASTER BRUCE.
SOMETIMES YOU SIMPLY HAVE TO SIT DOWN TO A CUP OF HOT CHOCOLATE AND DECIDE IT WAS ONE OF THOSE DAYS WHERE EVERYTHING WENT WRONG.
WHEN EVERYTHING WENT WRONG? NO, I DON'T SEE IT THAT WAY, ALFRED.
AFTER ALL, EVERYBODY GOT THEIR BELONGINGS BACK... THE BAD GUY WENT TO JAIL...
...AND NOBODY GOT HURT.
THE END

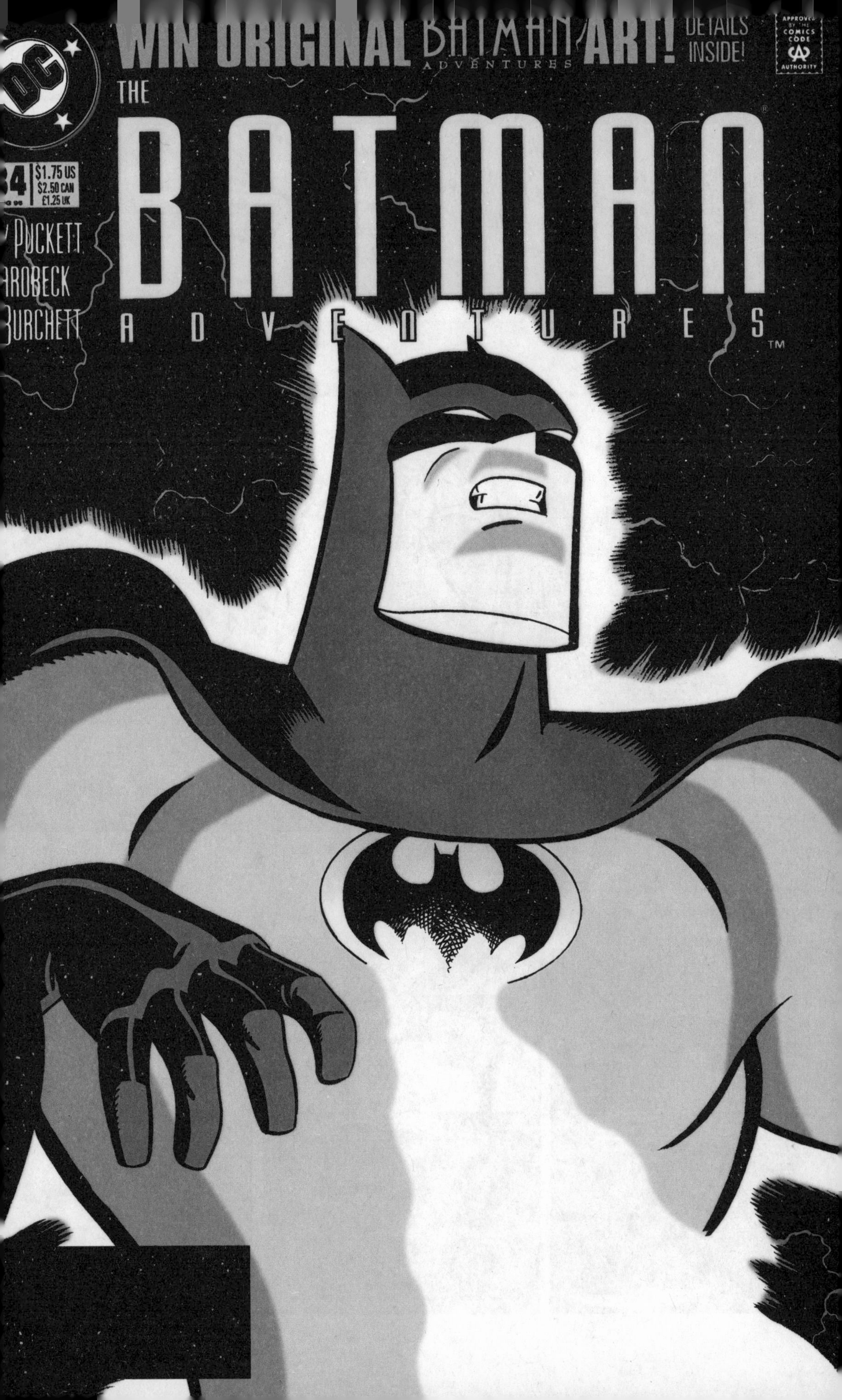

WIN ORIGINAL BATMAN ADVENTURES ART!
DETAILS INSIDE!
APPROVED BY THE COMICS CODE AUTHORITY
THE BATMAN ADVENTURES
$1.75 US
$2.50 CAN
£1.25 UK
PUCKETT

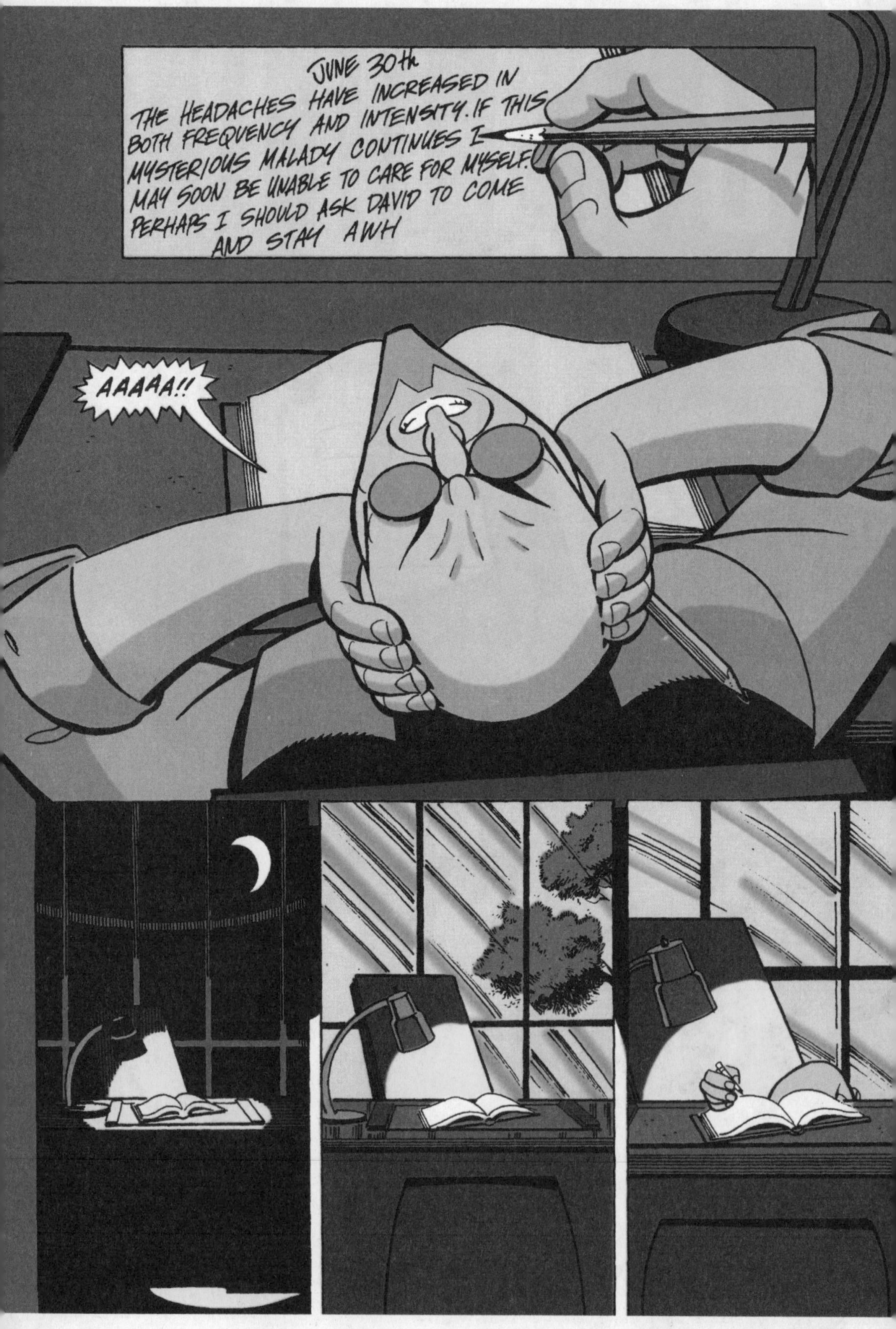
JUNE 30th
THE HEADACHES HAVE INCREASED IN BOTH FREQUENCY AND INTENSITY. IF THIS MYSTERIOUS MALADY CONTINUES I MAY SOON BE UNABLE TO CARE FOR MYSELF. PERHAPS I SHOULD ASK DAVID TO COME AND STAY AWH
AAAAA!!

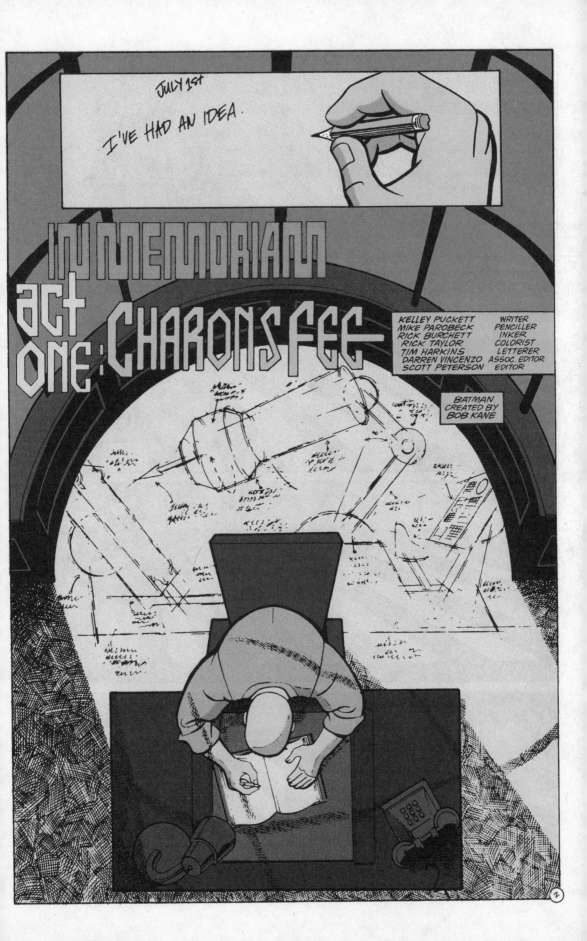

JULY 1st

I'VE HAD AN IDEA.

IN MEMORIAM

ACT ONE: CHARON'S FEE

KELLEY PUCKETT — WRITER
MIKE PAROBECK — PENCILLER
RICK BURCHETT — INKER
RICK TAYLOR — COLORIST
TIM HARKINS — LETTERER
DARREN VINCENZO — ASSOC. EDITOR
SCOTT PETERSON — EDITOR

BATMAN
CREATED BY
BOB KANE

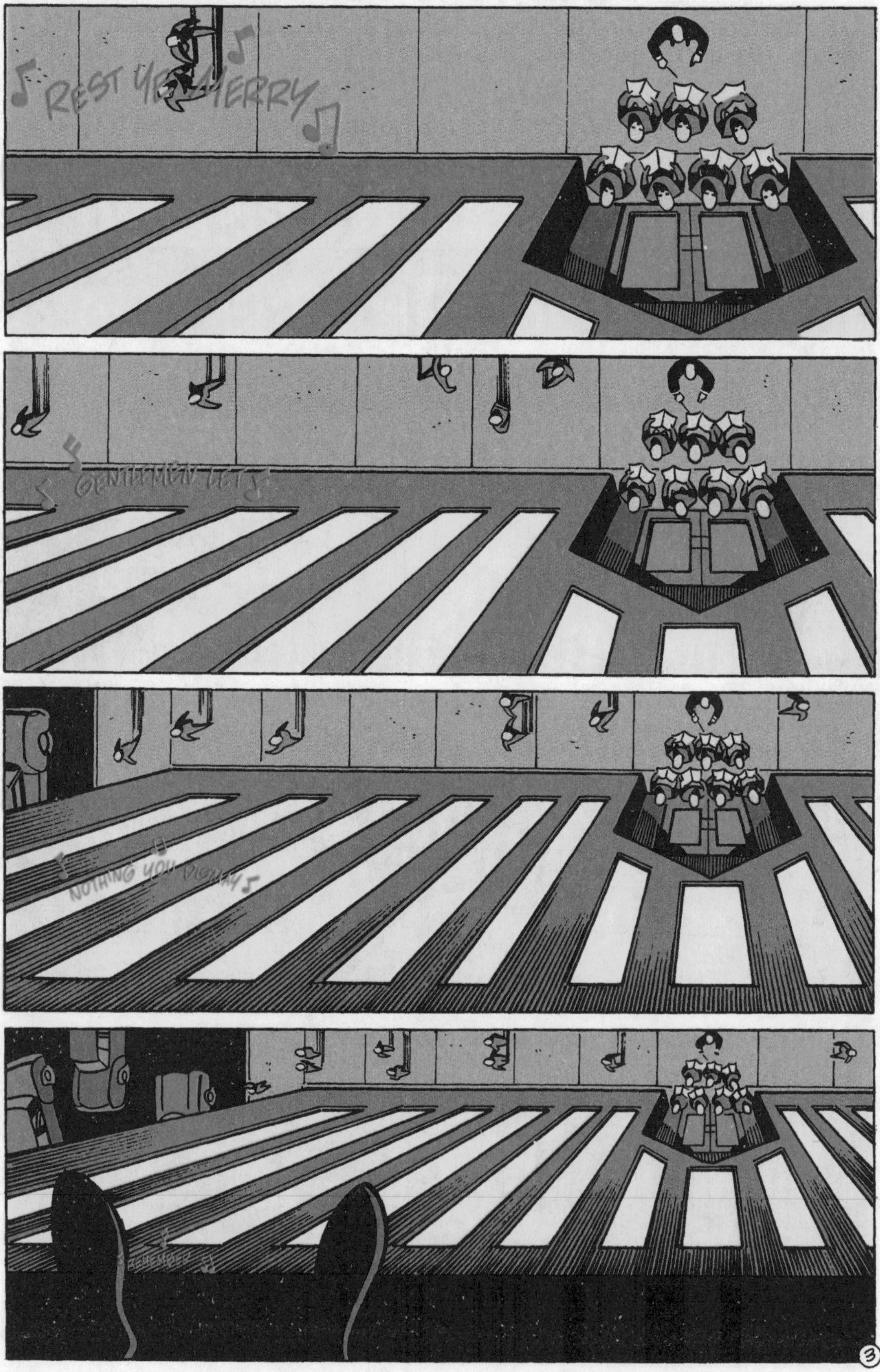
REST YE MERRY
GENTLEMEN LET'S
NOTHING YOU DISMAY
REMEMBER

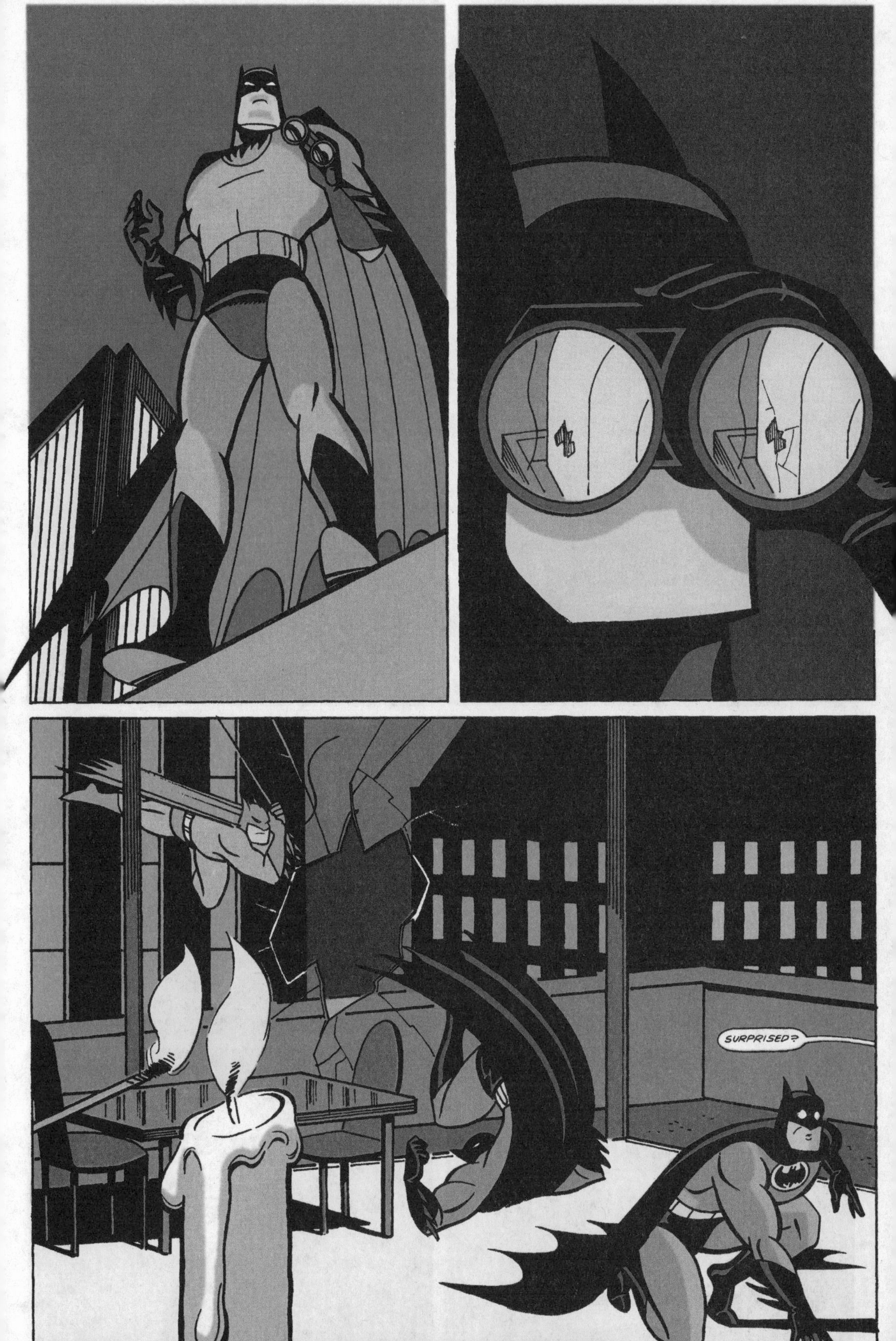
SURPRISED?

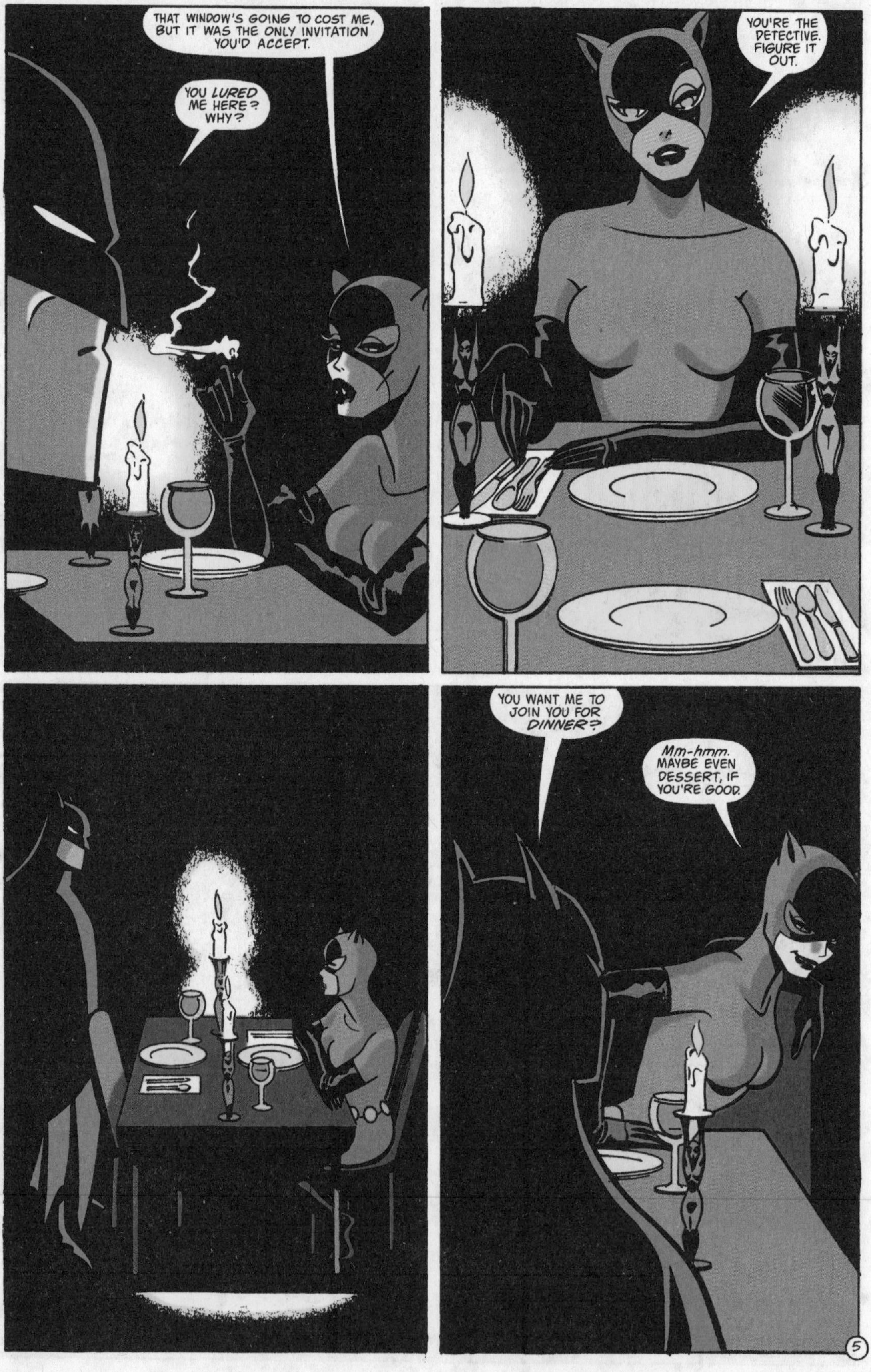
THAT WINDOW'S GOING TO COST ME, BUT IT WAS THE ONLY INVITATION YOU'D ACCEPT.
YOU *LURED* ME HERE? WHY?
YOU'RE THE DETECTIVE. FIGURE IT OUT.
YOU WANT ME TO JOIN YOU FOR *DINNER*?
Mm-hmm. MAYBE EVEN DESSERT, IF YOU'RE GOOD.

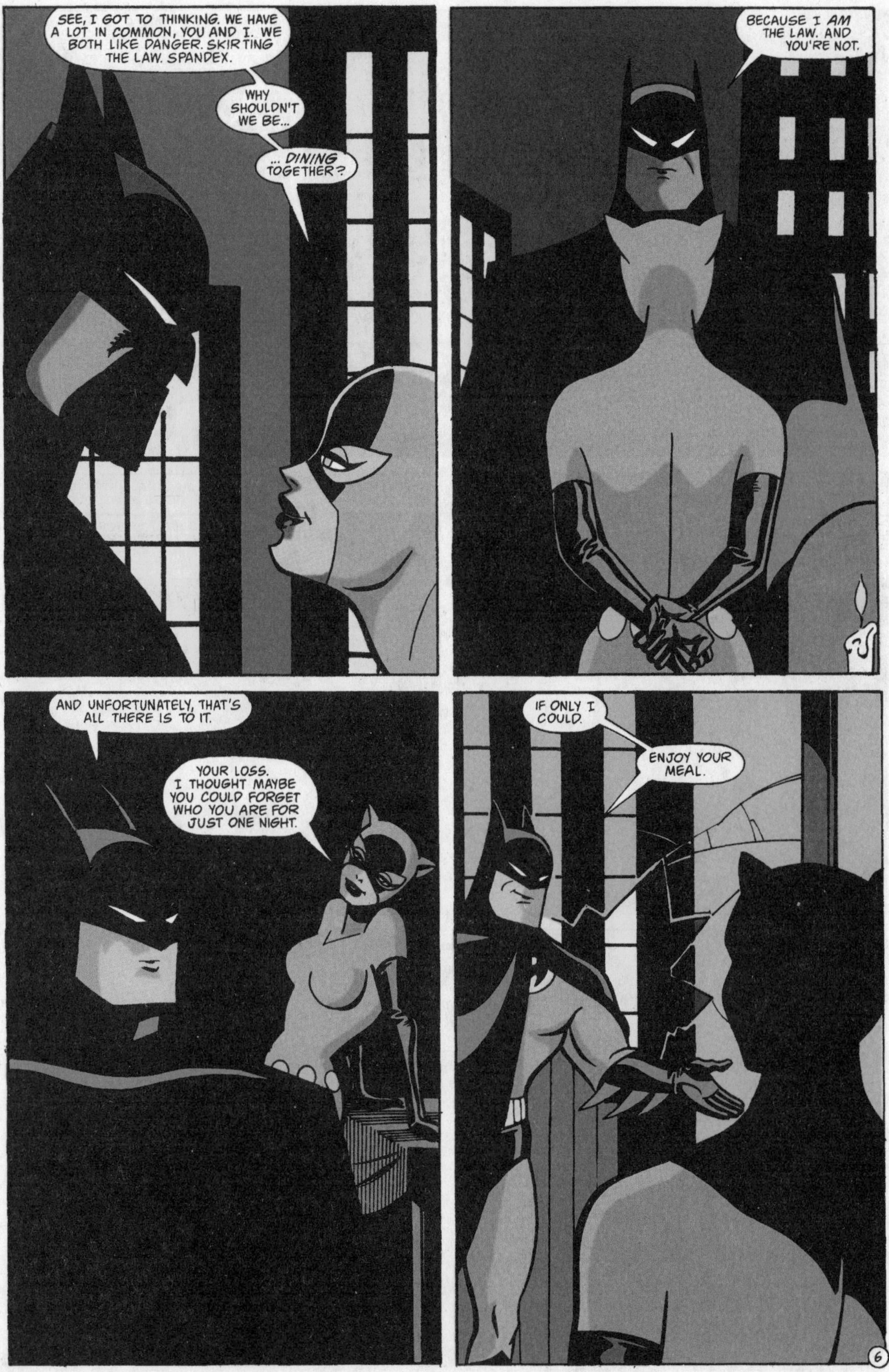
SEE, I GOT TO THINKING. WE HAVE A LOT IN COMMON, YOU AND I. WE BOTH LIKE DANGER. SKIRTING THE LAW. SPANDEX.
WHY SHOULDN'T WE BE...
...DINING TOGETHER?
BECAUSE I AM THE LAW. AND YOU'RE NOT.
AND UNFORTUNATELY, THAT'S ALL THERE IS TO IT.
YOUR LOSS. I THOUGHT MAYBE YOU COULD FORGET WHO YOU ARE FOR JUST ONE NIGHT.
IF ONLY I COULD.
ENJOY YOUR MEAL.

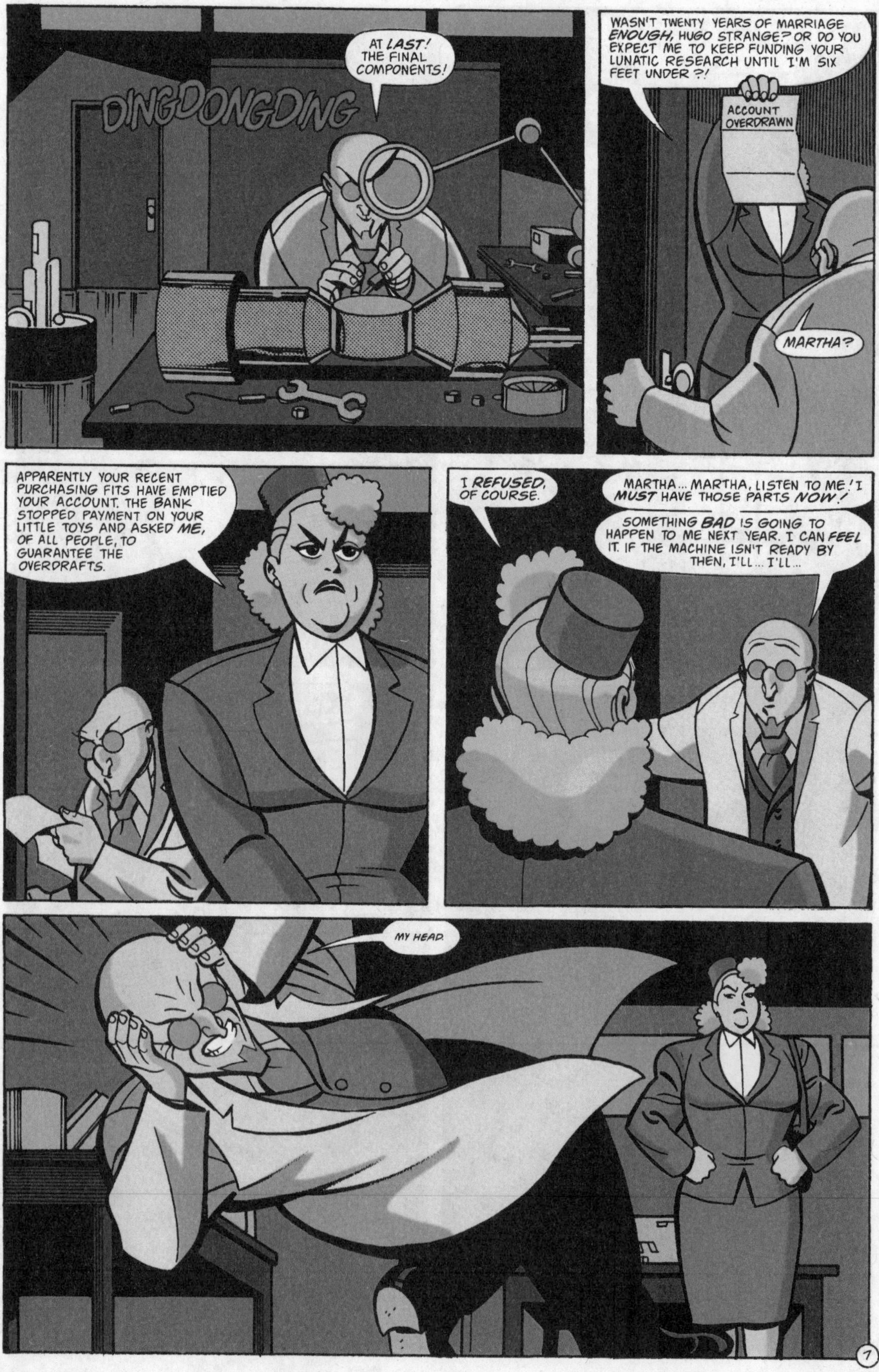
DINGDONGDING
AT LAST! THE FINAL COMPONENTS!
WASN'T TWENTY YEARS OF MARRIAGE ENOUGH, HUGO STRANGE? OR DO YOU EXPECT ME TO KEEP FUNDING YOUR LUNATIC RESEARCH UNTIL I'M SIX FEET UNDER?!
ACCOUNT OVERDRAWN
MARTHA?
APPARENTLY YOUR RECENT PURCHASING FITS HAVE EMPTIED YOUR ACCOUNT. THE BANK STOPPED PAYMENT ON YOUR LITTLE TOYS AND ASKED ME, OF ALL PEOPLE, TO GUARANTEE THE OVERDRAFTS.
I REFUSED, OF COURSE.
MARTHA... MARTHA, LISTEN TO ME! I MUST HAVE THOSE PARTS NOW!
SOMETHING BAD IS GOING TO HAPPEN TO ME NEXT YEAR. I CAN FEEL IT. IF THE MACHINE ISN'T READY BY THEN, I'LL... I'LL...
MY HEAD.

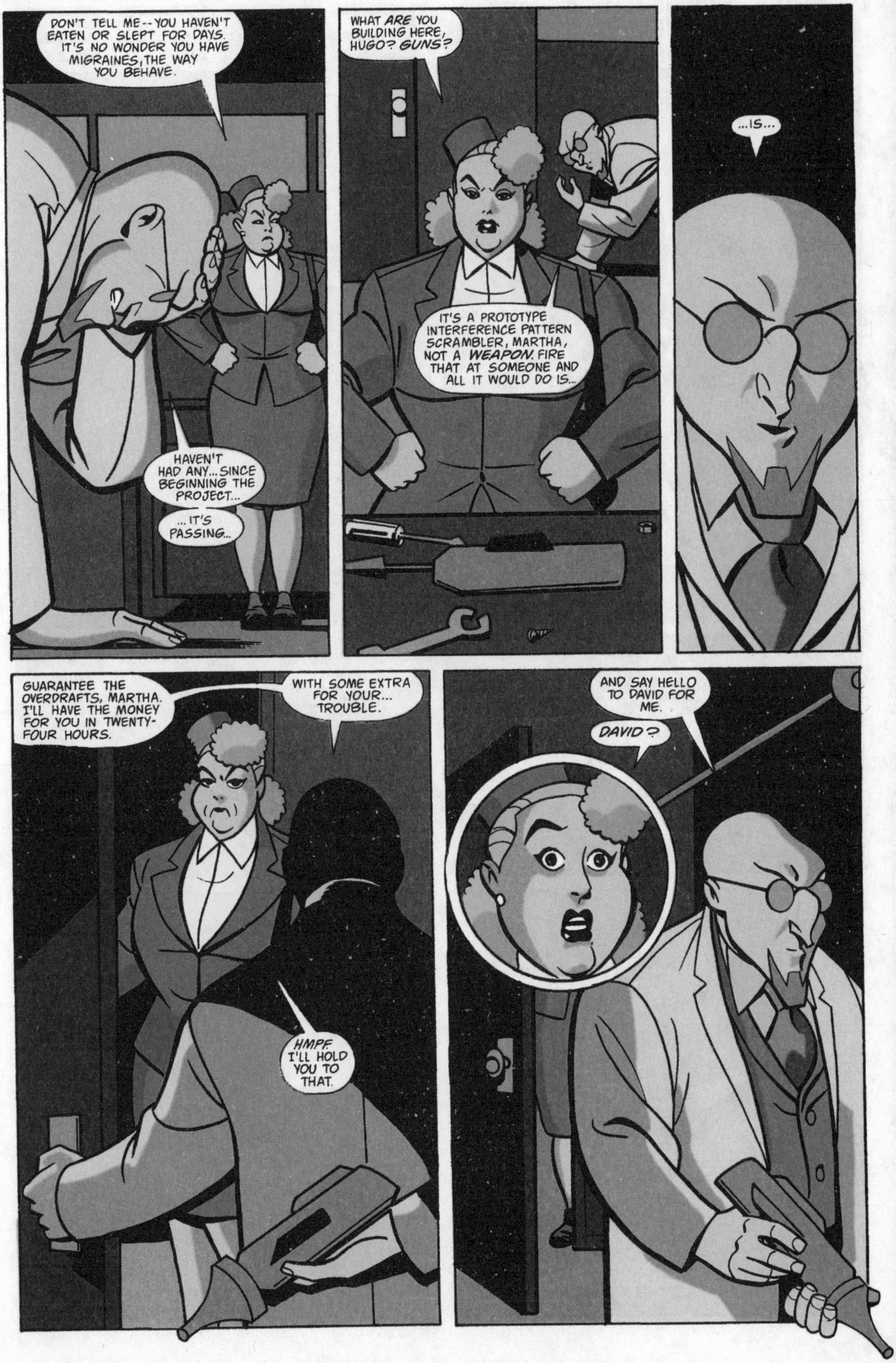

DON'T TELL ME--YOU HAVEN'T EATEN OR SLEPT FOR DAYS. IT'S NO WONDER YOU HAVE MIGRAINES, THE WAY YOU BEHAVE.
HAVEN'T HAD ANY...SINCE BEGINNING THE PROJECT...
...IT'S PASSING...
WHAT ARE YOU BUILDING HERE, HUGO? GUNS?
IT'S A PROTOTYPE INTERFERENCE PATTERN SCRAMBLER, MARTHA, NOT A WEAPON. FIRE THAT AT SOMEONE AND ALL IT WOULD DO IS...
...IS...
GUARANTEE THE OVERDRAFTS, MARTHA. I'LL HAVE THE MONEY FOR YOU IN TWENTY-FOUR HOURS.
WITH SOME EXTRA FOR YOUR... TROUBLE.
HMPF. I'LL HOLD YOU TO THAT.
AND SAY HELLO TO DAVID FOR ME.
DAVID?

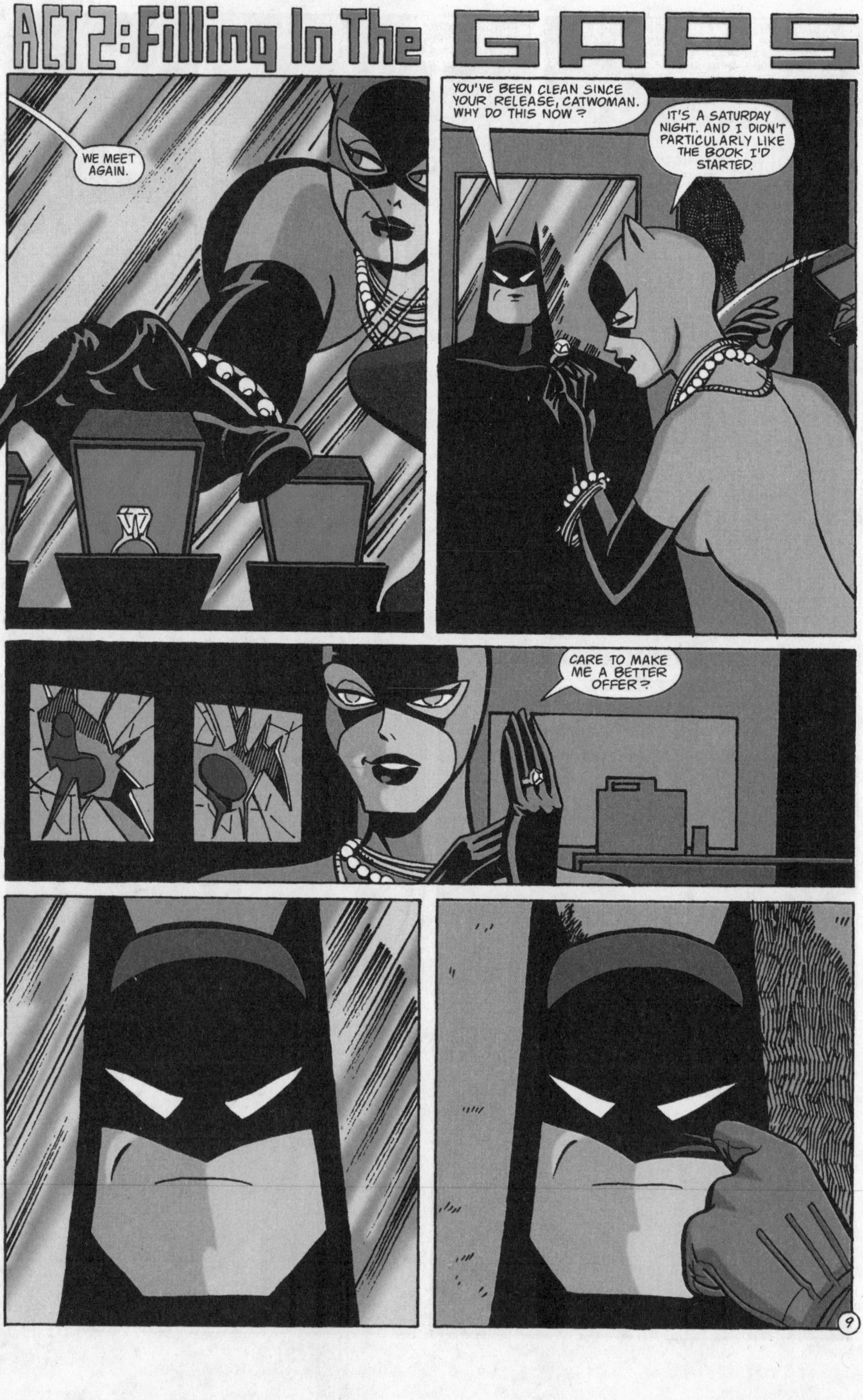
ACT 2: Filling In The GAPS
WE MEET AGAIN.
YOU'VE BEEN CLEAN SINCE YOUR RELEASE, CATWOMAN. WHY DO THIS NOW?
IT'S A SATURDAY NIGHT. AND I DIDN'T PARTICULARLY LIKE THE BOOK I'D STARTED.
CARE TO MAKE ME A BETTER OFFER?

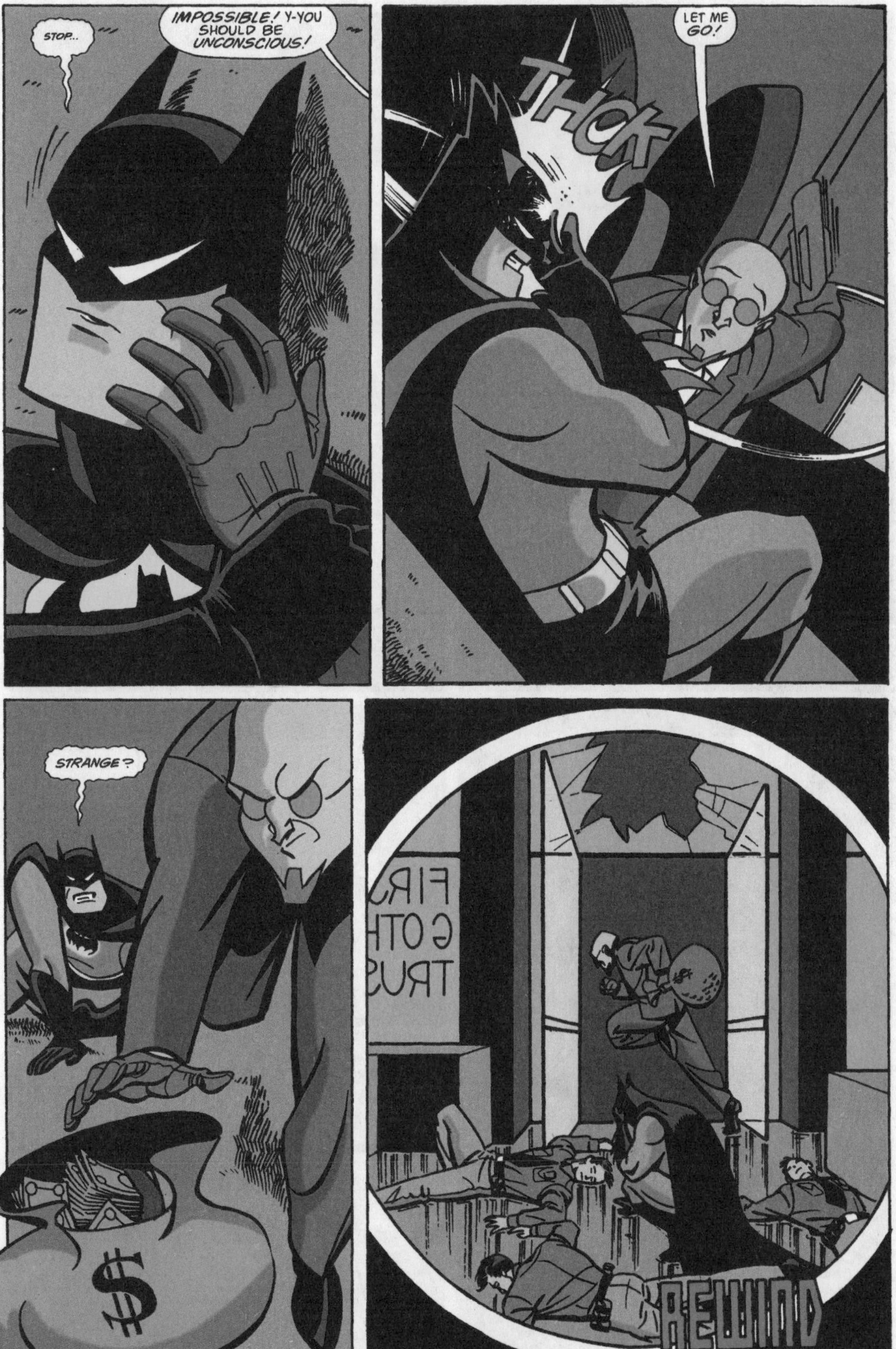

STOP..
IMPOSSIBLE! Y-YOU SHOULD BE UNCONSCIOUS!
THCK
LET ME GO!
STRANGE?
FIR
G OTH
TRUS
REWIND

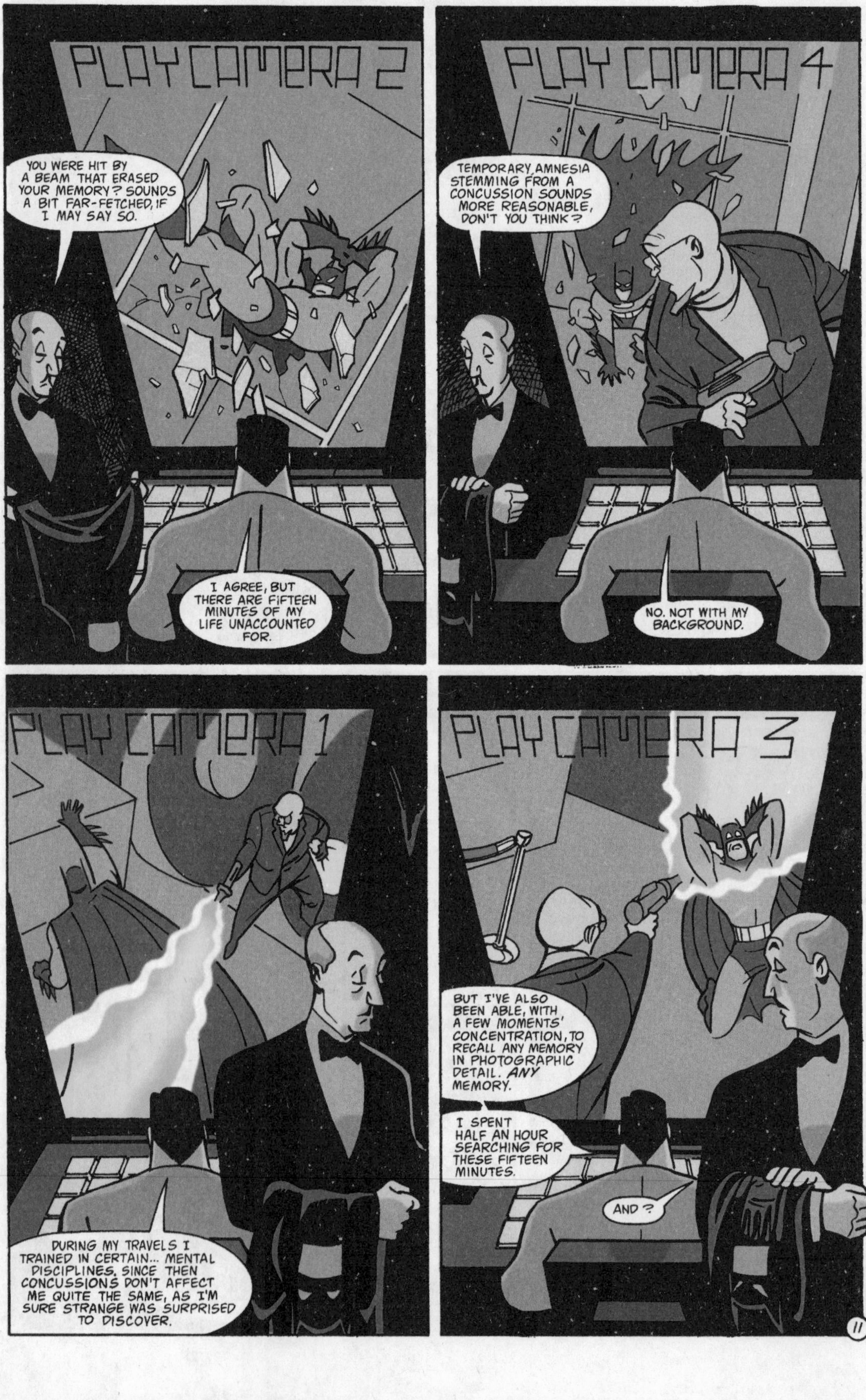
PLAY CAMERA 2
YOU WERE HIT BY A BEAM THAT ERASED YOUR MEMORY? SOUNDS A BIT FAR-FETCHED, IF I MAY SAY SO.
I AGREE, BUT THERE ARE FIFTEEN MINUTES OF MY LIFE UNACCOUNTED FOR.
PLAY CAMERA 4
TEMPORARY AMNESIA STEMMING FROM A CONCUSSION SOUNDS MORE REASONABLE, DON'T YOU THINK?
NO. NOT WITH MY BACKGROUND.
PLAY CAMERA 1
DURING MY TRAVELS I TRAINED IN CERTAIN... MENTAL DISCIPLINES. SINCE THEN CONCUSSIONS DON'T AFFECT ME QUITE THE SAME, AS I'M SURE STRANGE WAS SURPRISED TO DISCOVER.
PLAY CAMERA 3
BUT I'VE ALSO BEEN ABLE, WITH A FEW MOMENTS' CONCENTRATION, TO RECALL ANY MEMORY IN PHOTOGRAPHIC DETAIL. *ANY* MEMORY.
I SPENT HALF AN HOUR SEARCHING FOR THESE FIFTEEN MINUTES.
AND?

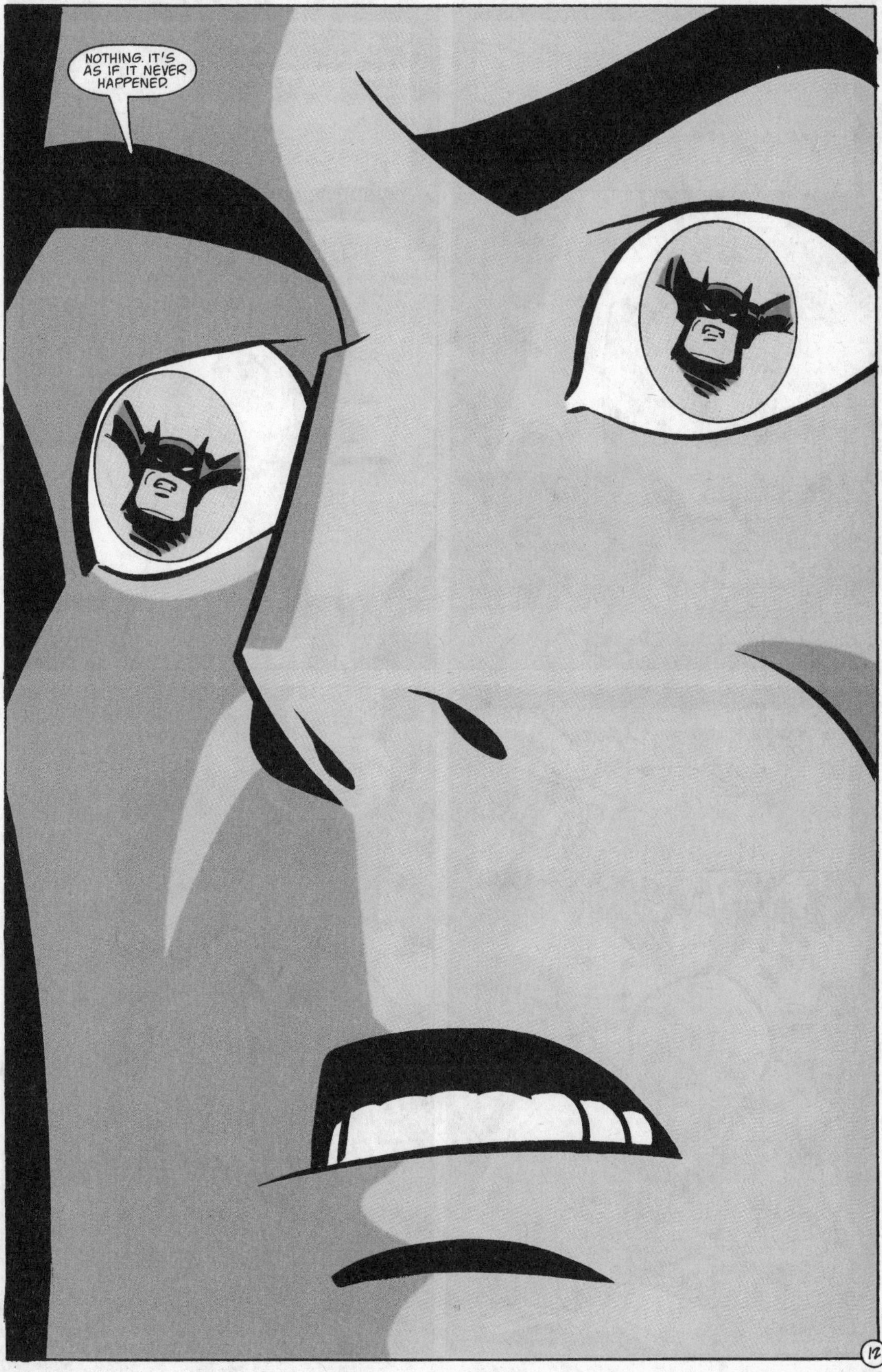
NOTHING. IT'S AS IF IT NEVER HAPPENED.

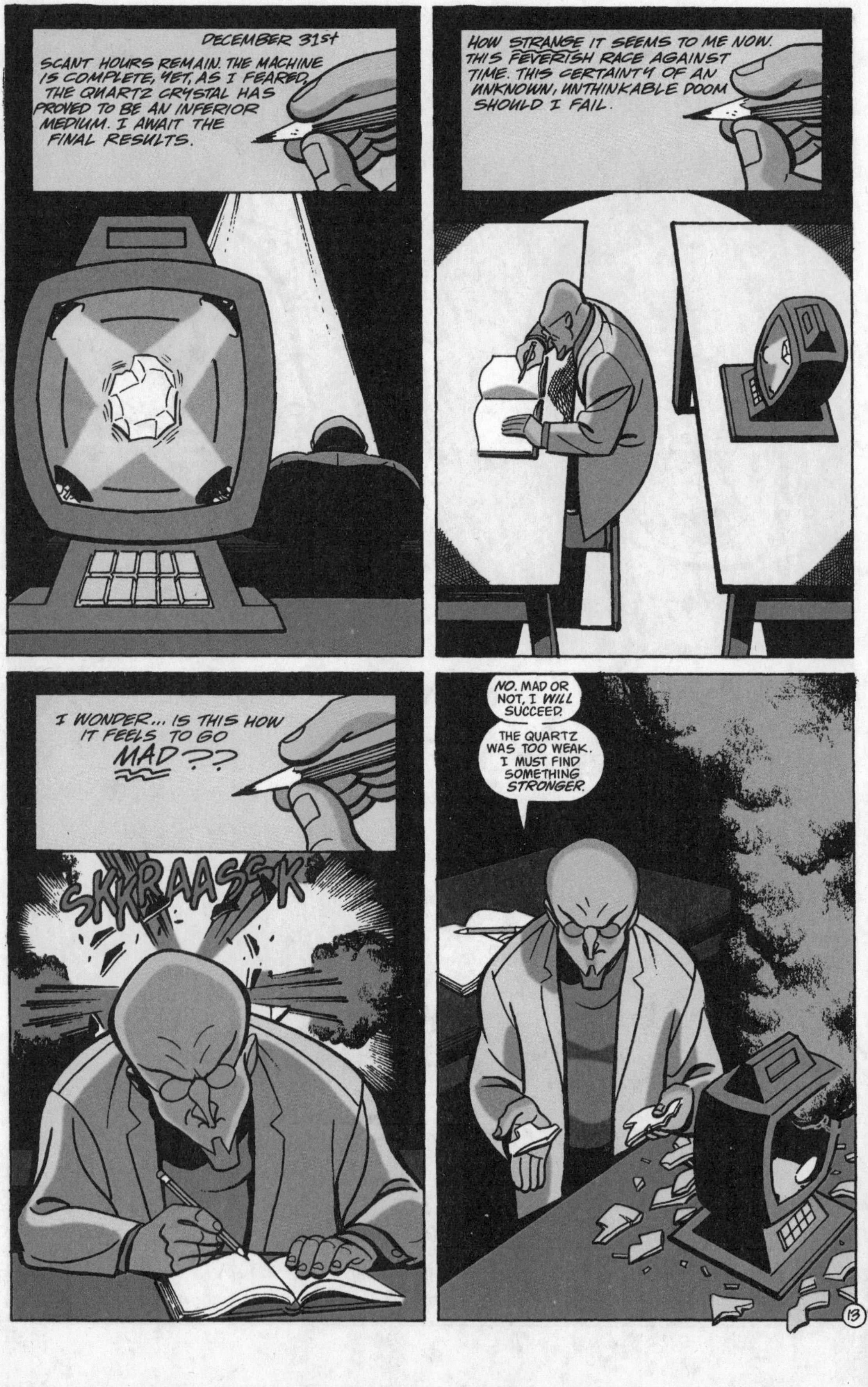
DECEMBER 31st
SCANT HOURS REMAIN. THE MACHINE IS COMPLETE, YET, AS I FEARED, THE QUARTZ CRYSTAL HAS PROVED TO BE AN INFERIOR MEDIUM. I AWAIT THE FINAL RESULTS.
HOW STRANGE IT SEEMS TO ME NOW. THIS FEVERISH RACE AGAINST TIME. THIS CERTAINTY OF AN UNKNOWN, UNTHINKABLE DOOM SHOULD I FAIL.
I WONDER... IS THIS HOW IT FEELS TO GO MAD??
SKKRAASSK
NO. MAD OR NOT, I WILL SUCCEED.
THE QUARTZ WAS TOO WEAK. I MUST FIND SOMETHING STRONGER.
13

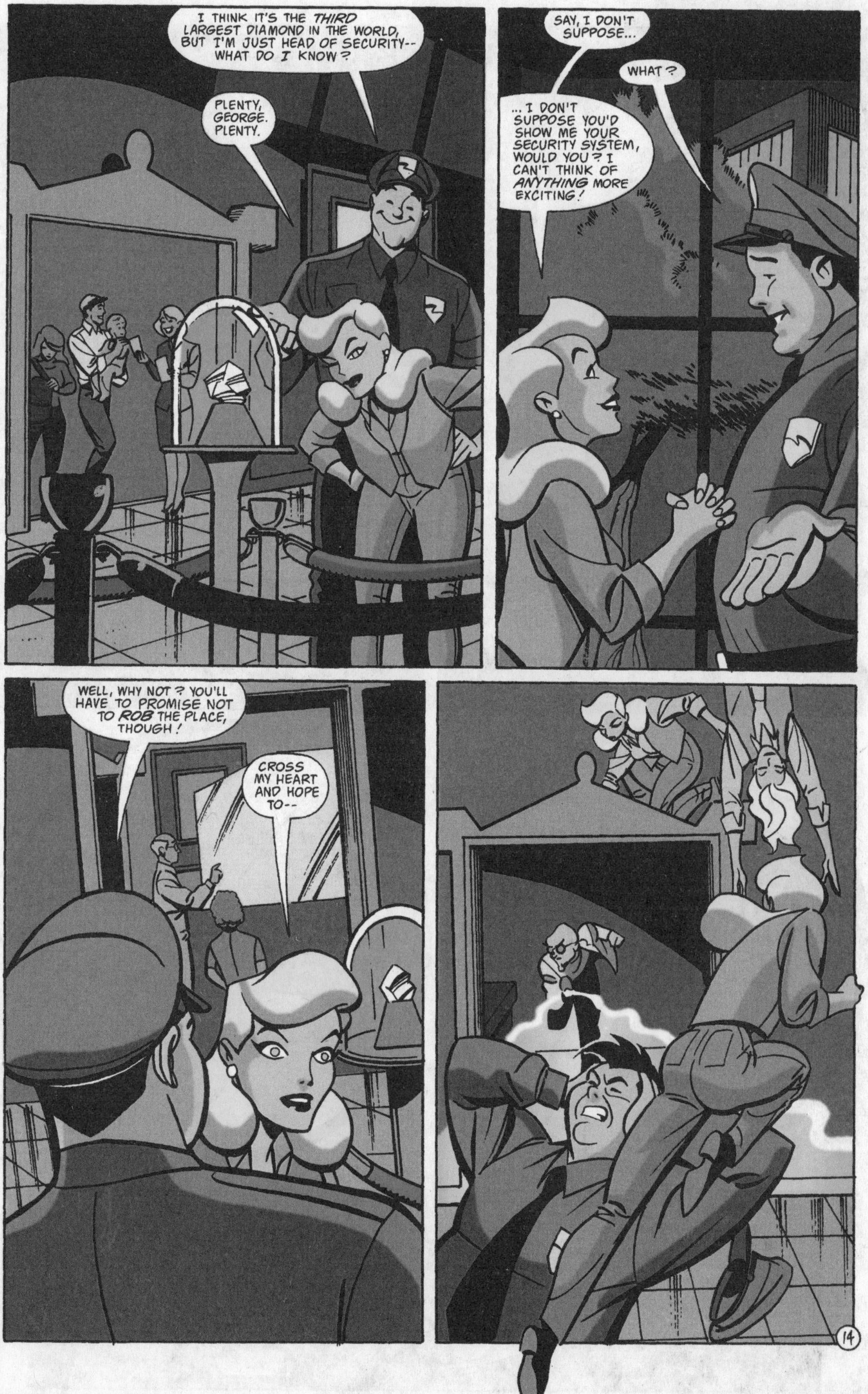

I THINK IT'S THE THIRD LARGEST DIAMOND IN THE WORLD, BUT I'M JUST HEAD OF SECURITY-- WHAT DO I KNOW?
PLENTY, GEORGE. PLENTY.
SAY, I DON'T SUPPOSE...
WHAT?
...I DON'T SUPPOSE YOU'D SHOW ME YOUR SECURITY SYSTEM, WOULD YOU? I CAN'T THINK OF ANYTHING MORE EXCITING!
WELL, WHY NOT? YOU'LL HAVE TO PROMISE NOT TO ROB THE PLACE, THOUGH!
CROSS MY HEART AND HOPE TO--

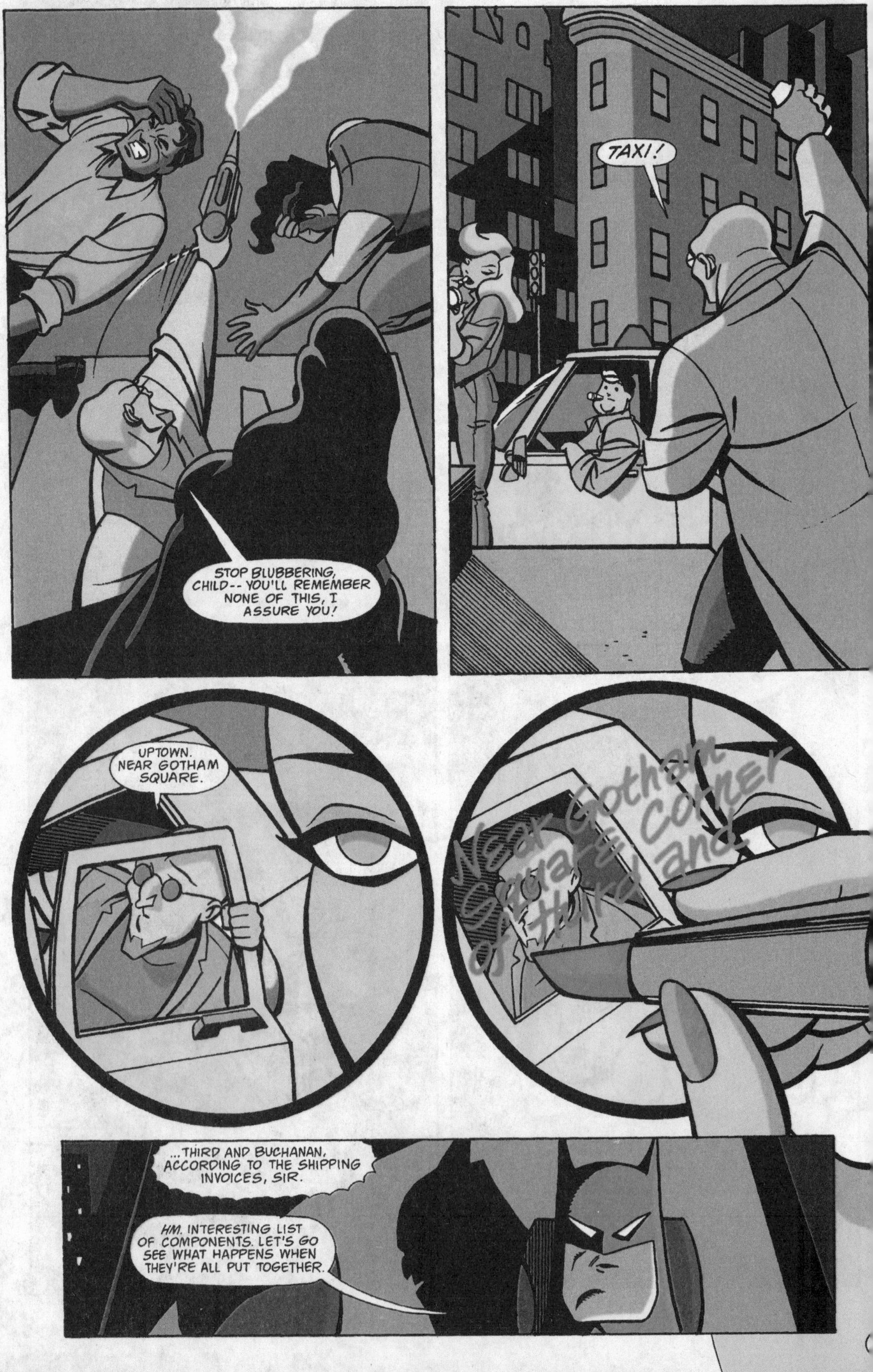
STOP BLUBBERING, CHILD-- YOU'LL REMEMBER NONE OF THIS, I ASSURE YOU!
TAXI!
UPTOWN. NEAR GOTHAM SQUARE.
Near Gotham Square Corner of third and
...THIRD AND BUCHANAN, ACCORDING TO THE SHIPPING INVOICES, SIR.
HM. INTERESTING LIST OF COMPONENTS. LET'S GO SEE WHAT HAPPENS WHEN THEY'RE ALL PUT TOGETHER.

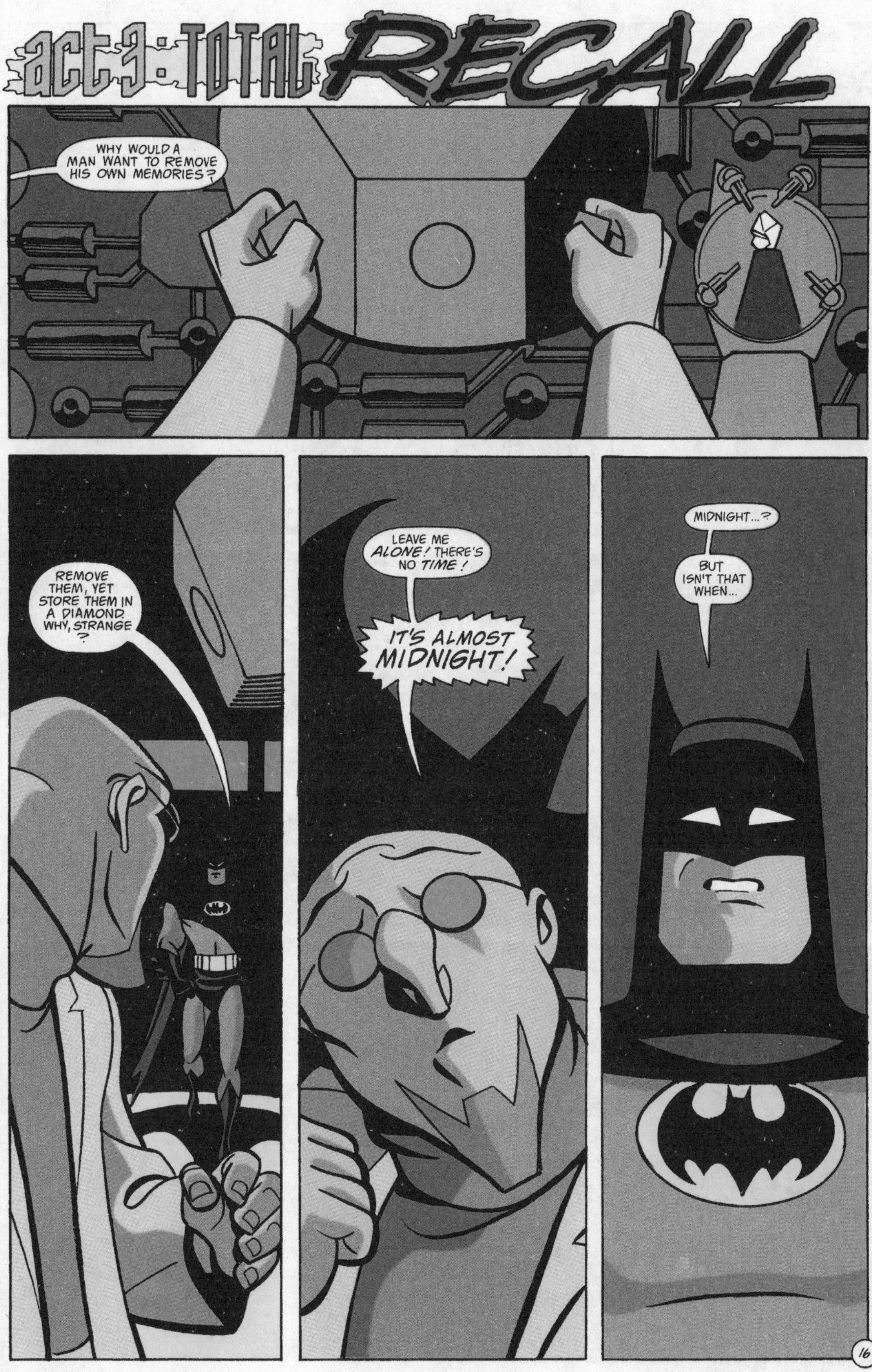
act 3: TOTAL RECALL
WHY WOULD A MAN WANT TO REMOVE HIS OWN MEMORIES?
REMOVE THEM, YET STORE THEM IN A DIAMOND. WHY, STRANGE?
LEAVE ME ALONE! THERE'S NO TIME!
IT'S ALMOST MIDNIGHT!
MIDNIGHT...?
BUT ISN'T THAT WHEN...

GOOD LORD, STRANGE. THIS IS ABOUT YOUR SON, ISN'T IT?

eh?

AAAAAAAAA!

NO!

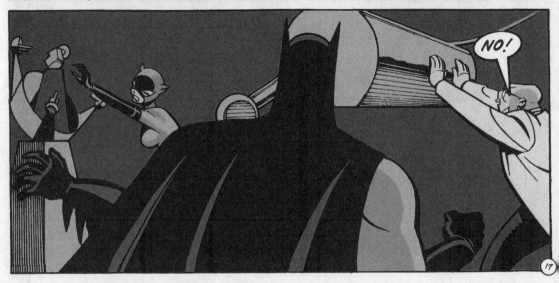

17

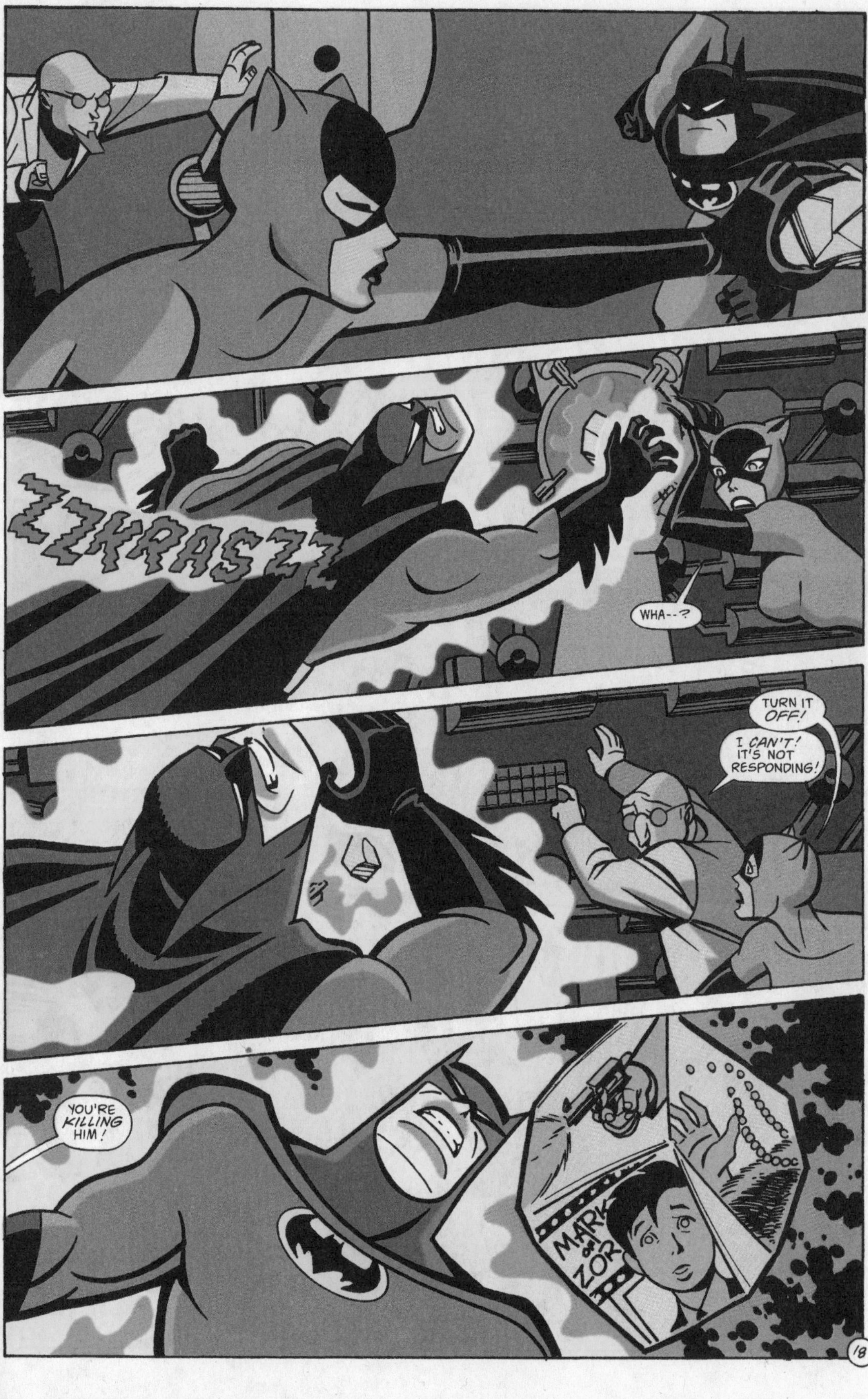
ZZKRASZZ
WHA--?
TURN IT OFF!
I CAN'T! IT'S NOT RESPONDING!
YOU'RE KILLING HIM!
MARK ZOR

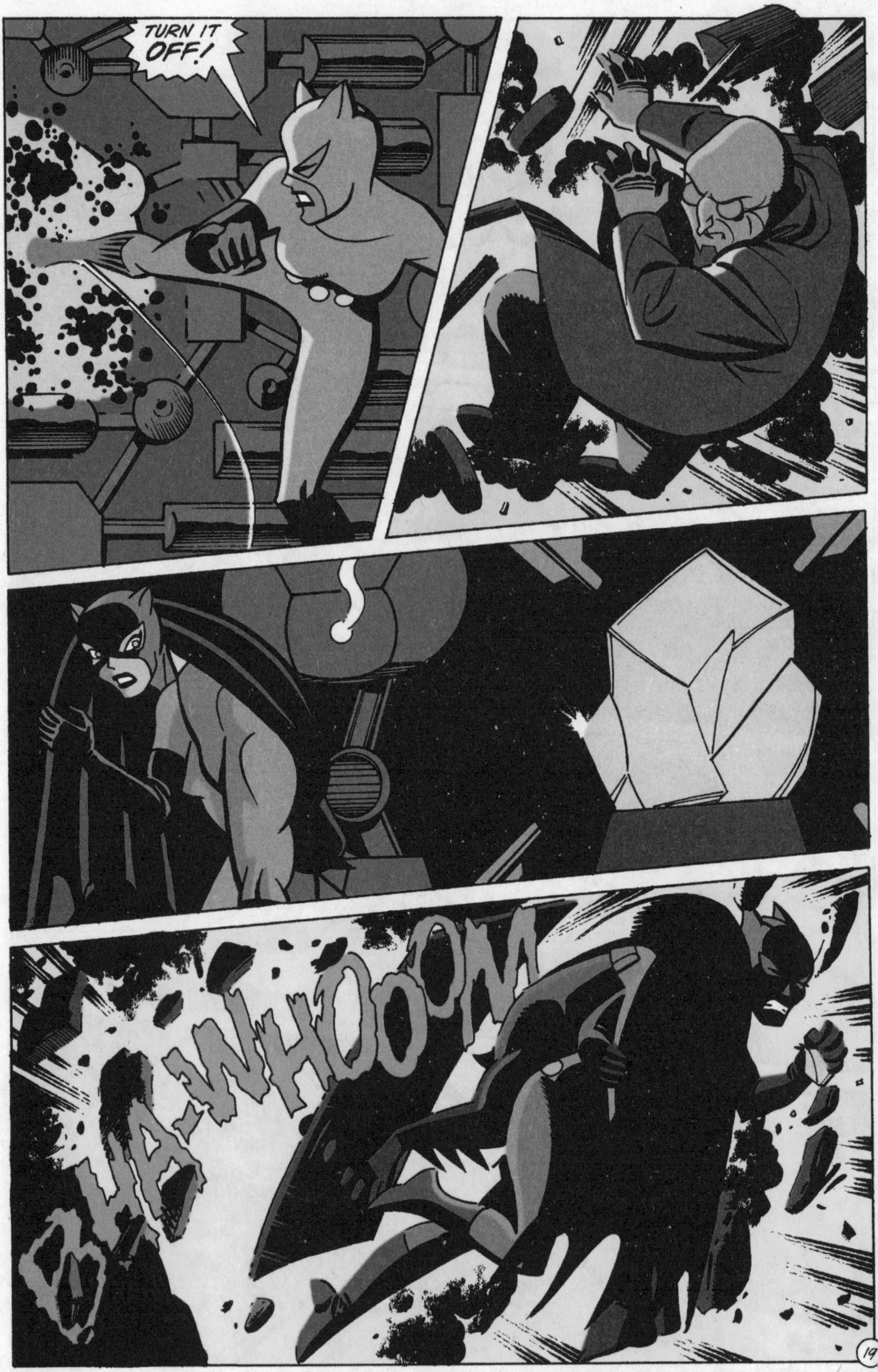

TURN IT OFF!
BA-WHOOOM

HELP ME... PLEASE...
IS... IS ANYONE THERE...?
ARE YOU PEOPLE READY FOR THE COUNTDOWN?!
2ND ANNUAL GOTHAM'S NEW YEAR'S COUNTDOWN
HERE WE GO!
2ND 2ND
1st 1st
NO

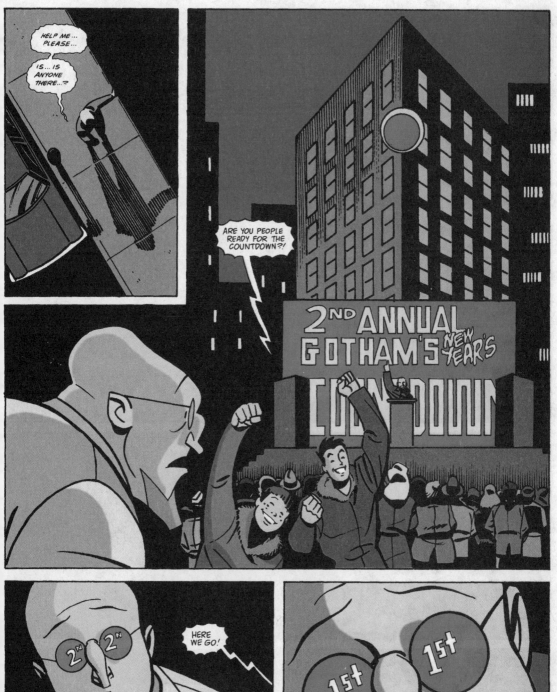

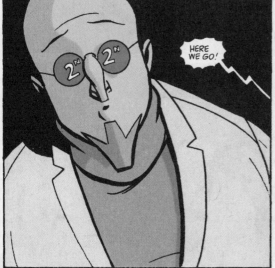

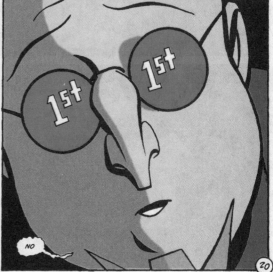

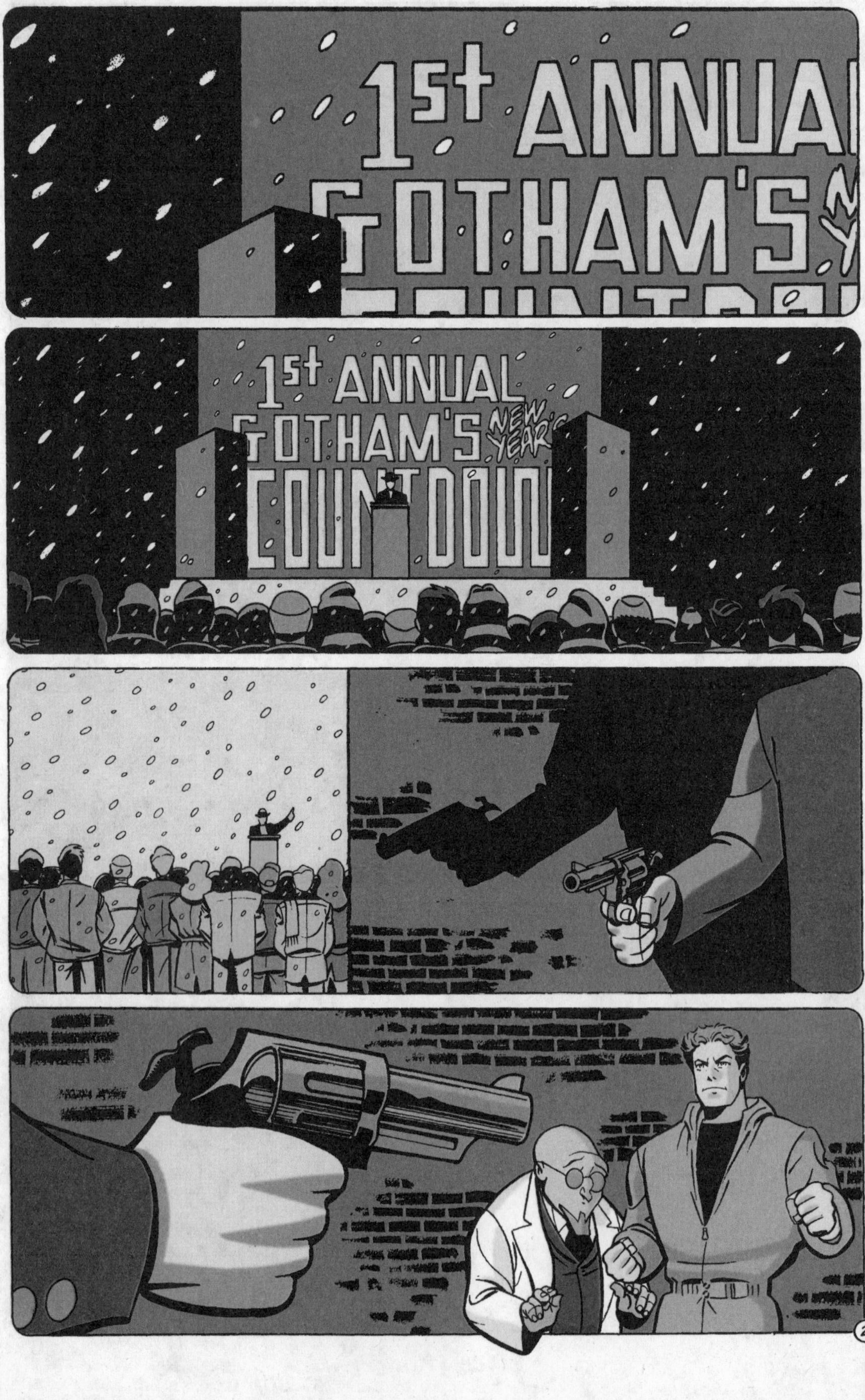

1st ANNUAL GOTHAM'S NEW YEAR'S COUNTDOWN

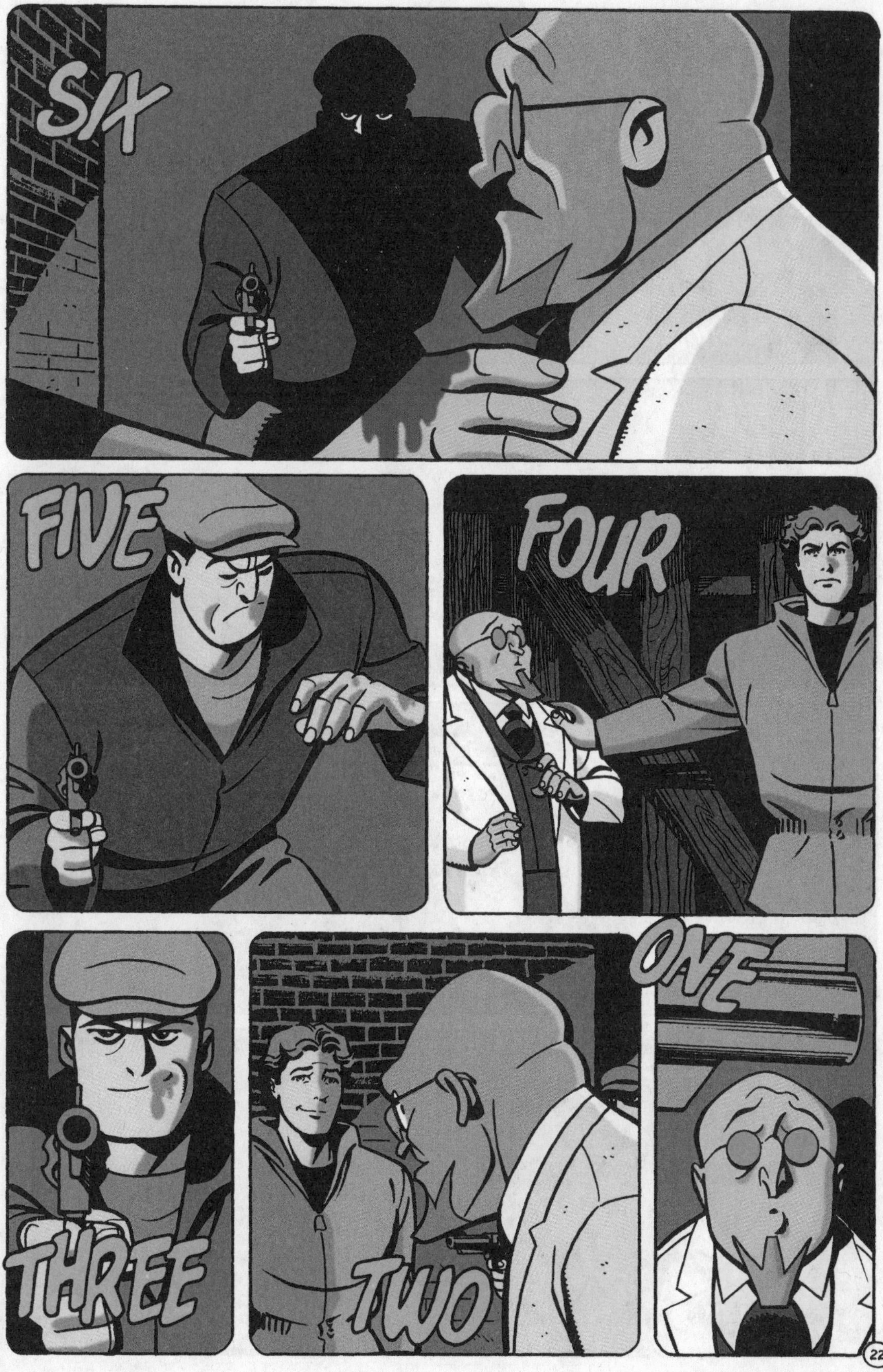
SIX
FIVE
FOUR
THREE
TWO
ONE

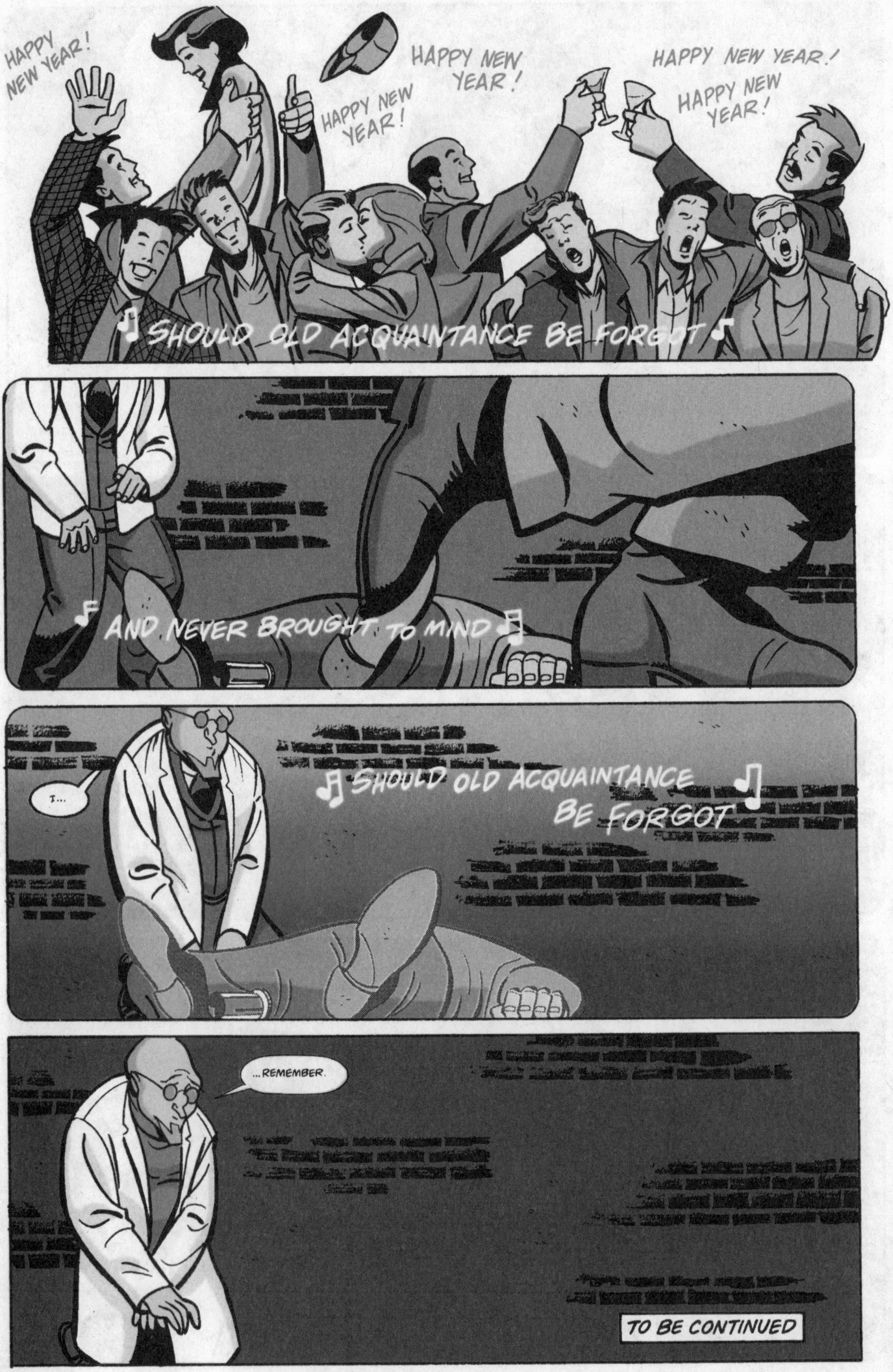
HAPPY NEW YEAR!
HAPPY NEW YEAR!
HAPPY NEW YEAR!
HAPPY NEW YEAR!
HAPPY NEW YEAR!
SHOULD OLD ACQUAINTANCE BE FORGOT
AND NEVER BROUGHT TO MIND
I...
SHOULD OLD ACQUAINTANCE BE FORGOT
...REMEMBER.
TO BE CONTINUED

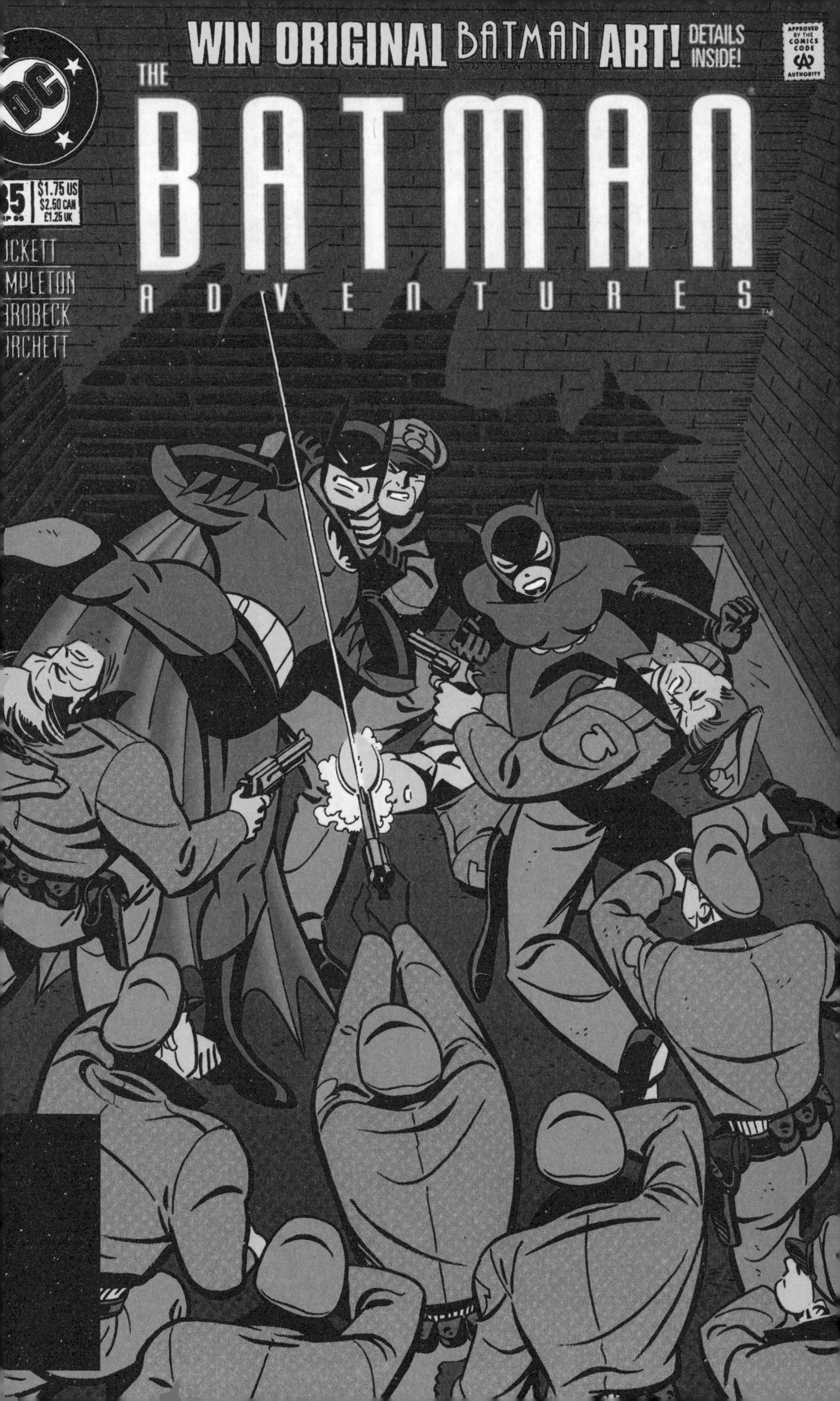

WIN ORIGINAL BATMAN ART! DETAILS INSIDE!
APPROVED BY THE COMICS CODE AUTHORITY
DC
THE BATMAN ADVENTURES
$1.75 US
$2.50 CAN
£1.25 UK

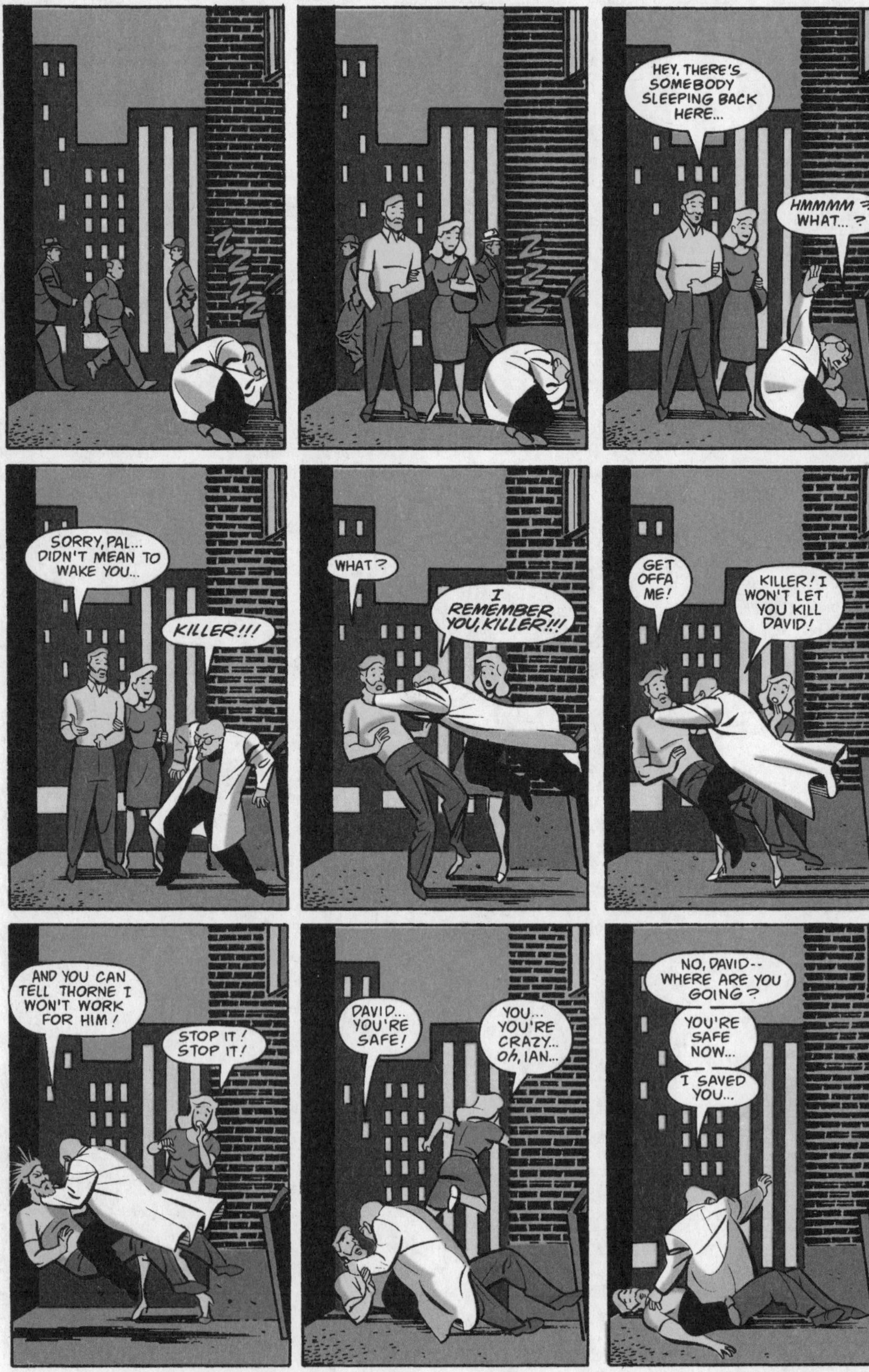
Z Z Z
Z Z Z
HEY, THERE'S SOMEBODY SLEEPING BACK HERE...
HMMMM? WHAT...?
SORRY, PAL... DIDN'T MEAN TO WAKE YOU...
KILLER!!!
WHAT?
I REMEMBER YOU, KILLER!!!
GET OFFA ME!
KILLER! I WON'T LET YOU KILL DAVID!
AND YOU CAN TELL THORNE I WON'T WORK FOR HIM!
STOP IT! STOP IT!
DAVID... YOU'RE SAFE!
YOU... YOU'RE CRAZY... Oh, IAN...
NO, DAVID-- WHERE ARE YOU GOING?
YOU'RE SAFE NOW...
I SAVED YOU...

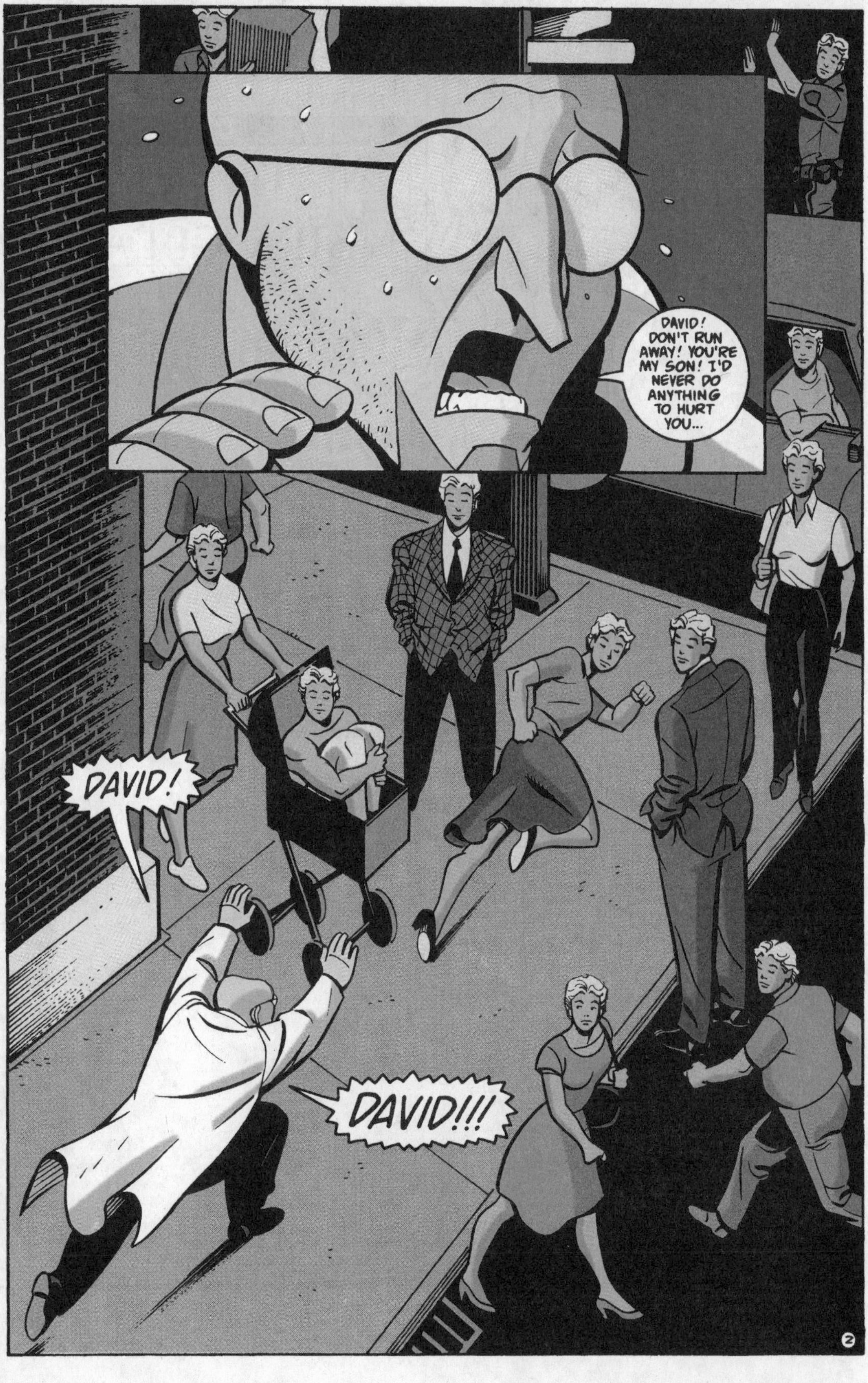
DAVID! DON'T RUN AWAY! YOU'RE MY SON! I'D NEVER DO ANYTHING TO HURT YOU...
DAVID!
DAVID!!!

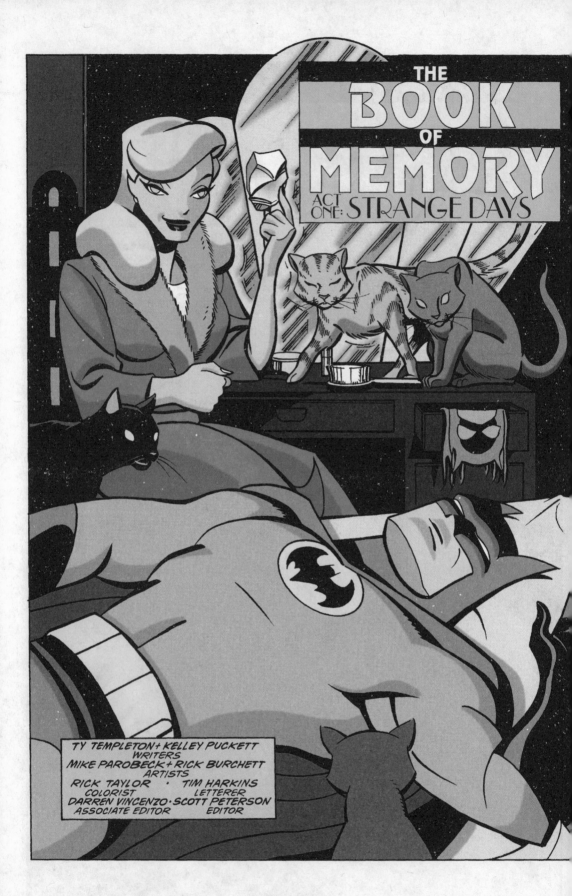

THE BOOK OF MEMORY
ACT ONE: STRANGE DAYS

TY TEMPLETON + KELLEY PUCKETT
WRITERS
MIKE PAROBECK + RICK BURCHETT
ARTISTS
RICK TAYLOR • TIM HARKINS
COLORIST LETTERER
DARREN VINCENZO • SCOTT PETERSON
ASSOCIATE EDITOR EDITOR

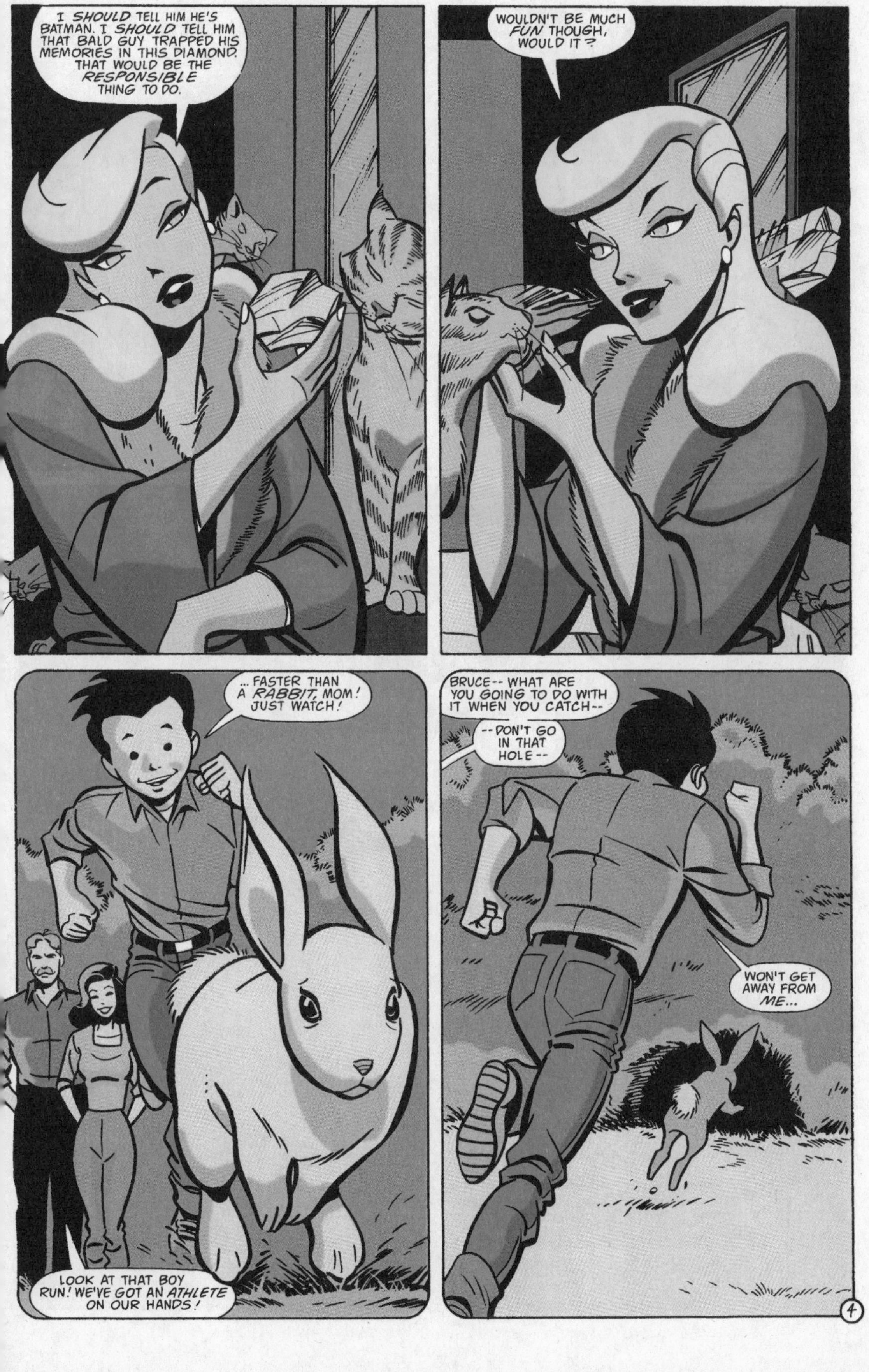
I SHOULD TELL HIM HE'S BATMAN. I SHOULD TELL HIM THAT BALD GUY TRAPPED HIS MEMORIES IN THIS DIAMOND. THAT WOULD BE THE RESPONSIBLE THING TO DO.
WOULDN'T BE MUCH FUN THOUGH, WOULD IT?
...FASTER THAN A RABBIT, MOM! JUST WATCH!
LOOK AT THAT BOY RUN! WE'VE GOT AN ATHLETE ON OUR HANDS!
BRUCE-- WHAT ARE YOU GOING TO DO WITH IT WHEN YOU CATCH--
--DON'T GO IN THAT HOLE--
WON'T GET AWAY FROM ME...
4

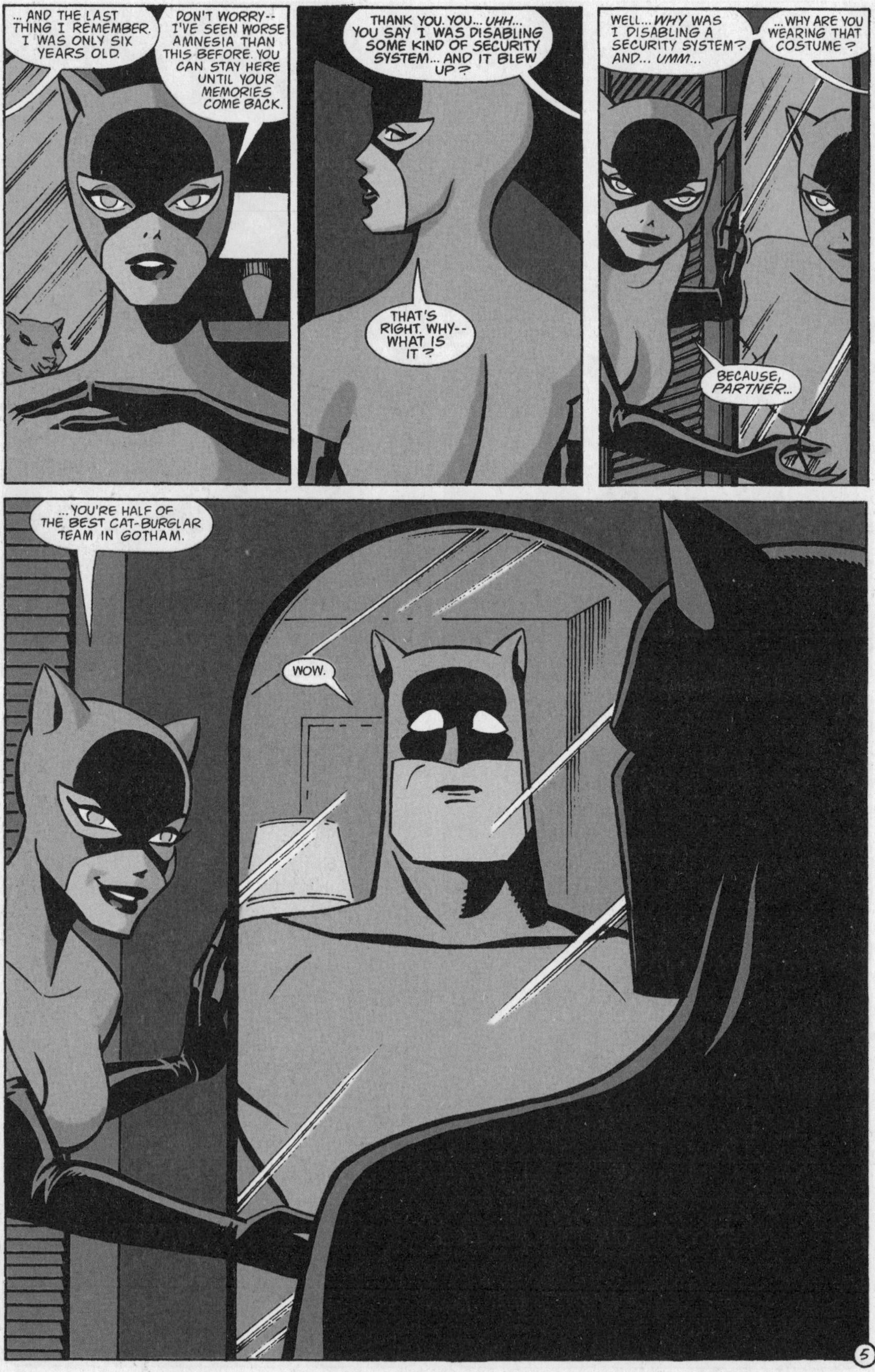

... AND THE LAST THING I REMEMBER. I WAS ONLY SIX YEARS OLD.
DON'T WORRY-- I'VE SEEN WORSE AMNESIA THAN THIS BEFORE. YOU CAN STAY HERE UNTIL YOUR MEMORIES COME BACK.
THANK YOU. YOU... *UHH*... YOU SAY I WAS DISABLING SOME KIND OF SECURITY SYSTEM... AND IT BLEW UP?
THAT'S RIGHT. WHY-- WHAT IS IT?
WELL... *WHY* WAS I DISABLING A SECURITY SYSTEM? AND... *UMM*...
...WHY ARE YOU WEARING THAT COSTUME?
BECAUSE, *PARTNER*...
...YOU'RE HALF OF THE BEST CAT-BURGLAR TEAM IN GOTHAM.
WOW.

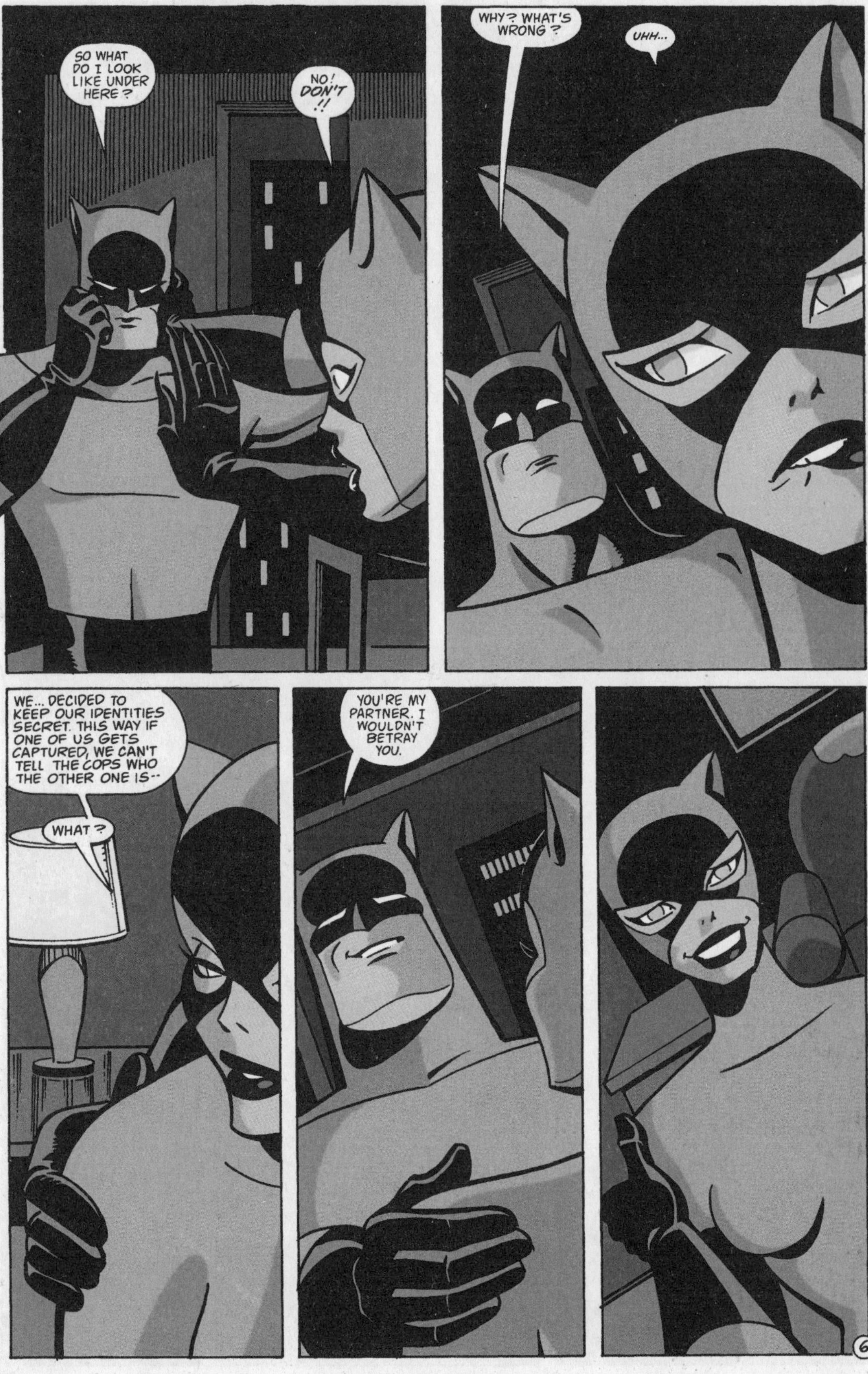
SO WHAT DO I LOOK LIKE UNDER HERE?
NO! DON'T !!
WHY? WHAT'S WRONG?
UHH...
WE... DECIDED TO KEEP OUR IDENTITIES SECRET. THIS WAY IF ONE OF US GETS CAPTURED, WE CAN'T TELL THE COPS WHO THE OTHER ONE IS--
WHAT?
YOU'RE MY PARTNER. I WOULDN'T BETRAY YOU.
6

OKAY-- THE IDEA'S SIMPLE. GET FROM HERE TO THERE WITHOUT TOUCHING A BEAM. NOW, WITH A FIELD THIS COMPLEX, YOU HAVE TO GO *VERY* SLOWLY AND TAKE IT ONE STEP AT A TIME.

HERBERT ROTHSCHILD MEMORIAL EXH

WHY BOTHER?

WHAT? HEY!

PIECE OF CAKE.

THIS IS *GREAT.* IT'S LIKE... I JUST *KNOW* WHAT TO DO. I DON'T EVEN HAVE TO *THINK* ABOUT IT!

IN *FACT...*

WAIT! WHAT'RE YOU --?

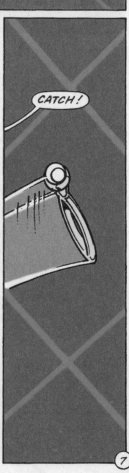

CATCH!

7

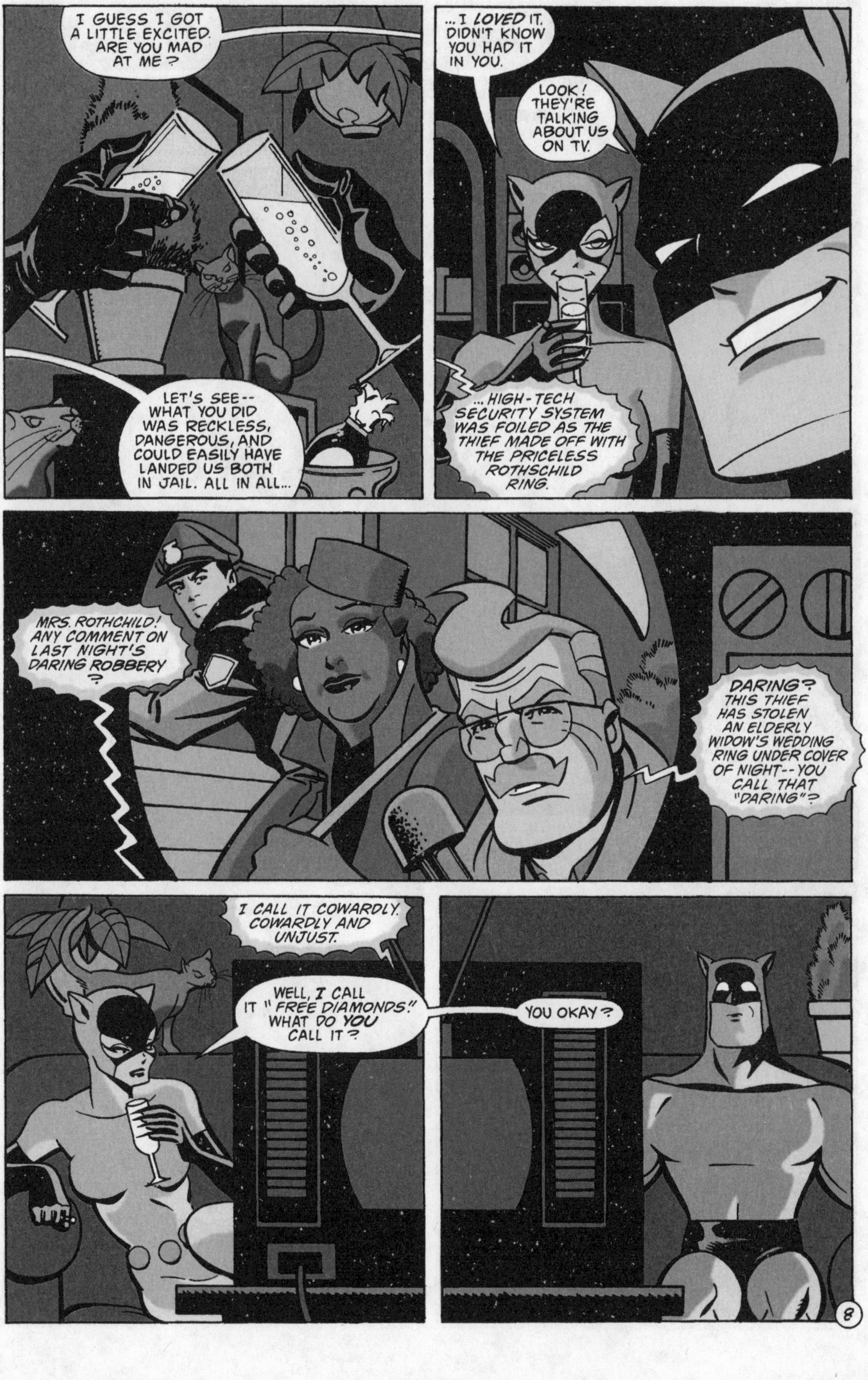
I GUESS I GOT A LITTLE EXCITED. ARE YOU MAD AT ME?
LET'S SEE-- WHAT YOU DID WAS RECKLESS, DANGEROUS, AND COULD EASILY HAVE LANDED US BOTH IN JAIL. ALL IN ALL...
...I LOVED IT. DIDN'T KNOW YOU HAD IT IN YOU.
LOOK! THEY'RE TALKING ABOUT US ON TV.
...HIGH-TECH SECURITY SYSTEM WAS FOILED AS THE THIEF MADE OFF WITH THE PRICELESS ROTHSCHILD RING.
MRS. ROTHCHILD! ANY COMMENT ON LAST NIGHT'S DARING ROBBERY?
DARING? THIS THIEF HAS STOLEN AN ELDERLY WIDOW'S WEDDING RING UNDER COVER OF NIGHT--YOU CALL THAT "DARING"?
I CALL IT COWARDLY. COWARDLY AND UNJUST.
WELL, I CALL IT "FREE DIAMONDS." WHAT DO YOU CALL IT?
YOU OKAY?
8

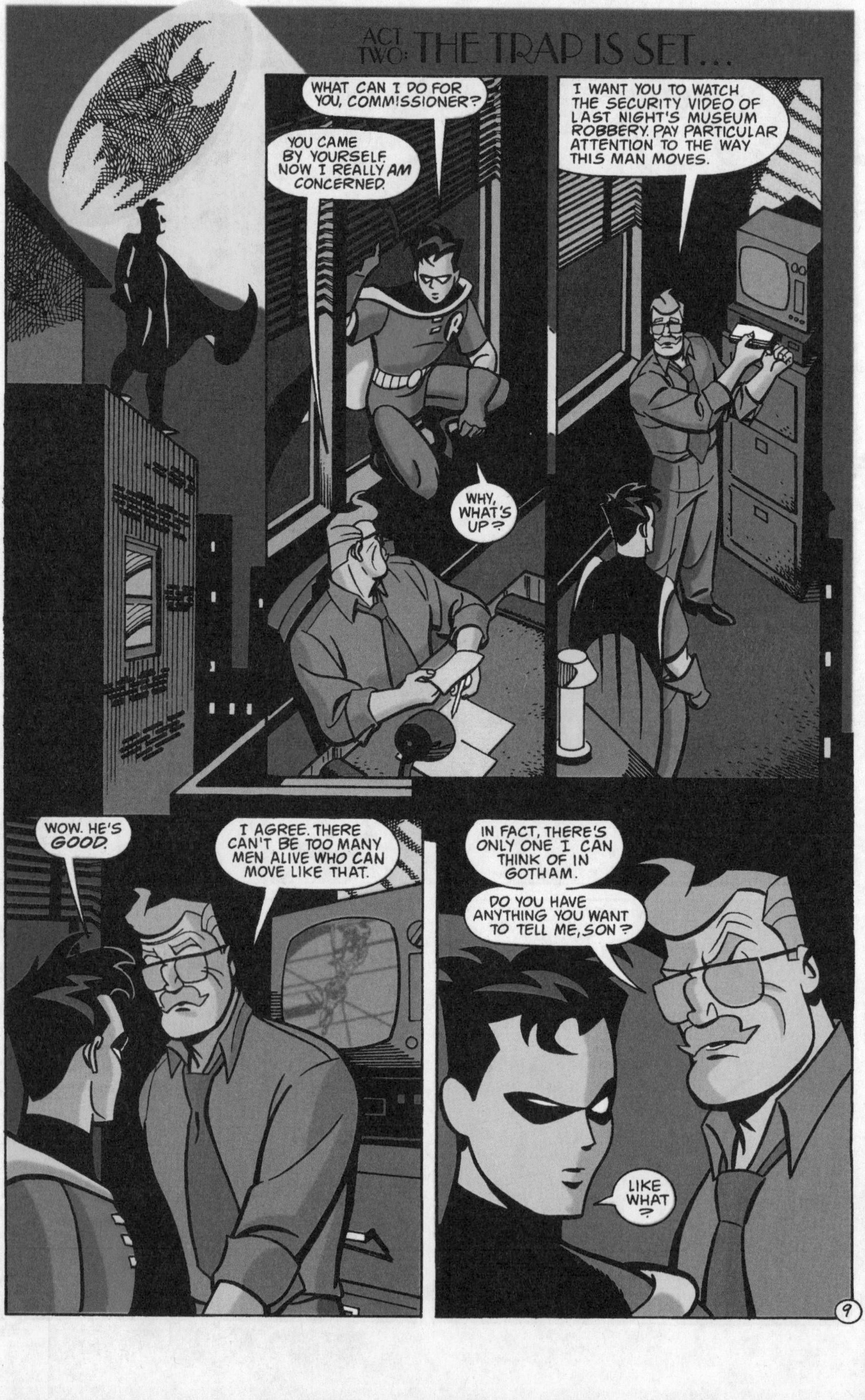

ACT TWO: THE TRAP IS SET...
WHAT CAN I DO FOR YOU, COMMISSIONER?
YOU CAME BY YOURSELF. NOW I REALLY AM CONCERNED.
WHY, WHAT'S UP?
I WANT YOU TO WATCH THE SECURITY VIDEO OF LAST NIGHT'S MUSEUM ROBBERY. PAY PARTICULAR ATTENTION TO THE WAY THIS MAN MOVES.
WOW. HE'S GOOD.
I AGREE. THERE CAN'T BE TOO MANY MEN ALIVE WHO CAN MOVE LIKE THAT.
IN FACT, THERE'S ONLY ONE I CAN THINK OF IN GOTHAM.
DO YOU HAVE ANYTHING YOU WANT TO TELL ME, SON?
LIKE WHAT?

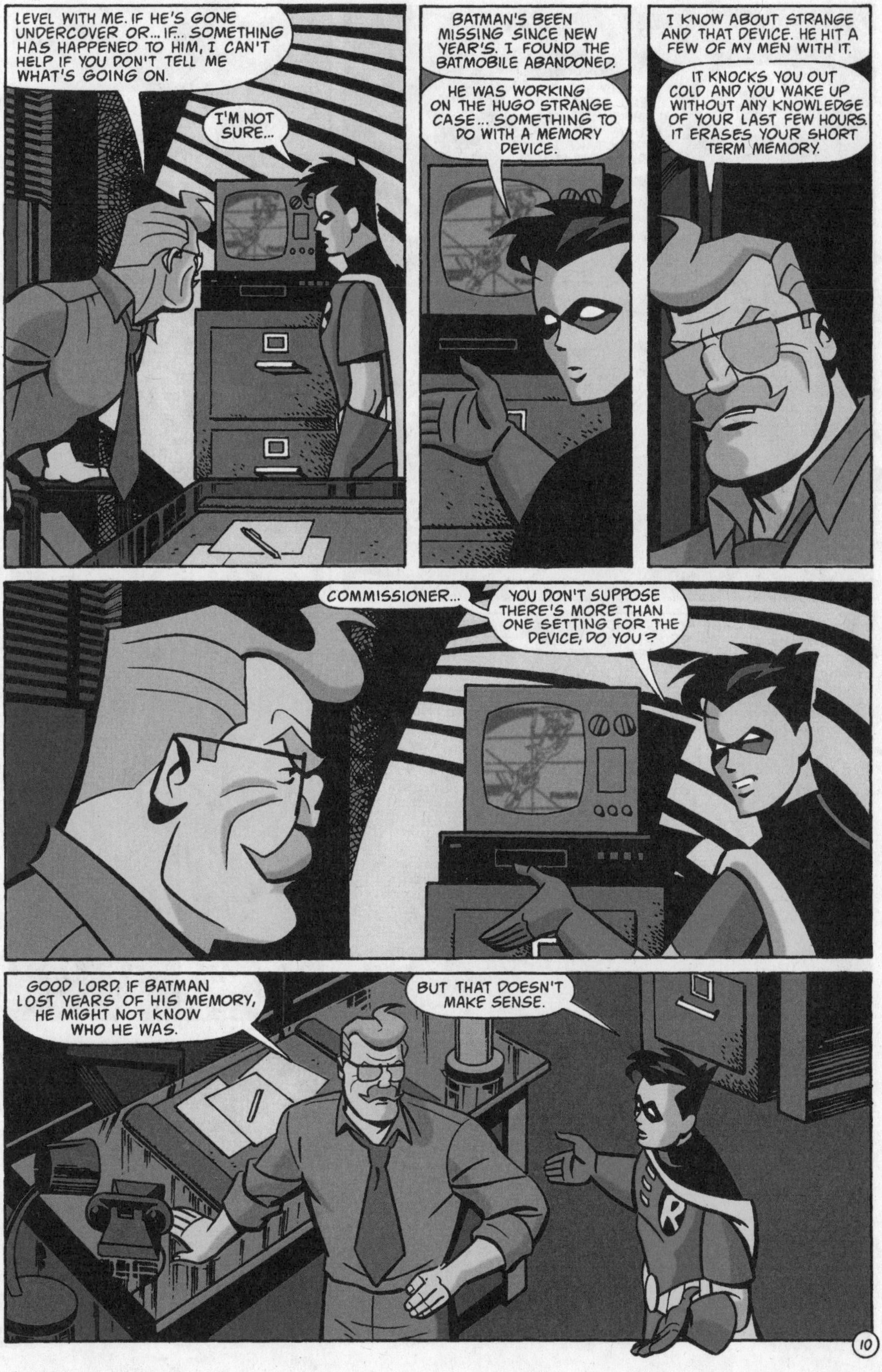

LEVEL WITH ME. IF HE'S GONE UNDERCOVER OR... IF... SOMETHING HAS HAPPENED TO HIM, I CAN'T HELP IF YOU DON'T TELL ME WHAT'S GOING ON.
I'M NOT SURE...
BATMAN'S BEEN MISSING SINCE NEW YEAR'S. I FOUND THE BATMOBILE ABANDONED.
HE WAS WORKING ON THE HUGO STRANGE CASE... SOMETHING TO DO WITH A MEMORY DEVICE.
I KNOW ABOUT STRANGE AND THAT DEVICE. HE HIT A FEW OF MY MEN WITH IT.
IT KNOCKS YOU OUT COLD AND YOU WAKE UP WITHOUT ANY KNOWLEDGE OF YOUR LAST FEW HOURS. IT ERASES YOUR SHORT TERM MEMORY.
COMMISSIONER...
YOU DON'T SUPPOSE THERE'S MORE THAN ONE SETTING FOR THE DEVICE, DO YOU?
GOOD LORD. IF BATMAN LOST YEARS OF HIS MEMORY, HE MIGHT NOT KNOW WHO HE WAS.
BUT THAT DOESN'T MAKE SENSE.

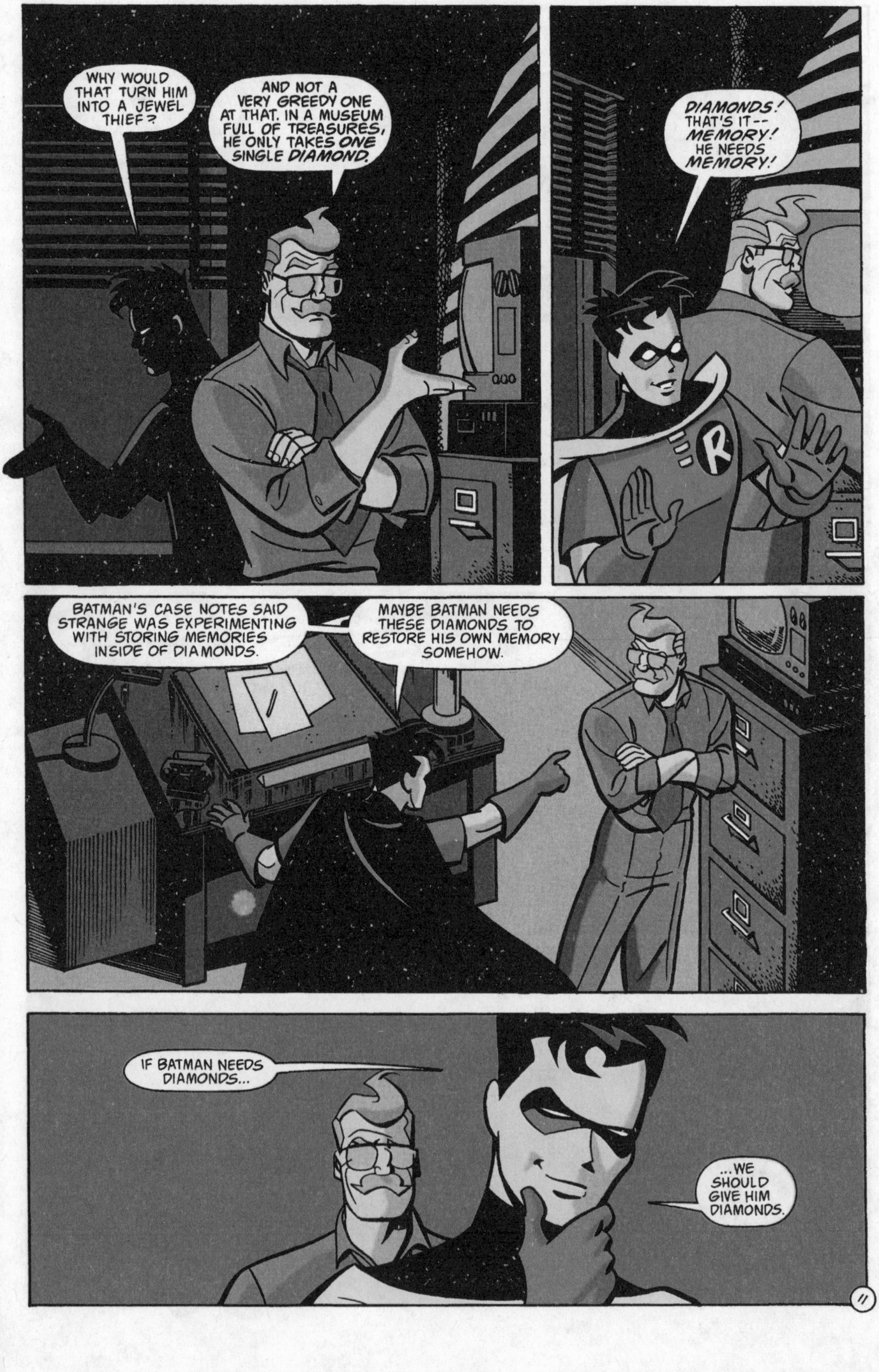

WHY WOULD THAT TURN HIM INTO A JEWEL THIEF?
AND NOT A VERY GREEDY ONE AT THAT. IN A MUSEUM FULL OF TREASURES, HE ONLY TAKES ONE SINGLE DIAMOND.
DIAMONDS! THAT'S IT-- MEMORY! HE NEEDS MEMORY!
BATMAN'S CASE NOTES SAID STRANGE WAS EXPERIMENTING WITH STORING MEMORIES INSIDE OF DIAMONDS.
MAYBE BATMAN NEEDS THESE DIAMONDS TO RESTORE HIS OWN MEMORY SOMEHOW.
IF BATMAN NEEDS DIAMONDS...
...WE SHOULD GIVE HIM DIAMONDS.

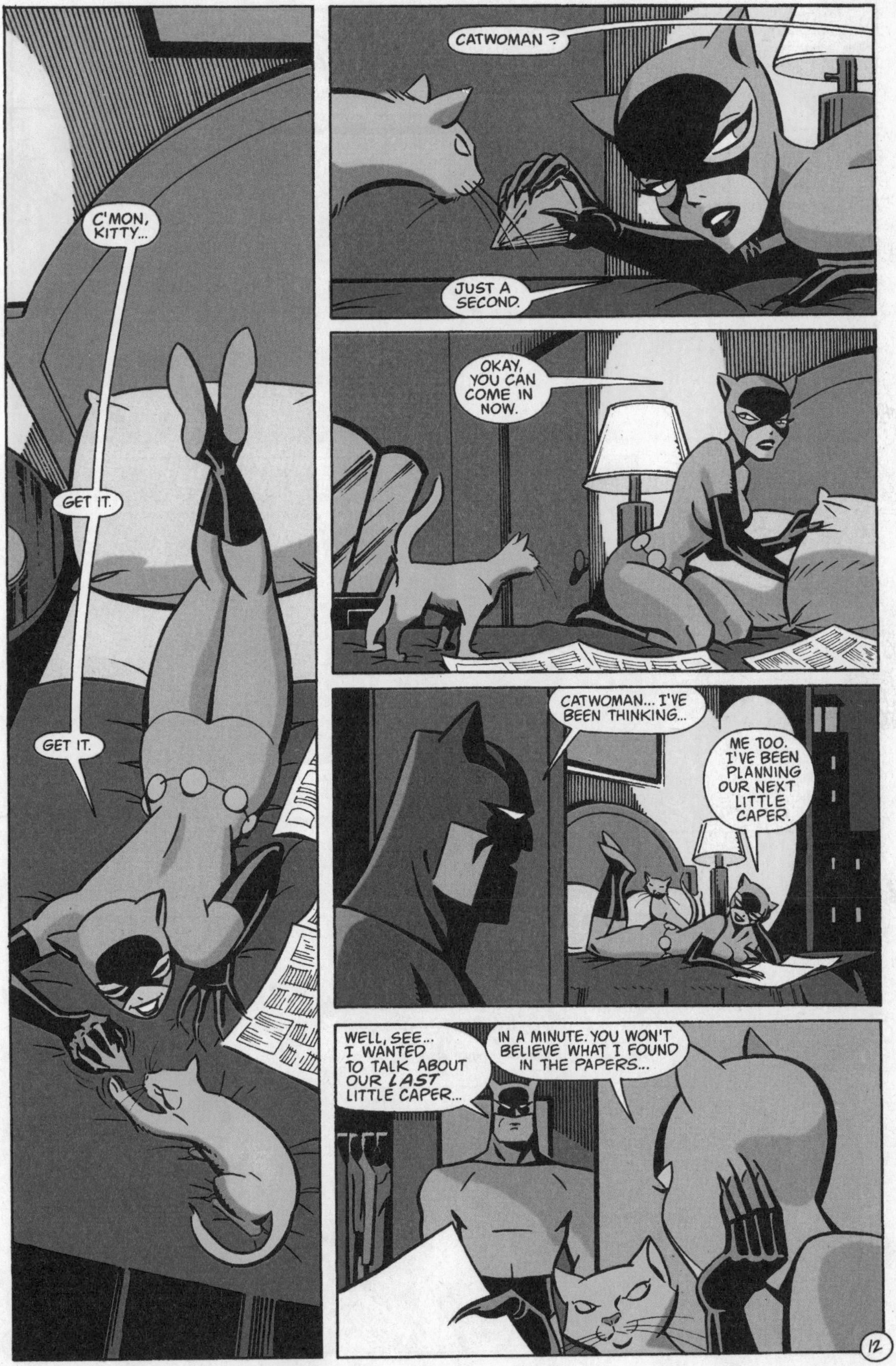
C'MON, KITTY...
GET IT.
GET IT.
CATWOMAN?
JUST A SECOND.
OKAY, YOU CAN COME IN NOW.
CATWOMAN... I'VE BEEN THINKING...
ME TOO. I'VE BEEN PLANNING OUR NEXT LITTLE CAPER.
WELL, SEE... I WANTED TO TALK ABOUT OUR *LAST* LITTLE CAPER...
IN A MINUTE. YOU WON'T BELIEVE WHAT I FOUND IN THE PAPERS...
12

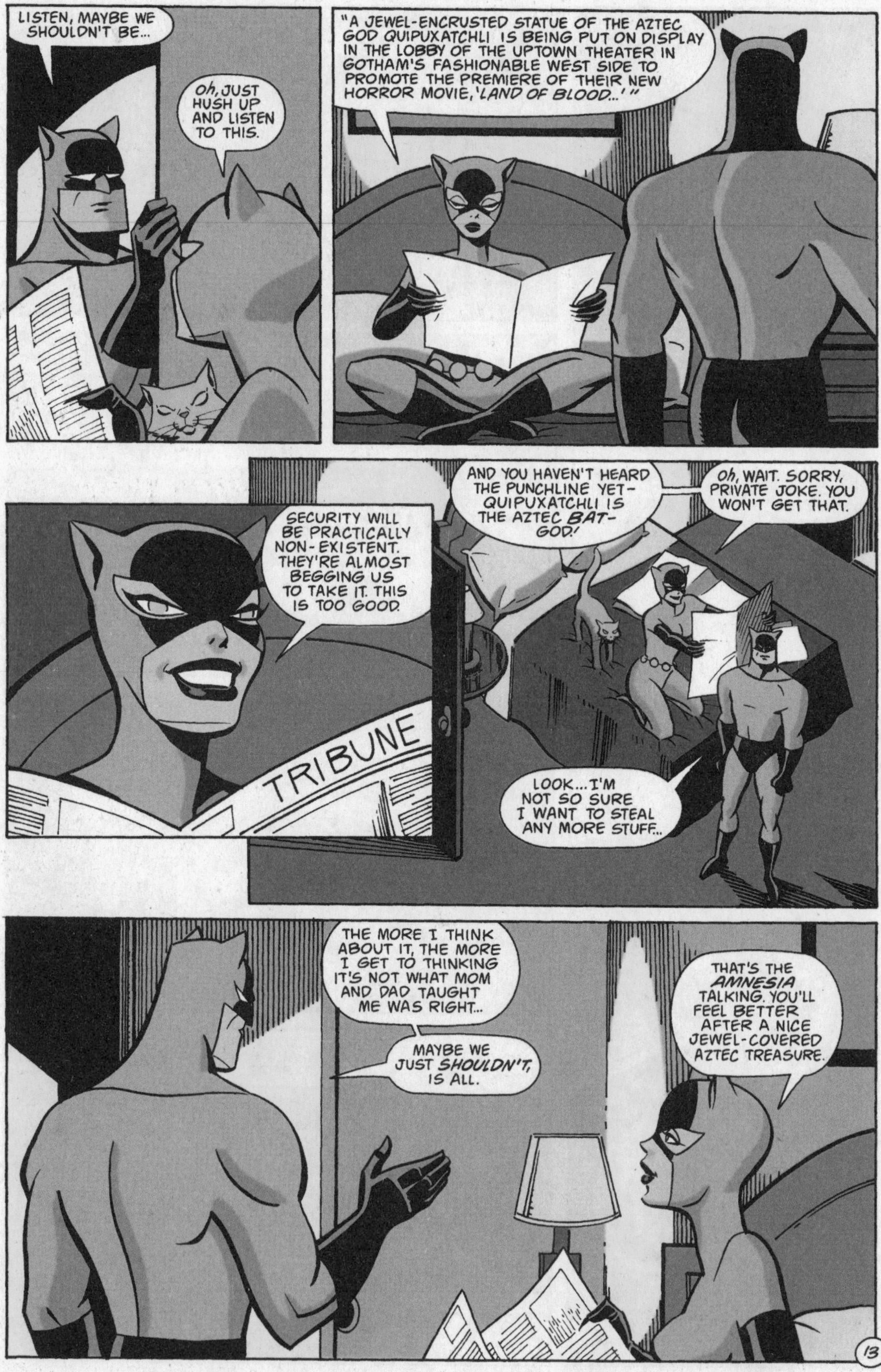

LISTEN, MAYBE WE SHOULDN'T BE...
Oh, JUST HUSH UP AND LISTEN TO THIS.
"A JEWEL-ENCRUSTED STATUE OF THE AZTEC GOD QUIPUXATCHLI IS BEING PUT ON DISPLAY IN THE LOBBY OF THE UPTOWN THEATER IN GOTHAM'S FASHIONABLE WEST SIDE TO PROMOTE THE PREMIERE OF THEIR NEW HORROR MOVIE, 'LAND OF BLOOD...' "
SECURITY WILL BE PRACTICALLY NON-EXISTENT. THEY'RE ALMOST BEGGING US TO TAKE IT. THIS IS TOO GOOD.
TRIBUNE
AND YOU HAVEN'T HEARD THE PUNCHLINE YET- QUIPUXATCHLI IS THE AZTEC BAT-GOD!
Oh, WAIT. SORRY, PRIVATE JOKE. YOU WON'T GET THAT.
LOOK... I'M NOT SO SURE I WANT TO STEAL ANY MORE STUFF...
THE MORE I THINK ABOUT IT, THE MORE I GET TO THINKING IT'S NOT WHAT MOM AND DAD TAUGHT ME WAS RIGHT...
MAYBE WE JUST SHOULDN'T, IS ALL.
THAT'S THE AMNESIA TALKING. YOU'LL FEEL BETTER AFTER A NICE JEWEL-COVERED AZTEC TREASURE.

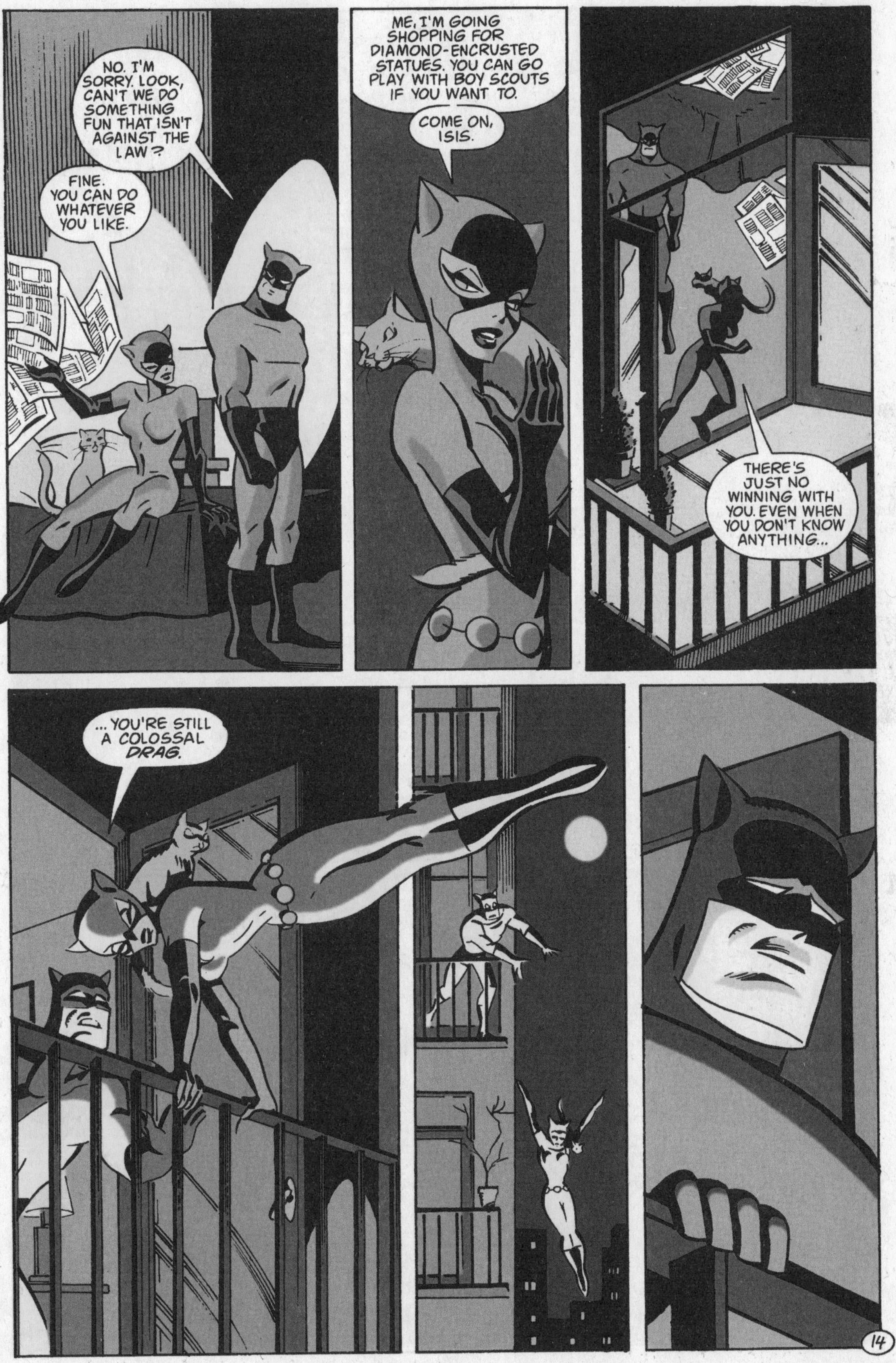
NO. I'M SORRY. LOOK, CAN'T WE DO SOMETHING FUN THAT ISN'T AGAINST THE LAW?
FINE. YOU CAN DO WHATEVER YOU LIKE.
ME, I'M GOING SHOPPING FOR DIAMOND-ENCRUSTED STATUES. YOU CAN GO PLAY WITH BOY SCOUTS IF YOU WANT TO.
COME ON, ISIS.
THERE'S JUST NO WINNING WITH YOU. EVEN WHEN YOU DON'T KNOW ANYTHING...
...YOU'RE STILL A COLOSSAL DRAG.

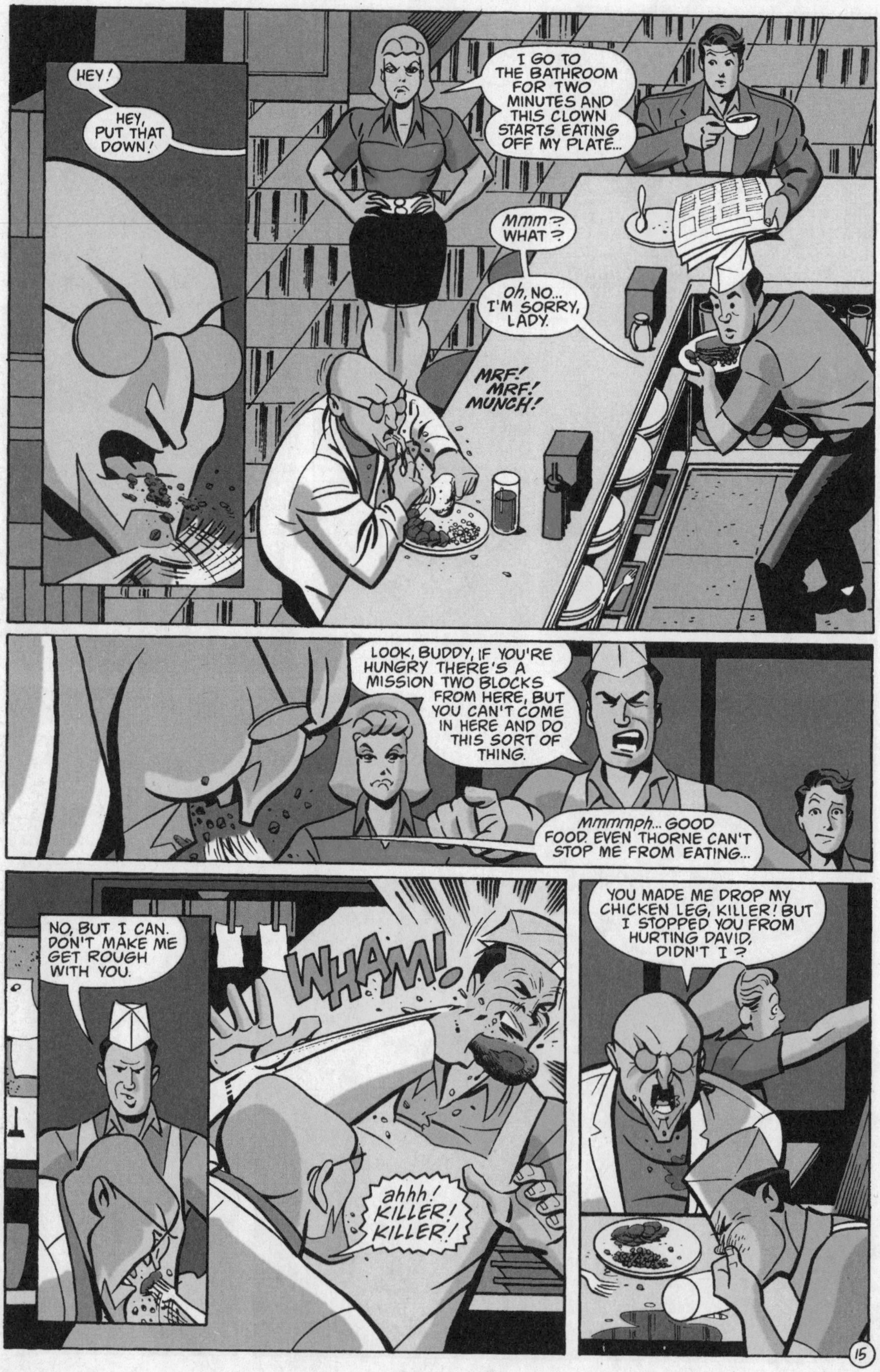

HEY!
HEY, PUT THAT DOWN!
I GO TO THE BATHROOM FOR TWO MINUTES AND THIS CLOWN STARTS EATING OFF MY PLATE...
Mmm? WHAT?
Oh, NO... I'M SORRY, LADY.
MRF! MRF! MUNCH!
LOOK, BUDDY, IF YOU'RE HUNGRY THERE'S A MISSION TWO BLOCKS FROM HERE, BUT YOU CAN'T COME IN HERE AND DO THIS SORT OF THING.
Mmmmph... GOOD FOOD. EVEN THORNE CAN'T STOP ME FROM EATING...
NO, BUT I CAN. DON'T MAKE ME GET ROUGH WITH YOU.
WHAM!
ahhh! KILLER! KILLER!
YOU MADE ME DROP MY CHICKEN LEG, KILLER! BUT I STOPPED YOU FROM HURTING DAVID, DIDN'T I?

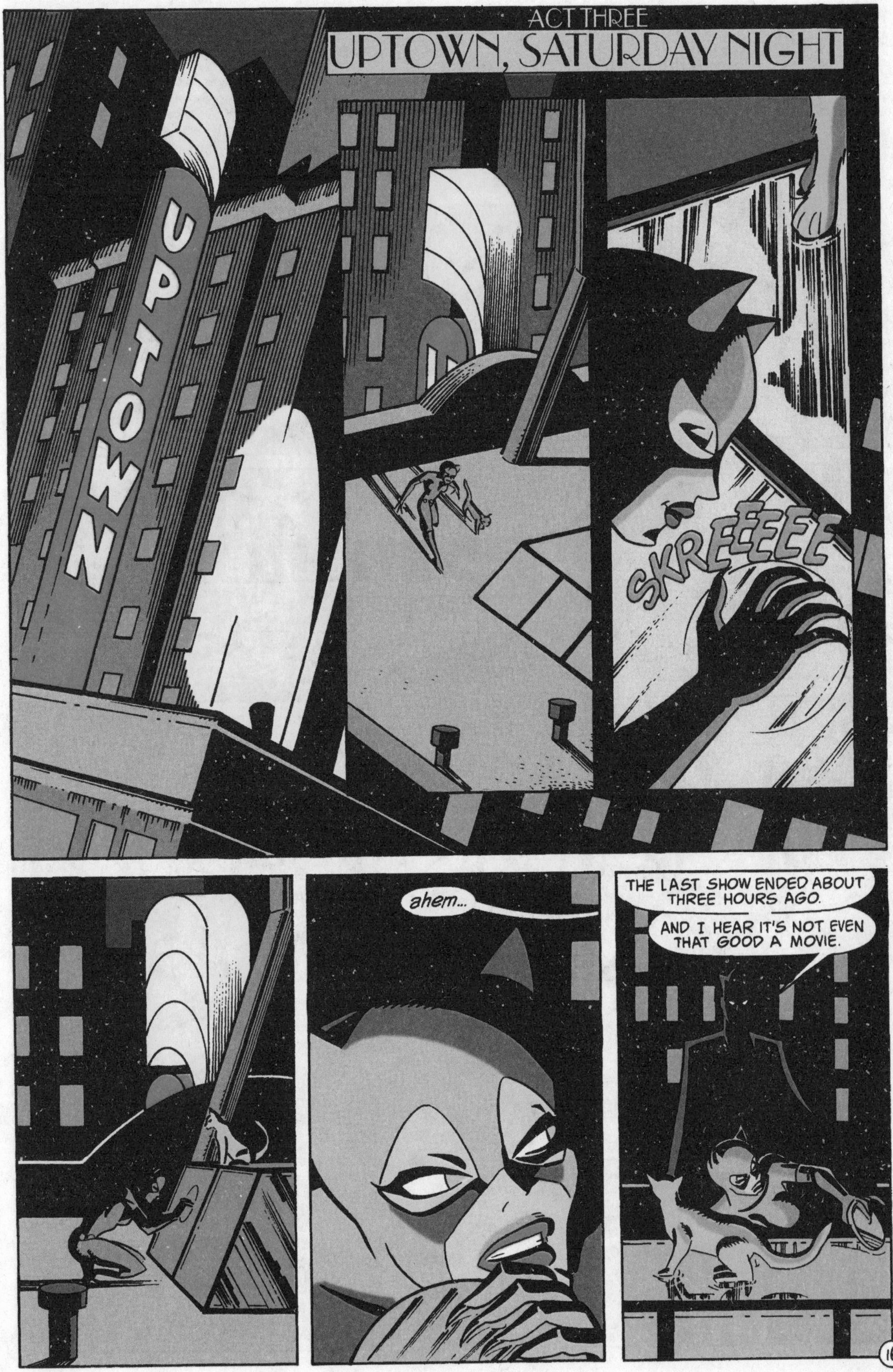

ACT THREE
UPTOWN, SATURDAY NIGHT
UPTOWN
SKREEEEE
ahem...
THE LAST SHOW ENDED ABOUT THREE HOURS AGO.
AND I HEAR IT'S NOT EVEN THAT GOOD A MOVIE.

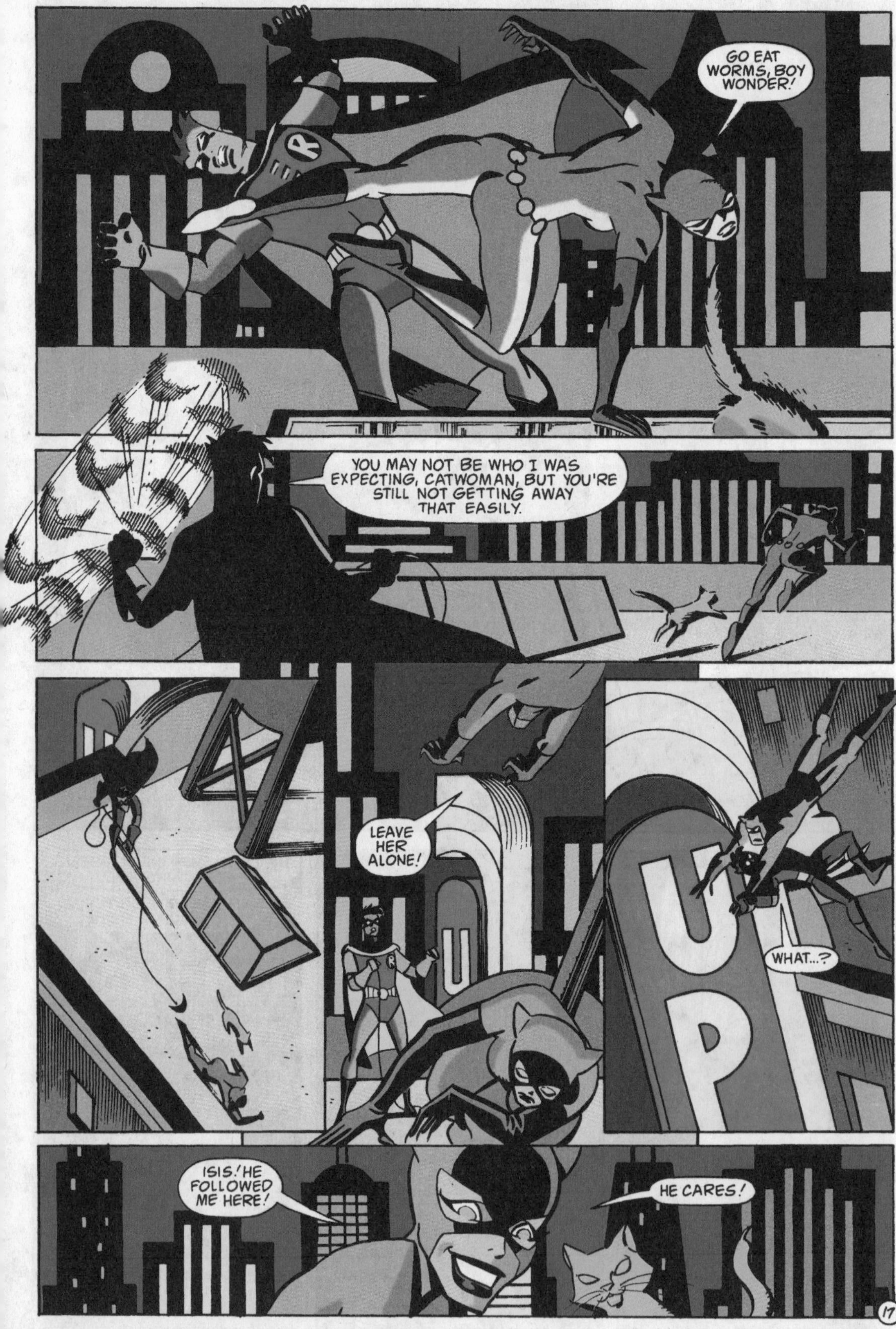
GO EAT WORMS, BOY WONDER!
YOU MAY NOT BE WHO I WAS EXPECTING, CATWOMAN, BUT YOU'RE STILL NOT GETTING AWAY THAT EASILY.
LEAVE HER ALONE!
WHAT...?
ISIS! HE FOLLOWED ME HERE!
HE CARES!

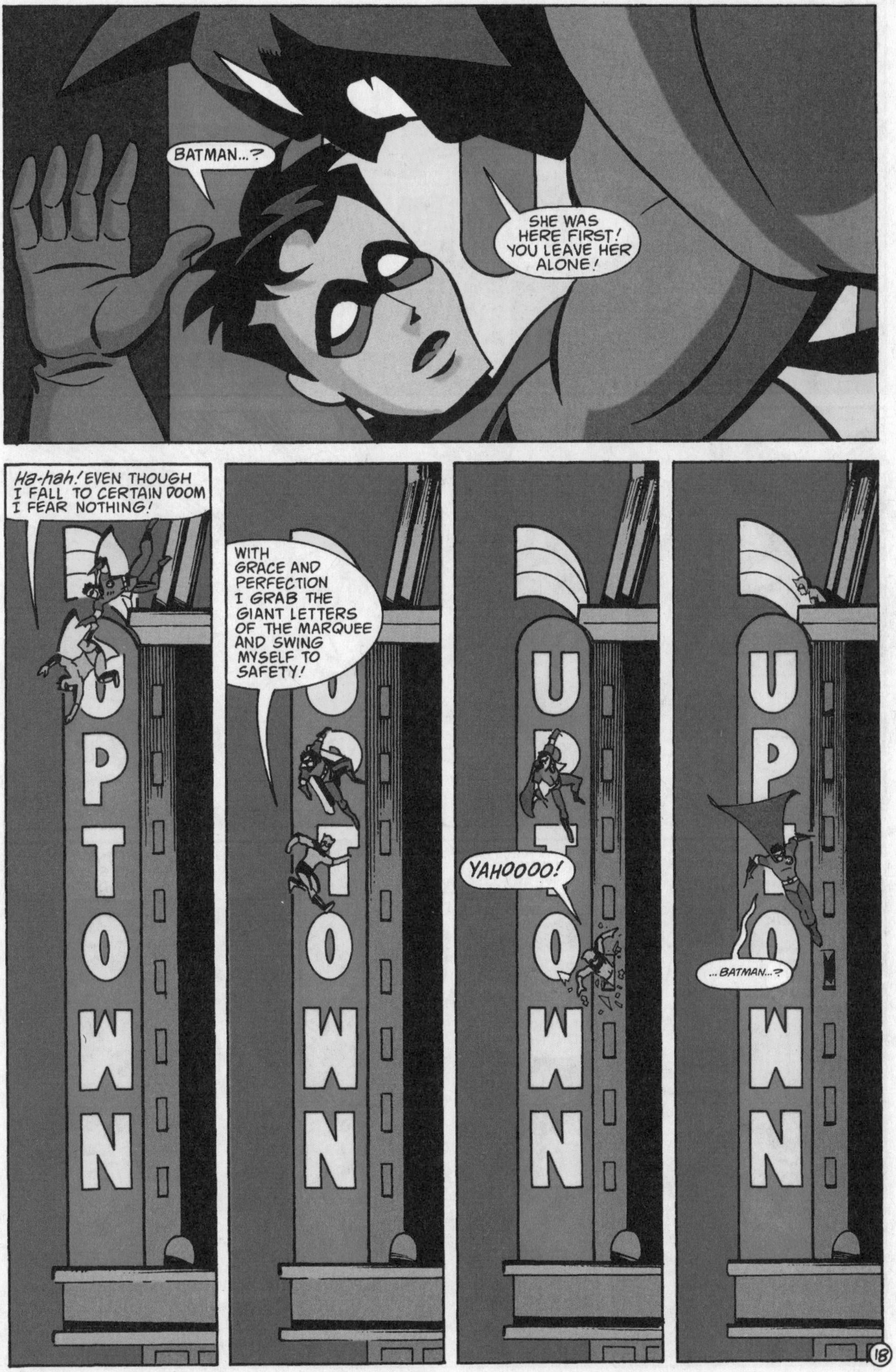
BATMAN...?
SHE WAS HERE FIRST! YOU LEAVE HER ALONE!
Ha-hah! EVEN THOUGH I FALL TO CERTAIN DOOM I FEAR NOTHING!
UPTOWN
WITH GRACE AND PERFECTION I GRAB THE GIANT LETTERS OF THE MARQUEE AND SWING MYSELF TO SAFETY!
YAHOOOO!
...BATMAN...?

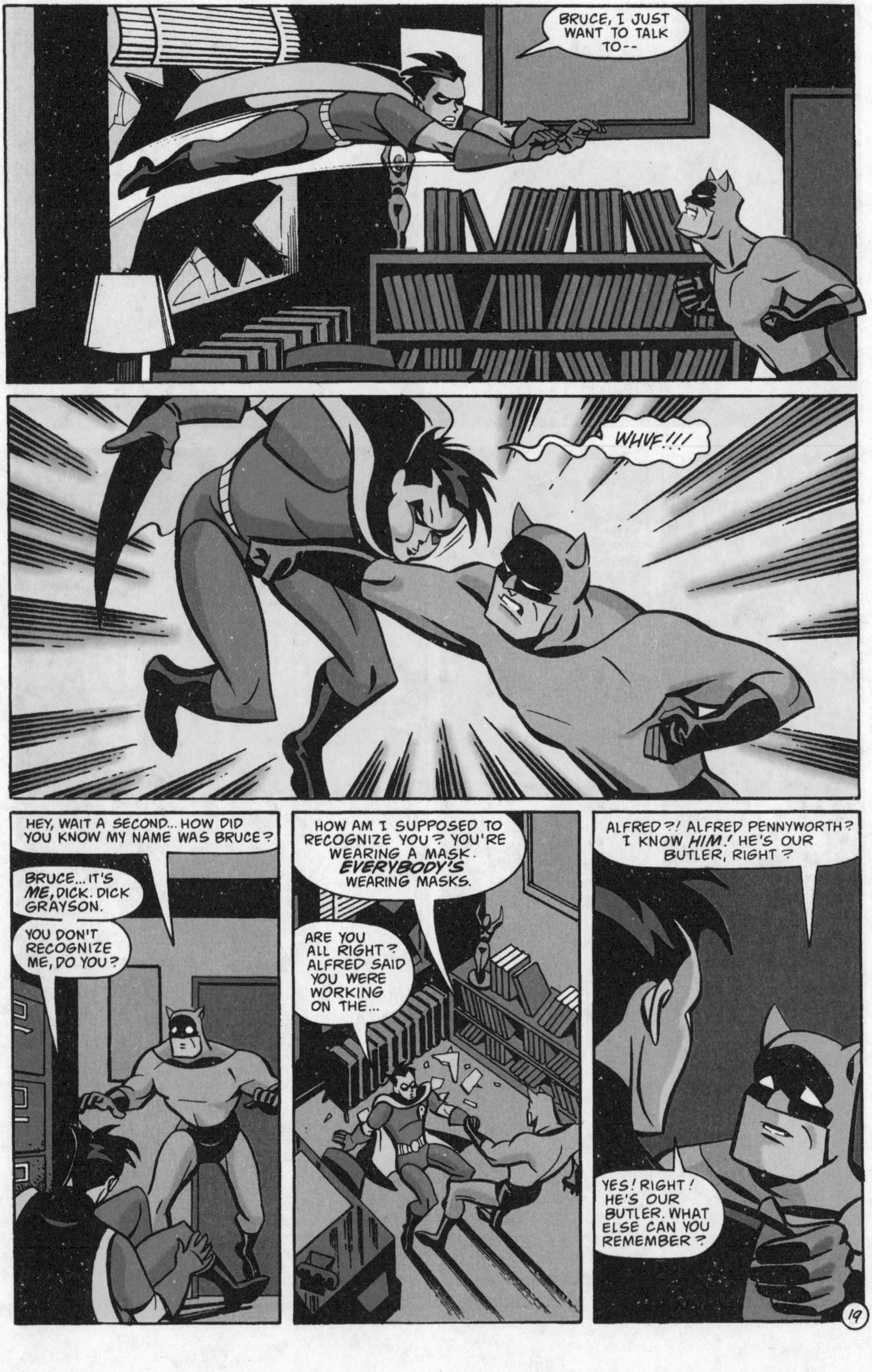
BRUCE, I JUST WANT TO TALK TO--
WHUF!!!
HEY, WAIT A SECOND... HOW DID YOU KNOW MY NAME WAS BRUCE?
BRUCE... IT'S ME, DICK. DICK GRAYSON.
YOU DON'T RECOGNIZE ME, DO YOU?
HOW AM I SUPPOSED TO RECOGNIZE YOU? YOU'RE WEARING A MASK. EVERYBODY'S WEARING MASKS.
ARE YOU ALL RIGHT? ALFRED SAID YOU WERE WORKING ON THE...
ALFRED?! ALFRED PENNYWORTH? I KNOW HIM! HE'S OUR BUTLER, RIGHT?
YES! RIGHT! HE'S OUR BUTLER. WHAT ELSE CAN YOU REMEMBER?

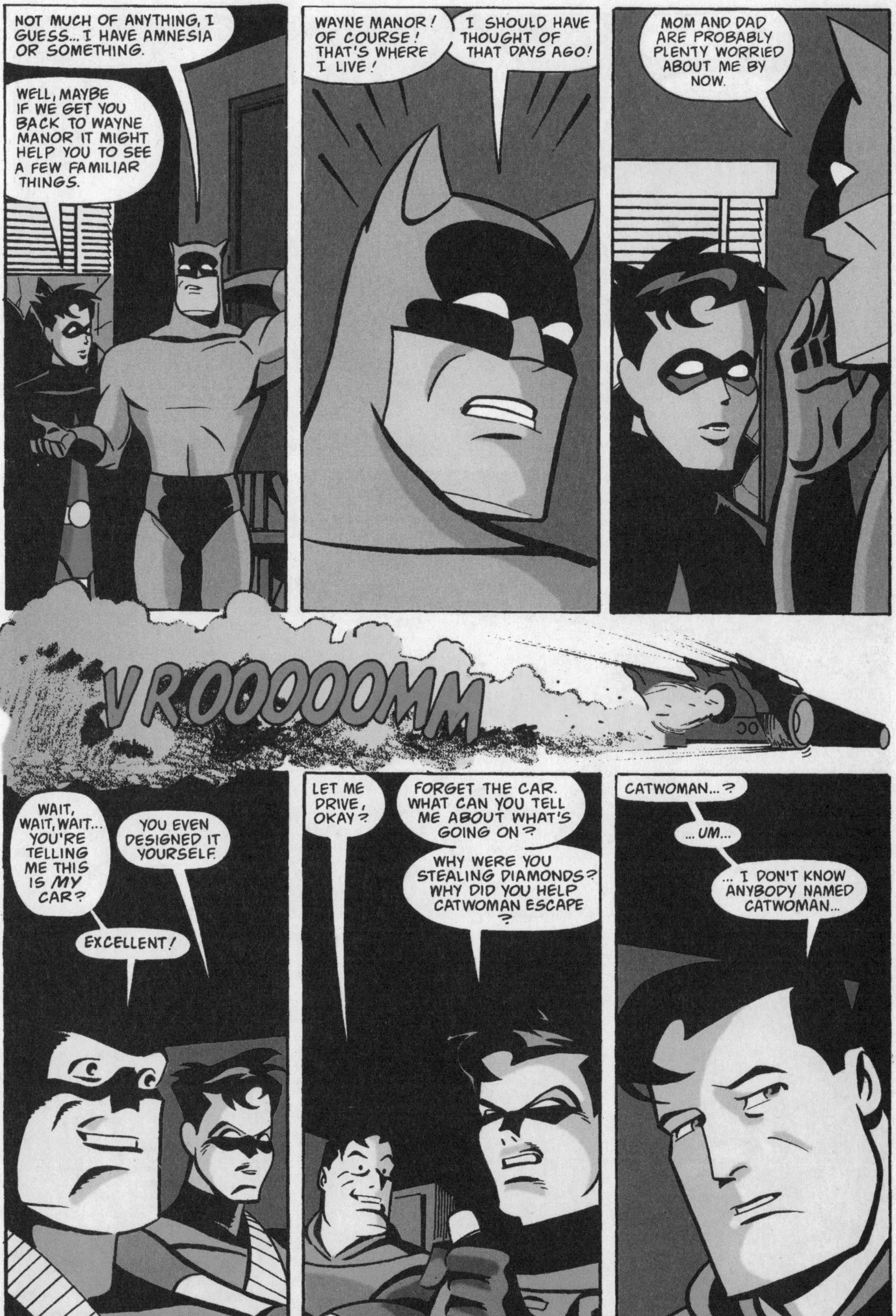
NOT MUCH OF ANYTHING, I GUESS... I HAVE AMNESIA OR SOMETHING.
WELL, MAYBE IF WE GET YOU BACK TO WAYNE MANOR IT MIGHT HELP YOU TO SEE A FEW FAMILIAR THINGS.
WAYNE MANOR! OF COURSE! THAT'S WHERE I LIVE!
I SHOULD HAVE THOUGHT OF THAT DAYS AGO!
MOM AND DAD ARE PROBABLY PLENTY WORRIED ABOUT ME BY NOW.
VROOOOOMM
WAIT, WAIT, WAIT... YOU'RE TELLING ME THIS IS MY CAR?
YOU EVEN DESIGNED IT YOURSELF.
EXCELLENT!
LET ME DRIVE, OKAY?
FORGET THE CAR. WHAT CAN YOU TELL ME ABOUT WHAT'S GOING ON?
WHY WERE YOU STEALING DIAMONDS? WHY DID YOU HELP CATWOMAN ESCAPE?
CATWOMAN...?
...UM...
... I DON'T KNOW ANYBODY NAMED CATWOMAN...

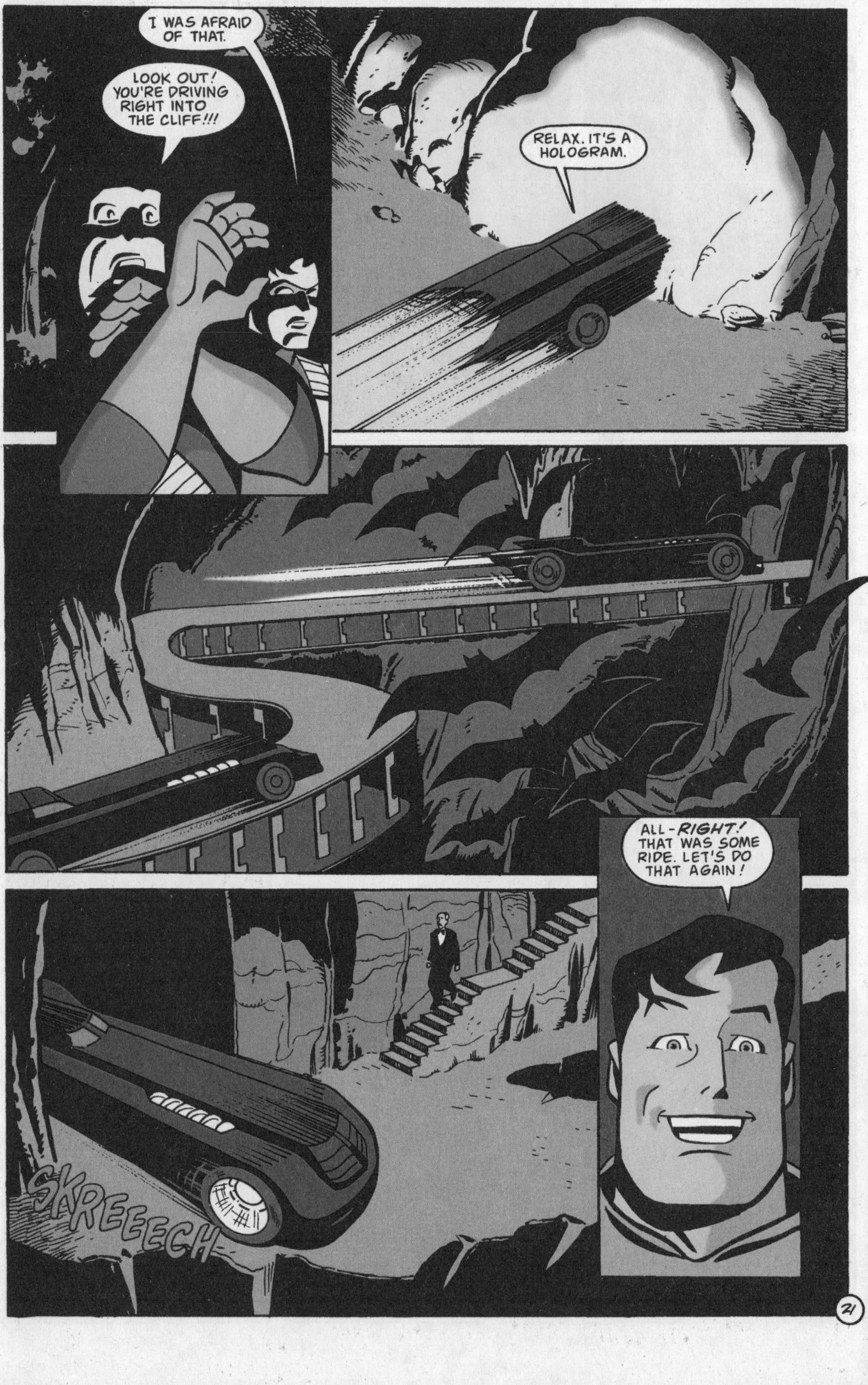
I WAS AFRAID OF THAT.
LOOK OUT! YOU'RE DRIVING RIGHT INTO THE CLIFF!!!
RELAX. IT'S A HOLOGRAM.
ALL-RIGHT! THAT WAS SOME RIDE. LET'S DO THAT AGAIN!
SKREEEECH

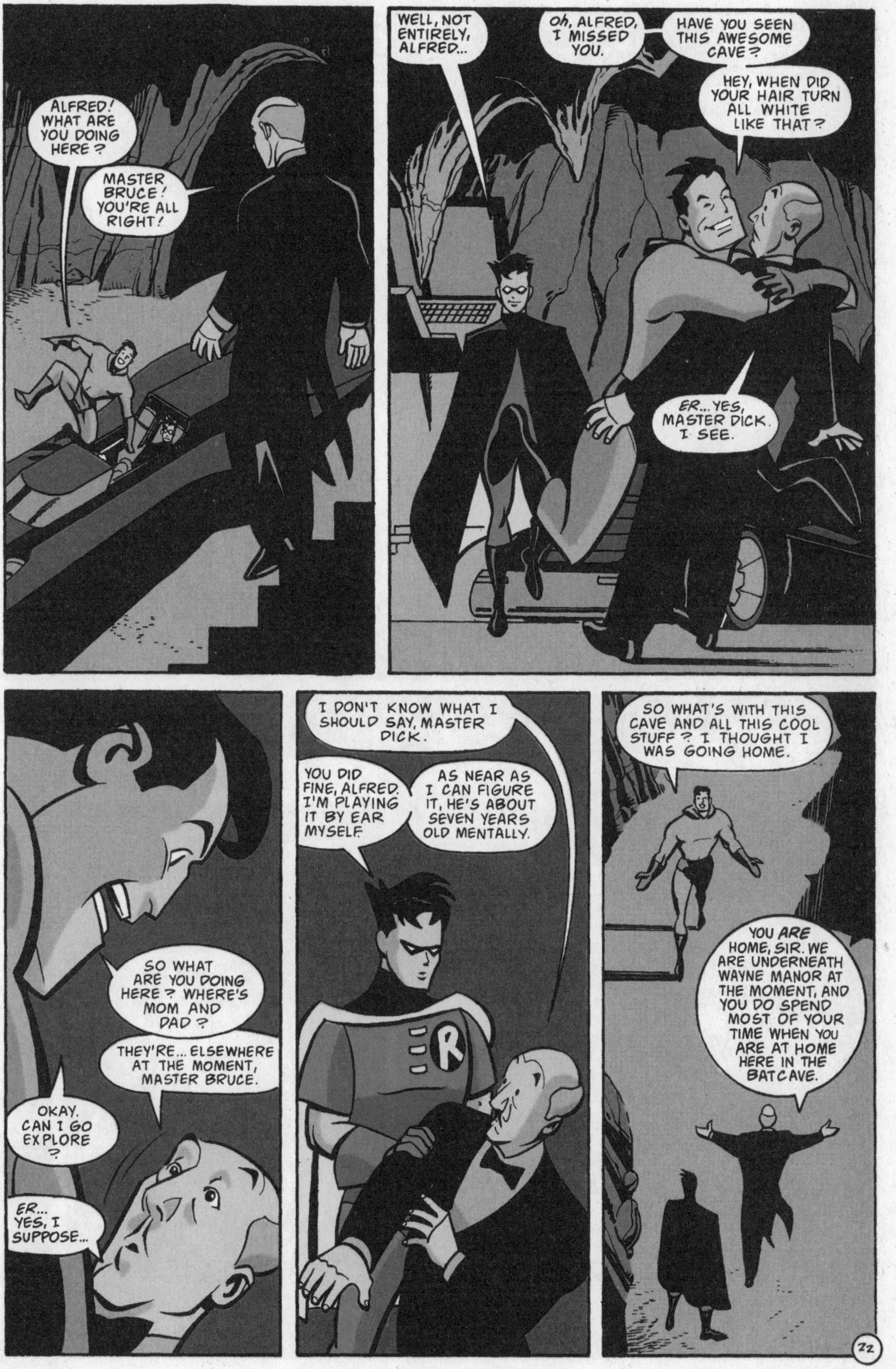
ALFRED! WHAT ARE YOU DOING HERE?
MASTER BRUCE! YOU'RE ALL RIGHT!
WELL, NOT ENTIRELY, ALFRED...
Oh, ALFRED, I MISSED YOU.
HAVE YOU SEEN THIS AWESOME CAVE?
HEY, WHEN DID YOUR HAIR TURN ALL WHITE LIKE THAT?
ER... YES, MASTER DICK. I SEE.
SO WHAT ARE YOU DOING HERE? WHERE'S MOM AND DAD?
THEY'RE... ELSEWHERE AT THE MOMENT, MASTER BRUCE.
OKAY. CAN I GO EXPLORE?
ER... YES, I SUPPOSE...
I DON'T KNOW WHAT I SHOULD SAY, MASTER DICK.
YOU DID FINE, ALFRED. I'M PLAYING IT BY EAR MYSELF.
AS NEAR AS I CAN FIGURE IT, HE'S ABOUT SEVEN YEARS OLD MENTALLY.
SO WHAT'S WITH THIS CAVE AND ALL THIS COOL STUFF? I THOUGHT I WAS GOING HOME.
YOU ARE HOME, SIR. WE ARE UNDERNEATH WAYNE MANOR AT THE MOMENT, AND YOU DO SPEND MOST OF YOUR TIME WHEN YOU ARE AT HOME HERE IN THE BATCAVE.
22

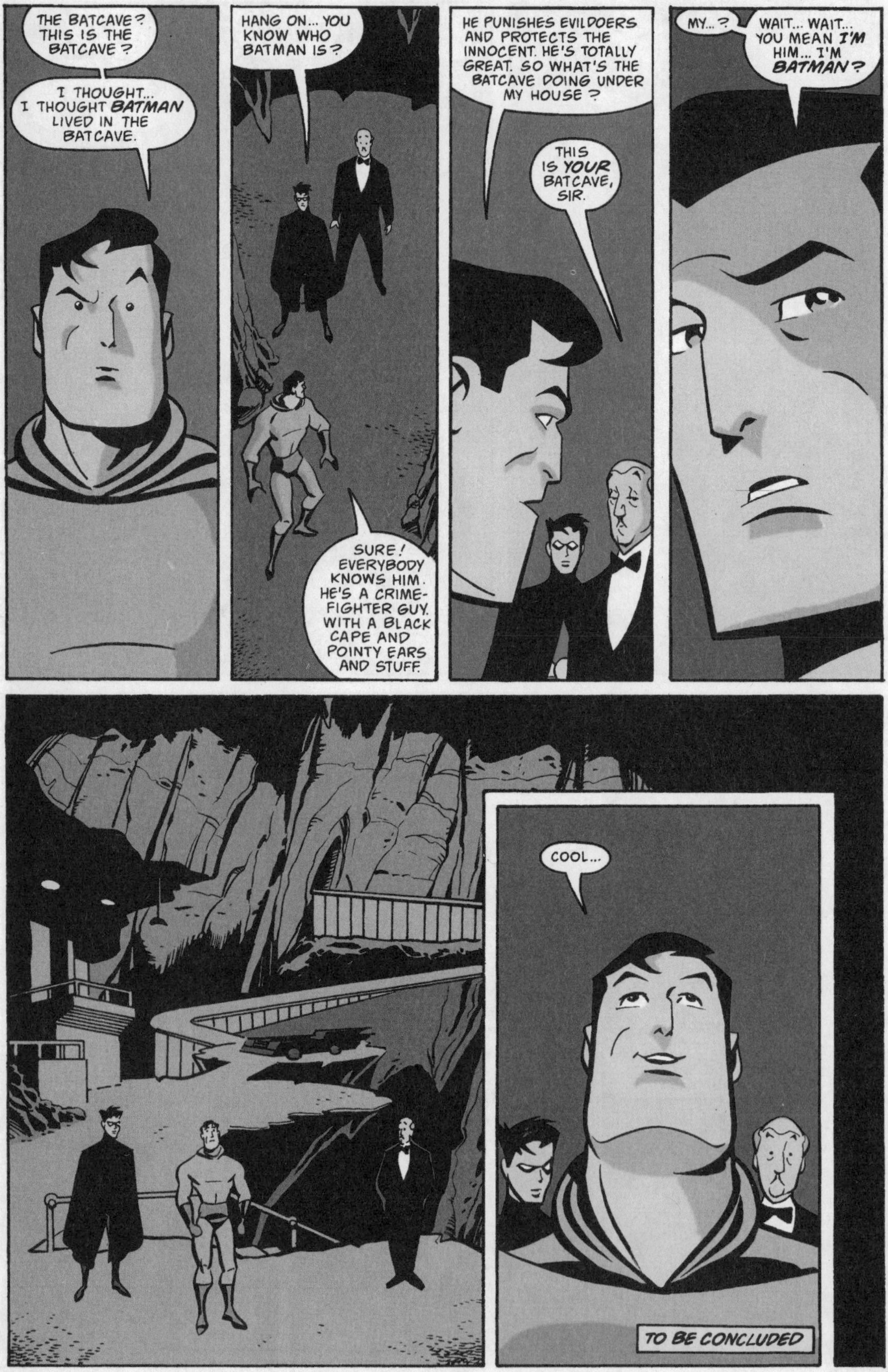
THE BATCAVE? THIS IS THE BATCAVE?
I THOUGHT... I THOUGHT BATMAN LIVED IN THE BATCAVE.
HANG ON... YOU KNOW WHO BATMAN IS?
SURE! EVERYBODY KNOWS HIM. HE'S A CRIME-FIGHTER GUY. WITH A BLACK CAPE AND POINTY EARS AND STUFF.
HE PUNISHES EVILDOERS AND PROTECTS THE INNOCENT. HE'S TOTALLY GREAT. SO WHAT'S THE BATCAVE DOING UNDER MY HOUSE?
THIS IS YOUR BATCAVE, SIR.
MY...?
WAIT... WAIT... YOU MEAN I'M HIM... I'M BATMAN?
COOL...
TO BE CONCLUDED

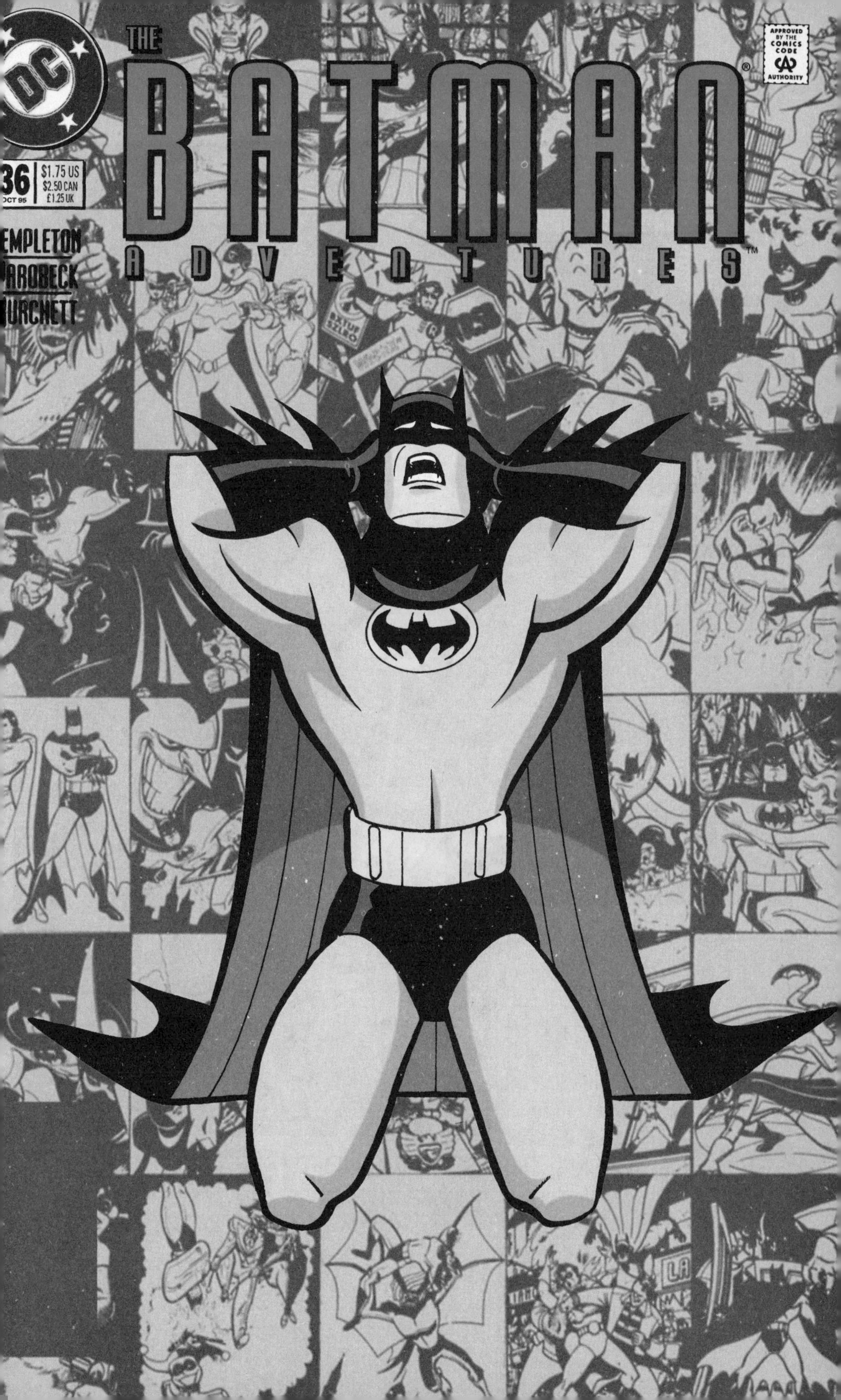
DC
THE
BATMAN
ADVENTURES
36
OCT 95
$1.75 US
$2.50 CAN
£1.25 UK
EMPLETON
AROBECK
URCHETT
APPROVED BY THE COMICS CODE AUTHORITY

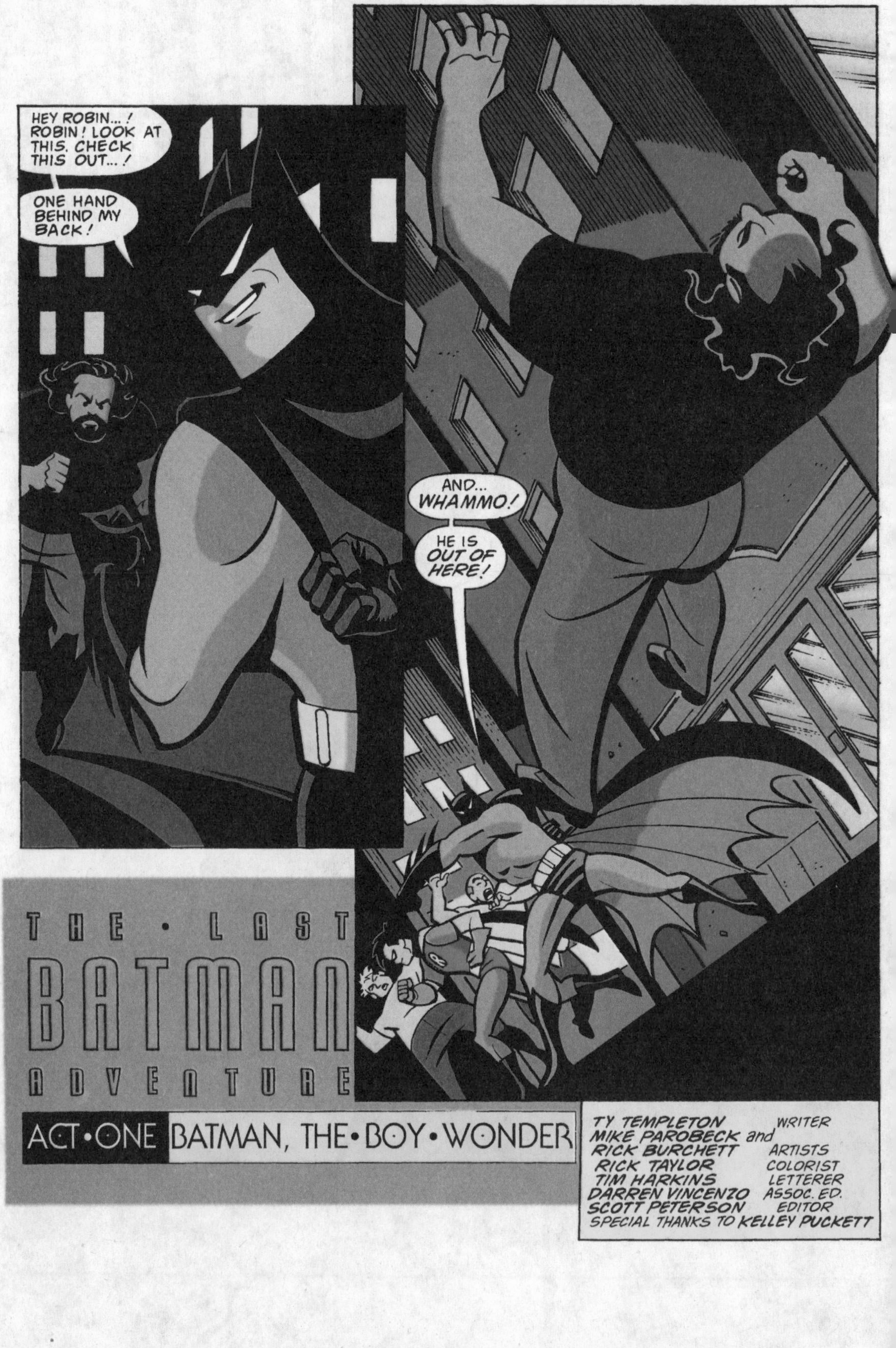
HEY ROBIN...! ROBIN! LOOK AT THIS. CHECK THIS OUT...!
ONE HAND BEHIND MY BACK!
AND... WHAMMO!
HE IS OUT OF HERE!
THE · LAST BATMAN ADVENTURE
ACT·ONE BATMAN, THE·BOY·WONDER
TY TEMPLETON WRITER
MIKE PAROBECK and RICK BURCHETT ARTISTS
RICK TAYLOR COLORIST
TIM HARKINS LETTERER
DARREN VINCENZO ASSOC. ED.
SCOTT PETERSON EDITOR
SPECIAL THANKS TO KELLEY PUCKETT

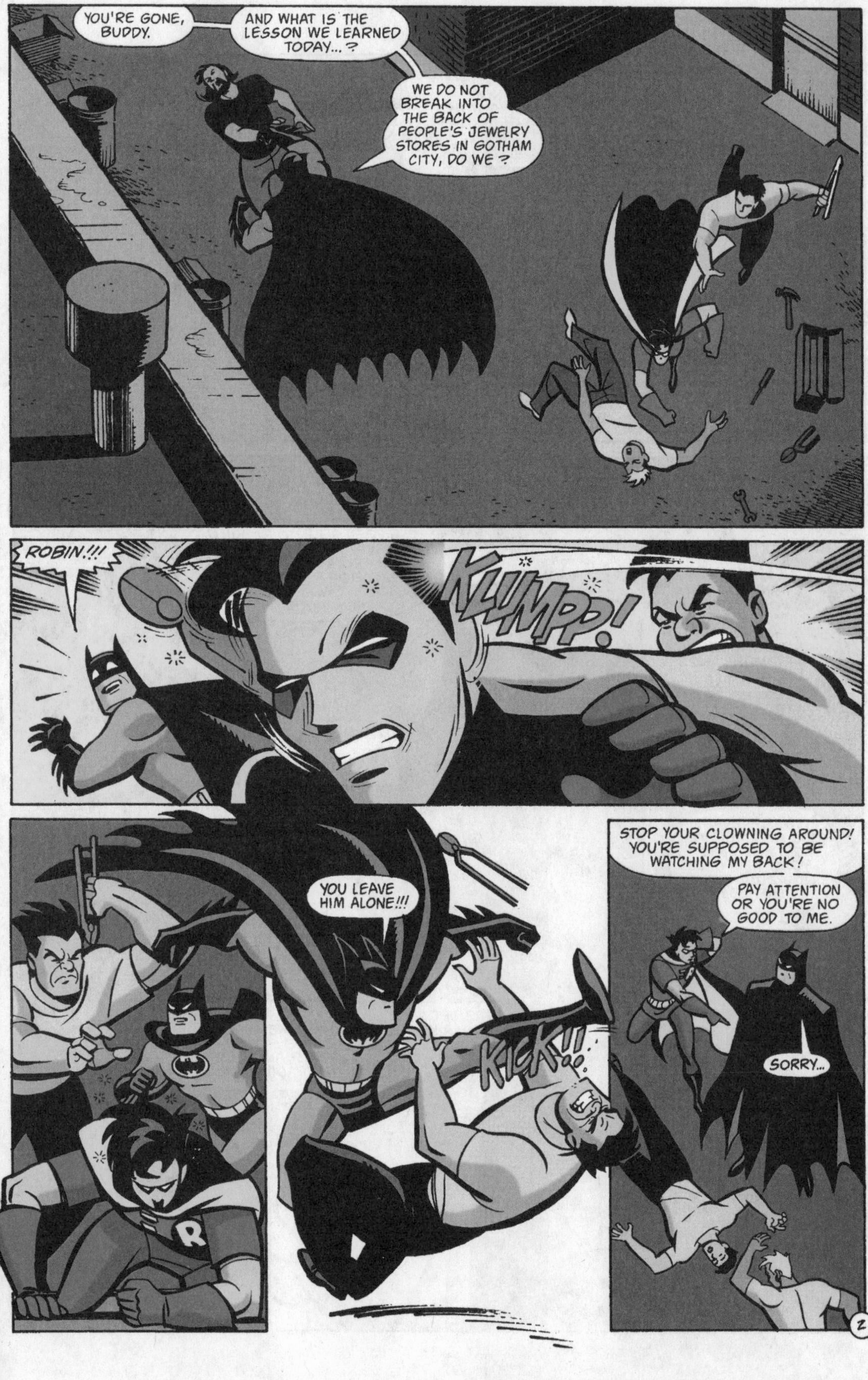

YOU'RE GONE, BUDDY.
AND WHAT IS THE LESSON WE LEARNED TODAY...?
WE DO NOT BREAK INTO THE BACK OF PEOPLE'S JEWELRY STORES IN GOTHAM CITY, DO WE?
ROBIN!!!
KLUMPP!
YOU LEAVE HIM ALONE!!!
KICK!!
STOP YOUR CLOWNING AROUND! YOU'RE SUPPOSED TO BE WATCHING MY BACK!
PAY ATTENTION OR YOU'RE NO GOOD TO ME.
SORRY...

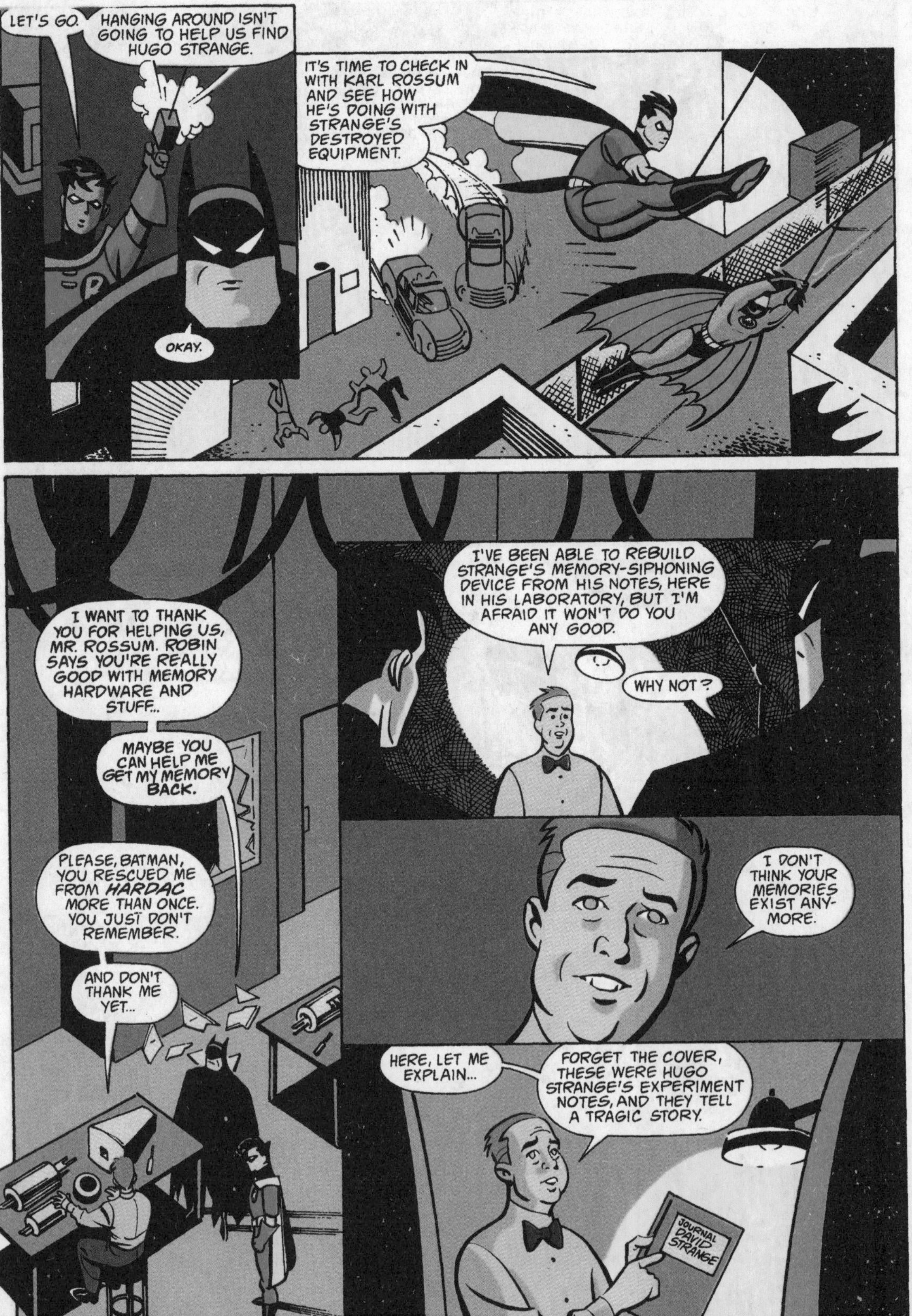
LET'S GO.
HANGING AROUND ISN'T GOING TO HELP US FIND HUGO STRANGE.
OKAY.
IT'S TIME TO CHECK IN WITH KARL ROSSUM AND SEE HOW HE'S DOING WITH STRANGE'S DESTROYED EQUIPMENT.
I WANT TO THANK YOU FOR HELPING US, MR. ROSSUM. ROBIN SAYS YOU'RE REALLY GOOD WITH MEMORY HARDWARE AND STUFF...
MAYBE YOU CAN HELP ME GET MY MEMORY BACK.
PLEASE, BATMAN, YOU RESCUED ME FROM HARDAC MORE THAN ONCE. YOU JUST DON'T REMEMBER.
AND DON'T THANK ME YET...
I'VE BEEN ABLE TO REBUILD STRANGE'S MEMORY-SIPHONING DEVICE FROM HIS NOTES, HERE IN HIS LABORATORY, BUT I'M AFRAID IT WON'T DO YOU ANY GOOD.
WHY NOT?
I DON'T THINK YOUR MEMORIES EXIST ANY-MORE.
HERE, LET ME EXPLAIN...
FORGET THE COVER, THESE WERE HUGO STRANGE'S EXPERIMENT NOTES, AND THEY TELL A TRAGIC STORY.
JOURNAL DAVID STRANGE
DAVID WAS HUGO'S SON.

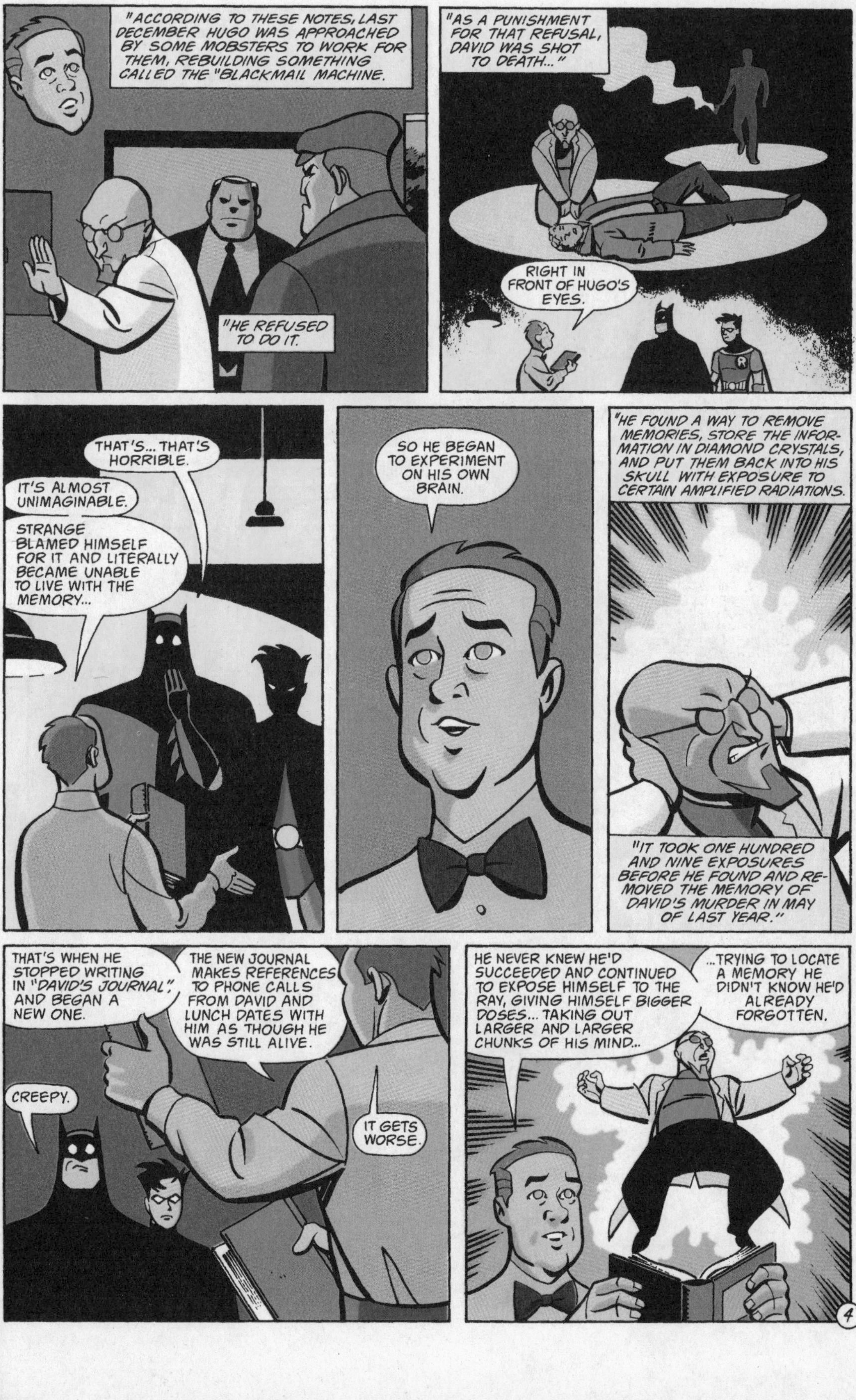

"ACCORDING TO THESE NOTES, LAST DECEMBER HUGO WAS APPROACHED BY SOME MOBSTERS TO WORK FOR THEM, REBUILDING SOMETHING CALLED THE "BLACKMAIL MACHINE.
"HE REFUSED TO DO IT.
"AS A PUNISHMENT FOR THAT REFUSAL, DAVID WAS SHOT TO DEATH..."
RIGHT IN FRONT OF HUGO'S EYES.
THAT'S... THAT'S HORRIBLE.
IT'S ALMOST UNIMAGINABLE.
STRANGE BLAMED HIMSELF FOR IT AND LITERALLY BECAME UNABLE TO LIVE WITH THE MEMORY...
SO HE BEGAN TO EXPERIMENT ON HIS OWN BRAIN.
"HE FOUND A WAY TO REMOVE MEMORIES, STORE THE INFORMATION IN DIAMOND CRYSTALS, AND PUT THEM BACK INTO HIS SKULL WITH EXPOSURE TO CERTAIN AMPLIFIED RADIATIONS.
"IT TOOK ONE HUNDRED AND NINE EXPOSURES BEFORE HE FOUND AND REMOVED THE MEMORY OF DAVID'S MURDER IN MAY OF LAST YEAR."
THAT'S WHEN HE STOPPED WRITING IN "DAVID'S JOURNAL", AND BEGAN A NEW ONE.
THE NEW JOURNAL MAKES REFERENCES TO PHONE CALLS FROM DAVID AND LUNCH DATES WITH HIM AS THOUGH HE WAS STILL ALIVE.
CREEPY.
IT GETS WORSE.
HE NEVER KNEW HE'D SUCCEEDED AND CONTINUED TO EXPOSE HIMSELF TO THE RAY, GIVING HIMSELF BIGGER DOSES... TAKING OUT LARGER AND LARGER CHUNKS OF HIS MIND...
...TRYING TO LOCATE A MEMORY HE DIDN'T KNOW HE'D ALREADY FORGOTTEN.

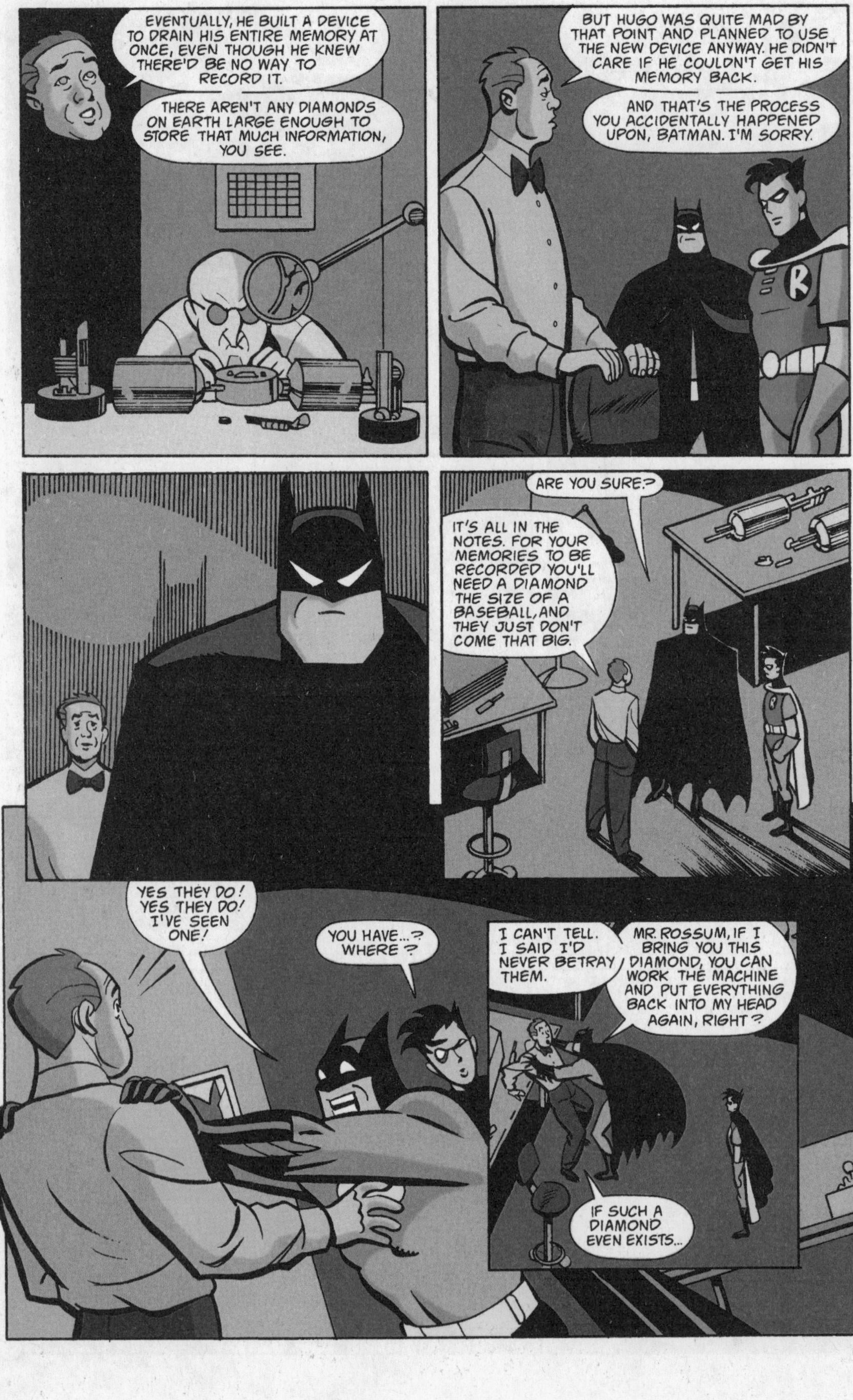

EVENTUALLY, HE BUILT A DEVICE TO DRAIN HIS ENTIRE MEMORY AT ONCE, EVEN THOUGH HE KNEW THERE'D BE NO WAY TO RECORD IT.
THERE AREN'T ANY DIAMONDS ON EARTH LARGE ENOUGH TO STORE THAT MUCH INFORMATION, YOU SEE.
BUT HUGO WAS QUITE MAD BY THAT POINT AND PLANNED TO USE THE NEW DEVICE ANYWAY. HE DIDN'T CARE IF HE COULDN'T GET HIS MEMORY BACK.
AND THAT'S THE PROCESS YOU ACCIDENTALLY HAPPENED UPON, BATMAN. I'M SORRY.
ARE YOU SURE?
IT'S ALL IN THE NOTES. FOR YOUR MEMORIES TO BE RECORDED YOU'LL NEED A DIAMOND THE SIZE OF A BASEBALL, AND THEY JUST DON'T COME THAT BIG.
YES THEY DO! YES THEY DO! I'VE SEEN ONE!
YOU HAVE...? WHERE?
I CAN'T TELL. I SAID I'D NEVER BETRAY THEM.
MR. ROSSUM, IF I BRING YOU THIS DIAMOND, YOU CAN WORK THE MACHINE AND PUT EVERYTHING BACK INTO MY HEAD AGAIN, RIGHT?
IF SUCH A DIAMOND EVEN EXISTS...

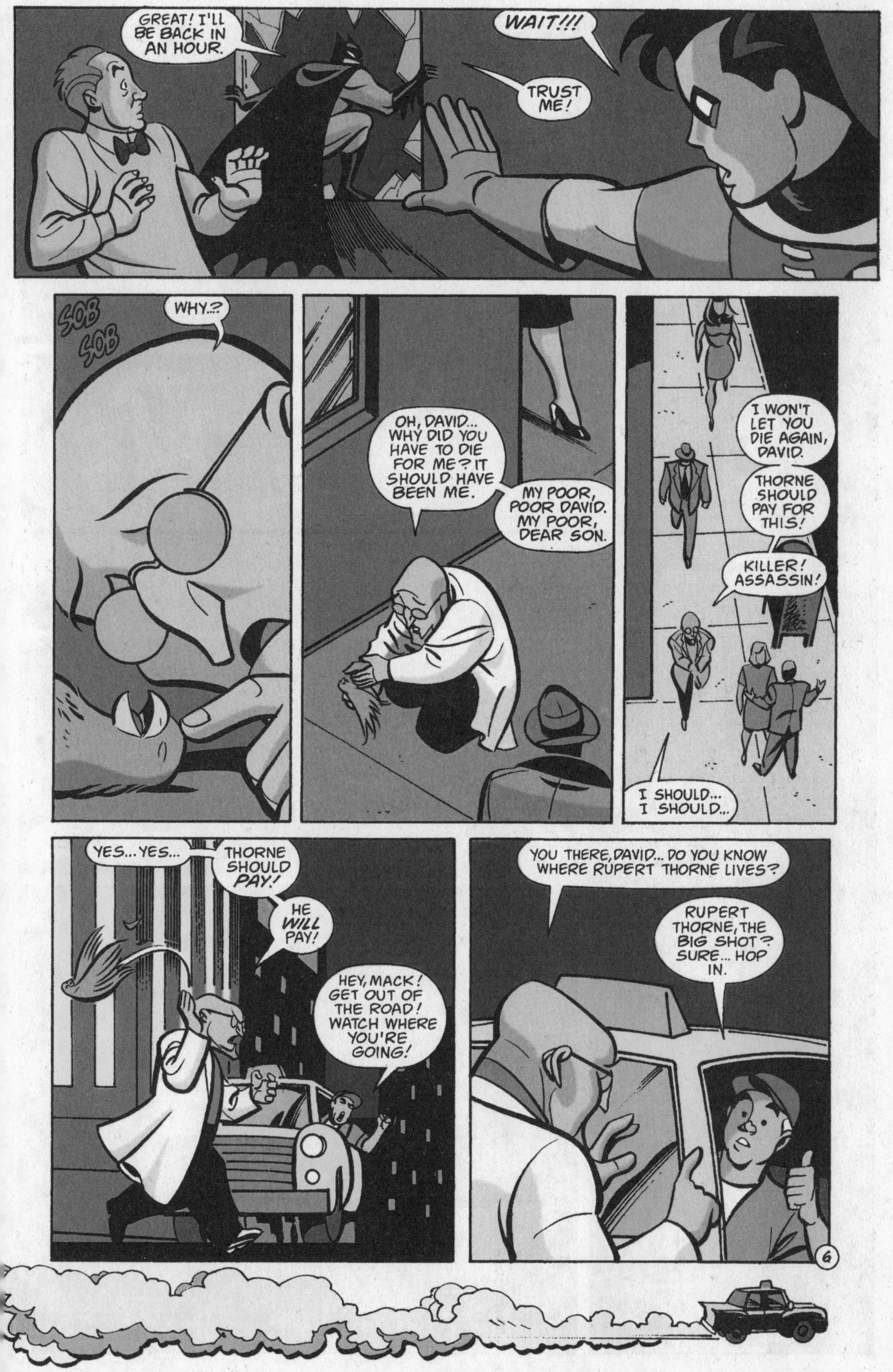
GREAT! I'LL BE BACK IN AN HOUR.
WAIT!!!
TRUST ME!
SOB SOB
WHY..?
OH, DAVID... WHY DID YOU HAVE TO DIE FOR ME? IT SHOULD HAVE BEEN ME.
MY POOR, POOR DAVID. MY POOR, DEAR SON.
I WON'T LET YOU DIE AGAIN, DAVID.
THORNE SHOULD PAY FOR THIS!
KILLER! ASSASSIN!
I SHOULD... I SHOULD...
YES... YES...
THORNE SHOULD PAY!
HE WILL PAY!
HEY, MACK! GET OUT OF THE ROAD! WATCH WHERE YOU'RE GOING!
YOU THERE, DAVID... DO YOU KNOW WHERE RUPERT THORNE LIVES?
RUPERT THORNE, THE BIG SHOT? SURE... HOP IN.
6

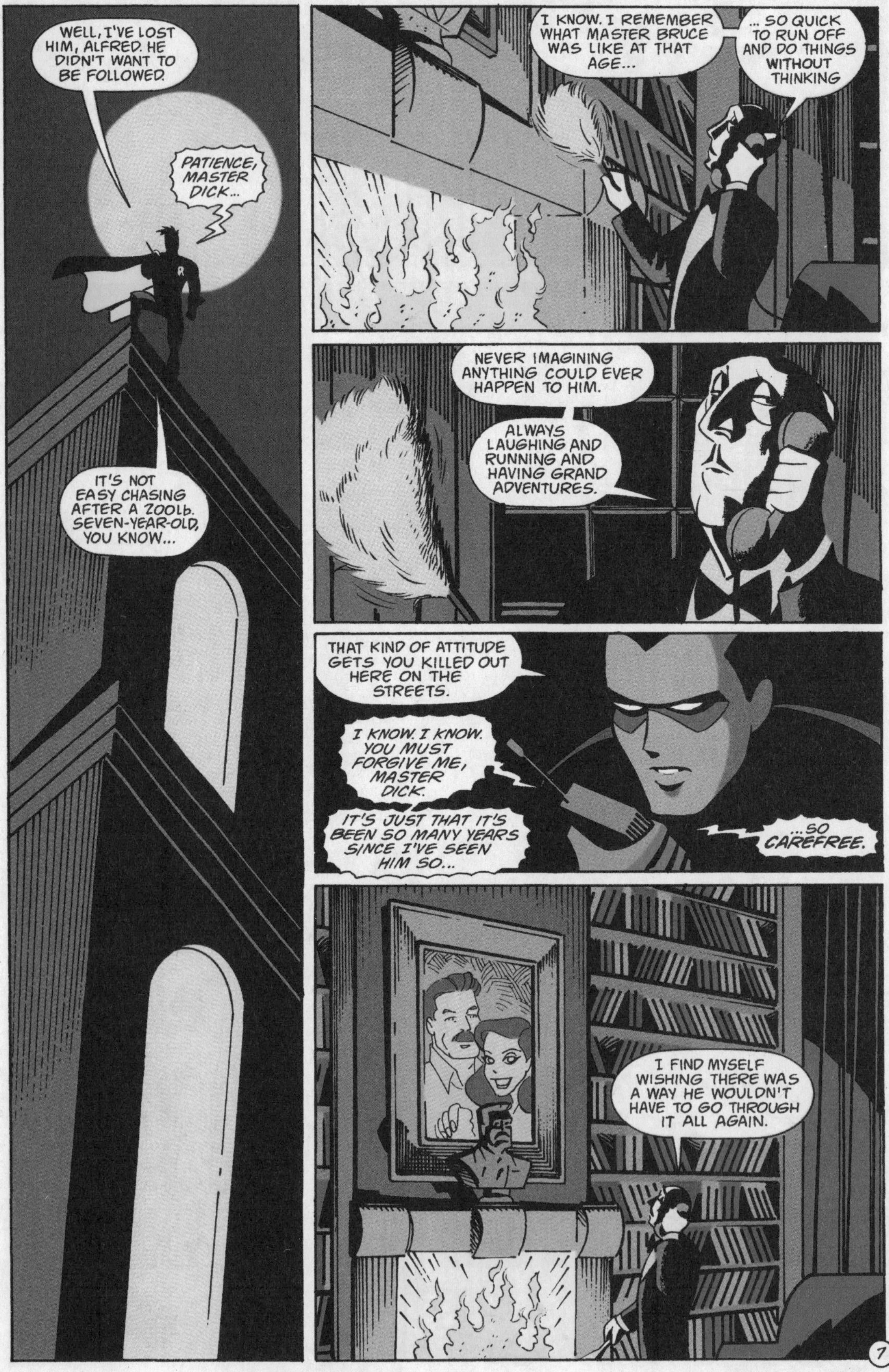
WELL, I'VE LOST HIM, ALFRED. HE DIDN'T WANT TO BE FOLLOWED.
PATIENCE, MASTER DICK...
IT'S NOT EASY CHASING AFTER A 200lb. SEVEN-YEAR-OLD, YOU KNOW...
I KNOW. I REMEMBER WHAT MASTER BRUCE WAS LIKE AT THAT AGE...
... SO QUICK TO RUN OFF AND DO THINGS WITHOUT THINKING
NEVER IMAGINING ANYTHING COULD EVER HAPPEN TO HIM.
ALWAYS LAUGHING AND RUNNING AND HAVING GRAND ADVENTURES.
THAT KIND OF ATTITUDE GETS YOU KILLED OUT HERE ON THE STREETS.
I KNOW. I KNOW. YOU MUST FORGIVE ME, MASTER DICK.
IT'S JUST THAT IT'S BEEN SO MANY YEARS SINCE I'VE SEEN HIM SO...
...SO CAREFREE.
I FIND MYSELF WISHING THERE WAS A WAY HE WOULDN'T HAVE TO GO THROUGH IT ALL AGAIN.

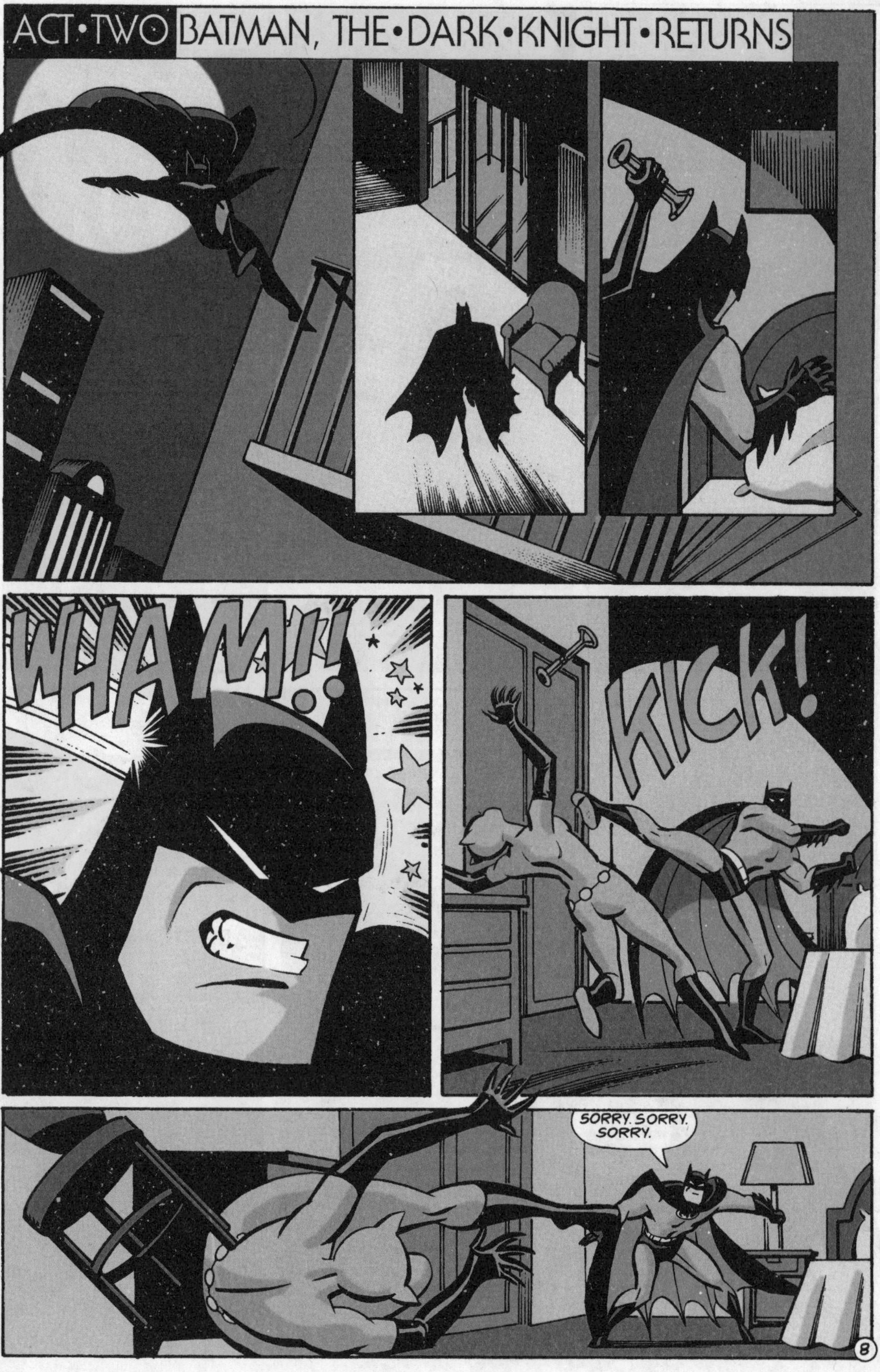
ACT·TWO BATMAN, THE·DARK·KNIGHT·RETURNS
WHAM!!
KICK!
SORRY. SORRY. SORRY.
8

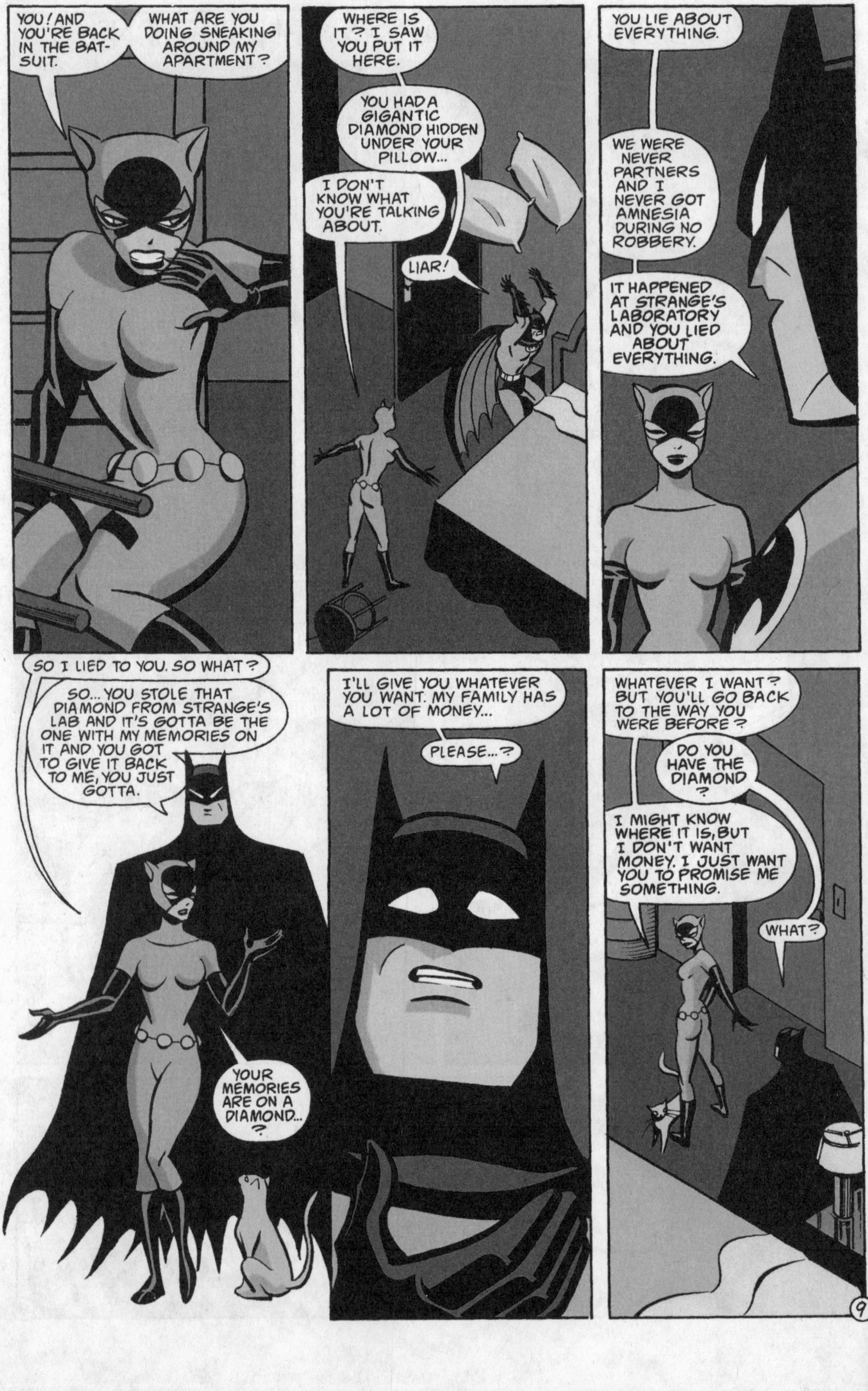
YOU! AND YOU'RE BACK IN THE BAT-SUIT.
WHAT ARE YOU DOING SNEAKING AROUND MY APARTMENT?
WHERE IS IT? I SAW YOU PUT IT HERE.
YOU HAD A GIGANTIC DIAMOND HIDDEN UNDER YOUR PILLOW...
I DON'T KNOW WHAT YOU'RE TALKING ABOUT.
LIAR!
YOU LIE ABOUT EVERYTHING.
WE WERE NEVER PARTNERS AND I NEVER GOT AMNESIA DURING NO ROBBERY.
IT HAPPENED AT STRANGE'S LABORATORY AND YOU LIED ABOUT EVERYTHING.
SO I LIED TO YOU. SO WHAT?
SO... YOU STOLE THAT DIAMOND FROM STRANGE'S LAB AND IT'S GOTTA BE THE ONE WITH MY MEMORIES ON IT AND YOU GOT TO GIVE IT BACK TO ME, YOU JUST GOTTA.
YOUR MEMORIES ARE ON A DIAMOND...?
I'LL GIVE YOU WHATEVER YOU WANT. MY FAMILY HAS A LOT OF MONEY...
PLEASE...?
WHATEVER I WANT? BUT YOU'LL GO BACK TO THE WAY YOU WERE BEFORE?
DO YOU HAVE THE DIAMOND?
I MIGHT KNOW WHERE IT IS, BUT I DON'T WANT MONEY. I JUST WANT YOU TO PROMISE ME SOMETHING.
WHAT?

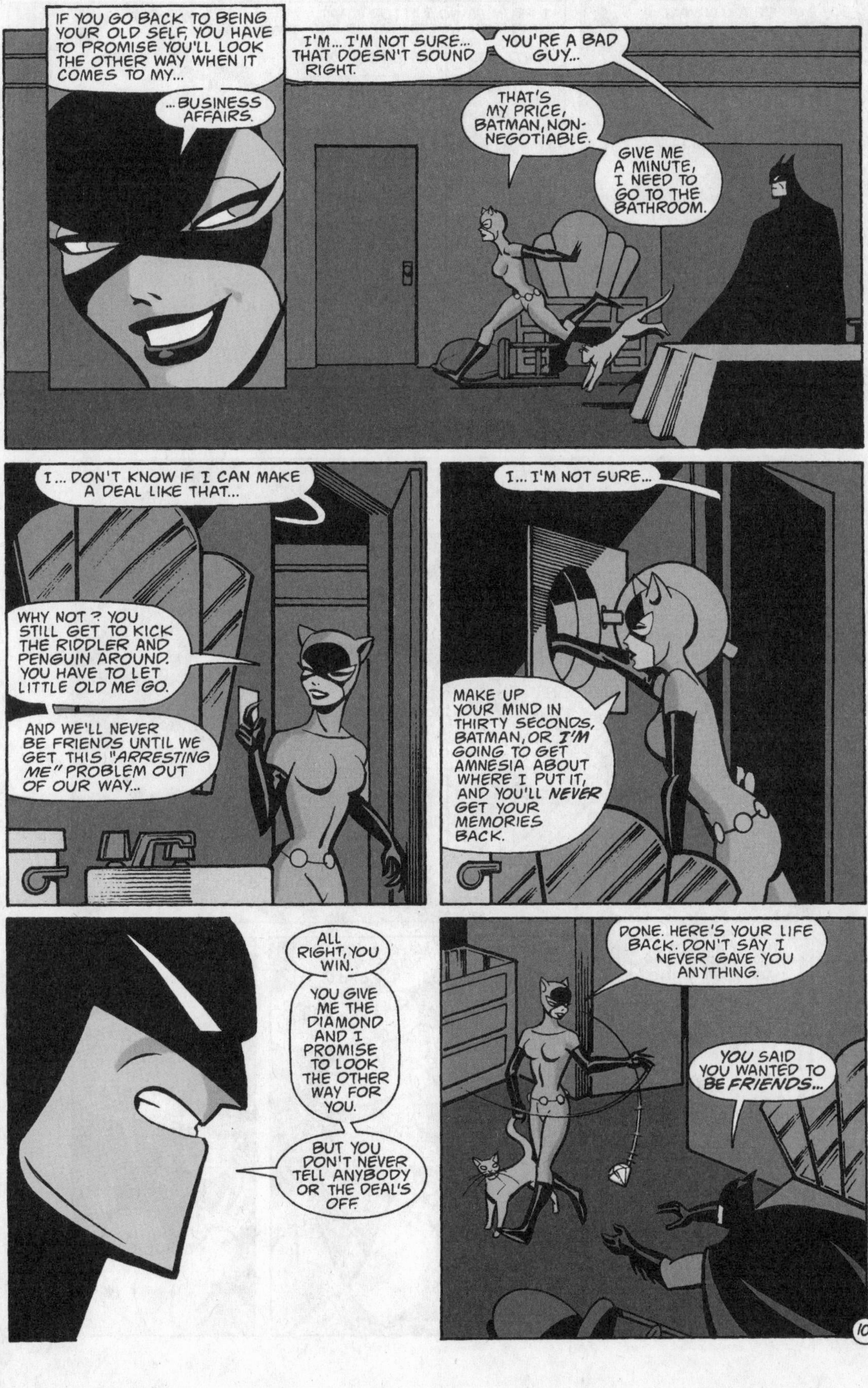

IF YOU GO BACK TO BEING YOUR OLD SELF, YOU HAVE TO PROMISE YOU'LL LOOK THE OTHER WAY WHEN IT COMES TO MY...
...BUSINESS AFFAIRS.
I'M... I'M NOT SURE... THAT DOESN'T SOUND RIGHT.
YOU'RE A BAD GUY...
THAT'S MY PRICE, BATMAN, NON-NEGOTIABLE.
GIVE ME A MINUTE, I NEED TO GO TO THE BATHROOM.
I... DON'T KNOW IF I CAN MAKE A DEAL LIKE THAT...
WHY NOT? YOU STILL GET TO KICK THE RIDDLER AND PENGUIN AROUND. YOU HAVE TO LET LITTLE OLD ME GO.
AND WE'LL NEVER BE FRIENDS UNTIL WE GET THIS "ARRESTING ME" PROBLEM OUT OF OUR WAY...
I... I'M NOT SURE...
MAKE UP YOUR MIND IN THIRTY SECONDS, BATMAN, OR I'M GOING TO GET AMNESIA ABOUT WHERE I PUT IT, AND YOU'LL NEVER GET YOUR MEMORIES BACK.
ALL RIGHT, YOU WIN.
YOU GIVE ME THE DIAMOND AND I PROMISE TO LOOK THE OTHER WAY FOR YOU.
BUT YOU DON'T NEVER TELL ANYBODY OR THE DEAL'S OFF.
DONE. HERE'S YOUR LIFE BACK. DON'T SAY I NEVER GAVE YOU ANYTHING.
YOU SAID YOU WANTED TO BE FRIENDS...

BUT YOU'RE A LIAR AND A CHEATER AND YOU TOOK ADVANTAGE OF ME.

AND I MAY HAVE TO KEEP MY PROMISE, BUT I WILL PROMISE YOU SOMETHING ELSE...

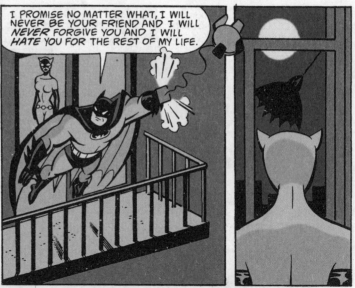

I PROMISE NO MATTER WHAT, I WILL NEVER BE YOUR FRIEND AND I WILL *NEVER* FORGIVE YOU AND I WILL *HATE* YOU FOR THE REST OF MY LIFE.

SCREEECH!

THORNE.

I'M NOT AFRAID.

I'VE GOT TO...

THORNE...

I'LL STOP...

I'LL STOP YOU, KILLER...

THAT WAS SOME KINDA CAR WRECK TO JUST WALK AWAY FROM LIKE THAT.

YES... YES, DAVID, IT WAS.

THE NAME AIN'T DAVID.

Ha Ha. WHATEVER YOU SAY, YOU SILLY CHILD...

RUPERT THORNE... HE LIVES HERE, YES?

YEAH, BUT YOU SHOULDN'T BE CONCERNIN' YOURSELF WIT' THAT...

NO, PLEASE, DAVID... YOU *MUST* TELL HIM I'M HERE. I *MUST* SEE HIM.

HUGO STRANGE, YOU SAY?

BY ALL MEANS, SEND HIM UP, SEND HIM UP.

THIS SHOULD BE INTERESTING. I WONDER WHAT THE OLD WEIRDO WANTS...

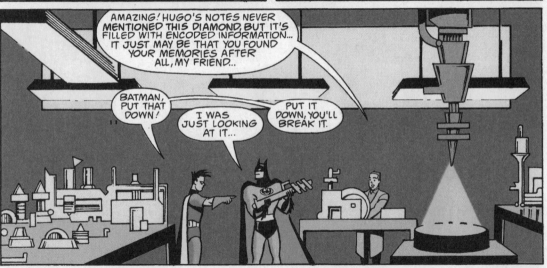

AMAZING! HUGO'S NOTES NEVER MENTIONED THIS DIAMOND, BUT IT'S FILLED WITH ENCODED INFORMATION... IT JUST MAY BE THAT YOU FOUND YOUR MEMORIES AFTER ALL, MY FRIEND...

BATMAN, PUT THAT DOWN!

I WAS JUST LOOKING AT IT...

PUT IT DOWN, YOU'LL BREAK IT.

uh, LISTEN, MR. ROSSUM... NOT EVERYTHING BATMAN'S GOING TO REMEMBER IS GOING TO BE THAT... NICE.

CAN HE HANDLE IT ALL COMING BACK AT ONCE LIKE THIS?

I DON'T KNOW. THIS HAS NEVER BEEN TRIED BEFORE...

I'M NOT SCARED, MR. ROSSUM, I DON'T MIND THE RISK...

I'M A PRETTY LOUSY BATMAN WITH MY MIND LIKE THIS.

I DON'T KNOW ANYTHING... I KEEP MESSING UP...

12

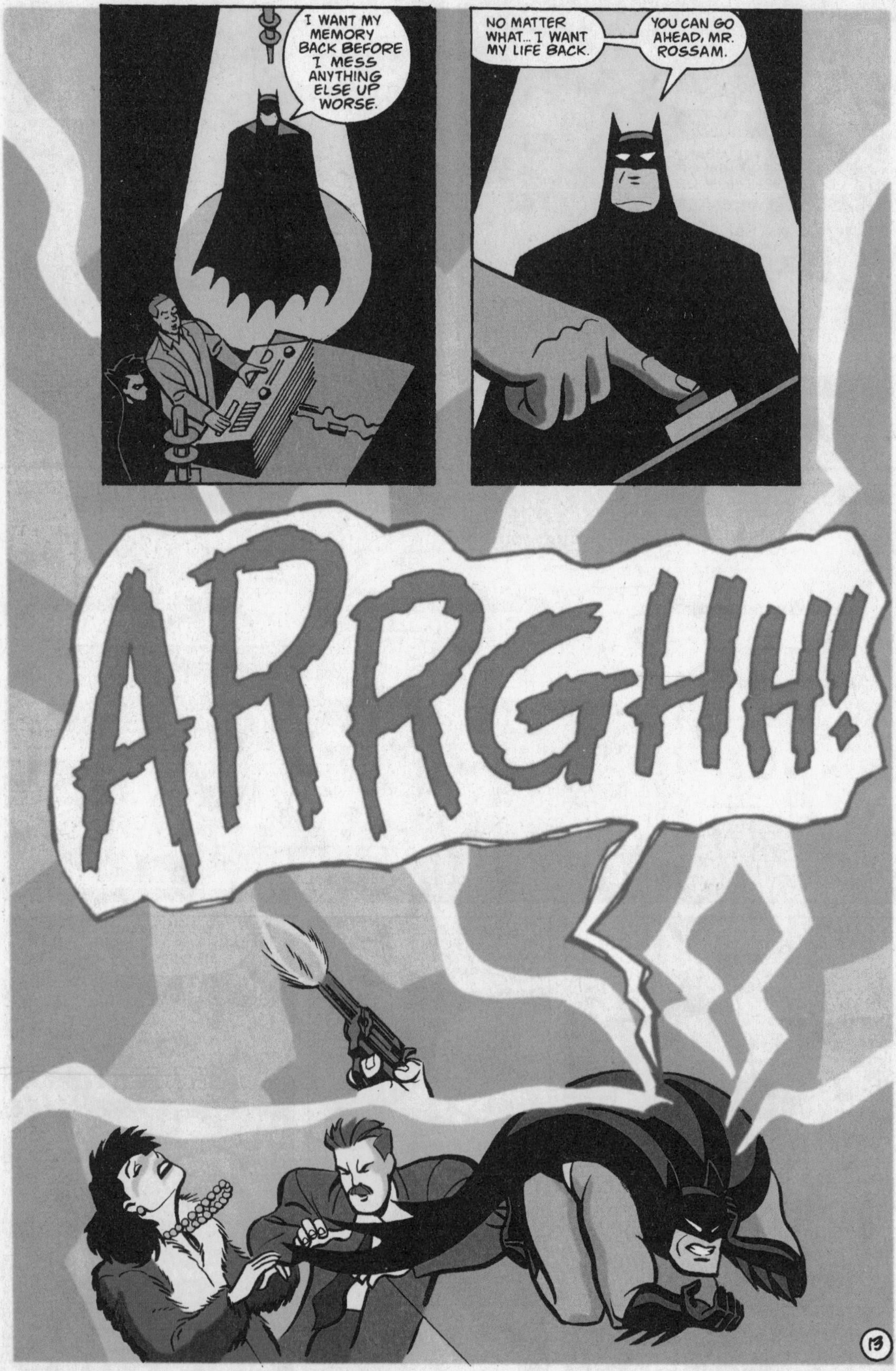
I WANT MY MEMORY BACK BEFORE I MESS ANYTHING ELSE UP WORSE.
NO MATTER WHAT... I WANT MY LIFE BACK.
YOU CAN GO AHEAD, MR. ROSSAM.
ARRGHH!
13

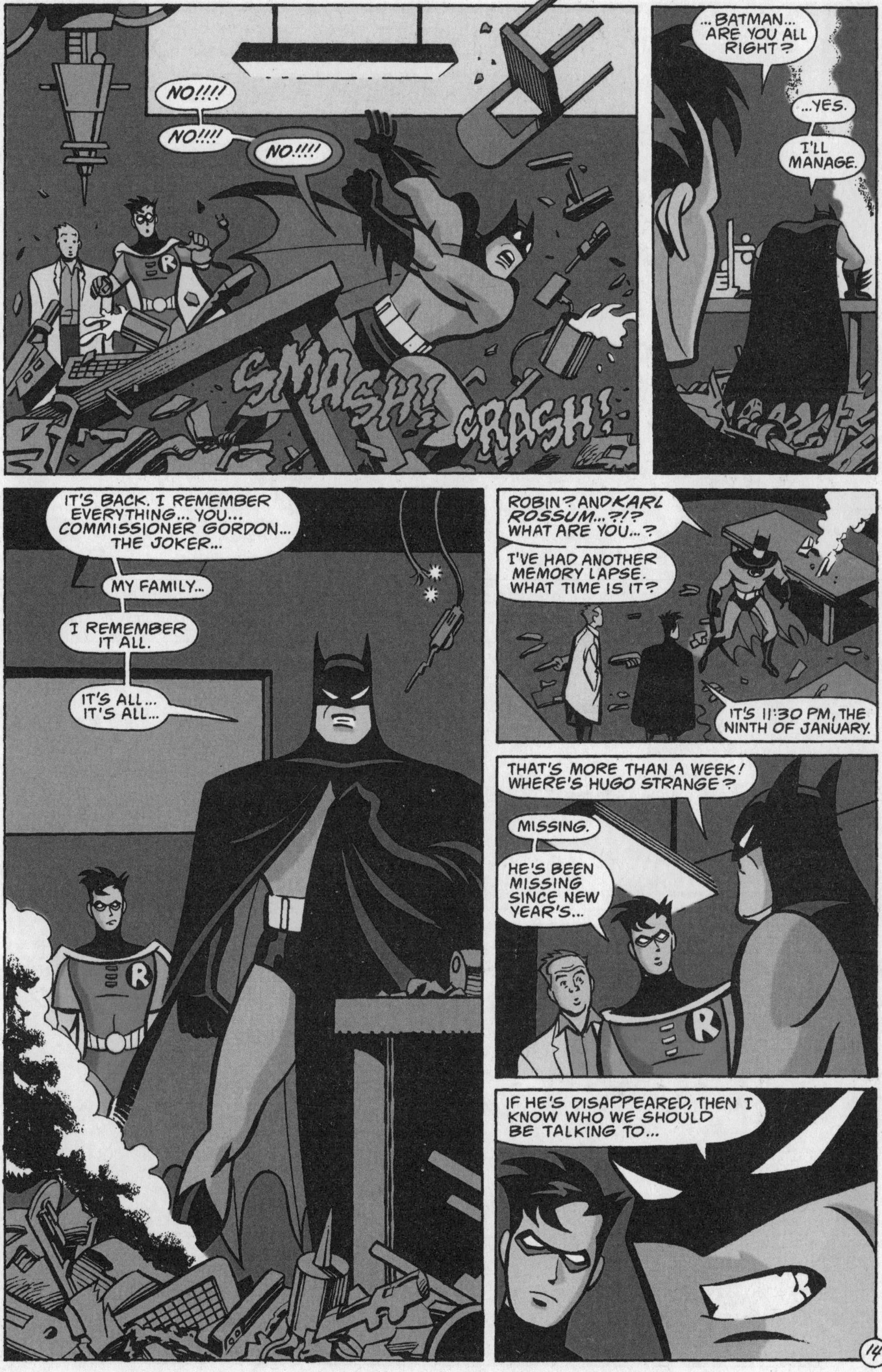
NO!!!!
NO!!!!
NO!!!!
SMASH!
CRASH!
...BATMAN... ARE YOU ALL RIGHT?
...YES.
I'LL MANAGE.
IT'S BACK. I REMEMBER EVERYTHING... YOU... COMMISSIONER GORDON... THE JOKER...
MY FAMILY...
I REMEMBER IT ALL.
IT'S ALL... IT'S ALL...
ROBIN? AND KARL ROSSUM...?!? WHAT ARE YOU...?
I'VE HAD ANOTHER MEMORY LAPSE. WHAT TIME IS IT?
IT'S 11:30 PM, THE NINTH OF JANUARY.
THAT'S MORE THAN A WEEK! WHERE'S HUGO STRANGE?
MISSING.
HE'S BEEN MISSING SINCE NEW YEAR'S...
IF HE'S DISAPPEARED, THEN I KNOW WHO WE SHOULD BE TALKING TO...

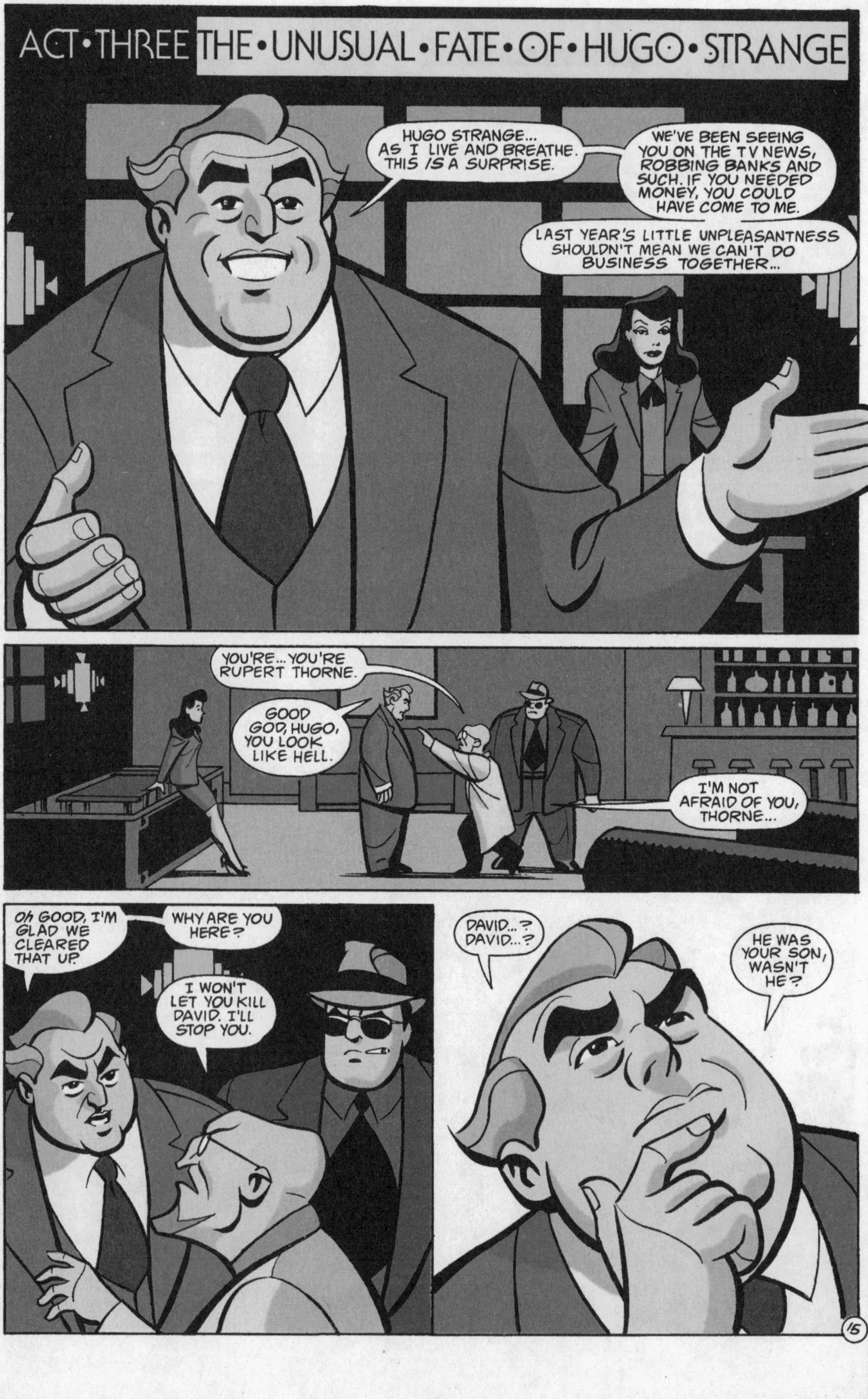
ACT•THREE THE•UNUSUAL•FATE•OF•HUGO•STRANGE
HUGO STRANGE... AS I LIVE AND BREATHE. THIS IS A SURPRISE.
WE'VE BEEN SEEING YOU ON THE TV NEWS, ROBBING BANKS AND SUCH. IF YOU NEEDED MONEY, YOU COULD HAVE COME TO ME.
LAST YEAR'S LITTLE UNPLEASANTNESS SHOULDN'T MEAN WE CAN'T DO BUSINESS TOGETHER...
YOU'RE... YOU'RE RUPERT THORNE.
GOOD GOD, HUGO, YOU LOOK LIKE HELL.
I'M NOT AFRAID OF YOU, THORNE...
Oh GOOD, I'M GLAD WE CLEARED THAT UP.
WHY ARE YOU HERE?
I WON'T LET YOU KILL DAVID. I'LL STOP YOU.
DAVID...? DAVID...?
HE WAS YOUR SON, WASN'T HE?

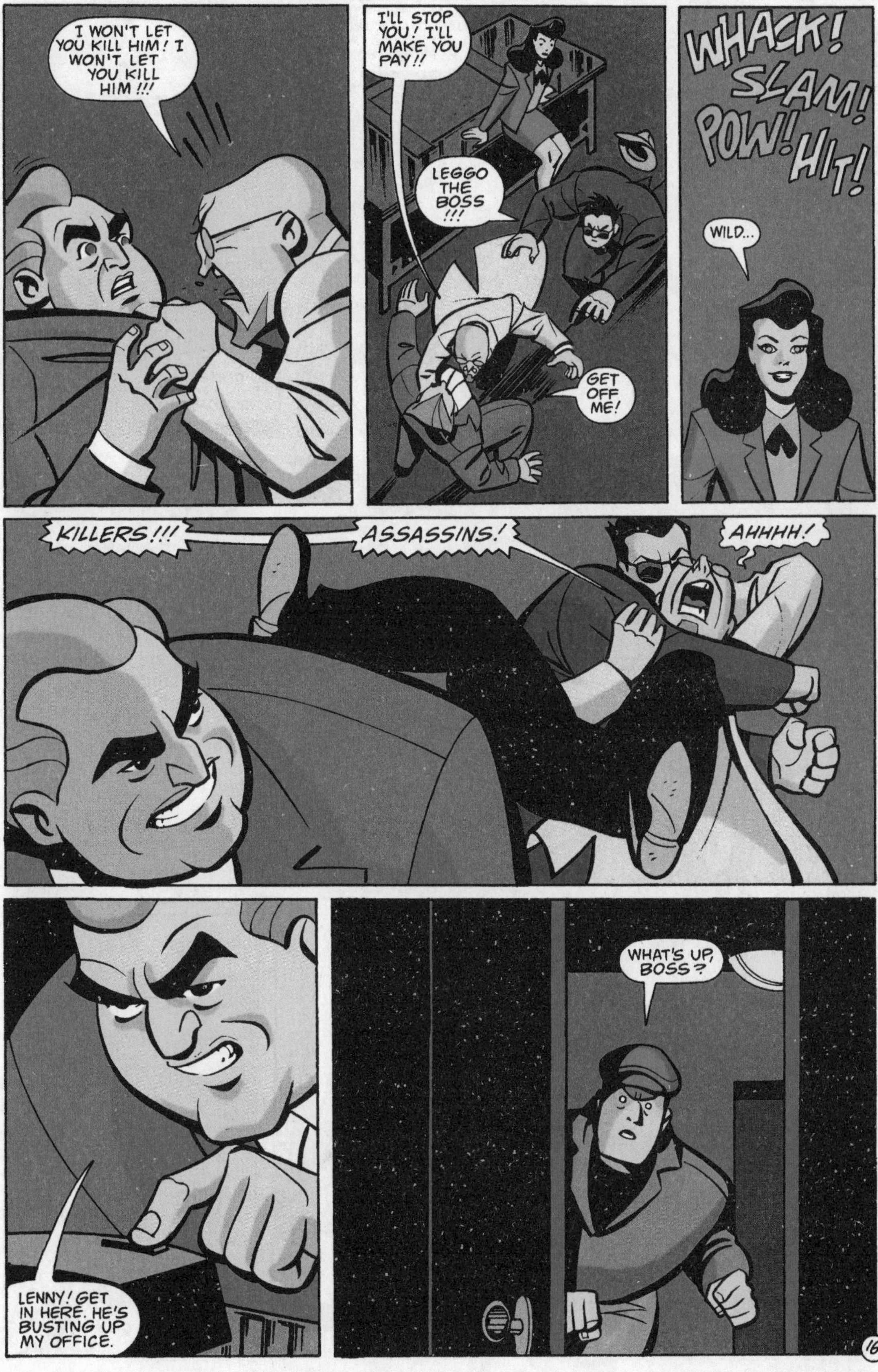
I WON'T LET YOU KILL HIM! I WON'T LET YOU KILL HIM!!!
I'LL STOP YOU! I'LL MAKE YOU PAY!!
LEGGO THE BOSS!!!
GET OFF ME!
WHACK! SLAM! POW! HIT!
WILD...
KILLERS!!!
ASSASSINS!
AHHHH!
LENNY! GET IN HERE. HE'S BUSTING UP MY OFFICE.
WHAT'S UP, BOSS?

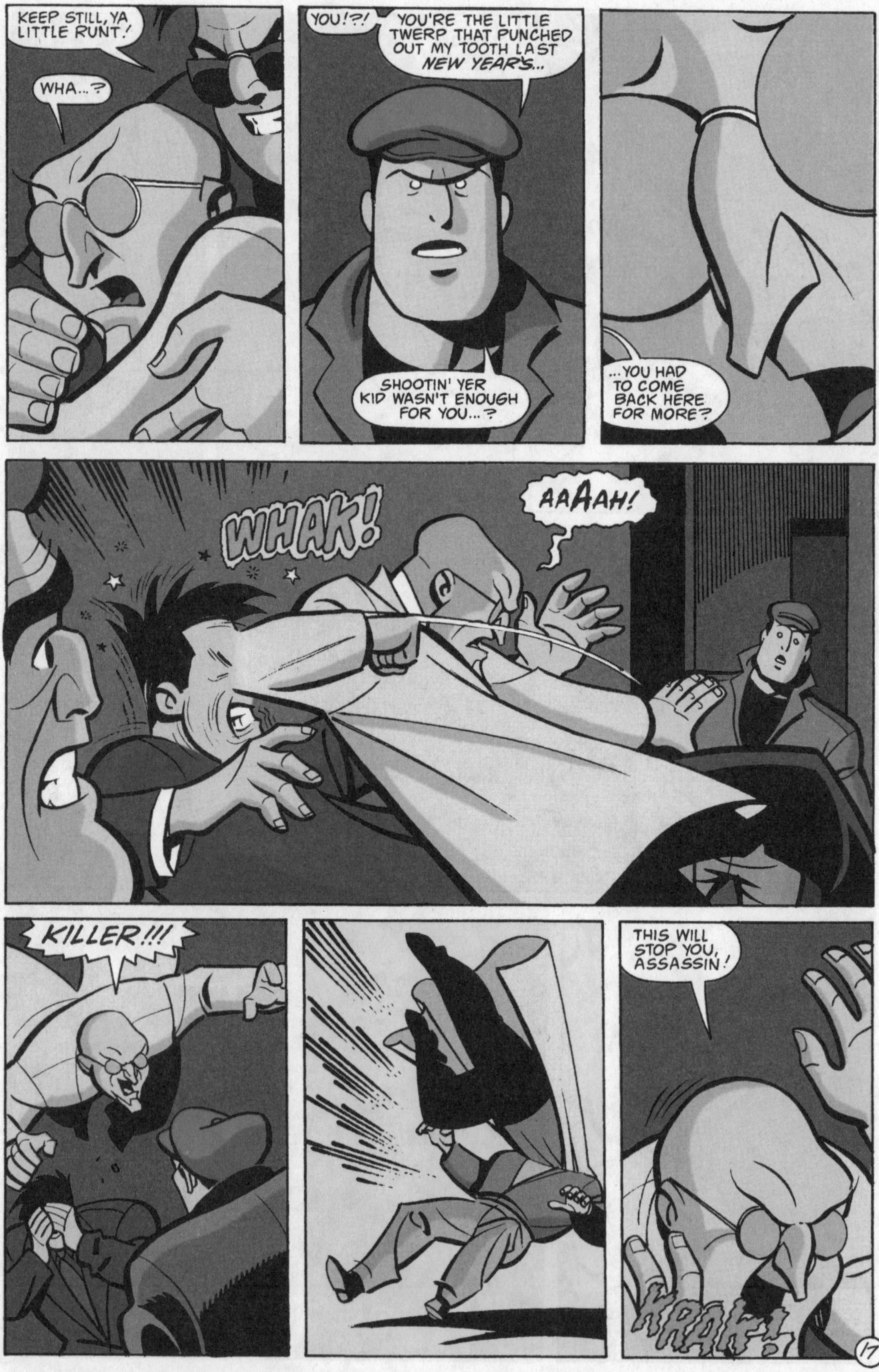

KEEP STILL, YA LITTLE RUNT!
WHA...?
YOU!?!
YOU'RE THE LITTLE TWERP THAT PUNCHED OUT MY TOOTH LAST NEW YEAR'S...
SHOOTIN' YER KID WASN'T ENOUGH FOR YOU...?
...YOU HAD TO COME BACK HERE FOR MORE?
WHAK!
AAAAH!
KILLER!!!
THIS WILL STOP YOU, ASSASSIN!
KRAK!

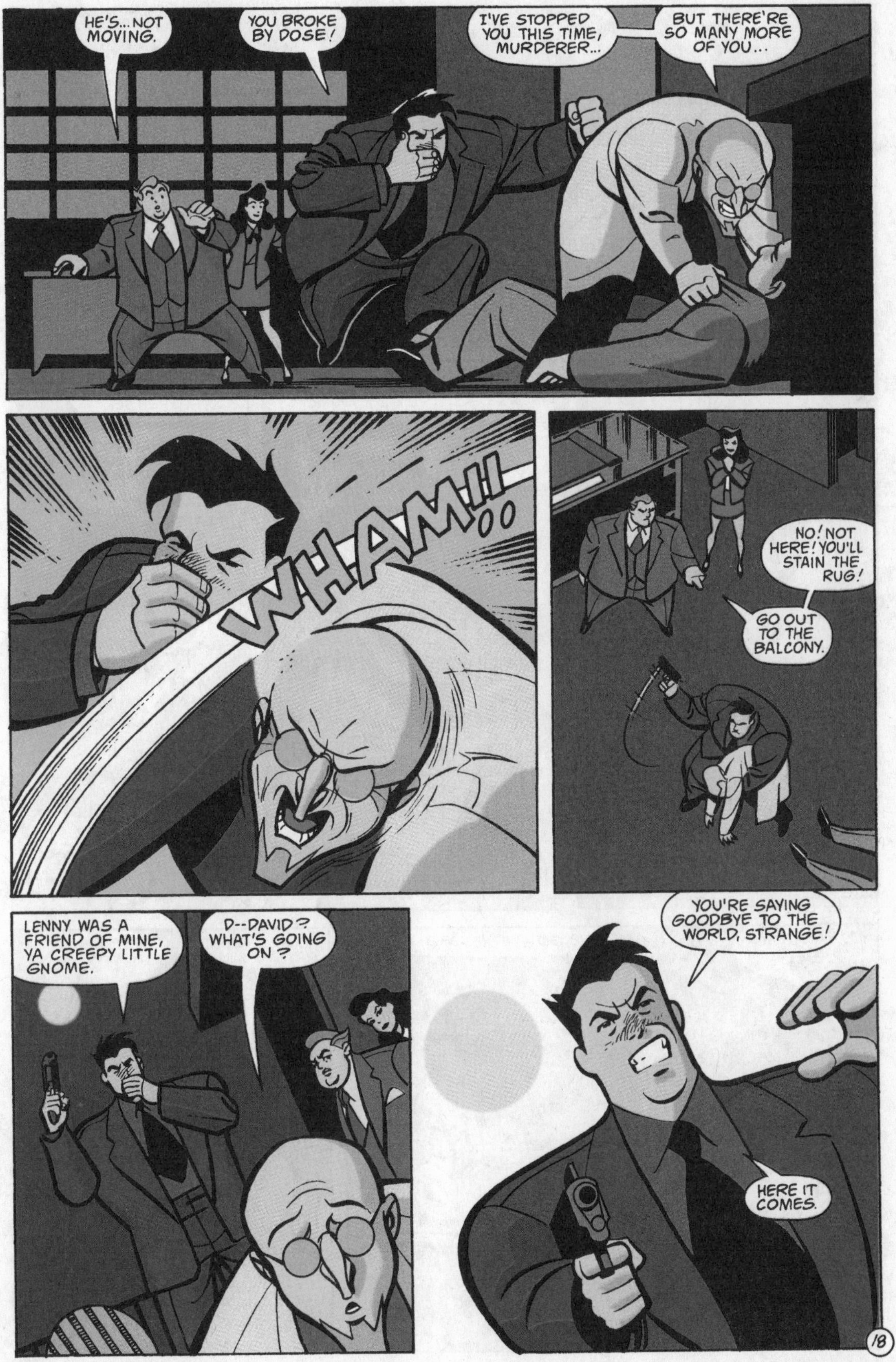

HE'S...NOT MOVING.
YOU BROKE BY DOSE!
I'VE STOPPED YOU THIS TIME, MURDERER...
BUT THERE'RE SO MANY MORE OF YOU...
WHAM!!
NO! NOT HERE! YOU'LL STAIN THE RUG!
GO OUT TO THE BALCONY.
LENNY WAS A FRIEND OF MINE, YA CREEPY LITTLE GNOME.
D--DAVID? WHAT'S GOING ON?
YOU'RE SAYING GOODBYE TO THE WORLD, STRANGE!
HERE IT COMES.

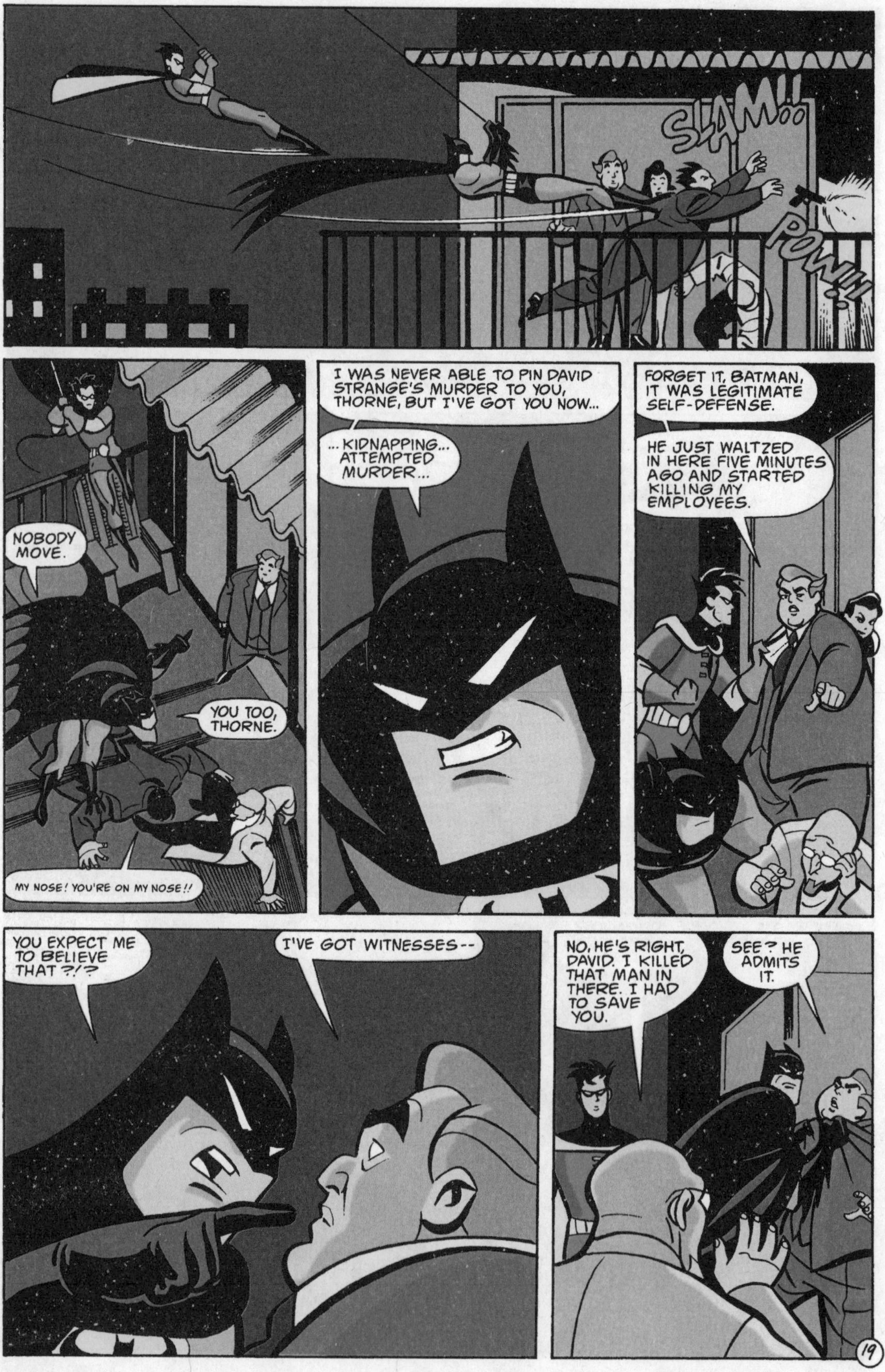

SLAM!!
POW!!
NOBODY MOVE.
YOU TOO, THORNE.
MY NOSE! YOU'RE ON MY NOSE!!
I WAS NEVER ABLE TO PIN DAVID STRANGE'S MURDER TO YOU, THORNE, BUT I'VE GOT YOU NOW...
...KIDNAPPING... ATTEMPTED MURDER...
FORGET IT, BATMAN, IT WAS LEGITIMATE SELF-DEFENSE.
HE JUST WALTZED IN HERE FIVE MINUTES AGO AND STARTED KILLING MY EMPLOYEES.
YOU EXPECT ME TO BELIEVE THAT?!?
I'VE GOT WITNESSES--
NO, HE'S RIGHT, DAVID. I KILLED THAT MAN IN THERE. I HAD TO SAVE YOU.
SEE? HE ADMITS IT.

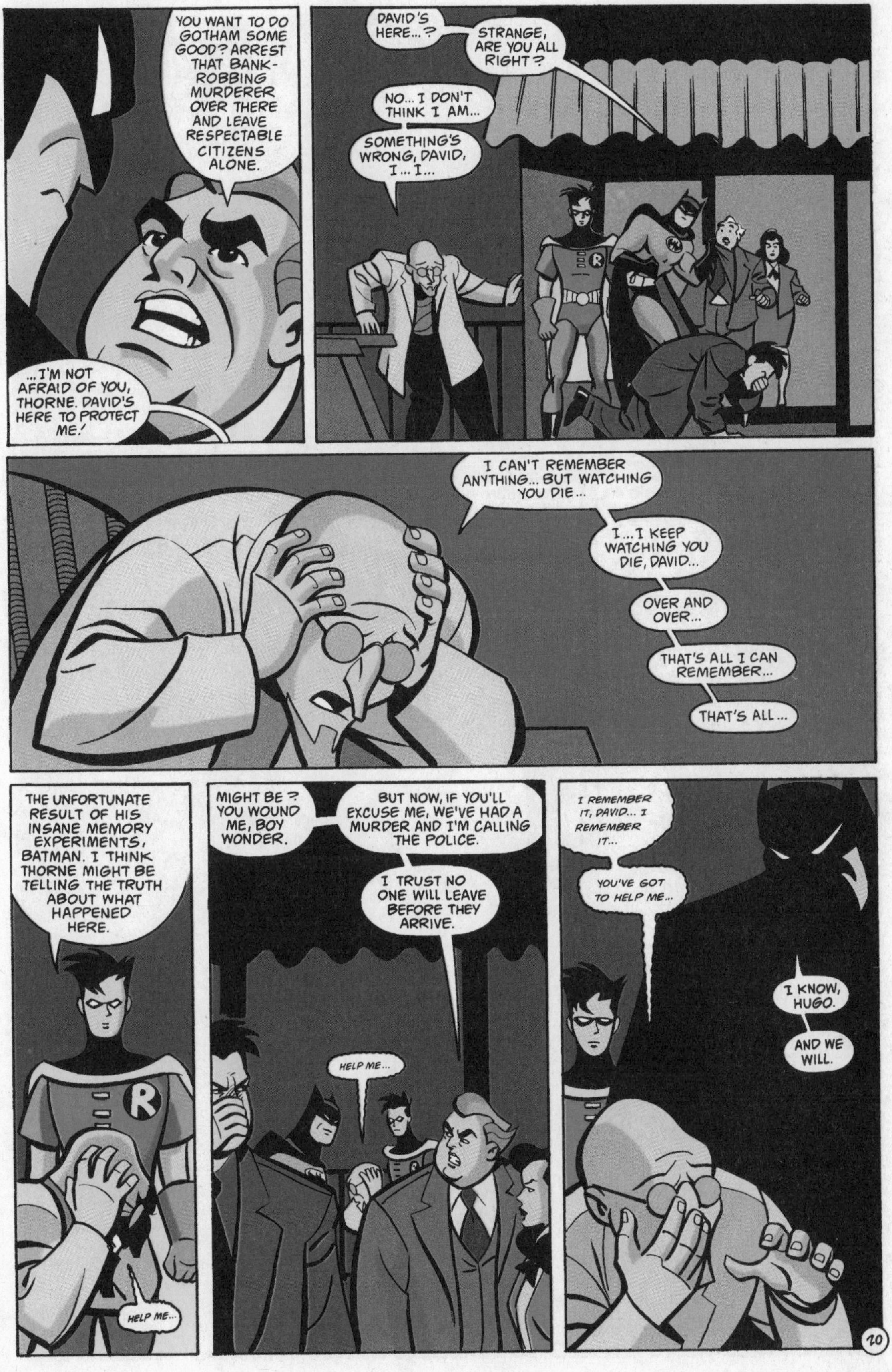
YOU WANT TO DO GOTHAM SOME GOOD? ARREST THAT BANK-ROBBING MURDERER OVER THERE AND LEAVE RESPECTABLE CITIZENS ALONE.
...I'M NOT AFRAID OF YOU, THORNE. DAVID'S HERE TO PROTECT ME!
DAVID'S HERE...?
STRANGE, ARE YOU ALL RIGHT?
NO... I DON'T THINK I AM...
SOMETHING'S WRONG, DAVID, I... I...
I CAN'T REMEMBER ANYTHING... BUT WATCHING YOU DIE...
I... I KEEP WATCHING YOU DIE, DAVID...
OVER AND OVER...
THAT'S ALL I CAN REMEMBER...
THAT'S ALL...
THE UNFORTUNATE RESULT OF HIS INSANE MEMORY EXPERIMENTS, BATMAN. I THINK THORNE MIGHT BE TELLING THE TRUTH ABOUT WHAT HAPPENED HERE.
HELP ME...
MIGHT BE? YOU WOUND ME, BOY WONDER.
BUT NOW, IF YOU'LL EXCUSE ME, WE'VE HAD A MURDER AND I'M CALLING THE POLICE.
I TRUST NO ONE WILL LEAVE BEFORE THEY ARRIVE.
HELP ME...
I REMEMBER IT, DAVID... I REMEMBER IT...
YOU'VE GOT TO HELP ME...
I KNOW, HUGO.
AND WE WILL.
20

YOU'RE GOING TO HAVE TO FIND LESS DESTRUCTIVE WAYS OF GETTING MY ATTENTION...

I SEE YOU GOT YOUR PERSONALITY BACK.

DON'T WORRY, IT'S WATER-SOLUBLE PAINT. ONE RAINSTORM AND *PHHHT!*

I'VE BEEN THINKING A LOT ABOUT WHAT YOU SAID THE OTHER DAY... ABOUT NEVER FORGIVING ME.

I'D LIKE TO SEE IF I COULD CHANGE YOUR MIND...

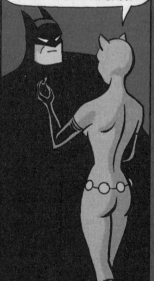

HERE. THE ROTHSCHILD RING.

I KNOW IT'S THE KIND OF THING THAT WOULD PLAY ON YOUR CONSCIENCE, SO NOW YOU CAN GIVE IT BACK, NO STRINGS ATTACHED.

ROBIN MENTIONED I HAD STOLEN THIS WHILE UNDER THE INFLUENCE OF STRANGE'S DEVICE...

BUT HOW DID *YOU* GET IT?

21

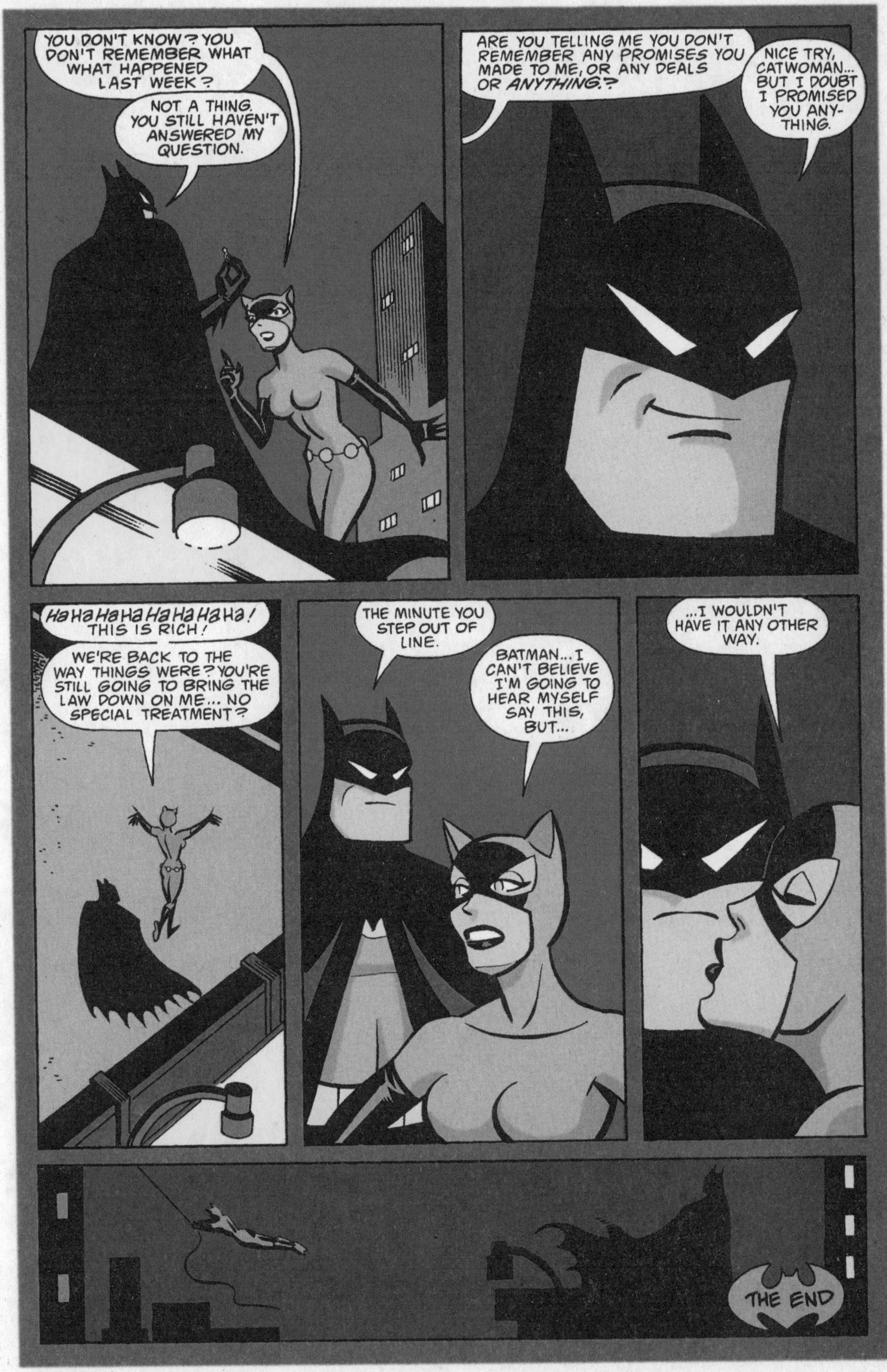
YOU DON'T KNOW? YOU DON'T REMEMBER WHAT WHAT HAPPENED LAST WEEK?
NOT A THING. YOU STILL HAVEN'T ANSWERED MY QUESTION.
ARE YOU TELLING ME YOU DON'T REMEMBER ANY PROMISES YOU MADE TO ME, OR ANY DEALS OR ANYTHING.?
NICE TRY, CATWOMAN... BUT I DOUBT I PROMISED YOU ANY-THING.
HaHaHaHaHaHaHaHaHa! THIS IS RICH!
WE'RE BACK TO THE WAY THINGS WERE? YOU'RE STILL GOING TO BRING THE LAW DOWN ON ME... NO SPECIAL TREATMENT?
THE MINUTE YOU STEP OUT OF LINE.
BATMAN... I CAN'T BELIEVE I'M GOING TO HEAR MYSELF SAY THIS, BUT...
...I WOULDN'T HAVE IT ANY OTHER WAY.
THE END

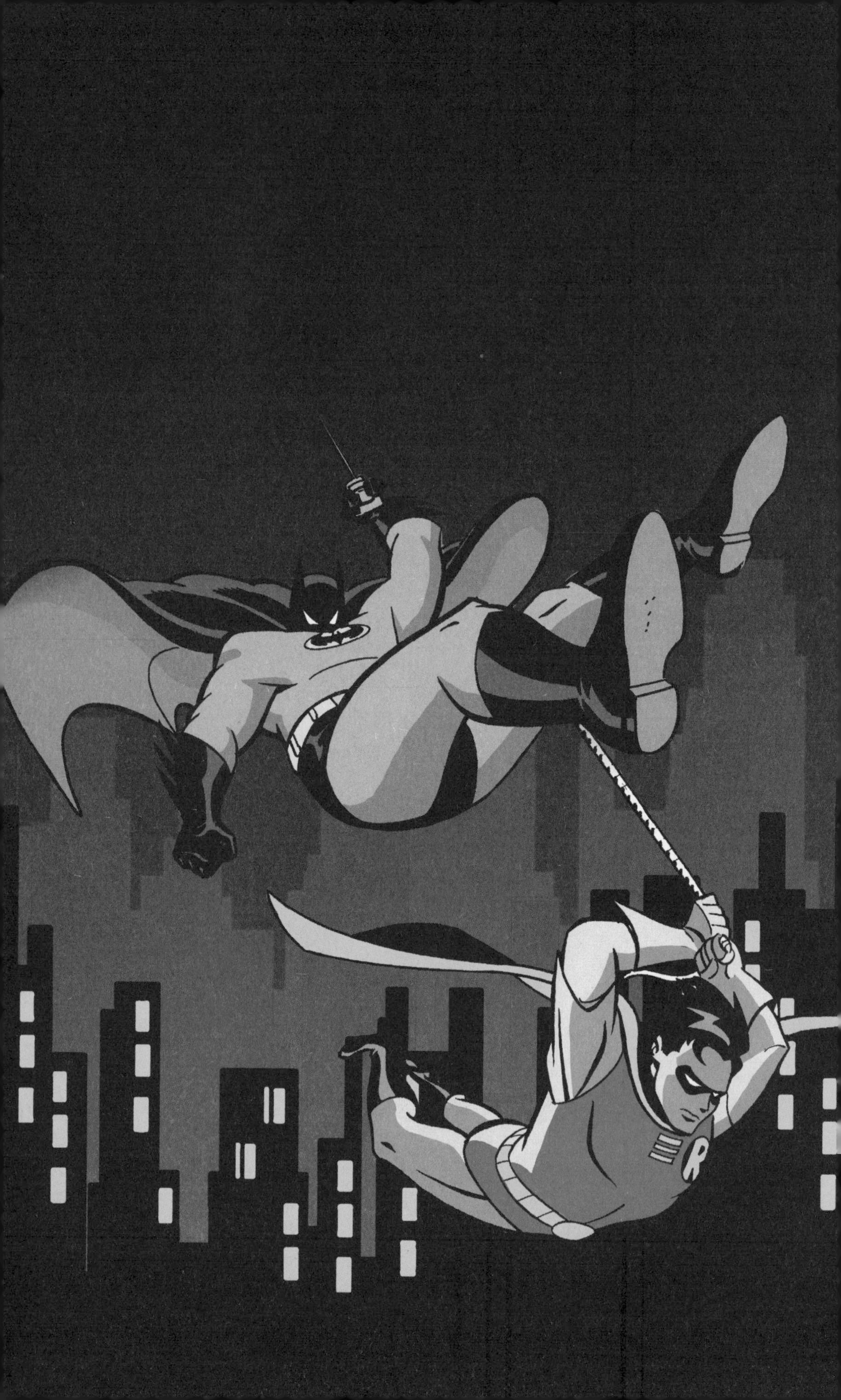

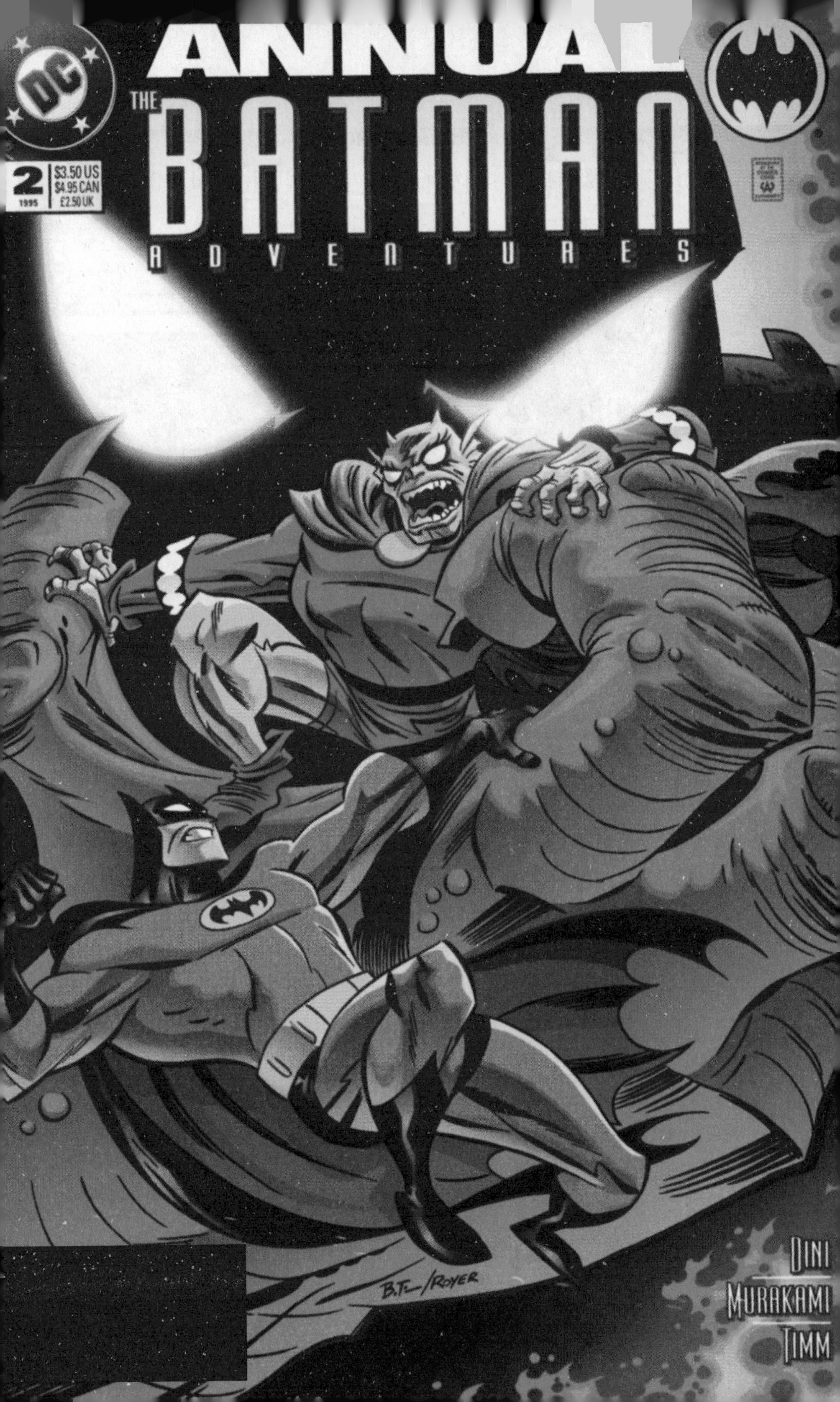
ANNUAL
DC
THE BATMAN ADVENTURES
2
$3.50 US
$4.95 CAN
£2.50 UK
1995
B.T./ROYER
DINI
MURAKAMI
TIMM

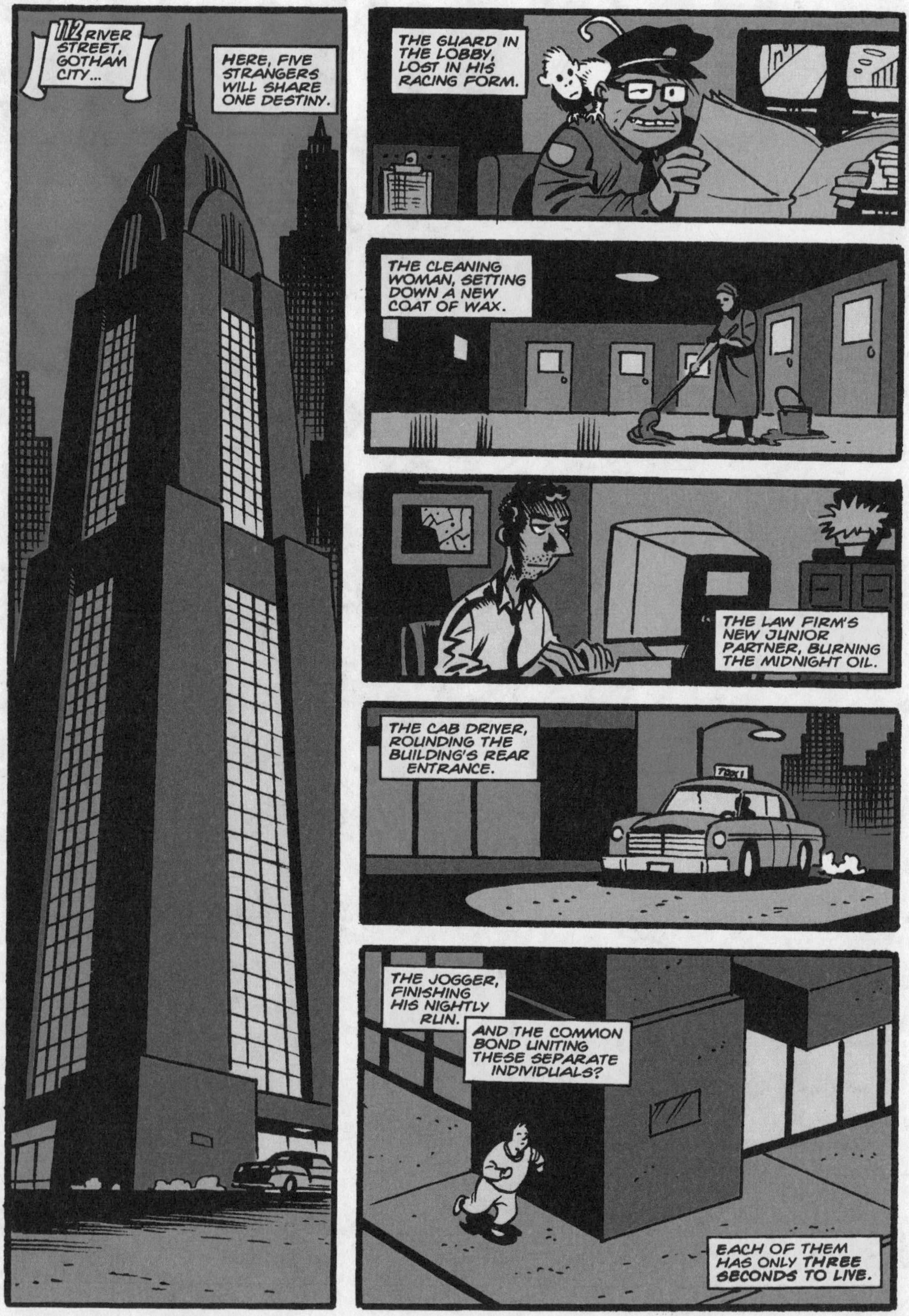
112 RIVER STREET, GOTHAM CITY...
HERE, FIVE STRANGERS WILL SHARE ONE DESTINY.
THE GUARD IN THE LOBBY, LOST IN HIS RACING FORM.
THE CLEANING WOMAN, SETTING DOWN A NEW COAT OF WAX.
THE LAW FIRM'S NEW JUNIOR PARTNER, BURNING THE MIDNIGHT OIL.
THE CAB DRIVER, ROUNDING THE BUILDING'S REAR ENTRANCE.
TAXI
THE JOGGER, FINISHING HIS NIGHTLY RUN.
AND THE COMMON BOND UNITING THESE SEPARATE INDIVIDUALS?
EACH OF THEM HAS ONLY THREE SECONDS TO LIVE.

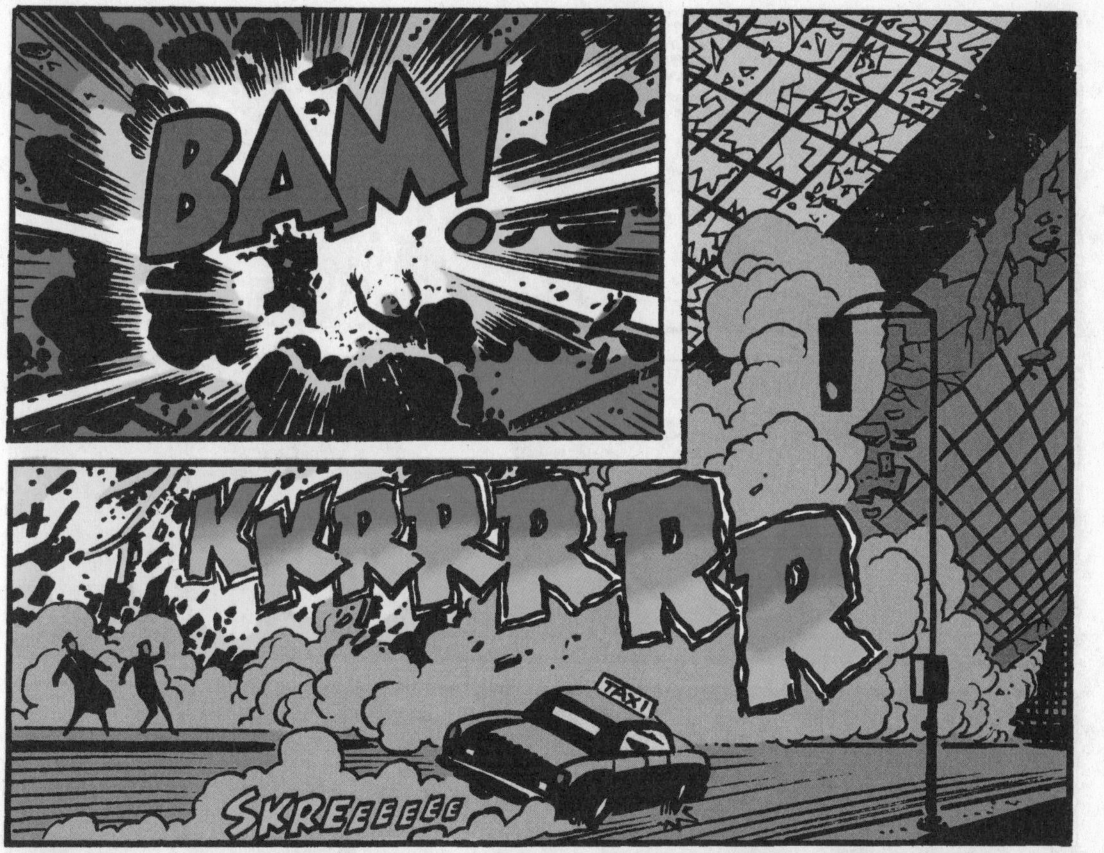
BAM!
KRRRRR
TAXI
SKREEEEEEE

DEMONS

PAUL DINI
CO-PLOT/WRITER

GLEN MURAKAMI & BRUCE TIMM
CO-PLOT/ART

GLEN MURAKAMI
COLOR

STARKINGS/COMICRAFT
LETTERING

DARREN VINCENZO
ASSOC. EDITOR

SCOTT PETERSON
EDITOR

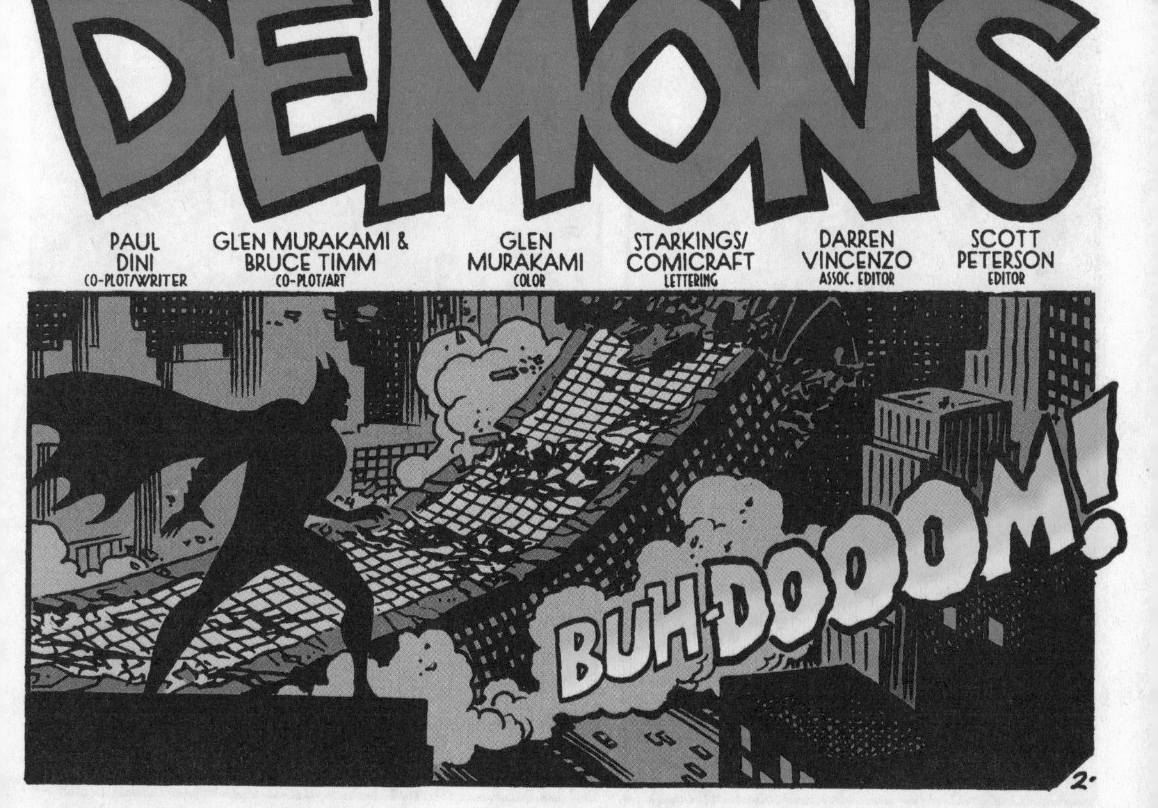
BUH-DOOOM!

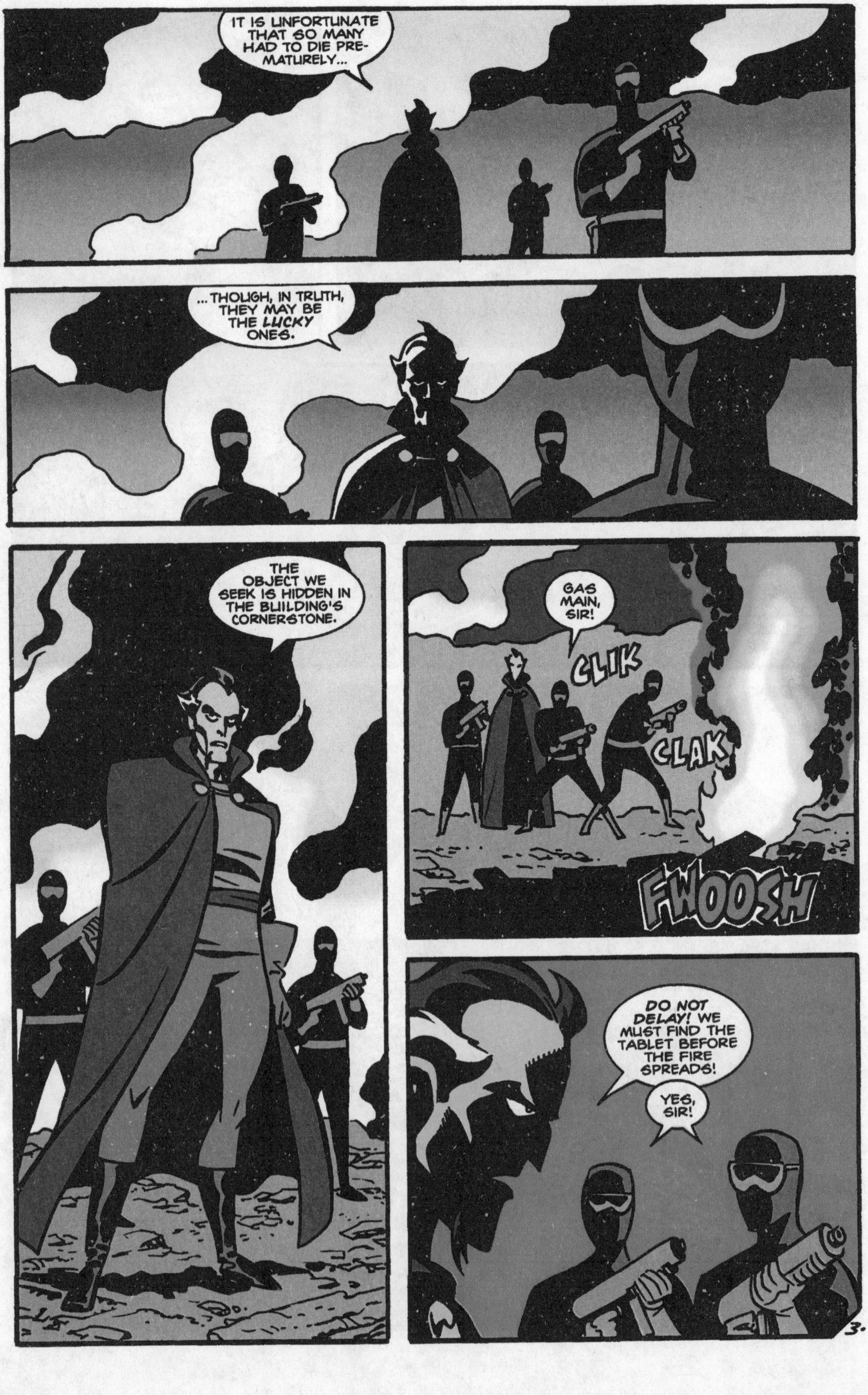
IT IS UNFORTUNATE THAT SO MANY HAD TO DIE PRE-MATURELY...
...THOUGH, IN TRUTH, THEY MAY BE THE *LUCKY* ONES.
THE OBJECT WE SEEK IS HIDDEN IN THE BUILDING'S CORNERSTONE.
GAS MAIN, SIR!
CLIK
CLAK
FWOOSH
DO NOT DELAY! WE MUST FIND THE TABLET BEFORE THE FIRE SPREADS!
YES, SIR!
3.

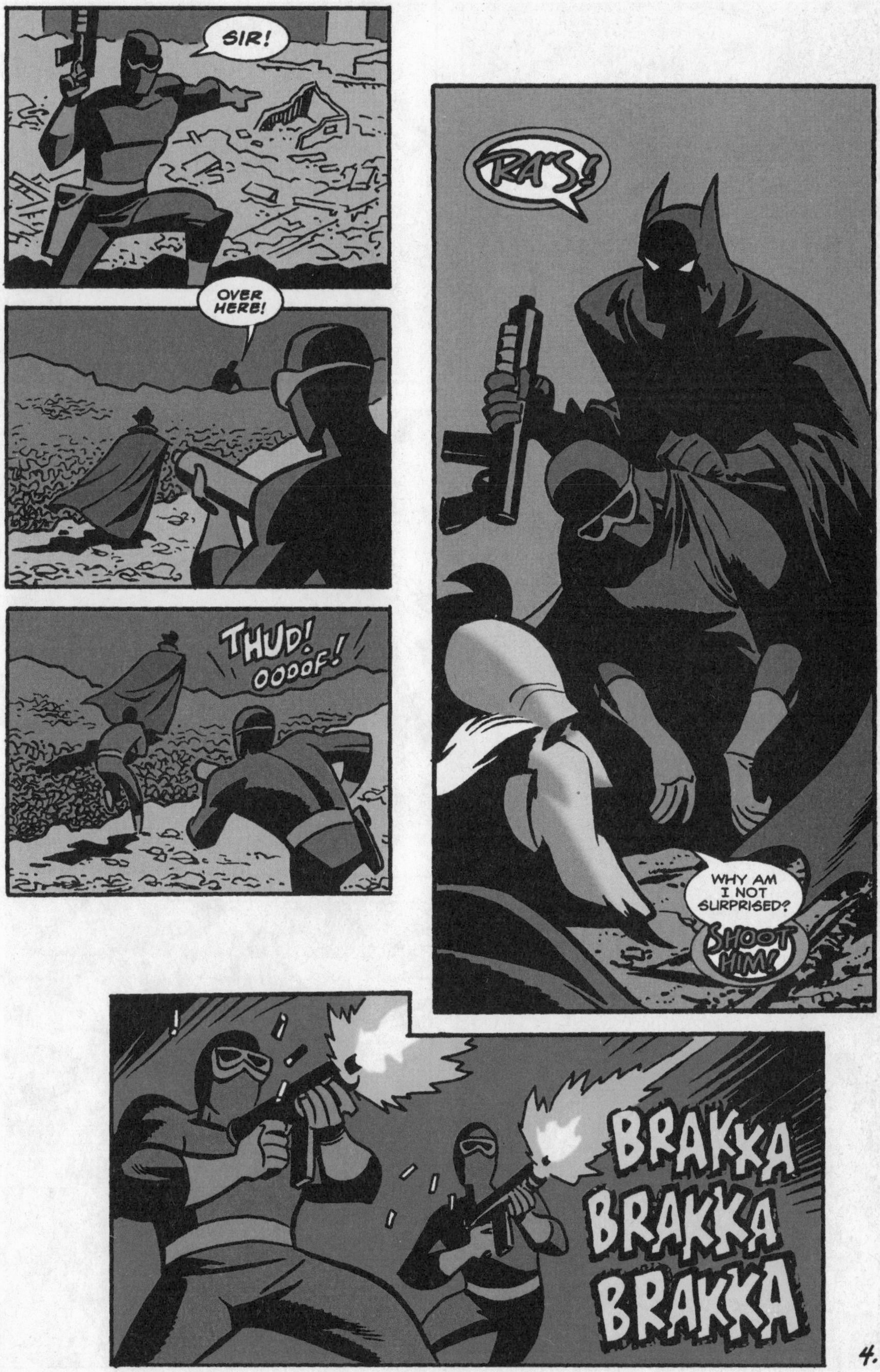

SIR!
OVER HERE!
THUD! OOOOF!
RA'S!
WHY AM I NOT SURPRISED?
SHOOT HIM!
BRAKKA BRAKKA BRAKKA

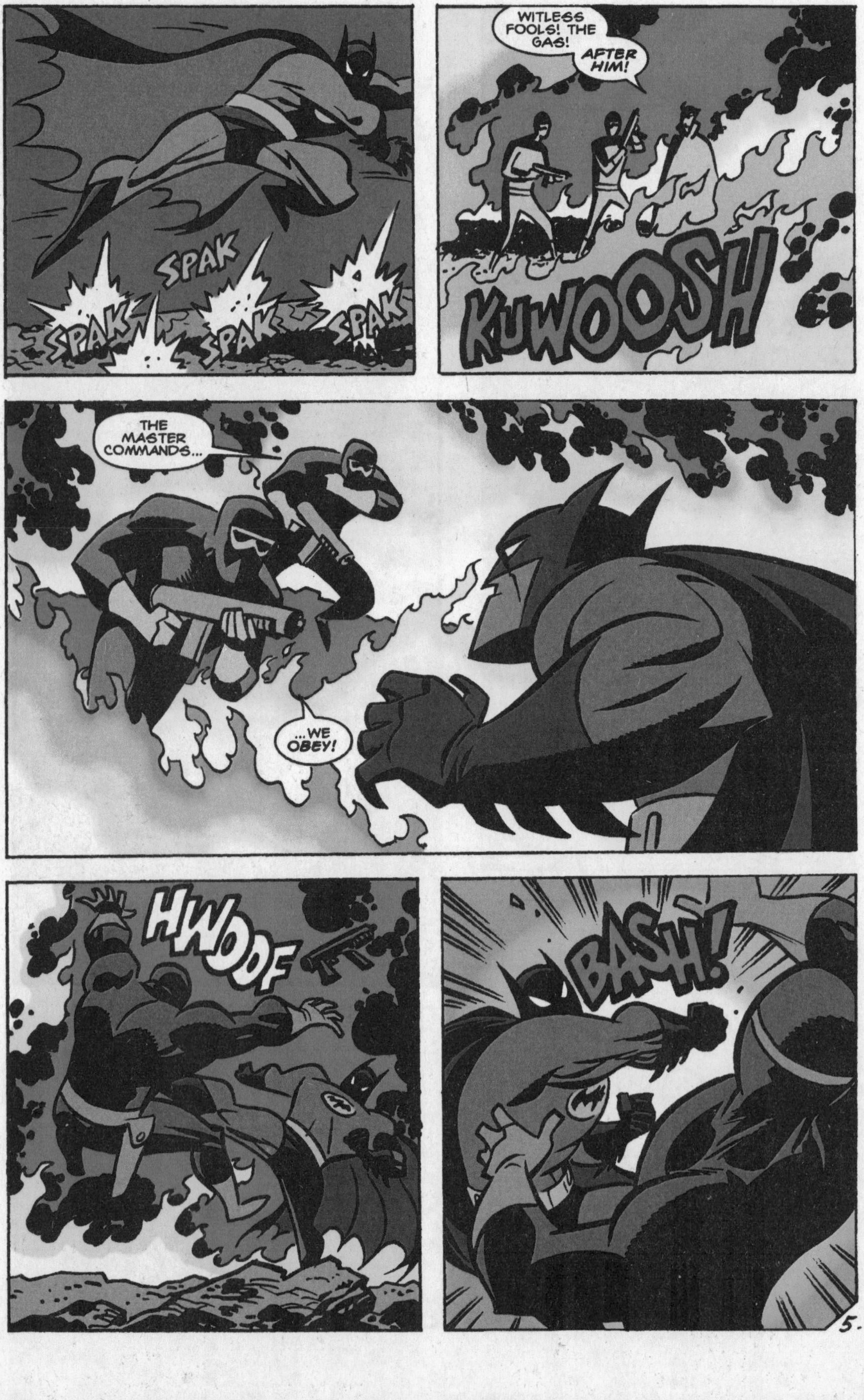
SPAK
SPAK
SPAK
SPAK
WITLESS FOOLS! THE GAS!
AFTER HIM!
KUWOOSH
THE MASTER COMMANDS...
...WE OBEY!
HWOOF
BASH!

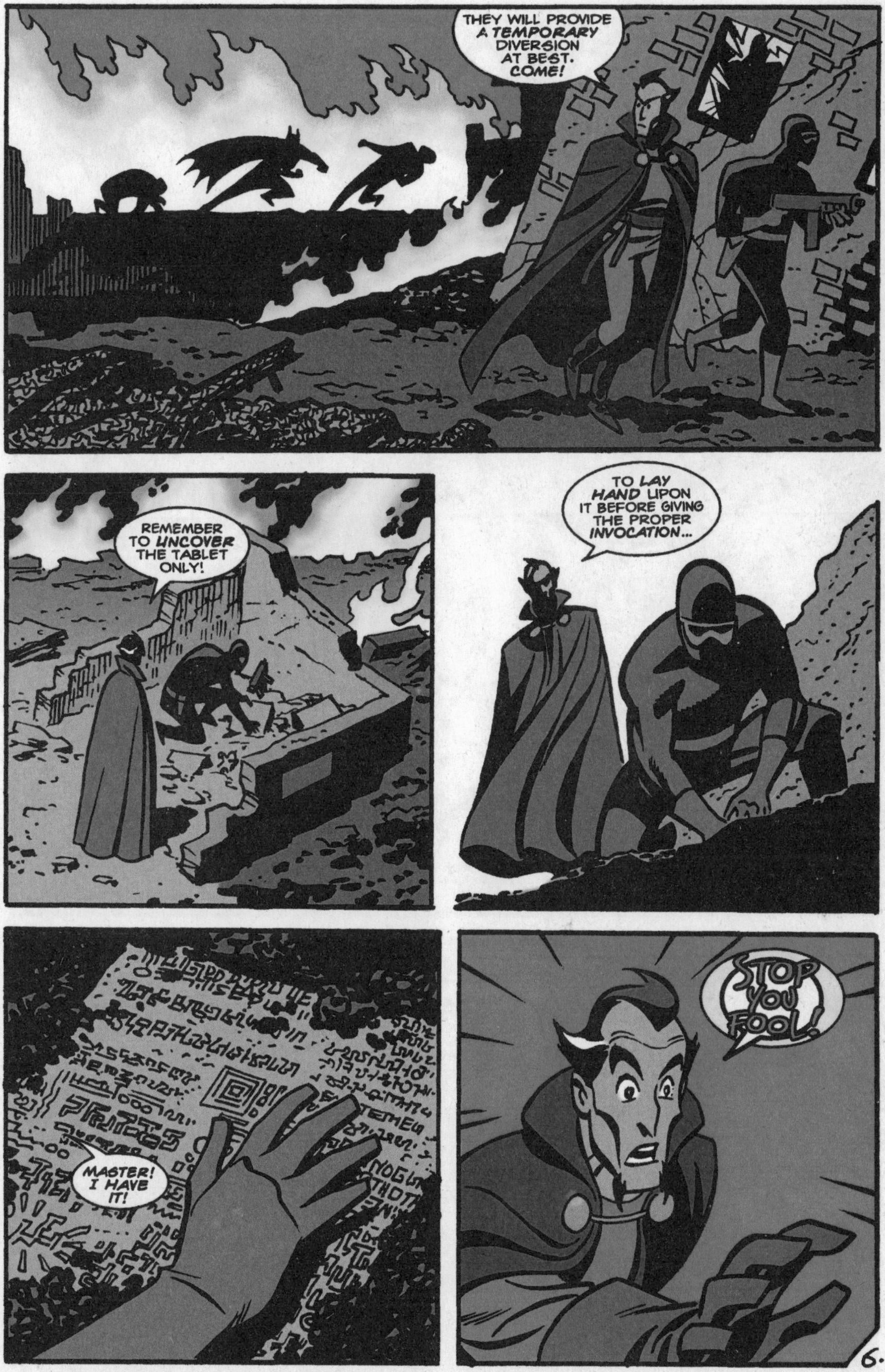
THEY WILL PROVIDE A TEMPORARY DIVERSION AT BEST. COME!
REMEMBER TO UNCOVER THE TABLET ONLY!
TO LAY HAND UPON IT BEFORE GIVING THE PROPER INVOCATION...
MASTER! I HAVE IT!
STOP YOU FOOL!

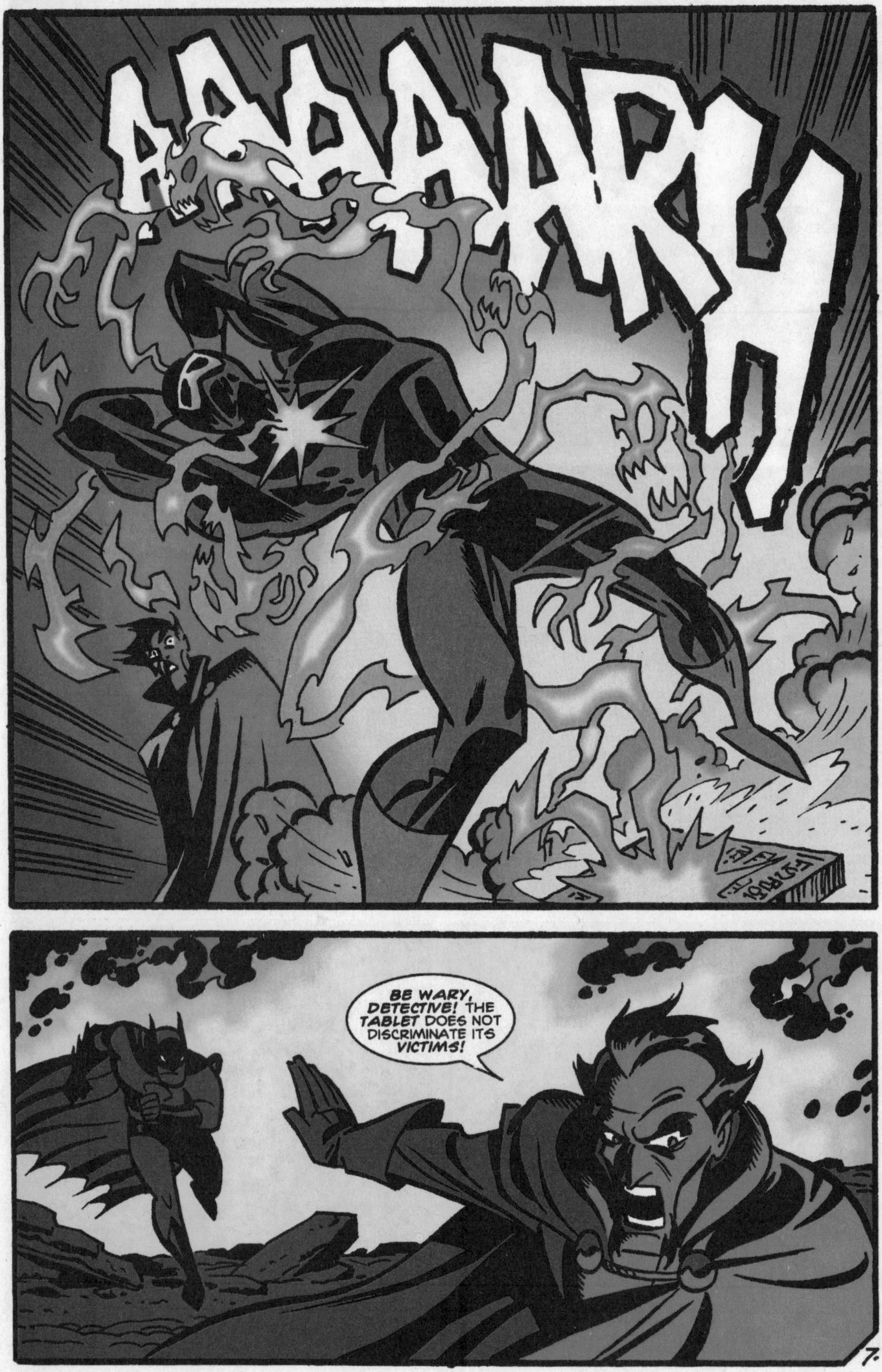
AAAAARH
BE WARY, DETECTIVE! THE TABLET DOES NOT DISCRIMINATE ITS VICTIMS!

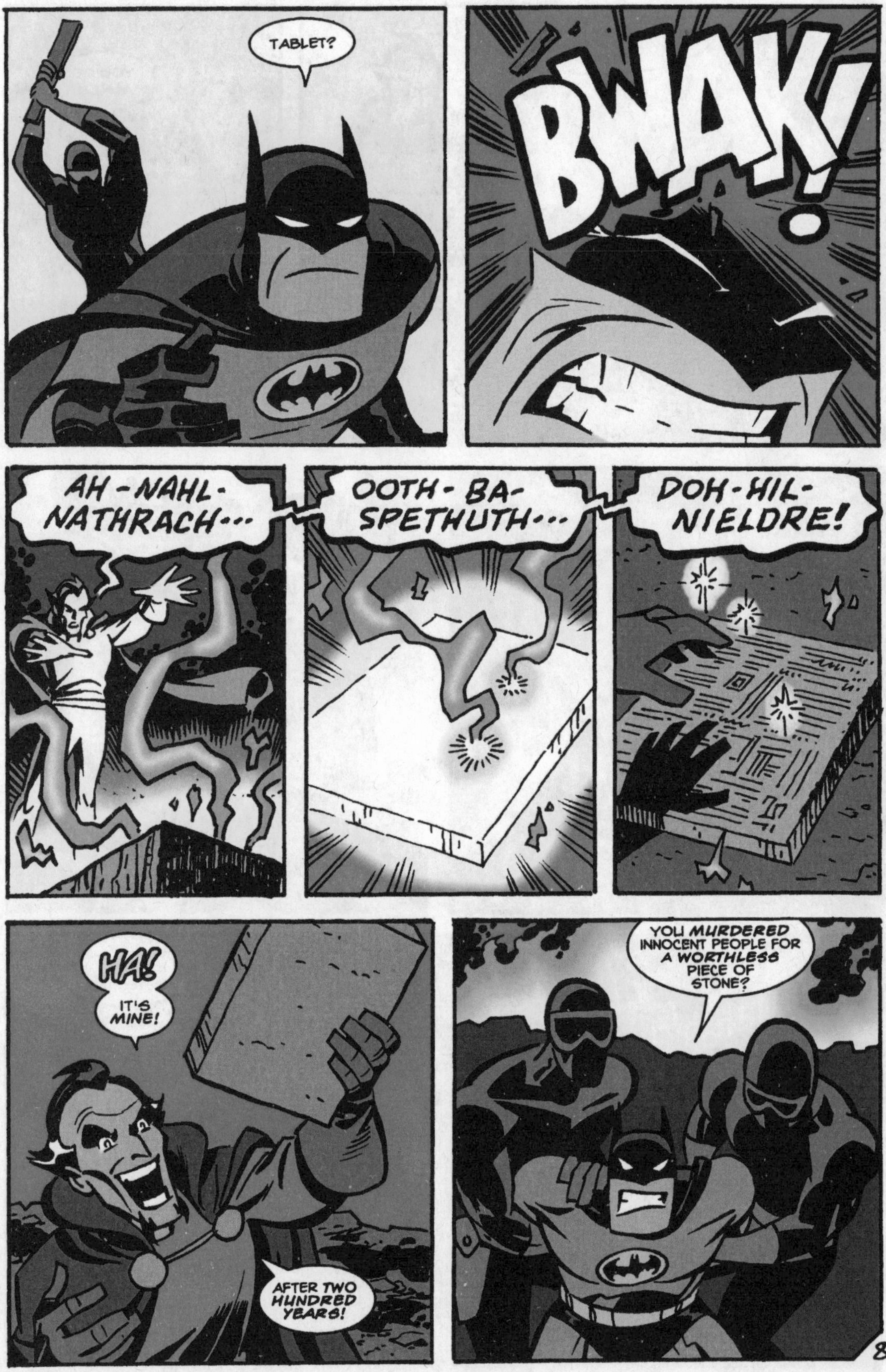
TABLET?
BWAK!
AH-NAHL-NATHRACH...
OOTH-BA-SPETHUTH...
DOH-HIL-NIELDRE!
HA!
IT'S MINE!
AFTER TWO HUNDRED YEARS!
YOU MURDERED INNOCENT PEOPLE FOR A WORTHLESS PIECE OF STONE?

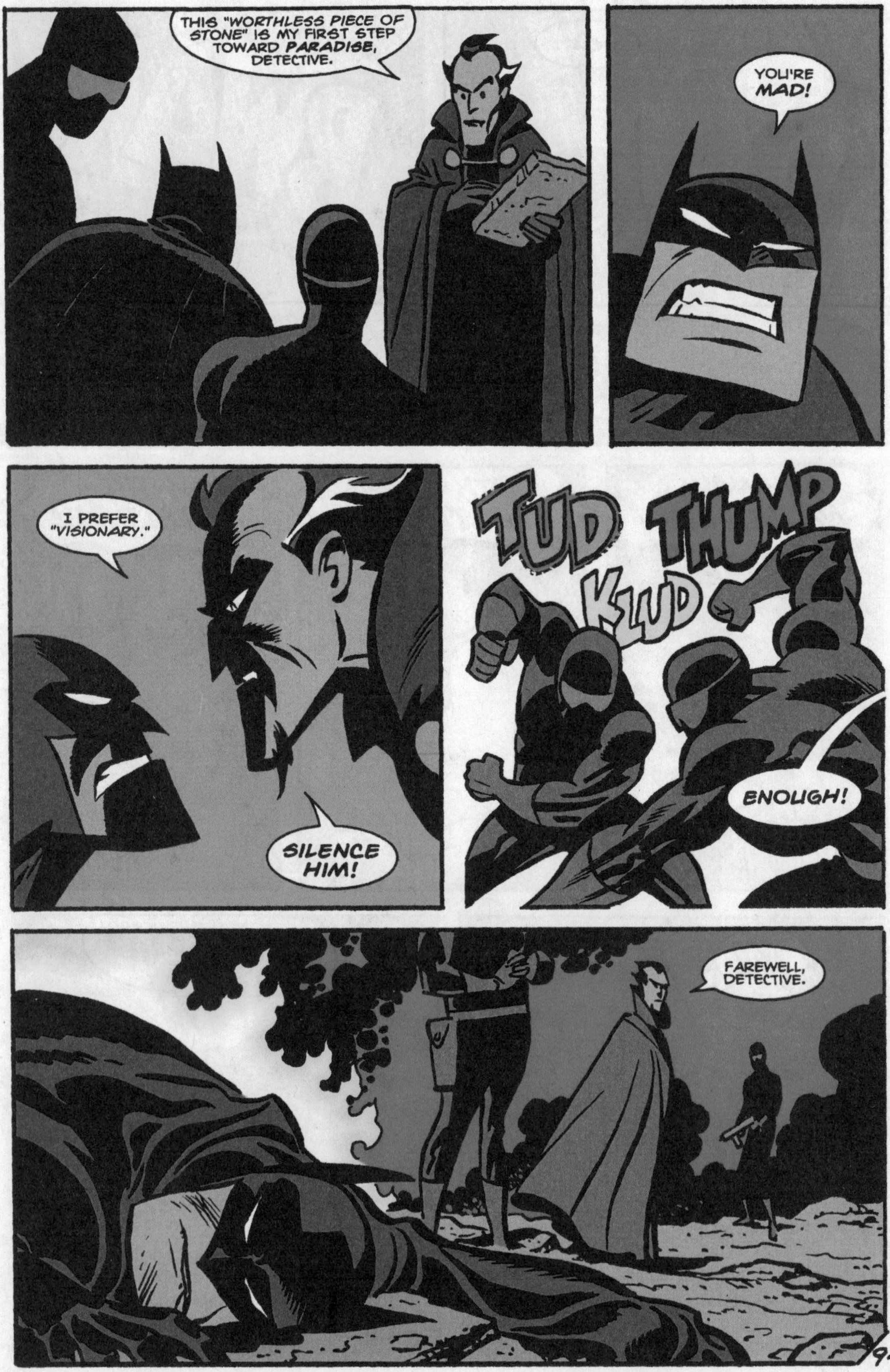
THIS "WORTHLESS PIECE OF STONE" IS MY FIRST STEP TOWARD PARADISE, DETECTIVE.
YOU'RE MAD!
I PREFER "VISIONARY."
SILENCE HIM!
TUD
THUMP
KLUD
ENOUGH!
FAREWELL, DETECTIVE.

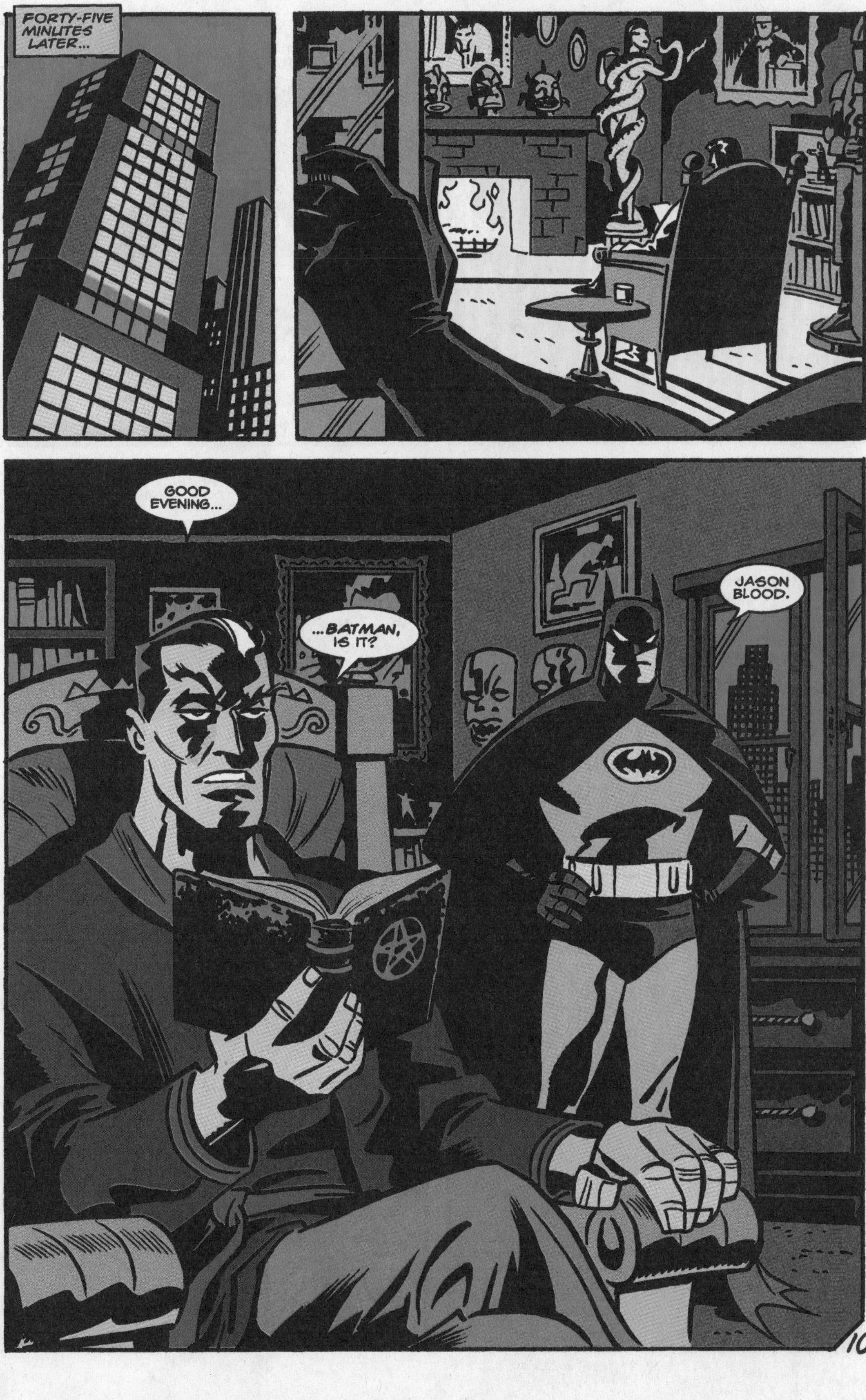
FORTY-FIVE MINUTES LATER...
GOOD EVENING...
...BATMAN, IS IT?
JASON BLOOD.

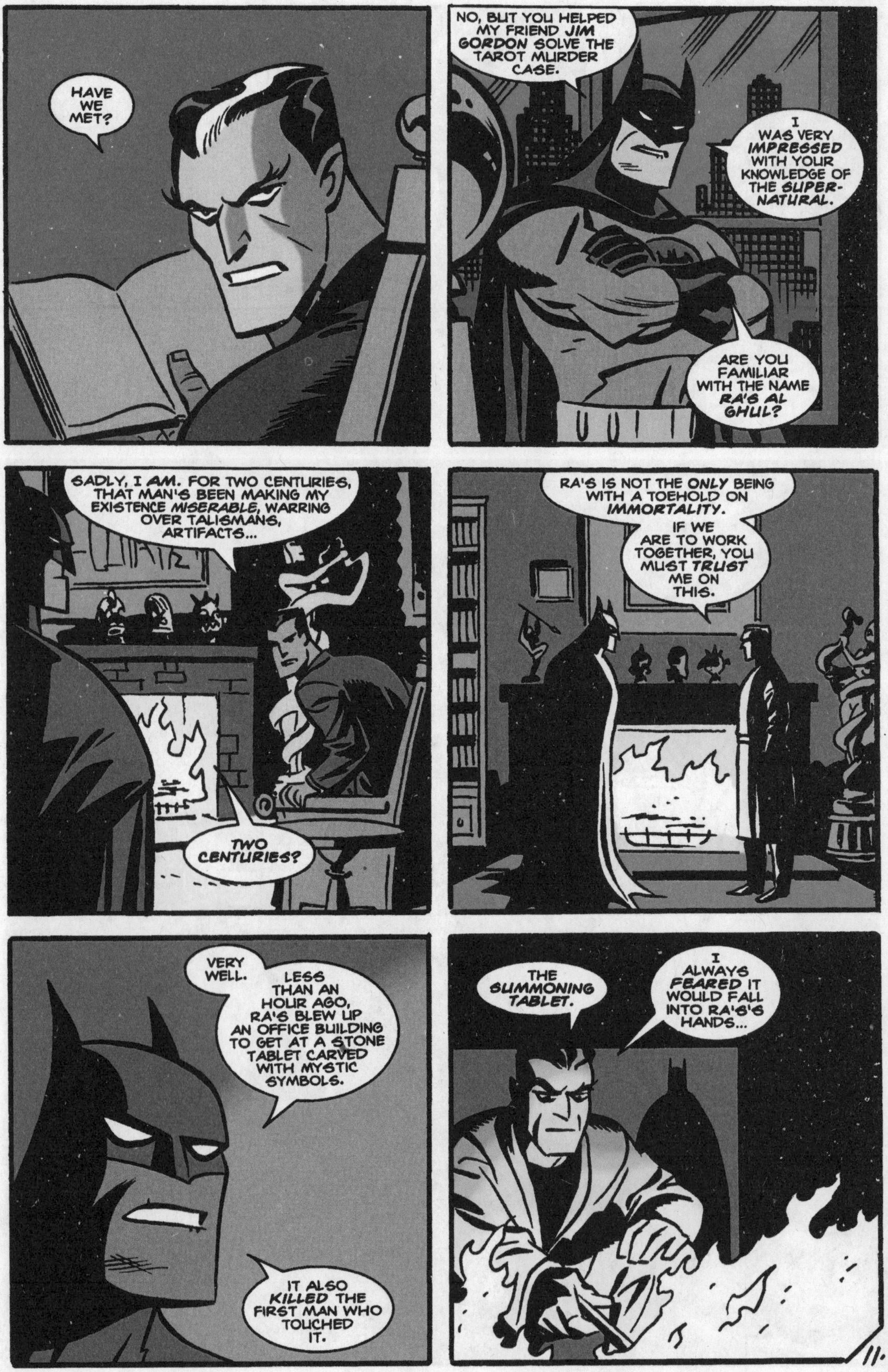
HAVE WE MET?
NO, BUT YOU HELPED MY FRIEND JIM GORDON SOLVE THE TAROT MURDER CASE.
I WAS VERY IMPRESSED WITH YOUR KNOWLEDGE OF THE SUPER-NATURAL.
ARE YOU FAMILIAR WITH THE NAME RA'S AL GHUL?
SADLY, I AM. FOR TWO CENTURIES, THAT MAN'S BEEN MAKING MY EXISTENCE MISERABLE, WARRING OVER TALISMANS, ARTIFACTS...
TWO CENTURIES?
RA'S IS NOT THE ONLY BEING WITH A TOEHOLD ON IMMORTALITY.
IF WE ARE TO WORK TOGETHER, YOU MUST TRUST ME ON THIS.
VERY WELL.
LESS THAN AN HOUR AGO, RA'S BLEW UP AN OFFICE BUILDING TO GET AT A STONE TABLET CARVED WITH MYSTIC SYMBOLS.
IT ALSO KILLED THE FIRST MAN WHO TOUCHED IT.
THE SUMMONING TABLET.
I ALWAYS FEARED IT WOULD FALL INTO RA'S'S HANDS...
11.

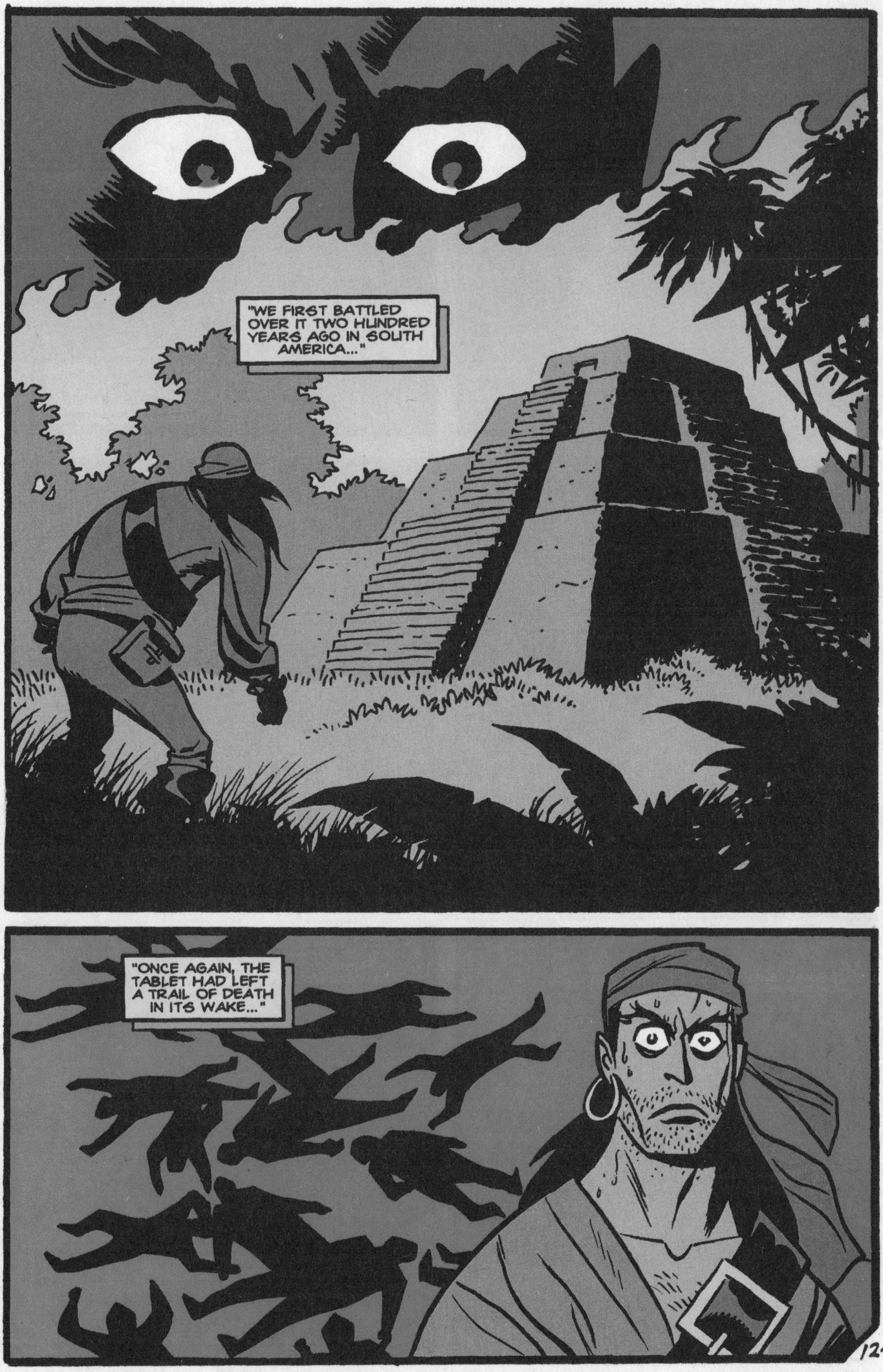
"WE FIRST BATTLED OVER IT TWO HUNDRED YEARS AGO IN SOUTH AMERICA..."
"ONCE AGAIN, THE TABLET HAD LEFT A TRAIL OF DEATH IN ITS WAKE..."

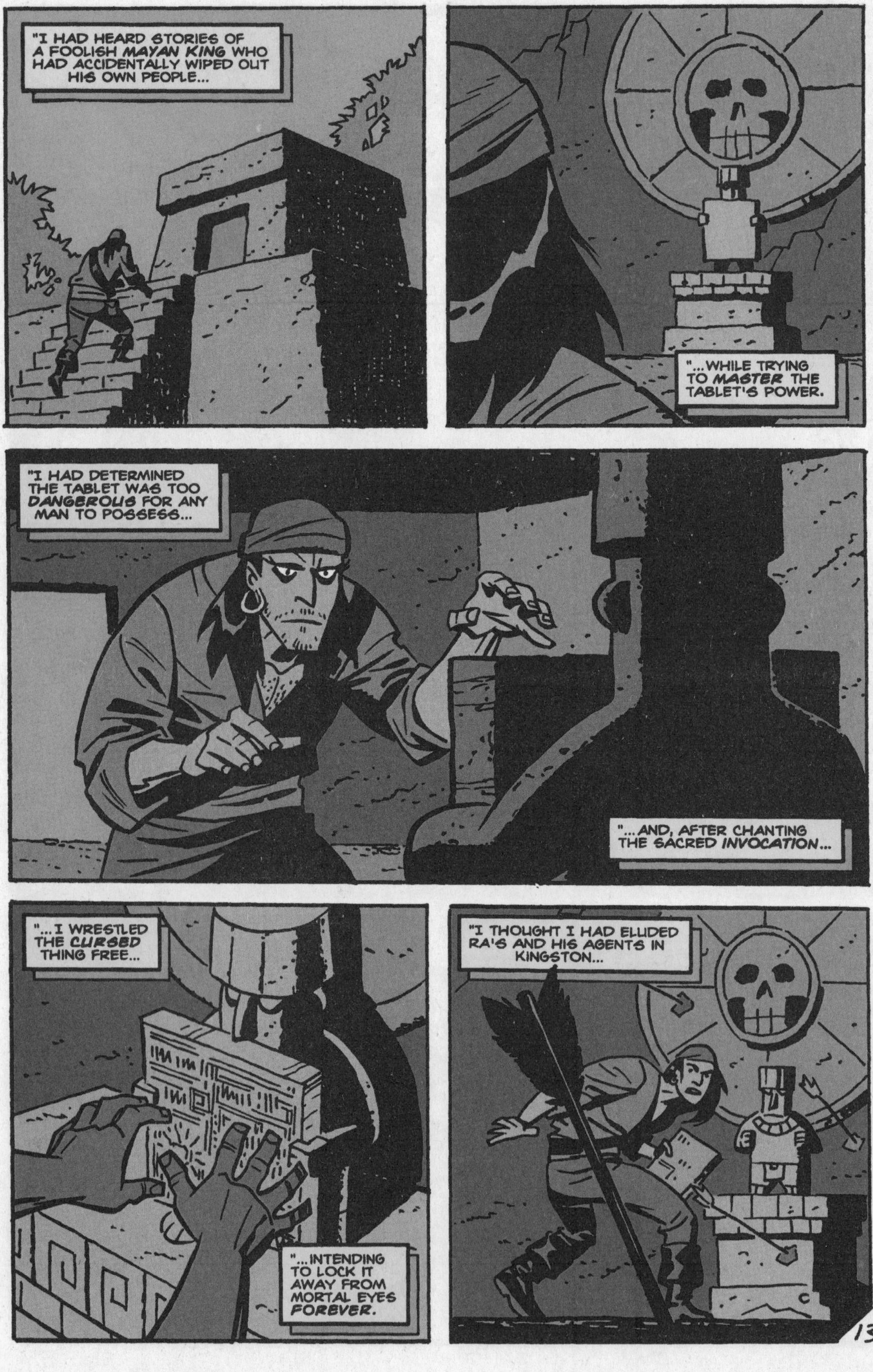
"I HAD HEARD STORIES OF A FOOLISH MAYAN KING WHO HAD ACCIDENTALLY WIPED OUT HIS OWN PEOPLE...
"...WHILE TRYING TO MASTER THE TABLET'S POWER.
"I HAD DETERMINED THE TABLET WAS TOO DANGEROUS FOR ANY MAN TO POSSESS...
"...AND, AFTER CHANTING THE SACRED INVOCATION...
"...I WRESTLED THE CURSED THING FREE...
"...INTENDING TO LOCK IT AWAY FROM MORTAL EYES FOREVER.
"I THOUGHT I HAD ELUDED RA'S AND HIS AGENTS IN KINGSTON...

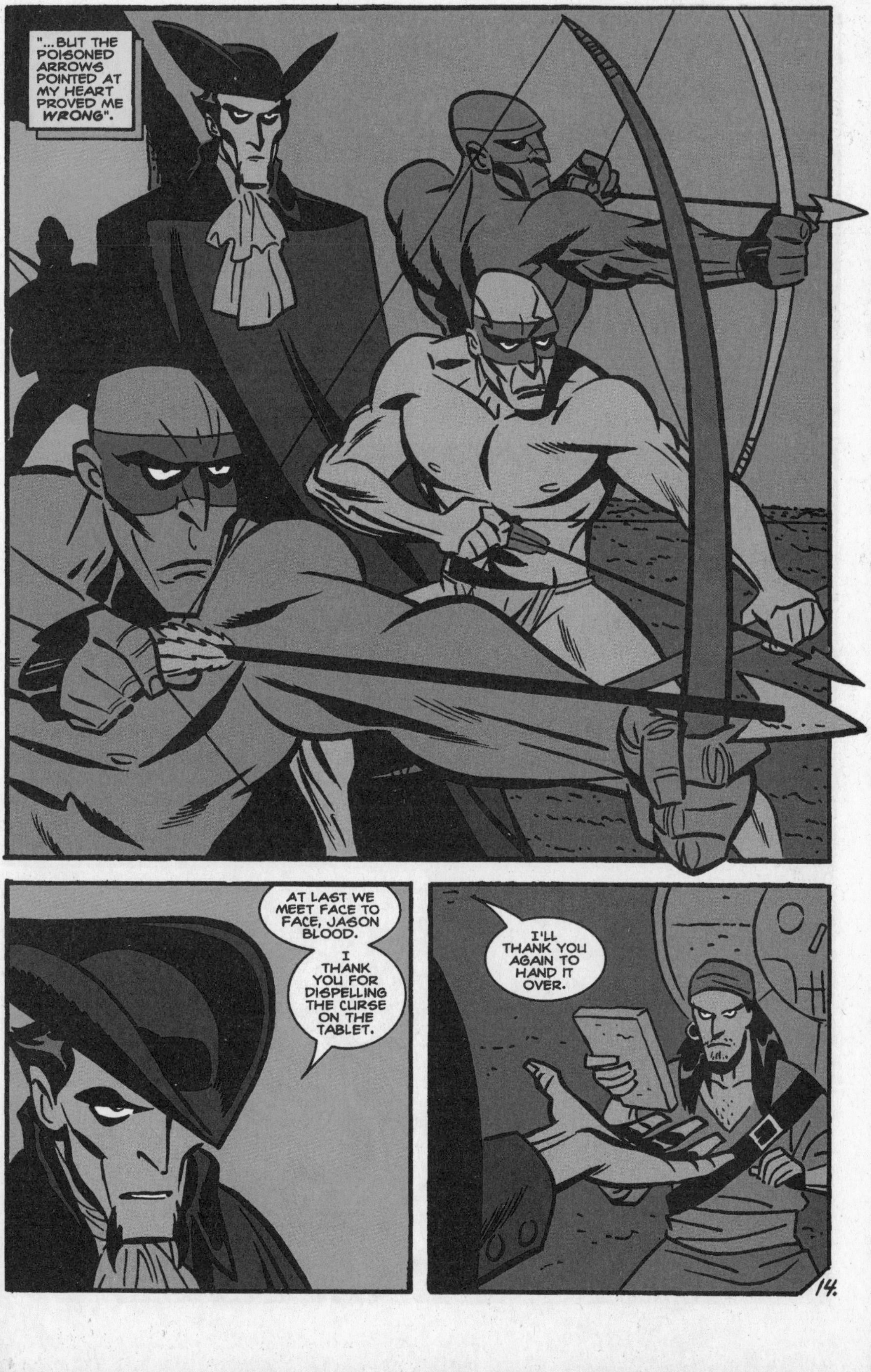
"...BUT THE POISONED ARROWS POINTED AT MY HEART PROVED ME WRONG".
AT LAST WE MEET FACE TO FACE, JASON BLOOD.
I THANK YOU FOR DISPELLING THE CURSE ON THE TABLET.
I'LL THANK YOU AGAIN TO HAND IT OVER.

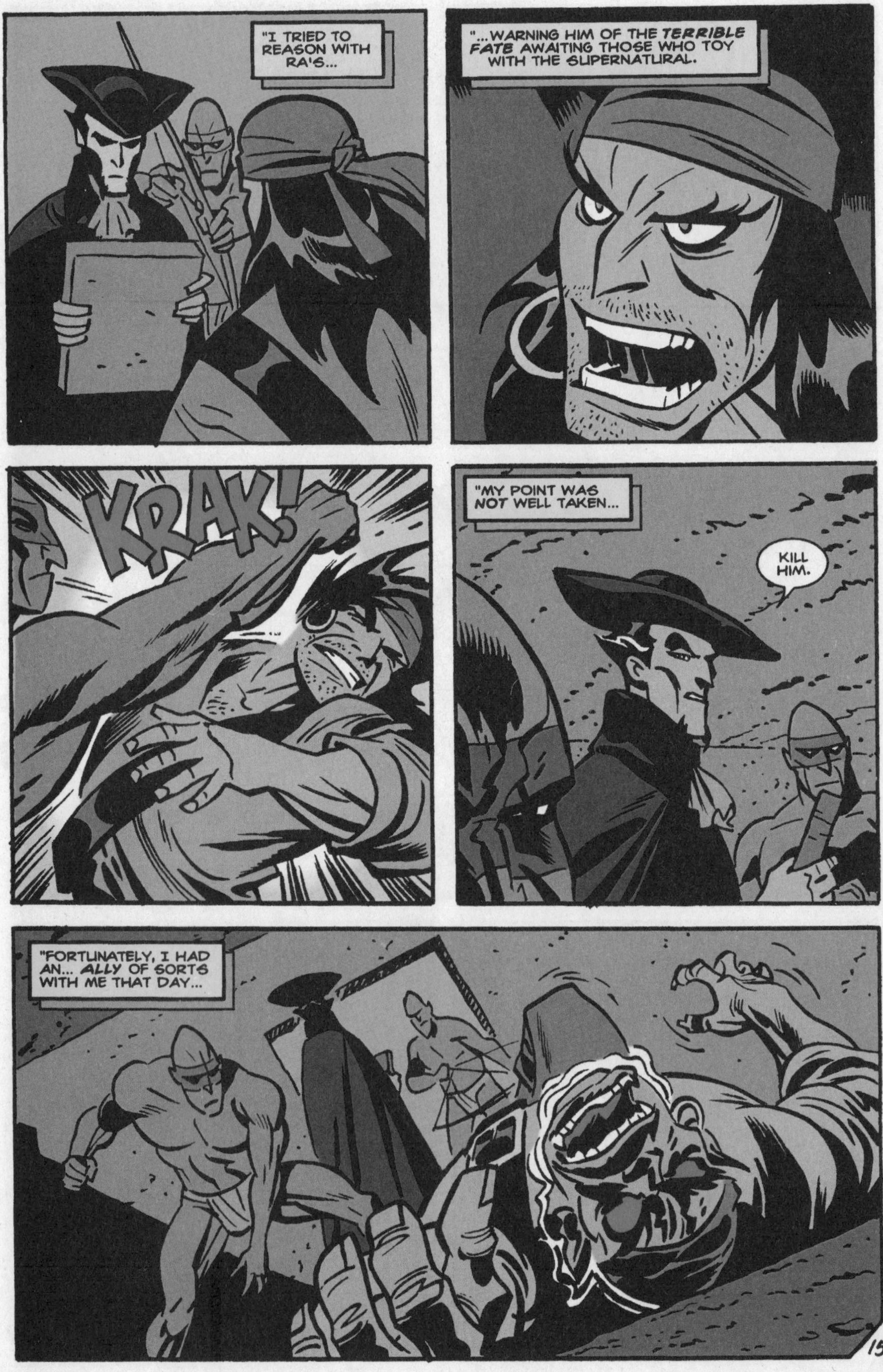
"I TRIED TO REASON WITH RA'S...
"...WARNING HIM OF THE TERRIBLE FATE AWAITING THOSE WHO TOY WITH THE SUPERNATURAL.
KRAK!
"MY POINT WAS NOT WELL TAKEN...
KILL HIM.
"FORTUNATELY, I HAD AN... ALLY OF SORTS WITH ME THAT DAY...

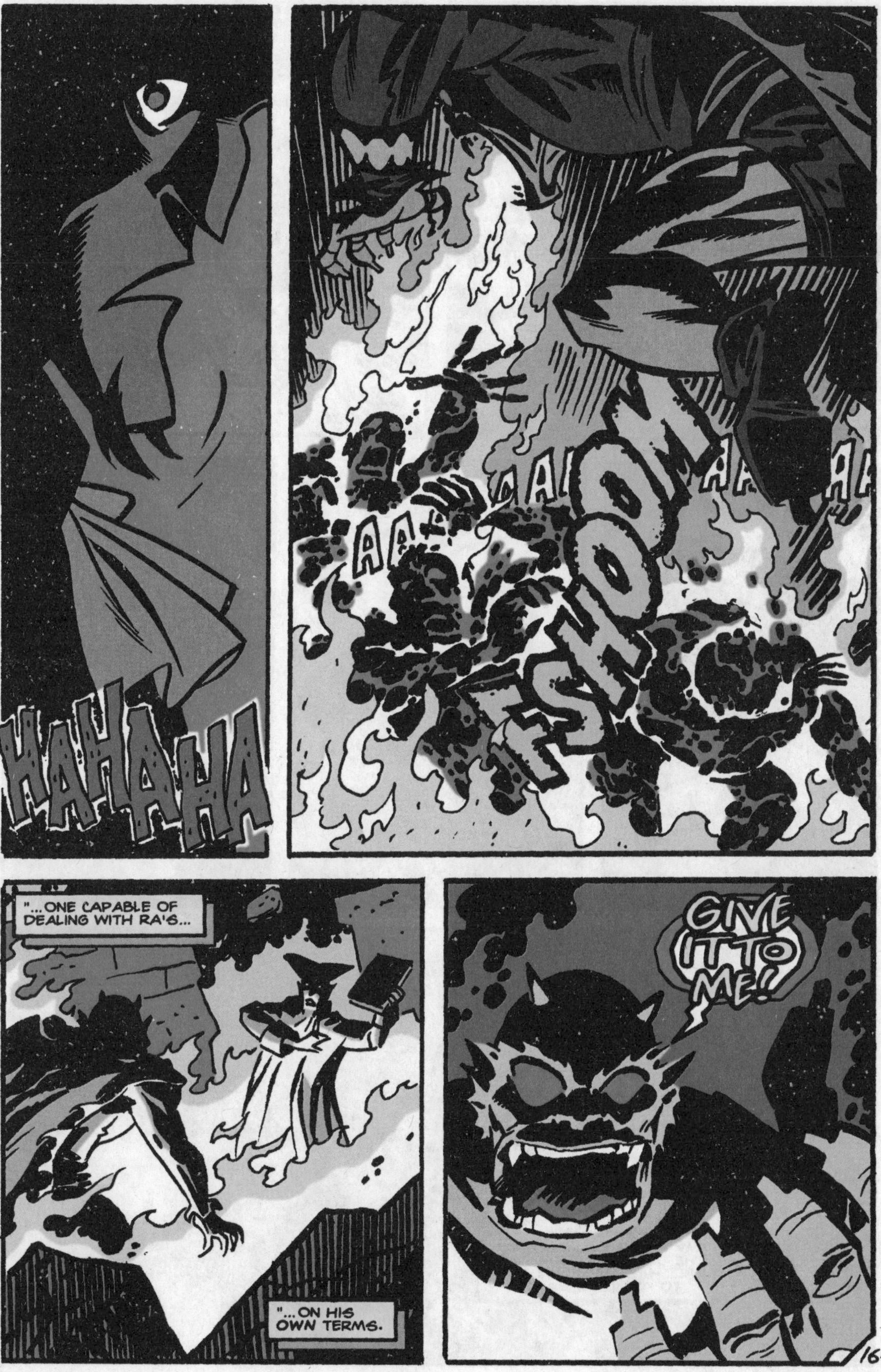
HAHAHA
FSHOOM
AAA
"...ONE CAPABLE OF DEALING WITH RA'S...
"...ON HIS OWN TERMS.
GIVE IT TO ME!

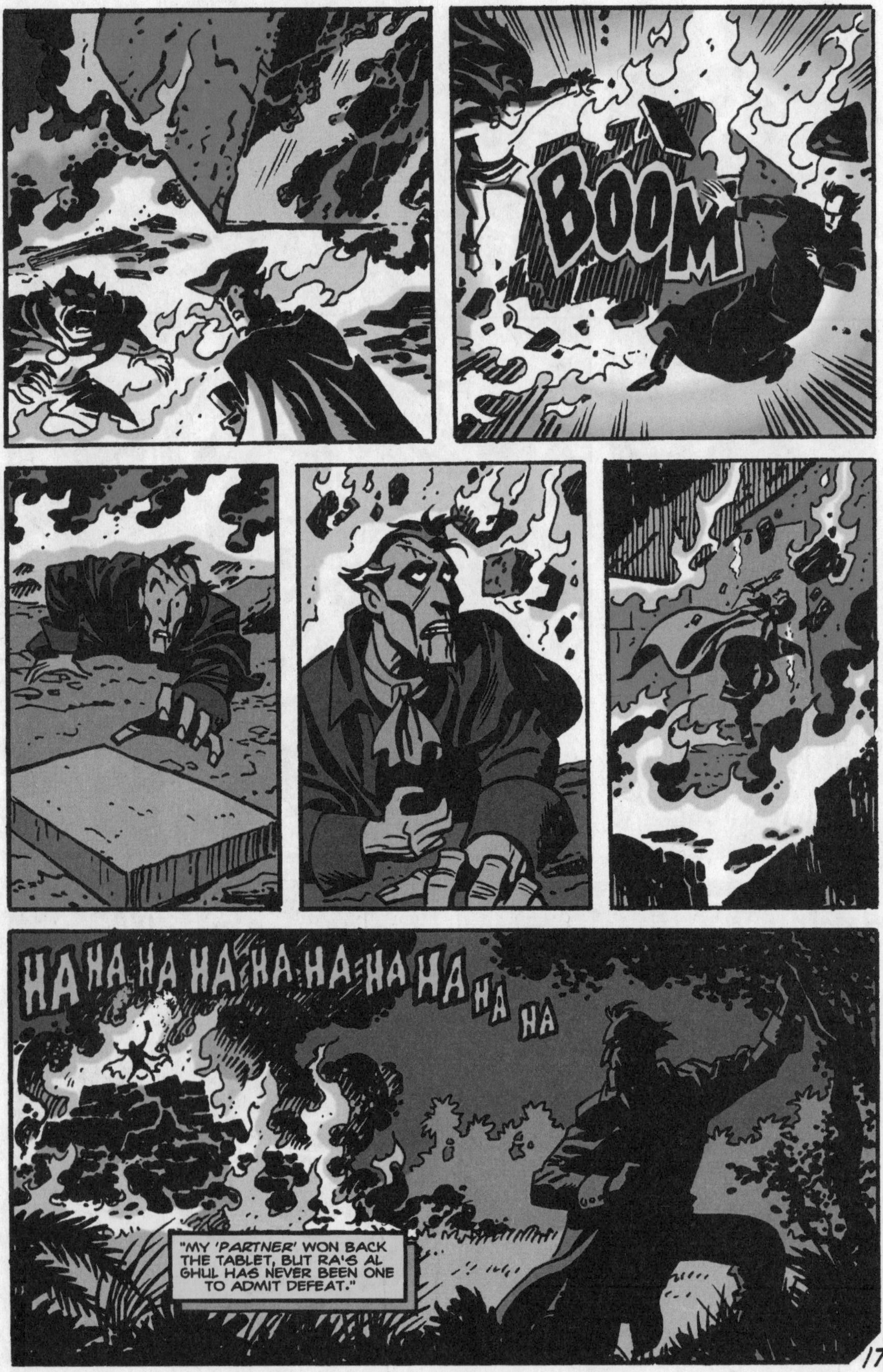
BOOM
HA HA HA HA HA HA HA HA HA HA HA
"MY 'PARTNER' WON BACK THE TABLET, BUT RA'S AL GHUL HAS NEVER BEEN ONE TO ADMIT DEFEAT."

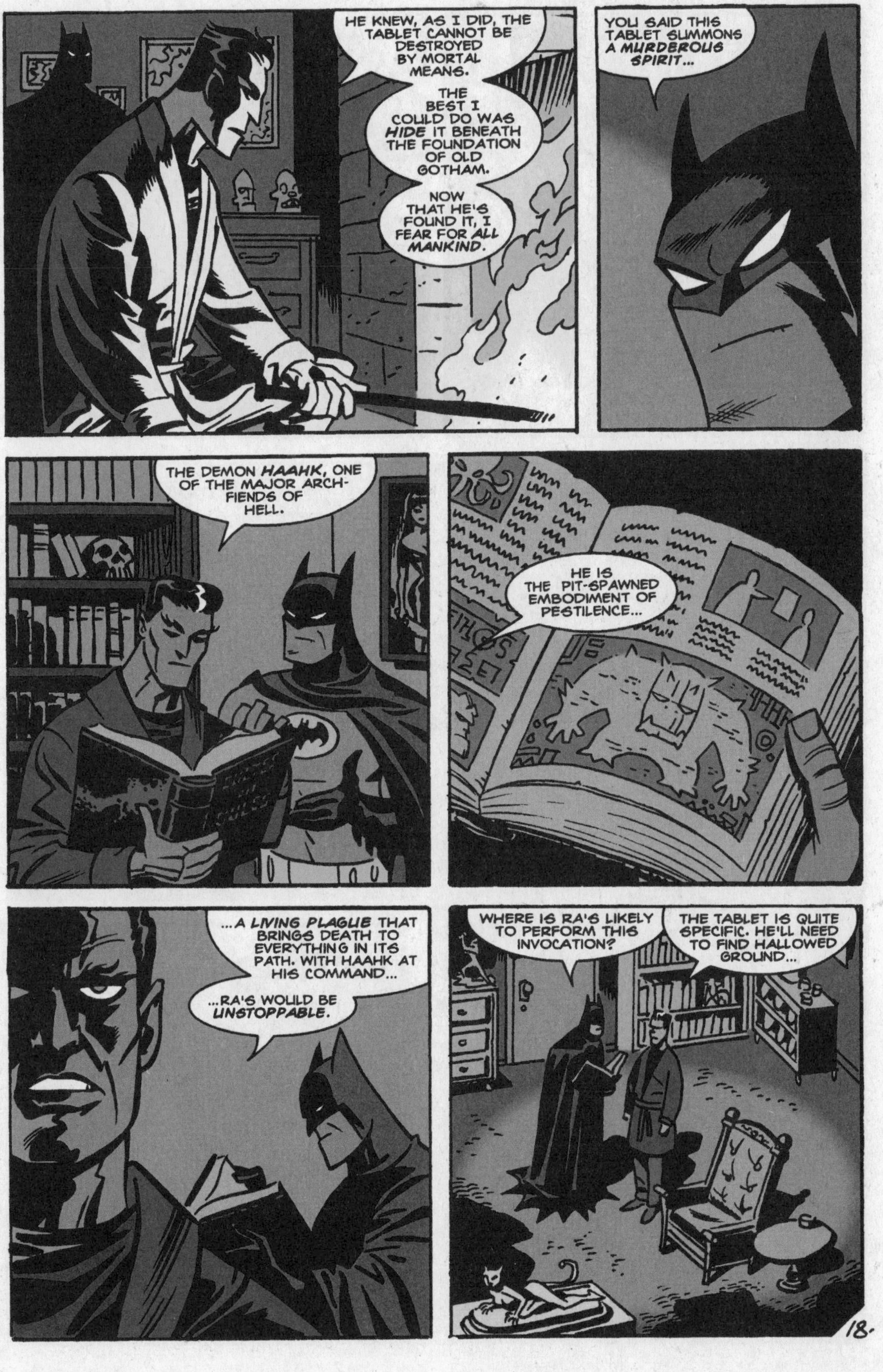
HE KNEW, AS I DID, THE TABLET CANNOT BE DESTROYED BY MORTAL MEANS.
THE BEST I COULD DO WAS HIDE IT BENEATH THE FOUNDATION OF OLD GOTHAM.
NOW THAT HE'S FOUND IT, I FEAR FOR ALL MANKIND.
YOU SAID THIS TABLET SUMMONS A MURDEROUS SPIRIT...
THE DEMON HAAHK, ONE OF THE MAJOR ARCH-FIENDS OF HELL.
HE IS THE PIT-SPAWNED EMBODIMENT OF PESTILENCE...
...A LIVING PLAGUE THAT BRINGS DEATH TO EVERYTHING IN ITS PATH. WITH HAAHK AT HIS COMMAND...
...RA'S WOULD BE UNSTOPPABLE.
WHERE IS RA'S LIKELY TO PERFORM THIS INVOCATION?
THE TABLET IS QUITE SPECIFIC. HE'LL NEED TO FIND HALLOWED GROUND...

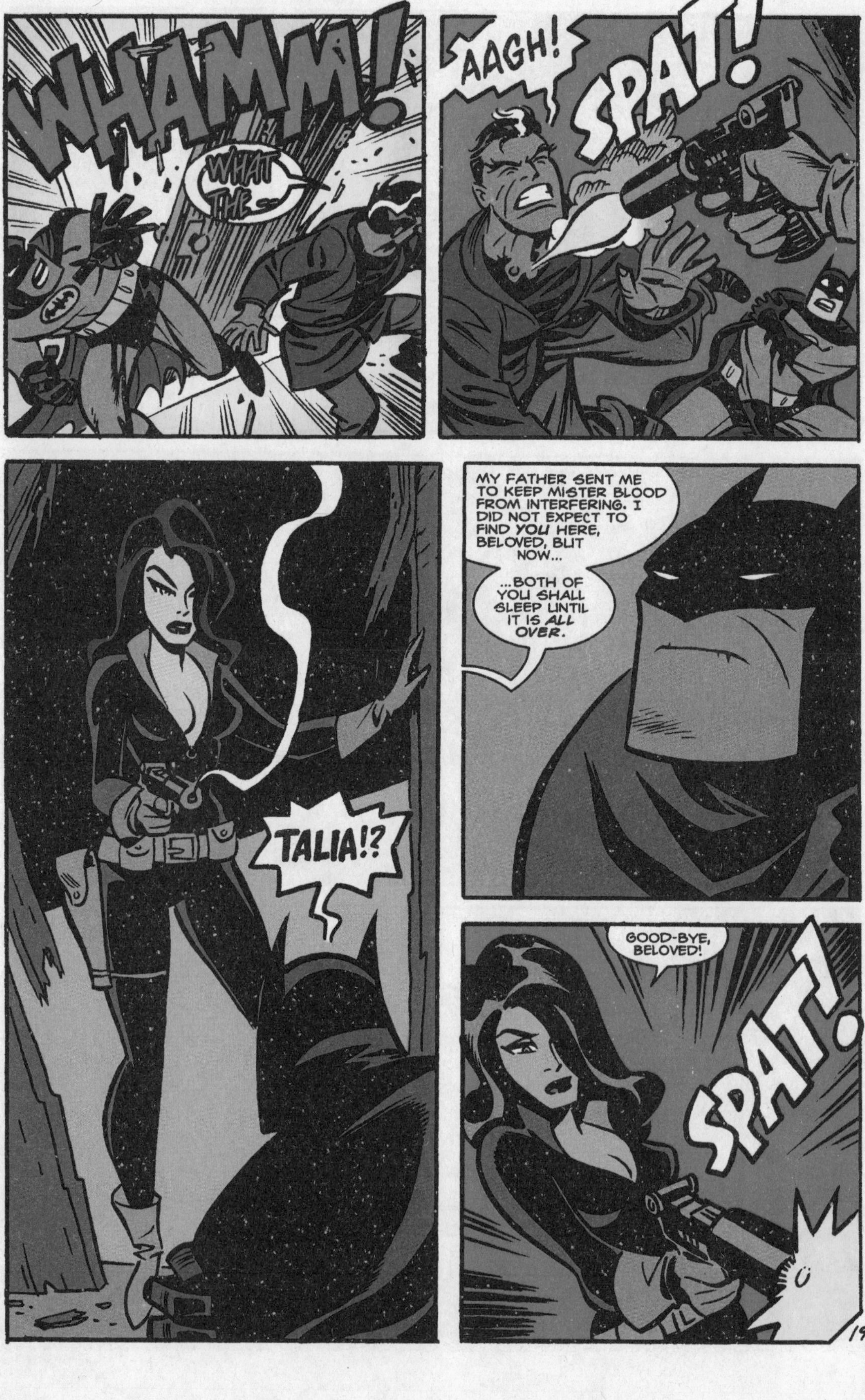
WHAMM!
WHAT THE--
AAGH!
SPAT!
TALIA!?
MY FATHER SENT ME TO KEEP MISTER BLOOD FROM INTERFERING. I DID NOT EXPECT TO FIND YOU HERE, BELOVED, BUT NOW...
...BOTH OF YOU SHALL SLEEP UNTIL IT IS ALL OVER.
GOOD-BYE, BELOVED!
SPAT!

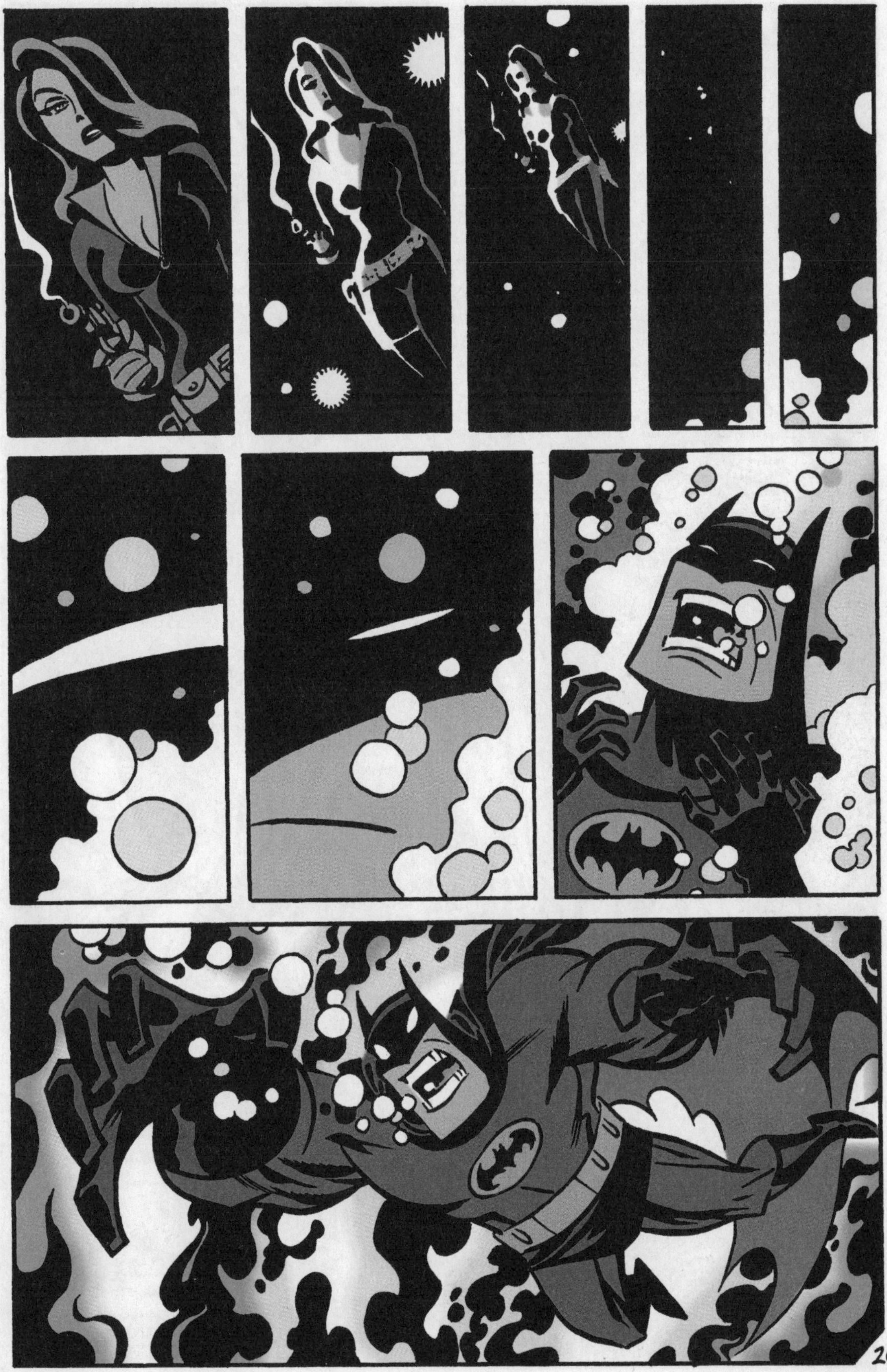

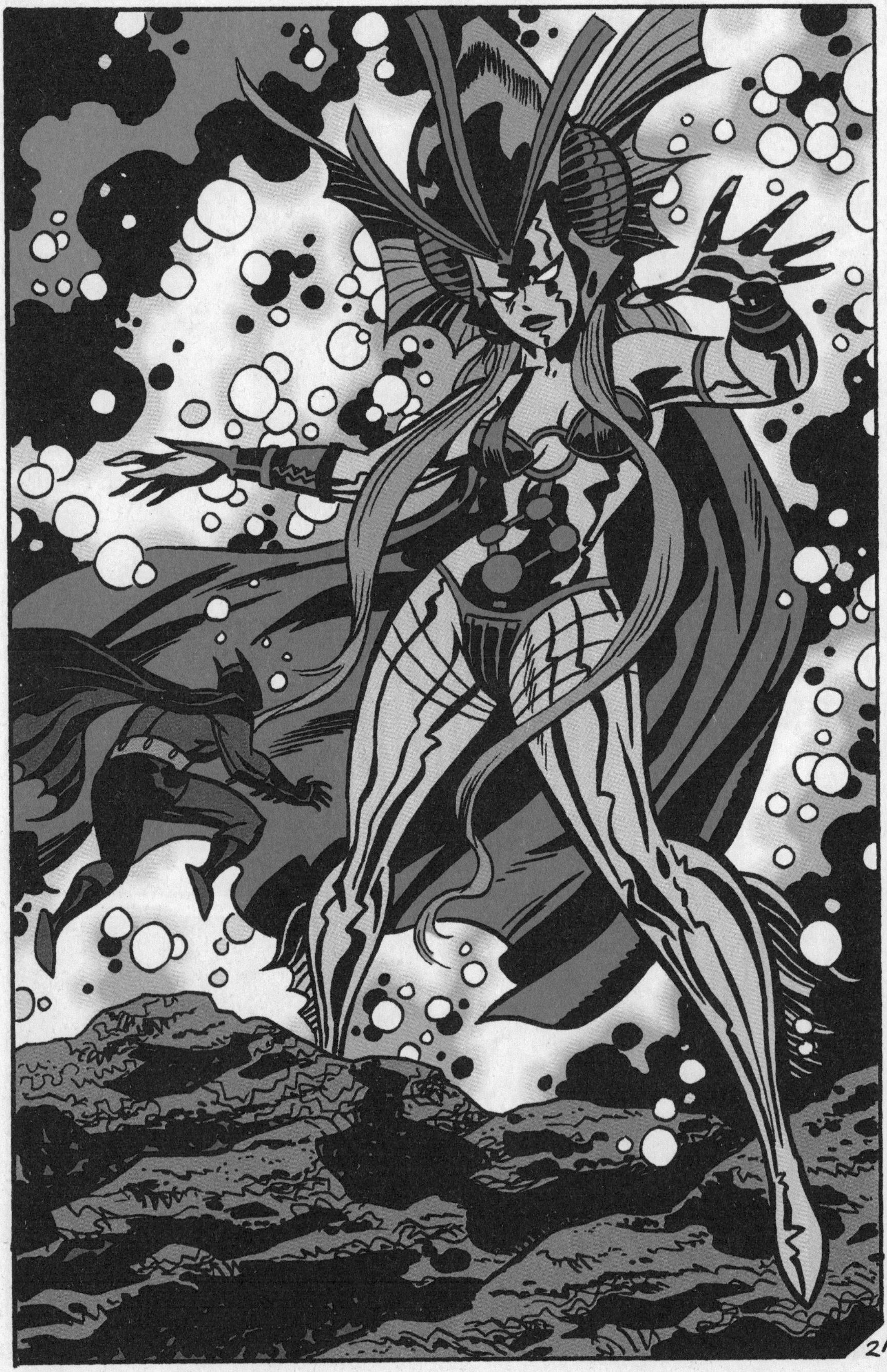

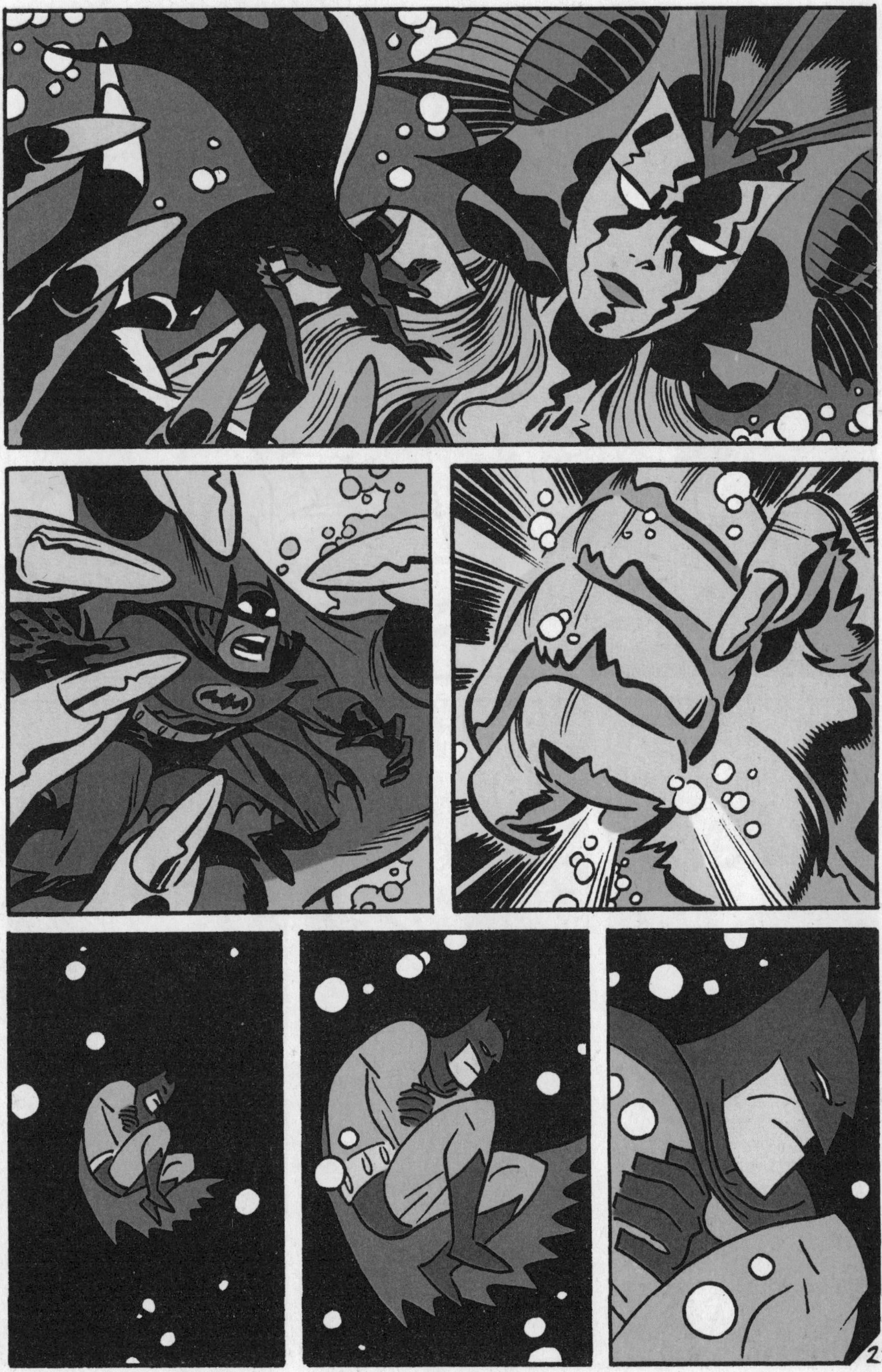

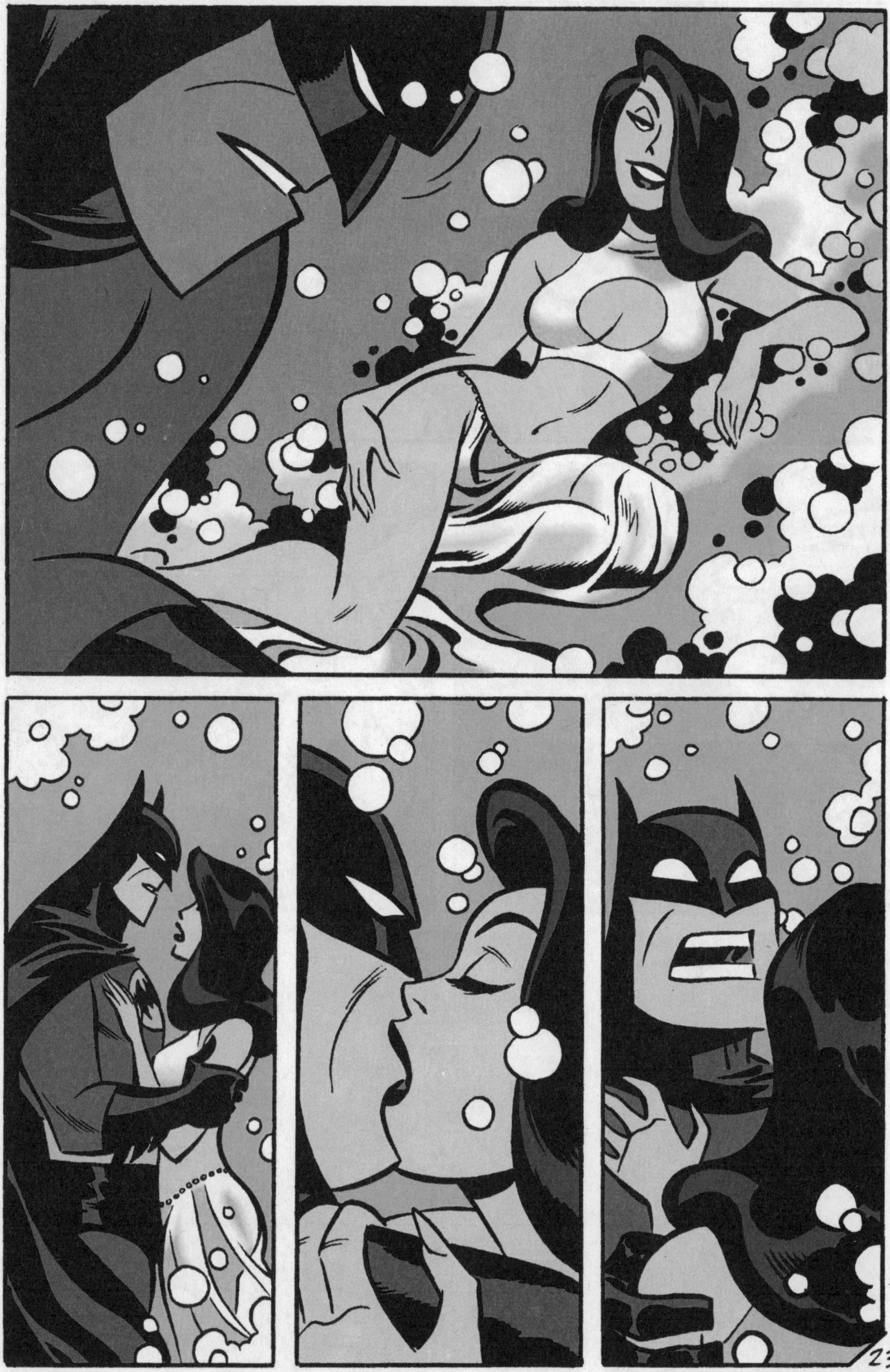

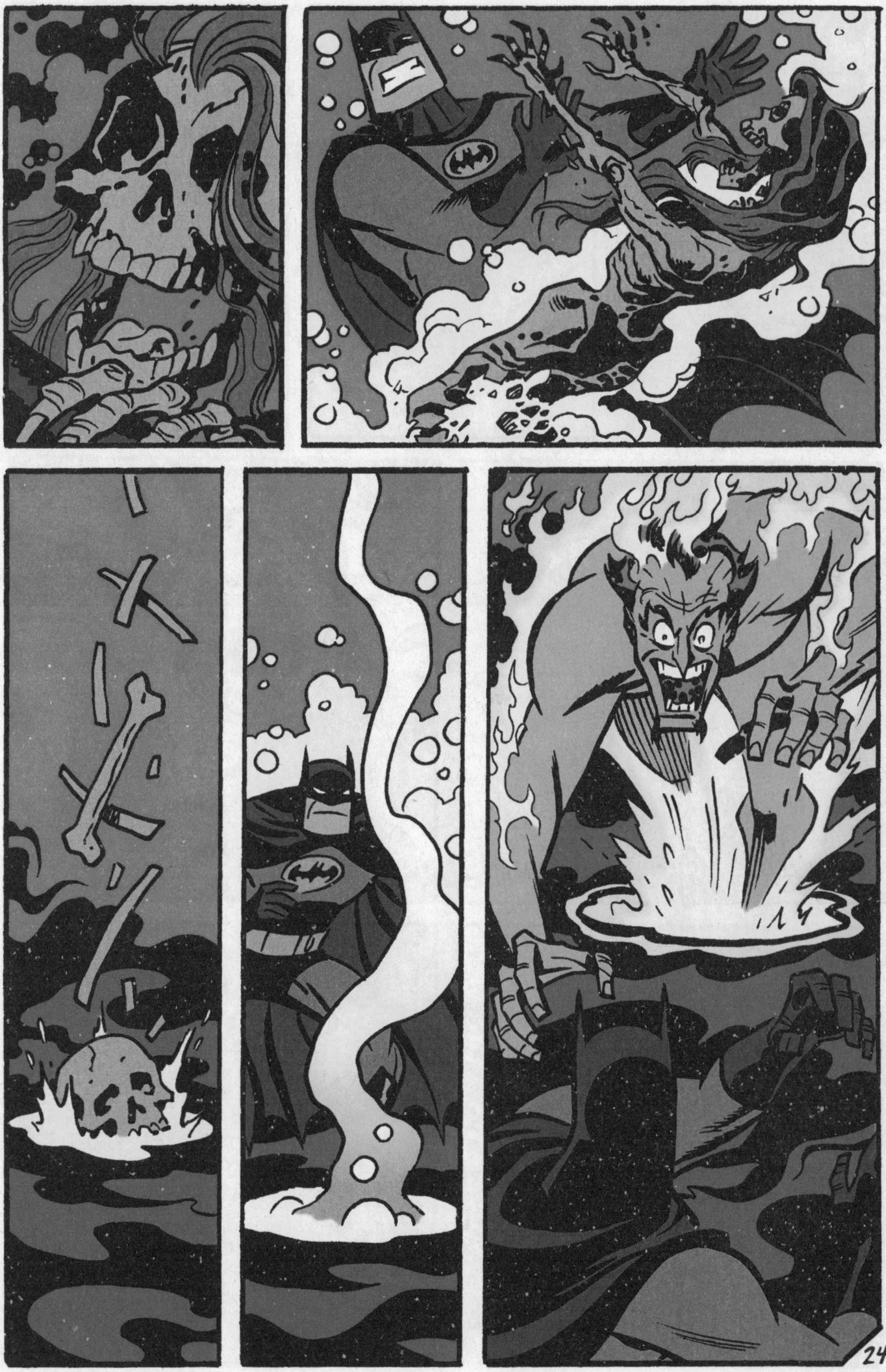

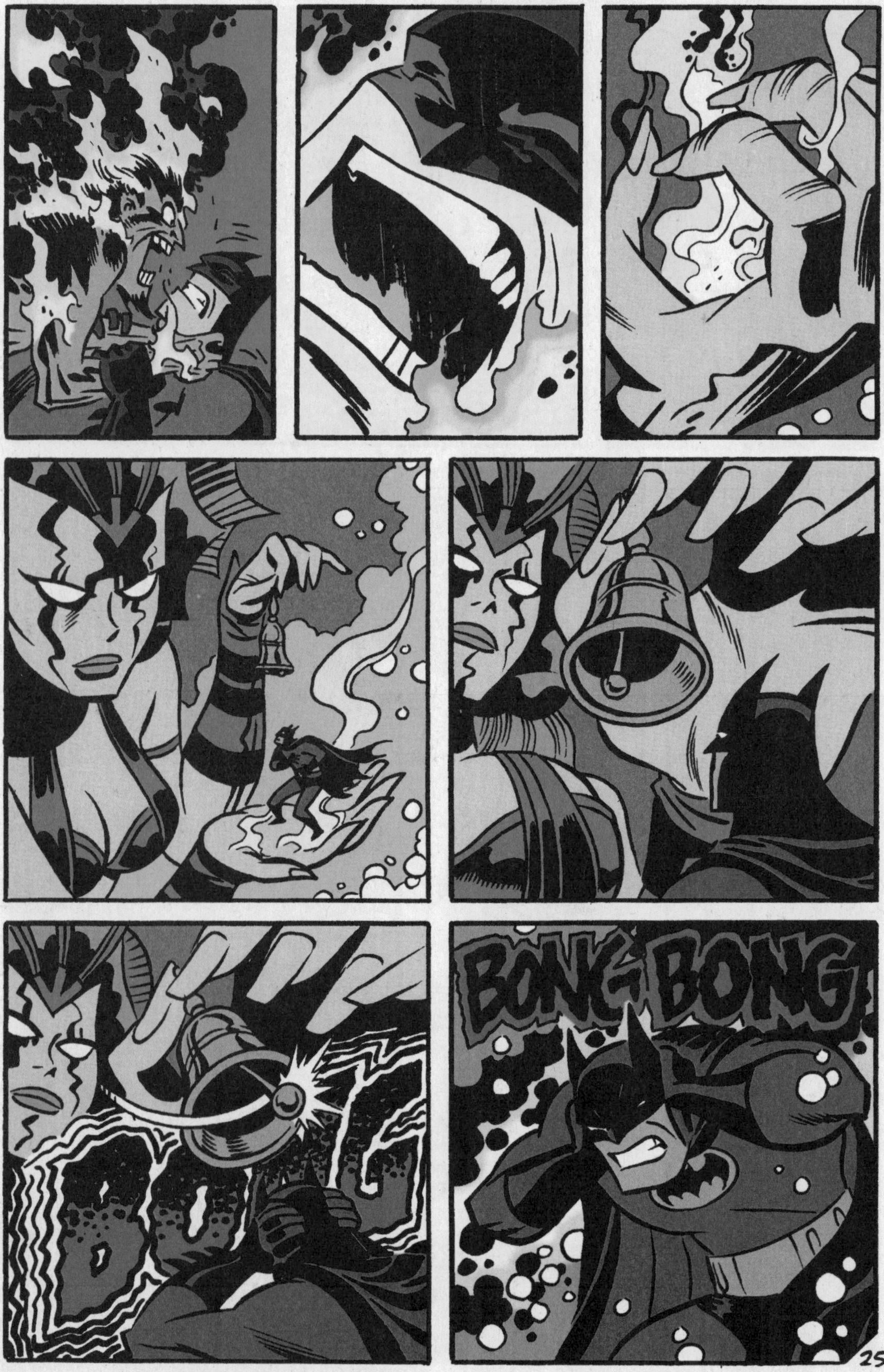
BONG BONG

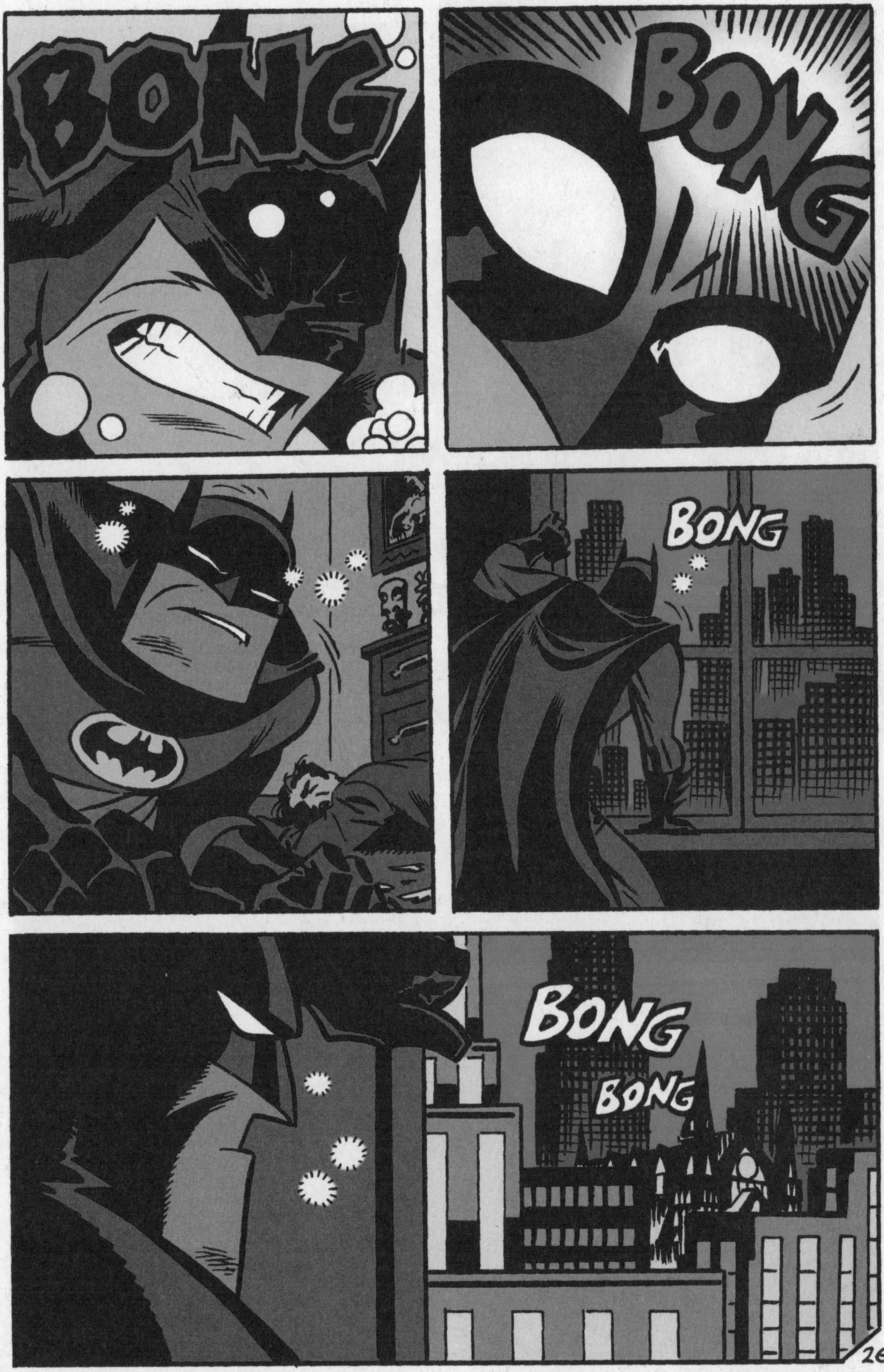
BONG
BONG
BONG
BONG
BONG

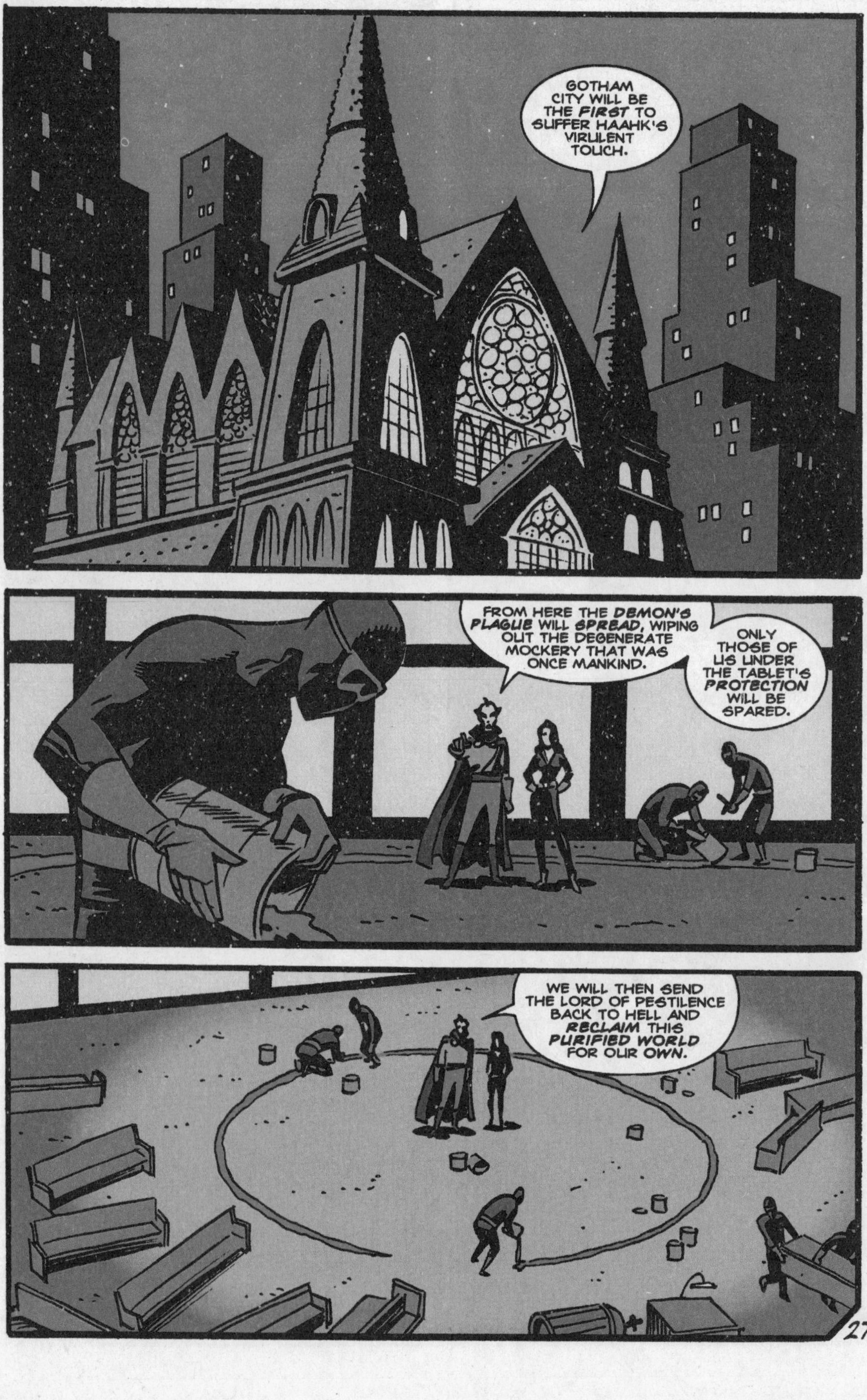
GOTHAM CITY WILL BE THE FIRST TO SUFFER HAAHK'S VIRULENT TOUCH.
FROM HERE THE DEMON'S PLAGUE WILL SPREAD, WIPING OUT THE DEGENERATE MOCKERY THAT WAS ONCE MANKIND.
ONLY THOSE OF US UNDER THE TABLET'S PROTECTION WILL BE SPARED.
WE WILL THEN SEND THE LORD OF PESTILENCE BACK TO HELL AND RECLAIM THIS PURIFIED WORLD FOR OUR OWN.

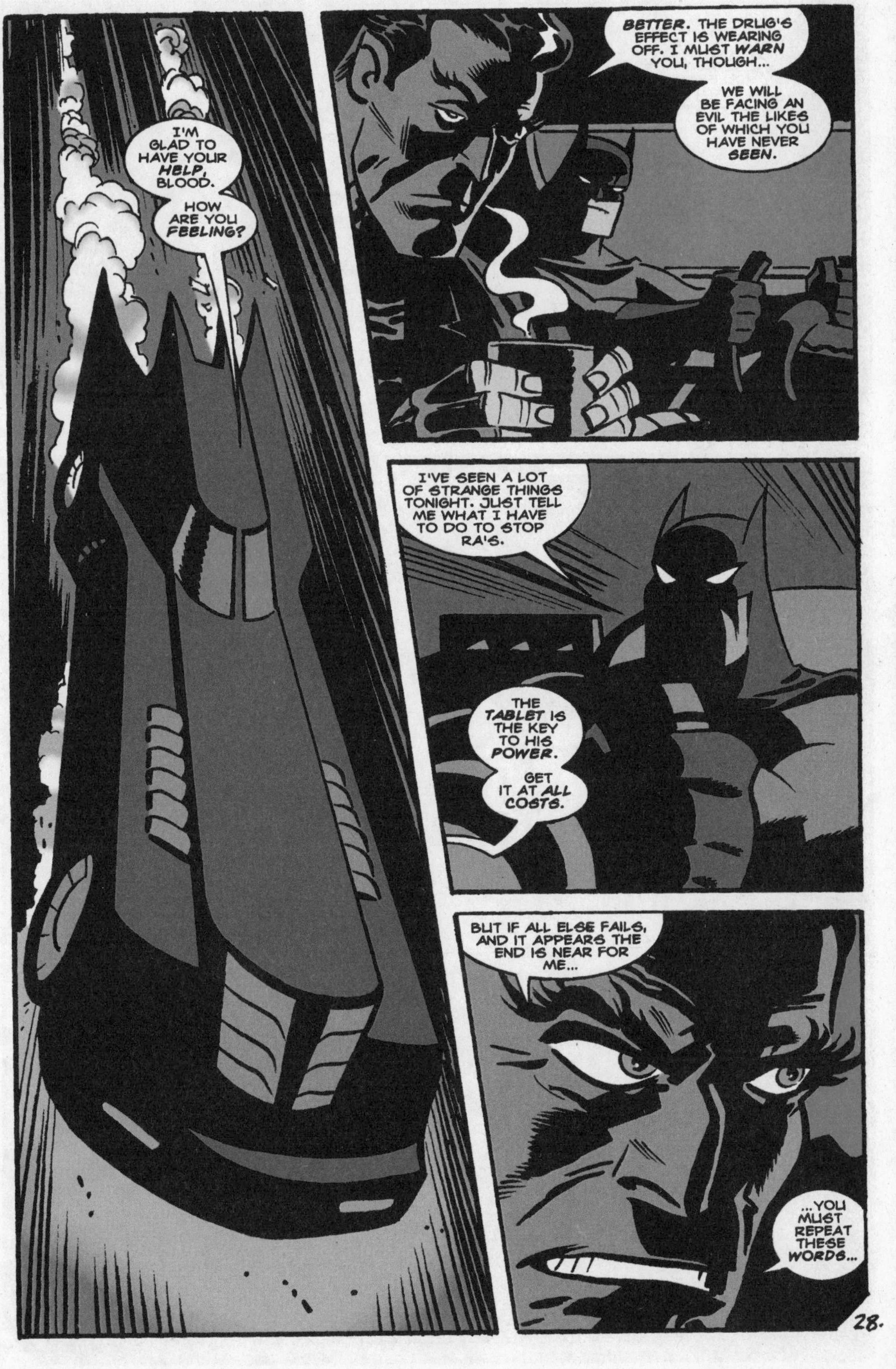

I'M GLAD TO HAVE YOUR HELP, BLOOD.
HOW ARE YOU FEELING?
BETTER. THE DRUG'S EFFECT IS WEARING OFF. I MUST WARN YOU, THOUGH...
WE WILL BE FACING AN EVIL THE LIKES OF WHICH YOU HAVE NEVER SEEN.
I'VE SEEN A LOT OF STRANGE THINGS TONIGHT. JUST TELL ME WHAT I HAVE TO DO TO STOP RA'S.
THE TABLET IS THE KEY TO HIS POWER.
GET IT AT ALL COSTS.
BUT IF ALL ELSE FAILS, AND IT APPEARS THE END IS NEAR FOR ME...
...YOU MUST REPEAT THESE WORDS...

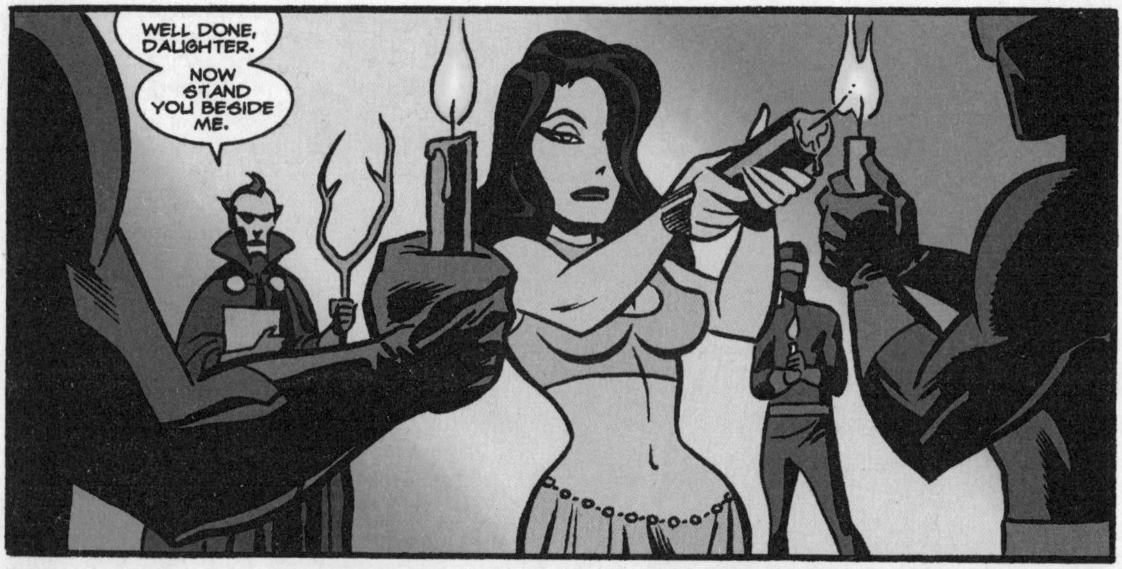
WELL DONE, DAUGHTER.
NOW STAND YOU BESIDE ME.

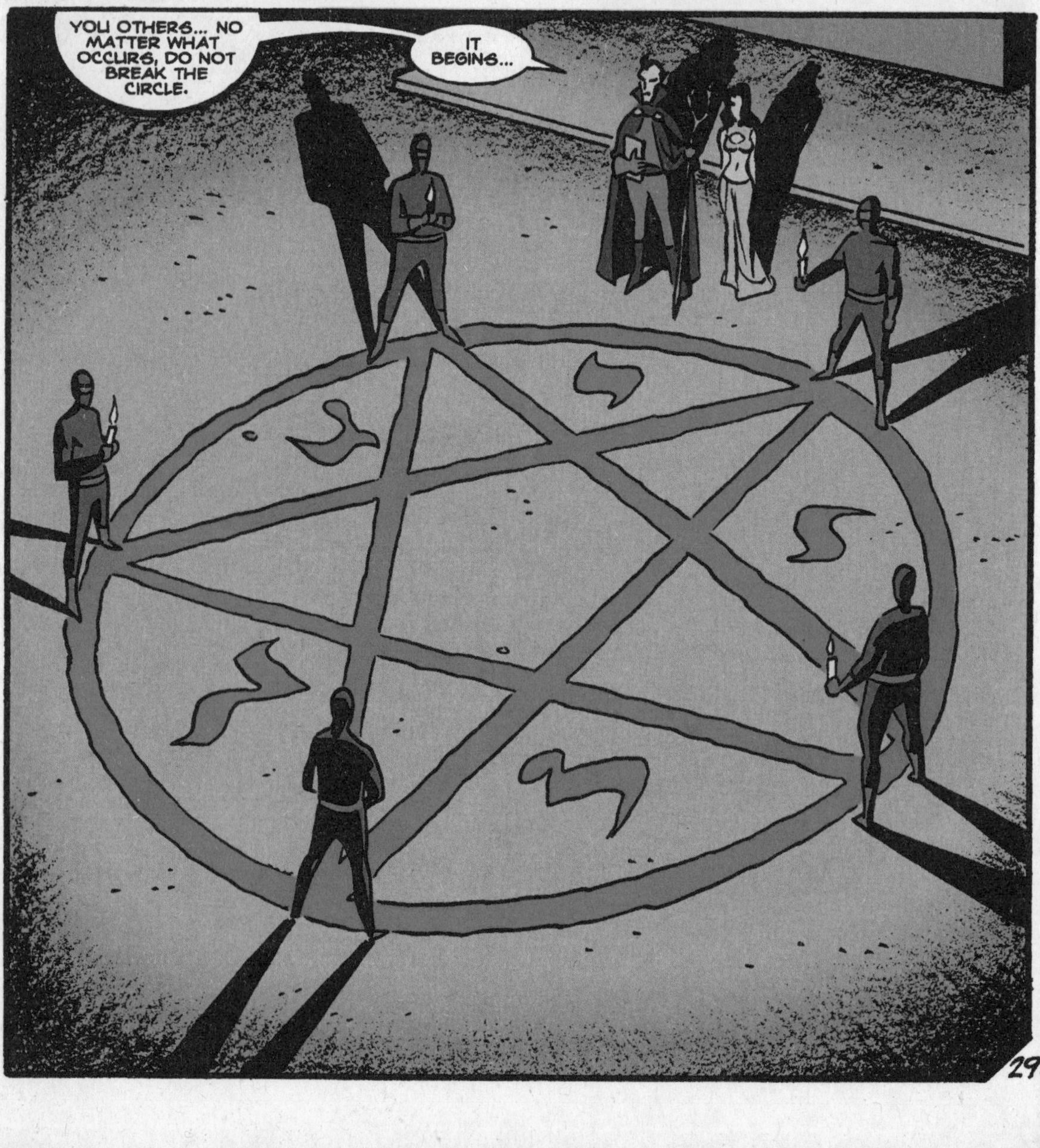
YOU OTHERS... NO MATTER WHAT OCCURS, DO NOT BREAK THE CIRCLE.
IT BEGINS...

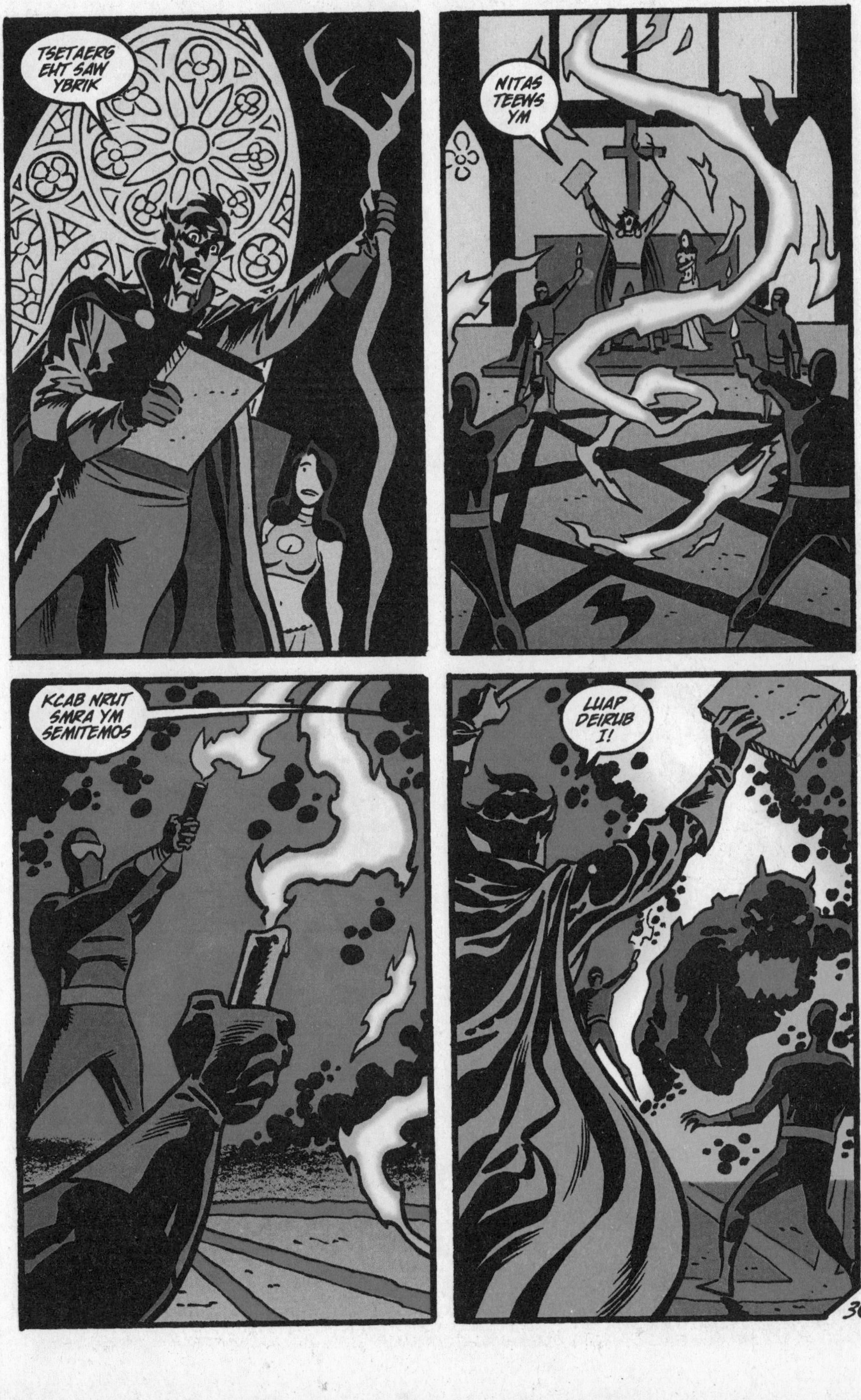
TSETAERG EHT SAW YBRIK
NITAS TEEWS YM
KCAB NRUT SMRA YM SEMITEMOS
LUAP DEIRUB I!

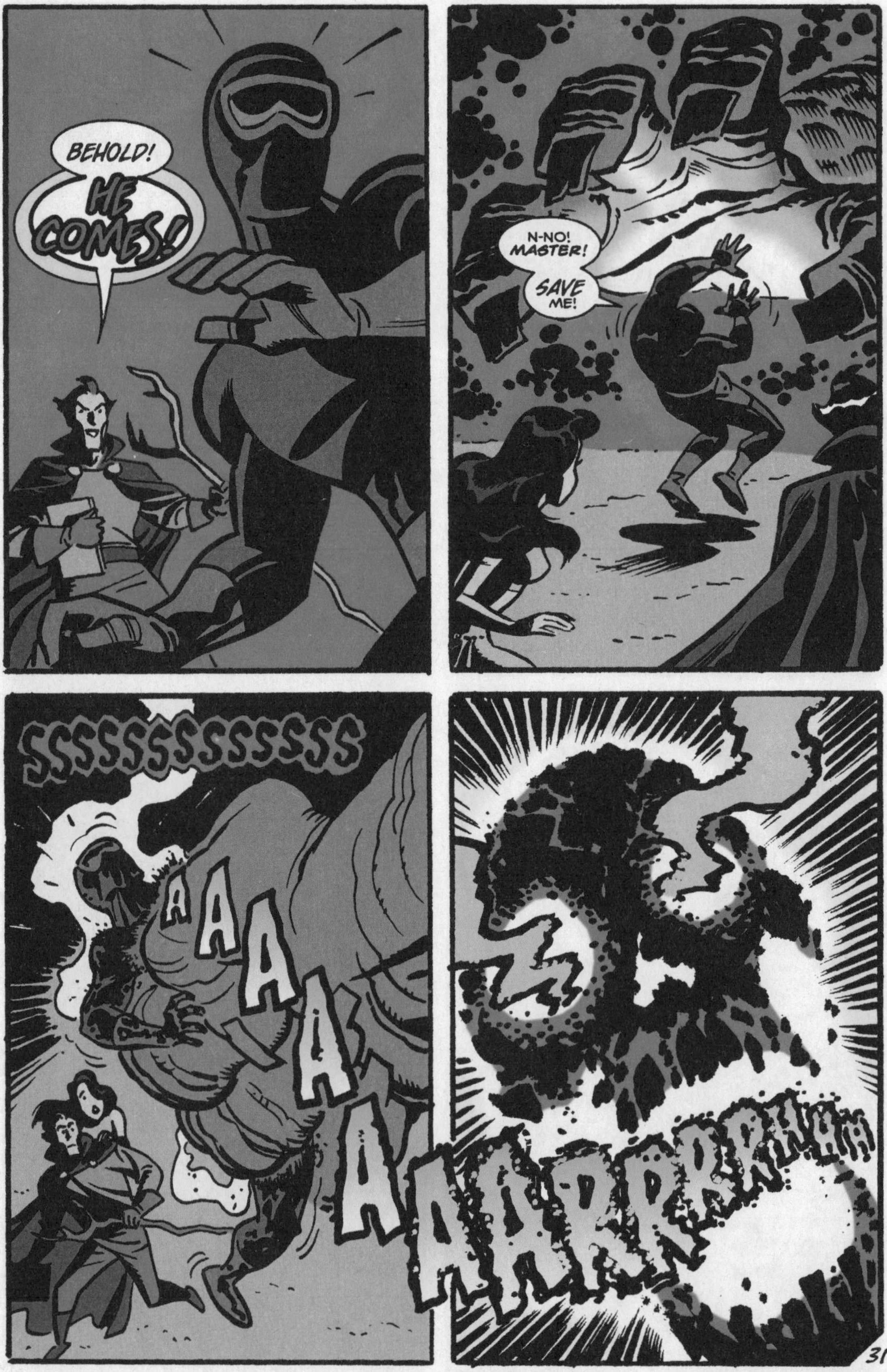
BEHOLD! HE COMES!
N-NO! MASTER!
SAVE ME!
SSSSSSSSSSSSSS
AAAAAAA
AARRRRRHHH

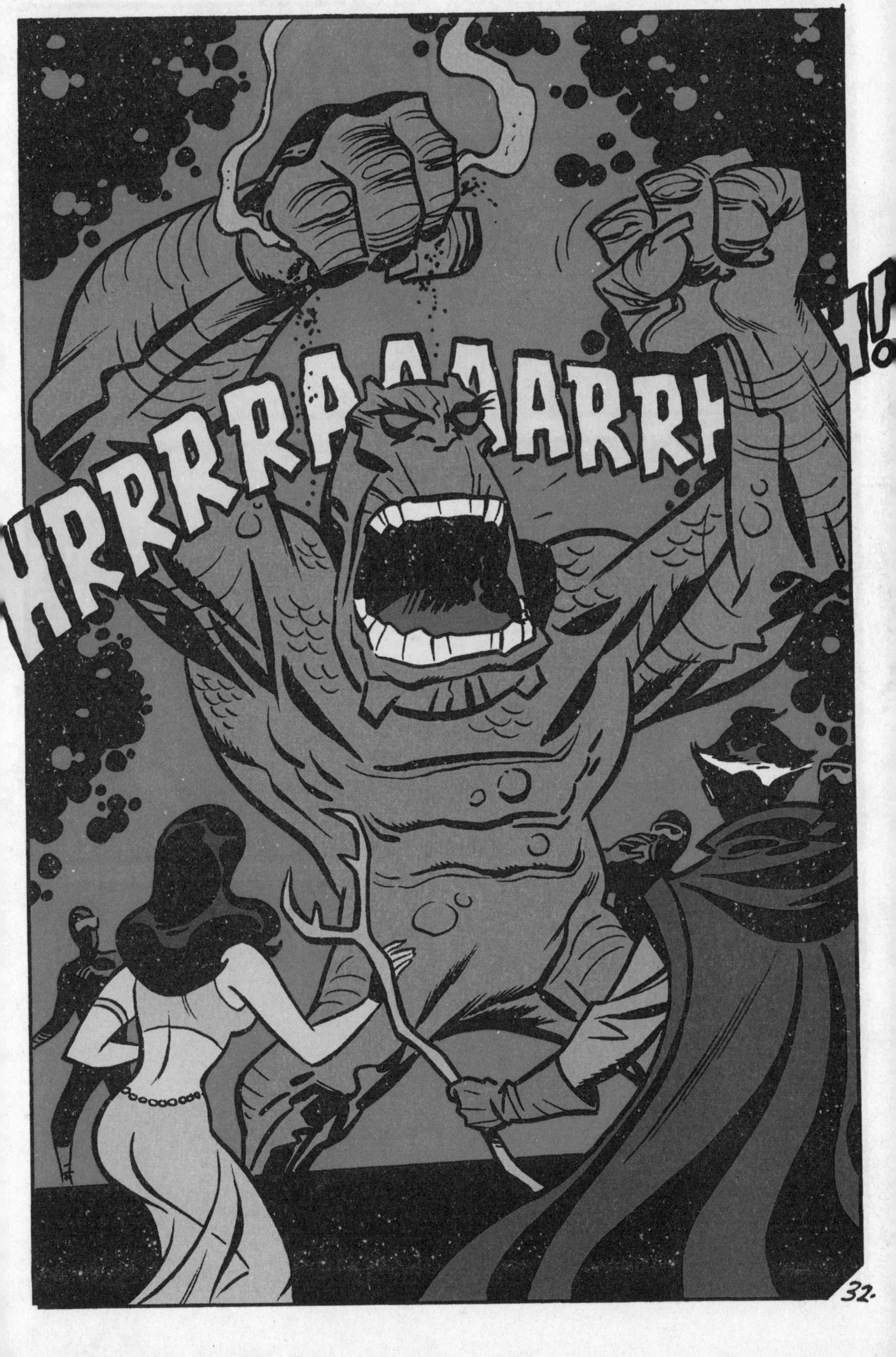
HRRRRAAAAARRH!

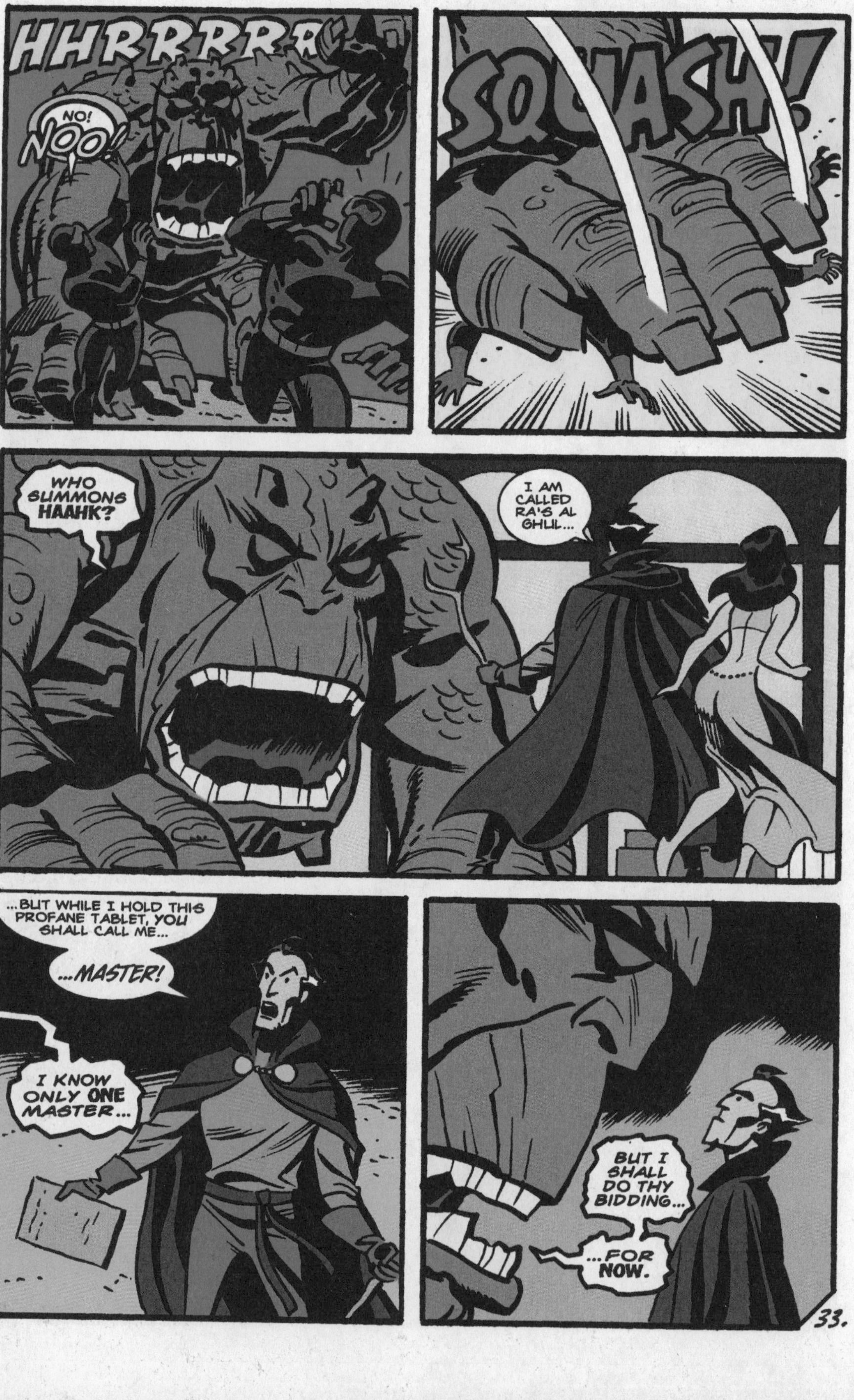
HHRRRRR
NO! NOO!
SQUASH!
WHO SUMMONS HAAHK?
I AM CALLED RA'S AL GHUL...
...BUT WHILE I HOLD THIS PROFANE TABLET, YOU SHALL CALL ME...
...MASTER!
I KNOW ONLY ONE MASTER...
BUT I SHALL DO THY BIDDING...
...FOR NOW.

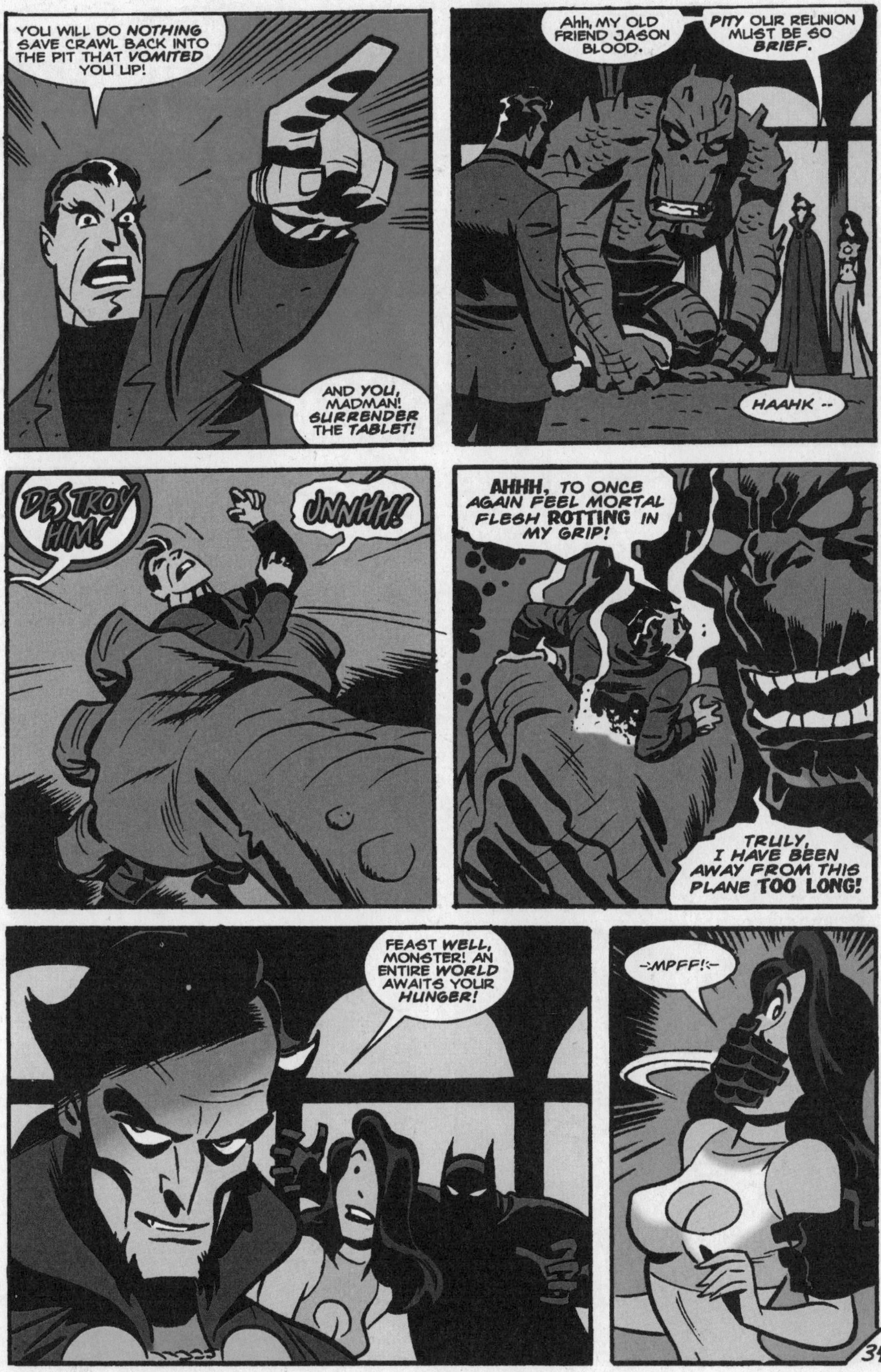

YOU WILL DO NOTHING SAVE CRAWL BACK INTO THE PIT THAT VOMITED YOU UP!
AND YOU, MADMAN! SURRENDER THE TABLET!
Ahh, MY OLD FRIEND JASON BLOOD.
PITY OUR REUNION MUST BE SO BRIEF.
HAAHK --
DESTROY HIM!
UNNHH!
AHHH, TO ONCE AGAIN FEEL MORTAL FLESH ROTTING IN MY GRIP!
TRULY, I HAVE BEEN AWAY FROM THIS PLANE TOO LONG!
FEAST WELL, MONSTER! AN ENTIRE WORLD AWAITS YOUR HUNGER!
-MPFF!-
34.

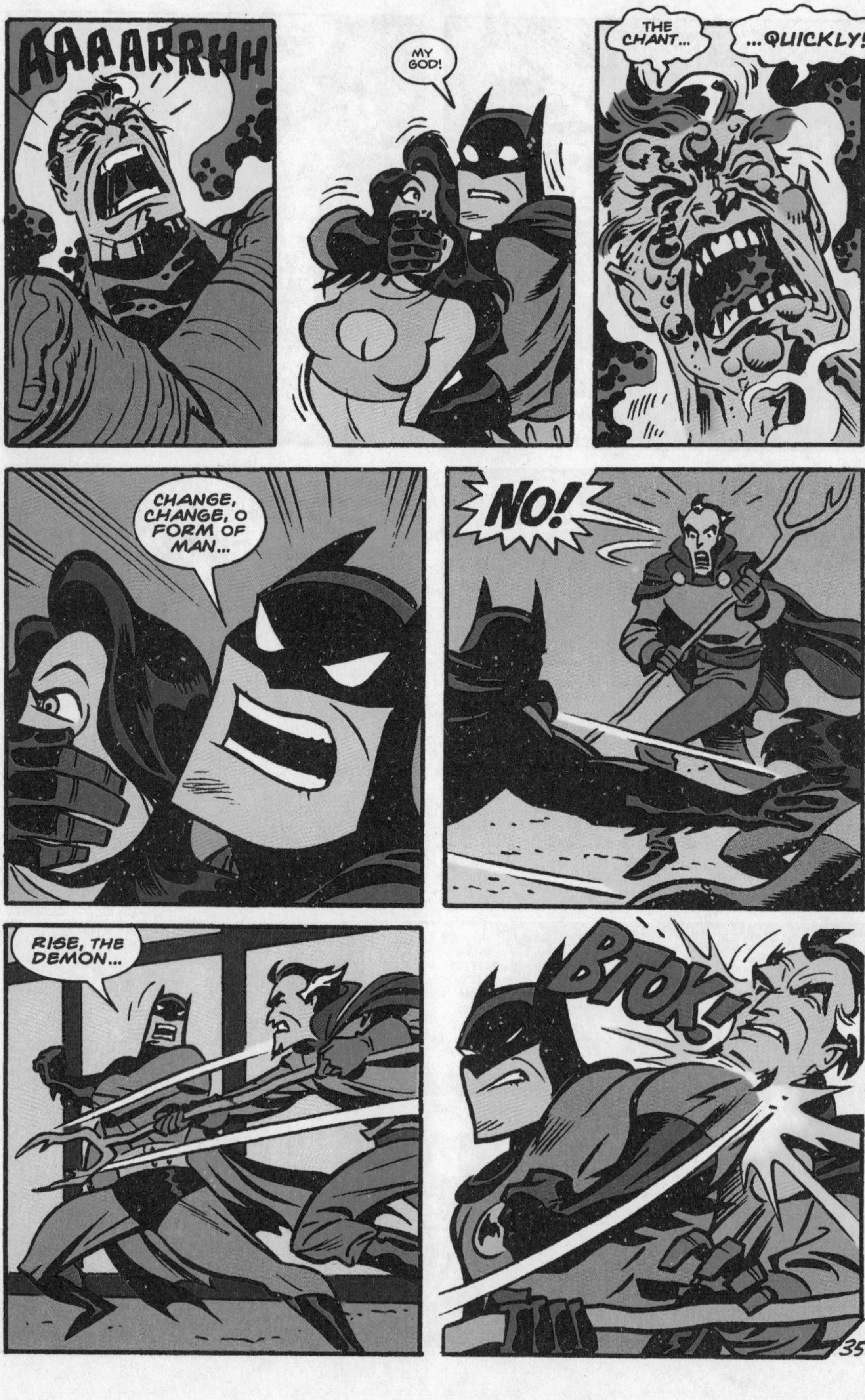
AAAARRHH
MY GOD!
THE CHANT...
...QUICKLY!
CHANGE, CHANGE, O FORM OF MAN...
NO!
RISE, THE DEMON...
BTOK!

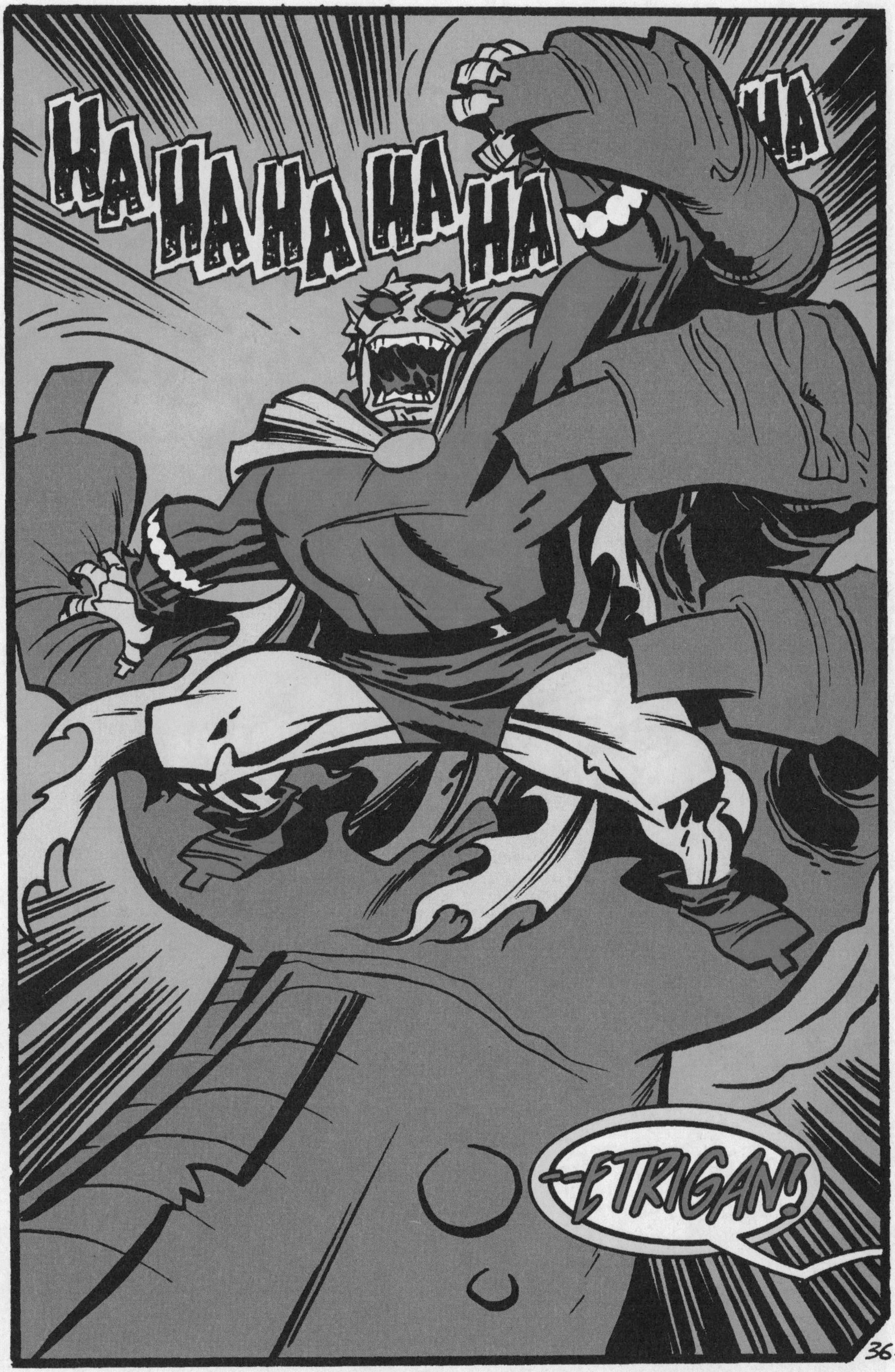
HA HA HA HA HA HA HA HA
--ETRIGAN!

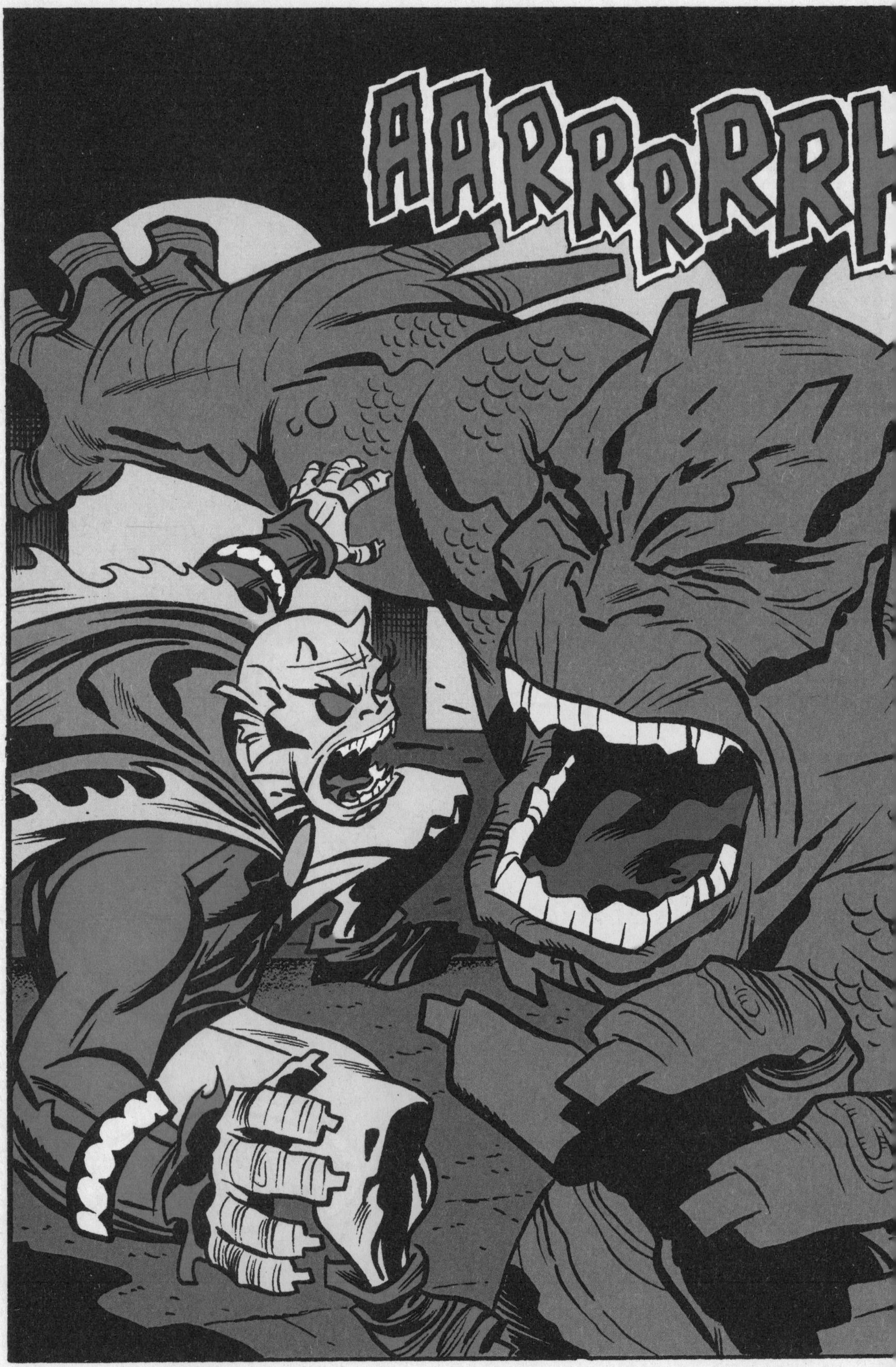
AARRRRRH

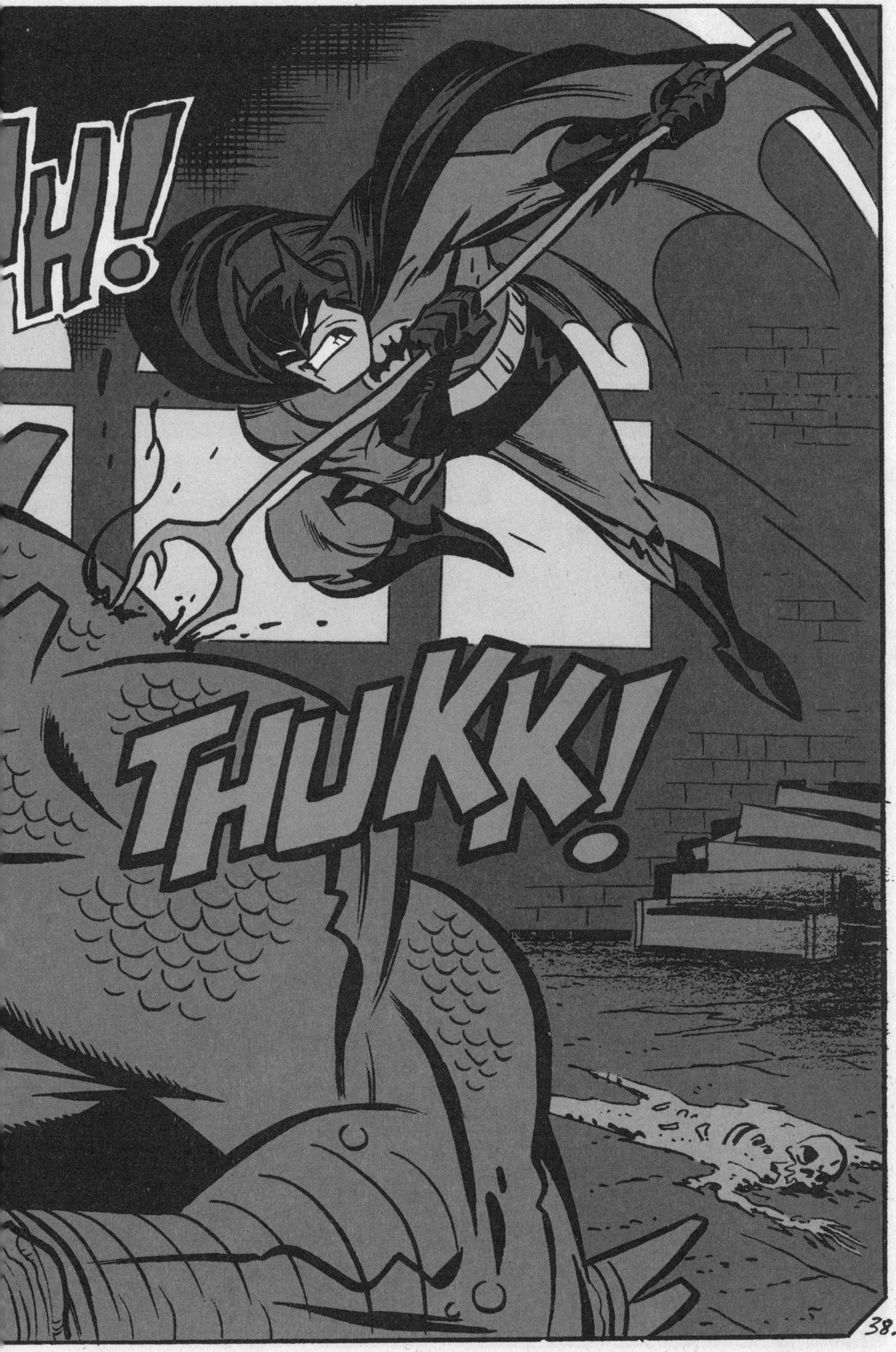

H!
THUKK!

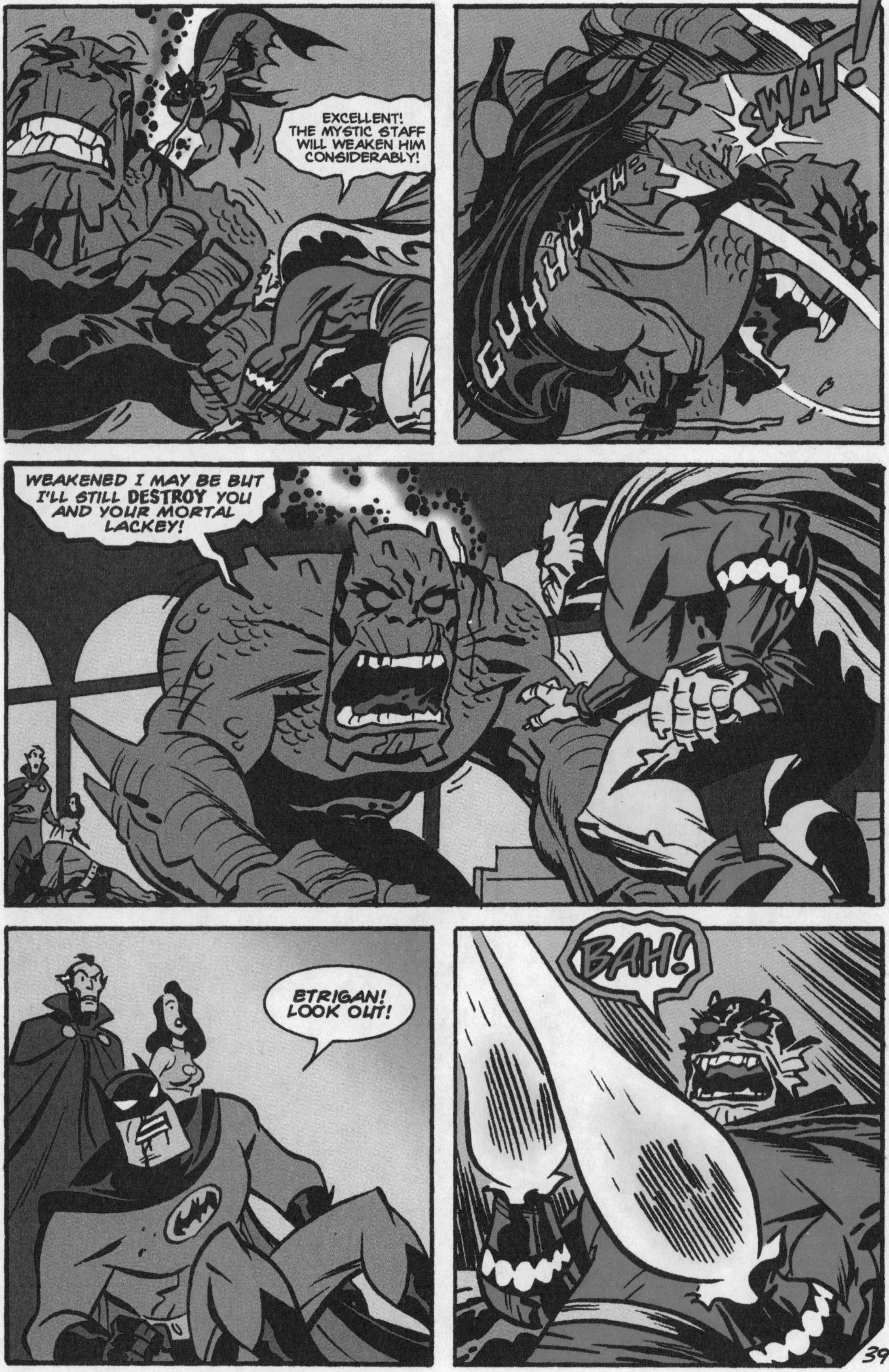
EXCELLENT! THE MYSTIC STAFF WILL WEAKEN HIM CONSIDERABLY!
SWAT!
GUHHHHHH-
WEAKENED I MAY BE BUT I'LL STILL DESTROY YOU AND YOUR MORTAL LACKEY!
ETRIGAN! LOOK OUT!
BAH!

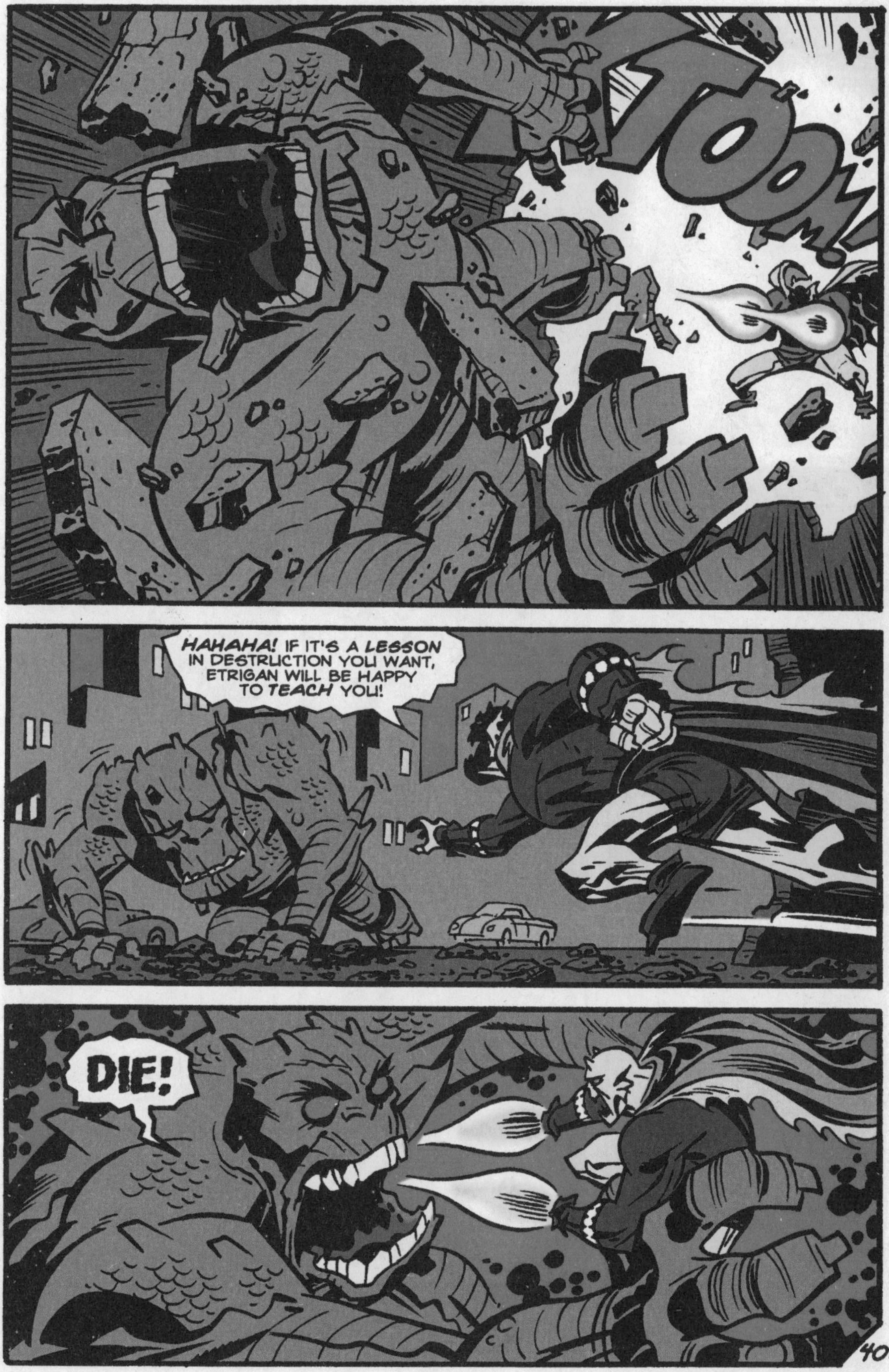
TOOOM!
HAHAHA! IF IT'S A LESSON IN DESTRUCTION YOU WANT, ETRIGAN WILL BE HAPPY TO TEACH YOU!
DIE!

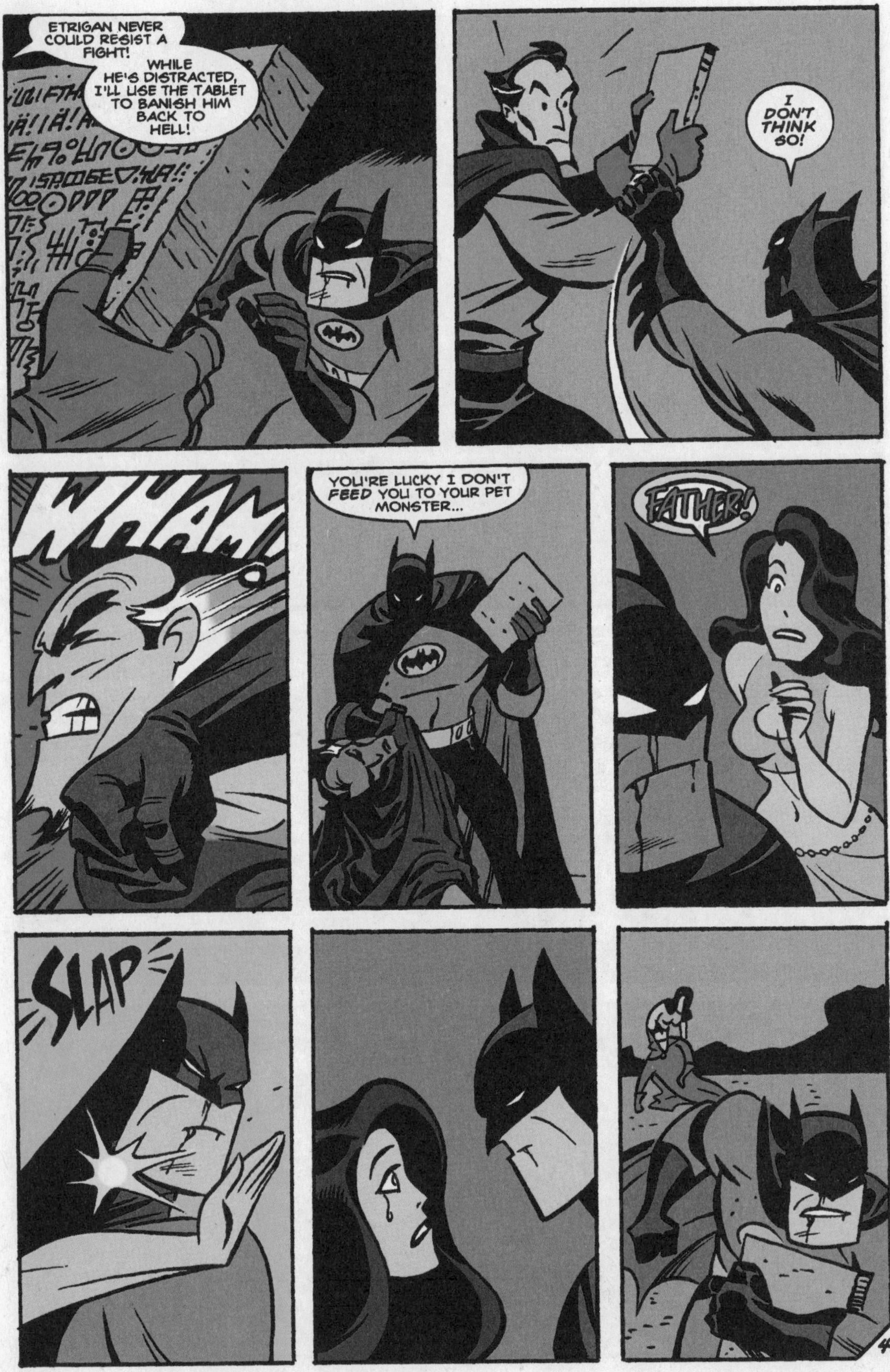
ETRIGAN NEVER COULD RESIST A FIGHT!
WHILE HE'S DISTRACTED, I'LL USE THE TABLET TO BANISH HIM BACK TO HELL!
I DON'T THINK SO!
WHAM
YOU'RE LUCKY I DON'T FEED YOU TO YOUR PET MONSTER...
FATHER!
SLAP

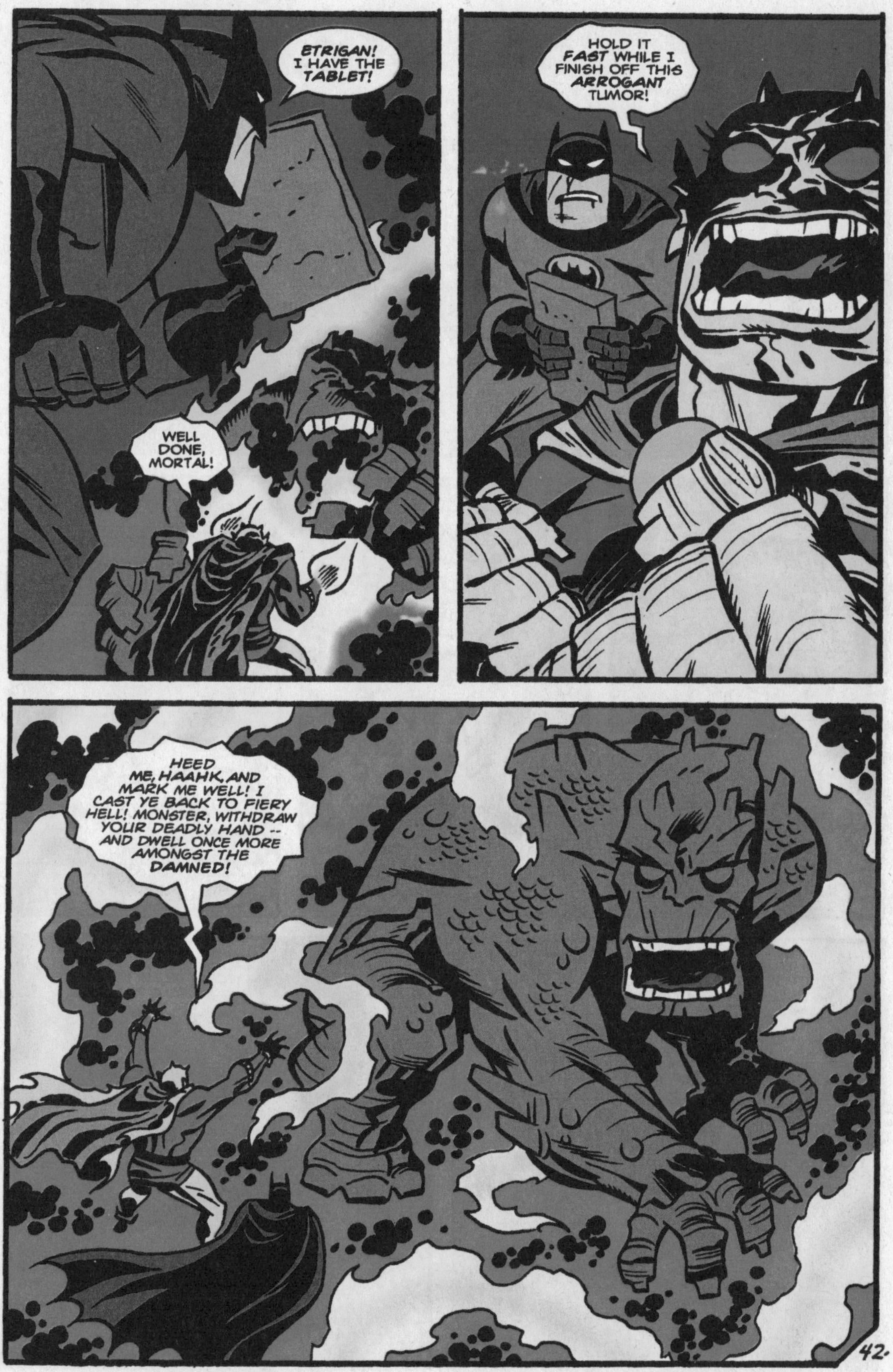
ETRIGAN! I HAVE THE TABLET!
WELL DONE, MORTAL!
HOLD IT FAST WHILE I FINISH OFF THIS ARROGANT TUMOR!
HEED ME, HAAHK, AND MARK ME WELL! I CAST YE BACK TO FIERY HELL! MONSTER, WITHDRAW YOUR DEADLY HAND -- AND DWELL ONCE MORE AMONGST THE DAMNED!
42.

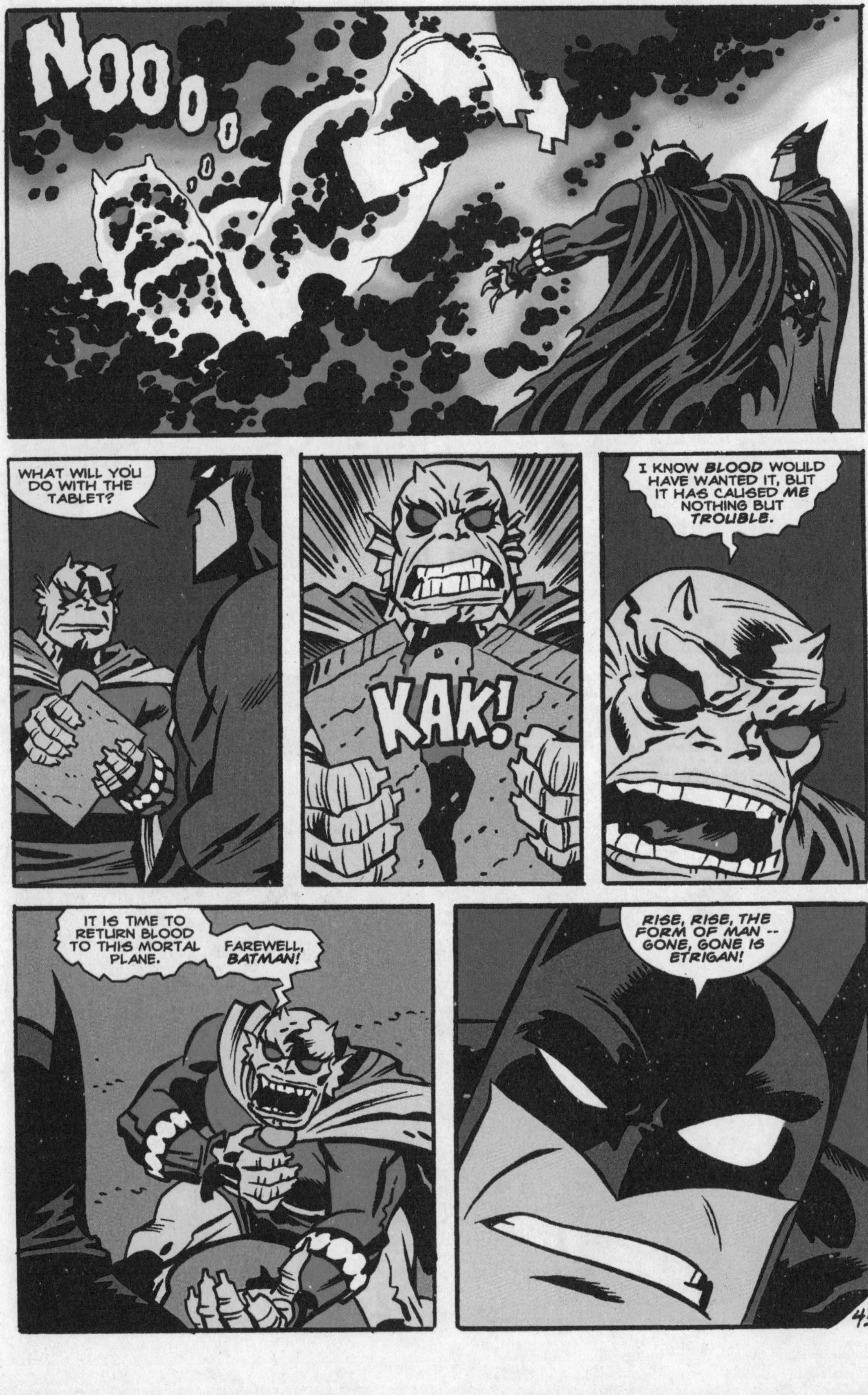
NOOOOO
WHAT WILL YOU DO WITH THE TABLET?
KAK!
I KNOW BLOOD WOULD HAVE WANTED IT, BUT IT HAS CAUSED ME NOTHING BUT TROUBLE.
IT IS TIME TO RETURN BLOOD TO THIS MORTAL PLANE.
FAREWELL, BATMAN!
RISE, RISE, THE FORM OF MAN -- GONE, GONE IS ETRIGAN!

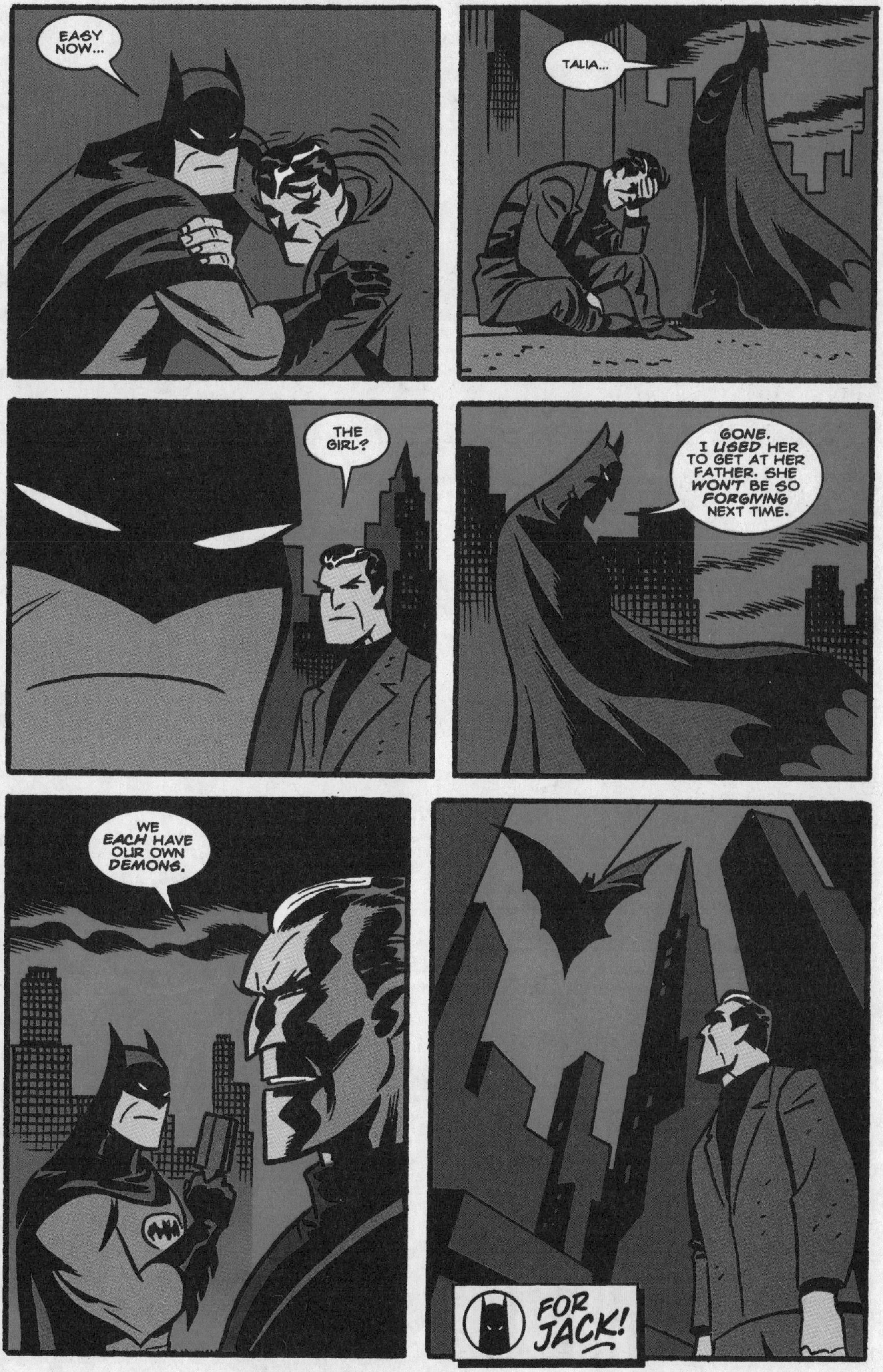
EASY NOW...
TALIA...
THE GIRL?
GONE. I USED HER TO GET AT HER FATHER. SHE WON'T BE SO FORGIVING NEXT TIME.
WE EACH HAVE OUR OWN DEMONS.
FOR JACK!

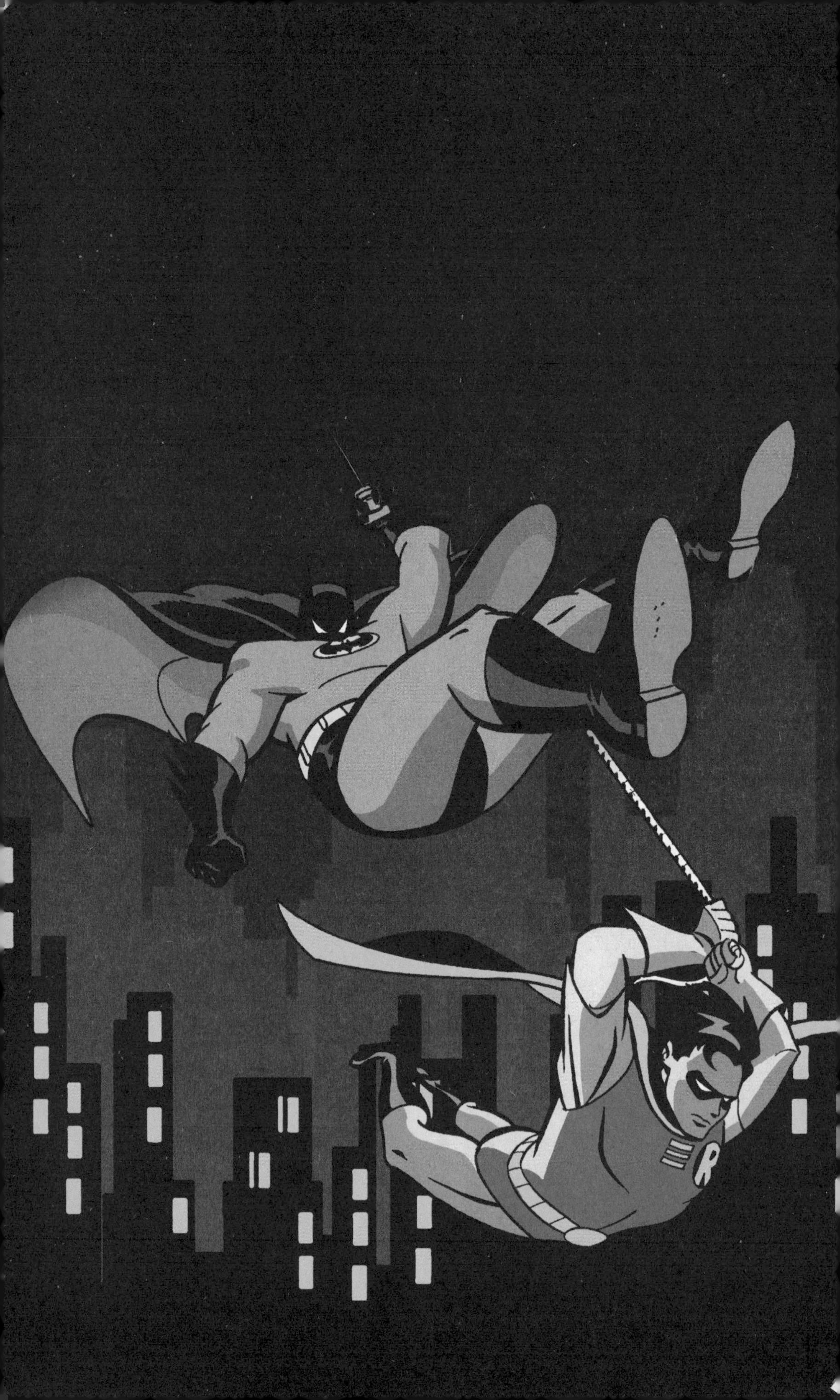

DC COMICS™

READ THE GRAPHIC NOVELS INSPIRED BY THE HIT CARTOON NETWORK SERIES!

THE ALL-NEW BATMAN: THE BRAVE AND THE BOLD

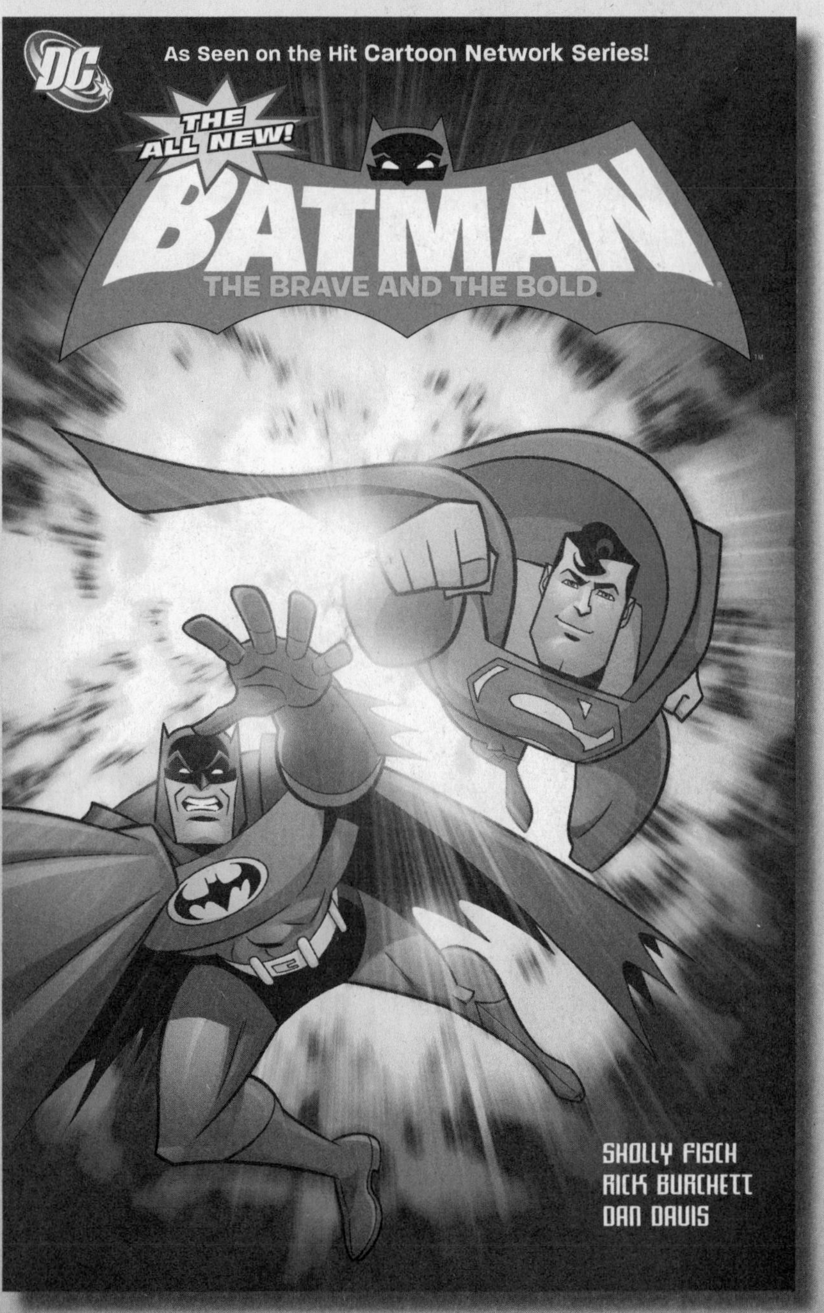
As Seen on the Hit Cartoon Network Series!
THE ALL NEW!
BATMAN
THE BRAVE AND THE BOLD
SHOLLY FISCH
RICK BURCHETT
DAN DAVIS

BATMAN: THE BRAVE AND THE BOLD: THE FEARSOME FANGS STRIKE AGAIN

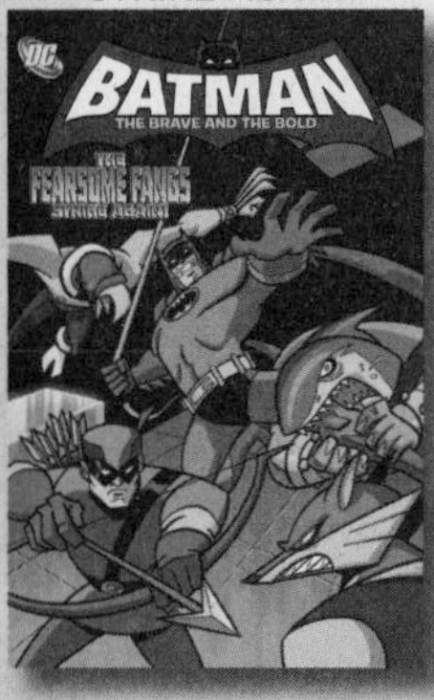
BATMAN
THE BRAVE AND THE BOLD
FEARSOME FANGS

BATMAN: THE BRAVE AND THE BOLD: EMERALD KNIGHTS

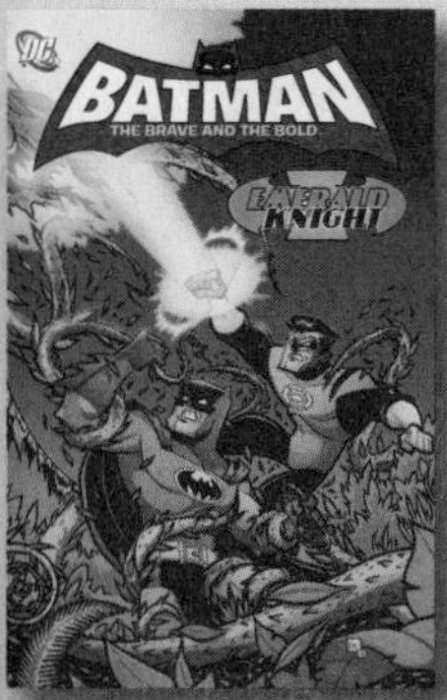
BATMAN
THE BRAVE AND THE BOLD

BATMAN: THE BRAVE AND THE BOLD: HELP WANTED

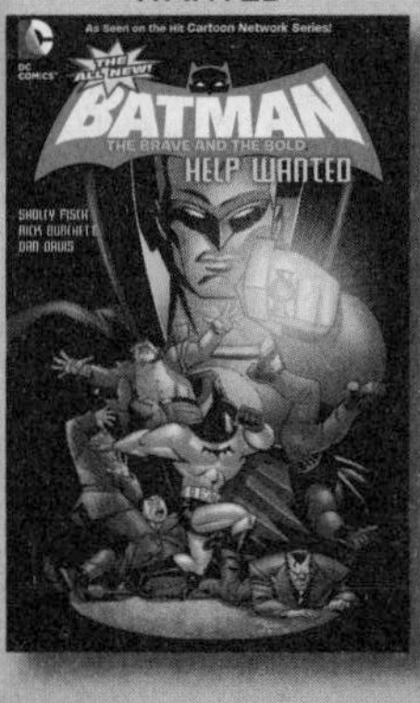
As Seen on the Hit Cartoon Network Series!
THE ALL NEW!
BATMAN
THE BRAVE AND THE BOLD
HELP WANTED

THE DARK KNIGHT. THE MAN OF STEEL. TOGETHER.

SUPERMAN/BATMAN: PUBLIC ENEMIES

JEPH LOEB & ED McGUINNESS

SUPERMAN/BATMAN:
SUPERGIRL

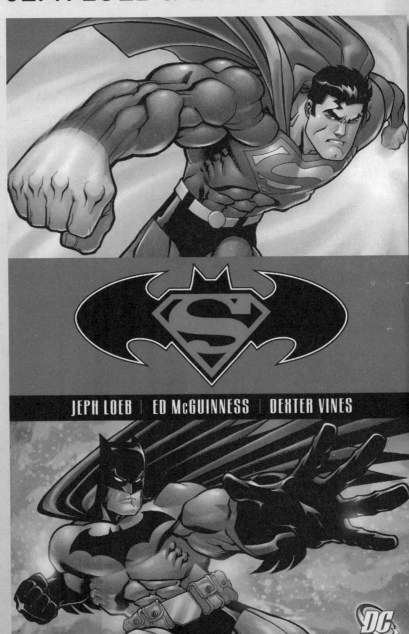

JEPH LOEB | ED McGUINNESS | DEXTER VINES